Dorence Atwater, Clara Barton

A List of the Union Soldiers Buried at Andersonville

Vol. 3

Dorence Atwater, Clara Barton

A List of the Union Soldiers Buried at Andersonville
Vol. 3

ISBN/EAN: 9783337307240

Printed in Europe, USA, Canada, Australia, Japan

Cover: Foto ©ninafisch / pixelio.de

More available books at **www.hansebooks.com**

A LIST

OF THE

UNION SOLDIERS

BURIED AT ANDERSONVILLE.

COPIED FROM THE OFFICIAL RECORD IN THE SURGEON'S OFFICE AT ANDERSONVILLE.

By DORENCE ATWATER.

Not more honorably die they who fall on the field in the moment of Victory!

NEW YORK:
PUBLISHED BY THE TRIBUNE ASSOCIATION.
154 NASSAU STREET.
1868.

TO THE

SURVIVING RELATIVES AND FRIENDS OF THE MARTYRED "DEAD" AT ANDERSONVILLE, GEORGIA.

THIS Record was originally copied for you because I feared that either you nor the Government of the United States would ever otherwise learn the fate of your *loved ones* whom I saw daily dying before me. I could do nothing for them, but I resolved that I would at least try to let you sometime know when and how they died. This at last I am now able to do.

So many conflicting rumors have been in circulation in regard to these *rolls* and myself, that I deem it prudent to give a brief statement of my entire connection with this Death Register, and to show how and why it has been so long withheld from you.

On the seventh day of July, 1863, I was taken prisoner near Hagerstown, Md., and taken to Belle Island, Richmond, Va., via Staunton, where I remained five months. I then went to Smith's Tobacco Factory, Richmond, where I kept the account of supplies received from our Government, and issued to Federal prisoners of war. In the latter part of February, 1864, I was sent to Andersonville with a squad of four hundred other prisoners from Belle Isle, arriving there on the first day of March. I remained inside the stockade until the middle of May, when I was sent to the hospital. On the 15th of June I was paroled and detailed as a clerk in Surgeon . H. White's office, to keep the daily record of deaths of all Federal prisoners of war. I also made monthly and quarterly abstracts of the deaths, the latter one was said to be for the Federal Government, which I have since learned was never received.

The appalling mortality was such that I suspected that it was the design of the Rebel Government to kill and maim our prisoners by exposure and starvation so that they would forever be totally unfit for military service, and that they withheld these facts. Accordingly, in the latter part of August, 1864, I began to secretly copy the entire list of our dead, which I succeeded in doing, and brought safely through the lines with me in March, 1865. Arriving at Camp Parole, at Annapolis, Md., I learned that I could not get a furlough on account of my term of service having expired some seven months before. I immediately wrote to the Secretary of War, asking for a furlough of thirty days, for the purpose of having my Death Register published for the relief of the many thousands anxious in regard to the fate of their dead. Before an answer could have returned, I received a furlough from the Commandant of the Camp. I then went to my home in Terryville, Connecticut, where I was taken sick the next day after my arrival, which confined me for three weeks. On the twelfth of April, I received a telegram from the War Department, requesting me to come immediately to Washington and bring my rolls, and if they were found acceptable, I should be suitably rewarded. I started the next day for Washington. Arriving there, I went to the War Department, and learned that the person (Col. Breck) with whom I was to make arrangements was absent at the Fort Sumter celebration. I left my rolls with the chief clerk for safe keeping. In a day or two Colonel Breck returned, and he informed me that the Secretary of War had authorized him to pay me three hundred dollars ($300) for the rolls. I told him I did not wish to sell the rolls, that they ought to be published for the benefit of the friends of the dead, for whom chiefly they had been copied. He told me if I went to publish them, the Government would confiscate them, that I could have until 9 o'clock the next morning to decide whether I would take the three hundred dollars or not. The rolls were then in his possession. I told him if I could have a clerkship in the department which he had described to me, three hundred dollars, and the *rolls back again as soon as copied*, I should consider it satisfactory. To this he agreed. He then informed me that it would be necessary for me to enlist in the General service in order to get the clerkship. To this I objected, but in no other way was it available, and I accepted. I was then mustered out of my original enlistment, and given permission to visit home, and return for duty by the first of June. While in New York in the latter part of May, I telegraphed to Colonel Breck, asking if my rolls were copied, to which I received a reply, "Not yet."

Soon after my arrival in Washington in June, I called on Colonel Breck, and asked the privilege of taking sheets of my rolls out after business hours, to copy and return them the next morning. He said he would have to ask General Townsend's consent. I again met him in a few days, he told me he had been unable to see General Townsend. I then wrote to Colonel Breck, asking if he did or did not intend to return my rolls, that I had promised that the rolls should be published for the benefit of the friends of the deceased. He returned my letter endorsed as follows: "I have fully explained the matter to General Townsend, and he says the rolls shall not be copied for any traffic whatever." I had never spoken of trafficking in them; I only wished to give them to the people for whom I had copied them at some personal risk. Nothing more was said in regard to the rolls until after my return from Andersonville in August.

Miss Clara Barton, of Washington, D. C., upon learning the condition of the Cemetery at Andersonville, and that the graves could be identified, had reported the facts to the Secretary of War, who ordered the necessary arrangements to be made for the marking of the graves. A party charged with this duty left Washington on the eighth day of July, consisting of Miss Clara Barton, Capt. J. M. Moore, myself, and forty-two letterers, painters, and clerks, arriving at Andersonville on the twenty-fifth of July.

Before leaving Washington it was found that the original Register, captured by Gen. Wilson, was deficient in one book containing about twenty-four hundred names, and my rolls were sent to supply this deficiency. The original was also found in many places blurred and imperfect, through want of care, and my rolls were frequently needed to aid this defect. They were therefore publicly and constantly in the hands of all who had occasion to consult them, and so came into my hands in the course of duty. They had been copied at Washington, according to my agreement with Colonel Breck, and were mine, and lawfully in my possession. I proposed to retain and give them to you as soon as I could. I did not propose to injure any one, to do anything unlawful or improper with them, much less to traffic or speculate on the information they contained, but I did retain them. When the originals were needed in the Wirz trial at Washington, they and my copy were in my tent when the messenger arrived in Andersonville. He took the original and left my copy.

When we started home I placed these rolls, with my other property, in my trunk and brought them to Washington. Upon my arrival I reported to Colonel Breck, at the War Department. He asked if I knew where my rolls were. I said "I have them; will you allow me to keep them, now you have them copied here."

He told me "We might as well come to an understanding about these rolls. This is the last conversation we shall have about them; if you will pay back three hundred dollars you can keep the rolls otherwise you must return them." I asked him "If he did not agree to give them back when copied;" he said "Yes, but you were going to set yourself up in business by publishing them, and we do not consider ourselves held to our agreement." I told him "I had a right to publish them (if he called that setting myself up in business), and it was my duty to do so." I then turned to leave, intending to see Secretary Stanton. He said, "I infer that you do not intend to give up the rolls." I said "Not yet; I must go farther to see about them." He said, "You will go to the 'Old Capitol' if you do not give them up," and then sent for a guard and had me arrested. My room and trunk were searched, but the rolls could not be found. I was then put in the guard house for two days, and then transferred to the "Old Capitol Prison," and in a few days I was arraigned and tried by court martial on the following charges and specifications:

Charge I. Conduct prejudicial to good military discipline. II. Larceny. Specifications in this that private Dorence Atwater, of the General Service of the United States Army, did seize and unlawfully take from the tent or quarters of Capt. J. M. Moore, assistant quartermaster U. S. army, certain property of the United States then and there in the proper charge and custody of the said Capt. J. M. Moore, to wit: a certain document, consisting of a list written upon about 21 sheets of paper, of Federal prisoners of war who had died at Andersonville, Georgia, the same having been prepared by said Atwater, while a prisoner of war at said Andersonville, and sold and disposed of by him to the United States, for the sum and price of three hundred dollars, and did appropriate and retain the said property to his own use. This at Andersonville, Georgia, on or about the 16th day of August, 1865.

I was convicted, and sentenced as follows: "To be dishonorably discharged from the United States Service, with loss of all pay and allowances now due; to pay a fine of three hundred dollars; to be confined at hard labor for the period of eighteen months, at such place as the Secretary of War may direct; to furnish to the War Department the property specified in the second specification as the property stolen from Capt. J. M. Moore, and stand committed at hard labor until the said fine is paid, and the said stolen property is furnished to the War Department."

On the 26th day of September I arrived at Auburn State Prison, New York, where I remained over two months at hard labor, when I was released under a general pardon of the President of the United States.

I reached New Haven, Ct., on the following day, and learned that the record had not yet been furnished you. I immediately set about preparing it for publication, and have arranged to have it printed and placed within your reach at the cost of the labor of printing and material, having no means by which to defray these expenses myself.

I regret that you have waited so long for information of so much interest to you.

DORENCE ATWATER.

REPORT

OF AN EXPEDITION TO ANDERSONVILLE, GEORGIA, JULY, 1865, FOR THE PURPOSE OF IDENTIFYING THE GRAVES AND ENCLOSING THE GROUNDS OF A CEMETERY CREATED THERE DURING THE OCCUPATION OF THAT PLACE AS A PRISON FOR UNION SOLDIERS IN REBEL HANDS.

To the People of the United States of America:

HAVING, by official invitation, been placed upon an expedition to Andersonville, for the purpose of identifying and marking the graves of the dead contained in those noted prison grounds, it is perhaps not improper that I make some report of the circumstances which induced the sending of such an expedition, its work, and the appearance, condition, and surroundings of that interesting spot, hallowed alike by the sufferings of the martyred dead, and the tears and prayers of those who mourn them.

During a search for the missing men of the United States Army, commenced in March, 1865, under the sanction of our late lamented President Lincoln, I formed the acquaintance of Dorence Atwater, of Connecticut, a member of the 2d New York cavalry, who had been a prisoner at Belle Isle and Andersonville 22 months, and charged by the rebel authorities with the duty of keeping the Death Register of the Union prisoners who died amid the nameless cruelties of the last-named prison.

By minute inquiry, I learned from Mr. Atwater the method adopted in the burial of the dead; and by carefully comparing his account with a draft which he had made of the grounds appropriated for this purpose by the prison authorities, I became convinced of the possibility of identifying the graves, simply by comparing the numbered post or board marking each man's position in the trench in which he was buried, with the corresponding number standing against his name upon the register kept by Mr. Atwater, which he informed me was then in the possession of the War Department.

Assured by the intelligence and frankness of my informant of the entire truthfulness of his statements, I decided to impart to the officers of the Government the information I had gained, and accordingly brought the subject to the attention of General Hoffman, Commissary General of prisoners, asking that a party or expedition be at once sent to Andersonville for the purpose of identifying and marking the graves, and enclosing the grounds; and that Dorence Atwater, with his register, accompany the same as the proper person to designate and identify. The subject appeared to have been not only unheard, but unthought of; and from the generally prevailing impression that no care had been taken in the burial of our prisoners, the idea seemed at first difficult to be entertained. But the same facts which had served to convince me, presented themselves favorably to the good understanding and kind heart of General Hoffman, who took immediate steps to lay the matter before the Hon. Secretary of War, upon whom, at his request, I called the following day, and learned from him that he had heard and approved my proposition, and decided to order an expedition, consisting of materials and men, under charge of some government officer, for the accomplishment of the objects set forth in my request, and invited me to accompany the expedition in person—which invitation I accepted.

Accordingly, on the 8th of July, the propeller Virginia, having on board fencing material, head-boards, the prison records, forty workmen, clerks and letterers, under command of Capt. James M. Moore, A. Q. M., Dorence Atwater and myself, left Washington for Andersonville, via Savannah, Georgia, arriving at the latter place July 12th. Having waited at Savannah seven days, and then resumed the journey by way of Augusta, Atlanta, and Macon, the entire party reached its destination in safety about noon on the 25th of July.

We found the prison grounds, stockade, hospital sheds, and the various minor structures, almost in the same condition in which they had been evacuated; and care is taken to leave these historic monuments undisturbed, so long as the elements will spare them.

There is not, and never was, any town or village at this place except what grew out of its military occupation. Anderson Station, on the railroad from Macon to Eufala, was selected as a depot for prisoners, probably on account of its remoteness and possible security, and the prison itself, with the buildings which sprang up around it, constituted all there was of Andersonville.

The land around is broken and undulating, and at the time of the occupation was covered with forests, mostly of the long-leafed pine, common to the uplands of the South. The bases of the hills are lined with oozy springs, which unite to form little rivulets, one of which winds sluggishly through each of the intervening marshy valleys.

The original enclosure of nineteen acres was made in the unbroken woods; and the timber was only removed as it was wanted for the necessities of the prison. The enclosure was made in January, 1864, and enlarged, during the summer, to 25½ acres—being a quadrangle of 1,295 by 865 feet. The greatest length is from north to south, the ground rising from the middle towards each end in rather a steep, rounded hill—the northern one being at once the highest and of the greatest extent. A small stream, rising from springs a little to the eastward, flows across it through a narrow valley filled with a compost washed down by the rains. The enclosing stockade is formed of pine logs, twenty feet in length, and about eight inches in diameter, sunk five feet in the ground, and placed close together. This is again surrounded by two successive, and precisely similar, palisades—a portion of the last of which is gone. It seems never to have been completed. The two inner walls remain entire. Within the interior space, at the distance of about seventeen feet from the stockade, runs the famous dead-line, marked by small posts set in the ground, and a slight strip of pine board nailed on the tops of them. The gates, of which there are two, situated on the west side, were continuations of the stockade, enclosing spaces of thirty feet square, more or less, with massive doors at either end. They were arranged and worked on the principle of canal locks. Upon the inner stockade were fifty-two sentry boxes, raised above the tops of the palisades, and accessible to the guard by ladders. In these stood fifty-two guards, with loaded arms, so near that they could converse with each other. In addition to these, seven forts mounted with field artillery, commanded the fatal space and its masses of perishing men.

Under the most favorable circumstances, and best possible management, the supply of water would have been insufficient for half the number of persons who had to use it. The existing arrangements must have aggravated the evil to the utmost extent. The sole establishments for cooking and baking were placed on the bank of the stream immediately above, and between the two inner lines of palisades. The grease and refuse from them were found adhering to the banks at the time of our visit. The guards, to the number of about 3,600, were principally encamped on the upper part of the stream, and when the heavy rains washed down the hill-sides, covered with 30,000 human beings, and the outlet below failed to discharge the flood which backed and filled the valley, the water must have become so foul and loathsome, that every statement I have seen of its offensiveness must be considered as falling short of the reality. And yet, within rifle-shot of the prison, there flowed a stream fifteen feet wide and three feet deep, of pure, delicious water. Had the prison been placed so as to include a section of the "Sweet Water Creek," the inmates might have drank and bathed to their hearts' content.

During the occupation, a beautiful spring broke out like the waters of Meribah from the solid ground, near the foot of the northern slope, just under the western dead line. It is still there—cool and clear—the only pleasing object in this horrid place.

The scarcity of water, the want of occupation, and perhaps the desire to escape by tunneling, impelled the prisoners to dig wells. Forty of these, finished and unfinished, remain. Those on the highest ground being sunk in the hard soil to the depth of eighty feet. The work was done with knives, spoons, sticks, and other tools but little better. The diggers brought up the earth in their pockets and blouses, and sprinkled it about the grounds to conceal the quantity. In some wells, excellent water was reached, and in others, horizontal galleries were attempted, for escape. In at least one instance, a tunnel was carried entirely through the hill, and a few prisoners are said to have got through.

The steep face of the northern hill is burrowed throughout its whole extent. The little caves are scooped out and arched in the form of ovens, floored, ceiled, and strengthened so far as the owners had means, with sticks and pieces of boards, and some of them are provided with fire-places and chimneys. It would seem that there were cases, during long rains, where the house would become the grave of its owner, by falling in upon him in the night. In these burrows are still found remnants of the wretched food, and rude utensils of the occupants—drinking cups made of sections of horns, platters and spoons wrought from parts of old canteens, kettles and pans made, without solder, from stray pieces of old tin or sheet iron. I brought away a considerable number of these articles, which may one day be of interest to the curious.

Five sheds stand on the top of the northern hill, erected in the early part of the occupation, and five more on the opposite height, built a short time before the evacuation.

Like nearly all southern land, the soil is liable to be washed away by the rains; and on the slopes of the hills, ravines are now formed, gullied to the depth of twelve feet. It seems impossible that men could have kept their footing on these hill-sides, when slippery with rain.

Outside of the enclosure, and nearly parallel with its south end, is the hospital stockade—800 feet by 250. It contains twenty-two sheds, for the most part without sides, erected about three months before the place was abandoned. The old hospital, occupied up to that time, in which so many brave men died, consisted only of tents enclosed by a board fence, and surrounded by a guard. Confused heaps of rubbish alone mark the place it occupied.

About half a mile from the main prison, and near Anderson Station, is the officers' stockade—a small enclosure, in which were never imprisoned more than 250 officers—and it was chiefly used for the confinement of rebel offenders.

The cemetery, around which the chief interest must gather, is distant about 300 yards from the stockade in a northwesterly direction. The graves, placed side by side in close continuous rows, cover nine acres, divided into three unequal lots by two roads which intersect each other nearly at right angles. The fourth space is still unoccupied, except by a few graves of "Confederate" soldiers.

No human bodies were found exposed, and none were removed. The place was found in much better condition than had been anticipated, owing to the excellent measures taken by Major-General Wilson, commanding at Macon, and a humane public-spirited citizen of Fort Valley, Georgia—a Mr. Griffin, who, in passing on the railroad, was informed by one of the ever faithful negroes, that the bodies were becoming exposed, and were rooted up by animals. Having verified this statement, he collected a few negroes, sank the exposed bodies, and covered them to a proper depth. He then reported the facts to General Wilson, and requested authority to take steps for protecting the grounds. That patriotic officer visited Andersonville in person, appointed Mr. Griffin temporary Superintendent, and gave him such limited facilities as could be furnished in that destitute country. It was determined to enclose a square of fifty acres; and, at the time of our arrival, the fence was nearly one-third built—from old lumber found about the place. He had also erected a brick kiln, and was manufacturing brick for drains to conduct the water away from the graves, and protect and strengthen the soil against the action of heavy rains. We found Mr. Griffin, with a force of about twenty negroes and a few mules, at work on the grounds. I have understood that that gentleman furnished the labor at his own cost, while General Wilson issued the necessary rations.

The part performed by our party was to take up and carry forward the work so well commenced. Additional force was obtained from the military commandant at Macon for completing the enclosure and erecting the head-boards. It seems that the dead had been buried by Union prisoners, paroled from the stockade and hospital for that purpose. Successive trenches, capable of containing from 100 to 150 bodies each, thickly set with little posts or boards, with numbers in regular order carved upon them, told to the astonished and tear-dimmed eye the sad story of buried treasures. It was only necessary to compare the number upon each post or board with that which stands opposite the name on the register, and replace the whole with a more substantial, uniform and comely tablet, bearing not only the original number, but the name, company and regiment and date of death of the soldier who slept beneath.

I have been repeatedly assured by prisoners that great care was taken at the time by the men to whom fell the sad task of originally marking this astonishing number of graves, to perform the work with faithfulness and accuracy. If it shall prove that the work performed by those who followed, under circumstances so much more favorable, was executed with less faithfulness and accuracy than the former, it will be a subject of much regret—but fortunately not yet beyond the possibility of correction. The number of graves marked is 12,920. The original records, captured by General Wilson, furnished about 10,500; but as one book of the record had not been secured, over 2,000 names were supplied from a copy (of his own record) made by Mr. Atwater in the Andersonville prison and brought by him to Annapolis on his return with the paroled prisoners.

Interspersed throughout this Death Register were 400 numbers against which stood only the dark word "unknown." So, scattered among the thickly designated graves, stand 400 tablets, bearing only the number and the touching inscription "Unknown Union Soldier."

Substantially, nothing was attempted beyond enclosing the grounds, identifying and marking the graves, placing some appropriate mottoes at the gates and along the spaces designed for walks, and erecting a flagstaff in the centre of the cemetery. The work was completed on the 17th of August, and the party took the route homeward by way of Chattanooga, Nashville, and Cincinnati, arriving at Washington on the morning of August 24th.

The health of the party during the expedition was remarkably good, when the season of the year, the fatigue, and the want of customary accommodations are taken into consideration. Cases of slight chills and fevers were not unfrequent; but, during the entire time, we had only one case of severe illness, and that, to our grief, terminated fatally. Edward Watts, of Georgetown, D. C., a clerk in the Q. M. Department in this city, sickened of typhoid fever during the passage up the Savannah river, and died on the 16th day of August. His remains were taken home to his friends. Mr. Watts was a young man of education and refinement, and of the highest type of moral and religious character; he suffered patiently, and died nobly and well. I have thought that he might be regarded as the last martyr of Andersonville.

The future of this historic spot cannot fail to constitute a subject of deep and abiding interest to the people of this entire country, and it would seem fitting that it should be preserved as one of the sanctuaries of the nation, and be in due time decorated with appropriate honors. Its susceptibility of internal improvement is very great. Water can be had for irrigation, and the climate will produce nearly all the flora of the temperate zones. Both national gratitude and personal affection will suggest the erection of a suitable monument within the cemetery, where, if desirable, may be preserved in durable form the names of the martyrs who sleep around. And as the land on which all these interesting associations are clustered, is still the property of private individuals, never having passed from the hands of the original owners, it would seem desirable that the cemetery at least, and its immediate surroundings, become the property of the nation. A mile square will embrace all points of general and historic interest.

There are numerous smaller burial-places in the State of Georgia which, from their seeming lesser importance, will scarcely be kept up as national cemeteries and in reference to which, without venturing to suggest, I would merely remark, that the fifty acres enclosed at Andersonville would afford ample space for all whom it might ever be deemed advisable to remove to that point.

During the occupation of Andersonville as a prison, it was a punishable offence for a colored man or woman to feed, shelter, aid, or even converse with the prisoners on parole. To others they had no access. I have been informed that they were not allowed about the prison grounds; and so great was their superstitious horror of the cruelties perpetrated upon the prisoners that only a comparatively small number had ever found the courage to visit the cemetery up to the time of our arrival. But the presence of so many northern people on such an errand, and especially a lady, entirely overcame their fears, and they visited the cemetery and myself by scores, men, women, and children, sometimes a hundred in a day. It was no uncommon occurrence, upon opening my tent in the morning, to find a group standing in front of it, who had walked fifteen or twenty miles to see the "Yankee lady," and ask her "if it were true that Abraham Lincoln was dead, and they were free," and "how Massa Lincoln's great paper read," and "what they ought to do," and tell her how the "poor Yankee prisoners" ran before the dogs, "like us," and they could not save them—starved, and they could not feed them—died, and they could not see them.

Remember, mothers, that the pitying tear of the old-time slave, whom your son helped to freedom, is the only tear that falls upon his distant grave to-day.

I have endeavored to point out to you, as faithfully as I am able, the various objects of interest, painful or otherwise, which presented themselves to my observation during the time occupied in the work of the expedition; and while I would not dwell upon the terribleness of the sufferings imposed upon our prisoners, nor stir the hearts already sunk in grief to deeper woe, still we owe it alike to the living and the dead, that a proper knowledge and a realization of the miseries which they endured be entertained by all. We are wont to attribute their chief suffering to insufficiency of food, and while this is probably just, still, to the mind of one who has looked over the scanty, shelterless, pitiful spot of earth to which they were confined, and takes into consideration the numberless trials which must have grown out of the privation of space and the necessary conveniences of life, the conviction will force itself that these latter were fall but little short of the former. It is to be remembered that during thirteen long months, they knew neither shelter nor protection from the changeable skies above, nor the pitiless, unfeeling earth beneath.

The treacherous nature of the soil, parching to seams in the sun, and gullying and sliding under their feet with every shower, must have augmented their ills almost beyond conception. I watched the effect of a heavy fall of rain upon the enclosed grounds, and in thirty minutes the entire hill-sides, which had constituted their sole abiding-place, were one rolling mass of slippery mud, and this the effect of a mere summer shower. What of the continued rains of autumn? Think of thirty thousand men penned by close stockade upon twenty-six acres of ground, from which every tree and shrub had been uprooted for fuel to cook their scanty food, huddled like cattle, without shelter or blanket, half-clad and hungry, with the dreary night setting in, after a day of autumn rain. The hill-tops would not hold them all, the valley was filled with the swollen brook; seventeen feet from the stockade ran the fatal dead line beyond which no man might step and live. What did they do? I need not ask where did they go, for on the face of the whole green earth there was no place but this for them; but where did they place themselves? how did they live? Ay! how did they die? But this is only one feature of their suffering; and perhaps the lightest. Of the long dazzling months when gaunt famine stalked at noon-day, and pestilence walked by night; and upon the seamed and parching earth the cooling rains fell not, I will not trust me to speak. I scarce dare think. If my heart were strong enough to draw the picture, there are thousands upon thousands all through our land too crushed and sore to look upon it. But after this, whenever any man who has lain a prisoner within the stockade of Andersonville, would tell you of his sufferings, how he fainted, scorched, drenched, hungered sickened, was scoffed, scourged, hunted and persecuted, though the tale be long and twice told, as you would have your own wrongs appreciated, your own woes pitied, your own cries for mercy heard, I charge you, listen and believe him. However definitely he may have spoken, know that he has not told you all. However strongly he may have outlined, or deeply he may have colored his picture, know that the reality calls for a better light, and a nearer view than your clouded, distant gaze will ever get. And your sympathies need not be confined to Andersonville, while similar horrors glared in the sunny light, and spotted the flower-girt garden fields of that whole desperate, misguided, and bewildered people. Wherever stretched the form of a Union prisoner, there rose the signal for cruelty and the cry of agony, and there, day by day, grew the skeleton graves of the nameless dead.

But, braving and enduring all this, some thousands have returned to you. And you will bear with me, and these noble men will pardon me, while, in conclusion, I speak one word of them.

The unparalleled severities of our four years' campaigns have told upon the constitutional strength even of the fortunate soldier, who alone marched to the music of the Union, and slept only beneath the folds of the flag for which he fought. But they whom fickle fortune left to crouch at the foot of the shadowless palmetto, and listen to the hissing of the serpent, drank still deeper of the unhealthful draught. These men bear with them the seeds of disease and death, sown in that fatal clime, and ripening for an early harvest. With occasional exceptions, they will prove to be short-lived and enfeebled men, and whether they ask it or not, will deserve at your hands no ordinary share of kindly consideration. The survivor of a rebel prison has endured and suffered what you never can, and what, I pray God, your children never may. With less of strength, and more of sad and bitter memories, he is with you now, to earn the food so long denied him. If he ask "leave to toil," give it him before it is too late; if he need kindness and encouragement, bestow them freely, while you may; if he seek charity at your hands, remember that "the poor you have always with you," but him you have not always, and withhold it not. If hereafter you find them making organized effort to provide for the widow and orphan of the Union prisoner, remember that it grows out of the heart sympathy which clusters around the memories of the comrades who perished at their side, and a well-grounded apprehension for the future of their own, and aid them.

In conclusion, tremulously, lest I assume too much, let me hasten to commend to the grateful consideration of this noble, generous people, alike the soldier who has given his strength, the prisoner who has sacrificed his health, the widow who has offered up her husband, the orphan that knows only that its father went out to battle and comes no more forever, and the lonely, distant grave of the martyr, who sleeps alone in a stranger soil, that freedom and peace might come to ours.

One word of explanation, in conclusion, and I have done. You have long and justly felt that some report of this expedition, embracing a record of the graves identified and reclaimed, was due you. And three thousand letters addressed to me upon the subject, have revealed only too plainly and painfully the bitter anxiety with which you have watched and waited.

A mere report, unaccompanied by the "record," seemed but a hollow mockery, which I would not impose upon you, and this is my first opportunity for such accompaniment. For the record of your dead, you are indebted to the forethought, courage, and perseverance of Dorence Atwater, a young man not yet twenty-one years of age; an orphan; four years a soldier; one tenth part of his whole life a prisoner, with broken health and ruined hopes, he seeks to present to your acceptance the sad gift he has in store for you; and, grateful for the opportunity, I hasten to place beside it this humble report, whose only merit is its truthfulness, and beg you to accept it in the spirit of kindness in which it is offered.

CLARA BARTON.

A LIST

OF THE

UNION SOLDIERS BURIED AT ANDERSONVILLE.

All Persons numbered below 12367, died in 1864; above that number, in 1865. All names with a *, denote Corporal; those with a †, Sergeant.

ALABAMA.

No. of Grave.

7524, Barton, Wm, 1 cav, Co L, died Sept 1, scorbutus.
2111, Berry, J M, †, 1 cav, Co A, died May 17, diarrhea c.
4622, Belle, Robt, 1 cav, Co A, died Aug 3, dysentery.
6505, Bonbur, Wm, 1 cav, Co E, died Aug 13, diarrhea.
8425, Brice, J C, 1 cav, Co L, died Sept 11, scorbutus.

8147, Guthrie, J, 1 cav, Co I, died Sept 8, scorbutus.

2514, Henry, P, 1 cav, Co F, died June 26, pneumonia.

993, Jones, Jno F, 1 cav, Co K, died Mar 15, anasarca.

No. of Grave.

4715, Mitchel, Jno D, 1, Co A, died Aug 4, scorbutus.

5077, Ponders, J, 1 cav, Co H, died Aug 8, diarrhea.
5763, Pauter, R, 1, Co L, died Aug 15, diarrhea c.
6586, Patterson, W D, 1, Co K, died Aug 25, diarrhea a.
2504, Prett, J R, 1, Co F, died June 26, diarrhea a.

10000, Redman, W R, 1 cav, Co G, died Oct 14, scorbutus.

4731, Stubbs, W, 1, Co I, died Aug 4, bronchitis.

CONNECTICUT.

2380, Anderson, A, 14, Co K, died June 23, diarrhea c.

3161, Batchelder, Benj, 16, Co C, died July 17, diarrhea a.
3664, Baty, John, 16, Co C, died July 19, diarrhea c.
7306, Brunkissell, H, 14, Co D, died Aug 30, dysentery.
2833, Brennon, M, 14, Co B, died July 3, dysentery c.
3224, Burns, John, 7, Co I, died July 12, diarrhea.
10414, Blumly, E, 8, Co D, died Oct 6, scorbutus.
545, Bigelow, Wm, 7, Co B, died April 14, diarrhea.
11965, Bill, H A, 3, Co B, died Nov 11, scorbutus.
12089, Brookmeyer, T W, 8, Co H, died Nov 18, scorbutus.
12152, Burke H, 16, Co D, died Nov 24, scorbutus.
12209, Bone, A, 1, Co E, died Dec 1, scorbutus.
10682, Burnham F,* 14, Co I, died Oct 11, dysentery c.
10690, Barlow, O L, 16, Co E, died Oct 11, dysentery a.
10876, Bennett, N, 18, Co H, died Oct 13, scorbutus.
5806, Brown, C H, 1, Co H, died Aug 15, dysentery.
6919, Boyce, Wm, 7, Co B, died Aug 17, dysentery.
6083, Bishop, B H, 1 cav, Co I, died Aug 18, dysentery.
6191, Bushnell, Wm, 14, Co D, died Aug 19, cerebritis.
7763, Bailey, F, 16, Co E, died Sept 4, dysentery.
2054, Brewer, G E, 21, Co A, died June 16, diarrhea c.
5594, Burns, B, 6, Co G, died Aug 14, bronchitis.
5632, Balcomb, 11, Co B, died Aug 14, diarrhea.
5754, Beers, James C, 16, Co A, died Aug 15, dysentery.
11036, Bidsell, D, 16, Co B, died Oct 28, scorbutus.
4206, Blakeslee, H, 1 cav, Co L, died July 30, anasarca.
3909, Bishop, A, 18, Co A, died July 24, dysentery.
1491, Beamnon, Peter, 14, Co B, died June 2, diarrhea.
2720, Babcock, H, 30, Co A, died July 1, scorbutus.
2818, Baldwin, Thomas, 1 cav, Co L, died July 3, pneumonia.
2156, Bosworth, A M, 16, Co D, died June 21, diarrhea c.
5132, Baugh, John, 11, Co C, died Aug 8, dysentery.
5151, Brooks, Wm D,* 18, Co F, died Aug 9, dysentery.
5318, Bower, John, 16, Co F, died Aug 11, scorbutus.
5452, Bently, F, 6, Co H, died Aug 12, diarrhea.

5464, Bently, James, 1 cav, Co I, died Aug 12, scorbutus.
4839, Blackman, A,* 2 artil, Co C, died Aug 6, scorbutus.
7742, Banning, J. F, 16, Co E, died Sept 3, dysentery.
8018, Ballentine, Robert, 16, Co A, died Sept 6, dysentery.
12408, Bassett, J B, 11, Co B, died Jan. 6, '65, scorbutus.
12540, Bolrne C, 2, Co E, died Jan 27, '65, rheumatism.
12620, Bemis Charles, 7, Co K, died Feb 8, scorbutus.

3707, Chapin, J L, 16, Co A, died July 21, '64, fever intermittent.
3949, Cottrell, P, 7, Co C, died July 25, diarrhea c.
3941, Clarkson, —, 11, Co H, died, July 25, scorbutus.
4367, Culler, M, 7, Co E, died July 31, diarrhea.
4419, Connor, D, 18, Co F, died Aug 1, scorbutus.
4848, Carrier, D B, 16, Co D, died Aug 6, diarrhea c.
6060, Cook, W H, 1 cav, Co G, died Aug 18, cerebritis.
6153, Clark, H H, 16, Co K, died Aug 19, cerebritis.
6846, Clark, W, 6, Co A, died Aug 25, diarrhea.
5799, Champlain, H, 10, Co F, died Aug. 15, dysentery.
336, Cane, John, 9, Co H, died April 2, diarrhea.
620, Christian, A M, 1, Co A, died April 13, dysentery.
775, Crawford, James, 14, Co. A, died April 25, diarrhea a.
7316, Chapman M, 16, Co E, died Aug 30, scorbutus.
7348, Cleary, P, 1 cav, Co B, died Aug 31, scorbutus.
7395, Campbell, Rob't, 7, Co E, died Aug 31, diarrhea.
7418, Culler, M, 16, Co K, died Aug 31, diarrhea a.
7685, Carver, John G, 16, Co D, died Sept 3, dysentery.
7780, Cain, Thomas, 14, Co G, died Sept 4, diarrhea.
9981, Crossley, B, 8, Co G, died Sept 20, scorbutus.
10272, Coltier, W, 16, Co B, died Oct 3, diarrhea.
11175, Callahan, J, 11, Co I, died Oct 19, scorbutus.
11361, Caudee, D. M, 2 artil, Co A, died Oct 23, scorbutus.

25, Dowd, F, 7, Co I, died March 8, pneumonia.
7325, Davis, W, 1 cav, Co L, died Aug 30, dysentery.
2813, Davis, W, 10, Co E, died July 3, anasarca.
3614, Damery, John, 6, Co A, died July 20, diarrhea.

No. of Grave.
7597, Diebenthal, H, 11, Co C, died Sept 2, diarrhea.
8508, Donoway, J, 1 Cav, Co A, died Sept 12, dysentery.
8709, Dutton, W H, 16, Co K, died Sept 14, dysentery.
6446, Dugan, Chas, 16, Co K, died Aug 12, scorbutus.
11329, Dean E, 15, Co H, died Oct 22, scorbutus.
11481, Dennings, G A, 15, Co I, died Oct 24 scorbutus.
11880, Downer, S, 18, Co C, died Nov 7, scorbutus.
11991, Demming, B J, 16, Co G, died Nov 13, diarrhea.

8482, Esmonds, A, 13, Co K, died July 17, fever typhoid.
4157, Eastery, Thomas, 14, Co G, died July 31, diarrhea c.
4508, Earnest, H C, 6, Co I, died Aug 2, gangrene.
5346, Ensworth, John, 16, Co C, died Aug 31, scorbutus.
7603, Edwards, O. J,* 8, Co G, died Sept 2, diarrhea.
8364, Evans, N L, 16, Co I, died Sept 15, scorbutus.
11608, Emmett, W, 15, Co K, died Oct 28, scorbutus.
12142, Eaton W, 6, Co F, died Jan 12, '65, diarrhea c.

185, Fuit, C W, 14, Co G, died March 27, diarrhea.
1277, Frinceel, Otto, 6, Co C, died May 22, diarrhea.
2612, Fry, S, 7, Co D, died June 28, diarrhea c.
4444, Fairfield, H, 16, Co G, died Aug 1, diarrhea.
4465, Fisher, H, 1, Co L, died Aug 1, dysentery.
6122, Flanders, J,* 16, Co C, died Aug 5, dysentery.
6382, Fuller, H S, 24, Co H, died Aug 11, scorbutus.
5913, Frisble, Levi, 1 cav, Co G, died Aug 17, dysentery.
6556, Foze, C † 7, Co K, died Aug 13, dysentery.
8628, Feely, M, 7, Co I, died Sept 6, scorbutus.
9089, Finy, A, 14, Co C, died Sept 18, diarrhea c.
10235, Frederick, John, 7, Co A, died Oct 3, scorbutus.
12188, Fagan, P D, 11, Co A, died Nov 28, dysentery.

8028, Gordon, John, 14, Co G, died July 7, diarrhea.
4296, Gray, Pat, 9, Co H, died July 27, phthisis.
4974, Grammon, Jas, 1 cav, Co K, died Aug 7, scorbutus.
4015, Galterman, J, 10, 1, Co E, died July 26, debilitas.
5173, Gilmore, J, 16, Co C, died Aug 9, diarrhea.
7057, Gallagher, P, 16, Co D, died Aug 28, diarrhea.
7337, Gott, G, musician, 18, died Aug 30, dysentery.
7592, Goodrich, J W, 16, Co C, died Sept 2, scorbutus.
7646, Griggs, W, 16, Co B, died Sept 3, dysentery.
9423, Guinn, H M, 11, Co G, died Sept 21, diarrhea.
10304, Grady, M, 11, Co B, died Oct 4, scorbutus.
10397, Gladstone, Wm, 6, Co K, died Oct 6, dysentery.

49, Holt, Thomas, 1 cav, Co A, died Mch 15, pleuritis.
2339, Hughes, Ed, 14, Co D, died June 22, diarrhea.
3195, Hitchcock, Wm A, 16, Co C, died July 12, diarrhea.
3448, Hall, Wm G, 1, Co K, died July 17, dysentery.
3559, Holcomb, D, 14, Co D, died July 18, diarrhea.
1350, Hilenthal, Jas, 14, Co C, died May 25, diarrhea.
3033, Haskins, Jas, 16, Co D, died July 8, diarrhea c.
5029, Hollister, A, 1 cav, Co L, died Aug 8, diarrhea.
6162, Hally, Thomas, 16, Co F, died Aug 9, diarrhea.
5352, Hanson, F A, 15, Co I, died Aug 11, anasarca.
6695, Hodges, Geo, 1 cav, Co H, died Aug 24, diarrhea c.
4937, Harwood, G, 15, Co A, died Aug 7, anasarca.
6964, Hoyt, E S, 17, Co B, died Aug 27, diarrhea.
7012, Hull, M, 16, Co E, died Aug 27, scorbutus.
7380, Holcomb, A A, 16, Co E, died Aug 31, diarrhea.
7642, Haly, W, 16, Co D, died Sept 3, dysentery.
7757, Hubbard, H D, 16, Co D, died Sept 4, gangrene.
8148, Hubbard, B, 16, Co A, died Sept 8, dysentery.
8403, Haywood, 18, Co E, died Sept 11, diarrhea c.
8613, Heath, J, 16, Co K, died Sept 13, scorbutus.
9129, Hall, B, 16, Co G, died Sept 18, anasarca.
9369, Heart, W, 11, Co F, died Sept 20, scorbutus.
9981, Harley, R A, 16, Co I, died Sept 29, diarrhea.
12086, Hibbard, A, 18, Co D, died Nov 18, scorbutus.
12117, Hancock, W, 14, Co G, died Nov 22, dysentery.
12163, Hudson, Chas, 11, Co C, died Nov 26, scorbutus.

9319, Islay, H, 11, died Sept 4, scorbutus.

737, Jamleson, Charles, 7, Co D, died Apl 26, diarrhea.
6221, Johnson, John, 16, Co E, died Aug 10, dysentery.
7083, Johnson, G W, 11, Co G, died Aug 28, dysentery.
7365, Jamison, John S, q. m. s, 1 cav, died Aug 31, diarrhea c.
7579, Jones, John J, 16, Co B, died Sept 2, diarrhea.
7961, Jones James R, 6, Co G, died Sept 6, diarrhea.
8502, Johnson, F, 1, Co D, died Sept 12, gangrene
11970, Johnson, C S, 16, Co E, died Nov 12, scorbutus.
12043, Johnson, W, 16, Co E, died Dec 20, scorbutus.

1500, Kingsbury, C, 14, Co K, died June 3, pneumonia.
6186, Kilbolund, L, 11, Co C, died Aug 9, scorbutus.
6374, Kempton, B F, 8, Co G, died Aug 21, diarrhea c.
6795, Kershoff B, 6, Co H, died Aug 25, diarrhea a.
6748, Kelley, F, 14, Co I, died Aug 25, rheumatism.
7749, Kelly, J, 1 cav, Co L, died Sept 3, diarrhea a.
8305, Kimball, H H, 7, Co H, died Sept 7, diarrhea a.

No. of Grave.
8806, Kohlenburg, C, 7, Co D, died Sept 15, scorbutus.
10233, Kearn, T, 16, Co A, died Oct 2, diarrhea a.

3401, Lendon, H, 16, Co D, died July 16, diarrhea c.
5883, Lastry, J, 10, Co I, died Aug 16, diarrhea c.
5499, Lewis, J, 8, Co E, died Aug 12, diarrhea c.
6124, Leonard, W, 14, Co H, died Aug 19, diarrhea a.
7912, Levanaugh, Wm O, † 16, Co C, died Sept 5, dysentery.
7956, Linker, C, 8, Co G, died Sept 6, diarrhea a.
9219, Lewis, G H, 7, Co G, died Sept 19, scorbutus.
10228, Lee,—farrier, 1 cav, Co F, died Oct 2, diarrhea c.

74, Miles, W J, 6, Co D, died March 20, rheumatism.
1119, McCaulley, Jas, 14, Co D, died March 20, diarrhea.
2295, Miller, Charles, 14, Co I, died June 21, diarrhea a.
3516, McCord, P, 16, Co G, died July 18, fever typhoid.
3644, Miller, A, 14, Co D, died July 19, scorbutus.
3410, Mould, James, 11, Co E, died July 16, fever typhoid
3932, McGinnis, J W, 15, Co E, died Aug 17, enteritis.
4079, Miller, D, 1 cav, Co E, died July 27, diarrhea.
4417, Messenger, A, 16, Co G, died July 31, diarrhea.
4492, McLean, Wm, 11, Co F, died Aug 1, scorbutus.
4365, Marshall, B, 8, Co H, died Aug 3, diarrhea.
6238, Mcghllis, F, 10, Co F, died Aug 10, diarrhea a.
5328, Miller, H, 16, Co A, died Aug 11, dysentery.
6342, Malone, John, 16, Co B, died Aug 22, diarrhea.
6428, Messey, M, 7, Co E, died Aug 22, scorbutus.
6451, McGee, Thomas, 11, Co D, died Aug 22, dysentery
6570, McDavid, Jas, 1, Co K, died Aug 23, ictus solis.
6800, Meal, John, 11, Co D, died Aug 25, dysentery.
6902, Mape, George, 11, Co B, died Aug 25, diarrhea a.
6240, Marshall, L, 8, Co H, died July 24, scorbutus.
7547, Moore, A P,* 1 cav, Co H, died Sept 2, diarrhea c.
7852, Miller, F D, 16, Co B, died Sept, 5, debilitas.
8150, Modger, A, 10, Co I, died Sept 8, wounds.
8446, Mathews, S J, 16, Co K, died Sept 11, scorbutus
8501, Meyers, L, 1 cav, died Sept 12, scorbutus.
9170, Merts, C, 11, Co C, died Sept 18, scorbutus.
9321, Miler, W, 14, Co F, died Sept 20, diarrhea.
10595, McCreieth, A, 14, Co H, died Oct, 10, scorbutus
10914, McKeon, J, 7, Co H, died Oct 14, scorbutus.
11487, Murphy, W, 16, Co C, died Oct 26, scorbutus.
11558, McDowell, J, 11, Co D, died Oct 27, dysentery.
12134, Montjoy, T, 5, Co C, died Nov 23, diarrhea.

5044, Nichols C, 16, Co G, died Aug 8, dysentery.
6222, Northrop, John, 7, Co D, died Aug 20, cerebritis.
7331, North, S S, † 1 cav Co D, died Aug 30, fever congestive.
10895, Nichols, M, 7, Co I, died Oct 14, scorbutus.

4565, Orton, H C, 6, Co I, died Aug 9, rheumatism.
7511, Olena, R, 1 cav, Co E, died Sept 1, scorbutus.
8276, Orr A, 14, Co H, died Sept 14, scorbutus.

2960, Pendalton, W, 14, Co C, died July 6, scorbutus.
3205, Pompey, C, 14, Co B, died July 24, diarrhea.
4356, Parker, S B, 10, Co B, died July 31, diarrhea a.
3803, Phelps, S G, 1, Co H, died July 22, fever typhoid.
4924, Pimble, A, 16, Co I, died Aug 7, diarrhea c.
5002, Plum, James, 11, Co G, died Aug 8, debilitas.
5384, Patchey, J, 1 cav, Co I, died Aug 12, diarrhea.
7487, Post, C,* 16, Co K, died Sept 1, diarrhea a.
7688, Potache, A, 7, Co G, died Sept 3, diarrhea a.
9248, Phillips, J I, 8, Co B, died Sept 19, scorbutus.
9444, Padfrey, Sylvanus, 8, Co H, died Sept 21, diarrhea.
9533, Painter, N P, 7, Co C, died Sept 22, scorbutus.
10676, Puritan, O, 1 cav, Co L, died Oct 11, scorbutus.
11646, Peir, A, 7, Co D, died Oct 28, wounds.
2804, Ruther, J,* 1 cav, Co E, died July 3, pneumonia.
2871, Reed, H H, 2 artil, Co H, died July 4, diarrhea.
3674, Risley, E,* 10, Co B, died July 20, diarrhea.
4636, Reins, Wm, 11, Co I, died Aug 5, diarrhea.
5912, Ross, D, 10, Co K, died Aug 16, diarrhea c.
6400, Robinson, H, 21, Co K, died Aug 21, scorbutus.
6796, Ringwood, R, 14, Co J, died Aug 25, diarrhea.
8078, Reed, John, 7, Co B, died Sept 7, diarrhea a.
8170, Richardson, C S, 16, Co E, died Sept 9, scorbutus.
8345, Ray, A, 11, Co G, died Sept 10, scorbutus.
7310, Reed, Robt K, 7, Co A, died Aug 30, diarrhea.
8662, Roper, H, 16, Co G, died Sept 13, anasarca.
10029, Robinson, J W, 18, Co D, died Sept 29, diarrhea.
10196, Richardson, D F, 16, Co G, died Oct 2, scorbutus.
10416, Reynolds, E, 1, Co E, died Oct 6, diarrhea.
12031, Rathbone, B, 2, Co A, died Nov 15, '64, scorbutus.

4, Stone, H J, 1 cav, Co A, died March 3, dysentery.
224, Smith, Horace, 7, Co D, died March 29, dysentery.
2405, Seward, G H, 11, Co A, died June 24, dysentery c.
2474, Stephens, E W, 1 cav, Co L, died June 25, fever typhoid.
2010, Scott W, 14, Co D, died July 7, scorbutus
3026, Sutcliff, B, 21, Co G, died July 7, diarrhea c.

No. of Grave.

8041, Stuart J. 7, died July 8.
3522, Smith, J, 14, Co I, died July 18, diarrhea c.
3598, Sherwood D. 1, Co D, died July 18, diarrhea a.
4212, Smith, C E, * 1 cav, Co L, died July 27, diarrhea.
4316, Straubell, L, 11, Co C, died July 30, diarrhea c.
4555, Straum, James, 2 artil, Co D, died Aug 2, diarrhea.
4722, Sullivan, M, 16, Co D, died Aug 4, diarrhea.
4892, Steele, Sam, 14, Co C, died Aug 6, diarrhea c.
5385, Shults, C T, 14, Co L, died Aug 12, dysentery.
5562, St no, P, 10, Co K, died Aug 13, diarrhea.
5712, Steele Sam, 16, Co C, died Aug 15, diarrhea.
5725, Smith S, 7, Co B, died Aug 15, scorbutus.
6734, Steele, James M, 16, Co F, died Aug 25, diarrhea.
7070, Stephens, B H, 14, died Aug 28, diarrhea.
7975, Smith, Henry, 5, Co H, died Sept 6, scorbutus.
8088, Short, L C, 18, Co K, died Sept 7, scorbutus.
8235, Smally, L, 16, Co E, died Sept 9, scorbutus.
9304, Starkweather, E M, 1 cav, Co L, died Sept 20, dysentery.
9435, Sutliff, J, 16, Co C, died Sept 21, diarrhea.
9643, See, L, 1, Co G, died Sept 24, gangrene.
9987, Sling, D, 7, Co F, died Sept 29, diarrhea.
10188, Schubert, K, 16, Co K, died Oct 1, diarrhea.
10347, Sparring, T, 7, Co K, died Oct 3, diarrhea.
10476, Steele, H, 16, Co F, died Oct 7, dysentery.
10787, Stauff, J, 1 cav, Co L, died Oct 12, diarrhea.
12005, Swift, J, 1, Co K, died Nov 14, diarrhea.
12288, Smith, J T, 7, Co D, died Dec 13, scorbutus.

No. of Grave.

541, Taylor, Moses, 14, Co E, died April 14, bronchitis.
4443, Thompson, Wm T, 14, Co I, died Aug 1, diarrhea.
5427, Thompson, F, 14, Co A, died Aug 12, diarrhea c.
5479, Tibbels, Wm, 16, Co G, died Aug 12, diarrhea.
7723, Treadway, J H, * 15, Co E, died Aug 3, diarrhea a.
10035, Tisdale, E F, 1 cav, Co B, died Sept 29, scorbutus.
10142, Taylor, J, 14, Co I, died Oct 1, scorbutus.
11059, Turner, H, 11, Co A, died Oct 18, scorbutus.

8107, Valter, H, 14, Co A, died July 13, anasarca.

401, Winship, J H, 18, Co G, died Apr 16, dysentery.
2158, Weldon, Henry, 7, Co E, died June 19, diarrhea a.
2601, Warner, E, 1 cav, Co E, died June 28, diarrhea.
5543, Wickert, Henry, 14, Co C, died Aug 13, dysentery.
5722, Wright, C, 15, Co B, died Aug 19, dysentery.
4649, Wheely, James, 10, Co G, died Aug 3, diarrhea.
5675, Wenchell, John L, 16, Co E, died Aug 14, gangrene.
6138, Way, H C, 16, Co K, died Aug 19, diarrhea.
6918, Wigglesworth, M L, 2 artil, Co H, died Aug 26, scorbutus.
8024, West, Chas H, 16, Co I, died Sept 6, fever typhus.
9028, Williams, H D, * 16, Co F, died Sept 17, scorbutus.
9255, Wheeler, J, 1 cav, Co M, died Sept 19, scorbutus.
9512, Ward, Gilbert, 1 H, died Sept 22, dysentery.
10033, Weins, John, 6, Co K, died Sept 29, diphtheria.
12600, Ward, G W, 18, Co C, died Feb 6, '65, scorbutus.

6394, Young, C S, * 16, Co C, died Aug 21, '64, pneumonia.

DELAWARE.

6812, Aiken, Wm, 7, Co G, died Sept 15, scorbutus.

5529, Boice, J, 4, died Aug 13, diarrhea.
7016, Brown, J H, 2 Co I, died Aug 27, diarrhea a.

1709, Callihan, Jno, 1, Co B, died June 7, diarrhea c.
2698, Conoway, F, 1, Co K, died June 30, diarrhea c.
4394, Conley, J H, 2, Co F, died July 31, diarrhea a.
12253, Conner, G, 1 cav, Co D, died Dec 9, scorbutus.
10868, Conner, C, 2, Co F, died Oct 13, scorbutus.
11245, Cunningham, K, 1, Co F, died Oct 13, scorbutus.

6217, Donahue, H, 2, Co D, died Aug 20, scorbutus.

6677, Emmett, W, 1, Co K, died Aug 24, anasarca.

2091, Field, S, 2, Co D, died June 17, anasarca.

9004, Hanning, H, drum, 2, Co F, died Sept 17, scorbutus.
8346, Hills, W, 2, Co K, died Sept 10, diarrhea c.
5504, Hobson, W, 1 cav, Co E, died Aug 13, diarrhea a.
9839, Hudson, G W, † 2, died Sept 27, scorbutus.
11634, Hussey, J R, 1 cav, Co D, died Oct 28, scorbutus.

790, Joseph, W C.* 1, Co E, died Apr 28, diarrhea c.
5346, Jones, H, 2, Co B, died Aug 11, diarrhea.

11410, Kinney, M, 1, Co D, died Oct 24, scorbutus.

8292, Laughlin, R M, 1, Co C, died Sept 9, scorbutus.
483, Lampkins, J H, 2, Co D, died Apr 9, diarrhea c.

6956, Malam, Jas, 2, Co C, died Aug 17, fever typhoid.
8972, Moxworthy, Geo, 2, Co D, died Sept 16, diarrhea.
9589, Martin, J, 1, Co G, died Sept 23, diarrhea.
9947, Manner, C, 2, Co K, died Sept 28, diarrhea.
1671, McCracklin, H, 1, Co B, died June 6, dysentery.
11570, McKinney, J, 1, Co F, died Oct 27, scorbutus.
12407, McBride, 2, Co F, died Jan 6, '65, scorbutus.

9450, Norris, Clarence, 1 cav, Co L, died Sept 21, diarrhea.

6397, Peterson, P, 4, Co F, died Aug 20, diarrhea.
5743, Puffer, W, 2, Co F, died Aug 14, debility.

7551, Retter, G, 2, Co F, died Sept 2, dysentery.
11534, Riddon, H A, 1, Co H, died Oct 27, scorbutus.

6018, Sturet, John, 2, Co E, died Aug 23, diarrhea a.
6479, Sholder, Ed, 2, Co H, died Aug 22, diarrhea c.
6593, Simble, Wm, 1 cav, Co C, died Aug 22, diarrhea a.
12707, Sill, James, 2, Co K, died Feb 28, '65, scorbutus.
5764, Smith, E E, 2, Co E, died Aug 15, diarrhea a.

276, Taylor, Rob't, 1, Co G, died Mar 31, pneumonia.
8682, Thorn, H I, 2, Co D, died Sept 8, dysentery.
9324, Tilbrick, E L, 1 cav, Co L, died Sept 20, diarrhea c.

11981, Warner, G, 2, Co K, died Nov 13, scorbutus.
10392, Wilds, J, 2, Co K, died Oct 4, scorbutus.
198, Wilburn, Geo, 2, Co G, died Mar 27, bronchitis.

DISTRICT OF COLUMBIA.

8449, Boissonnault, F M, 1 cav, Co H, died Sept 11, scorbutus.

11700, Clark, Theodore, 1 cav, Co I, died Oct 31, scorbutus.

11180, Farrell, C, 1 cav, Co E, died Oct 19, scorbutus.

5736, Gray, G S, 1 cav, Co K, died Aug 15, dysentery.

9403, Pillman, John, 1 cav, Co D, died Sept 21, scorbutus.

6973, Ridley, A C, 1 cav, Co M, died Aug 20, dysentery.

11716, Russell, T, 1 cav, Co D, died Nov 1, scorbutus.

6847, Stretch, J, 1 cav, Co G, died Aug 25, debilitas.
8189, Sergeant, L, 1 I, Co G, died Sept 8, dysentery.
11742, Stanhope, W H, 1, Co I, died Nov 2, diarrhea.

12457, Veazie, F, 1 cav, Co K, died Jan 15, '65, diarrhea.

8172, Winworth, G, 1 cav, Co G, died Sept 5, dysentery.
8807, Wiggin, Nat, 1 cav, Co M, died Sept 15, scorbutus.
10301, Wilson, W, 1 cav, Co E, died Oct 3, scorbutus.

ILLINOIS.

8402, Adams, H F, † 17, Co E, died Sept 11, scorbutus.
12430, Adder, W, 30, Co C, died Jan 4, '65, diarrhea.
3840, Adlet, John, 119, Co K, died July 23, diarrhea c.
8219, Adrian, F, 9 cav, Co E, died Sept 9, scorbutus.
6876, Akens, C, * 78, Co F, died Aug 16, diarrhea.
8581, Albany, D, 22, Co D, died Sept 10, scorbutus.
1264, Aldridge, A, 16 cav, Co L, died May 20, diarrhea.
8127, Alexander, P, 123, Co B, died Sept 8, scorbutus.
1424, Allen, E C, 17, Co I, died May 29, diarrhea.

10762, Alf, H, 89, Co A, died Oct 10, dysentery.
2400, Allison, L J, 21, Co B, died June 24, dysentery.
6710, Anderson, A, 19, Co F, died Aug 25, scorbutus.
10242, Anderson, A, 98, Co F, died Oct 2, scorbutus.
9946, Anderson, W, 59, Co C, died Sept 28, scorbutus.
1271, Anthony, E, 3, Co E, died Oct [illegible], diarrhea.
7320, Armstrong, R, 89, Co A, died Aug 31, scorbutus.
12702, Arnold, L, 137, Co I, March 12, '65, scorbutus.
10979, Atkins, E, 6, Co C, died Oct 15, scorbutus.

No. of Grave.
9733, Atkinson, James, 14 cav, Co D, died Sept 25, dysentery
11777, Atwood, A, 23, Co G, died Nov 3, scorbutus.
8046, Augustine, J, 100, Co I, died Sept 6, anasarca.

3700, Babbitt, John, 7, Co K, died July 21, scorbutus.
2598, Babcock, F, 44, Co G, died June 28, pneumonia.
3781, Bailey, P, † 38, Co B, died July 22, anasarca.
12530, Baker, James, 25, Co H, died Jan 26, '65, scorbutus.
2802, Baker, John, 89, Co B, died July 4, pneumonia.
3308, Baker, Thomas, 16 cav, Co M, died July 14, diarrhea.
1031, Bales, Thomas, 2 artil, Co M, died May 11, anasarca.
6848, Barber, C F, 112, Co I, died Aug 10, debilitas.
3829, Barclay, P, 42, Co I, died July 23, diarrhea c.
12758, Barnard, W, 14, Co F, died March 12, '65, diarrhea c.
10480, Barnes, Thomas, 135, Co F, died Oct 7, diarrhea.
8458, Barnet, J, 120, Co I, died Sept 11, gangrene.
8702, Barrett, A, * 25, Co A, died Sept 14, diarrhea.
12687, Bass, J, 2 cav, Co C, died Feb 22, '65, diarrhea.
977, Basting, C, 47, Co B, died May 9, diarrhea.
3275, Bathrick, J, 1 cav, Co A, died July 14, diarrhea.
4818, Batsdorf, M, 93, Co F, died Aug 3, fever intermittent.
3600, Bayley, Frank, 16 cav, Co E, died July 19, diarrhea a.
11917, Beaver, M, 29, Co B, died Nov 8, scorbutus.
11652, Beard, J, 14, Co K, died Oct 30, scorbutus.
1870, Beal, John, 78, died June 12, diarrhea c.
6644, Bear, D, 93, Co B, died Aug 23, scorbutus.
4573, Beck, J, 21, Co G, died Aug 2, dysentery.
411, Beliskey, J, 16 cav, Co D, died April 7, diarrhea.
1230, Bender, George, 12, Co C, died May 20, diarrhea.
6242, Bennet, A, 16, Co B, died Aug 10, diarrhea.
6412, Benning, John, 6 cav, Co O, died Aug 22, diarrhea.
3345, Benstill, John, 27, Co H, died July 15, diarrhea.
10653, Benton, C W, 29, Co B, died Oct 11, scorbutus.
8189, Berlizer, B, 16 cav, Co F, died Sept 8, scorbutus.
10681, Best, William, 88, Co E, died Oct 11, scorbutus.
4315, Black, John, † 31, Co A, died July 30, wounds.
2904, Black, J H, 21, Co E, died July 5, scorbutus.
1665, Blanchard, L, * 16 cav, Co D, died June 6, anasarca.
1983, Bloss, P, 21, Co A, died June 15, pneumonia.
11085, Bolkins, E L, 103, Co D, died Oct 18, scorbutus.
2890, Bogley, J E, 21, Co D, died July 4, diarrhea.
12458, Bohem, J, 14 cav, Co B, died Jan 14, '65, scorbutus.
9899, Boles, William, 89, Co C, died Sept 27, scorbutus.
10795, Bolton, N P, 100, Co B, died Nov 4, scorbutus.
10791, Boman, J, 108, Co D, died Oct 12, scorbutus.
3008, Boorem, O, 64, Co B, died July 7, diarrhea.
12621, Borem, M, 75, Co G, died Feb 9, '65, pleuritis.
11921, Bouser, G, 89, Co F, died Nov 8, scorbutus.
6475, Bowden, W, 9, Co F, died Aug 13, scorbutus.
6046, Bowen, A O, 113, Co C, died Aug 6, dysentery.
6943, Bowman, E, 123, Co F, died Aug 17, scorbutus.
9323, Boyd, B F, 6 cav, Co D, died Sept 25, diarrhea.
11678, Boyd, H P, 14, Co I, died Oct 31, scorbutus.
1971, Boyd, J E, 84, Co B, died June 15, diarrhea.
10984, Boyer, J, † 14, Co H, died Oct 16, diarrhea.
11729, Boyle, F, 4, Co B, died Nov 2, scorbutus.
12840, Bradford, D, 85, Co C, died April 25, '65, diarrhea.
4259, Branch, J, 38, Co C, died July 29, scorbutus.
1815, Brandiger, F, 24, Co K, died June 10, diarrhea.
1619, Brannock, C, † 79, Co K, died June 4, diarrhea.
1578, Brayheyer, H, 7 cav, Co M, died June 3, pneumonia.
8940, Brett, James, 88, Co K, died July 24, scorbutus.
1669, Brewer, Henry, † 24, Co C, died June 6, diarrhea.
6421, Brewer, H, 78, Co F, died Aug 22, scorbutus.
3264, Bridges, W H, 30, Co K, died July 13, debilitas.
9570, Bridges, W J, 122, Co F, died Sept 23, diarrhea.
1613, Bridewell, H C, 78, Co D, died June 4, diarrhea.
2367, Brinkey, Morris, † 16, Cav, Co L, died June 25, catarrh
3056, Britenyder, J, 65, Co O, died July 9, diarrhea.
2927, Brockhill, J, 4 cav, Co M, died July 5, scorbutus.
3717, Brookman J E, * 44, Co I, died July 21, diarrhea.
8911, Brothers, D, 48, Co H, died Sept 16, scorbutus.
9350, Brown, A F, † 73, Co C, died Sept 20, diarrhea.
12450, Brown, H, 15, Co F, died Jan 14, '65, scorbutus.
6978, Brown, J, 73, Co B, died Aug 17, cerebritis.
9011, Brown, J H, 12, Co F, died Sept 17, diarrhea.
6924, Brown, J M, 29, Co B, died Aug 17, enteritis.
6836, Brown, William, 1 cav, Co O, died Aug 26, dysentery.
8962, Brown, William, 16, Co C, died Sept 16, anasarca.
6256, Bryant, William C, 107, Co A, died Aug 20, scorbutus.
10763, Briden, E, 35, Co E, died Oct 12, dysentery.
6785, Buck, B F, 30, Co I, died Aug 15, wounds.
4963, Buchman, 16 cav, Co H, died Aug 7, dysentery.
10888, Buckmaster, J, 79, Co C, died Oct 13, scorbutus.
12362, Bullington, B, 74, Co F, died Dec 30, diarrhea.
6457, Burbles, G, 89, Co A, died Aug 12, fever intermittent.
4299, Burrows, J, 93, Co L, died July 30, diarrhea.
7065, Burns, John, 109, Co K, died Aug 28, diarrhea.
6936, Burns, H, † 16 cav, Co D, died Aug 17, scorbutus.
626, Burr, W B, 112, Co E, died April 13, diarrhea.
11556, Burton, O L, 35, Co I, died Nov 6, scorbutus.

No. of Grave.
11858, Butler, H J, 89, Co D, died Oct 10, scorbutus.
10302, Butler, N, * 89, Co D, died Oct 5, scorbutus.
8776, Butler, J, 89, Co A, died Sept 14, diarrhea.
11668, Button, A R, 79, Co E, died Oct 30, scorbutus.
9824, Butts, John, 22, Co F, died Sept 27, diarrhea.
636, Byres, George, 65, Co B, died April 19, '65, diarrhea.

12348, Cadding, J. C, 89, Co B, died Dec 27, scorbutus.
6356, Callahan, C, 39, Co F, died Aug 21, diarrhea.
6505, Campbell, J M, 120 Co G, died Aug 22, '65, diarrhea.
10026, Capell, C, 87, Co D, died Sept 29, diarrhea.
10257, Capsey, J, * 90, Co D, died Oct 3, scorbutus.
3556, Carl, C C, 38, Co H, died July 18, diarrhea.
666, Carroll, J, 3, Co H, died April 22, fever typhus.
7037, Carroll, J Q, * 78, Co I, died Aug 27, scorbutus.
3393, Carren, O, 38, Co H, died July 16, anasarca.
6693, Carlrt, Robert, 113, Co D, died Aug 24, diarrhea.
446, Cault, Albert, 116, Co A, died April 9, pneumonia.
1844, Castle, F, 103, Co E, died June 10, diarrhea.
7502, Center, E R, 115, Co H, died Sept 1, dysentery.
3907, Charles, R J, 5 cav, Co M, died July 24, diarrhea.
6109, Chase, E S, 23, Co C, died Aug 18, scorbutus.
9095, Chattonay, S, 82, Co H, died Sept 18, scorbutus.
10469, Chenly, S, 79, Co A, died Oct 7, scorbutus.
4319, Chitwood, Thos C, 16 cav, Co H, died July 30, diarrhea.
3205, Chlunworth, Wm, 9, Co G, died July 12, diarrhea.
10551, Choate, Wm, 6 cav, Co D, died Oct 10, scorbutus.
9925, Chunberg, A, 89, Co G, died Sept 28, scorbutus.
6935, Christiansen, J, 82, Co F, died Aug 26, anasarca.
7808, Clancey, J W, 38, Co E, died Sept 5, gangrene.
504, Clark, A E, 16 cav, Co M, died April 12, pneumonia.
7760, Clark, C, 51, Co K, died Sept 4, diarrhea.
9560, Clark, C, 29, Co B, died Sept 23, dysentery.
8834, Clark, F J, 6 cav, Co B, died Sept 15, scorbutus.
12672, Clark, R, 114, Co F, died Feb 18, '65, diarrhea.
6143, Clark, Wm, 14 cav, Co K, died Aug 9, dysentery.
9925, Cleaver, M, 3 cav, Co H, died Sept 28, scorbutus.
8750, Cleggett, M*, 36, Co I, died Sept 14, dysentery.
5787, Cline, John, 12 cav, Co I, died Aug 15, diarrhea.
12726, Cline, M, 14, Co B, died March 4, '65, diarrhea.
12051, Cline, T, 15, Co E, died Nov 16, scorbutus.
2287, Clusterman, —— 16 cav, Co D, died June 21, diarrhea a.
2048, Coalman, H, 16 cav, June 15, diarrhea
2753, Colbern, M, 73, Co I, died July 1, diarrhea.
2344, Colburn, Thomas, 16 cav, Co G, died June 20, diarrhea
6597, Colburn, William, 16 cav, Co G, died Aug 14, scorbutus.
300, Cole, John, 112, Co E, died April 1, diarrhea.
7211, Cole, W H, 112, Co A, died Aug 29, diarrhea c.
6971, Culler, John, 8, Co B, died Aug 27, diarrhea.
256, Collins, Wm, 93, Co G, died March 30, fever typhus.
1108, Coddington, M J, 93, Co G, died May 18, dysentery.
11710, Compton, H H, 21, Co K, died Nov 1, scorbutus.
2033, Couret, D, 78, Co F, died July 5, diarrhea.
4683, Covey, J, 38, Co I, died Aug 4, scorbutus.
2759, Corey, O C, 108, Co D, died July 1, diarrhea.
6738, Cornelius, Jas, 9 cav, Co H, died Aug 24, diarrhea.
3856, Corwin, J, 7 cav, Co K, died July 24, diarrhea.
3077, Corwin, J V, 6 cav, Co L, died July 20, dysentery.
6091, Cotton, J*, 100, Co H, died Aug 18, ictus solis.
9704, Craig, G, 23, Co B, died Sept 25, scorbutus.
9307, Craig, J, 38, Co I, died Sept 20, scorbutus.
12506, Craig, J, 2 artil, Co B, died Jan 22, '65, diarrhea.
9704, Craig, S, 23, Co B, died Sept 25, scorbutus.
10087, Craig, F, 9, Co K, died Sept 30, scorbutus.
1974, Crandall, W M, 93, Co A, died June 15, diarrhea.
2329, Crane, M, 23, Co E, died June 23, diarrhea c.
2253, Crawford, Wm, 16 cav, Co K, died June 21, diarrhea.
10012, Crelley, C W, 29, Co B, died Oct 14, anasarca.
4879, Cook, G P, 16 cav, Co L, died Aug 6, diarrhea.
12433, Crosbey, J, 90, Co C, died Jan 11, '65, scorbutus.
1417, Cross E, 111, Co C, died May 27, bronchitis.
8859, Cross, J D, 14 cav, Co I, died Sept 15, wounds.
7082, Cross, J T, 21, Co D, died Sept 6, scorbutus.
6744, Crouse, J, † 16, Co I, died Aug 24, dysentery.
2092, Crube, J, 79, Co D, died June 15, diarrhea c.
2179, Croman, George, 24, Co C, died June 19, diarrhea.
10026, Cupell C, 82, Co D, died Sept 29, diarrhea.
10257, Cupsay, J, * 90, Co D, died Oct 3, scorbutus.
3877, Curtis, A, 16, Co D, died July 24, diarrhea.

8626, Dake, G, * 100, Co D, died Sept 13, dysentery.
4663, Dalby, James, 73, Co H, died Aug 3, dysentery.
1820, Darling, D W, 93, Co B, died June 10, scorbutus.
10961, Darum, J J, 112, Co I, died Oct 15, scorbutus.
358, Davis, And, 112, Co A, died Apr 2, diarrhea.
8553, Davis, C, 112, Co E, died Sept 12, scorbutus.
10603, Davis, J, 113, D, died Oct 10, scorbutus.
4150, Davis, W, 16 cav, Co M, July 28, diarrhea.
4048, Davis, H, † 38, Co A, died July 27, dysentery.
12311, Delancey, L D, 2 artil, Co F, died Dec 9, scorbutus.
7013, Day, W F, 111, Co H, died Aug 27, wounds.

No. of Grave.
9073, Decker, C, 7 cav, Co M, died Sept 17, diarrhea.
4038, Decker, J P, 119, Co G, died Aug 3, dysentery.
7150, Demos, B F, 78, Co F, died Aug 29, diarrhea c.
2497, Denhart, W, 16 cav, Co K, died June 26, dysentery.
4422, Denioo, E, † 79, Co B, died July 31, diarrhea.
7514, Deming, Joseph, 31, Co D, died Sept 1, scorbutus.
12660, Denton, E, * 15, Co B, died Feb 16, '65, diarrhea.
2231, Dereeman, D, † 41, Co E died June 20, scorbutus.
6165, DePay, J W, 16, Co C, died Aug 9, scorbutus.
354, Derans, G W, 21, Co B, died April 2, diarrhea a.
2365, Dicks, Henry, 89, Co C, died June 23, dysentery.
12547, Dilley, A, 15, Co E, died Jan 28, '65, pneumonia.
1311, Dobson M, 13 cav, Co H, died May 23, diarrhea.
8187, Dock, C, 9 cav, Co H, died Sept 8, scorbutus.
3844, Dodd, G W, 21, Co F, died July 23, fever typhus.
4207, Dodson, R B, 6 cav, Co B, died July 29, diarrhea.
2867, Dooley, James, 16 cav, Co L, died July 4, fever remittent.
1441, Doran, W H, 78, Co I, died May 28, anasarca.
1103, Doren, C, 6, Co I, died Mar 15, diarrhea.
1727, Dowd, J W, 38, Co G, died June 8, dysentery.
1343, Dowdy, John, 16, Co K, died May 24, bronchitis.
10143, Dowell, J W, 112, Co K, died Oct 1, scorbutus.
10496, Downer, A, 24, Co H, died Oct 8, scorbutus.
12436, Doyle, P, 65, Co H, died Jan 11, '65, wounds.
12476, Doyle, J, 112, Co I, died Jan 17, '65, wounds.
5053, Drake, R R, 34, Co H, died Aug 8, diarrhea c.
10632, Dresser, C, 24, Co G, died Oct 4, diarrhea c.
9678, Drum, G, 89, died Sept 24, scorbutus.
3123, Dudley, J W, 80, Co F, died July 10, anasarca.
2666, Dumond, P, 35, Co E, died June 29, diarrhea.
9947, Dunn, Alexander, 75, Co A, died Sept 28, scorbutus.
12496, Dunsing, A, 39, Co C, died Jan 21, diarrhea.
9057, Dyer, J C, 30, Co D, died Sept 17, scorbutus.
12656, Drew, E, 53, Co D, died Feb 29, '05, rheumatism.

209, Eadley Levi, 26, Co H, died Mch 28, dysentery.
8045, Easinbeck, M, 109, Co D, died Sept 6, diarrhea.
10909, Easley, W A, * 21, Co G, died Oct 14, scorbutus.
6992, Eastman, Wm, 36, Co F, died Aug 17, marasmus.
4962, Edwards, C D, 51, Co K, died Aug 7, dysentery.
8084, Elliott, E I, 92, Co B, died Sept 7, diarrhea.
9703, Ellis William, 26, Co G, died Sept 25, diarrhea.
9754, Ellison, W, 14 cav, Co F, died Sept 25, diarrhea.
2249 Elsllo, James, 112, Co E, died July 24, anasarca.
4502, Emery, J, 22, Co K, died Aug 1, diarrhea.
4979, Emerson, J, 16 cav, Co L, died Aug 7, scorbutus.
9717, Erb, J, 9, Co C died Sept. 25, diarrhea.
12028, Ermalos, F, 11 cav, Co M, died Feb 14, '65, diarrhea.
214, Errickson C, 16 cav, Co M, died March 28, catarrh.
2211, Esch, W, 29, Co H, died June 20, asphyxia.
11727, Enrow, W, 7 cav, Co M, died Nov 1, dysentery.
2936, Evans, J, 9, Co C, died Sept 25, diarrhea.
8373, Eydroner, R, 74, Co F, died July 15, diarrhea.

6208, Fagan, O, 28, Co G, died Aug 20, marasmus.
2436, Fandish, S, 1 artil, Co A, June 25, diarrhea.
2230, Farmer, F, 21, Co A, died June 20, diarrhea.
4991, Farnham, C A, 51, Co D, Aug 7, diarrhea.
10740, Ferguson Louis, * 115, Co K, died Oct 14, diarrhea.
2512, Fele, R, 11, Co K, died June 20, diarrhea.
12026, Fermer, J, 14, Co M, died Feb 20, '65, diarrhea.
3854, Finch, F M, 21, Co G, died July 24, diarrhea.
10097, Fink, J P, 53, Co F, died Sept 30, scorbutus.
11541, Fish, J, 65, Co G, died Oct 27, scorbutus.
8345, Fisher, S F, 123, Co F, died Sept 27, diarrhea.
2129, Fitzgerald, H, 10 cav, Co I, died June 18, pneumonia.
9092, Flanagan J, 42, Co H, died Sept 29, scorbutus.
6072, Floyd, A, 7, Co A, died Aug 27, diarrhea.
10881, Ford, W J, † 17, Co I, died Oct 13, diarrhea.
101, Folk, A P, 112, Co G, died March 26, fever typhoid.
2564, Forney, D, 91, Co G, died June 27, scorbutus.
8239, Foster, A J, 16 cav, Co M, died Sept 8, diarrhea.
7720, Foster, B B, 112, Co G, died Sept 3, diarrhea.
12473, Foster, E S, * 9, Co A, died Jan 17, '65, scorbutus.
681, Fowler, John, 14, Co D, died April 13, diarrhea.
12275, Frame, W, 120, Co K, died Dec 17, diarrhea.
12837, Francis, J F, 12, Co I, died April 19, diarrhea.
5933, Franklin, H, 81, Co F, died Aug 17, enteritis.
432, Frass, Louis, 16, Co E, died April 8, pneumonia.
4031, Freeman, D, 11 cav, Co L, died July 26, bronchitis.
2080, French J, 129, Co B, died June 17, '63, diarrhea.
2210, Fritz, P, † 38, Co C, died June 20, scorbutus.
1055 Fremont, James, 7 cav, Co B, died May 18, diarrhea.
405, Fuller, Ira B, 112, Co D, died April 11, diarrhea.
6114, Funks, Wm, 26, Co F, died Sept 8, scorbutus.
2021, Furlough, H, 23, Co B, died June 15, diarrhea.

9026, Gaines, C, 20, Co B, died Sept 28, wounds.
1347, Gallagher, P, 21, Co C, died May 24, dysentery.
579, Garim, John, † 59, died April 16, diarrhea.
12301, Gerlock, D, 30, Co C, died March 30, '65, rheumatism.
1340, German, P, 24, Co G, died May 24, diarrhea.

No. of Grave.
1410, Gibson, H D, 93, Co K, died May 27, diarrhea c.
4201, Gibson, L F, 76, Co I, died July 20, dysentery.
4485, Gichina, J, † 16 cav, Co G, died Aug 1, dysentery.
1652, Giles, J V, 89, Co H, died June 5, colitis.
7988, Giles, S P, 112, Co A, died Sept 6, diarrhea.
6141, Gillespie, J W, 84, Co H, died Aug 0, dysentery.
1499, Gillgrease, J, 16 cav, Co I, died May 30, diarrhea.
1898, Gilmore, James, 16 cav, Co E, died June 12, diarrhea.
12731, Gleason, G M, 14 cav, Co A, died March 4, '65, diarrhea c.
1850, Gladwell, F, * 73, Co K, died June 11, diarrhea.
2901, Goffinet, P, 51, Co D, died June 15, diarrhea.
10307, Goddard, H, 89, Co G, died Oct 4, scorbutus.
4203, Gooles, H F, † 47, Co B, died July 29, scorbutus.
12847, Gordon, I, 114, Co B, died April 25, '65, diarrhea.
7953, Gore, F, 36, Co I, died Sept 5, dysentery.
7761, Gore, N, 16, Co C, died Sept 4, diarrhea.
6111, Garrig J, 78, Co F, died Aug 18, scorbutus.
12461, Gott, H, 29, Co C, died Jan 15, '65, scorbutus.
9403, Graber, J, 24, Co H, died Sept 21, diarrhea c.
9312, Graber, J F, 81, Co D, died Sept 20, diarrhea.
2164, Grace, W, 21, Co D, died June 19, diarrhea.
6117, Graham, M J, 41, Co E, died Aug 23, diarrhea.
10998, Gravel, J, 51, Co C, died Oct 16, scorbutus.
2942, Greadley, H, 20, Co A, died July 6, dysentery.
4560, Greathouse, J, 6, Co I, died Aug 2, diarrhea.
783, Greaves, George, 16, Co K, died Apr 28, diarrhea.
12110 Green, C, 79, Co A, died Nov 22, scorbutus.
11155, Green, John, 23, Co H, died Oct 19, scorbutus.
7856, Green, M, 9, Co C, died Sept 4, gangrene.
3111, Greenwald, B, 16 cav, Co L, died July 11, diarrhea.
11778, Greer, George, * 120, Co D, died Nov 3, scorbutus.
10594, Gress, J, 29, Co B, died Oct 19, diarrhea.
12834, Grimmins, M A, 42, Co H, died Apr 17, '65, diarrhea c.
4033, Griswold, J P, 79, Co E, died July 27, fever typhus.
2591, Grogan, H, 66, Co B, died June 26, dysentery.
10460, Grower, H, 42, Co K, died Oct 7, diarrhea.
3730, Gulk, P, 79, Co B, died July 21, scorbutus.
5025, Guyon, William, 72, Co E, died Aug 8, dysentery.
5961, Gonder, H, 16 cav, Co B, died Aug 17, enteritis

5074, Hageman, James, 16 cav, Co E, died Aug 8, diarrhea.
4094, Haggard, E, 16 cav, Co K, died July 27, diarrhea.
11959, Hagnis, W, 89, Co B, died Nov 11, scorbutus.
2825, Haines, Theodore, 14 cav, Co M, died July 3, diarrhea.
63, Haks, William, 16, Co E, died Mar 19, pneumonia.
11572, Hall, G H, 7 cav, Co B, died Oct 27, scorbutus.
12314, Hall, H C, * 41, Co D, died Dec 20, scorbutus.
7194, Hall, J L, 9, Co C, died Aug 29, dysentery.
12223, Hall, J L, 89, Co G, died Dec 4, scorbutus.
11833, Hall, Peter, * 103, Co D, died Nov 5, scorbutus.
10061, Haley, C H, 22, Co H, died Sept 30, scorbutus.
1241, Hallam, Wm, 82, Co H, died May 20, diarrhea c.
2695, Hanna, P, 21, Co G, died June 28, diarrhea c.
187, Hannah, H, * 191, Co C, died Mar 21, diarrhea a.
11188, Hansom, D, 39, Co E, died Oct 19, diarrhea a.
318, Harkon, John, 65, Co E, died Apr 2, diarrhea.
6684, Harlin, J C, 7, Co L, died Aug 24, scorbutus.
6113, Harrell, O, 120, Co K, died Aug 19, dysentery.
2633, Harrington, S M, 112, Co A, died June 29, diarrhea a.
11725, Harris, E K, 79, Co C, died Nov 1, scorbutus.
10447, Harris, G W, 9, Co G, died Oct 7, scorbutus.
8715, Harshman, Peter, 84, Co H, died Sept 14, scorbutus.
2677, Hart, George, 16 cav, Co K, died June 30, anasarca.
2202, Hart, W, 16 cav, Co K, died June 19, fever remittent.
1980, Harvey, E, 39, Co B, died June 15, pneumonia.
10608, Hathaway, S, 15 cav, Co B, died Oct 10, scorbutus.
12791, Hauch, L, 15, Co D, died Mch 18, '65, diarrhea.
8603, Hawkins, J W, 79, Co I, died Sept 12, scorbutus.
2126, Hayward, W G, * 16, Co I, died June 22, diarrhea.
5192, Hayworth, F, 7 cav, Co I, died Aug 10, scorbutus.
1852, Hegenberg, W, 24, Co F, died June 11 scorbutus.
8798, Helch, S, 77, Co K, died Sept 15, dysentery.
6480, Hendson, Geo B, 31, Co C, died Aug 22, diarrhea a.
1162, Henry, Wm P, 23, Co A, died July 17, diarrhea c.
6035, Herdson, Wm H, 107, Co C, died Aug 18, cerebritis.
8429, Herrell, Wm, 14 Cav, Co K, died Sept 11, scorbutus.
2365, Hess, H, 84, Co G, died June 27, diarrhea.
1906, Hester, John, 38, Co G, died June 13, diarrhea c.
7869, Hicks, George W, 65, Co F, died Sept 6, diarrhea
8303, Hicks, H, 11, Co G, died Sept 10, dysentery.
1102, Hicks, W, 85 Co D, died May 15, diarrhea.
12070, Highland, C, 14 cav, Co C, died Nov 17, wounds.
725, Hilderbrand, N, 24, Co G, died April 25, pneumonia.
8830, Hill, Aaron, 115, Co C, died Sept 15, scorbutus.
67, Hill, David, * 36, Co A, died March 19, bronchitis.
8721, Hill, Henry, 11, died Sept 14, diarrhea.
4499, Hill, J, 9 cav, Co F, died Aug 1, scorbutus.
12383, Hinchcliff, J, 8, Co B, died Feb 29, '65, diarrhea.
6117, Hoeo, Peter, 112, Co H, died Aug 19, diarrhea.
8825, Hoffman, J, 7 cav, Co I, died July 23, dysentery.
11847, Hofman, R, 35, Co C, died Nov 5, diarrhea.

No. of Grave.

2098, Hoo[illegible], Jas J, † 93, Co E, died June 17, scorbutus.
3255, Ho[illegible]p[illegible], I, 112, Co F, died July 13, dysentery.
98[illegible], Hos[illegible]on, A F, 38, Co F, died Sept 27, diarrhea.
9211 H[illegible]ner J, 38, Co F, died Sept 19, diarrhea.
12[illegible] Ho[illegible], P, 84, Co A, died Nov 19, scorbutus.
[illegible], [illegible], W, 16 cav, Co I, died March 21, pneumonia.
5812, H[illegible], D S, † 79, Co E, died Aug 16, diarrhea.
1[illegible], [illegible]d, G S,* 127, Co K, died Nov 3, scorbutus.
[illegible], Howel, [illegible] W, 78, Co F, died July 12.
1[illegible], Hoge, [illegible], 110, Co A, died Oct 21, diarrhea c.
[illegible], [illegible], C, 24, Co F, died Aug 15, scorbutus.
[illegible], [illegible], W H, 115, Co C, died Aug 18, cerebritis.
[illegible], H[illegible], D S, 125, Co H, died Sept 28, diarrhea.
12[illegible], H[illegible]se, A E, 14, Co D, died March 12, '65, ulcus.
1[illegible], H[illegible]g[illegible]od, S, 108, Co I, died Oct 19, scorbutus.
[illegible], H[illegible]nt[illegible]e, R, 89, Co F, died Aug 18, anasarca.
11[illegible], Harm[illegible], D, 81, Co C, died May 10, wounds.
11[illegible]2, H[illegible]rey, W B, 23, Co A, died May 16, diarrhea.
5[illegible], H[illegible]ch[illegible]s, S, 101, Co A, died Aug 8, scorbutus.
4[illegible], H[illegible]n[illegible], G F, † 92, Co D, died Aug 2, dysentery.
4[illegible]91, H[illegible]er, John, [illegible] cav, Co A, died July 27, dysentery.

3312, Iverson, J S, 16 cav, Co I, died July 14, diarrhea.

4132, Jacoarls, S A, † 29, Co E, died July 28, anasarca.
2658, Jackson, H, 51, Co C, died June 29, diarrhea a.
10 8[illegible], Jackson, M, 125, Co F, died Oct 4, scorbutus.
1274[illegible], Jenks, J P, 3 cav, Co A, died March 18, '65, diarrhea.
36[illegible] Jer[illegible]s, J, 73, Co K, died July 20, fever remit.
6[illegible] Jennings[illegible]n, O B, 30, Co E, died Aug 24, diarrhea.
1815 Jenny, E H,* 79, Co F, died June 11, diarrhea c.
21[illegible] Jewett, F, 14, Co A, died June 18, diarrhea c.
19[illegible] Johnson, C W, 7 cav, Co F, died June 15, diarrhea c.
945[illegible], Johnson, Joseph, 125, Co K, died Sept 21, scorbutus.
1412, Johnson, J S, 7, Co C, died May 27, diarrhea c.
5395, Johnson, Samuel, 100, Co B, died Aug 12, scorbutus.
9827, Jones, G W, 27, Co E, died Sept 27, scorbutus.
89[illegible]1, Jones, J, 117, Co E, died Sept 16, scorbutus.
48[illegible], Jones, P, 41, Co G, died Aug 6, dysentery.
641, Jones, Thomas, 112, Co F, died April 12, pneumonia.
2567, Jones, Thomas, 1 cav, Co F, died June 27, diarrhea c.
20[illegible] Jones, Wm, 27, Co D, died July 7, scorbutus.
17[illegible], Jordan, B W, 84, Co D, died June 9, dysentery.
915[illegible], Jordan, M, 38, Co C, died Sept 18, diarrhea.
29[illegible]1, Joy, B, 16, Co I, died July 6, diarrhea.
2241, Joyce, A, 90, Co D, died June 20, anasarca.
10513, Jas[illegible]ee, H, 7 cav, Co H, died Oct 8, dysentery.

12052, Kane, H, 95, Co A, died Nov 16, scorbutus.
4[illegible]8, Kampel, H, 29, Co H, died July 30, ictus solis.
47[illegible], Keefe, James P, 2 artil, Co M, died Aug 5, diarrhea.
8348, Keez[illegible], E, 20, Co G, died Sept 10, diarrhea c.
18 K[illegible], M R,* 49, Co D, died March 7, pneumonia.
7183, Kelley, John, 75, Co F, died Aug 29, scorbutus.
6795, Kelley, William, 94, Co I, died Aug 25, diarrhea c.
5518, Kennedy, M, 38, Co C, died Aug 13, scorbutus.
12188, Kent, J, 14, Co F, died Jan 10, '65, pleuritis.
5707, Kersey, John, 93, Co H, died Aug 15, scorbutus.
396, Kiger, John, 22, Co E, died April 6, pneumonia.
105[illegible], Kirkreat[illegible], J, 42, Co A, died Oct 8, scorbutus.
82, Kimball, James, 25 artil, Co L, died March 20, anasarca.
158, Kinkie, John, 16, Co G, died March 25, fever remitting.
[illegible], Kinderman, G, 82, Co D, April 26, dysentery.
7807, Kingham, J, 38, Co G, died Sept 4, scorbutus.
688 Kinehaus, D, 65, Co G, died April 23, diarrhea.
47[illegible], Keniggo, A, 113, Co C, died Aug 5, debilitas.
49[illegible], Knight, J, 9, Co H, died Aug 6, anasarca.
11891 Knowe, P, 108, Co E, died Nov 7, scorbutus.
47[illegible], Knoh[illegible], J, 16 cav, Co H, died Aug 4, diarrhea c.
2754, Krail, J, 10 cav, Co I, died July 1, scorbutus.
12[illegible]85, Kreiger, J, 14, Co E, died Feb 20, '65, debilitas.
652, Kaiser, John, 10, Co D, died April 20, fever typhus.
18[illegible]9 Kyser, John, 32, Co I, died June 10, diarrhea.

7027, Lacost, J M, 89, Co E, died Sept 5, anasarca.
72[illegible] Lach[illegible], J, 100, Co H, died Aug 23, scorbutus.
7155 Lambert, C, 38, Co D, died Aug 29, diarrhea c.
10419, Lamsley, W H, 78, Co A, died Oct 6, scorbutus.
12[illegible], La[illegible]ce, V, 59, Co D, died Nov 16, scorbutus.
12[illegible], Langley, G H, Co K, died Dec 12, scorbutus.
[illegible]9[illegible]8, Lanner, W A, 9 cav, Co E, died Aug 10, diarrhea c.
1[illegible]3, Law, Henry, 93, Co G, died May 20, diarrhea c.
[illegible]5, Lawrence, L G, 89, Co G, died Sept 24, scorbutus.
1[illegible]9 Lape, J, 125, Co A, died Oct 1, diarrhea.
1[illegible] Leatherm[illegible], M, 93, Co E, died Oct 14, scorbutus.
[illegible] Leach, W, 115, Co B, died Sept 11, scorbutus.
[illegible]2 Lee, A, 112, Co B, died July 28, diarrhea.
[illegible] Lee, P,* 16, Co A, died Sept 12, scorbutus.
[illegible] Lee, Thomas, 8, Co E, died May 9, diarrhea.
12[illegible], Lee, W E, 16 cav, Co I, died May 23, dysentery.
11258, Lewis, Charles, 79, Co A, died Oct 21, scorbutus.
6238, Lewis, Thomas, 2, Co L, died Aug 20, cerebritis.

No. of Grave.

10149, Lickey, J B, † 96, Co F, died Oct 1, scorbutus.
8255, Liday, J, 113, Co I, died Sept 9, dysentery.
6295, Liken, John, † 112, Co I, died Aug 20, scorbutus.
1685, Linday, B, 57, Co H, died June 6, diarrhea.
7768, Linderman, H A, 93, Co B, died Sept 4, dysentery.
6414 Lindsay, A, 113, Co D, died Aug 22, scorbutus.
1818, Linebergh, I,* 16, Co F, died June 10, pneumonia.
11440, Linwood, J, 79, Co F, died Oct 25, scorbutus.
12358, Lipsey, D,* 2 cav, Co C, died Dec 30, scorbutus.
10405, Lord, L B,* 112, Co B, died Oct 26, debilitas.
11222, Lorsam, C, 89, Co C, died Oct 20, scorbutus.
2268, Loudon, L, 16 cav, Co D, died June 21, diarrhea c.
1017, Lowry, Frank, 35, Co E, died May 11, dysentery.
2342, Lusk, John, 29, Co B, died June 23, diarrhea c.
1456, Lutz, John, 23, Co H, died May 29, pneumonia.
8196, Lyman, J, 100, Co D, died Sept 8, scorbutus.
11167, Lynch, V,* 38, Co C, died Oct 26, scorbutus.

10849, Mack, J, 14 cav, Co G, died Oct 13, dysentery.
5390, Madden, L, 96, Co D, died Aug 12, scorbutus.
11358, Maddock, J W, † 79, Co A, died Oct 23, scorbutus.
10982, Madrill, A, 12, Co A, died Oct 15, scorbutus.
3935, Malcolm, J R, 38, Co K, died July 25, diarrhea a.
2868, Manning, A, 215, Co A, died July 4, debilitas.
953, Manty, P, † 16 cav, Co E, died May 8, diarrhea.
2050, Markman, Wm, 16 cav, Co K, died June 16, diarrhea c.
6333, Marritt, H, 16 cav, Co L, died Aug 21, scorbutus.
2762, Marshall, A,* 96, Co C, died July 2, diarrhea c.
8444, Martin, A, 16 cav, Co L, died May 28, pneumonia.
4071, Martin, I, 9, Co K, died July 27, diarrhea.
12757, Masman, S, 42, Co G, died March 12, '65, diarrhea.
863, Mason, Thos B, 93, Co B, died May 3, dysentery.
1428, Massey, W F, 111, Co D, died May 28, diarrhea c.
746, Master, Wm, 12, Co A, died April 26, dysentery.
429, Mathening, A D, † 79, Co I, died April 8, pneumonia.
12744, Matthews, F M, 32, Co G, died March 7, '65, diarrhea.
1061, Maxem, H C, 19, Co H, died May 13, diarrhea.
3280, Maxwell, S, 8 cav, Co C, died July 13, dysentery.
10019, May, M H, 89, Co I, died Sept 29, scorbutus.
3100, McCamphell, D, 104, Co B, died July 10, diarrhea a.
56, McCleary, Thos, 16 cav, Co L, died March 17, pneumonia.
1315, McClusky, James, 16 cav, Co K, died May 27, diarrhea.
4850, McCray, A, 103, Co A, died Aug 6, dysentery.
1617, McCready, Wm, 96, Co C, died June 4, anasarca.
6513, McCreary, J, 119, Co C, died Aug 22, pleuritis.
5724, McCone, R, 16 Cav, Co K, died Aug 15, scorbutus.
3050, McCunne, H, 13, Co C, died July 8, diarrhea c.
3470, McEntire, L, 10 cav, Co K, died July 17, dysentery.
5283, McGee, Wm, 30, Co D, died Aug 11, wounds.
11623, McGivens, J, 119, Co A, died Oct 28, scorbutus.
11[illegible]52, McLarens, B, 89, Co A, died Nov 10, scorbutus.
1634, McLaughlin, B, 90, Co I, died June 5, scorbutus.
3109, McLlug, Benj,* 23, Co E, died July 11, diarrhea.
4725, McMahon, M, 93, Co E, died Aug 4, diarrhea.
1337, McMillan, W B,* 112, Co E, died May 24, pleuritis.
9733, McMiller, W B, 78, Co D, died Sept 25, scorbutus.
692, McShaw, B, 80, Co B, died April 23, diarrhea.
9710, McWorthy, W M, 92, Co G, died Sept 25, diarrhea c.
3270, Mead, G, 19, Co H, died July 14, bronchitis.
4[illegible]48, Medler, H, 38, Co I, died Aug 3, scorbutus.
6266, Mee, William, 51, Co C, died Aug 20, ictus solis.
2177, Meher, Charles, 16 cav, Co F, died June 19, diarrhea a.
2019, Mercen[illegible]er, Chas, 93, Co A, died June 16, diarrhea c.
2637, Merritt, F, † 89, Co F, died June 29, scorbutus.
7464, Merg, F, 44, Co K, died Sept 1, diarrhea a.
9145, Meyors, A,* 24, Co H, died Sept 19, scorbutus.
5608, Meyers, J, 24, Co K, died Aug 14, diarrhea.
2297, Meyers, J K, 110, Co C, died June 17, diarrhea c.
5[illegible]2, Meyers, Samuel, 25, Co A, died Aug 12, fever intermittens.
9188, Miller, F,* 16, Co B, died Sept 18, scorbutus.
3159, Miller, H, 92, Co F, died July 10, pneumonia.
11721, Miller, J, 21, Co C, died Nov 1, scorbutus.
2257, Miller, J M, † 31, Co I, died June 21, diarrhea c.
9795, Miller, M, 92, Co A, died Sept 27, scorbutus.
4515, Miller, Mac, 16 cav, Co C, died Aug 18, diarrhea a.
3955, Mills, N, 11, Co K, died July 25, scorbutus.
10721, Mills, S, 14 cav, Co F, died Oct 14, wounds.
7989, Mind, D, 6, Co D, died Sept 6, diarrhea a.
381, Mitchan, A, 92, Co E, died April 5, diarrhea.
11617, Mitchell, J R, 89, Co G, died Oct 27, scorbutus.
9753, Mix, C, 22, Co C, died Sept 25, scorbutus.
4680, Mixwell, L B, 38, Co F, died Aug 4, dysentery.
4526, Moneeal, J, 21, Co G, died Aug 2, diarrhea a.
2640, Morehead, J, 9, Co E, died June 29, diarrhea c.
2539, Morley, H, 16 cav, Co M, died June 26, diarrhea c.
9187, Moran, F, 89, Co C, died Sept 18, diarrhea.
7428, Moran, W, 11, Co C, died Aug 31, anasarca.
10615, Morbly, B, 48, Co H, died Oct 11, diarrhea a.
6402, Mountz, R, 6, Co B, died Aug 21, diarrhea.
3293, Morris, B, 8 cav, Co F, died July 13, pneumonia.
816, Morris, J, 15, Co H, died April 30, dysentery.

ILLINOIS.

No. of Grave.

1320, Morris, James, 66, Co K, died May 23, diarrhea.
12757, Mossman, S, 42, Co O, died March 12, '65, diarrhea c.
2933, Mulford, W R,‡ 23, died July 7, diarrhea c.
2844, Munkey, D, 69, Co D, died July 3, dysentery.
11900, Munz, P, 14, Co I, died Nov 7, wounds.
59, Myers, Charles, 16 cav, Co B, died March 16, pleuritis.
3080, Myers, C H,* 24, Co F, died July 9, anasarca.
5038, Myers, F, 16 cav, Co L, died Aug 8, dysentery.
1407, Meyers, P, 24, Co F, died May 27 diarrhea c.

438, Nashen, Ed, 65, Co A, died April 8, diarrhea c.
283, Neal Joseph, 10, Co K, died April 1, diarrhea.
7450, Needham, [illegible] H,† 42, Co K, died Sept 1, diarrhea.
9531, Nelson, J,* 3, Co K, died Sept 22, scorbutus.
8160, Newberg, H, 22, Co F, died Sept 8, diarrhea.
299, Newbery, Wm, 2 art, Co M, died April 1, pneumonia.
6778, Newby, E, 123, Co A, died Aug 15, diarrhea c.
8129, N[illegible]w[illegible]n, H, 25, Co B, died Sept 8, scorbutus.
4896, Nicely, F, 82, Co A, died Aug 6, diarrhea.
6945, Nichols, L C, 14, Co F, died Aug 26, scorbutus.
7847, Nicholson, R H, 123, Co B, died Sept 4, diarrhea a.
7086, Nugent, T, 108, Co E, died Aug 28, diarrhea c.
12460, Nully, C, 120, Co A, died Jan 15, '65, scorbutus.

6519, Obevre, O B,* 112, Co C, died Aug 22, diarrhea a.
10551, O'Brian, D, 89, Co C, died Oct 13, scorbutus.
11274, Ochley, Wm, 24, Co K, died Oct 20, scorbutus.
3847, O'Connor, M, 2, Co F, died July 24, scorbutus.
1921, O'Dean, Thomas, 78, Co F, died June 14, diarrhea c.
1533, O'David J H, 9, Co A, died June 1, diarrhea c.
7751, O'Donnell, 34, Co I, died Sept 3, scorbutus.
[illegible]609, O[illegible]oin, W, 9, Co G, died July 19, scorbutus.
1592, Oglesby, D, 16 cav, Co M, died May 31, diarrhea c.
1214, O'Keefe, M, 2, artil, Co G, died May 19, diarrhea.
7856, Olderfield, J R, 6 cav, Co B, died Sept 5, debilitas.
9101, Oley, O S,* 21, Co I, died Sept 18, diarrhea c.
10142, Omny, A, 108, Co K, died Sept 29, diarrhea a.
9885, Olson, J, 112, Co K, died Sept 27, scorbutus.
6098, Olson, J, 89, Co D, died Aug 18, diarrhea c.
39, O'Neil, D, 16 cav, Co K, died April 19, small pox.
10469, Osborn, J W, 9, Co H, died Oct 7, diarrhea c.
6774, Oss, 89, Co D, died Aug 25, diarrhea a.
4123, Otway, D, 8 cav, Co A, died July 28, dysentery.
8414, Owens, C, 120, died Sept 11, diarrhea.
10279, O'M[illegible]oc, D J,* 9 cav, Co E, died Oct 3, scorbutus.

5541, Padon C, 12, Co F, died Aug 13, diarrhea.
6005, Paine, S, 84, Co B, died Aug 18, scorbutus.
3408, Paisley, F F, 120, Co E, died July 16, dysentery.
6301, Parshall, J M, 114, Co A, died Aug 20, diarrhea c.
6303, Partridge, W J,† 30, Co F, died Aug 20, wounds.
12357, Parkhurst, B, 14, Co H, died Dec 30, scorbutus.
12677, Patterson, F J, 14, Co F, died Feb 19, '65, diarrhea c.
393, Penoy, James, 14 cav, Co D, died April 6, diarrhea c.
12707, Penny, W, 114, Co F, died Feb 26, '65, diarrhea c.
7700, Peeter, H M, 107, Co C, died Sept 3, diarrhea.
2621, Perkins, A E, 89, Co A, died June 28, fever typhus.
4853, Perry George, 89, Co G, died Aug 6, fever intermittent.
9313, Perry, J, 9 cav, Co G, died Sept 20, diarrhea c.
8953, Perry, N, 1 cav, Co B, died July 18, debilitas.
12179, Peterson, J B, 112, Co I, died Nov 27, anasarca.
1686, Pettias, Wm, 65, Co I, died June 6, diarrhea c.
6880, Pettijohn, J, 21, Co F, died Aug 16, diarrhea.
12694, Phillbrook, A,† 17 cav, Co F, died Feb 5, '65, diarrhea c.
410, Phillips, Wm,* 16 cav, Co L, died April 6, diarrhea.
4587, Pierce, Charles,* 16 cav, Co H, died Aug 6, scorbutus.
1506, Pierce, W B, 8, cav, Co H, died May 31, diarrhea c.
3764, Place, S, 44, Co F, died July 22, dysentery.
10059, Plamerly, H, 14, Co D, died Sept 30, scorbutus.
3679, Porterlinge, Wm, 24, Co K, died July 24, diarrhea.
1862, Pollard, F, 127, Co A, died June 12, diarrhea c.
9602, Post, George, 7 cav, Co L, died Sept 23, diarrhea a.
6783, Powell, A, 122, Co C, died Aug 15, diarrhea.
3058, Powell, D, 16 cav, Co K, died July 9, diarrhea a.
3422, Powers, James, 44, Co C, died July 16, diarrhea.
23, Preston, C W, 8 cav, Co M, died March 8, pneumonia.
6007, Price, J M, 79, Co D, died Aug 17, diarrhea c.
9159, Prickett, F, 30, Co E, died Sept 17, scorbutus.
12591, Pratt, W, 16, Co F, died Feb 6, '65, diarrhea c.
10863, Prime, D, 103, Co K died Oct 14, scorbutus.
7972, Puck, John, 122, Co D, died Sept 5, scorbutus.
1143, Pulfer, Fred, 27, Co A, died May 16, diarrhea.
10412, Pyoer, T, 89, Co D, died Oct 6, scorbutus.

10531, Quinn, P, 52, Co A, died Oct 8, scorbutus.

3039, Ralston, John, 79, Co I, died July 8, fever remittent.
1011, Ramsay, J, C, 21, Co B, died May 10, diarrhea.
1765, Ramsey, A B, 45, Co K, died June 9, diarrhea.
12763, Ramsey, T J, 79, Co A, died Mar 12, '65, scorbutus.
10772, Randall, C F, 124, Co I, died Oct 12, scorbutus.

8578, Rankin, W A,* 3 cav, Co I, died Sept 12, diarrhea a.
12680, Ransom, J, 4 cav, Co B, died Feb 19, '65, diarrhea a.
7604, Renny, J H,‡ 6 cav, Co B, died Sept 2, diarrhea c.
6968, Redmont, John, 112, Co H, died Aug 17, diarrhea a.
8571, Reed, A, 98, Co I, died Sept 12, dysentery.
3496, Reed, D, 26, Co H, died July 18, scorbutus.
12324, Richardson, T, 34, Co E, died Dec 23, scorbutus.
1616, Richards, H, 79, Co I, died June 4, scorbutus.
3809, Rickold, W, 16, Co G, died July 23, scorbutus.
2836, Rictor, Charles,* 82, Co H, died July 3, diarrhea.
8632, Ripley, J, 9, Co B, died Sept 13, gangrene.
7748, Ritter, D, 14 art, Co D, died Sept 3, diarrhea a.
2074, Roberts, W W, 16 cav, Co I, died June 17, anasarca.
8416, Robinson, E, H, 36, Co A, died Sept 11, anasarca.
4460, Robinson, H B,‡ 6 cav, Co B, died Aug 1, diarrhea.
6080, Robinson, J B, 79, Co A, died Aug 18, cerebritis.
10751, Roder, F, 16 cav, Co G, died Oct 12, scorbutus.
2596, Rodenberger, N, 96, Co E, died June 29, scorbutus.
10184, Roferty, J O, 6 cav, Co H, died Oct 1, diarrhea a.
747, Rodgers, O, 12, Co A, died Apr 25, dysentery.
1807, Rogers, Silas, 65, Co D, died June 10, diarrhea c.
7228, Rogers, George, 16 cav, Co G, died June 29, diarrhea c.
528, Rolls, E J, 103, Co G, died Apr 13, diarrhea.
4389, Rosecrans, H, 113, Co A, died July 31, anasarca.
11473, Ross, J W, 45, Co F, died Oct 26, dysentery.
8465, Ross, Thomas, 113, Co K, died Sept 11, scorbutus.
306, Rudd, Ernst, 100, Co K, died Apr 2, diarrhea.
1204, Rudd, F, 16 cav, Co L, died May 23, diarrhea c.
2557, Ryan, M, 89, Co A, died June 27, phthisis.

2000, Saddle, M, 27, Co G, died June 15, anasarca.
9245, Saler, J B,† 14, Co F, died Sept 20, diarrhea a.
10512, Saudler, L,* 19, Co D, died Oct 8, diarrhea.
11289, Sargeant, M,† 14, Co K, died Oct 22, scorbutus.
1902, Savage, P P, 13, died June 13, diarrhea c.
9915, Sauin, B, 30, Co C, died Sept 28, scorbutus.
7558, Schrider, D, 23, Co A, Sept 2, dysentery.
7163, Schrider, John, 44, Co K, died Aug 29, diarrhea c.
3493, Schannoller, C, 24, Co H, died July 17, dysentery.
10359, Schurtz, W, 44, Co F, died Oct 5, scorbutus.
1573, Scitaz, Victor, 16 cav, Co L, died June 3, dysentery.
11077, Scott, H, 28, Co G, died Oct 17, scorbutus.
4524, Scuyner, N,* 64, Co O, died Aug 2, wounds.
12034, See, S, 11, Co G, died Oct 15, scorbutus.
1757, Seeley, Charles, 44, Co G, died June 10, diarrhea c.
9325, Sem, C, 8 cav, Co D, died Sept 20, diarrhea c.
4972, Serens, R B, 112, Co I, died Aug 6, dysentery.
1333, Setters, Geo H, 38, Co G, died May 24, diarrhea c.
12827, Seward, R, 61, Co E, died Apr 8, '65, diarrhea.
5350, Seybert, A J, 39, Co E, died Aug 11, scorbutus.
9322, Shadrach, G H, 7 cav, Co C, died Sept 20, diarrhea c.
1661, Shaobach, Ed, 44, Co E, died June 6, anasarca.
8861, Shark, L F, 113, Co D, died Sept 15, diarrhea a.
12149, Sharp, A, 7 cav, Co B, died Nov 24, scorbutus.
2579, Sharp, A H, 22, Co A, died June 27, dysentery.
1899, Sharp, E D T, 89, died June 15, diarrhea.
2647, Shaw, J, 89, Co E, died June 29, dysentery.
7315, Shaw, Joseph, 98, Co D, died Aug 30, scorbutus.
4135, Sheehy, John,‡ 42, Co G, died July 28, diarrhea c.
8386, Sherwood, J F, 16 cav, Co I, died Sept 10, diarrhea c.
7270, Shields, J A, 6 cav, Co E, died Aug 30, scorbutus.
12046, Siebert, H C, 7 cav, Co M, died Nov 16, scorbutus.
10441, Siffle, H, 7 cav, Co M, died Oct 7, scorbutus.
2430, Silkwood, H M, 89, Co D, died June 24, epilepsy.
1777, Silter, John, 16 cav, Co I, died June 9, anasarca.
12713, Simmons, W D, 42, Co H, died March 1, '65, diarrhea.
7680, Simpson, C, 14, Co D, died Sept 2, diarrhea c.
12834, Simmons, M A, 42, Co H, died April 17, '65, diarrhea.
309, Sipple, A, 107, Co E, died April 2, diarrhea.
12390, Skinner, H, 14, Co C, died Jan 4, '65, diarrhea c.
10082, Skinner, Wm, 16, Co G, died Sept 30, scorbutus.
2585, Slasher, H,* 96, Co E, died June 28, scorbutus.
10663, Slick, P, 9, Co E, died Oct 11, diarrhea c.
9402, Smith, C W, 16, Co K, died Sept 24, diarrhea.
6960, Smith, George, 63, Co E, died Aug 17, dysentery.
362, Smith, John B, 7 cav, Co L, died April 2, diarrhea.
12566, Smith, J S, 115, Co D, died Feb 1, '65, debilitas.
10866, Smith, N P, 28, Co G, died Oct 13, scorbutus.
10975, Smith, O, 114, Co H, died Oct 15, scorbutus.
4650, Smith, William, 16 cav, Co M, died Aug 3, gastritis.
8223, Snyder, B, 6 cav, Co B, died Sept 8, diarrhea.
8079, Sommers, W, 40, Co F, died Sept 7, diarrhea.
2165, Soma, C, 82, Co A, died June 10, diarrhea c.
4283, Spangler, H J, 16 cav, Co L, died July 30, diarrhea.
9092, Spindler, W, 113, Co F, died Sept 18, diarrhea.
11259, Sprulock, A, 70, Co E, died Oct 23, scorbutus.
4598, Sprague, W, 8 cav, Co K, died Aug 3, diarrhea.
1667, Springer, M, 112, Co E, died June 6, diarrhea c.
12132, Stellhoult, A, 92, Co H, died Nov 23, wounds.
2532, Standsfield, H, 96, Co H, died June 26, diarrhea.
1718, Stark, F, 78, Co H, died June 8, dysentery.

No. of Grave.
1018, Stegall, J, 16 cav, Co L, died May 11, diarrhea.
10757, Stevens, S, 44, Co D, died Oct 11, diarrhea c.
6292, Stewart, F, 78, Co I, died Aug 20, scorbutus.
4878. Stillwell, F H, 79, Co L, died Aug 6, scorbutus.
1640, Stillwell, James, 38, Co I, died June 5, fever remittent.
10828, Stine, A, 14, Co H, died Oct 13, scorbutus.
4724, Stopes, S W, 80, Co E, died Aug 4, scorbutus.
8151, Storem, A, 89, Co D, died Sept 11, scorbutus.
12199, Storem, C, 98, Co C, died Nov 29, scorbutus.
10440, Strand, John, 9, Co H, died Oct 6, diarrhea.
8519, Striker, J, 11, Co K, died Sept 12, scorbutus.
12822, Stringer, P, 15, Co B, died April 5, '65, diarrhea.
9515, Strong, S M, 93, Co B, died Sept 17, diarrhea.
865, Strue, S L, 40, Co O, died May 3, diarrhea c.
8615, Sullivan J, 16 cav, Co I, died Sept 13, diarrhea.
12482, Sullivan M, 15, Co E, died Jan 17, '65, debilitas.
9625, Sunn, C, 8 cav, Co D, died Sept 20, diarrhea.
11808, Suter, B F, 4 cav, Co L, died Nov 4, scorbutus.
5515, Sutton, M, 9 cav, Co M, died Aug 13, diarrhea.
4442, Swanson, P, 9, Co K, died July 31, dysentery.
12725, Steinhaus, J, 15, Co B, died March, 3, '65, diarrhea.
6292, Steward F, 78, Co I, died Aug 20, scorbutus.
12557, Swarts, E, * 24, Co G, died Jan 30, '65, scorbutus.
6105, Swartz, A, 7 cav, Co M, died Aug 18, diarrhea.
535, Sweet, Wm, 89, Co E, died April 12, rheumatism.

10515, Turner, J, ——, Co A, died Oct 8, scorbutus.
502, Taylor, George, 16 cav, Co M, died April 12, pneumonia.
10036, Taylor, H, * 7 cav, Co I, died Sept 29, scorbutus.
809, Taylor James, 4 cav, Co F, died April 30, diarrhea.
12526, Taylor, M P, 14, Co I, died Jan 26, '65, rheumatism.
1825, Temple, I, 100, Co H, died June 10, diarrhea.
4466, Terry, John, 16 cav, Co M, died Aug 1, diarrhea c.
12437, Thayer, D, 64, Co E, died Jan 12, '65, rheumatism.
2415, Thomas, A, 10, Co A, died June 24, debilitas.
10411, Thompson, D, 24, Co K, died Oct 6, scorbutus.
6191, Thompson, F, 10, Co B, died Aug 22, diarrhea.
7128, Thompson, G O, 1 cav, Co M, died Aug 28, '63, scorbutus.
2453, Thompson, John, 16 cav, Co I, died June 25, diarrhea.
6831, Thompson, T, 2, Co M, died Aug 25, scorbutus.
10347, Thomsburg, N C, 79, Co A, died Oct 5, fever typhus.
8803, Thorn, J, 16 cav, Co K, died Sept 15, dysentery.
9833, Thurman, J, 84, Co E, died Sept 27, scorbutus.
46, Tuler, W, 16 cav, Co D, died March 15, pneumonia.
2064, Topp, A, 19, Co C, died July 9, anasarca.
547, Trafler, Van Buren, 16 cav, Co I, died April 14, pneumonia.
11550, Trask J J, 7 cav, Co B, died Oct 27, scorbutus.
751, Trowbridge, L, 16 cav, Co M, died April 20, diarrhea.
1915, Trout, E, 21, Co F, died June 14, diarrhea.
2502, Turnerholm, S H, 19, Co K, died June 26, diarrhea c.
3032, Tucker, E, 38, Co B, died July 8, diarrhea.
12736, Tucker, J, 7, Co F, died March 6, '65, debilitas.
10832, Tucker, J P, 8 cav, Co G, died Oct 13, scorbutus.
10958, Turner, S, 120, Co A, died Oct 16, gangrene.

11091, Underwood, D, 11, Co E, died Oct 18, diarrhea.

5183, Vase, ——, 16 cav, Co H, died Aug 9, dysentery.
1078, Vaugh, James, 16 cav, Co L, died May 14, diarrhea.
7765, Vincent, L D, 7 cav, Co G, died Sept 4, diarrhea.
1026, Voris, Rose, 16 cav, Co I, died May 11, diarrhea c.
3271, Volter, George, 9, Co C, died July 13, diarrhea c.
2015, Vought, Wm, 24, Co H, died July 15, diarrhea.

No. of Grave.
5638, Vox, Wm, 24, Co E, died Aug 14, diarrhea.

6767, Waddle, J, † 112, Co C, died Aug 24, scorbutus.
2964, Wahl, M, 16 cav, Co I, died July 8, diarrhea c.
9218, Walker, George, 31, Co K, died Sept 10, scorbutus.
12072, Ward, R S, 15, Co C, died Nov 18, fever intermittent.
11345, Ward, G B, 7 cav, Co E, died Nov 23, scorbutus.
2488, Ward, W J, 16 cav, Co M, died June 26, diarrhea.
12392, Wareck, N, 120, Co D, died Jan 4, '65, scorbutus.
7895, Warkwich, J, 93, Co C, died Sept 5, scorbutus.
5898, Watts, Wm, 16 cav, Co L, died Aug 16, diarrhea.
11619, Waterman, L, 95, Co D, died Nov 28, scorbutus.
6173, Weaver, G, 16 cav, Co L, died Aug 19, scorbutus.
9317, Weaver, Alex, 93, Co A, died Sept 20, diarrhea.
742, Weeks, Benj, 16 cav, Co L, died Apr 26, diarrhea.
10765, Weedman, J. W, * 38, Co I, died Oct 12, scorbutus.
4911, Weinmuller, John, † 56, Co G, died Aug 7, debilitas.
10001, Welch, John, 7, Co E, died Sept 29, diarrhea.
11751, Welch, L, 24, Co F, died Nov 2, scorbutus.
10085, Welch, G, † 95, Co A, died Sept 20, scorbutus.
4758, Wentworth, Charles, 27, Co D, died July 31, fever remittent.
7426, Westbrook, B D, 6 cav, Co B, died Aug 31, gangrene.
3967, Whalin, M, 23, Co E, died July 9, scorbutus.
5910, Wham, T, 21, Co G, died July 24, scorbutus.
9184, Wheeler, J, 61, Co F, died Sept 18, diarrhea.
992, Wheelock, A, 96, Co H, died May 10, anasarca.
1496, Whitmore, B, 16 cav, Co D, died May 31, anasarca.
1699, Whitmore, L, 104, Co I, died June 7, diarrhea.
5998, Whitney, J F, 89, Co G, died Aug 17, diarrhea.
8713, Whipp, Charles, 9 cav, Co E, died Sept 14, scorbutus.
5613, Wildberger, P, 6 cav, Co B, died Aug 14, diarrhea.
5158, Wiley, T, 7, Co M, died May 15, dysentery.
12732, Wiley, W P, 32, Co C, died March 5, '65, scorbutus.
12071, Wilkes, R, 81, Co A, died Feb 18, '65, diarrhea.
7840, Wilhelm, G A, 9, Co C, died Sept 4, gangrene.
90, Will, Gustavus, 16 cav, Co E, died March 21, pneumonia.
9785, Will, J, 36, Co B, died Sept 26, diarrhea c.
8310, Williams, A, 22, Co H, died Sept 10, scorbutus.
3254, Williams, E, 49, Co D, died July 13, pneumonia.
10899, Williams, G W, 15 battery, died Oct 14, scorbutus.
11497, Williams, G B, 15, Co B, died Oct 26, diarrhea.
12780, Willis, A P, 84, Co A, died March 15, '65, diarrhea.
4737, Wilson, D, 16 cav, Co M, died Aug 4, scorbutus.
9551, Wilson, J, * Co K, died Sept 22, scorbutus.
11712, Wilson, W, † 89, Co F, died Nov 15, diarrhea.
1130, Wimmer, G, 16 cav, Co I, died May 15, pneumonia.
969, Wink, Lewis, 16 cav, Co C, died May 10, fever remittent.
8755, Winning, D, 125, Co C, died Sept 14, diarrhea.
6079, Winters, Wm, 24, Co H, died Aug 18, scorbutus.
3743, Wismer, J, * 74, Co G, died July 21, scorbutus.
2301, Wing, John, 7 cav, Co H, died June 22, diarrhea.
8815, Wood, 21, Co G, died Sept 15, dysentery.
1042, Woodcock, H, 16 cav, Co L, died May 12, diarrhea.
3695, Workman, James, 7, Co G, died July 21, diarrhea.
10582, Worthy, A A, 21, Co K, died Oct 10, dysentery.
2064, Wright, J W, 35, Co C, died June 28, diarrhea c.
6205, Wright, M, 69, Co E, died Aug 10, fever intermittent.

12309, Yates, J, 120, Co E, died Dec 19, diarrhea.
10766, Yagle, C, 24, Co B, died Oct 12, scorbutus.

2301, Zimmerman, Philip, 1 artil, died June 24, diarrhea.
72, Zoran, Philip, 44, Co I, died March 20, pneumonia.

INDIANA.

671, Allen, Jessie, * 116, Co K, died April 16, dysentery c.
1937, Adkins, George, 6 cav, Co D, died June 14, scorbutus.
3991, Andrews, E L, 6 cav, Co K, died July 26, anasarca.
4270, Anderson, D, 76, Co E, died July 29, diarrhea.
6680, Ault, J W, 40, Co D, died Aug 14, diarrhea.
6921, Alexander, S, 93, Co D, Aug 26, scorbutus.
7124, Alexander, J D, 5 cav, Co K, died Aug 28, scorbutus.
9292, Auburn, C, 65, Co H, died Sept 19, diarrhea.
9445, Atkins, J F, 2 cav, Co H, died Sept 21, diarrhea.
9584, Adams, H, 35, Co A, died Sept 23, diarrhea.
9643, Allen, D B, † 29, died Sept 24, gangrene.
9759, Alfred, W J, 117, Co K, died Sept 25, scorbutus.
10473, Allyn, D, 88, Co K, died Oct 7, scorbutus.
10793, Atland, C, 32, Co C, died Oct 12, scorbutus.
11190, Albin, I, 89, Co D, died Oct 19, diarrhea.
12183, Austin, Alfred, 5, Co K, died Nov. 27, scorbutus.
12513, Amick, W, 82, Co B, died Jan 23, '65, scorbutus.
513, Bush, David, 117, Co C, died April 2, pneumonia.
676, Bee, Thomas, cav, died April 16, dysentery c.
696, Bock, Samuel, 75, Co I, died April 17, dysentery c.
839, Brown, T, 66, Co D, died May 1, diarrhea.
1514, Barrey, Henry, 84, Co D, died May 31, dysentery.
1603. Boley, A J, 66, Co C, died June 4, diarrhea c.
1759, Barra, John, 65, Co H, died June 9, diarrhea c.
2610, Burnett, Wm, 6 cav, Co G, died June 15, diarrhea.
2191, Buckhart, E, 27, Co F, died June 19, diarrhea.
2222, Brasler, S, musician, 10, Co I, died June 20, diarrhea.
2299, Bumgardner, 44, Co D, died June 22, diarrhea.
2458, Barrett, E, 42, Co I, died June 25, diarrhea c.
2874, Bowman, John, 42, Co C, died July 4, diarrhea.
3044, Bruce, J W, 5 cav, Co M, died July 8, diarrhea c.
3359, Broughton, D, 7 cav, Co K, died July 15, dysentery.
3366, Bricker, J, 68, Co C, died July 15, diarrhea c.
4027, Barton, J F, 52, Co G, died July 26, diarrhea c.
4035, Ballinger, Robert, 39, Co I, died July 26, scorbutus.
4251, Bonly, James, 81, Co C, died July 29, diarrhea.
4479, Baker, J, 9, Co G, died Aug 1, scorbutus.
4563, Baker, D W, 13, Co B, died Aug 2, diarrhea.
4948, Bayer, F, 129, Co H, died Aug 7, dysentery.
5059, Brenton, J W, 29, Co I, died Aug 6, scorbutus.
5093, Bowlin, Wm, 58, Co G, died Aug 8, wounds.
6220, Barton, E, 2 cav, Co G, died Aug 10, scorbutus.
5275, Beick, W A, * 101, Co F, died Aug 10, diarrhea.
5442, Bryer, P, 81, Co K, died Aug 12, scorbutus.
5590, Bohems, Philip, 79, Co A, died Aug 14, diarrhea.
5690, Baker, I P, 7 cav, Co H, died Aug 15, diarrhea.

No. of Grave.
5794, Boom W P, 31, Co F, died Aug 15, scorbutus.
5981, Barton, George, 130, Co F, died Aug. 17, diarrhea c.
6163, Brookers, J M, 112, Co E, died Aug 10, dysentery.
6410, Brown, J M, 66, Co F, died Aug 22, scorbutus.
6518, Bartholomew, I, 93, Co A, died Aug 22, dysentery.
7370, Bamgroover, J A, 101, Co H, Aug 31, diarrhea.
7794, Barnes, Thomas M, 5 cav, Co B, died Sept 4, dysentery.
8314, Babbitt, W H, 29, Co I, died Sept 10, dysentery.
8397, Bassinger, H, 14, Co C, died Sept 10, diarrhea.
8519, Boyd, W F, 125, Co F, died Sept 12, anasarca.
9098, Bartley, S, 38, Co I, died Sept 18, scorbutus.
9548, Bray, T E, 79, Co K, died Sept 23, scorbutus.
9706, Brown, J, † 1 cav, Co A, died Sept 24, diarrhea.
9777, Birch, T A, 58, Co L, died Sept 26, scorbutus.
9793, Bozell J F, 40, Co B, died Sept 26, scorbutus.
9846, Baxter, D, 6, Co B, died Sept 27, scorbutus.
10350, Blackaber, Wm H, 42, Co I, died Oct 6, scorbutus.
10939, Benton, L, 80, Co H, died Oct 14, scorbutus.
11559, Bennett, R N, 72, Co D, died Oct 27, scorbutus.
11604, Demis, J M, * 87, Co F, died Oct 28, scorbutus.
11919, Brown, D, 128, Co B, died Nov 8, dysentery.
11930, Bailey, George, 72, Co A, died Nov 8, scorbutus.
12019, Bennett, A, 29, Co G, died Nov 16, scorbutus.
12128, Booth, J, 32, Co E, died Nov 22, scorbutus.
12294, Bennett, C, 6, Co H, died Dec 15, scorbutus.
12480, Barrey, H, 66, Co I, died Jan. 19, '65, scorbutus.
12504, Balstrum, J, 93, Co F, died Jan 22, '65, scorbutus.
12596, Branson, E, 57, Co A, died Feb 6, '65, pneumonia.

301, Charles, James, 6, Co G, died April 1, diarrhea.
625, Connell, P, 6 cav, Co M, died April 19, dysentery c.
634, Claycome, S A, †, 66, Co G, died April 20, diarrhea.
1117, Cox, Joseph, † 42, Co B, died May 15, diarrhea.
1146, Carter, Henry, 2, Co C, died May 16, pneumonia.
1172, Curry, J W, 30, Co F, died May 17, diarrhea c.
1463, Currier, Wm, 87, Co K, died May 30, diarrhea.
1523, Crest, J D, 31, Co F, died May 31, diarrhea c.
2254, Carpenter, O C, * 29, Co D, died June 21, diarrhea.
2307, Cottrell, M, † 6 cav, Co G, died June 22, anasarca.
2776, Cooley, A, 38, Co C, died July 2, pneumonia.
3043, Clark, W, 82, Co C, died July 8, dysentery.
3922, Connolley, D, 9, Co I, died July 26, diarrhea.
4192, Cox, S, 66, Co E, died July 28, diarrhea.
4917, Clifford, H C, 7 cav, Co I, died Aug 6, scorbutus.
5202, Courtney, J F, 2 cav, Co L, died Aug 10, dysentery.
5654, Collar, E, 130, Co G, died Aug 14, scorbutus.
5660, Crews, E M, 5 cav, Co A died Aug 14, dysentery.
5901, Clark, A, 64, Co A, died Aug 16, diarrhea c.
6208, Chrichfuls, S, 93, Co A, died Aug 19, gangrene.
6477, Croane, J J, 22, Co C, died Aug 22, scorbutus.
6646, Cornelius, E, 58, Co B, died Aug 23, scorbutus.
6926, Carnaban, A W, † 6, Co E, died Aug 26, dysentery.
7383, Carpenter, S, 66, Co I, died Aug 31, scorbutus.
7726, Callinge, W, 120, Co F, died Sept 3, diarrhea.
7737, Cramer, A, 30, Co H, died Sept 3, debilitas.
7899, Cheny, James, 7 cav, Co I, died Sept 5, dysentery.
8051, Crumton, R, 101, Co I, died Sept 6, diarrhea.
8108, Crazer, J, 53, Co G, died Sept 7, scorbutus.
8133, Crager, J, 13, Co C, died Sept 8, fever conges.
8144, Cooper, J, 80, Co E, died Sept 8, diarrhea.
9294, Christman, J E, 6 cav, Co G, died Sept 19, scorbutus.
9535, Collins, G, 56, Co F, died Sept 22, diarrhea.
9980, Connell, Daniel, 130, Co F, died Sept 28, scorbutus.
10084, Conel, J, 13, Co D, died Sept 30, diarrhea.
10905, Callan, M, 35, Co B, died Oct 13, diarrhea.
11423, Cafer, J H, 87, Co K, died Oct 24, scorbutus.
11631, Cummings, J W, 93, Co F, died Oct 28, scorbutus.
12062, Clark, M, 101, Co B, died Nov 17, diarrhea.
12178, Cannon, A, 42, Co F, died Nov 26, scorbutus.
12213, Crega, Wm, 5 cav, Co E, died Dec 3, scorbutus.
12415, Collins, W A, † 5, Co G, died Jan 8, '65, scorbutus.
12559, Calvert, G F, 8 cav, Co I, died Jan 30, '65, diarrhea c.
4234, Curry, W F, 4 cav, Co I, died July 29, diarrhea c.

426, Dummond, J H, 65, Co F, died April 7, diarrhea c.
608, Davis, J M, 66, Co I, died April 12, diarrhea.
964, Darker, Wm, 12, Co C, died May 8, anasarca.
2205, Denny, John, 44, Co K, died June 19, diarrhea.
3157, Detrich, C, 29, Co K, died July 11, diarrhea.
3419, Dusan, J, 6, Co D, died July 16, diarrhea c.
4021, Develin, E, 35, Co B, died July 26, pneumonia.
4029, Decer, P, 32, Co K, died July 26, scorbutus.
4124, Dill, C P, 42, Co F, died July 27, diarrhea.
5255, Davis, K, 13, Co D, died Aug 10, diarrhea.
5367, Dunben, M, 36, Co E, died Aug 11, scorbutus.
5420, Delup, Z S, 13, Co D, died Aug 12, scorbutus.
5581, Dallinger, W C, 38, Co E, died Aug 14, diarrhea.
6147, Denton, Philip, 81, Co D, died Aug 19, '65, scorbutus.
6834, Downey, S M, 116, Co I, died Aug 25, scorbutus.
6944, Dowell, W L, 6, Co C, died Aug 26, dysentery.
9638, Dunlap, W, 30, Co A, died Sept 24, scorbutus.

No. of Grave.
10010, Downs, J R, 5 cav, Co I, died Sept 29, dysentery.
10435, Dane, Andrew, 36, Co I, died Oct 6, scorbutus.
10446, Dignon, L, 35, Co B, died Oct 7, diarrhea.
10916, Dawson, L F, 29, Co I, died Oct 14, scorbutus.
10954, Dial, R, 1, Co B, died Oct 14, diarrhea c.
12087, Daffendall, P H, 63, Co D, died Nov 18, scorbutus.
12172, Davenport, J, 6 cav, Co I, died Nov 24, scorbutus.
12236, Delashment, F, † 14, Co B, died Dec 6, scorbutus.
12533, Duckworth, J, 86, Co F, died Jan 27, '65, scorbutus.
12545, Dawley, J, 73, Co I, died Jan 27, '65, rheumatism.
12580, Dawson, J, 124, Co D, died Feb 3, '65, pleuritis.
9236, Diver, O, 19, Co F, died Sept 10, gastritis.

916, Evans, G H, 1 cav, Co A, died May 6, diarrhea c.
917, Edwards, G H, musician, 6, Co G, died May 7, diarrhea c.
1093, Ellis, H C, 6 cav, Co D, died May 14, diarrhea.
1279, Evans, W, 75, Co I, died May 22, fever remit.
1346, Eskridge, Oakley, 29, Co D, died May 24, diarrhea c.
1994, Edwards, J W, 38, Co G, died June 15, diarrhea c.
2481, Esenthal, F, 5 cav, Co D, died June 25, diarrhea c.
4075, Eaton, W H, 68, Co B, July 27, diarrhea c.
4953, Ecker, J, 30, Co I, Aug 17, anasarca.
5076, Evans, J, 6 cav, Co I, Aug 8, diarrhea.
7917, Ells, D, 20, Co I, died Sept 5, diarrhea c.
11320, Elston, F, 9, Co B, died Oct 22, scorbutus.
11420, Estelle, E W, † 2 cav, Co L, died Oct 24, scorbutus.
11712, Eldridge, E, 38, died Nov 1, scorbutus.
11774, Earl, D, * 2 cav, Co B, died Nov 3, scorbutus.
12285, Emmons, W, 5, Co D, died Dec 14, scorbutus.

1482, Frecks, F, 35, Co D, died May 30, diarrhea.
1808, Fitter, B, 66, Co I, died June 10, diarrhea.
2143, Fike, Tobias, 30, Co D, died June 18, diarrhea.
3014, Fitzgerald, I, 30, Co D, died July 7, diarrhea.
3453, Feacher, D, 32, Co E, died July 17, scorbutus.
3637, Fuget W, 3 cav, Co C, died July 20, dysentery.
8379, Fields, N, 6 cav, Co F, died Sept 10, scorbutus.
8547, Fenton, I, 72, Co D, died Sept 12, scorbutus.
8766, Forward, S, 8 cav, Co I, died Sept 14, anasarca.
9847, Forshua, W, 25, Co H, died Sept 27, scorbutus.
10509, Farmingham, W C, 14 cav, Co K, died Oct 8, scorbutus.
11311, Fanier, F, 6 cav, Co I, died Oct 22, scorbutus.
11526, Fish, C, 2 cav, Co H, died Oct 26, scorbutus.
12012, Falkerson, J, † 93, Co B, died Nov 14, fever intermit.
12144, Francis, F, musician, 93, died Nov 24, scorbutus.
12320, Frose, John, † 5 cav, Co D, died Dec 24, scorbutus.
12728, Feloich, H, 10, Co F, died March 4, '65, diarrhea c.

98, Graham, Wm, 6, Co G, died March 22, pneumonia.
322, Gladman, H, 110, Co B, died April 2, pneumonia.
1048, Goodwin, Wm, 2 cav, Co M, died May 12, anasarca.
1165, Grimes, F O, 66, Co I, died May 17, dysentery.
1215, Garver, John, 20, Co F, died May 19, diarrhea c.
1312, Gulisen, William, 7 cav, Co L, died May 23, diarrhea c.
1594, Griffin, William, 6 cav, Co I, died June 8, rheumatism.
2337, Gray, D L, 22, Co I, died June 22, fever typhus.
2386, Guthrie, W B, 80, Co C, died June 24, diarrhea c.
2418, Gillard, Wm, 120, Co C, died June 24, fever remittent.
3573, Gibbons, W T, 128, Co I, died July 19, diarrhea.
4179, Gould, Wm, 66, Co E, died July 28, scorbutus.
4273, Gilbert, H A, † 2 cav, Co K, died July 29, diarrhea.
4347, Galliger, Wm, 7, Co B, died July 31, diarrhea.
4901, Gerard, H, 35, Co G, died Aug 6, anasarca.
6189, Goodwin, I, 20, Co F, died Aug 19, diarrhea.
6398, Gordon, W M, 74, Co G, died Aug 21, scorbutus.
6493, Goodridge, E, * 94, Co H, died Aug 22, diarrhea c.
7298, Grass, C, 32, Co H, died Aug 30, scorbutus.
7321, Gray, H F, 2 cav, Co H, died Aug 30, scorbutus.
7698, Gerber, I, 30, Co C, died Sept 3, diarrhea.
8546, Galliger, P, 58, Co C, died Sept 12, scorbutus.
8791, Gagham, Wm, 35, Co K, died Sept 14, scorbutus.
9112, Green, S, 72, Co E, died Sept 18, wounds.
9114, Gillan, J, 20, Co F, died Sept 18, scorbutus.
10782, Griswold, Thomas, 2, Co F, Oct 12, scorbutus.
11409, Gordon, J W, 13, Co D, died Oct 24, scorbutus.
11581, Greenwood, W, 3, Co C, died Oct 28, scorbutus.
12216, Grant, H G, 5, Co G, died Dec 3, diarrhea.
12398, Garnett, T, 6, Co E, died Jan 5, '65, scorbutus.
12488, Green, Wm, 39, Co E, died Jan 19, '65, scorbutus.

630, Hollar, John, 6 cav, Co I, died April 19, diarrhea c.
879, Henick, Wm, 30, Co F, died May 4, dysentery.
1953, Hall, L S, 117, Co C, died June 14, dysentery.
2118, Hilliard, J, 116, Co D, died June 17, diarrhea c.
2130, Hodges, J, 7, Co C, died June 18, pneumonia.
2379, Hustin, James, 74, Co B, died June 23, diarrhea.
2392, Hodges, S, 9, Co F, died June 24, diarrhea.
2629, Humphrey, I, 8, Co C, died June 28, diarrhea.
2768, Hendricks, J, 2 cav, Co C, died July 2, rheumatism.
2768, Higgins, M P, 3 cav, Co C, died July 2, dysentery.
2793, Hodges, W J, 5, Co F, died July 2, scorbutus.

No. of Grave.

2812, Hillman, H. 65, Co G, died July 3, anasarca.
2974, Hamilton, James, 7, Co K, died July 7, diarrhea.
3280, Hine, S, 68, Co A, died July 14, diarrhea.
3507, Hodgen, J W, 80, Co G, died July 18, debilitas.
4487, Haeger, L S, 65, Co A, died Aug 1, diarrhea.
5302, Hart, J R, 88, Co H, died Aug 11, scorbutus.
5078, Hittle, B, 6 cav, Co L, died Aug 14, scorbutus.
5658, Helville, N C, 23, Co F, died Aug 15, diarrhea.
5872, Heath, Jacob, 20, Co G, died Aug 16, diarrhea.
6076, Hearne, John, 5 cav, Co F, died Aug 18, scorbutus.
6198, Hershton, A, 4, Co M, died Aug 19, dysentery.
6491, Hendrick, I, 129, Co H, died Aug 22, scorbutus.
7031, Hartsock, I, 30, Co A, died Aug 27, diarrhea.
7790, Hunter, J M, 42, Co F, died Sept 4, debilitas.
7837, Hammond, G W,* 65, Co D, died Sept 4, diarrhea.
7963, Halfre, J A, 32, Co A, died Sept 5, diarrhea.
7971, Hamilton, P S, 7, Co E, died Sept 6, scorbutus.
8091, Hughes, W H,* 81, Co D, died Sept 7, dysentery.
8317, Hart, A, 7, Co A, died Sept 10, diarrhea.
8541, Huff, M, 4 battery, died Sept 12, anasarca.
8681, Hunter, H, 42, Co F, died Sept 13, scorbutus.
8778, Haynes, W, 30, Co G, died Sept 14, anasarca.
8836, Higgins, John W, 3 cav, Co C, died Sept 15, scorbutus.
8967, Holloway, J, 5 cav, Co M, died Sept 16, diarrhea.
9083, Hubbner, F, 4 cav, Co E, died Sept 18, diarrhea c.
9329, Hurst, R V,* 36, Co B, died Sept 20, scorbutus.
9429, Higgins, W E, 53, Co H, died Sept 21, wounds.
9911, Haghton, J, 2, Co D, died Sept 28, anasarca.
9933, Harrington, O, 20, Co I, died Sept 28, dysentery.
10123, Hoffman, J, 80, Co C, died Oct 1, pneumonia.
10293, Hunstler, W H,† 38, Co E, died Oct 4, scorbutus.
10522, Ho.gler, N C, 79, Co E, died Oct 8, scorbutus.
10613, Harris, W C, 13, Co D, died Oct 10, diarrhea c.
10820, Hector, E, 13, Co D, died Oct 12, scorbutus.
11221, Hoskins, H, 90, Co A, died Oct 20, scorbutus.
11243, Hasde, J, musician, 1, Co F, died Oct 21, scorbutus.
11790, Hill, R, 14, Co D, died Nov 4, scorbutus.
12249, Hamilton D, 13, Co B, died Dec 9, scorbutus.
12536, Hall, H H, 2, Co E, died Jan 27, '65, diarrhea.

6444, Ilin, C, 129, Co B, died Aug 22, '64, scorbutus.
8263, Igo, T,* 4, Co E, died Sept 16, diarrhea,

670, Johnson, Isaac, 5, Co C, died Apr 22, dysentery.
1931, Jennings, C,* 6 cav, Co I, died June 14, diarrhea c.
2212, Jackson, John, 22, Co C, died June 20, diarrhea.
2553, Jones, Wm M, 63, Co D, died June 23, diarrhea c.
3311, Jasper, Wm, 38, Co I, died July 10, scorbutus.
5243, Judd, Henry,† 2, Co D, died Aug 10, scorbutus.
6172, Julerson, H, 2 cav, Co D, died Aug 19, marasmus.
6311, Jones, H C, 5, Co C, died Aug 20, scorbutus.
7100, Jones, A, 88, Co I, died Aug 28, diarrhea.
9048, Johnson, J, 7 cav, Co A, died Sept 28, scorbutus.
12517, Jones, J, 130, Co C, died Jan 24, '65, rheumatism.
12799, Johnson, H, 49, Co C, died Mar 19, '65, diarrhea c.

417, Kistner, George, 42, Co B, died Apr 7, debilitas.
618, Kinman, A, 56, Co G, died Apr 18, diarrhea.
858, Ketchum, G W,† 5 cav, Co I, died May 3, diarrhea.
2056, Kelley, John,† 5 cav, died June 15, diarrhea.
2407, Kennedy, Amos, 2, Co H, died June 24, diarrhea c.
1998, Kelso, E O, 3 cav, Co C, died June 17, diarrhea c.
2527, Kange, J, 74, Co E, died June 26, fever remittent.
3047, Kennedy, J W,* 3, Co I, died July 8, diarrhea.
4024, Keys, Wm, 72, Co E, died July 26, debilitas.
5149, Keller, W J,† 4 cav, Co H, died Aug 9, dysentery.
5253, Kosher, T, 29, Co I, died Aug 10, scorbutus.
5722, Kern, W, 25, Co H, died Aug 15, enteritis.
6596, Kelly, John, 32, Co C, died Aug 23, scorbutus.
7085, Kames, J, 128, Co F, died Aug 28, diarrhea.
8621, King, D, 81, Co A, died Sept 13, scorbutus.
10689, Keller, I, 40, Co B, died Oct 11, diarrhea c.
12276, Kuling, I, 79, Co A, died Dec 12, scorbutus.
12587, Keef, P,* 10 cav, Co C, died Feb 4, '65, diarrhea.

1041, Lewis, J, 6, Co H, died May 12, '64, diarrhea c.
1239, Lawrence, R J, 30, Co G, died May 20, diarrhea c.
1261, Lower, N G, 118, Co I, died May 21, diarrhea.
2615, Lewis, James, 65, Co F, died June 29, diarrhea c.
2745, Luff, C, 58, Co I, died July 1, diarrhea c.
2729, Lewis, J, 3 cav, Co C, died July 7, scorbutus.
3767, Lannon, J S, 128, Co F, died July 22, debilitas.
3893, Lawrence, D, 80, Co A, died July 24, diarrhea.
4548, Lyons, Wm, 35, Co A, died Aug 2, scorbutus.
5011, Lee, John, 3 cav, Co C, died Aug 8, dysentery c.
5685, Lawson, William, 75, Co A, died Aug 14, scorbutus.
5618, Lawyer, James, 80, Co B, died Aug 14, dysentery.
6775, Lyons, Wm, 1, Co E, died Aug 25, diarrhea.
7162, Lowery, D, 2 cav, Co G, died Aug 29, diarrhea.
8007, Langer, A, 7 cav, Co M, died Sept 12, scorbutus.
9264, Ligger, —— 82, Co G, died Sept 16, scorbutus.
10508, Lewis, R, 7 cav, Co C, died Oct 8, diarrhea c.
11152, Lush, J, 101, Co B, died Oct 18, scorbutus.
11715, Lakin, A, 7 cav, died Nov 1, scorbutus.
12250, Lawrence, B T, 42, Co D, died Dec 9, scorbutus.

130, McCarty, John, 66, Co D, died March 23, fever intermit.
631, Mullen, James, 6 cav, Co G, died April 19, diarrhea.
746, Masters, Wm, 65, Co G, died April 26, diarrhea.
841, Milton, John, 18, Co C, died May 1, dysentery.
903, Mythaker, Wm, 117, Co F, died May 5, diarrhea c.
954, Milburn, J, 6, Co K, died May 8, diarrhea.
1090, Moore, Peter, 6, Co I, died May 14, diarrhea c.
1405, Miller, Jacob, 74, Co E, died May 27, diarrhea.
1516, Martin, George,† 3 cav, Co C, died May 31, diarrhea.
1860, Merritt, H, 30, Co G, died June 12, diarrhea, c.
2240, Mitchell, J J, 30, Co D, died June 20, diarrhea.
2397, Milliken, S L, 1 cav, Co G, died June 24, phthisis.
2511, Moneyhon B, 38, Co D, died June 26, diarrhea c.
2608, Marsh, J, 88, Co D, died June 28, diarrhea c,
5, Moodie, Z, 117, Co K, died March 31, small pox.
3387, Mauk, E, 80, Co E, died July 10, diarrhea c.
3633, Marlit, J, 80, Co H, died July 20, scorbutus.
3884, Mulcey, J, 35, Co A, died July 24, diarrhea c.
4010, Mercer, John, 12, Co F, died July 26, dysentery.
4388, Malshy, F, 14 cav, Co A, died July 31, diarrhea.
4959, McDale, R, 19, Co A, died Aug 7, diarrhea.
5502, Manihan, J, 38, Co D, died Aug 13, diarrhea.
5618, Mageson, J, 7 cav, Co A, died Aug 14, fever typhus.
5703, Mensome, S,† 42, Co E, died Aug 15, dysentery.
5713, Monroe, S, 30, Co F, died Aug 15, scorbutus.
5767, Montgomery, R, 80, Co F, died Aug 15, dysentery c.
5803, Michael, S, 7, Co I, died Aug 16, diarrhea,
6461, Mitchell, J H, 30, Co I, died Aug 22, scorbutus.
6521, Monroe, H J,† 44, Co G, died Aug, 22, scorbutus.
6566, Mathews, M, 42, Co K, died Aug 23, ictus solis.
7043, Milsker, J, 5, Co D, died Aug 27, diarrhea.
7238, Matheny, N,† 42, Co A, died Aug 29, diarrhea.
7272, McQuerston, J O, 13, Co B, died Aug 30, diarrhea.
7510, Myers, A, 29, Co E, died Sept 1, scorbutus.
7820, Moore, G,* 101, Co F, died Sept 4, dysentery c.
7973, Mine, John N, 2, Co H, died Sept 6, scorbutus.
8007, Miller, W W, 101, Co B, died Sept 6, diarrhea c.
8176, McCoy, W,† 66, Co B, died Sept 8, diarrhea.
8389, Murphy, J, 9, Co E, died Sept 10, diarrhea.
8851, McElvain, J, 93, Co E, died Sept 15, diarrhea c
8925, Myers, J, 143, Co D, died Sept 16, scorbutus.
9575, Morrison, J, 4, Co B, died Sept 23, diarrhea c.
9590, Miller, J, 7 cav, Co G, died Sept 23, scorbutus.
9858, Murgu, A, 35, Co D, died Sept 27, scorbutus.
10231, Monay, G W, 7, Co E, died Oct 2, diarrhea.
10245, McFarney, J, 93, Co B, died Oct 3, scorbutus.
10394, Manles, H, 29, Co H, died Oct 6, scorbutus.
10891, Murphy, J, 35, Co B, Oct 13, scorbutus.
10995, McDonald, I, 74, Co B, died Oct 16, scorbutus.
11166, Mills, M Rem, 26, Co D, died Oct 18, scorbutus.
11271, Mitchell, I, 7, Co K, died Oct 21, scorbutus.
11585, McCarty, A, 7, Co A, died Oct 28, scorbutus.
11665, McBeth, I C, 28, Co K, died Oct 30, diarrhea.
11680, Murphy, F, 35, Co C, died Oct 31, scorbutus.
11746, McCarty, A, 7, Co A, died Nov 2, diarrhea.
11857, McCarty, I, 6, Co A, died Nov 6, scorbutus.
11946, Miller, F B, 30, Co C, died Nov 10, scorbutus.
12548, Mallener, L, 12, Co K, died Jan 27, '65, diarrhea c.
12563, McFall, I, 30, Co A, died Jan 31, '65, scorbutus
12624, Mainfold, W, 6 cav, Co I, died Feb 9, rheumatism.
12639, Montgomery, W, 5 cav, Co G, died Feb 17, '65, diarrhea c.
12709, Maloy I, 11 cav, Co O, died Feb 28, diarrhea c.

2007, Norsman, G, 117, Co G, died June 15, diarrhea.
3205, Newcomb, George, 22, Co A, died July 12, anasarca.
3519, Nuckn, S, 8 cav, Co I, died July 18, diarrhea.
4627, Napper, W H,† 6, Co I, died Aug 3, scorbutus.
6528, Norton, N A, 38, Co B, died Aug 23, dysentery.
10187, Note John H, 30, Co F, died Oct 1, scorbutus.
12226, Nichols, J, 38, Co G, died Dec 5, scorbutus.
9494, Newbery, M, 7 cav, Co L, died Sept 21, diarrhea.

342, O'Niel, Thomas, 6, Co G, died April 2, diarrhea c.
1874, Oliver, John,* 42, died June 12, diarrhea c.
2778, Oliver, H H, 5 cav, Co M, died July 2, diarrhea
5226, Oliver, J, 120, Co K, died Aug 10, scorbutus.
5361, Osborn, J, 73, Co E, died Aug 11, diarrhea.
7863, Oliver, J, 19, Co D, died Sept 5, diarrhea.
7911, O'Conner, Thomas, 5 cav, Co B, died Sept 5, diarrhea.
10940, Olinger, E, 65, Co A, died Oct 14, scorbutus.
12544, Ortell, M, 35, Co O, died Jan 27, '65, scorbutus.
12590, Ousley, W I, 7, Co A, died Feb 5, diarrhea c.

287, Peache, Cyrus, 66, Co D, died April 1, diarrhea.
559, Pashby, John, 6 cav, Co C, died April 15, dysentery c.
3434, Pavy, W, 123, Co A, died July 11, diarrhea.

No. of Grave.
3738, Palmer, A, 42, Co F, died July 21, dysentery.
4068, Parker, E,† 29, Co A, died July 27, diarrhea.
4171, Park, John, 129, Co B, died July 28, fever remittent.
4551, Pettis, H, 53, Co C, died Aug 2, dysentery.
4553, Pruitt, H C, 7 cav, Co K, died Aug 2, scorbutus.
5627, Prentice, J M, 22, Co K, died Aug 14, wounds.
6159, Peust, Alexander, 38, Co B, died Aug 19, dysentery.
6278, Patterson, E, 4 cav, Co G, died Aug 20, marasmus.
6874, Parten, D R, 65, Co F, died Aug 26, diarrhea.
7710, Plough, J W,† 63, Co D, died Sept 3, scorbutus.
8601, Pratt, William, 29, Co F, died Sept 13, anasarca.
9196, Plunier, A, 2, Co D, died Sept 18, scorbutus.
9705, Pope, I T,† 5 cav, Co G, died Sept 24, scorbutus.
9709, Patterson, N S, 93, Co G, died Sept 24, diarrhea.
10128, Packett, T C,† 39, Co F, died Oct 1, scorbutus.
11880, Pangburn, —,† 20, Co B, died Nov 6, gangrene.
12572, Potts I, 99, Co H, died Feb 2, '65, scorbutus.
12588, Phepps, A, 30, Co D, died Feb 4, '65, scorbutus.
1249, Packer, Samuel B, 6 cav, Co D, died May 20, dysentery

872, Remy, John, 66, Co B, died May 4, fever remittent.
944, Reed, R, 57, Co F, died May 7, diarrhea.
1005, Remcett, L, 65, Co H, died May 13, diarrhea.
1558, Roll, N C, 117, Co F, died June 2, diarrhea c.
1690, Reose, L, 110, Co I, died June 7, diarrhea c.
2140, Robinson, L, 7, Co I, died June 18, fever remittent.
4039, Rogman, —, 38, Co I, died July 26, diarrhea.
4165, Reiggs, K N, 39, Co K, died July 28, scorbutus.
4406, Richardson, I, 35, Co I, died July 31, diarrhea.
6180, Rawlings, J W, 117, Co F, died Aug 9, dysentery.
6250, Rains, G D, 4, Co G, died Aug 10, dysentery.
6434, Ritter, Benjamin, 29, Co K, died Aug 12, scorbutus.
6542, Ralph, G, 63, Co F, died Aug 13, dysentery.
6247, Roundbush, Daniel, 6, Co B, died Aug 20, diarrhea.
6383, Redyard, A, 65, Co F, died, Aug 21, diarrhea.
6754, Russell, J, 7, Co K, died Aug 24, diarrhea.
7677, Ringold I, 7 cav, Co I, died Sept 8, diarrhea.
8468, Russmore, E, 2 cav, Co C, died Sept 11, scorbutus.
8577, Redman, N E, 80, Co F, died Sept 12, scorbutus.
9521, Richardson, John, 86, Co D, died Sept 21, diarrhea.
9547, Riggs, L, 19, Co E, died Aug 23, scorbutus.
10829, Reeves, Wm, 42, Co F, died Oct 13, scorbutus.
11416, Riordon, M D, 5 battery, died Oct 24, scorbutus.
11451, Rutger, W,* 44, Co D, died Oct 25, scorbutus.
11935, Russell, W H, 13, Co C, died Nov 9, scorbutus.
12454, Robinson, R, 8, Co G, died Jan 14, '65, wounds.
12523, Richardson, E, 127, Co E, died Jan 26, '65, scorbutus.
1440, Ryan, Martin, 35, Co B, died May 28, dysentery c.
6707, Rawlings, E,† 66, Co C, died Aug 24, diarrhea.

86, Smilley, —, 65, Co I, died March 21, diarrhea.
129, Stein, Thomas, 66, Co D, died March 23, dysentery.
205, Stouts, —, 65, Co I, died March 28, diarrhea c.
768, Sanderson, H, 6 cav, Co G, died April 27, diarrhea.
817, Sears, I, 63, Co I, died April 30, diarrhea c.
901, Slack, Eli, 20, Co C, died May 5, diarrhea c.
1039, Smith, M C,* 24 battery, died May 12, fever typhus.
1331, Smith, H, 80, Co A, died May 24, dysentery.
1400, Sapp, A J, 44, Co H, died May 26, anasarca.
1450, Swindle, T O,† 82, Co A, died May 28, diarrhea c.
1501, Smith, L, 116, Co A, died May 31, anasarca.
1611, Schroder, W, 42, Co A, died June 4, diarrhea.
1690, Sparks, L D, 66, Co D, died June 7, diarrhea.
1732, Search, C, 6 cav, Co D, died June 8, diarrhea.
2079, Shigley, T W, 10, Co H, died June 17, pneumonia.
2083, Stinit, D, 6 cav, Co L, died June 17, pneumonia.
2218, Smudley, W, 5, Co E, died June 20, scorbutus.
2318, Swain, J W, 30, Co A, died June 22, diarrhea c.
2420, Snow, J, 5 cav, Co G, died June 24, diarrhea c.
2447, Stafford, J W, 68, Co I, died May 25, diarrhea c.
2749, Smith, J, 65, Co H, died July 1, diarrhea.
2799, Stanchley, Wm, 5, Co K, died July 2, scorbutus.
2923, Stofer, L,† 29, Co B, died July 5, diarrhea.
3416, Spencer, M, 80, Co K, died July 16, diarrhea c.
4014, Shields, J, 128, Co F, died July 26, dysentery.
4054, Smith, J W, 38, Co G, died July 27, diarrhea.
4062, Smith, H, 79, Co H, died July 27, '65, diarrhea.
4088, Schneider, S A, 3 cav, died July 27, diarrhea.
4229, Sollman, C,† 35, Co D, died July 29, diarrhea.
4418, Stevens, M, 6 cav, Co M, died July 31, diarrhea.
4630, Solder, D, 117, Co K, died Aug 3, scorbutus.
4799, Summersvolt, V, 29, Co A, died Aug 5, scorbutus.
5254, Scott, B, 9 Co D, died Aug 10, scorbutus.
5418, Smith, Samuel E, 9, Co C, died Aug 12, scorbutus.
5513, Shoemaker, E W, 5 cav, Co I, died Aug 13, scorbutus.
5514, Sims, S, 101, Co B, died Aug 13, diarrhea.
5571, Sackett, I, 8 cav, Co G, died Aug 14, fever typhus.
5611, Stockman, L M, 68, Co E, died Aug 14, diarrhea.
5884, Standish, M, 68, Co B, died Aug 16, diarrhea c.
5977, Stockhoff, G, 19, Co I, died Aug 17, diarrhea c.
6044, Stout, H, 7, Co G, died Aug 18, diarrhea.

No. of Grave.
6736, Sipe, J, 82, Co A, died Aug 24, diarrhea.
6830, Strong, L, 9, Co F, died Aug 25, scorbutus.
7120, Spellman, J, 80, Co F, died Aug 28, scorbutus.
7264, Shaver, F, 129, Co I, died Aug 30, scorbutus.
7583, Snyder, L, 6 cav, Co A, died Sept 3, diarrhea.
7822, Sanders, D, 7, Co I, died Sept 4, diarrhea.
8058, Sutheen, J H, 66, Co E, died Sept 7, diarrhea.
8107, Starkey, I, 6 cav, Co I, died Sept 7, scorbutus.
8262, Sizeman, I, 123, Co B, died Sept 9, scorbutus.
8313, Stegewald, J M,† 22, Co K, died Sept 10, scorbutus.
8623, Swillenbarger, F, 21, Co I, died Sept 13, scorbutus.
8666, Sylvanus, J J, 35, Co G, died Sept 13, scorbutus.
8727, Sonel, J P, 30, Co B, died Sept 14, scorbutus.
8910, Storm, L M,† 6, Co A, died Sept 16, scorbutus.
9098, Simmons, J, 84, Co I, died Sept 18, diarrhea.
9252, Sharp, D M, 13, Co E, died Sept 19, scorbutus.
9546, Sharpless, W, 43, Co G, died Sept 23, diarrhea.
9623, Smith, S B, 17, Co F, died Sept 24, diarrhea.
9807, Skeels, W, 65, Co A, died Sept 26, diarrhea.
10790, Smith, George, 131, Co D, died Oct 12, dysentery.
10949, Smith, I, 39, Co I, died Oct 14, scorbutus
11006, Stout, G W,† 44, Co B, died Oct 16, scorbutus.
11187, Seagford, G H, 4 cav, Co I, died Oct 19, diarrhea.
11427, Switzer, J, 2, Co G, died Oct 24, scorbutus.
11842, Shaw, W R, 99, Co B, died Nov. 5, wounds.
11969, Shoe, G W, 74, Co E, died Nov 12, scorbutus.
11984, Steamer F, 29, Co F, died Nov 13, scorbutus.
12115, Scarff, F, 6 cav, Co D, died Nov 21, scorbutus.
12381, Starke, M S, 93, Co D, died Jan 2, '65, debilitas.
12492, Saits, H C, 4 cav, Co F, died Jan 20, '65, diarrhea c.
12582, Smith, D H, 12 cav, Co H, died Feb 3, '65, diarrhea c.
12615, Sides G, 66, Co A, died Feb 8, '65, pleuritis.
12666, Smure, C, 2 cav, Co G, died Feb 17, '65, diarrhea c.
12724, Stewart, E B, 36, Co E, died March 3, '65, scorbutus.
12809, Staley, G W, 72, Co A, died March 24, '65, diarrhea c.
2625, Satterthwait A, 62, Co I, died June 28, scorbutus.

619, Teeher, James, 117, Co I, died April 13, diarrhea c.
3778, Tandlora, B, 65, Co B, died July 22, diarrhea.
3791, Thompson, T, 6 cav, Co C, died July 22, dysentery a.
4733, Tooley, G W, 42, Co H, died Aug 4, scorbutus.
5065, Truman, L H,† 6 cav, Co G, died Aug 6, scorbutus.
5463, Taylor, N, 63, Co I, died Aug 12, wounds.
6509, Toohey, W R,* 42, Co H, died Aug 22, dysentery.
6719, Todd, T, 6, Co B, died Aug 24, hepatitis.
7096, Thomas, H D, 42, Co I, died Aug 28, anasarca.
7442, Taylor, George H, 4 cav, Co M, died Sept 1, diarrhea c.
8495, Tramble, D A, 20, Co A, died Sept 11, diarrhea.
8525, Taylor, E, 25, Co I, died Sept 12, diarrhea.
10458, Thomas, M, 2 cav, died Oct 6, dysentery.
12237, Tucey, B, citizen, died Nov 26, scorbutus.
12669, Terlinne, C, 9 cav, Co A, died Feb 7, '65, pleuritis.
10219, Tasnabet, Charles,† 33, Co E, died Oct 2, scorbutus.

10356, Underwood, P, 7 cav, Co C, died Sept 5, scorbutus.
10760, Upton, F M, 52, Co A, died Oct 12, scorbutus.

1717, Voit, T, 6 cav, Co K, died June 8, diarrhea c.
5363, Venome, James, 30, Co K, died Aug 11, diarrhea.
6250, Vanose, J, 93, Co B, died Aug 20, cerebritis.
7691, Verhouse, D, 42, Co A, died Sept 3, scorbutus.

135, Windinger, J, 117, Co G, died March 24, fever remittent.
586, Walters, J H*, 6 cav, Co G, died May 5, fever intermittent.
634, Williams, A, 6, Co G, died May 7, diarrhea c.
1194, Wright, Samuel, 6 cav, Co I, died May 18, diarrhea.
1776, White, P, 6 cav, Co C, died June 9, diarrhea c.
1812, Wise, Eli, 88, Co D, died June 10, diarrhea.
1918, Warren, E, 65, Co H, died June 14, diarrhea.
2107, Williams, F, 38, Co F, died June 17, diarrhea c.
2232, West, E, 7 cav, Co H, died June 20, diarrhea.
2283, Woodward, W W, 20, Co A, died June 23, diarrhea c.
2417, Wilson, J N, 76, Co G, died June 24, diarrhea c.
2467, Worden, I, 44, Co B, died June 25, diarrhea a.
2554, Warren, E, 37, Co I, died June 27, pneumonia.
2670, Ward, J, 79, Co F, died June 29, anasarca.
2890, Wynn, W E, 13, Co D, died July 5, diarrhea.
2929, Wislake, I, 116, Co I, died July 6, dysentery c.
2934, Wicks, L, 6 cav, Co H, died July 6, diarrhea.
4528, Whitehead, J, 29, Co I, died Aug 2, diarrhea.
4639, Winship, James, 36, Co K, died Aug 4, scorbutus.
4826, Witt, T, 125, Co D, died Aug 5, diarrhea.
5399, Wade, C, 81, Co K, died Aug 12, dysentery.
5547, Wayman, J H, 4 cav, Co I, died Aug 13, diarrhea.
6132, Washburn, R H, 6 cav, Co A, died Aug 19, scorbutus.
6405, Winders, A, 120, Co I, died Aug 21, debilitas.
6524, Wagner, M, 8 cav, Co I, died Aug 22, scorbutus.
7184, Winters, F W, 84, Co C, died Aug 29, diarrhea.
7161, Wagoner, E, 42, Co A, died Aug 29, scorbutus.
7349, Witzgall, John, 2, Co D, died Aug 31, scorbutus.
8943, Weber, Charles, 13, Co F, died Sept 16, scorbutus.

No. of Grave.

9228, White, W, 7, Co E, died Sept 19, diarrhea.
9316, Watkins, J, 81, Co A, died Sept 20, diarrhea c.
6418, Wellington, H, 129, Co I, died Sept 21, diarrhea c.
9501, Wilson, J B, 6, Co E, died Sept 21, diarrhea.
9998, Wagner, F, 7, Co D, died Sept 29, diarrhea.
10648, Ward, J, 29, Co G, died Oct 11, scorbutus.
11141, Whitehead, N B, 5 cav, Co L, died Oct 18, scorbutus.
11424, White, R B, 6, Co D, died Oct 24, scorbutus.
11692, Walters, J, 5, Co I, died Oct 28, scorbutus.
12708, Winebrook, P, 35, Co B, died Nov 18, scorbutus.
12316, Werper, J, 32, Co E, died Dec 20, scorbutus.
12341, White, J, 7, Co A, died Dec 26, scorbutus.

No. of Grave.

12462, Wells, J M, 13, Co D, died Jan 16, '65, scorbutus.
12497, What, J, 93, Co B, died Jan 21, '65, pleuritis.
12737, Wade, W, 10 cav, Co M, died Mar 6, '65, diarrhea c.
3837, Weltz, Ira, † 4, Co E, died July 28, diarrhea c.
6000, West, S N,* 7, Co B, died Aug 17, diarrhea.
9920, Williams, J A, † 33, Co C, died Sept 29, scorbutus.

6055, Younce, Charles A, 7 cav, Co I, died Aug 8, dysentery.
6838, Yorker, Daniel, 28, Co B, died Aug 16, enteritis.

1540, Zuot, J, 65, Co H, died June 1, debilitas.

IOWA.

6560, Allen, N, 3 Co K, died Aug 13, diarrhea.
8974, Ankobus, L,* 6, Co I, died Sept 17, diarrhea c.
9472, Ashford, A W, 11, Co C, died Sept 21, wounds.
11784, Alderman, W W, 31, Co F, died Nov 4, scorbutus.
11896, Austin, Wm, 3 Cav, Co A, died Nov 7, diarrhea.

1293, Bartche, C P, 5, Co K, died May 23, diarrhea.
1570, Bingman, W H, 39, Co H, died June 3, diarrhea.
6276, Blanchard, A, 7, Co A, died Aug 10, diarrhea c.
6164, Bursford, M, 7, Co F, died Aug 19, diarrhea.
7779, Baird, J J, 26, Co H, died Sept 4, diarrhea.
8265, Buckmaster, F, 15, Co K, died Sept 9, diarrhea.
9301, Buell, J, 4, Co D, died Sept 20, diarrhea.
9450, Boylan, C, 14, Co G, died Sept 21, diarrhea.
9691, Boles, M B, —, Co I, died Sept 24, diarrhea.
10749, Bellinge, J, 5, Co B, died Oct 12, scorbutus.
11334, Blakely, Geo, 3, Co G, died Oct 23, wounds.

167, Collins, Henry,† 4, Co O, died March 28, diarrhea.
328, Chenworth, Wm, 4, Co K, died April 2, dysentery.
4582, Cromwell, G W, 27, Co F, died Aug 2, diarrhea.
5101, Cooper, S. 5, Co B, died Aug 9, scorbutus.
5244, Cox, E E,* 5, Co G, died Aug 9, dysentery.
5920, Cox, W A, 5, Co G, died Aug 14, diarrhea.
6099, Coder, E, 31, Co E, died Aug 17, diarrhea.
6378, Cox, H, 5, Co I, died Aug 21, scorbutus.
6604, Clameson, Henry, 26, Co I, died Aug 23, diarrhea c.
6848, Collins, M, 3, Co L, died Aug 25, diarrhea.
8062, Culbertson, S,* 5, Co H, died Sept 7, diarrhea.
8352, Crow, B, 4, Co E, died Sept 10, dysentery.
9784, Coles, J W, † 8, Co K, died Sept 26, diarrhea c.
9820, Cobb, E, 3 cav, Co C, died Sept 26, diarrhea c.
10037, Cramer, J M, 5 cav, Co B, died Sept 29, diarrhea c.
10901, Chapman, J, 3, Co G, died Oct 14, gangrene.
12230, Chamberlain, J B, 8 cav, Co A, died Dec 8, wounds.

2903, Davis, S, 3, Co E, died June 30, diarrhea c.
4206, Davis, J, 15, Co D, died July 29, wounds.
9229, Davis, H, 17, Co A, died Sept 19, scorbutus.
4075, Dermott, L, 5, Co G, died Aug 4, scorbutus.
6849, Discol, S, 26, Co I, died Aug 25, dysentery.
9852, Dingman, W, 31, Co D, died Sept 27, scorbutus.
11098, Denoya, W H, 5, Co M, died Oct 18, debilitas.
11753, Dutlin, S, 6 cav, Co C, died Nov 2, scorbutus.
12245, Durochis, Wm, 12 Co H, died Dec 8, scorbutus.
12657, Derickson, W W,* 8 cav, Co M, died Feb 16, '65, diarrhea c.

262, Ennis, Wm, 4, Co B, died March 31, dysentery a.
11414, England, G, 9, Co F, died Oct 24, scorbutus.

3705, Field, Jacob, 5, Co K, died July 21, dysentery.
4503, Farnsworth, S, 2, Co H, died Aug 1, anasarca.
1316, Forney, James M, 10, Co K, died May 23, diarrhea.
7715, Frul, J, 10, died Sept 3, diarrhea.
7878, Frederick, J A, 16, Co C, died Sept 5, diarrhea.
8380, Frussell, G W, 6, Co D, died Sept 10, scorbutus.
10048, Fordson, Michael, 16, Co H, died Sept 29, diarrhea.
11078, Fenor, J W, 3 cav, Co B, died Oct 17 scorbutus.
12711, Ferguson, A W, 15, Co A, died Feb 28, '65, ulcus.

750, Gain, L, 6, Co C, died April 20, fever typhus.
1484, Gender, Jacob, 5, Co I, died May 30, diarrhea c.
5004, Gentle, G, 4, Co G, died Aug 8, diarrhea c.
5836, Gunshaw, O, 26, died Aug 18, marasmus.
10511, Gray, J, 11, Co C, died Oct 7, dysentery.
10366, Gotbard, J, 8, Co G, died Oct 11, scorbutus.

6461, Harris, J, 8 cav, Co H, died Aug 13, dysentery.
8106, Hastings, J, † 11, Co B, died Sept 7, diarrhea.
9379, Hird, D, * 3, Co G, died Sept 20, wounds.
9417, Hudson, M, 16, Co B, died Sept 21, diarrhea.
2168, Huffman, R J, 5, Co H, died June 19, dysentery.
862, Hecller, A, 5, Co D, died May 3, bronchitis.
1633, Harper, D, 7, Co K, died June 5, debilitas.
1816, Hurlay, J, 8, Co H, died June 11, diarrhea c.

12740, Hubanks, C, † 17, Co H, died March 8, '65, debilitas.

10360, Ireland, J S, 5 cav, Co H, died Oct 5, '64, wounds.

4461, Jones, C, 4, Co B, died Aug 1, scorbutus.
8656, Jenks, G A, † 8, Co C, died Sept 13, diarrhea c.
9401, Jones, J, 5, Co C, died Sept 21, diarrhea c.

3204, Kolenbrander, H, 17, Co K, died July 12, diarrhea.
7, King, Alexander, 17, Co H, died April 5, small pox.
6464, King, E, 2 cav, Co C, died Aug 22, wounds.
3560, Kesler, F, 4, Co B, died July 18, scorbutus.
5378, Kennedy, B, 16, Co I, died Aug 11, wounds.
11281, Knight, J H, † 9, Co I, died Oct 22, gangrene.

892, Lambert, Chas, * 30, Co K, died May 5, bronchitis.
2045, Littleton, J, 5, died June 15, diarrhea.
7959, Lord, L, 13, Co G, died Sept 6, debilitas.
8263, Lanning, A, 13, Co I, died Sept 9, scorbutus.
9438, Lowdenbeck, N, 5, Co B, died Sept 21, anasarca.
10224, Lowelenbuck, D R, 5, Co B, died Oct 2, diarrhea.
10881, Layers, W, 5, Co E, died Oct 14, scorbutus.
11752, Luther, J, * 9, Co B, died Nov 2, scorbutus.
12620, Littlejohn, L D, 4 cav, Co B, died Feb 10, '65, diarrhea c.

257, Monre, John, 30, Co H, died March 31.
307, Myers, M, 4, Co K, died April 2, diarrhea.
450, Moon, James, 30, Co H, died April 9, dysentery.
1192, McMullen, James, 4, Co C, died May 18, fever intermittent.
1317, Miller, F, 5, Co H, died May 23, diarrhea.
1472, McCameron, W, 4, Co A, died May 30, fever remittent.
2027, McAllister, A P, 14, Co E, died June 15, diarrhea.
3423, McNeil, J W, 11, Co I, died July 16, diptheria.
4804, Moore, Wm, 18, Co A, died Aug 5, scorbutus.
5445, Murray, J J, 17, Co I, died Aug 12, scorbutus.
6167, McCall, Thos, 8 cav, Co M, died Aug 19, marasmus.
6815, Merchant, Wm, 13, Co O, died Aug 25, diarrhea.
6878, Maynard, J D, 4, Co B, died Aug 26, dysentery.
7143, McDonald, D B, † 5 cav, Co M, died Aug 29, diarrhea.
8120, McClure, Z, † 16, Co C, died Sept 8, scorbutus.
9274, Martin, S S, 11, Co G, died Sept 19, scorbutus.
9585, Mann, J, 16, died Sept 23, scorbutus.
10110, Miller, J, 5, Co D, died Oct 1, scorbutus.
10827, McCoy, G B, * 5, Co G, died Oct 13, diarrhea.
10950, Mercer, John, 4, Co C, died Oct 14, scorbutus.
11745, Miller, E, * 31, Co D, died Nov 2, scorbutus.
12484, Martin, J B, 5, Co B, died Jan 19, '65, rheumatism.
12561, Macy, O S, 8 cav, Co C, died Jan 31, '65, diarrhea.

6959, O'Conner, P, 26, Co D, died Aug 27, diarrhea.
9509, O'Verturf, F W, 5, Co H, died Sept 22, scorbutus.
12169, Osborn, F L, 16, Co A, died Nov 26, scorbutus.

1972, Peterson, J, 70, Co E, died June 15, anasarca.
2869, Palmer, L H, 9, Co D, died July 4, anasarca.
6209, Philpot, C P, 31, Co B, died Aug 19, diarrhea.
9370, Putnam, G, 27, Co F, died Aug 20, scorbutus.
10270, Pitts, J, 16, Co I, died Oct 3, diarrhea.
10297, Pugh, A, * 8, Co M, died Oct 3, scorbutus.
10413, Parker, D, 4, Co I, died Oct 6, scorbutus.

18, Rule, Y A, 10, Co A, died April 12, small pox.
1796, Ryan, Charles, 5, Co G, died June 10, pleuritis.
1820, Richardson, John, 2 cav, Co I, died June 11, diarrhea.
1951, Ratcliff, J, 4, Co I, died June 14, debilitas.
5878, Reed, R, 16, Co I, died Aug 16, diarrhea c.
6572, Robinson, D, 13, Co O, died Aug 23, wounds.
7400, Rice, H M, suttler's clerk, 9, died Aug 31, scorbutus.
9413, Riley, M, 5, Co A, died Sept 21, fever typhus.
9483, Reeves, S J, 9, Co D, died Sept 21, debilitas.
10015, Reed, C, 2, Co C, died Sept 29, scorbutus.
10017, Rogers, L, 4, Co F, died Sept 29, scorbutus.
12264, Russel, E, 4, Co G, died Dec 12, scorbutus.
12287, Raiser, A, 8, Co C, died Dec 14, scorbutus.

No. of Grave.
451, Stout, John, 5, Co A, died April 9, pneumonia.
599, Shuffleton, J, 5, Co H, died April 17, pneumonia.
641, Seeley, Norman, 9, Co B, died April 20, pneumonia.
2712, Smith, R F,* 10, Co H, died July 1, diarrhea.
2845, Shutter, J, 30, Co K, died July 3, dysentery.
3060, Sparks, M J, 5, Co K, died July 9, dysentery.
4176, Sutton, S, 5, Co H, died July 28, anasarca.
4773, Smith, Charles,* 20, Co F, died Aug 4, scorbutus.
5410, Starr, C F, 30, Co H, died Aug 12, pneumonia.
5892, Sneddle, G, 10, Co C, died Aug 16, diarrhea c.
7951, Sains, Wm, 3, Co D, died Sept 6, diarrhea c.
8210, Smith, J, 13, Co A, died Sept 6, dysentery.
9209, Smith, O, 5, Co D, died, Sept 19, scorbutus.
9125, Sherman, J W, 3, Co I, died Sept 17, diarrhea c.
9234, Spears, J, 5 cav, Co H, died, Sept 19, scorbutus.
9367, Smith, D, 3 cav, Co B, died Sept 20, diarrhea.
11789, Shaw, W W, 5 Co H, died Nov 4, scorbutus.
12729, Snice, W, 16, Co E, died March 4, '65, diarrhea c.
10834, Sayres, W, 5, Co E, died Oct 14, scorbutus.

1981, Talplog, Wm, 5, Co K, died June 15, pneumonia.
3986, Thopson, M, 5, Co G, died July 25, dysentery.

6687, Tivis, C, 5, Co A, died Aug 24, scorbutus.
9720, Tonune, B, 4 cav, Co M, died Sept 25, scorbutus.
11706, Thier, A F, 3, died Nov 1, scorbutus.

10351, Voke, John C,* 5, Co E, died Oct 5, scorbutus.

1674, Whitman, O R,* 5, Co E, died June 6, diarrhea c.
2161, Welte, F,† 5, Co I, died June 19, diarrhea c.
2213, Withsrick, A K, 9, Co K, died June 20, scorbutus.
2855, Wolf, B F, 8, Co E, died July 4, diarrhea.
4016, Wolfe, J H, 2, Co C, died Aug 6, scorbutus.
6934, Wheelan, J,† 26, Co D, died Aug 26, dysentery.
8101, Walworth, C,† 5, Co K, died Sept 7, scorbutus.
8131, Woolston, S P,† 13, Co H, died Sept 8, diarrhea.
9221, Ward, O R, 3, Co E, died Sept 19, anasarca.
9485, Wagner, Joseph, 13, Co E, died Sept 21, scorbutus.
9727, Werahrol, Y, 31, Co A, died Sept 25, scorbutus.
10848, Wilson, P D, 10, Co G, died Oct 13, scorbutus.
10942, Woodward, J, sutler, 9, died Oct 14, scorbutus.
11114, Whiting, J, 5, Co H, died Oct 18, scorbutus.
11141, Whitehead, N B, 5 cav, Co L, died Oct 19, scorbutus.
12741, Weu, C, 57, Co C, died March 6, '65, dysentery.

KANSAS.

1614, Freeman, F J,† 8, Co F, died June 4, diarrhea c.

1935, Gensardo, Thos, 8, Co A, died June 14, diarrhea c.

12127, Sweeney, M, 1, Co H, died Nov 22, scorbutus.
11139, Weidman, W, 8, Co B, died Oct 19, diarrhea c.
1663, Williams, C A, 8, Co A, died June 6, dysentery.

KENTUCKY.

329, Allen, Sam'l S,* 13, Co F, died Apr 2, diarrhea c.
674, Alford, George, 11 cav, Co B, died April 22, syphilis.
1575, Anderson, S, 11 cav, Co D, died May 3, diarrhea.
3385, Adams, J D, 1 cav, Co I, died July 16, diarrhea.
3759, Ashley, J M, 1 cav, Co L, died July 22, scorbutus.
4723, Allen, Wm,* 11 cav, Co C, died Aug 4, scorbutus.
4994, Atkins, A, 39 cav, Co H, died Aug 6, anasarca.
6093, Aughlin, J, A,* 18 cav, Co B, died Aug 18, scorbutus.
6720, Arnett, H S, 13 cav, Co A, died Aug 24, diarrhea.
10514, Adamson, Wm, 15 cav, Co K, died Oct 8, scorbutus.
11759, Adams, J L, 27, Co G, died Nov 3, scorbutus.
12426, Arthur, D, 4, Co G, died Jan 9, '65, diarrhea c.
12528, Ayers, E, 52, Co A, died Jan 26, '65, pleuritis.
12703, Ayers, S, 52, Co A, died Jan 26, '65, diarrhea c.
12593, Arnett, T, 4 cav, Co F, died Jan 5, '65, diarrhea c.

193, Bow, James, 1 cav, died Mar 27, '64, pleuritis.
261, Burrows, Wm, 1 cav, Co K, died Mar 31, diarrhea c.
306, Byerly, Wm, 11 cav, Co E, died Apr 2, rubeola.
379, Baker, Isaac, 1 cav, Co H, died Apr 5, diarrhea c.
413, Bisham, S, 12 cav, Co E, died Apr 7, diarrhea c.
419, Button, E I, 11 cav, Co D, died Apr 7, diarrhea c.
608, Burritt, B, 6 cav, Co D, died Apr 18, diarrhea.
639, Bloomer, H, 4 cav, Co G, died Apr 18, diarrhea.
813, Baker, A W, 3 cav, Co C, died Apr 29, diarrhea c.
832, Bailey, Peter, 12, Co L, died May 1, diarrhea.
891, Bird, W T, 11 cav, Co H, died May 5, diarrhea.
857, Bailey, A W, 14, Co G, died May 2, diarrhea c.
1167, Burton, Tillman, 1 cav, Co F, died May 17, scorbutus.
1200, Butner L B,† 6 cav, Co I, died May 18, diarrhea.
1203, Bell, P B, 11 cav, Co I, died May 21, dysentery.
1362, Barnett, James, 8 cav, Co H, died May 25, dysentery.
1566, Baird, Sam'l J, 12 cav, Co D, died June 2, diarrhea.
1789, Bishop, D L, 11 cav, Co A, died June 10, diarrhea.
2022, Bowman, G, 11 cav, Co D, died June 15, diarrhea c.
2428, Bray, H N,* 9 cav, Co H, died June 24, phthisis.
2529, Buchanan, S, 12 cav, Co F, died June 26, diarrhea c.
2760, Ball, David, 11 cav, Co B, died July 2, diarrhea c.
3087, Beard, John C,† 1 cav, Co C, died July 9, diarrhea c.
3228, Brophy, M, 5 cav, Co I, died July 12, dysentery.
3433, Bailey, F M, 4 cav, Co G, died July 17, scorbutus.
3000, Banner, J, 11 cav, Co C, died July 24, diarrhea c.
3998, Brdell, S,* 8 cav, Co F, died July 26, dysentery.
4563, Booth, Z,† 16 cav, Co E, died Aug 2, scorbutus.
4653, Barger, George, 5 cav, Co I, died Aug 3, diarrhea.
4835, Baker, Wm, 3 cav, Co I, died Aug 6, anasarca.
4971, Bigler A, 6 cav, Co B, died Aug 7, scorbutus.
5471, Bailey, J H, 11 cav, Co A, died Aug 12, diarrhea c.
5644, Branan, H, 1 cav, Co G, died Aug 14, dysentery.
6576, Boston, J, 27 cav, Co E, died Aug 23, scorbutus.
6727, Bottoms, J M, 1 cav, Co H, died Aug 24, dysentery.
9551, Branton, W J,† 11 cav, Co C, died Sept 23, anasarca.
9568, Barnett, A, 12 cav, Co K, died Sept 23, scorbutus.
9628, Brown, J, 10 cav, Co I, died Sept 24, diarrhea.
9740, Boyd, M, 13 cav, Co A, died Sept 25, diarrhea.
10141, Batt, W, 5, Co G, died Oct 1, diarrhea.
10202, Byron, H M,† 1 cav Co I, died Oct 2, scorbutus.

10451, Bill, B S, 1 cav, Co K, died Oct 7, pneumonia.
10810, Bodkins, P,* 1 cav, Co K, died Oct 12, diarrhea c.
10859, Bagley, T, 11 cav, died Oct 13, scorbutus.
11052, Brickey, W L, 4, Co F, died Oct 17, gangrene.
12256, Baldwin, J W, 11, Co H, died Oct 21, diarrhea.
11303, Brown, E W, 4, Co F, died Oct 22, scorbutus.
11491, Barber, T, 4 cav, Co H, died Oct 26, scorbutus.
12006, Brannon, J, 3, Co B, died Nov 13, scorbutus.
12304, Beatty, R, 5, Co B, died Dec 18, diarrhea.
12333, Barnes, J, 11, Co D, died Dec 25, scorbutus.
12360, Brodus, O, 11 cav, Co A, died Dec 30, scorbutus.
12421, Britton, J, 45, Co F, died Jan 9, '65, scorbutus.
5098, Bowman, Henry, 11 cav, Co F, died Aug 9, diarrhea c.
12777, Baleon, L, 12, Co B, died March 15, '65, diarrhea a.

11483, Cranch, J P, 10, Co D, died Oct 26, '64, scorbutus.
240, Conler, Wm, 14, Co I, died March 30, '64, diarrhea.
484, Caldwell, Wm, 12, cav, Co I, died April 9, diarrhea.
609, Cook, Theodore, 12 cav, Co D, died April 12, diarrhea c.
672, Colvin, George, 11 cav, Co D, died April 22, diarrhea.
877, Christmas, J, 11 cav, Co F, died May 4, diarrhea.
966, Collague, M, 12 cav, Co E, died May 8, diarrhea.
1298, Cash, Philip, 1 cav, Co I, died May 21, pneumonia.
1600, Cole, W C, 1 cav, Co C, died June 4, diarrhea.
1670, Christenburg, R I,† 12 cav, Co G, died June 6, dysentery.
1687, Callihan, Pat, 11 cav, Co A, died June 6, scorbutus.
1856, Clane, H, 11 cav, Co E, died June 12, diarrhea c.
2152, Clinge, W H, 40, Co A, died June 18, debilitas.
2293, Cox, A B, 6 cav, Co I, died June 21, fever intermittent.
2339, Chippendale, C, 1 cav, Co B, died June 22, diarrhea c.
2446, Carlisle, J, 6 cav, Co I, died June 26, diarrhea c.
2823, Cumminge, J, 11, Co F, died July 3, diarrhea.
2912, Cleming, Thos, 13, Co I, died July 5, diarrhea c.
3184, Carter, W, 11 cav, Co H, died July 11, dysentery.
60, Cristian, John, 4 cav, Co C, died July 4, small pox.
4044, Clark, A H, 11, Co I, died July 27, diarrhea.
4809, Chapman, 11, Co H, died Aug 5, diarrhea.
6367, Coulter, M, 23, Co B, died Aug 21, pneumonia.
9835, Conrad, R P, 4, Co B, died Sept 27, scorbutus.
11179, Clun, W H, 11 cav, Co L, died Oct 10, scorbutus.
11498, Chatsin, W M, 6 cav, Co H, died Oct 26, scorbutus.
12447, Carcunright, 4, Co C, died Jan 13, '65, scorbutus.
12700, Cook, J P, 4, Co G, died Jan 26, '65, anasarca.
2223, Corbitt, Thos, 5, Co A, died June 20, '64, diarrhea.
6113, Coyle, C, 11 cav, Co I, died Sept 7, scorbutus.
4740, Chance, A J, 1 cav, Co C, died Aug 5, anasarca.

491, Dupon, F, 12, Co G, died April 7, pneumonia.
1388, Delaney, M, 11 cav, Co I, died May 26, diarrhea.
1414, Dugean, J R,† 12 cav, Co K, died May 27, dysentery.
1508, De Barnes, P M, 11 cav, Co C, died June 2, diarrhea.
1627, Demody, Thos, 1 cav, Co H, died June 4, diarrhea c.
1867, Drake, J H, 12 cav, Co G, died June 12, anasarca.
2736, Davis, B, 5, Co C, died July 1, diarrhea c.
23, Duncan, E, 12 cav, Co G, died April 15, small pox.
3023, Dodson, E, 30, Co H, died July 20, scorbutus.
27, Derine, George, 1 cav, Co I, died April 17, small pox.

No. of Grave.

3924, Davis, G C, 12 cav, Co F, died July 25, debilitas.
3066, Derringer, H, 11 cav, Co I, died July 25, diarrhea c.
4510, Dulrebeck, H, 11, Co E, died Aug 1, diarrhea c.
4556, Delaney, H, 4 cav, Co H, died Aug 2, dysentery.
5088, Dounty, P, 5, Co F, died Aug 8, dysentery.
6899, Dooel, R, 9, Co F, died Aug 16, diarrhea c.
11405, Disone, F, 6 cav, Co G, died Oct 24, scorbutus.
12280, Durand, D W, 8, Co K, died Dec 13, scorbutus.
12523, Dannard, W, 4, Co D, died Feb 9, '65, diarrhea c.
12684, Dipple, S, 4, Co E, died Feb 21, '65, diarrhea c.
1109, Dinsman, H, 4 cav, Co E, died May 15, '64, diarrhea c.
2805, Davis, J P, 13, Co A, died July 3, diarrhea.
2117, Davis, C, 6 cav, Co D, died June 21, scorbutus.

639, Eodus, James, 1 cav, Co F, died April 29, diarrhea.
1174, Edmiston, J W, 11 cav, Co A, died May 17, diarrhea c.
1450, Edwards, H S,* 8 cav, Co K, died May 27, diarrhea c.
2544, Emery, J, 10, Co G, died June 27, fever typhus.
5341, Errbanks, J, 1 cav, Co A, died Aug 11, diarrhea.
12277, Estell, J, 1 cav, Co L, died Oct 22, diarrhea.
1447, East, R, 1 cav, Co G, died May 20, diarrhea.

354, Falconburg, I K, 1 cav, Co A, died April 5, pneumonia.
2540, Fleming, R, 4 cav, Co D, died June 27, diarrhea c.
3640, Forteen, John, 8, Co A, died July 20, diarrhea.
4344, Funkstine, M, 1, Co D, died July 30, diarrhea.
6763, Featherstone, J, 6 Co C, died Aug 25, fever intermittent.
7069, Fritz, J, 4 cav, Co G, died Aug 28, dysentery.
10260, Funk, L, 1 cav, Co I, died Oct 4, wounds.
11640, Frazier, C R, 23, Co H, died Oct 27, wounds.
11720, Fletcher, T, 17, Co E, died Nov 1, diarrhea, c.

1612, Gritton, G, 11 cav, Co D, died June 4, diarrhea c.
1618, Graves, G, 18, Co C, died June 4, diarrhea c.
1841, Gritton, M, 11 cav, Co B, died June 11, diarrhea c.
2583, Gibson, John, 6 cav, Co L, died June 27, dysentery.
3630, Griffin, B, 11, Co E, died July 20, diarrhea.
3663, Glassman, P, 4 cav, Co B, died July 20, diarrhea.
3888, Gouns, J M, 4, Co H, died July 24, diarrhea.
4438, Gather, M, 4 cav, Co F, died July 31, diarrhea.
5779, Gullett, A, 45, Co K, died Aug 15, anasarca.
7197, Green, J B,† 11, Co I, died Aug 20, diarrhea.
7817, Grabul, B, 1, Co F, died Sept 4, anasarca.
8049, Gury, J, 4, Co H, died Sept, 6, scorbutus.
8903, Gray, C D, 29, Co G, died Sept 18, scorbutus.
9318, Gett, John,† 40, Co G, died Sept 20, diarrhea.
9950, Gill, W J, 11 cav, Co H, died Sept 28, scorbutus.
10053, Gower, J C, 13, Co A, died Sept 30, scorbutus.
10651, Gibson, A, 8 cav, Co K, died Oct 10, scorbutus.
10831, Grubach, J,† 4, Co K, died Oct 13, scorbutus.
11910, Grimstead, J R, 1, Co E, died Nov 8, scorbutus.
12022, Griffin, R, 11, Co E, died Nov 15, scorbutus.
1235, Gregory, H, 12 cav, Co D, died May 20, diarrhea.

81, Hanns, J B, 12, Co K, died March 20, pneumonia.
237, Holloway, Richard, 4, Co I, died March 29, fever typhus
289, Harley, Alfred, 40, Co K, died April 1, diarrhea c.
292, Hood, G, 5 cav, Co F, died April 1, diarrhea.
348, Hammond, J W, 1 cav, Co G, died April 2, diarrhea c.
376, Harper, J, 1 Co C, died April 5, diarrhea a.
402, Harlow, Harvey, 13, Co I, died April 6, dysentery.
614, Hess, Wm F, 12 cav, Co M, died April 18, dysentery.
643, Hendree, A,† 11, Co F, died April 20, bronchitis.
1023, Hillard, Geo, 11, Co D, died May 11, fever typhus.
1127, Hoffman, C, 11 cav, Co E, died May 15, dysentery.
1584, Hughes, Thomas,† 9 Co G, died June 3, anasarca.
1760, Hennesy, J, 28, Co D, died June 9, diarrhea c.
1878, Hundly, Geo W, 4 cav, died June 12, diarrhea.
1956, Hazlewood, J H, 18, Co G, died June 14, dysentery.
1990, Hamner, A, 9, Co B, died June 15, diarrhea.
2490, Hudson, J W,† 9, Co B, died June 26, pneumonia.
2705, Hillard, S, 1 cav, Co I, died June 30, diarrhea c.
3239, Henderson, J, 15, Co B, died July 12, dysentery
26, Hooper, Samuel, 11 cav, Co D, died April 10, small pox
3944, Hooper, J, 1 cav, Co D, died July 25, scorbutus.
3904, Hickworth, J, 45, Co D, died July 26, diarrhea
4313, Hall, J H, 1 cav, Co C, died July 30, diarrhea.
4420, Hammontine, P, 6 cav, Co L, died June 31, diarrhea c.
4970, Hayner, E, 1 cav, Co D, died Aug 7, scorbutus.
5059, Haines, J, 12 cav, Co D, died Aug 8, scorbutus.
6091, Harrington, C, 15, Co K, died Aug 8, scorbutus.
5793, Hatfield, L, 1, Co F, died Aug 15, anasarca.
6193, Hendrie, Wm, 11 cav, Co F, died Aug 19, scorbutus.
6801, Hardison, G, 28, Co I, died Aug 25, fever remittent.
8032, Hise, P, 4, Co I, died Sept 6, diarrhea.
8111, Hicks, P, 11 cav, Co F, died Sept 7, scorbutus.
8181, Heglin, C, 4 cav, Co I, died Sept 8, dysentery.
9376, Hacker, R, 18, Co F, died Sept 20, scorbutus.
9 9, Hyronimus James, 11 cav, Co D, died Sept 23, diarrhea.
10683, Holton, S M, 2, Co K, died Oct 11, scorbutus.
11054, Halligan, J, 4, Co A, died Oct 17, anasarca.

No. of Grave.

11095, Hall, F, 1 cav, Co F, died Oct 15, scorbutus.
11132, Hazer, John, 11, Co I, died Oct 16, scorbutus.
11251, Hartor, F, 12 cav, Co M, died Oct 21, diarrhea c.
12283, Hays, J F, 5, Co A, died Dec 15, scorbutus.
12518, Hasting, J, 4, Co H, died Jan 24, '65, scorbutus.
12638, Hudson, B F, 4, Co A, died Feb 11, '65, diarrhea c.

5734, Inman, John, 24, Co A, died, Aug 15, '64, diarrhea.
9757, Isabell, J M, 3, Co H, died Sept 25, scorbutus.
11392, Inman, W, 11 cav, Co D, died Oct 24, scorbutus.
12203, Isabel, A, 1, Co K, died Dec 1, scorbutus.

649, Jackson, John, 45, Co D, died April 20, anasarca.
2670, Jeffries Wm, 1 cav, Co A, died June 30, diarrhea.
5229, Jacobs, John W, 4 cav, Co I, died Aug 10, scorbutus.
7294, Johnson, A, 10, Co H, died Aug 31, scorbutus.
7371, Jenkins S, 6 cav, Co A, died Aug 31, diarrhea.
7594, Justin, J, 39, Co F, died Sept 2, anasarca.
7754, James, W, 5, Co K, died Sept 4, diarrhea.
9054, Jarvis, W P, 12, Co D, died Sept 24, diarrhea.
11000, Jordan, J, 5 cav, Co B, died Oct 16, dysentery c.
11143, Jones, D, 1 cav, Co L, died Oct 18, scorbutus.
12541, Jones, J, 16, Co E, died Jan 27, '65, diarrhea.

87, Kennedy, James, 11 cav, Co E, died March 21, '64, diarrhea c.
191, Knotts, Fred, 11 cav, Co E, died March 27, fever typhus.
926, Kessmer, John, 12 cav, Co I, died May 7, diarrhea.
1045, Kennedy, S B, 39, Co B, died May 12, diarrhea.
1173, Keiling, M, 11 cav, Co D, died May 17, pneumonia.
3928, Keystone, C, 6, Co E, died July 25, diarrhea.
4921, Kenndey, A,* 1 cav, Co A, died July 6, diarrhea.
5553, Knapp, Thomas, 6 cav, Co M, died July 13, scorbutus.
5925, Kressler, P, 4 cav, Co K, died July 17, diarrhea.
12265, Knapp, J, 5 cav, Co B, died Dec 12, scorbutus.

48, Lenniert, L, 1, Co K, died March 15, bronchitis.
310, Lambert, R, 11 cav, Co F, died April 2, diarrhea.
1135, Lay, Wm, 11 cav, Co D, died May 16, pleuritis.
1726, Lossman, A, 4 cav, Co E, died June 8, diarrhea.
1802, Larger, W, 1 cav, Co L, died June 10, dysentery.
1912, Ledford, J A, 16, Co B, died June 13, diarrhea c.
2109, Little, J, 1, Co D, died June 17, fever congestive.
2352, Lononey, B, 1 cav, Co K, died June 23, anasarca.
2654, Lutherland, H, 32, Co G, died June 29 dysentery.
2668, Lasper, Otto, 15, Co H, died June 29, diarrhea c.
2837, Lublett, M L, 13, Co E, died July 3, typhus fever.
3340, Leville, Thomas, 4, Co D, died July 15, dysentery.
3398, Lee, S, 1 cav, Co A, died July 16, scorbutus.
3658, Loy, W B, 8 cav, Co L, died July 20, anasarca.
3770, Lanhart, J, 6 cav, Co G, died July 22, diarrhea.
3839, Lowry, Jas W, 12 cav, Co G, died July 23, diarrhea c.
6024, Lewis T, 2 cav, Co C, died Aug 18, scorbutus.
7132, Landers, —,* 36, Co I, died Aug 28, diarrhea.
7934, Luster, W, 1 cav, Co B, died Sept 5, diarrhea.
8487, Lutton, Thomas, 6, Co K, died Sept 11, scorbutus.
8634, Little, J F, 12 cav, Co D, died Sept 13, diarrhea.
11870, Lindusky, G, 11, Co G, died Nov 8, scorbutus
12175, Ledwick, A, 7, Co C, died Nov 27, scorbutus.
9175, Lord, Wm, 28, Co G, died Sept 18, scorbutus.

271, McMannus, Samuel, 11, Co D, died March 31, diarrhea c.
360, Miller, John, 3, Co A, died April 5, pleuritis.
525, McDougal, W C, 14, Co K, died April 13, hydrocele.
796, Mills, John, 1, Co H, died April 29, diarrhea c.
991, McClure, P, 11 cav, Co C, died May 10, dysentery.
1222, Marshall, Wm, 5 cav, Co I, died May 19, diarrhea c.
1380, Montgomery, W A, 5 cav, Co H, died May 26, diarrhea c
1301, Moreland, H, 1 cav Co F, died May 26, diarrhea a.
1969, Merix, J, 45 cav, Co D, died June 14, diarrhea c.
2024, Morton, W, 7 cav, Co I, died June 15, anasarca.
2137, Meldown, D, 11 cav, Co E, died June 18, diarrhea a.
2669, Miller, W C, 27 cav, Co A, died June 29, diarrhea.
3152, Mitchell, James, 12 cav, Co C, died July 11, diarrhea.
64, Mullins, W W, 1 cav, Co H, died Aug 8, small pox.
3418, Morgan J, 4 cav, Co D, died July 17, diarrhea c.
4513, Masters, J, 11 cav, Co A, died Aug 1, scorbutus.
4550, McDonald, J, 4 cav, Co I, died Aug 2, dysentery.
4646, Mitchell, R M, 17 cav Co E, died Aug 3, dysentery.
5691, Mooney, Pat, 11 Cav, Co G, died Aug 15, diarrhea.
7951, McCarty, E, 5 cav, Co K, died Sept 6, diarrhea.
8455, McCarty, John, 6 cav, Co K, died Sept 9, scorbutus.
8685, McCarter, W, 9 cav, Co B, died Sept 13, scorbutus.
9239, Munch, J, 28 cav, Co F died Sept 19, catarrh.
9408, Macury, C, 11 cav, Co M, died Sept 21, gangrene.
9711, Moore, Wm, 12 cav, Co D, died Sept 24, diarrhea.
7336, Martin F P, 12 cav, Co D, died Aug 30, scorbutus.
10170, Marshall, L, 1 cav, Co F, died Oct 1, diarrhea.
10460, Mills, George, 4 cav, Co H, died Oct 7, scorbutus.
11455, Murphy, W M, 2 cav, Co H, died Oct 25, scorbutus.
11478, Miller, E, 4 cav, Co I, died Oct 26, scorbutus.
12406, Miller, J, 4 cav, Co K, died Jan 16, '65, rheumatism.

No. of Grave.

12491, Meyers, J, 4 cav, Co C, died Jan 20, '65, diarrhea.
12520, Meach, A J, 1 cav, Co A, died March 3, '65, debilitas.
12764, Morgan F,* 3, Co I, died March 12, '65, wounds.

212, New, Geo W, 1 cav, Co F, died March 28, pneumonia.
447, Neely, B W, 1 cav, Co G, died April 9, dysentery.
63, Nelson, John, 1 cav, Co D, died July 19, small pox.
7693, Northcraft, J, 6 cav, Co H, died Sept 3, scorbutus.
9230, Newton A,* 4 cav, Co H, died Sept 19, diarrhea c.

2499, O'Bannon, Wm, 11 cav, Co B, died June 20, diarrhea c.
2513, Oper, L, 4 cav, Co B, died June 26, diarrhea c.
11943, Owen, W,* 1 cav, Co L, died Nov 9, scorbutus.

1178, Pott, J, 7 cav, Co C, died May 17, scorbutus.
1905, Porter, J F, 18 cav, died June 13, pneumonia.
3654, Pulliam, J, 2, died July 20, dysentery.
4220, Plyman, Wm, 39, Co D, died July 27, diarrhea c.
5761, Pally, S C,† 12 cav, Co B, died Aug 15, diarrhea c.
6616, Phelps, Wm E, 6 cav, Co F, died Aug 23, diarrhea.
6632, Pruils, W H, 1 cav, Co F, died Aug 23, scorbutus.
7222, Pope, Frank,* 5 cav, Co B, died Aug 29, scorbutus.
8070, Pott, Samuel, 4 cav, Co G, died Sept 7, dysentery.
8207, Patterson, J, 2 cav, Co B, died Sept 8, dysentery.
9299, Phelps, F, M,† 11 cav, Co I, died Sept 20, diarrhea.
10240, Partis, J R, 1 cav, Co F, died Oct 3, scorbutus.
12220, Price, John, 3 cav, Co G, died Dec 4, scorbutus.
12327, Purcell, J, 1 cav, Co G, died Dec 23, scorbutus.

2144, Questa, J, 11 cav, Co E, died June 18, diarrhea.

452, Reeves, E,† 4 cav, Co F, died April 9, debilitas.
577, Roberts, R, 12 cav, Co H, died April 16, diarrhea.
590, Ramay, Lester, 39 cav, Co H, died April 17, dysentery.
637, Raberle, Geo, 1 cav, Co A, died April 20, pneumonia.
825, Richardson, M,* 3, Co H, died May 1, pneumonia.
1097, Ruos, T, 11 cav, Co H, died May 14, diarrhea.
1193, Russell, Jacob, 12 cav, Co B, died May 18, diarrhea.
1355, Ritter, B B, 6 cav, Co L, died May 25, diarrhea.
1555, Rose, R C,* 6 cav, Co B, died June 2, scorbutus.
1571, Rogers, W, 1, Co F, died June 3, diarrhea c.
2463, Reve, F N, 11, Co F, died June 25, diarrhea.
2751, Reilly, Thos, 1, Co D, died July 1, diarrhea c.
4018, Ramsay, Robert, 45, Co A, died July 26, dysentery.
4482, Robertson, H, 11 cav, Co D, died Aug 1, debilitas.
4549, Rodes, James, 1 cav, Co F, died Aug 2, diarrhea.
4919, Rockwell, W W,* 1 cav, Co C, died Aug 6, anasarca.
5775, Roberts, L, 1 cav, Co K, died Aug 15, scorbutus.
5967, Rieff, R, 1 artil, died Aug 17, scorbutus.
5976, Roberts, Andrew, 1 cav, Co K, died Aug 17, diarrhea a.
6274, Readman, W, 11 cav, Co I, died Aug 20, marasmus.
7215, Rogers, Henry, 12 cav, Co A, died Aug 29, diarrhea.
10124, Robuy, F, 15 cav, Co E, died Oct 1, scorbutus.
11369, Racine, P, 12 cav, Co M, died Oct 21, scorbutus.
11583, Ryan, W, 1 cav, Co I, died Oct 28, scorbutus.
11642, Riddle, J H, 1 cav, Co I, died Oct 30, scorbutus.
11644, Rogers, Wm, 2 cav, Co I, died Oct 30, scorbutus.
11873, Rushy, J, 2 cav, Co F, died Nov 6, scorbutus.
12828, Rice P D,† 3, Co I, died April 9, '65, diarrhea c.
1202, Ruble, Leander,* 11 cav, Co D, died May 19, diarrhea a.
4106, Rankin, J H,† 18 cav, Co G, died July 27, diarrhea.

213, Simpson, W, 1 cav, Co C, died Mar 28, pneumonia.
277, Sims, Geo,† 40, Co I, died Mar 31, pneumonia.
567, Summers, W H, 11 cav, Co D, died Apr 15, pneumonia.
797, Smith, Geo, 13 cav, Co G, died April 29, anasarca.
925, Sallac, Geo,* 11 cav, Co C, died May 7, diarrhea c.
995, Smith, Wm A, 4 cav, Co K, died May 10, diarrhea.
1003, Smith, H, 16 cav, Co B, died May 10, dysentery.
1101, Smith, R C, 1 cav, Co I, died May 14, dysentery.
1180, Schafer, J E, 4 cav, Co A, died May 18, diarrhea.
1500, Stempf, Lewis, 12 cav, Co G, died May 31, dysentery.
1659, Sutherland, J E,† 1 cav, Co C, died June 6, dysentery.
1681, Sebastian, J W, 45, Co C, died June 6, diarrhea.
1691, Sanders, J S, 12 cav, Co E, died June 7, diarrhea.
1708, Stine, C, 4 cav, Co K, died June 7, dysentery.
1716, Sandifer, Jno, 11 cav, Co B, died June 8, diarrhea c.
1811, Summers, Wm, 11 cav, Co D, died June 10, diarrhea.
1827, Sweeney, M, 5 cav, Co I, died June 11, diarrhea.
1952, Shirley, John, 28 cav, Co E, died June 14, diarrhea a.
1964, Stanley, C O, 17 cav, Co E, died June 14, diarrhea c.
2063, Salmoud, P, 18 cav, Co H, died June 16, scorbutus.
2094, Shanks, W L, 6 cav, Co B, died June 17, diarrhea.
2766, Show, J, 11 cav, Co I, died July 6, diarrhea c.
44, Smith, John, 2 cav, Co I, died May 10, small pox.
51, Shaggs, I P, 11 cav, Co G, died June 2, small pox.
3402, Shunran, J, 4 cav, Co A, died July 16, diarrhea.
4258, Smith, B,* 5 cav, Co A, died July 29, diarrhea c.
4529, Sohmal, Andrew, 4 cav, Co B, died Aug 6, dysentery.
4531, Schottsman, F,* 1 cav, Co D, died Aug 6, diarrhea.
4976, Snyder, H M, 10 cav, Co B, died Aug 7, scorbutus.
5297, Smith, W H,* 27, Co E, died Aug 11, dysentery.
6260, Stevens, P L,† 12 cav, Co G, died Aug 20, fever typhus.
6280, Schrausburg, R, 1 cav, Co K, died Aug 20, scorbutus.
8226, Stimett, J, 6 cav, Co K, died Sept 6, scorbutus.
8487, Sutton, Thomas, 6 cav, Co A, died Sept 11, scorbutus.
8827, Shulds, J, 2 cav, Co K, died Sept 15, scorbutus.
10154, Sanders, B, 4 cav, Co F, died Oct 1, diarrhea.
10673, Sheppard, T L, 5 cav, Co H, died Oct 11, diarrhea.
11456, Sapp, B, 1 cav, Co B, died Oct 25, scorbutus.
11598, Selors, W H, 1 cav, Co C, died Nov 7, scorbutus.
12556, Stewart, E, 4 cav, Co A, died Jan 30, '65, scorbutus.
10197, Sawcey, Wm, 5 cav, Co H, died Oct 2, '64, scorbutus.

253, Taylor, Thos,* 11 cav, Co H, died March 30, diarrhea.
391, Thrope, H, 1 cav, Co B, died April 6, diarrhea c.
781, Tucker, Wm, 12 cav, Co I, died April 28, diarrhea c.
1009, Travis, Geo, 16 cav, Co E, died May 10, diarrhea.
1628, Tranney, J, 11 cav, Co C, died June 4, diarrhea c.
2116, Tutune, J,† 11 cav, Co A, died June 17, scorbutus.
2371, Tudor, Abraham,* 11 cav, Co A, died June 23, diarrhea a.
3701, Tullor, G W, 28, Co A, died July 21, catarrh.
6424, Tabu, Silas, 27, Co D, died Aug 12, diarrhea.
6234, Templeton, W H,* 11 cav, Co B, died Aug 20, dysentery.
6257, Tapp, George, 13 cav, Co I, died Aug 20, scorbutus.
6508, Tracy, Jas, 11 cav, Co L, died Aug 22, diarrhea.
6956, Thorp, J, 4 cav, Co K, died Aug 26, scorbutus.
7205, Tucker, Robt, 17 cav, Co G, died Aug 29, scorbutus.
10028, Tucker, J A, 15 cav, Co A, died Sept 29, scorbutus.
10338, Thornburg, B, 2 cav, Co G, died Oct 6, fever typhus.
10588, Tussey, E D, 24 cav, Co A, died Oct 10, scorbutus.
10809, Terry, Wm, 1 cav, Co A, died Oct 12, scorbutus.
10892, Thomas, W E,† 11 cav, Co G, died Oct 14, scorbutus.

10657, Vandevier, J, 11 cav, Co C, died Oct 11, diarrhea.

278, West, John C, 11 cav, Co E, died Mar 31, fever typhus.
494, White, A, 6 cav, Co K, died Apr 12, dysentery.
735, Wallar, M R, 16 cav, Co C, died Apr 24, dysentery.
1125, White, John, 11 cav, Co D, died May 15, dysentery c.
1706, Westfall, J, 4 cav, Co D, died June 7, dysentery c.
1734, Wickles, John, 40, Co K, died June 8, diarrhea c.
1745, Walsh, J E, 6 cav, Co L, died June 8, diarrhea.
1894, Wright, John E,* 1 cav, died June 13, diarrhea.
2199, Wheelan, Jas, 18 cav, Co C, died June 19, diarrhea.
2584, White, C, 1 cav, Co H, died June 27, anasarca.
2901, Wiser, R M, 1 cav, Co B, died July 5, diarrhea.
40, Ward, F W, 1 cav, Co A, died May 3, small pox.
4374, Warren, W P, 34 cav, Co K, died July 31, diarrhea.
4624, Wallace, H, 14 cav, Co E, died Aug 3, dysentery.
4697, West, P H, 6 cav, Co K, died Aug 3, diarrhea.
5057, Webb, J, 6 cav, Co F, died Aug 8, scorbutus.
5762, Welch, T C, 5 cav, Co G, died Aug 15, diarrhea.
5790, Walsh, John, 6 cav, Co H, died Aug 15, scorbutus.
6101, Winter, H, 11 cav, Co E, died Aug 18, diarrhea c.
6121, Winfries, W S, 3 cav, Co A, died Aug 19, dysentery.
6893, White, S A, 17 cav, Co G, died Aug 28, dysentery.
7038, Willser, J, 11 cav, Co I, died Aug 27, scorbutus.
7694, Wells, John W, 12 cav, Co C, died Sept 3, wounds.
8533, Wallace, J,† 11 cav, Co K, died Sept 12, diarrhea.
9258, Warner, D, 12 cav, Co A, died Sept 19, scorbutus.
9541, Wicog, S, 4 cav, Co I, died Sept 23, diarrhea.
9630, Wagoner, H,* 4 cav, Co I, died Sept 24, scorbutus.
10710, Warner, Thos, 15 cav, Co F, died Oct 12, scorbutus.
10898, Walton, J J, 8 cav, Co A, died Oct 14, scorbutus.
11749, Willit, M, 4 cav, Co I, died Nov 2, scorbutus.
12279, Weasett, A, 1 cav, Co D, died Nov 13, scorbutus.

934, Yocombe, H, 11 cav, Co D, died May 5, phthisis.
1168, Yoam, J, 10 cav, Co D, died May 17, catarrh.
2489, Yeager, L,† 11 cav, Co C, died June 30, diarrhea.
3757, Yeast, R, 1 cav, Co I, died July 22, catarrh.

5257, Zerles, O, 4 cav, Co G, died Aug 10, anasarca.

LOUISIANA.

6778, Kimball, Jas, 2 cav, Co A, died Aug 25, constipatio.

MAINE.

No. of Grave.

2604, Anderson, John, 19, Co I, died June 28, diarrhea c.
8093, Allen A, 32, Co K, died July 10, diarrhea c.
7024, Arnold, E W, 17, Co G, died Aug 27, diarrhea c.

22, Butler, C A, 3, Co K, died March 7, pneumonia.
269, Brown, E M, 5, Co G, died March 31, diarrhea.
8958, Buner, A E, 31, Co E, died July 25, scorbutus.
6211, Bachelor, P, † 3, Co K, died Aug 19, diarrhea c.
9162, Baker, James, 17, Co H, died Sept 18, diarrhea c.
10669, Ballast, J, 19, Co G, died Oct 11, scorbutus.
7683, Bartlett, H, 17, Co C, died Sept 8, ictus solis.
7255, Barney, G S, 32, Co I, died Aug 30, scorbutus.
6683, Bean, G W, 8, Co C, died Aug 24, debilitas.
6603, Bennett, L, 1 artil, died Aug 23, diarrhea.
9097, Berry, C H, 6, Co H, died Sept 18, scorbutus.
7615, Bigelow, C, 19, Co H, died Sept 8, scorbutus.
5290, Blaizdell, H, S, Co F, died Aug 11, scorbutus.
12055, Boren, W, 16, Co I, died Nov 16, diarrhea.
9408, Bowden, ——, 7, Co A, died Sept 21, diarrhea.
4776, Braley, J, 3, Co E, died Aug 4, diarrhea.
6015, Briggs, J C, 19, Co F, died Aug 8, scorbutus.
8512, Brinkerman, L 9, Co D, died Sept 11, scorbutus.
8247, Broadstreet, C B, 1 cav, Co B, died Sept 9, diarrhea c.
6811, Brown, J, 3, Co G, died Aug 25, diarrhea c.
11980, Bryant, C D, 16, Co E, died Nov 18, diarrhea c.
5719, Bullsen, E T, † 5 cav, Co B, died Aug 15, enteritis.
5757, Bunker, S A, 1 artil, Co A, died Aug 15, scorbutus.
8474, Burgen, A, 4, Co I, died Sept 11, scorbutus.

7017, Cardoney, C, 17, Co G, died Aug 27, diarrhea.
7746, Carlen, M, 1 cav, Co F, died Sept 3, diarrhea.
8374, Carr, J, 19, Co E, died Sept 10, scorbutus.
6246, Carlton, J S, 31, Co D, died Aug 19, diarrhea c.
6089, Chase, F W, 1 artil, Co D, died Aug 17, diarrhea.
2316, Clark, James, 1 cav, Co C, died June 22, diarrhea.
8143, Clark, P M, † 1 cav, Co C, died Sept 6, diarrhea c.
10376, Clark L, 19, Co D, died Oct 5, diarrhea.
10421, Clayton, E B, 1, Co F, died Oct 6, scorbutus.
28, Cohan, D, 3, Co K, died March 7, pneumonia.
6950, Conder, W H, 16, Co G, died Aug 26, bronchitis.
8087, Conley W, 5, Co F, died Sept 6, diarrhea.
8943, Cook, James, 4, Co D, died July 25, fever typhus.
8488, Conlon, D H, 20, Co K, died Sept 11, scorbutus.
425, Craw, H, 3, Co B, died April 7, pneumonia.
12061, Cressy, N F, 11, Co G, died Nov 17, scorbutus.
10936, Cromwell, S R, * 1 artil, Co M, died Sept 14, scorbutus.
11211, Cromwell, W H, 19, Co D, died Oct 20, scorbutus.
6625, Curtiss, John, 16, Co I, died Sept 13, scorbutus.
12367, Cutts, O M, 16, Co D, died Jan 1, '65 scorbutus.
80, Cutter, A, 20, Co E, died March 20, dysentery.
5171, Cross, Noah, 1 artil, Co A, died Aug 9, ictus solis.
8581, Crosby, W, 4, Co A, died Sept 12, dysentery.

8445, Davis, D, 3, Co C, died Sept 11, scorbutus.
227, Davis, Wm L, 20, Co E, died March 29, diarrhea.
6615, Dougherty, Thomas, 8, Co G, died Aug 14, dysentery.
6612, Donnell, F, 8, Co E, died Aug 23, diarrhea.
9624, Downes J, S, Co G, died Sept 23, diarrhea.
1359, Doyle, Wm, 6, Co D, died May 25, diarrhea c.
5481, Drisdale, F, 1, Co H, died Aug 13, diarrhea.
4425, Duffy, A, 8, Co G, died July 31, anasarca.
6415, Dugan, D, 32, Co A, died Aug 21, scorbutus.
6438, Dunning, S P, 29, Co G, died Aug 21, diarrhea.
7240, Dunnie, G, 5, Co G, died Aug 29, anasarca.
6857, Dye, John, 1 cav, Co E, died Aug 21, scorbutus.
5085, Dittener, H, 20, Co A, died Aug 8, scorbutus.

10609, Eckhard, H, 7, Co C, died Sept 10, scorbutus.
7212, Edwards, N S, 1 cav, Co F, died Aug 29, diarrhea.
8518, Ellis, A, 2 artil, Co H, died Sept 11, diarrhea.
1677, Emerson, H H, 8, died June 12, scorbutus.

2628, Farewell, E, 31, Co E, died June 23, dysentery.
8401, Ferrell, P, 6, Co H, died Sept 10, scorbutus.
4765, Fish, Wm, 7, Co A, died Aug 5, dysentery.
5243, Flagg, J B, 5, Co K, died Aug 10, dysentery.
69, Flanders, L O, 20, Co E, died March 19, diarrhea.
1989, Foley, John, 19, Co E, died June 15, diarrhea.
2362, Forrest, Thomas, 1 cav, Co E, died June 23, diarrhea.
2482, Foster, A, * 6, Co K, died June 25, diarrhea c.
8145, Foster, E R, 16, Co C, died Sept 8, diarrhea.
7073, Foster, Sam'l C, 16, Co K, died Aug 28, fever remittent.
6191, Frisbie L, 7, Co C, died Aug 19.
10957, Fitzgerald, Joseph, 8, Co E, died Oct 14, scorbutus.

5907, Gardner, W H, † 4, died Aug 16, scorbutus.
12515, Gibbs, R, 19, Co K, died Jan 28, '65, diarrhea.

2906, Gilgan, W, 7, Co C, 5, died July 5, dysentery.
6107, Goodward, A, 1 artil, Co I, died Aug 18, diarrhea.
5580, Goodwin, M T, 8, Co F, died Aug 14, diarrhea.
4141, Grant, G, 1 artil, Co F, died July 28, diarrhea.
7391, Grant, Frank, 16, Co F, died Aug 30, catarrh.
8892, Griffith, S, 6, Co G, died Sept 20, diarrhea c.
9190, Gunney, C, 31, Co A, died Sept 18, diarrhea.
10081, Gunney, J F, † 1, Co I died Sept 29, scorbutus.
11533, Gilgrist, ——, 31, Co E, died Nov 5, scorbutus.

8306, Hammond, J, 19, Co G, died Sept 10, anasarca.
12343, Harris, J S, 1, Co F, died Dec 26, dysentery.
5506, Hassen, H, 7 Co G, died July 18, diarrhea.
8274, Hatch, J S, 8, Co O, died July 13, dysentery.
6112, Hatch, S, † 8, Co F, died Aug 19, scorbutus.
9311, Heath, B, 3, Co F, died Sept 20, diarrhea.
4174, Heninger, 19, died July 28, debilitas.
12349, Hopes, H, 19, Co D, died Dec 27, scorbutus.
7474, Howard, D H, 17, Co D, died Sept 1, dysentery.
3844, Howe, Sam'l W, 1, Co K, died July 23, diarrhea.
7186, Hoyt, A D, 8, Co K, died Aug 29, diarrhea.
8287, Hudson, W, 17, Co E, died July 12, diarrhea.
8797, Hughes, Wm, 31, Co K, died Sept 15, scorbutus.
9652, Humphrey, ——, 8 cav, Co L, died Sept 24, scorbutus.
3484, Hunkey, E B, 1, Co L, died July 17, diarrhea c.
4703, Henley, D, 8, Co G, died Aug 4, dysentery.

5835, Ingols, L, 16, Co H, died Aug 11, '64, ictus solis.
9359, Ingerson, P, 7, Co J, died Sept, 20th '64, diarrhea.

11489, Jackson, A J, 17, Co J, died Oct 26, '64, scorbutus.
10619, Jackson, R, 7, Co B, died Oct 10, '64, scorbutus.
10710, Jackson, R W, 7, Co D, died Oct 11, '64, diarrhea.
12602, Jerdan, J, 19, Co F, died Feb 6, '65, rheumatism.
7385, Johnson, B, 7, Co K, died Aug 30, '64, scorbutus.
5849, Jones, Wm, 19, Co E, died Aug 16, '64, enteritis.
10243, Jory, G F, 8, Co F, died Oct 3, '64, scorbutus.

11586, Kellar, J, 19, Co J, died Oct 29, '64, scorbutus.
8237, Kelley, L, 11, Co D, died Sept 9, '64, diarrhea.
8813, Kennedy, W, 17, Co G, died July 14, '64, diarrhea.
6169, Kilpatrick, C, 8, Co C, died Aug 19, '64, debilitas.

5866, Ladd, C, 6, Co I, died Aug 11, '64, diarrhea c.
8350, Lamber, W, 17, Co K, died Sept 10, '64, diarrhea.
11707, Levitt, H, 19, Co A, died Nov 1, '64, scorbutus.
7967, Lincoln, A, 16, Co I, died Sept 6, '64, scorbutus.
10981, Littlefield, C, 1 cav, Co F, died Oct 14, scorbutus.
6340, Lord, Geo H, 8, Co B, died Aug 21, '64, diarrhea.
5549, Ludovloe, F, 13, Co F, died Aug 13, '64, scorbutus.
490, Lowell, B, 4, Co G, died April 12, '64, diarrhea c.

9426, Macon, L, 8, Co A, died Sept 21, diarrhea.
709, Malcolm, H M, 16, Co A, died April 24, '64, erysipelas.
6606, Marshall, B F, 1, Co H, died 23 Aug, '64, diarrhea.
12122, Maston, A, 19, Co D, died Nov 22, '64, scorbutus.
10392, Mathews, James 32, Co F, died Oct 14, '64, scorbutus.
12011, Maxwell, J, 9, Co E, died Nov 14, scorbutus.
3679, McFarland, O, 3, Co G, died July 21, anasarca.
9536, McGinley, J, 7, Co A, died Sept 22, scorbutus.
2200, McKinney, G, 3, Co I, died June 19, diarrhea.
12084, McFarland, E S, 8, Co I, died Nov 13, '65, scorbutus.
4391, Medcalf, Oliver, 8, Co H, died July 31, diarrhea c.
12768, McFarland, W, * 19, Co K, died March 13, scorbutus.
5200, Melgar, J, 7, died Aug 10, diarrhea.
5614, Messer, O R, 7, Co F, died Aug 14, scorbutus.
9399, Miller, C J, 1 cav, Co B, died Sept 21, scorbutus.
2002, Miller, J O, 2, Co D, died June 15, diarrhea.
7573, Mills, M, 1, died Sept 2, diarrhea.
2508, Moore, Charles W, 3, Co B, died July 8, dysentery.
11042, Moore, G, 18, Co D, died Oct 17, scorbutus.
7278, Moore, J D, 1 cav, Co B, died Aug 30, scorbutus.
6940, Moore, W C, 7, Co A, died Aug 26, scorbutus.
8118, Moyes, F, 32, Co F, died Sept 8, diarrhea.

7046, Newton, C, 9, Co K, died Aug 27, anasarca.
1507, Nickerson, D, 4, Co F, died May 31, diarrhea c.
6020, Nolton, H, 7, Co B, died Sept 6, anasarca.

2131, O'Brion, W, 16, Co A, died June 18, diarrhea c.
6325, Opease, S, 19, died Aug 21, debilitas.
148, Osborn, A, J, 3, died March 24, dysentery.
10666, Owens, O H, 10, died Nov 6, scorbutus.

3710, Parker, A, 1 cav, Co E, died July 21, diarrhea.
7979, Parsons, James W, 16, Co D, died Sept 6, diarrhea.
9362, Patrick, F, 14, Co F, died Sept 23, diarrhea.
2272, Peabody, F S, 15, Co I, died June 20, diarrhea.
12543, Pequette, P, 4, Co G, died Jan 26, '65 scorbutus.

No. of Grave.
1498, Perkins, D, 1 cav, Co I, died May 31, diarrhea.
5197, Perkins, T, 1, Co H, died Aug 10, scorbutus.
6911, Peters, H, 4, Co E, died Aug 26, scorbutus.
12056, Chillbrook, F, 1 artil, Co A, died Nov 17, diarrhea.
2064, Phelps, W H, 1 cav, Co H, died June 16, diarrhea.
8486, Pinkham, U W, 1 artil, Co A, died July 17, diarrhea.
1861, Pottle, A E, 1 cav, Co I, died May 25, diarrhea.
5698, Pratt, A M, 1 cav, Co L, died Aug 15, wounds.
8441, Poterman, G, 16, Co D, died Sept 11, scorbutus.
12410, Prescott, C, 19, Co H, died Jan 7, '65, diarrhea.

7785, Richardson, C, 31, Co L, died Sept 4, scorbutus.
6762, Richardson, J K, 8, Co G, died Aug 24, scorbutus.
10465, Richardson, W M,* 1 cav, Co B, died Oct 7, dysentery.
5522, Ricker, Wm,* 1 cav, Co D, died Aug 13, dysentery.
6480, Ridlon, N, 7, Co D, died Sept 11, scorbutus.
900, Risees, K, 3, Co I, died May 5, anasarca.
8921, Roberts, H, 19, Co K, died July 25, diarrhea.
6236, Rowe, L, 1, Co A, died Aug 10, diarrhea.
166, Rosmer, Frank, 4, Co C, died March 26, diarrhea.
5796, Rust, H, 2, Co H, died Aug 15, dysentery.
8557, Russell, G A, 1 cav, Co E, died Sept 12, scorbutus.

5150, Sampson, E, 1, Co F, died Aug 12, scorbutus.
4532, Sawyer, Enos, 1 artil, Co H, died Aug 2, diarrhea.
9182, Sawyer, John, 31, Co K, died July 11, ictus solis.
11462, Shorey, S, 1 cav, Co K, died Oct 20, scorbutus.
2243, Simmons, G F, 6, Co K, died 20 June, diarrhea.
8159, Smith, W, 9, Co K, died July 11, diarrhea c.
3381, Smith, W A, 6, Co F, died July 14, diarrhea.
1782, Snowdale, F, 4, Co C, died June 10, diarrhea c.
9974, Snower, S C, 19, Co A, died Sept 28, diarrhea.
1998, Springer, H W, 36, Co A, died June 15, diarrhea.
4596, Steward, G, 20, Co H, died Aug 9, diarrhea.
11562, St Peter, F, 19, Co F, died Oct 27, scorbutus.
7001, Swaney, P, 19, Co F, died Aug 27, diarrhea.
199, Swan, H R,* 3, Co F, died March 28, dysentery.
1936, Swan, F, 3, Co F, died June 14, anasarca.

No. of Grave.
8682, Thompson, F, 9, Co F, died Sept 18, scorbutus.
10455, Thompson, John, 8, Co E, died Oct 7, diarrhea.
621, Thorn, E, 9, Co I, died April 19, dysentery.
10925, Toothacre, J, 7, Co G, died Oct 14, scorbutus.
1106, Turner, C C, 4, Co E, died May 16, diarrhea c.
5080, Tufts, J, 32, Co C, died Aug 8, diarrhea.
11875, Taylor, G, 9, Co C, died Nov 16, scorbutus.
12322, Tuttle, D L, 32, Co F, died Dec 20, scorbutus.
12196, Tuttle, L S*, 32, Co F, died Nov 30, diarrhea.
12706, Thorndie, W B,* 19, Co I, died March 2, '65, scorbutus.

6245, Valley, F, 32, Co K, died Aug 19, diarrhea.
3835, Venill, C, 32, Co G, died July 15, diarrhea.

7226, Walker, A B,* 1, Co K, died Aug 29, diarrhea.
3894, Walker, M C, 5, Co I, died July 24, debilitas.
7722, Wall, A, 1 cav, Co K, died Sept 4, diarrhea.
5942, Walsh, Thomas, 20, Co H, died Aug 17, scorbutus.
6750, Watson, B, 7, Co K, died Aug 24, dysentery.
10559, Webber, Oliver, 3, Co A, died Oct 9, diarrhea.
4559, Whiteman, A M,* 5, Co I, died Aug 2, scorbutus.
1643, Whitcomb, T O, 4, Co F, died June 5, diarrhea c.
6251, Whittier, J K P, 32, Co C, died Aug 19, bronchitis.
10445, Willard, W, 20, Co B, died Oct 7, scorbutus.
7711, Williams, C, 6, Co G, died Sept 8, debilitas.
6900, Wilson, George, 32, Co C, died Aug 26, diarrhea.
8639, Wilson, G W, 16, Co H, died July 20, anasarca.
3132, Wiley, D H, 19, Co E, died July 10, dysentery.
8860, Winslow, E, 1, 4, Co B, died July 24, scorbutus.
5512, Winslow, N L, 4, Co K, died Aug 18, debilitas.
6372, Wyman, A, 32, Co C, died Aug 21, scorbutus.
2095, Wyman, J, 16, Co A, died June 17, diarrhea.
12470, Wyer, R, 8, Co K, died Jan 16, '65, diarrhea.
12043, Wright C, 1, Co G, died Nov 16, scorbutus.

178, Young, E W,† 3, Co H, died March 26, debilitas.
6369, Young, J, 8, Co H, died Aug 21, scorbutus.
8140, Young, J W,* 8, Co I, died Sept 6, scorbutus.

MARYLAND.

850, Allen, W H, 1, Co H, died May 8, dysentery.
1028, Anderson, Wm, 2, Co C, died May 11, dysentery.
1379, Aikens, A, 1 cav, Co I, died May 26, diarrhea c.
1928, Adams, Jas T, 6, Co H, died May 14, diarrhea.
10283, Abbott, D E, 2, Co D, died Oct 4, scorbutus.
12325, Archer, H, 1, Co I, died Dec 24, scorbutus.

112, Babb, Samuel, 8, Co I, died March 28, bronchitis.
283, Berlin, Jas, 2 cav, Co F, died April 1, pneumonia.
472, Beltz, W W, 2, Co H, died April 9, diarrhea c.
1056, Bowers, A, 1, Co I, died May 14, diarrhea c.
1455, Brown, Augustus, 2, Co G, died May 29, diarrhea c.
1487, Braddock, Wm, 2, Co D, died May 30, diarrhea.
1549, Buck, H, 1 cav, Co H, died June 1, diarrhea c.
1644, Buckley, Geo, 9, Co B, died June 5, diarrhea c.
2404, Bennett, C B, 1, Co D, died June 24, diarrhea c.
3269, Brant, D B, 2, Co H, died July 18, diarrhea c.
4602, Betson James, 1 battery, Co A, died Aug 8, scorbutus.
5261, Ball, J A, 2, Co B, died Aug 10, scorbutus.
5525, Brown, J C, 1 artil, Co B, died Aug 13, scorbutus.
6540, Brown, E R, 2, Co C, died Aug 28, scorbutus.
7727, Brown, E, 2, Co D, died Sept 3, dysentery.
6975, Buckley A M, 1, Co B, died Sept 17, diarrhea.
11184, Beale, R, 1 cav, Co D, died Sept 19, scorbutus.
11761, Buckner, George, 2, Co K, died Nov 8, scorbutus.
11620, Bell, J R, 8, Co D, died Oct 28, scorbutus.
12373, Bloom, J,* 7, Co F, died Jan 1, '65, pleuritis.
12679, Book, C, 8, Co G, died Feb 19, '65, diarrhea.

54, Carpenter, Wm, 2 cav, Co I, died March 17, diarrhea.
804, Cook, Lewis, 9, Co E, died April 1, dysentery.
469, Coombs, E A, 9, Co I, died April 9, diarrhea.
524, Carter, Wm, 2, Co C, died April 13, pneumonia.
728, Cury, W H, 9, Co F, died April 25, diarrhea.
1357, Carl, J M, 6, Co E, died May 25, diarrhea c.
1871, Cabhage, C H, 2, Co H, died May 25, dysentery.
2012, Cullin, John, 2, Co D, died June 15, diarrhea.
4182, Crasby, M, 1, Co G, died July 28, dysentery.
4620, Carter, John, 2, Co C, died Aug 8, diarrhea.
5088, Carr, Wm, 1 cav, Co D, died Aug 8, diarrhea c.
5063, Childs, G A, 9, Co I, died Aug 5, diarrhea c.
5826, Criste, J, 6, Co G, died Aug 16, dysentery.
8098, Crouse, W A, Coles' cav, Co E, died Sept 6, diarrhea.
8085, Conway, Wm E, 4, Co E, died Sept 6, diarrhea.
8266, Crabb, H, 4, Co E, died Sept 9, diarrhea c.
8357, Corn, H S, 1, Co E, died Sept 10, diarrhea.
8619, Crouse, J A, 1 cav, Co A, died Sept 18, diarrhea c.
10600, Cullins, D, 1, Co C, died Sept 10, diarrhea a.

12395, Callabao, P, 1, Co F, died Jan 4, '65, diarrhea.

181, Duff, Chas,* 8, Co A, died March 27, pneumonia.
1410, Dunn, John,* 9, Co H, died May 27, diarrhea c.
2896, Davis, Thomas, 9, died June 24, scorbutus.
3912, Drew, C, 85, Co B, died July 24, diarrhea.
4188, Dennis, Benj, 2, Co A, died July 28, diarrhea.
4211, Davis, G, 1 cav, Co F, died July 29, scorbutus.
6510, Dickwall, Wm, 2, Co F, died Aug 22, diarrhea.
8199, Deller, F, 1, Co E, died Sept 8, diarrhea.
6758, Dennisseo, T, 42, Co I, died Aug 25, diarrhea.

8428, Ellis, C, 4, Co D, died Sept 12, scorbutus.
10410, Eli, W, 7, Co C, died Oct 6, scorbutus.

3849, Fecker, L, 2, Co I, died July 24, scorbutus.
1321, Fairbanks, J E, 9, Co C, died May 23, diarrhea c.
2559, Francis J,* 2, Co K, died June 27, fever remittent.
2600, Fenge, F J, 2, Co H, died June 28, diarrhea.
2824, Farrnas, Jas, 7, Co G, died July 2, dysentery.
6016, Frantz, F, 2, Co H, died Aug 17, anasarca.
7404, Fink, L, 2, Co H, died Aug 31, debilitas.
9290, Frederick, J E, 9, Co I, died Sept 19, scorbutus.
12752, Freaere, W, 3, Co A, died March 10, '65, scorbutus.

1271, Gordon, A B, 9, Co E, died May 22, dysentery.
2188, Gerard, Fred, 1 cav, Co B, died June 18, diarrhea c.
8018, Green, Thos, 2, Co D, died July 7, diarrhea.
8789, Gregg, F, 2, Co I, died July 22, diarrhea.
6072, Gilson, J E,† 1 cav, Co C, died Aug 18, scorbutus.
6781, Ganon, J W, 2, Co K, died Aug 21, diarrhea.
12785, Guff, John, 1, Co I, died March 6, '65, diarrhea c.

1767, Hoock, J,* 2, Co H, died April 27, diarrhea.
826, Hickley, John, 9, Co G, died May 1, anasarca.
1625, Howell, L H, 1 cav, Co M, died June 4, diarrhea c.
1720, Hoop H, 2, Co I, died June 6, scorbutus.
2857, Hickley, J S, 2, Co H, died June 28, diarrhea c.
2494, Hidderick, H, 1, Co I, died June 26, diarrhea.
2978, Hite, J E, 2, Co I, died July 7, diarrhea c.
8864, Hering, P,† 2, Co C, died July 24, scorbutus.
4767, Hank, Thomas, 1 battery, Co D, died Aug 5, scorbutus.
5292, Hilligar, J, Co E, died Aug 11, diarrhea.
5408, Hood, John, 6, Co C, died Aug 12, scorbutus.
5917, Holmes, L, 2, Co H, died Aug 17, dysentery.
6184, Hone, S, 8, Co E, died Aug 22, diarrhea.
6504, Harris, J E, 1, Co A, died Aug 22, diarrhea.
7434, Hazel, J, 9, Co C, died Sept 1, dysentery.

No. of Grave.

6165, Hlmick, F, 1 cav, Co E, died Sept 8, fever remittent.
8398, Hall, J, 7, Co D, died Sept 10, diarrhea c.
9932, Holden, J R, 9, Co C, died Sept 28, dysentery.
11109, Hukalon, F, 2, Co K, died Oct 13, scorbutus.
12422, Hoover, J, 2 cav, Co C, died Jan 9, '65, scorbutus.

2895, Issac, Henry, 2, Co H, died July 4, diarrhea c.

93, Jones, David, 1 battery, Co A, died March 22, diarrhea.
669, Jenkins, M, 2, Co A, died April 22, diarrhea c.

460, Keplinger, J, 2, Co H, died April 9, diarrhea.
511, Keefe, Lewis, 7, Co F, died April 14, pneumonia.
7242, Kirby, J, 9, Co F, died Aug 29, dysentery.

1019, Laird, Corbin, 1 cav, Co F, died May 11, diarrhea c.
1056, Lees, W H, 2, Co C, died May 13, fever intermittent.
8918, Loois J, †2, Co B, died July 24, dysentery.
11385, Little, D, 2 cav, Co K, died Oct 24, scorbutus.
12361, Lebud, J, 1 cav, Co D, died Dec 30, scorbutus.
12067, Lambert, W, 1, Co I, died Feb 17, '65, scorbutus.

206, McCarle, Jas, 1 cav, Co B, died March 28, diarrhea c.
471, Moland, B, 2, Co F, died April 9, diarrhea c.
896, Myers, Noah, 9, Co G, died May 5, diarrhea.
1190, McGuigen, S K, 1 battery, Co D, died May 18, diarrhea.
1847, Myers, L S, 1, Co B, died May 28, diarrhea c.
1797, Moore, Frank, 9, Co A, died June 10, congestive chill.
1898, Moffitt, Thos, 6, died June 13, diarrhea c.
2059, Maitz, G H, 2, Co H, died June 16, anasarca.
3129, Mechler, C S, 1 battery, Co A, died July 17, diarrhea.
3797, McKinsay, Jno, 2, Co I, died July 22, diarrhea.
4051, Miller, F, 6, Co C, died July 27, scorbutus.
4146, Mathews, F, 8, Co G, died July 28, diarrhea.
4881, Macomber, John, 1 cav, Co B, died Aug 6, diarrhea.
5170, Marvin, J, 2, Co H, died Aug 9, scorbutus.
6757, Moon, J J, 1, Co D, died Aug 25, scorbutus.
7281, McCullough, J, 1, Co I, died Aug 30, scorbutus.
7327, McLamos, J, 7, Co C, died Aug 30, dysentery.
8043, Markell, S, 2, Co H, died Sept 6, diarrhea.
10150, Munroe, J, *4, Co H, died Oct 1, dysentery.
10861, Markin, W, 1, Co F, died Oct 18, scorbutus.
11517, Mathews, J, 8, died Oct 27, scorbutus.
12608, McMiller, J A, 1, Co E, died Feb 7, '65, scorbutus.

91, Nice, Jacob, 5 cav, Co M, died March 21, pneumonia.
871, Nace, Harrison, 9, Co H, died April 5, pneumonia.
9752, Norris, N, 1, Co I, died Sept 25, scorbutus.

158, Pool, Hanson, 2, Co H, died March 25, phthisis.
7590, Porter, G, 1, Co I, died Sept 2, diarrhea.
7941, Pindiville, M, 7, Co H, died Sept 6, scorbutus.
5069, Papple, D, *2, Co H, died Aug 8, dysentery.

252, Rusk, John, 9, Co E, died March 30, diarrhea.
918, Russell, A P, 2, Co C, died May 6, dysentery.
1606, Raub Simon, 9, Co E, died June 4, diarrhea.
1901, Robinson, J, 9, died June 18, diarrhea c.
2850, Rynedollar, Wm, 1 cav, Co D, died June 23, diarrhea c.
6599, Reed, Thos P, 1 artil, Co B, died Aug 23, diarrhea c.

155, Seberger, F, 9, Co F, died March 25, fever congestive.
817, Scarboro, Rob't, 9, Co I, died April 8, pneumonia.
478, Suffecol, S, 1, Co I, died April 9, diarrhea c.
718, Sinder, John, 2, Co H, died April 24, diarrhea.
899, Snooks, W, 9, Co E, died May 5, diarrhea c.
1205, Spence, Levi, 9, Co D, died May 19, anasarca.
1272, Scarlett, Jas, 1, Co D, died May 22, dysentery.
1926, Smith, Ed, †9, Co I, died June 14, diarrhea c.
2004, Stafford, John, 9, Co G, died June 15, diarrhea.
2361, Shipley, W, 9, Co G, died June 28, diarrhea c.
2489, Schineder, J, 1 battery, Co B, died June 26, diarrhea.
5797, Smith, John, 1 cav, Co B, died Aug 15, dysentery.
6751, Shelley, B, 2, Co F, died Aug 24, scorbutus.
6816, Shiver, G H, *1, Co C, died Aug 25, scorbutus.
6919, Stull, G E, 1 cav, Co D, died Aug 26, diarrhea c.
7580, Shilling, Wm, 2, Co K, died Sept 2, diarrhea c.
7843, Stolz, 7, Co K, died Sept 4, diarrhea c.
8296, Smitzer, J, 1, Co D, died Sept 9, scorbutus.
8716, Segar, Chas, 6, Co F, died Sept 14, scorbutus.
9309, Snyder, F, 2, Co, K, died Sept 20, diarrhea.
9451, Straiten, J A, 1 artil, Co C, died Sept 21, diarrhea.
10215, Shafer, J N, 1 cav, Co A, died Oct 22, diarrhea.
11159, Samon, L W, 1, Co I, died Oct 19, diarrhea c.
11160, Speaker, H, 1, Co F, died Oct 19, scorbutus.
12195, Spaulding, J, 4, Co C, died Nov 29, diarrhea.
12704, Smith, G C, 1, Co I, died Feb 26, '65, scorbutus.

149, Tyson, J T, 9, Co D, died March 25, pneumonia.
1022, Tysen, J T, 9, Co I, died May 11, diarrhea c.
677, Turner, Wm F, 1 cav, Co D, died April 22, dysentery.
1029, Turner, A, 1 cav, Co B, died May 11, pneumonia.
1356, Tindle, E, *9, Co G, died May 25, diarrhea c.
1377, Turner, C, 9, Co E, died May 26, diarrhea c.
7872, Thompson, J, 13, Co I, died Sept 5, scorbutus.
8689, Thompson, John, 2, Co S, died Sept 14, diarrhea.
9246, Tucker, 2, Co D, died Sept 19, scorbutus.
9335, Tindell, Wm, 11, Co B, died Sept 20, scorbutus.
11450, Tilton, J, 1 cav, Co F, died Oct 25, diarrhea.

1583, Ulrich, Daniel, 9, Co I, died June 8, diarrhea.

1805, Veach, Jesse, 2, Co H, died May 28, diarrhea c.
8269, Viscounts, A J, 1 artil, Co E, died Sept 9, diarrhea c.

78, Wise, John, 8, Co D, died March 20, diarrhea.
21, White, Wm, 9, Co C, died March 7, dysentery.
553, Widdons, D, 1, Co E, died April 14, diarrhea.
597, Webster, Samuel, *9, Co G, died April 17, diarrhea.
1171, Wharton, Samuel, 2, Co F, died May 17, diarrhea c.
2275, Worthen, Wm, 9, Co C, died June 20, diarrhea c.
4748, West, M, 4, Co D, died Aug 5, scorbutus.
9409, Weaver, George, 1, Co B, died Sept 21, diarrhea.
11578, Witman, D, 18, Co D, died Sept 28, scorbutus.
12147, Wolfe, H, 1, Co B, died Nov 24, scorbutus.

455, Yieldhan, E, 9, Co C, died April 9, pneumonia.

1060, Zeck, Wm J, *7, Co E, died May 18, debilitas.
3228, Zimmerman, Chas, 9, Co E, died July 12.

MASSACHUSETTS.

11286, Adams, I B, 16, Co G, died Oct 22, scorbutus.
9561, Adams, S B, 18, Co G, died Sept 23, scorbutus.
6860, Akers, H H, 2, Co I, died Aug 21, scorbutus.
4290, Aldrich, H, 86, Co G, died July 30, diarrhea.
10973, Aldrich, H W, 27 Co I, died Oct 15, scorbutus.
5650, Alger, W A, *15, Co D, died Aug 14, diarrhea.
8730, Allen, Francis, 1 artil, Co M, died Sept 14, scorbutus.
5381, Allen, G H, 2, Co E, died Aug 11, dysentery.
9748, Allen, John, 19, Co B, died Sept 25, diarrhea.
2286, Ames, H, 35, Co A, died June 25, anasarca.
8319, Ames, M L, 32, Co G, died Sept 10, diarrhea c.
8378, Anaistine, 54, died Sept 10, scorbutus.
1054, Anchey, J, 61, Co F, died May 4, diarrhea.
8589, Armington, H, 18, Co C, died Sept 12, scorbutus.
10693, Armstrong, G, 28, Co A, died Oct 11, scorbutus.
9781, Atmore, C, 2 cav, Co A, died Sept 25, diarrhea.
4005, Avery, John W, 1 artil, Co G, died July 27, dysentery.
5372, Avigron, F, 56, Co I, died Aug 11, dysentery.

10767, Bacey, Wm, 27, Co H, died Oct 12, scorbutus.
7116, Baggard, F, 1 artil, Co B, died Aug 28, scorbutus.
8438, Bace, G A, 27, Co G, died Sept 10, dysentery.
6624, Barley, R, 20, Co A, died Aug 23, scorbutus.
6785, Baker, E E, 84, Co C, died Aug 25, diarrhea.
11435, Baldwin, W, 35, Co A, died Oct 24, scorbutus.
9078, Banuer, M, 20, Co B, died Sept 17, scorbutus.
642, Barge, Henry, 20, Co E, died April 20, fever typhus.
6974, Barnes, L A, 19, Co F, died Aug 27, anasarca.
1697, Barnes, W L, 2 cav, Co M, died June 7, diarrhea c.
7653, Barlen, E F, 18, Co E, died Sept 5, scorbutus.
3841, Barneh, John, 17, Co H, died July 28, diarrhea.
6952, Barnett, G H, 25, Co G, died Aug 26, dysentery.
8546, Bassett, B C, 1 artil, Co I, died Sept 15, diarrhea.
4355, Batten, Geo C, †2 artil, Co G, died July 31, diarrhea.
8603, Baxton, H, 2 artil, Co G, died Sept 12, scorbutus.
2525, Bear, G W, 56, Co I, died June 26, diarrhea.
6856, Beannian, Wm, 2 artil, Co G, died Aug 21, dysentery.
6499, Beavey, Henry, 59, Co B, died Aug 22, diarrhea.
3801, Beele, H, 59, Co C, died July 22, diarrhea.
8110, Bell, Wm, 2 cav, Co M, died Sept 7, scorbutus.
8442, Bemis, Albert, 57, Co B, died Sept 11, scorbutus.
11955, Berry, George, 18, Co K, died Nov 10, diarrhea.
6403, Besson, Wm, 2 cav, Co H, died Aug 21, dysentery.
8657, Biglow, G, 84, Co E, died Sept 18, scorbutus.
5321, Biglow, John, 22, Co F, died Aug 11, fever remittent.
2908, Black, James, 9, Co E, died July 5, diarrhea.
109, Blanchard, Oscar, 2 cav, Co E, died March 28, diarrhea.
4067, Blanchard, O S, 52, Co G, died July 27, dysentery.
3837, Blair, J W, 27, Co C, died July 15, diarrhea.
3973, Blair, D, 27, Co B, died July 25, dysentery.
10758, Blake, Wm, 19, Co K, died Oct 12, scorbutus.
7166, Blodgett, A Z, 34, Co A, died Aug 29, debilitas.

No. of Grave.
187, Blood, T B, 18, Co F, died March 24, anasarca.
4470, Bodge, S D, 18, Co D, died Aug 1, dysentery.
8080, Bosworth, H, 23, Co B, died July 8, diarrhea.
7166, Bowler, H A, 1 artil, Co C, died Sept 10, scorbutus.
12013, Boyd, F, 18, Co A, died Nov 10, diarrhea.
1798, Boynton, Henry, 32, Co A, died June 10, diarrhea.
1851, Bracketts, L, 23, Co C, died June 12, pleuritis.
4059, Brackin, Denis, 46, died July 27, diarrhea.
6512, Bradford, J, 2 cav, Co F, died Aug 22, wounds.
8178, Brady, F, 27, Co G, died July 11, diarrhea.
11902, Bradish, F, 19, Co B, died Nov 11, scorbutus.
12030, Branagan, C, 2 artil, Co H, died Nov 15, scorbutus.
4070, Brand, S C, 37, Co K, died Oct 12, scorbutus.
2565, Briggs, W, 2 artil, Co G, died July 2, bronchitis.
993, Briggs, W W, 38, Co H, died May 10, fever typhus.
5799, Brumley, A, 1, Co K, died Sept 15, dysentery.
465, Broadley, James, 17, Co A, died April 9, scorbutus.
8581, Bronagan, M, 17, Co E, died July 19, dysentery.
11982, Brotherton, W H, * 29, Co G, died Aug 26, dysentery.
2641, Brown, A, 56, Co D, died June 29, diarrhea.
6051, Brown, D, 18, Co K, died Aug 13, diarrhea.
6177, Brown, J, 25, Co A, died Aug 19, scorbutus.
9660, Brown, J, 11, Co E, died Sept 24, diarrhea.
10819, Brown, John, * 57, Co E, died Oct 12, dysentery.
7440, Brown, L, 27, Co I, died Sept 1, dysentery.
8780, Brown, Samuel, 56, Co E, died Sept 14, diarrhea.
5339, Brown, Wm, 2 artil, Co H, died Aug 11, diarrhea.
6942, Brownell, A G, 58, Co B, died Aug 25, scorbutus.
6903, Bryant, W A, 2 artil, Co H, died Aug 26, scorbutus.
7756, Buchanan, J, 27, Co A, died Sept 4, diarrhea.
5775, Buldas, L, 56, Co I, died Aug 9, diarrhea.
10746, Bullen, J W, 60, Co C, died Oct 11, diarrhea.
11517, Bubler, J W, 40, Co C, died Oct 26, scorbutus.
1784, Bullock, W D, 24, Co K, died July 22, diarrhea.
11154, Burns, W H, * 2 artil, Co H, died Oct 19, scorbutus.
2907, Burt, C E, † 2 artil, Co K, died July 5, diarrhea.
7184, Burgan, L, 25, Co G, died Aug 28, scorbutus.
8699, Burgess, W F, 16, Co H, died July 21, scorbutus.
5540, Burnham, J, 12, Co I, died Aug 18, scorbutus.
7717, Burton, John, 19, Co E, died Sept 4, dysentery.
2429, Butler, A, 72, Co H, died June 24, diarrhea.
4956, Buxton, Thomas, 1 artil, Co G, died Aug 7, dysentery.
9368, Byerns, I, 1 artil, Co I, died Sept 27, scorbutus.

7230, Callihan, J, 57, Co B, died Aug 29, diarrhea.
3159, Callihan, P, 57, Co A, died July 11, bronchitis.
12663, Campbell, D A, 15, Co G, died Feb 16, '65, diarrhea.
4081, Carr, Wm, * 1 artil, Co B, died July 27, scorbutus.
4156, Carroll, J, 2 artil, Co D, died Aug 1, diarrhea.
4866, Carroll, O J, 2 artil, Co G, died July 31, dysentery.
4168, Casey, M, 28, Co C, died July 29, diarrhea.
4509, Casey, M, 17, Co H, died Aug 2, scorbutus.
4226, Castle, M, 22, Co H, died July 29, dysentery.
6724, Caughlin, B, 58, Co E, died Aug 24, diarrhea.
7070, Caswell, James, 18, Co F, died Aug 18, diarrhea.
7818, Chase, John, 25, Co F, died Aug 30, diarrhea.
8696, Chase, M M, 2 artil, Co G, died Sept 13, scorbutus.
6280, Child, A F, 1 cav, Co E, died Aug 20, cerebritis.
8844, Chiselson, P, 1 cav, Co B, died July 15, scorbutus.
1684, Church, W H, 1 cav, Co E, died June 6, diarrhea.
2416, Churchill, F J, 39, Co G, died June 24, diarrhea.
1674, Chute, A M, 23, Co B, died June 11, diarrhea.
4516, Claflin, F G, 1 artil, Co F, died Aug 1, diarrhea.
11178, Claug, J H, 1 artil, Co E, died Oct 19, scorbutus.
8016, Clausky J,* 17, Co E, died July 1, diarrhea.
10699, Clark,* 21, Co A, died Sept 30, diarrhea.
3649, Clark, E, 27, Co H, died July 20, diarrhea.
4295, Clark, George, 16, Co I, died July 30, diarrhea.
6492, Clark, S, 27, Co I, died Aug 27, diarrhea.
7928, Clemens, J, 19, Co B, died Sept 5, diarrhea.
12825, Cloonan, P, 1 artil, Co E, died April 7, '65, diarrhea.
5815, Coffin, A R, 2 cav, Co M, died Aug 11, diarrhea.
11590, Cohash, John, 23, Co L, died Oct 25, scorbutus.
8099, Cole, W H, 16, Co K, died Sept 7, dysentery.
8, Coleman, Leonard, 1 cav, Co A, died March 5, pneumonia.
10778, Coalman, C S, 37, Co I, died Oct 12, scorbutus.
11658, Collins, A J, 2 artil, Co D, died Nov 6, scorbutus.
6714, Collins, C R, 27, Co D, died Aug 24, diarrhea.
5409, Colt, J, 20, Co K, died Aug 12, anasarca.
9081, Colyer, B, 1 artil, Co G, died Sept 18, scorbutus.
6042, Coney, C W, 1 artil, Co L, died Aug 18, fever typhus.
6591, Congden, E, 2 cav, Co G, died Aug 23, anasarca.
9382, Connell, J D, 24, Co E, died Sept 19, scorbutus.
1849, Conner, D, 17, Co H, died June 11, diarrhea.
6678, Conner, John, 11, Co F, died Aug 24, scorbutus.
11892, Conner, P, 2 cav, Co H, died Nov 7, scorbutus.
11575, Conner, F, 9, Co C, died Oct 25, scorbutus.
4547, Conlin, Tim, 1 artil, Co L, died Aug 2, dysentery.
7693, Cook, W H, 37, Co H, died Sept 2, scorbutus.
8841, Coombs, George, 2 artil, died Sept 15, diarrhea.
1068, Coones, J M, 1 cav, Co K, died May 14, diarrhea.

No. of Grave.
11174, Copeland, J, 15, Co D, died Oct 19, scorbutus.
7802, Corbet, W M, 1 artil, Co M, died Sept 4, diarrhea.
4210, Cox, D O, 59, Co F, died July 29, diarrhea.
687, Cox, Joseph, 7, Co G, died May 23, diarrhea.
11080, Cox, P,† 1 artil, Co G, died Oct 16, diarrhea.
4453, Crockett, A W, 17, Co K, died Aug 1, diarrhea.
174, Crofts, E P, 17, Co E, died March 26, pneumonia.
7619, Cromlan, John, 1 artil, Co E, died Sept 2, diarrhea.
9026, Crominshield, T, 37, Co I, died Sept 17, scorbutus.
6812, Crosby, E, 40, Co A, died Aug 25, diarrhea.
15, Cross, Ira M, 16, Co G, died March 6, dysentery.
8592, Cross, George W, 1 artil, Co L, died July 19, dysentery.
5248, Crosser, E P, 9, Co C, died Aug 10, diarrhea.
5150, Crossman, E J, 20, Co L, died Aug 9, scorbutus.
1290, Cummings, A B,† 29, Co C, died May 22, dysentery.
8746, Culligan, Joseph, 2 cav, Co A, died July 22, diarrhea c.
574, Cunell, H G, 39, Co C, died April 16, diarrhea.
7858, Curren, F, 58, Co I, died Sept 5, diarrhea.
1869, Cushing, C E, 12, died June 12, diarrhea.
10172, Cutler, C F, 2 artil, Co G, died Oct 1, diarrhea.

8579, Dalber, S A, 17, Co B, died July 19, diarrhea.
737, Daly, John, 23, Co F, died April 28, diarrhea.
9421, Davis, C, 27, Co H, died Sept 21, diarrhea.
7180, Davis, C A, 58, Co I, died Aug 29, diarrhea.
1518, Davis, Thomas, 1 cav, Co H, died May 31, diarrhea.
12031, Davidson, W, 27, Co H, died Nov 16, scorbutus.
7289, Day, D B, 25, died Aug 29, debilitas.
2390, Decker, C, 1 artil, Co E, died June 24, diarrhea.
11768, Delano, E, 19, Co E, died Nov 8, scorbutus.
7849, Densmore, Wm, 9, Co F, died Sept 4, scorbutus.
6983, Dewry, L A, 27, Co C, died Aug 26, dysentery.
4012, Dexter, G, 2 cav, Co M, died July 27, scorbutus.
7069, Dill, Z, 59, Co A, died Aug 28, dysentery.
10961, Dimmick, George H, 27, Co I, died Oct 15, scorbutus.
8180, Dodge, Thomas A, 1 cav, Co A, died Sept 11, scorbutus.
8059, Downing, G, 14 bat, died July 9, dysentery.
5501, Doggett, L, 22, Co L, died Aug 13, diarrhea.
9577, Dolan, J, 1 cav, Co D, died Sept 23, diarrhea.
8782, Dulo, Charles H, 10, Co H, died Sept 4, diarrhea.
6676, Dones, S M, 58, Co A, died Aug 24, dysentery.
12004, Douglass, B, 10, Co H, died Sept 14, diarrhea.
12529, Dow, H A,* 1 artil, Co E, died April 10, '65, diarrhea.
6678, Dowlin, J, 27, Co H, died July 20, scorbutus.
1677, Downey, Joel, 2 artil, Co M, died June 6, diarrhea.
2676, Drake, E C, 57, Co E, died June 30, diarrhea.
12778, Drake, T, 4, Co D, died March 14, '65, rheumatism.
7115, Danfield, John, 19, Co E, died Aug 28, scorbutus.
5856, Drawn, George, 32, Co C, died Aug 16, marasmus.
2717, Drickerm, L, 1 cav, Co K, died July 1, dysentery.
8294, Dromantle, W, 25, Co G, died Sept 9, scorbutus.
3570, Drum, R, 19, Co G, died July 19, diarrhea.
9251, Duffey, J, 2 artil, Co H, died Sept 19, scorbutus.
1512, Duffey, James, 18, Co A, died May 31, diarrhea.
4618, Dull, W, 2 artil, Co H, died Aug 31, dysentery.
11666, Duninell, S, 4, Co D, died Oct 30, diarrhea.
10660, Dunn, J, 2 artil, Co G, died Oct 11, scorbutus.
11819, Dunn, I, 20, Co H, died Oct 22, scorbutus.
4471, Dunn, P, 2 artil, Co H, died Aug 1, scorbutus.
4964, Dyer, G W, 2 artil, Co H, died Aug 7, dysentery.

8212, Eaff, N, 56, Co H, died Sept 8, diarrhea.
8616, Earl, G W,† 1 artil, Co I, died Sept 18, scorbutus.
8157, Eastman, D, 35, Co I, died Sept 8, dysentery.
10006, Eaton, F W, 5, Co D, died Sept 29, scorbutus.
7254, Edes, W,* 11, Co F, died Aug 29, scorbutus.
11809, Edwards, C, 19, Co A, died Nov 4, scorbutus.
6351, Edwards, C F, 2 artil, Co H, died Aug 21, diarrhea.
171, Egan, Charles, 11, Co K, died March 26, pneumonia.
10622, Elbers, Henry, 19, died Oct 13, scorbutus.
6994, Emerson, G W, 51, Co A, died Aug 27, diarrhea.
418, Emerson, Wm, 12, Co D, died April 7, pleuritis.
5619, Emery, J, 1 artil, Co F, died Aug 14, scorbutus.
5589, Emmerson, F F, 1 artil, Co B, died Aug 13, diarrhea.
8800, Empay, Robert, 25, Co E, died July 14, diarrhea.
10542, Emuslo, D G, 21, Co B, died Oct 8, diarrhea.
5286, Evans, H, 1 cav, Co K, died Aug 10, scorbutus.
2785, Evans, J, 17, Co H, died July 2, diarrhea.
7689, Ester, W A, 1 artil, Co A, died Sept 5, dysentery.
4399, Everts, T P, 2 artil, Co G, died July 31, diarrhea.

8558, Farmer, G. S, † 1 artil, Co H, died Sept 12, scorbutus.
11909, Farralle, G, 19, Co K, died Nov 7, scorbutus.
9449, Farledale, H, 1 artil, Co G, died Sept 21, diarrhea.
6926, Fearing, J I, 1 artil, Co F, died July 25, diarrhea.
4987, Feamloy, Wm, 25, Co E, died Aug 7, scorbutus.
6450, Fegan, John, 2 artil, Co H, died Aug 21, diarrhea.
12812, Fellows, H, 15, Co E, died March 19, '65, scorbutus.
7803, Felyor, Wm, 20, Co E, died Sept 4, diarrhea.
7611, Fenis, J, 1 cav, Co C, died Sept 2, diarrhea.
5795, Fields, E, 87, Co F, died Aug 15, diarrhea.
11401, Finjay, W, 1 cav, Co K, died Oct 24, scorbutus.

No. of Grave.

6723, Finigan, B, 19, died Aug 21, diarrhea.
8974, Fisher, C. B, 2 artil, Co G, died July 25, diarrhea.
441, Fisher, John, 2 cav, Co E, died April 9, pneumonia.
8451, Flanders, Charles, 1 artil, Co E, died July 17, scorbutus.
286, Fleming, M, 17, Co E, died April 1, pneumonia.
2176, Floyd, George E, 2 artil, Co H, died June 25, diarrhea.
4187, Forbs, H, 1 artil, Co B, died July 29, diarrhea.
70, Fosgate, Henry S, 17, Co K, died March 19, diarrhea.
5649, Fowler, Samuel, 1 artil, Co M, died Aug 11, scorbutus.
10601, Fralmr, P, 2 artil, Co D, died Oct 10, scorbutus.
11135, Frazier, L, 20, Co C, died Oct 18, dysentery.
8848, Fray, Patrick, 17, Co G, died July 21, scorbutus.
4267, Frederick, C, 28, Co A, died July 29, scorbutus.
8186, Frisby, A, 12, Co G, died Sept 8, scorbutus.
9502, Frost, B, 16, Co H, died Sept 21, diarrhea.
102 5, Frost, B, 16, Co H, died Oct 2, scorbutus.
7170, Fuller, A, 2 cav, Co G, died Aug 29, debilitas.
12081, Fuller, H, 15, Co E, died Feb 20, '65, rheumatism.
6467, Fuller, S, 27, Co D, died Aug 13, dysentery.
7392, Fuller, Geo A, 2 artil, Co G, died Aug 31, dysentery.
7154, Funold, C G, 24, Co G, died Aug 29, diarrhea.

9304, Gadkin, G. H, 21, Co H, died Sept 22, diarrhea.
4338, Gaffering, John, 11, Co F, died July 30, diarrhea.
8927, Galligher, F, 18, Co B, died Sept 19, diarrhea.
2787, Galse, I. E, * 27, Co B, died July 2, diarrhea c.
7569, Gardner, D, 25, Co E, died Sept 2, diarrhea.
12630, Garland, W, 1 artil, Co M, died Feb 10, '65, scorbutus.
8882, Garmon, E, 2 artil, died Sept 16, diarrhea c.
11470, Gay, C, 1 cav, Co K, died Oct 6, scorbutus.
7910, Gay, George C, 2 artil, Co G, died Sept 5, diarrhea.
9312, Gibson, D K, 33, Co F, died Sept 10, diarrhea.
8364, Gibson, H H, 25, Co B, died Sept 10, scorbutus.
4464, Gifford, J, 40, Co A, died Aug 1, diarrhea.
4250, Gilbert, S, 2 artil, Co H, died July 29, diarrhea.
159, Gilchrist, J R, * 17, Co A, died March 25, fever remittent.
11157, Gilliland, J, 17, Co H, died Oct 19, scorbutus.
7110, Gilsby, P, 36, Co G, died Aug 28, diarrhea.
10918, Glancey, P, 59, Co A, died Oct 18, scorbutus.
9471, Goanney, G, 2 artil, Co G, died Sept 21, diarrhea.
2414, Godbold, F A, 29, Co K, died June 24, scorbutus.
8585, Gosling, N, 54, Co C, died July 19, wounds.
9202, Goodman, J, 25, died Sept 18, scorbutus.
5988, Goodman, S, 2 artil, Co B, died Aug 17, diarrhea.
9817, Goodrich, G J, 1 artil, Co F, died Sept 25, diarrhea.
12844, Gonler, D, 4, Co D, died April 23, '65, diarrhea.
179, Gordon, Charles, 17, Co C, died March 26, pneumonia.
8486, Gordon, W L, 2 artil, Co H, died July 17, dysentery.
10501, Gorlebe, H, 2 artil, Co G, died Oct 8, scorbutus.
693, Gould, Wm, 17, Co G, died May 5, diarrhea.
9092, Gove, J, 2 artil, Co G, died Sept 7, dysentery.
8839, Gowen, J, 11, Co C, died Sept 10, dysentery.
7885, Grant, George W, 1 artil, Co E, died Sept 5, diarrhea.
6277, Grant, J, 15, Co E, died Sept 9, scorbutus.
10191, Grant, Wm, 15, Co E, died Oct 7, diarrhea.
8898, Gray, C, 28, Co D, died Sept 16, scorbutus.
2018, Green, John, 18, Co A, died June 15, diarrhea.
9417, Gayson, C W, 25, Co I, died Sept 21, diarrhea.
5168, Guild, C, 2 artil, Co C, died Aug 9, diarrhea.
12568, Guilford, J, 1 artil, Co I, died Feb 1, '65, debilitas.
10109, Gutherson, G, 1 artil, Co B, died Sept 30, scorbutus.

6056, Haggert, P, * 2 cav, Co M, died Sept 7, scorbutus.
7408, Haley, Wm, 16, Co F, died Aug 31, scorbutus.
151, Halstead, J W, * 2 cav, Co M, died March 25, pneumonia.
11096, Hall, G H, 1 artil, Co E, died Oct 18, scorbutus.
1742, Hamlin, H P, 2 cav, Co M, died June 8, diarrhea.
9342, Hammond, George, * 77, Co G, died Sept 19, scorbutus.
7374, Handy, George, 1 artil, Co K, died Aug 31, diarrhea.
10126, Handy, Moses, 59, Co A, died Oct 1, scorbutus.
6273, Hane, J H, 1 artil, Co I, died Sept 9, diarrhea.
8804, Hanks, Nelson, 98, Co D, died Sept 15, scorbutus.
6382, Hanley, M, 1 cav, Co L, died Aug 28, anasarca.
12276, Hare, F, 27, Co H, died Dec 18, scorbutus.
8697, Harding, C, 58, Co G, died Sept 14, scorbutus.
556, Harrison, Henry, 12, Co I, died April 14, diarrhea.
7626, Hamesworth, F, 27, Co A, died Sept 2, diarrhea.
8901, Harrington, F, 12, Co H, died July 24, dysentery.
7957, Hart, W, 15, Co G, died Sept 6, diarrhea.
6928, Hartret, M, 84, Co I, died Aug 26, anasarca.
766, Harty, John, * 2 cav, Co M, died April 27, diarrhea.
8505, Harvey, S J, 2 artil, Co G, died July 17, anasarca.
10024, Hash, Wm, 1 artil, Co H, died Sept 29, scorbutus.
3212, Hay, Wm, 2 artil, Co H, died July 13, fever typhus.
5189, Haymouth, N, 2 cav, Co M, died Aug 15, scorbutus.
4209, Haynes, Charles E, 2 artil, Co H, died July 29, diarrhea.
9604, Hayes, P, 37, Co A, died Sept 23, diarrhea.
3508, Heart, John, 28, Co G, died July 15, diarrhea.
7418, Hebban, Thomas, 28, Co B, died Aug 31, diarrhea.
8168, Henrie, E W, 17, Co H, died July 14, diarrhea.
5606, Henry, D, 16, Co H, died Aug 14, dysentery.

No. of Grave.

4604, Henry, J, 2 artil, Co K, died Aug 3, diarrhea.
1093, Hermans, John, 11, Co G, died May 24, dysentery.
7297, Hervey, George W, * 33, Co I, died Aug 30, scorbutus.
6242, Higgin, A, 23, Co B, died Aug 20, fever typhus.
4906, Hill, F, 9, Co I, died Aug 6, diarrhea.
1740, Hills, J B, 2 cav, Co G, died June 8, diarrhea.
11762, Hillman, G, 16, Co H, died Nov 8, scorbutus.
6056, Hines, S, 59, Co C, died Aug 10, dysentery.
9223, Hitchcock, J C, 27, Co C, died Sept 19, diarrhea.
6907, Hogan, Pat, 2 artil, Co G, died Aug 26, dysentery.
6067, Hogan, S, 19, Co E, died Aug 18, diarrhea.
9260, Holt, D, 19, Co B, died Sept 19, scorbutus.
4811, Hott, J F, 2 artil, Co D, died Aug 5, diarrhea.
6228, Holbrook, Charles, 2 artil, Co H, died Aug 20, anasarca.
6826, Holden, Pat, 2 artil, Co G, died Aug 25, fever remittent.
1986, Holland, P, 17, Co I, died June 15, diarrhea.
905, Holland, Pat, 11, Co C, died May 5, diarrhea.
4816, Holmes, S, 12, Co I, died Aug 5, scorbutus.
8712, Holt, E K, 1 artil, died Sept 14, scorbutus.
6716, Holt, T K, 22, Co H, died Aug 24, anasarca.
8575, Howard, C, 24, Co C, died Sept 12, diarrhea.
10864, Howard, James, 59, Co D, died Oct 13, scorbutus.
7025, Howe, C H, 36, Co G, died Aug 27, scorbutus.
222, Howe, E H, 36, Co H, died May 29, diarrhea.
8871, Howe, John W, 24, Co B, died July 21, scorbutus.
5978, Hubbard, E, 34, Co B, died Aug 17, diarrhea.
11045, Hubert, G W, 27, Co I, died Oct 17, scorbutus.
11960, Hunt, J, 84, Co D, died Nov 11, scorbutus.
4323, Hunting, John W, 25, Co I, died July 20, diarrhea.
12299, Hartshaw, L E, 56, Co A, died Dec 16, diarrhea.
6161, Hyde, N L, 2 cav, Co B, died Aug 19, scorbutus.
5470, Hyde, Richard, 39, Co E, died Aug 13, scorbutus.

3187, Jackson, N S, 1 artil, Co K, died July 17, dysentery.
8501, Jackson, N S, 17, Co K, died July 17, diarrhea.
8429, Jackson, Wm B, 2 cav, Co B, died Sept 11, scorbutus.
5788, Jaquirins, C, 57, Co D, died Aug 15, diarrhea.
2308, Jaynes, H, 59, Co G, died June 22, anasarca.
10561, Jeff, M, 16, Co I, died Oct 9, scorbutus.
5915, Jeffrey, A, 58, Co B, died Aug 17, debilitas.
9951, Jewett, E, 27, Co I, died Sept 28, diarrhea.
12820, Jewett, G, 4, Co A, died April 11, '65, diarrhea.
5473, Johnson, M, 84, Co G, died Aug 13, scorbutus.
5850, Johnson, R A, 19, Co G, died Aug 16, dysentery.
3684, Johnson, Wm, 2 artil, Co H, died July 21, diarrhea.
10702, Jones, J, 59, Co E, died Oct 11, diarrhea.
608, Jones, John, 2 cav, Co M, died April 18, dysentery.
6875, Jones, N P, 82, Co F, died Sept 16, diarrhea.
6054, Jones, Thomas, 11, Co A, died Aug 18, scorbutus.

6183, Kavanaugh, Jas, 32, Co K, died Aug 19, debilitas.
8658, Kelley, Charles, 3 artil, Co C, died Sept 13, scorbutus.
6579, Kelley, Henry, 20, Co E, died Aug 23, scorbutus.
9988, Kelley, M, 2 artil, Co H, died Sept 17, scorbutus.
6275, Kelsey, E, 27, Co D, died Aug 20, marasmus.
6712, Kempton, E, 2 artil, Co G, died Aug 24, pleuritis.
5708, Kennedy, Wm, 59, Co F, died Aug 15, scorbutus.
6529, Kenny, J, 3 cav, Co G, died Aug 23, scorbutus.
8252, Kent, S, 27, Co H, died Sept 9, diarrhea.
12490, Kerr, Wm, † 56, Co D, died Jan 20, '65, scorbutus.
6086, Keyes, J C, 2 artil, Co G, died Aug, 18, scorbutus.
868, Kice, Thomas, 2 cav, Co B, died May 3, fever remittent.
296, Kilan, M, † 17, Co I, died April 1, pneumonia.
4514, Kimball, A, 1 artil, Co B, died Aug 2, debilitas.
1754, Kinnely, F, † 17, Co E, died June 9, diarrhea.
12818, Kluener, F, 27, Co A, died March 25, '65, diarrhea.
554, Knapp, David, 2 cav, Co M, died April 14, diarrhea.
3842, Knight, ——, 25, Co A, died July 28, wounds.
11119, Keephart, M, 2 artil, Co E, died Oct 18, scorbutus.
5087, Kuppy, H, 1 artil, Co K, died Aug 8, diarrhea.
8648, Krote, Huer, 20, Co G, died Sept 13, scorbutus.

12549, Langley, L F, † 29, Co B, died Jan 28, '65, scorbutus.
6735, Lain, S, 12, Co I, died Aug 24, diarrhea.
10885, Lane, J H, † 28, died Oct 13, scorbutus.
9738, Latham, W, 25, Co K, died Sept 25, diarrhea.
8835, Lathrop, W O, 58, Co C, died Sept 15, scorbutus.
2175, Laurens, John, 23, Co E, died June 15, diarrhea.
9621, Leach, C W, 20, Co I, died Sept 28, diarrhea.
2781, Leary, D, 2 cav, Co A, died July 2, diarrhea.
7707, Leavey, W H, 12, Co A, died Sept 3, dysentery.
7210, Lecraw, W P, 1 artil, Co G, died Aug 29, diarrhea.
7548, Leonard, W E, 59, Co H, died Sept 2, diarrhea.
7725, Leonard, I G, 1 artil, Co K, died Sept 3, scorbutus.
7798, Lewin, Charles, 19, Co I, died Sept 3, dysentery.
2448, Lewis, F, 2 artil, Co G, died June 25, diarrhea.
10068, Lewis, G G, 2 artil, Co G, died Sept 30, scorbutus.
4082, Lewis, L, 5 cav, Co L, died July 27, diarrhea.
10750, Lewis, L, 1 artil, Co A, died Oct 12, dysentery.
5401, Lindsay, J, 18, Co A, died Aug 12, scorbutus.
12418, Liswell, L, 27, Co F, died Jan 8, '65, diarrhea.

No. of Grave.
8748, Livingston, R, 89, Co C, died Sept 14, diarrhea.
1156, Lochlen, Joel, 1 cav, Co E, died May 16, diarrhea.
480, Loheim, E D, 18, Co H, died April 9, dysentery.
8163, Lombard, B K, 58, Co A, died July 11, catarrh.
12256, Loring, G, 24, Co A, died Dec 10, scorbutus.
10744, London, Ed, 22, Co G, died Oct 11, scorbutus.
8487, Lovely, Francis, 25, Co I, died Sept 11, scorbutus.
8217, Lovell, A W, 89, Co E, died July 12, scorbutus.
8175, Lowell, George, 22, Co E, died July 11, dysentery.
9957, Lucier, J, 2, Co G, died Sept 23, diarrhea.
4099, Lugby, Z, 2 artil, Co G, died July 27, diarrhea.
6593, Lyons, E, 2, Co I, died Sept 12, scorbutus.
8083, Lynch, John, 56, Co K, died July 21, diarrhea.

7521, Macey, Charles, 18, Co I, died Sept 1, dysentery.
4261, Macomber, J, 20, Co H, died July 29, diarrhea.
4034, Mahan, E, 56, Co L, died July 26, diarrhea.
8383, Marinthe, G H, 18, Co I, died July 16, dysentery.
9940, Mann, N C, 16, saddler, Co F, died Sept 28, scorbutus.
6320, Mansfield, D E, 58, Co G, died Aug 20, cerebritis.
503, Marden, O O, 17, Co I, died April 12, fever intermittent.
1350, Marland, W H, 17, Co D, died May 25, diarrhea.
7147, Marchet, C, 23, Co F, died Aug 22, diarrhea.
8430, Martin, C M, 2 artil, Co H, died Sept 11, anasarca.
6272, Maxwell, M, 1 artil, Co I, died Aug 20, marasmus.
5060, McAllister, J, * 17, died Aug 8, dysentery.
7828, McCaffrey, J, 27, Co E, died Sept 4, diarrhea.
8835, McCloud, J, 56, Co K, died July 28, diarrhea.
9942, McCord, J G, 32, Co H, died Sept 28, scorbutus.
12176, McCorner, J, 19, Co F, died Nov 27, scorbutus.
8905, McDavis, J, 3 artil, Co M, died Sept 15, diarrhea.
6162, McDermott, J, 2 artil, Co B, died Aug 19, scorbutus.
4409, McDevitt, Wm, 25, Co E, died July 31, diarrhea.
9439, McDonald, R, 18, Co D, died Sept 21, diarrhea.
430, McDonnell, P, 2, Co B, died April 3, pneumonia.
7459, McDonough, P, * 25, Co E, died Sept 1, diarrhea.
1954, McGlven, J, 22, Co K, died June 15, diarrhea.
6375, McGovern, B, 34, Co D, died Aug 21, diarrhea.
2652, McGowen, John, 2 artil, Co H, died June 29, dysentery.
5290, McGowen, Wm, 12, Co A, died Aug 11, dysentery.
4260, McGoneyal, R, 16, Co K, died July 29, diarrhea.
5124, McGuire, A, 58, Co D, died Aug 9, dysentery.
6460, McHenry, James, 2 artil, Co G, died Aug 21, scorbutus.
6544, McIntire, H, 1 artil, Co K, died Aug 23, diarrhea.
10591, McKarren, E, 1 artil, Co I, died Oct 26, scorbutus.
11849, McKenny, R, 84, Co A, died Nov 5, dysentery.
6358, McKinzie, George, 27, Co I, died Aug 5, scorbutus.
6223, McKnight, B, 8 cav, Co G, died Aug 10, scorbutus.
8174, McLaughlin, E, † 9, Co C, died July 11, fever typhus.
10030, McMasters, 57, Co A, died Sept 29, diarrhea.
8675, McMillan, Jas, 24, Co B, died July 20, dysentery.
522, McNamara, 17, Co I, died April 18, dysentery.
6185, McNaury, P, 27, Co I, died Aug 9, diarrhea.
11381, McNulty, P, 2 artil, Co G, died Oct 24, scorbutus.
5194, McWilliams, W, 77, Co D, died Aug 10, scorbutus.
7586, Medren, W, 20, Co G, died Sept 2, scorbutus.
5308, Mehan, B, 2 artil, Co H, died Aug 16, anasarca.
1434, Melun, A, 16, Co F, died May 29, diarrhea.
9785, Melvin, S, 1 artil, Co K, died Sept 25, diarrhea.
2263, Meritt, M, 27, Co C, died June 20, pneumonia.
1358, Merriman, W H, 17, Co D, died May 25, diarrhea c.
9117, Messera, W, 1 artil, Co B, died Sept 18, diarrhea.
9597, Mesters, E, 84, Co H, died Sept 28, scorbutus.
6286, Meyer, J, 1 cav, Co K, died Aug 20, diarrhea.
8631, Miland, John, 2 artil, Co H, died Sept 18, scorbutus.
11514, Millard, P S, 19, Co G, died Oct 26, scorbutus.
1219, Miller, A, 28, Co F, died May 19, diarrhea.
4329, Miller, J M, 11, Co A, died July 30, fever typhus.
10169, Miller, L, 20, died Oct 1, scorbutus.
4050, Miller, Joseph, † 57, Co C, died July 27, diarrhea.
7178, Millrean, M W, * 2 cav, Co E, died Aug 29, anasarca.
9539, Milton, C, 21, Co A, died Sept 22, diarrhea.
8506, Mitchell, W C, 23, Co A, died Sept 11, scorbutus.
11567, Mitchell, F, 14, Co A, died Nov 6, scorbutus.
11771, Mitchell, John, 19, Co G, died Nov 3, diarrhea.
8348, Mittance, L, 20, Co G, died Sept 10, scorbutus.
4053, Mixter, G L, 1 cav, Co E, died July 27, diarrhea.
6295, Monroe, J, 3 artil, Co M, died Aug 20, diarrhea.
2450, Morgan, C H, 27, Co H, died June 25, fever remittent.
8077, Morgan, Pat, 28, Co B, died Sept 7, scorbutus.
8160, Moore, A, 56, Co C, died July 11, dysentery.
6490, Moore, C A, musician, 2 artil, Co H, died Aug 13, diarrhea.
10593, Moore, M, 57, Co A, died Oct 10, diarrhea.
8411, Moore, P, 18, Co F, died July 16, diarrhea.
8990, Morris, N G, 1 artil, died July 26, dysentery.
1004, Morris, R, † 28, Co F, died May 10, dysentery.
9627, Mortimer, L, 19, Co E, died Sept 24, scorbutus.
8272, Morton, G H, 42, Co C, died Sept 9, diarrhea.
5360, Morton, J, 84, Co A, died Aug 11, diarrhea.
6982, Moss, Charles, 2 artil, Co H, died Aug 27, diarrhea.
12516, Moulton, H, 15, Co F, died Jan 24, '65, diarrhea.

No. of Grave.
12619, Murdock, A B, * 27, Co D, died Feb 8, '65, diarrhea.
321, Morley, D, 9, Co D, died April 2, diarrhea.
7862, Morphy, C, 17, Co D, died Sept 5, anasarca.
5488, Murphy, F, 17, Co D, died Aug 18, scorbutus.
1080, Murphy, Michael, 12, Co K, died June 6, debilitas.
12783, Murphy, P, 27, Co H, died March 15, '65, scorbutus.
6041, Murray, Thomas, 19, Co A, died Aug 6, scorbutus.

9241, Needham, J A, 1 artil, Co B, died Sept 19, scorbutus.
9278, Nelson, J, 2 artil, died Sept 19, scorbutus.
7006, Newcomb, John E, 2 artil, Co G, died Aug 27, scorbutus.
9694, Nitchman, A, 19, Co B, died Sept 24, scorbutus.
1282, Noble, David, 17, Co D, died May 22, diarrhea.
12439, Norman, E, 1 artil, Co E, died Jan 12, '65, pleuritis.
850, Norton, F F, 39, Co H, died April 14, diarrhea.
10058, Nottage, I L, 2, Co F, died Sept 30, scorbutus.

7193, O'Brien, James, 2 art, Co G, died Aug 20, dysentery.
2509, O'Brien, John, 36, Co K, died June 26, diarrhea.
5117, O'Connell, J, 9, Co C, died Aug 9, scorbutus.
12189, O'Connell, J, 15, Co H, died Nov 28, wounds.
9759, O'Connell, M, 2, Co H, died Sept 26, diarrhea.
11050, O'Conner, Wm, 29, Co K, died Oct 17, diarrhea.
11493, O'Donnell, W, 11, Co G, died Oct 26, scorbutus.
10592, Oliver, J, 39, Co E, died Oct 10, scorbutus.
4640, Oliver, S E, 27, Co B, died Aug 3, diarrhea.
7161, O'Neil, Charles, 25, Co B, died Aug 29, diarrhea.
4854, O'Neil, D, 25, Co K, died Aug 6, diarrhea.
4975, Osborn, W, 19, Co K, died Aug 7, scorbutus.

5340, Packard, N M, 27, Co C, died Aug 11, scorbutus.
6029, Page, Wm, 16, Co D, died Aug 23, diarrhea.
598, Paisley, Wm, 17, Co D, died April 17, diarrhea.
10695, Palmer, T, 50, Co E, died Oct 11, diarrhea.
4714, Panier, J M, 17, Co K, died Aug 4, dysentery.
11059, Pantins, A J, 15, Co H, died Oct 17, scorbutus.
6899, Pandes, L, 2 artil, Co G, died Aug 26, diarrhea.
7811, Parrish, Charles, 1 cav, Co C, died Sept 4, dysentery.
6380, Paine, F, 2 artil, Co E, died Aug 12, scorbutus.
1074, Parker, D H, 36, Co C, died May 13, diarrhea.
2327, Parsons, W D, 23, Co E, died June 22, diarrhea.
6860, Pasco, J M, 58, Co D, died Aug 26, scorbutus.
1231, Patterson, H W, 33, Co G, died May 20, diarrhea.
8888, Payne, G A, 57, Co H, died Sept 16, scorbutus.
4967, Payne, Wm A, 1 artil, Co M, died Aug 7, dysentery.
7556, Peabody, W F, 37, died Sept 2, diarrhea.
6471, Peckham, A P, 15, Co B, died Aug 21, diarrhea.
5441, Peete, A, 26, Co A, died Aug 12, fever typhoid.
4003, Pennington, R A, 1 artil, died July 26, dysentery.
9605, Perry, N, 1 artil, Co F, died Sept 23, diarrhea.
274, Perry, Samuel, K, 39, Co D, died March 31, fever congestive.
4986, Pettie, C, 2 artil, Co H, died Aug 7, diarrhea.
7671, Phillbrook, J E, 56, Co F, died Sept 3, debilitas.
7708, Phillips, A, 50, Co B, died Sept 3, scorbutus.
10383, Phillips, L M, † 17, Co D, died, Oct 5, scorbutus.
6906, Phipps, H B, * 1 artil, Co B, died Aug 20, dysentery.
4763, Phipps, M M, 27, Co C, died Aug 4, diarrhea.
11079, Pierson, R, † 2 artil, Co H, died Oct 17, diarrhea.
20, Pilbuton, John, 11, Co E, died April 14, small pox.
5128, Piper, Charles, 28, Co G, died Aug 9, diarrhea.
6740, Piper, F, 25, Co E, died Aug 24, diarrhea.
7080, Polshon, F B, 17, Co D, died Aug 28, scorbutus.
703, Poole, Charles, * 1, Co G, died April 23, dysentery.
6583, Pratt, Daniel, 27, Co I, died Aug 27, dysentery.
12135, Pratt, D W, 2 artil, Co G, died Nov 25, scorbutus.
5742, Pratt, Henry, 23, Co C, died Aug 15, scorbutus.
2008, Price, Edward, 2 artil, Co M, died June 15, diarrhea.
12475, Prichard, J, * 2, Co G, died June 18, scorbutus.
6404, Prior, Michael, 56, Co I, died Aug 12, anasarca.
11975, Puller, E D, 34, Co A, died Nov 12, scorbutus.

4219, Quinn, James, 15, Co M, died July 29, anasarca.
12804, Quirk, M J, 1, Co D, died March 20, diarrhea.

12094, Ragan, C, * 27, Co H, died Nov 19, scorbutus.
10156, Ramstoll, H, 37, Co H, died Oct 1, diarrhea.
5500, Rand, M, 2 artil, Co G, died Aug 13, scorbutus.
3358, Randall, J, 2, Co F, died July 15, diarrhea c.
54, Raymond, C, 20, Co I, died June 12, small pox.
8072, Reed, Charles, 2 artil, Co H, died Sept 7, diarrhea.
1725, Rensseller, C N, 54, Co C, died June 8, diarrhea.
6122, Rapp, James, 28, Co A, died Aug 19, dysentery.
2970, Reynolds, N A, 36, Co C, died July 7, diarrhea.
3272, Rice, C A J, 2 artil, Co G, died July 13, diarrhea.
1285, Rich, C, 2, Co D, died May 22, diarrhea.
4233, Rich, Samuel, 27, Co B, died July 29, diarrhea.
4918, Richards, G, 16, Co I, died Aug 6, bronchitis.
3156, Richards, James, 27, Co C, died July 11, diarrhea.
11553, Richardson, L, 1 artil, Co G, died Oct 27, scorbutus.
4167, Richardson, S R, 1 artil, Co M, died July 28, diarrhea.
7546, Richard, Thomas, 20, Co B, died Sept 2, diarrhea.

No. of Grave.

7199, Ridlam, James, 19, Co C, died Aug 29, diarrhea.
10638, Riley, H J, 2 artil, Co G, died Oct 10, diarrhea.
8642, Riley, M, 59, Co K, died Sept 13, anasarca.
7203, Ripley, M A, 32, Co F, died Aug 29, diarrhea.
6650, Rippon, Wm, 58, Co G, died Aug 23, scorbutus.
6166, Roach, J, 35, Co F, died Aug 19, marasmus.
11552, Roberts, J H, 18, Co I, died Oct 27, scorbutus.
9148, Roberts, Joseph, 1 cav, Co K, died Sept 21, diarrhea.
12505, Roberts, L, 13, Co F, died Jan 22, '65, pleuritis.
11699, Robinson, J, 19, Co H, died Oct 31, scorbutus.
3833, Robinson, R, 27, Co F, died July 23, dysentery.
6659, Roe, Wm, 2 artil, Co H, died Aug 14, scorbutus.
4875, Roherty, John, 2, Co K, died Aug 6, diarrhea.
12393, Roma, R, 1, Co I, died Jan 4, '65, scorbutus.
4219, Rover, F, 4, Co E, died July 29, diarrhea.
6654, Rope, A R, 11, Co I, died Aug 23, dysentery.
6536, Rowe, Asa, 1 art, Co K, died Aug 11, fever intermittent.
11521, Rowley, Charles, 19, Co K, died Oct 26, scorbutus.
3155, Russell, —, 27, Co C, died July 17, fever typhoid.
9319, Rustar, E, 27, Co A, died Sept 19, diarrhea.
5987, Ruth, F, 36, Co C, died Aug 17, dysentery.
6036, Ryes, J C, 2 artil, Co G, died Aug 18, scorbutus.

5276, Sabines, Edward, 19, Co K, died Aug 11, diarrhea.
9465, Samlett, P V, 1, Co A, died Sept 21, scorbutus.
8074, Sanborn, G B, 2 cav, Co B, died Sept 7, diarrhea.
392, Sanborn, T, 17, Co D, died Apr 16, diarrhea.
8281, Sanders, F, 2 art, Co G, died Sept 9, dysentery.
10637, Sandwich, J, 1, Co G, died Oct 10, diarrhea.
3405, Sanford, J D, 40, Co A, died July 16, diarrhea.
10406, Savin, J H, 34, Co C, died Oct 6, scorbutus.
11888, Sawer, John, 33, Co F, died Nov 7, scorbutus.
4180, Sawyer, S F, 1 artil, Co B, died July 28, diarrhea.
11263, Sayer, G D, 11, Co I, died Oct 20, dysentery.
6834, Schaleter, S, 25, Co G, died Aug 16, marasmus.
5623, Seeley, Charles H, 2 artil, Co G, died Aug 14, diarrhea.
11731, Sergeant, J C, 19, Co E, died Nov 2, scorbutus.
11378, Shannock, I, 19, Co H, died Oct 23, scorbutus.
6782, Shaw, Andrew, 25, Co K, died Aug 25, diarrhea.
12313, Shaw, C L,* 15, Co E, died Dec 18, scorbutus.
7827, Shea, J, 2 art, Co H, died Sept 4, diarrhea.
7481, Sheehan, James, 2 art, Co G, died Sept 1, scorbutus.
2824, Sherman, P H, 37, Co E, died June 23, fever intermittent.
8822, Sherwood, F, 76, Co B, died Sept 15, diarrhea.
4954, Shindler, John, 1 art, Co I, died Aug 7, diarrhea.
6672, Shore, J J, 1, Co F, died Aug 24, diarrhea.
10946, Short, J, 2, Co B, died Oct 14, scorbutus.
7735, Shultes, A M, 28, Co B, died Sept 3, scorbutus.
10415, Shults, George, 28, Co H, died Oct 6, scorbutus.
1458, Simmonds, E, 17, Co D, died May 29, diarrhea.
6957, Simons, A, 2 art, Co M, died Aug 26, scorbutus.
4186, Simpson, D O, 31, Co D, died July 24, diarrhea.
9812, Simpson, W, 2 art, Co H, died Sept 27, scorbutus.
6141, Sinclair, A, 1, Co G, died Aug 19, diarrhea.
11189, Sloan, S, 20, Co K, died Oct 19, fever intermittent.
9375, Small, Z, 1 art, Co G, died Sept 17, scorbutus.
10404, Smalley, J H, 2, Co G, died Oct 6, scorbutus.
9, Smith, Warren, 12, Co F, died March 5, phthisis.
10256, Smith, C, 27, Co D, died Oct 3, scorbutus.
8002, Smith, C A, 1 art, Co G, died Sept 6, fever typhoid.
4952, Smith, D H, 1, Co I, died Aug 7, scorbutus.
12499, Smith, E, 27, Co G, died Jan 21, '65, diarrhea.
11804, Smith, E M, 1, Co D, died Nov 4, dysentery.
7158, Smith, H, 57, Co D, died Aug 29, diarrhea.
7463, Smith, J,* 20, Co E, died Sept 1, diarrhea.
967, Smith, John, 17, Co K, died May 8, diarrhea.
7538, Smith, J P, 1 art, Co A, died Sept 2, diarrhea.
5784, Smith, J H, 19, Co G, died Aug 15, debilitas.
8184, Smith, W, 24, Co B, died Sept 8, scorbutus.
154, Smith, W H, 12, Co I, died Mar 25, phthisis.
2064, Smith, Wm, 51, died June 22, dysentery.
12748, Smith, V, 57, Co K, died Mar 6, '65, pleuritis.
3745, Snow, W, 16, Co E, died July 21, scorbutus.
12063, Somers, F, 19, Co G, died Nov 17, diarrhea.
6316, Switzer, L, 16, Co E, died Aug 11, diarrhea.
8280, Southworth, J, 18, Co G, died Sept 9, dysentery.
2169, Southworth, John, 18, Co E, died June 25, dysentery.
2188, Spalding, J, 2, Co E, died June 19, diarrhea.
12160, Spor, H, 19, Co H, died Nov 25, scorbutus.
10442, Spellman, B F, 2 art, died Oct 4, scorbutus.
6179, Spence, David, 19, Co D, died Aug 19, cerebritis.
4153, Spooner, C L, 27, Co H, died July 23, anasarca.
5940, Spooner, E O, 27, Co A, died Aug 14, scorbutus.
4922, Spooner, F, 18, Co A, died Aug 8, dysentery.
8397, Stabler, E P, 17, Co H, died July 16, pneumonia.
9873, Stanf, J, 24, Co D, died Sept 27, scorbutus.
6591, Steadson, W, 16, Co G, died Aug 22, diarrhea.
5028, Stelle, F, 1 art, Co I, died Aug 8, scorbutus.
7991, Stevens, Henry, 28, Co F, died Sept 6, scorbutus.
9183, Stevens, N, 1, Co E, died Sept 18, anasarca.
2651, Stevens, Thomas, 2, Co M, died July 4, fever typhus.

1758, Steward, J, 11, Co H, died June 9, debilitas.
11291, Stewart, E, 52, Co D, died Oct 22, diarrhea.
12420, Stone, F P, 27, Co A, died Jan 9, '65, debilitas.
10181, Stone, A, 2 art, Co H, died Oct 1, diarrhea.
5937, Sullivan, John, 16, Co A, died Aug 17, scorbutus.
7401, Sullivan, John, 2, Co K, died Aug 31, scorbutus.
10890, Sullivan, M, 2, Co D, died Oct 4, scorbutus.
8203, Sullivan, P, 9, died Sep 8, diarrhea.
10792, Sullivan, P, 15, Co I, died Oct 12, rheumatism.
11671, Sullivan, F, 59, Co B, died Oct 30, scorbutus.
12788, Sylvester, D, 1, Co B, died Mar 17, '65, diarrhea.
6325, Sylvester, E, 2 art, Co H, died Sept 10, diarrhea.
12053, Sylvester, J, 4, Co A, died Nov 16, scorbutus.

11957, Tabor, B, 35, Co C, died Nov 11, scorbutus.
10697, Tabor, F J, 16, Co E, died Oct 11, scorbutus.
2067, Taggerd, John, 17, Co E, died June 10, diarrhea.
8368, Taylor, N, 37, Co D, died July 15, scorbutus.
2515, Taylor, Thomas, 2 cav, Co G, died June 26, dysentery.
8805, Temerts, T J, 110, Co D, died Sept 15, scorbutus.
4388, Tenney, William, 3, Co G, died July 31, fever typhoid.
3812, Thayer, J, 27, Co A, died July 23, dysentery.
8612, Thomas, J, 2 art, Co H, died Sept 13, diarrhea.
11124, Thomas, J A, 32, Co G, died Oct 18, scorbutus.
2121, Thomas, J W, 56, Co I, died June 24, diarrhea.
12527, Thompson, C, 1 art, Co B, died Jan 26, '65, scorbutus.
1890, Thompson, George, 16, died June 13, pneumonia.
4536, Thompson, George, 58, Co F, died Aug 2, scorbutus.
8908, Thompson, J M, 27, Co H, died July 24, dysentery.
3596, Thompson, W W, 58, Co G, died July 19, scorbutus.
4634, Tibbett, A, 23, Co F, died Aug 3, scorbutus.
7168, Tiffany, J, 4, Co F, died Sept 1, diarrhea.
6549, Tilden, A, 27, Co B, died Aug 23, diarrhea.
8828, Tillson, Chas E, 29, Co E, died July 24, diarrhea.
3749, Toomas, John, 25, Co E, died July 18, diarrhea.
407, Torey, L, 12, Co H, died Apr 7, dysentery.
6019, Torrey, C L, 7, Co G, died Aug 17, diarrhea.
10131, Townley, J J, 1, Co F, died Oct 1, scorbutus.
9308, Travern, W, 2 art, Co G, died Sept 18, diarrhea.
7850, Travis, H C,* 59, Co C, died Sept 5, diarrhea.
7996, Trescutt, W M, 15, Co I, died Sept 6, diarrhea.
8132, Turner, H, 31, Co F, died Sept 8, fever congestive.
12161, Tufts, F, 20, Co F, died Nov 25, scorbutus.
5128, Twichell, J, 17, Co K, died Aug 12, diarrhea.
6332, Twichell, 36, Co C, died Aug 21, debilitas.

9517, Usher, Samuel, 17, Co I, died Sept 22, diarrhea.

8466, Wade, A D L, 2 art, Co G, died Sept 11, scorbutus.
5959, Waldon, William, 36, Co B, died Aug 17, diarrhea.
12444, Walker, A, 19, Co F, died Jan 12, '65, scorbutus.
3457, Wallace, P, 57, Co B, died July 16, scorbutus.
11494, Walsh, M, 4, Co C, died Oct 26, dysentery.
5191, Walton, E A, 57, Co H, died Aug 10, dysentery.
8724, Walton, Nathaniel, 59, Co E, died Sept 14, scorbutus.
8834, Wanderfelt, 6, Co C, died Sept 10, diarrhea.
1738, Wardin, H, 17, Co I, died June 8, anasarca.
5217, Ware, Samuel, 1, Co H, died Aug 10, diarrhea.
8864, Warffender, J W, 25, Co C, died Sept 15, diarrhea.
12151, Warner, A F,* 19, Co D, died Nov 22, scorbutus.
6154, Washburne, W E, 27, Co I, died Aug 21, diarrhea.
4721, Weidan, H, 17, Co H, died Aug 4, anasarca.
1066, Welch, Frank, 17, Co B, died May 13, diarrhea.
6224, Weldon, Charles, 1 artil, Co D, died Aug 20, dysentery.
11796, Wells, S, 1, Co A, died Nov 14, scorbutus.
5214, Wellington, G W, 2, Co G, died Aug 10, scorbutus.
3647, Welworth, C W, 18, Co D, died July 18, diarrhea.
8347, Werdler, W, 58, Co G, died July 13, diarrhea.
1334, West, E, 24, Co A, died May 24, rheumatism.
7009, West, J G, 1 artil, Co E, died Aug 27, dysentery.
4577, White, F, 15, Co K, died Aug 2, diarrhea.
6807, White, Joseph, 2 artil, Co G, died Aug 25, dysentery.
7188, White, Joseph, 2, Co G, died Aug 29, diarrhea.
7962, Whiting, A, 27, Co H, died Sept 5, diarrhea.
6867, Whitney, F P, 1, Co G, died Aug 26, scorbutus.
635, Whittaker, S, 17, Co D, died April 20, diarrhea.
1115, Wiggard, George, 22, Co A, died May 15, diarrhea.
6715, Wilber, E, 27, Co G, died Aug 24, anasarca.
4589, Wilcox, Allen, 14 artil, Co C, died Aug 2, diarrhea.
5519, Wilder, L E, 2, Co G, died Aug 18, diarrhea.
7318, Wilkins, S O, 1, Co G, died Aug 30, diarrhea.
6661, Williams, Chas, 27, Co G, died Aug 21, diarrhea.
8668, Williams, J, 58, Co G, died Sept 13, diarrhea.
3469, Willis, C, 11, Co K, died July 17, dysentery.
7549, Wilson, J, 2 artil, Co H, died Sept 2, diarrhea.
6769, Wilson, Rob't, 34, Co A, died Aug 25, scorbutus.
6742, Wilson, S, 2 artil, Co G, died Aug 24, fever remittent.
10545, Wilson, W, 18, Co B, died Oct 9, diarrhea.
6213, Witherill, O, 47, Co C, died Aug 20, diarrhea.
6483, Woodbury, B, 17, Co A, died Aug 21, debilitas.
6561, Woodward, W A, 27, Co B, died Aug 23, ictus solis.

No. of Grave.
6368, Wright, C E, 27, Co D, died Aug 21, scorbutus.
6288, Wright, M E, 27, Co C, died Aug 20, diarrhea.
4928, Wyman, H C, 2 artil, Co H, died Aug 6, diarrhea c.
3362, Wright, W M, 3 artil, Co G, died July 18, diarrhea.

No. of Grave.
6862, Young, E, 2, died Sept 16, diarrhea.
6952, Young, G W, 2 artil, Co H, died Aug 26, diarrhea.
7152, Young, N C, 1, Co I, died Aug 29, diarrhea.

MICHIGAN.

2198, Ayres, J B, † 22, Co C, died June 17, dysentery.
2247, Acker, J, 22, Co K, died June 20, diarrhea.
2461, Atkinson, P, 22, Co C, died June 22, diarrhea c.
2546, Anderson, George, 23, Co E, died June 27, debilitas.
3257, Abbott, G M, 5, Co E, died July 13, dysentery.
4947, Ammermann, H H, 23, Co A, died Aug 7, scorbutus.
5472, Anlger, Geo, 10, Co F, died Aug 13, scorbutus.
5601, Ackler, W, 3 cav, Co C, died Aug 14, anasarca.
6119, Austin, D, 8, Co C, died Aug 19, scorbutus.
6713, Allen, A A, 14, Co I, died Aug 24, debilitas.
9156, Anderson, F, 1 cav, Co G, died Sept 18, scorbutus.
12850, Arsnoe, W, 7, Co E, died Dec 27, diarrhea.
12571, Allen, J, 9, Co H, died Feb 2, '65, rheumatism.
12606, Adams, A, 4, Co B, died Feb 7, '65, pleuritis.

121, Brockway, O, 11, Co K, died March 23, fever typhus.
1154, Banghart, J, 9 cav, Co G, died May 16, diarrhea c.
1288, Broman, C, 4, Co H, died May 22, paralysis.
1511, Beckwith, E,* 6 cav, Co I, died May 31, anasarca.
1513, Bishop, C, 27, Co F, died May 31, rheumatism.
1664, Beard, J, 6, Co E, died June 6, diarrhea.
2004, Bostwick, R S,* 2, Co F, died June 15, pneumonia.
2025, Bowerman, R,* 22, Co H, died June 17, diarrhea c.
2201, Bryant, Geo, 6 cav, Co H, died June 17, dysentery.
2271, Bush, Thomas, 9, Co A, died June 20, diarrhea c.
2303, Brigham, David, 22, Co D, died June 22, diarrhea c.
2381, Bowlen, J, 27, Co E, died June 23, dysentery.
2478, Briggs, I, 6, Co E, died June 25, diarrhea c.
2595, Berry, Henry, 15, Co E, died June 28, scorbutus.
2700, Bros, F, 22, Co I, died June 30, diarrhea c.
2946, Bailey, John, 4 cav, Co M, died July 6, diarrhea.
3149, Briggs, W H, 20, Co G, died July 11, diarrhea.
3215, Bibley, J, 9, Co C, died July 12, diarrhea c.
3479, Brannock, F, 3, Co C, died July 17, diarrhea.
3517, Brush, J, 16, Co E, died July 18, diarrhea.
3581, Bradley, Geo, 17, Co B, died July 18, diarrhea c.
3591, Bullt, F, 3 artil, Co A, died July 19, diarrhea.
3777, Gohomiller, J, 10 cav, Co H, died July 22, scorbutus.
3798, Beardslee, M A, † 22, Co D, died July 22, dysentery.
4179, Billiams, Jno, 2, Co K, died July 27, diarrhea.
4339, Binder, John, 2, Co A, died Aug 30, diarrhea c.
4395, Brown, G, 4 cav, Co E, died July 31, diarrhea.
4810, Baker, A, 5 cav, Co F, died Aug 5, diarrhea.
5573, Botts, P, 1, Co C, died Aug 14, dysentery.
8383, Brookinizer, F, 7, Co D, died Sept 10, scorbutus.
5930, Berton, L, 8 cav, Co B, died Aug 16, marasmus.
5970, Burnett, J, 7, Co G, died Aug 17, enteritis.
6013, Burkhart, C,* 22, Co G, died Aug 17, scorbutus.
6065, Brower, L F,* 17, Co H, died Aug 18, dysentery.
6290, Bilbey, Geo, 9, Co E, died Aug 20, scorbutus.
6388, Burcham, J, 5, Co B, died Aug 21, scorbutus.
6990, Burdick, Theo, 6 cav, Co I, died Aug 27, diarrhea.
7148, Beirs, S, 18, Co B, died Aug 29, scorbutus.
7227, Billingsby, J, 1 battery, died Aug 29, diarrhea.
7536, Bradley, B, 9 cav, Co E, died Sept 1, diarrhea.
7796, Blair, John, 7, Co E, died Sept 4, dysentery.
7912, Barr, W,† 8 cav, Co L, died Sept 5, bronchitis.
8191, Brown, H S, 8 cav, Co F, died Sept 10, diarrhea c.
8565, Bradley, E,† 11, Co K, died Sept 12, diarrhea.
8814, Blanchard, Jas, 7, Co G, died Sept 15, scorbutus.
8869, Brown, A, 8, Co G, died Sept 15, diarrhea.
9226, Beckley, W, 1 cav, Co E, died Sept 19, wounds.
9240, Brown, H, 13, Co A, died Sept 19, scorbutus.
9305, Beebe, John,* 1, Co A, died Sept 20, diarrhea c.
9430, Baker, John, 1 cav, Co H, died Sept 21, scorbutus.
9545, Elidsey, J, 7, Co D, died Sept 23, scorbutus.
9558, Barber, J M,* 26, Co C, died Sept 23, scorbutus.
9637, Baxter, S, 6 cav, Co L, died Sept 24, scorbutus.
9890, Batt, W H, 6 cav, Co L, died Sept 27, diarrhea c.
9834, Bunker, E B, 1, Co D, died Sept 27, scorbutus.
9858, Barnard, G,* 7 cav, Co M, died Sept 27, scorbutus.
9866, Beekley, L, 10, Co F, died Sept 27, scorbutus.
10044, Barney, H, 17, Co D, died Sept 29, scorbutus.
10340, Blackburn, Jas, 5, Co G, died Oct 4, diarrhea.
10490, Bentley, H, 24, Co I, died Oct 7, scorbutus.
10835, Bittman, J, 1 cav, Co C, died Oct 13, scorbutus.
11275, Baldwin, L A, 24, Co B, died Oct 22, scorbutus.
12180, Beck, G, 1 cav, Co H, died Nov 23, scorbutus.
12162, Bennett, W L, 26, Co G, died Nov 26, scorbutus.
12187, Barnett, L, 2, Co E, died Nov 28, diarrhea.
12745, Bourves, M, 15, Co G, died Oct 7, diarrhea c.

84, Colan, Fred, 17, Co F, died Feb 9, pneumonia.
210, Chilcote, Jas C, 20, Co G, died Feb 28, diarrhea c.
898, Chambers, J R,† 5 cav, Co K, died April 5, diarrhea c.
439, Cowill, Ed, 8 cav, Co G, died April 8, nephritis.
693, Cowell, John, 10 cav, Co H, died April 15, debilitas.
1037, Conrad, Edson, 5 cav, Co G, died May 12, dysentery.
1077, Cripper, G F, 5 cav, Co C, died May 14, anasarca.
1164, Costner, J D, 5 cav, Co L, died May 16, dysentery.
1330, Chapman, H, 5 cav, Co E, died May 24, pneumonia.
1351, Cameron, Jas,† 27, Co H, died May 25, scorbutus.
1505, Constank, John, 9, Co B, died May 31, diarrhea.
1692, Cronkwhite, John, 22, Co K, died June 7, diarrhea c.
1711, Cook, J, 4 cav, Co D, died June 7, diarrhea c.
1811, Churchward, A R, 9, Co C, died June 10, diarrhea c.
1948, Clear, James, 22, Co F, died June 14, diarrhea c.
2617, Cussick, B, 7, Co C, died June 28, dysentery.
3071, Collins, James, 5, Co I, died July 9, diarrhea c.
3462, Cartney, A, 2 cav, Co E, died July 17, anasarca.
3595, Cameron, D,† 1 cav, Co L, died July 19, dysentery.
3800, Commings, W, 2, Co F, died July 22, anasarca.
3959, Clements, Wm, 1 s s, Co C, died July 26, dysentery.
4032, Cook, J, 10, Co F, died July 26, diarrhea c.
4620, Cronk, James, 5 cav, Co G, died Aug 3, diarrhea.
4920, Cooper, J, 7, Co K, died Aug 6, diarrhea c.
4956, Curtis, M D, 5, Co G, died Aug 7, scorbutus.
5201, Crunch, J, 1 cav, died Aug 10, scorbutus.
5685, Cummings, D, 5 cav, Co I, died Aug 15, scorbutus.
5686, Churchill, G W, 3, Co A, died Aug 15, diarrhea.
5905, Carr, C B, 25, Co K, died Aug 16, diarrhea c.
6263, Coft, James, 20, Co F, died Aug 20, scorbutus.
6285, Cobb, G, 4, Co D, died Aug 20, diarrhea c.
6446, Cook, George, 10 cav, Co H, died Aug 22, debilitas.
6904, Cahon, W J, 1, Co H, died Aug 26, anasarca.
7094, Carp, J S,† 4, Co K, died Aug 28, phthisis.
7164, Caten, M, 7 cav, Co E, died Aug 29, dysentery.
7496, Cline, Jacob, 2, Co K, died Sept 1, scorbutus.
7534, Campbell, S B, 2, Co H, died Sept 1, diarrhea.
7583, Coldwell, W,* 124, Co H, died Sept 5, diarrhea.
8406, Cope, J B, 17, Co A, died Sept 11, diarrhea c.
8993, Cornice, J D, 7, Co F, died Sept 17, diarrhea.
9341, Carver, J H, 4 cav, died Sept 20, scorbutus.
10644, Cooley, G, 8, Co A, died Oct 9, dysentery.
10759, Clago, S,† 7, Co C, died Oct 12, scorbutus.
10788, Crain, R O, 17, Co A, died Oct 12, scorbutus.
10871, Cooley, Henry, 34, Co G, died Oct 13, scorbutus.
11143, Collins, C, 2, Co K, died Nov 2, scorbutus.
11973, Clark, G W,† 1 artil, Co C, died Nov 7, scorbutus.
12143, Cameron, F, 11, Co E, died Nov 24, scorbutus.
12258, Cook, N, 1, Co K, died Dec 10, scorbutus.
12391, Case, S,* 5 cav, Co L, died Jan 4, '65, scorbutus.
12474, Corse, E, 6 cav, Co C, died Jan 17, '65, diarrhea.
12634, Chambers, W, 3 cav, Co G, died Feb 10, '65, diarrhea c.

1345, Davis, Wilson, 8, Co A, died May 24, pneumonia.
48, Diets, John, 6 cav, Co I, died Feb 14, diarrhea.
195, Dunay, John, 6, Co C, died Feb 27, bronchitis.
815, Deas, Abe, 7 cav, Co L, died April 2, diarrhea.
716, Decker, L, 10, Co H, died April 24, diarrhea.
1270, Drummond, John, 27, Co E, died May 21, diarrhea.
1292, Dolf, Sylvanus, 27, Co G, died May 23, diarrhea.
1296, Dentor, W A, 5 cav, Co E, died May 23, diarrhea c.
1683, Dougherty, D, 8, Co C, died June 6, diarrhea.
2090, Demerie, D, 1 battery, died June 17, diarrhea.
2248, Dillingham, W O,* 20, Co I, died June 20, anasarca.
2683, Dennison, H, 5 cav, Co G, died June 30, debilitas.
2882, Dreal, D, 2 cav, Co B, died July 4, fever typhus.
3207, Dosalt, A, 17, Co H, died July 12, diarrhea c.
3314, Dyre, Wm, 17, Co B, died July 14, dysentery c.
3610, Davy, B, 22, Co C, died July 19, diarrhea c.
3619, De Reatt, F, 5, Co G, died July 20, dysentery.
4660, Decker, G S,* 5 cav, Co K, died Aug 3, dysentery.
4669, Deret, S, 5, Co I, died Aug 4, dysentery.
4670, Dugan, D, 21, Co I, died Aug 4, diarrhea.
5070, Dawson, D, 17, Co H, died Aug 8, diarrhea c.
5351, Dalzell, Wm, 6, Co A, died Aug 10, diarrhea.
5660, Dolph, S, 8, Co B, died Aug 14, scorbutus.
6225, Dulnz, G W, 5 cav, Co I, died Aug 20, dysentery.
6401, Denton, G, 5, Co E, died Aug 21, dysentery.
7654, Derffy, Wm, 1, Co H, died Sept 3, diarrhea.
7769, Dunmont, W, 86, Co H, died Sept 4, dysentery.
8651, Daly, A,* 7 cav, Co E, died Sept 13, diarrhea.

No. of Grave.
9995, Dyer, J, 5, Co I, died Sept 29, scorbutus.
10161, Dusp, M. 1 cav, Co L, died Oct 1, scorbutus.
10922, Dixon, John, 5 cav, Co L, died Oct 14, scorbutus.
11125, Dennis, C, 1, Co H, died Oct 18, diarrhea c.
12124, Dunroe, P I, 24, Co H, died Oct 22, scorbutus.
12574, Drake, O, 22, Co D, died Feb 2, '65, diarrhea.

2850, Eg-illin, P H, 22, Co K, died July 4, bronchitis.
6318, Eggleston, Wm, 7 cav, Co E, died Aug 10, diarrhea c.
8981, Elliot, J, 24, Co G, died July 20, scorbutus.
1210, Eaton, R, 22, Co H, died May 19, scorbutus.
1240, Ellis, E, 2 cav, Co B, died May 20, diarrhea c.
2788, Ensign, J, 11, Co A, died July 2, diarrhea.
7901, Edwards, S, 6, Co E, died Sept 5, diarrhea.
8255, Edmonds, B, 1, Co H, died Sept 9, diarrhea.
11065, English, James, 17, Co B, died Oct 17, scorbutus.
6817, Everett, J, 77, Co K, died Aug 16, diarrhea.

890, Force, F, 27, Co D, died May 5, diarrhea c.
1064, Fitzpatrick, M, 1 cav, Co B, died May 13, bronchitis.
1867, Folk, C, 14, Co E, died May 25, debilitas.
2197, Fitse, T, 1 cav, Co C, died June 19, diarrhea c.
2252, Fairbanks, J, 15 cav, Co G, died June 20, diarrhea c.
2343, Face, W H, 6, died June 23, diarrhea.
4194, Fisher, F, 22, Co G, died June 29, diphtheria.
5081, Farmer, M, 22, Co D, died Aug 8, diarrhea c.
5361, Flanigan, John, 5, Co D, died Aug 16, marasmus.
6185, Farnham, A, 5, Co A, died Aug 19, diarrhea.
6363, Fox, James, 8, Co H, died Aug 21, diarrhea.
6680, Fritchei, M, 22, Co G, died Aug 24, scorbutus.
6983, Fitzpatrick, M, 8, Co E, died Aug 27, diarrhea.
7027, Fox, Charles, 1, Co B, died Aug 27, diarrhea.
7060, Forsythe, H, 5, Co F, died Aug 28, phthisis.
7171, Forbs, C, 1 cav, Co B, died Aug 29, scorbutus.
6586, Fethlno, F, 1 cav, Co G, died Sept 12, scorbutus.
10275, Flidin, H, 27, Co F, died Oct 8, scorbutus.
11500, Freeman, B, 1 s s, died Oct 26, scorbutus.
11709, Fredenburg, F, 7, died Nov 1, diarrhea c.
12083, Findlater, H, 7 cav, Co C, died Feb 22, '65, diarrhea.
12845, Frederick, G, 9, Co G, died April 28, '65, diarrhea.
8250, Face, C, 1 s s, Co B, died Sept 9, scorbutus.
11509, Fox W, 22, Co E, died Oct 26, scorbutus.

745, Goodenough, G M, 23, Co K, died March 25, diarrhea c.
666, Grover, James, 20, Co H, died April 15, debilitas.
781, Grippman, J, 5 cav, Co M, died April 28, fever typhus.
956, Graham, Geo W, 5, Co C, died May 8, dysentery.
1049, Goodbold, Wm, 2 cav, Co L, died May 12, diarrhea.
1131, German, E,* 13, Co H, died May 16, ascites.
1284, Garrett, S H, 2 cav, Co G, died May 20, diarrhea c.
1927, Grimley, James, 22, Co D, died June 14, dysentery.
2192, Ganigan, J, 9 cav, Co L, died June 19, diarrhea c.
2614, Gorden, Jas, 1, Co D, died June 28, diarrhea.
2662, Gilbert, F, 8, Co K, died July 3, scorbutus.
2928, Gibbons, M, 6, Co C, died July 5, diarrhea c.
3863, Goodman, W, 5, Co I, died July 24, anasarca.
4092, Griffin, G, 11, Co H, died July 27, scorbutus.
4225, Green, E, 11, Co H, died July 29, dysentery c.
5716, Gatrin, M, 23, Co I, died Aug 15, scorbutus.
6482, Greek, C H, 1 cav, Co K, died Aug 22, diarrhea c.
6806, Gillis, Jno, 4 cav, Co F, died Aug 25, diarrhea c.
7476, Gaines, A, 22, Co F, died Sept 1, scorbutus.
7518, Gullz H, 1, Co A, died Sept 1, scorbutus.
7624, Griens, O D, 8, Co I, died Sept 2, diarrhea c.
7659, Graff, Jacob, 17, Co H, died Sept 3, diarrhea.
7741, Gibson, J, 1, Co K, died Sept 8, scorbutus.
7968, Grant, A H, 7, Co D, died Sept 6, scorbutus.
8628, Gray, George, 1 cav, Co E, died Sept 13, scorbutus.
10671, Gallett, L, 22, Co F, died Oct 9, scorbutus.
10726, Gibbs, J, 7, Co H, died Oct 11, scorbutus.
11207, Gask, I, 8 cav, Co C, died Oct 20, wounds.
11302, Gray, James, 6 cav, Co A, died Oct 22, scorbutus.
11352, Groucher, J, 6 cav, Co B, died Oct 23, scorbutus.
11647, Grabough, J, 5, Co G, died Oct 30, scorbutus.
12164, Gifford, L, 6, Co I, died Nov 26, scorbutus.
12443, Gowell, N, 19, Co F, died Jan 12, '65, scorbutus.
12578, Goodel, M, 5, Co C, died Feb 2, '65, diarrhea.
5918, Gurmane, B S,† 77, Co K, died Aug 16, diarrhea.
4511, Grasman, E, 23, Co I, died Aug 1, diarrhea c.
12207, Gabullsoo, J, 5 cav, Co F, died Dec 1, diarrhea c.

6, Hall William, 2 cav, Co M, died Feb 5, pneumonia.
839, Holton, S M, 1, Co B, died April 20, dysentery.
867, Henry, James, 9, Co A, died April 5, pneumonia.
409, Hartsell, Geo, 7 cav, Co B, died April 6, diarrhea c.
818, Hutton, S, 9 cav, Co G, died April 30, diarrhea c.
860, Hood, Jas D, 22, Co H, died May 3, diarrhea.
947, Hart, J R,* 6, Co E, died May 7, anasarca.
1422, Hannah, Jno, 22, Co C, died May 29, anasarca.
1519, Hunter, F A, 22, Co F, died May 31, anasarca.
1656, Herrimao, D, 23, Co D, died June 6, diarrhea.
1738, Huntley, W, 5 cav, Co E, died June 8, diarrhea c.
1813, Holnes, R, 9 cav, Co G, died June 10, diarrhea c.
1904, Hough, M, 22, died June 18, diarrhea c.
1910, Harty, J S, 16, Co F, died June 13, diarrhea c.
2660, Hays, C, 6, Co H, died June 29, diarrhea.
3015, Hardy, Jno, 4, Co H, died July 7, diarrhea.
3040, Hugbey, James, 17, Co B, died July 8, diarrhea c.
3206, Hopkins, N, 6 cav, Co E, died July 12, diarrhea c.
4, Hulson, David, 8 cav, Co A, died March 27, small pox.
3343, Hell, H, † 9, Co G, died July 15, scorbutus.
3483, Hoosgner, W L, * 7, Co C, died July 17, diarrhea c.
3889, Hatter, C, bugler, 7, Co D, died July 24, diarrhea c.
3927, Hawkins, George, 12, Co H, died July 25, diarrhea.
4166, Hunter, M W, * 22, Co D, died July 28, dysentery.
4286, Heron, Jno, * 5, Co F, died July 30, diarrhea.
4426, Heath, M, 21, Co C, died July 31, diarrhea.
4674, Hale, S B, 7 cav, Co D, died Aug 4, dysentery.
5332, Hollen, Geo, 1 cav, Co L, died Aug 11, diarrhea.
5370, Haynes, P, 1 cav, Co H, died Aug 11, dysentery.
5376, Husted, J, 10, Co C, died Aug 10, diarrhea.
5556, Henrich, J, 8 Co C, died Aug 13, scorbutus.
5930, Hall, W, 26, Co I, died Aug 17, diarrhea c.
6110, Holmes, J F, 42, Co H, died Aug 18, scorbutus.
6276, Hibler, A, * 9 cav, Co D, died Aug 20, marasmus.
6992, Henry, A, 27, Co B, died Aug 27, diarrhea.
6998, Hungerford, C, † 20, Co E, died Aug 27, diarrhea.
6999, Hunt, L, 2, Co C, died Aug 27, diarrhea c.
8100, Holcomb, J, 6 cav, Co K, died Sept 7, dysentery.
8624, Harrington, G, 6 cav, Co D, died Sept 18, diarrhea c.
9239, Hawley, C, 4, Co F, died Sept 19, diarrhea.
9886, Hartman, H, 29, Co A, died Sept 21, diarrhea.
9968, Hinkley, O C, 20, Co F, died Sept 28, diarrhea.
10348, Hong, J, M, 20, Co H, died Oct 5, scorbutus.
11027, Hankins, E, 5, Co E, died Oct 16, scorbutus.
11057, Hayes, James, 1, Co E, died Oct 17, scorbutus.
11070, Haywood, J B, 1 cav, Co H, died Oct 17, scorbutus.
11260, Hamlin, J H, 1 s s, Co K, died Oct 20, scorbutus.
11336, Hong, J M, 20, Co H, died Oct 23, scorbutus.
11412, Hill, W, 1 s s, died Oct 24, scorbutus.
11480, Howard, F S, † 8, Co E, died Oct 26, scorbutus.
11593, Hawk, H L, * 24, Co I, died Oct 28, scorbutus.
11757, Hodges, M, † 22, Co I, died Nov 3, scorbutus.
11835, Hilmer, C, 6 cav, Co M, died Nov 5, scorbutus.
12067, Howe, J, 7 cav, Co F, died Nov 17, scorbutus.
12612, Hicks, C, 8, Co B, died Feb 8, '65, diarrhea c.
9718, Harper, D, 3, Co E, died Sept 25, diarrhea.

5141, Ingraham, W L, 5 cav, Co B, died Aug 9, scorbutus.

1817, Jackson, James, 7, Co I, died June 7, diarrhea c.
2576, Jones, A, 6, Co E, died June 27, scorbutus.
3564, Jagnet, E B, 7 cav, Co C, died July 19, diarrhea c.
3621, Jackson, Geo G, 22, Co F, died July 20, scorbutus.
4736, Johnson, J H, 7, Co G, died Aug 4, scorbutus.
6578, Johnson, J, 24, Co I, died Aug 23, diarrhea c.
7520, Jump, D O, 1, Co A, died Sept 1, dysentery.
7788, Johnson, H, 9 cav, Co L, died Sept 2, diarrhea c.
9746, Jackland, C, 9 cav, Co E, died Sept 25, diarrhea c.
12010, Jamieson, H, 5 cav, Co H, died Nov 14, scorbutus.
12396, Jondro, M, 1, Co K, died Jan 5, '65, diarrhea.
12463, Johnson, A, 5, Co C, died Jan 16, '65, diarrhea.

868, King, Leander, 8, Co G, died April 5, diarrhea c.
488, Keintzler, R, 5 cav, Co F, died April 12, dysentery.
706, Karl, Wm, 2, Co A, died April 24, dysentery.
4140, Klunder, Charles, 5 cav, Co F, died July 28, diarrhea.
4397, Kennedy, H, 27, Co H, died July 31, scorbutus.
4424, Kinney, Jno, 17, Co H, died July 31, diarrhea.
4728, Kendall, W, 6, Co D, died Aug 4, diarrhea.
8289, Kessler, J, 17, Co G, died Sept 9, dysentery.
10789, Kinsell, George, 5 cav, Co B, died Oct 12, scorbutus.
10908, Kenkosin, H C, 5 cav, Co E, died Oct 14, scorbutus.
12431, Keaney, C, 5 cav, Co H, died Jan 11, '65, scorbutus.

1882, Lewis, F L, 9 cav, died June 12, diarrhea c.
223, Lossing, Jno, 8 cav, Co B, died March 29, pneumonia.
960, Loring, Jno, 27, Co E, died May 8, hepatitis.
1187, Lewis, P, 5, Co D, died May 18, dysentery.
1801, Lanereed, M, 14, Co B, died May 23, diarrhea c.
87, Lunner, Jno 17, Co F, died March 29, small pox.
3305, Landing, H B, 22, Co H, died July 14, diarrhea.
3700, Lyon, A D, * 5 cav, Co G, died July 21, anasarca.
4343, Looney, L, 1 cav, Co L, died July 29, diarrhea c.
4918, Luce, F, 1 artil, Co A, died Aug 6, scorbutus.
4992, La Duk, Jas, 17, Co G, died Aug 7, diarrhea.
5142, Larke, J A, 23, Co F, died Aug 9, scorbutus.
5216, Lowell, Jas, 1 cav, Co E, died Aug 10, diarrhea c.
5776, Laither, L, 8, Co H, died Aug 15, bronchitis.
5923, Loffer, E S, 17, Co H, died Aug 17, diarrhea.
6067, Lord, M, † 3, Co M, died Aug 24, dysentery.
8055, Lemmon, O, 8 cav, Co H, died Sept 7, scorbutus.

No. of Grave.

9685, Lard, H O, 22, Co D, died Sept 24, diarrhea.
9760, Lund, Jas, 6 cav, Co H, died Sept 25, scorbutus.
10877, Laidlum, G, 1 Co D, died Oct 18, diarrhea.
11969, Lutz, Wm, 6 cav, Co F, died Nov 11, scorbutus.

218, McCartney, H, 5 cav, Co K, died March 29, diarrhea c.
268, McGuire, Jas, 20, Co A, died March 31, fever typhus.
512, Markham, D, 5 cav, Co B, died April 14, pneumonia.
612, McCarter, Jas, 22, Co H, died April 18, diarrhea.
1059, Mann, A F, 27, Co F, died May 13, diarrhea.
1062, Miller, Charles, 5 cav, Co D, died May 13, diarrhea.
1710, Miller, J, 3, Co C, died June 7, diarrhea c.
2255, Moby, Ed, 8 cav, Co K, died June 20, debilitas.
2586, McDowell, J, 8 cav, Co F, died June 28, scorbutus.
2759, McSpoulding, W, 22, Co E, died July 2, diarrhea c.
2828, Manwaring, Wm, 22, Co D, died July 3, diarrhea c.
2976, Man, Thos G, 5, Co A, died July 7, diarrhea.
3090, Marshall, H E, 27, Co B, died July 9, anasarca.
3150, Morris, A T, 14, Co K, died July 9, diarrhea.
3567, Marvey, Andrew, 17, Co G, died July 18, dysentery.
3697, Miller, W E, 2, Co K, died July 21, fever typhus.
3936, McCabe, F, 22, Co H, died July 25, dysentery.
3954, Morgan, M, 22, Co E, died July 26, scorbutus.
4078, McFall, H, 17, Co E, died July 27, diarrhea c.
4144, Miller, G, 5, Co I, died July 28, diarrhea.
4301, Mottov, Jno, 5 cav, Co L, died July 30, diarrhea.
4783, Monroe, D, 6 cav, Co A, died Aug 4, diarrhea.
4942, Morgan, E C, 23, Co G, died Aug 7, scorbutus.
5158, Miller, L, 7, Co F, died Aug 9, scorbutus.
5630, Mench, C, †20, Co I, died Aug 14, diarrhea.
6219, McCarty, Charles, 26, Co I, died Aug 20, dysentery.
6329, Meyers, J, 6, Co H, died Aug 21, diarrhea.
6820, Myer, J, 4, Co I, died Aug 25, scorbutus.
7114, Moore, J, 27, Co B, died Aug 28, fever intermittent.
7269, Merrill, S H, 5, Co G, died Aug 30, scorbutus.
7279, McLaloe, Thos, 1, Co I, died Aug 30, diarrhea.
7478, McCloud, A, 21, Co I, died Sept 1, scorbutus.
7513, Mason, F, 7 cav, Co L, died Sept 1, scorbutus.
7918, Martin, Peter, 17, Co H, died Sept 5, dysentery.
7936, Musket, J, 4 cav, Co K, died Sept 5, diarrhea.
7962, Miller, F, 22, Co G, died Sept 6, diarrhea.
8025, Moody, E, 17, Co G, died Sept 6, fever typhus.
8387, McClure, R, 7, Co D, died Sept 9, diarrhea.
8519, Miles, C S, *1 cav, Co F, died Sept 12, scorbutus.
8590, McGinis, P, 16, died Sept 12, scorbutus.
8030, McKay, K, 10, died Sept 6, diarrhea.
8570, Munson, H C, 30, Co E, died Sept 16, scorbutus.
8897, Morrison, J, 21, Co F, died Sept 16, scorbutus.
8994, Maher, S L, 7 cav, Co I, died Sept 17, diarrhea.
9185, Marine, Wm, 22, Co E, died Sept 18, anasarca.
9750, McArthur, W, 17 cav, Co D, died Sept 25, scorbutus.
9791, Moore, John, 6, cav, Co G, died Sept 26, scorbutus.
10011, Moses, C, 5 cav, Co I, died Sept 29, scorbutus.
10134, Moses, A, 6 cav, Co M, died Oct 1, diarrhea.
10423, Migele, J, 9, Co A, died Oct 6, scorbutus.
10575, Mays, Thos, 6 cav, Co H, died Oct 9, diarrhea.
10958, McMillen, Alex, 5 cav, Co M, died Sept 14, scorbutus.
11126, Miller, Jno A, 10, Co F, died Oct 18, diarrhea c.
11536, Molosh, F, 3, Co D, died Oct 27, scorbutus.
11548, McMann, W, 17, Co A, died Oct 27, scorbutus.
11582, Moreby, D, 22, Co C, died Oct 28, scorbutus.
11798, Merrill, C, 4, Co K, died Nov 4, scorbutus.
12085, Miller, H, 9, Co A, died Nov 18, scorbutus.
12093, Mogram, J, 1 s s, died Nov 19, diarrhea.
12252, McCane, W, 7, Co B, died Dec 9, scorbutus.
12418, Morton, J, 1, Co I, died Jan 15, '65, diarrhea.
11511, Mackswarer, W, 1 s s, Co K, died Oct 26, scorbutus.
12674, Marshall, O, 4, Co M, died Feb 19, '65, diarrhea c.
12733, McNiell, C, 8 cav, Co M, died March 5, '65, diarrhea c.
8790, Major, Wm, 22, Co D, died July 22, scorbutus.
7916, Monroe, Jno, 7, Co I, died Sept 5, dysentery.
9791, Moor, Jno, 6 cav, Co G, died Sept 26, scorbutus.
9965, McClary, W, 7 cav, Co H, died Sept 28, diarrhea.

513, Nicholson, E, 6 cav, Co G, died April 12, diarrhea c.
1209, Newbury, Jas, 5 cav, Co A, died May 19, fever typhoid.
2077, Nash, Chas, 22, Co H, died June 17, diarrhea c.
8313, Noel, H, †9, Co F, died June 15, pneumonia.
4102, Neek, H, 4, Co K, died July 27, diarrhea.
5092, Nirthhammer, J, 20, Co D, died Aug 8, scorbutus.
5100, Nagle, C, 11, Co G, died Aug 11, scorbutus.
5493, Narrane, A, 17, Co E, died Aug 13, scorbutus.
11011, Noyes, Jas E, 1, died Oct 16, diarrhea c.
11911, Niland, H, 8, Co D, died Nov 9, diarrhea.
1005, Nurse, H W, 5 cav, Co L, died May 10, diarrhea.
9512, Northam, O H, 6, Co M, died Sept 26, diarrhea.

255, O'Brien, Austin, 9 cav, Co H, died April 1, pneumonia.
499, Oliver, Alex, 8 cav, Co G, died April 12, diarrhea c.
1158, Orrison, George, 9 cav, Co M, died May 18, dysentery.
2267, Olney, O W, 4 Co A, died June 20, diarrhea c.
4081, Osborn, S, 27, Co B, died July 31, scorbutus.
4874, Overmeyer, J F, 6 cav, Co E, died Aug 6, scorbutus.
5574, O'Neil, J, 22, Co K, died Aug 14, dysentery.
5846, Orcutt, C, 3, Co F, died Aug 16, enteritis.
8141, Orung, S W, 20, Co C, died Sept 8, diarrhea.
8511, O'Brian, W H, 17 cav, Co A, died Sept 12, diarrhea.
9011, Ogden, E S, 5 cav, Co M, died Sept 17, scorbutus.
11940, O'Leary, J, *1 s s, Co H, died Nov 9, diarrhea.
11999, Osborn, J L, 6, Co E, died Nov 13, scorbutus.
12500, Oathart, D, 18, Co C, died Jan 17, '65, diarrhea c.

413, Parsons, G, 7, Co I, died April 9, diarrhea.
615, Pullman, Geo, 5, Co I, died April 12, diarrhea c.
1038, Parker, H C, †8 cav, Co C, died May 12, dysentery.
1276, Perigo, John, 2 cav, Co D, died May 22, pleuritis.
1374, Parish, Thos, 6, Co I, died May 26, dysentery.
1892, Paisley, A G, †22, died June 13, diarrhea.
1997, Payne, E H, 6, Co I, died June 15, diarrhea c.
2533, Piller, J, 6 cav, Co I, died June 26, diarrhea.
3546, Pierson, Daniel, 8 cav, Co C, died July 18, diarrhea.
3594, Palmerly, J, 7 cav, Co C, died July 19, diarrhea c.
4100, Post, E L, 10, Co H, died July 27, diarrhea.
4253, Pratt, M, 22, Co E, died July 29, scorbutus.
4486, Pelton, A, *21, Co A, died Aug 1, pneumonia.
4662, Philbrook, F, 1 artil, died Aug 3, pthisis.
5056, Polroff, D, 13, Co D, died Aug 8, anasarca.
5546, Peck, J H, *1 cav, Co D, Aug 13, anasarca.
5612, Pond, C, 1, Co I, died Aug 14, diarrhea.
5745, Pettibone, E E, 7, Co D, Aug 15, dysentery.
4564, Porter, L, 1 s s, Co G, died Aug 2, pthisis.
5760, Pentecost, W G, 18, died Aug 15, scorbutus.
5852, Palmer, D, 5, Co D, died Aug 16, marasmus.
7389, Parks, V, 7, Co C, died Aug 31, scorbutus.
7351, Perrin, N, 8 cav, Co B, died Aug 31, fever congestive.
7960, Parks, F, 5 cav, Co E, died Sept 6, wounds.
8195, Pearmell, J, *23, Co B, died Sept 8, scorbutus.
8636, Pike, E H, *2 cav, Co C, died Sept 13, diarrhea.
6986, Plant, Wm, 16, Co G, died Sept 16, diarrhea c.
9231, Plurrett, Wm, 22, Co D, died Sept 20, scorbutus.
11046, Platt, R, 22, Co A, died Oct 17, scorbutus.
11177, Palmer, P, 5, Co H, died Oct 19, scorbutus.
11986, Preston, B, 7, Co K, died Nov 13, scorbutus.
12273, Pitts, Wm, 5 cav, Co C, died Dec 12, scorbutus.
12409, Preston, J, 6, Co C, died Jan 7, '65, scorbutus.
12578, Pratt, L, 8 cav, Co C, died Feb 3, '65, diarrhea c.
12762, Parmalee, C,* 5 cav, Co M, died Feb 12, '65, pleuritis.

77, Roloff, Jno, 5 cav, Co E, died Mar 23, fever typhus.
324, Russell, Peter, 23, Co G, died Apr 2, diarrhea.
623, Rowland, B, 6, Co M, died Apr 19, diarrhea.
922, Robinson, Wm, 2, Co H, died May 6, diarrhea.
1804, Rhinehart, D, 5 cav, Co C, died June 10, diarrhea c.
2291, Rolland, J, 6, Co G, died June 21, diarrhea c.
2402, Ruggles, O, 32, Co H, died June 24, diarrhea a.
3296, Rassan, A, 28, Co I, died July 14, dysentery.
3732, Riley, Charles, 6, Co I, died July 21, diarrhea.
3740, Riggs, J, 22, Co I, died July 21, diarrhea.
3876, Ross, W J,* 22, Co C, died July 24, diarrhea.
5176, Rood, C, 22, Co G, died Aug 9, diarrhea.
5885, Roman, John, 5, Co C, died Aug 16, diarrhea c.
6154, Rehn, A, 17, Co G, died Aug 19, scorbutus.
7507, Ryan, W, 1, Co E, died Sept 1, diarrhea.
7750, Robinson, H, 5 cav, Co L, died Sept 2, diarrhea.
7955, Rich, A, 11, Co B, died Sept 6, diarrhea.
8617, Riley, Miles,* 7 cav, Co F, died Sept 13, scorbutus.
9254, Rimer, J C, 1 cav, Co C, died Sept 19, scorbutus.
9914, Ryno, T, 22, Co I, died Sept 28, scorbutus.
10136, Robinson, T, 27, Co F, died Oct 1, scorbutus.
10380, Randall, H D, 6, Co D, died Oct 5, diarrhea.
11151, Raley, R,† 24, Co H, died Oct 19, dysentery.
11457, Ramsey, J, 15, Co H, died Oct 25, scorbutus.
11675, Raley, H, 24 cav, Co L, died Oct 30, scorbutus.
11705, Rhott, S, 1 s s, Co K, died Nov 1, scorbutus.
12553, Richardson, M B, 1, Co L, died Jan 29, '65, scorbutus.
12580, Rodgers, W, 26, Co G, died Feb 5, '65, debilitas.
12749, Robbins, A, 4 cav, Co H, died Mar 6, '65, pleuritis.
12745, Reaves, M, 15, Co G, died Mar 8, '65, diarrhea c.

134, Snyder, E, 17, Co F, died Mar 24, bronchitis.
172, Smith, Wm, 7 cav, Co L, died Mar 26, pneumonia.
236, Soper, Calvin, 27, Co H, died Mar 29, fever typhus.
350, Sheldon, H S, 1, Co A, died Apr 2, diarrhea.
520, Shannon, Jno, 20, Co H, died Apr 13, diarrhea c.
812, Smith, W W,* 5 cav, Co D, died May 2, diarrhea.
854, Stillman, L D, 6, Co M, died May 3, dysentery.
1082, Stuck, L H, 2 cav, Co B, died May 11, diarrhea c.
1328, Schemerhorn, J, 7 cav, Co C, died May 24, diarrhea.
1406, Samborg, H, 22, Co K, died May 27, diarrhea.
1446, Snow, Levi, 20, Co H, died May 28, anasarca.
1626, Smith, A, 1 cav, Co L, died June 4, anasarca.
1801, Smith, S, 17, Co C, died June 10, diarrhea c.

No. of Grave.

1741, Stevens, S,* 22, Co K, died June 9, diarrhea.
1918, Shafer, W, 22, Co G, died June 11, diarrhea.
19[illegible]6, Strickland, Thos, 10, Co E, died June 14, diarrhea.
2239, Sanborn, H, 22, Co K, died June 2[illegible], diarrhea.
2507, Smith, C, [illegible] 6, Co E, died June 26, diarrhea.
26[illegible], Symonds, C, 24, Co C, died June 29, diarrhea c.
2631, Stevens, L, 6 cav, Co M, died June 29, diarrhea.
2[illegible], Stewart, C A, 7, Co F, died June 30, diarrhea.
2[illegible], Sprague, W B, 11, Co I, died July 3, dysentery.
29[illegible]6, Shaw, [illegible] 2, Co K, died July 7, anasarca.
30[illegible], S[illegible], E, [illegible] 2 cav, Co C, died July 7, diarrhea c.
3[illegible], Snider, J E, 1, Co H, died July 9, diarrhea.
3[illegible], Stubbs, J, 9 cav, Co L, died July 15, pneumonia.
3518, Simpson, E T, 6 artil, Co G, died July 18, diarrhea.
3[illegible], Smith, G, 5, Co B, died July 18, diarrhea c.
3[illegible], S[illegible], Wm, 8 cav, Co L, died July 18, scorbutus.
3[illegible], Sears, F [illegible], 7, Co D, died July 25, scorbutus.
39[illegible], Sharp, Jas, 6, died July 25, scorbutus.
4[illegible], Stiles, H, 4, Co K, died July 27, diarrhea.
4311, Sprague, B, 7 cav, Co E, died July 30, diarrhea.
41[illegible], Sale, Thos, 17, Co G, died July 31, anasarca.
48[illegible], Smith, Wm, 17, Co H, died Aug 6, dysentery.
51[illegible], Swain, D, 6 cav, Co H, died Aug 10, dysentery.
507[illegible], Stow, George, 10, Co C, died Aug 17, enteritis.
6[illegible]23, Simpson, T, 8, Co I, died Aug 21, diarrhea.
6[illegible], Sanders, A, 17, Co B, died Aug 22, diarrhea c.
68[illegible], Sand[illegible], H [illegible], 6, Co H, died Aug 24, diarrhea.
71[illegible], Sullivan, Jno, 27, Co E, died Aug 27, syphilis.
750[illegible], Sherman, Fred, 22, Co G, died Aug 30, diarrhea.
7[illegible]50, Sayre, J M, 1, Co G, died Aug 31, diarrhea.
7528, Schofield, C, 27, Co G, died Sept 1, dysentery.
7676, Satter[illegible], H J, 6 cav, Co E, died Sept 2, diarrhea c.
8000, Sutherland, J, 1, Co I, died Sept 6, scorbutus.
6[illegible]80, Stanning, G W,* 5 cav, Co G, died Sept 12, diarrhea c.
9150, Sulphur, H W, 15, Co F, died Sept 18, diarrhea.
9469, Stewart, F, 6 cav, Co E, died Sept 21, scorbutus.
9481, Steward, W V, 5, Co E, died Sept 21, anasarca.
9629, Snyder, J, 5 cav, Co M, died Sept 24, diarrhea.
1008[illegible], Strant, C A, 5 cav, Co F, died Sept 30, diarrhea.
10117, Spencer, George, 21, Co H, died Oct 1, scorbutus.
10254, Simmonds, A, 17, Co E, died Oct 3, scorbutus.
10[illegible]8, Spencer, Jno, [illegible], Co I, died Oct 3, scorbutus.
10[illegible]7, Skull, Wm, 7, Co B, died Oct 6, diarrhea.
10411, Simpson, I P, 22, Co A, died Oct 7, scorbutus.
11138, Swart, M M, 3, Co E, died Oct 19, scorbutus.
11[illegible], Swesler, C, † [illegible], Co K, died Oct 19, scorbutus.
11[illegible], Sutton, H, 22, Co I, died Oct 21, wounds.
11265, Strander, A, 6, Co G, died Oct 21, diarrhea.
11[illegible], Stafford, S, 5 cav, Co F, died Oct 23, scorbutus.
117[illegible], Steadman, S, 10, Co H, died Oct 30, scorbutus.
11717, Smith, S, 7, Co H, died Nov 1, scorbutus.
11773, Stekles, M, 11, Co I, died Nov 3, diarrhea c.
120[illegible], Secor, H, 6 cav, Co B, died Nov 15, scorbutus.
12[illegible], Spendle, C, [illegible] cav, Co C, died Dec 5, dysentery.
12229, Sumner, H, 27, Co E, died Dec 6, scorbutus.
122[illegible], Stedman, S D, 10, Co H, died Dec 11, scorbutus.
12310, Smith, Peter, 1 s s, Co K, died Dec 19, diarrhea.
12[illegible]78, Smith, C B, 8 cav, Co L, died Feb 19, '65, diarrhea c.
128[illegible], Smith, Geo, 8, Co B, died March 20, '65, diarrhea.
12254, Stickner, J, 16, Co D, died Dec 10, scorbutus.
11[illegible]8, Seckom, A, 1 s s, Co K, died Oct 26, scorbutus.
11[illegible], Springer, J, 7 cav, Co K, died Oct 26, scorbutus.

1[illegible]01, Tarrell, Henry, 22, Co H, died May 23, diarrhea c.
29[illegible]5, Tubbs, F, 7, Co K, died July 6, diarrhea.
48, Tilt, George, 2 cav, Co D, died May 24, small pox.
81[illegible]8, Trateher, E H, 6 cav, Co F, died July 18, diarrhea.
6[illegible]3, Tompkins, N R, 1, Co B, died Aug 24, diarrhea.

No. of Grave.

7009, Tift, H, 5 cav, Co M, died Aug 27, diarrhea.
7544, Thompson, W, 8, Co F, died Sept 2, diarrhea c.
7599, Tracy, D, 7 cav, Co K, died Sept 2, diarrhea.
7797, Thompson, M C, 5 cav, Co I, died Sept 4, dysentery.
9108, Taylor, H, 32, Co F, died Sept 18, dysentery.
11118, Taylor, J M, 11, Co A, died Oct 18, scorbutus.
11149, Twesler, C, † 5, Co K, died Oct 19, scorbutus.

3945, Udell, W O, 2, Co D, died July 25, diarrhea.

731, Vanderhoof, Jas, 6 cav, Co G, died April 25, dysentery.
1126, Vangleson, L, † 5 cav, Co D, died May 15, nephritis.
1467, Vogle, Jacob, 27, Co D, died May 29, diarrhea.
2270, Van Dyke, Jno, 6 cav, Co D, died June 20, pneumonia.
2994, Van Brant, W H, 9 cav, Co E, died July 7, diarrhea c.
3278, Vonlin, C, † 6, Co F, died July 11, diarrhea.
6864, Vanstoten, W H, 6 cav, Co K, died Aug 26, diarrhea c.
7595, Vansickle, L, † 5 cav, Co G, died Sept 2, dysentery.
8958, Vanmaker, F, 16, Co G, died Sept 15, diarrhea c.
95[illegible]6, York, C, 5, Co K, died Sept 22, diarrhea.
9936, Vleight, A, 22, Co D, died Sept 28, scorbutus.
12166, Vaonlien, C, 27, Co K, died Nov 26, dysentery.
12690, Vincient, J, 6, Co K, died Feb 22, '65, diarrhea c.

840, Whittaker, J, 7, Co B, died April 2, diarrhea.
7[illegible]3, Whipple, G, 4, Co A, died April 25, diarrhea.
741, Wilson, Byron, 5 cav, Co D, died April 26, diarrhea.
749, Wright, Wm A, 7, Co K, died April 26, dysentery c.
957, Wilson, J, 22, Co K, died May 8, dysentery.
2102, Wilson, W, 11, Co I, died June 17, diarrhea c.
4961, Winegardner, A S, 1 cav, Co K, died Aug 7, dysentery.
12723, White, C, 5, Co F, died March 3, '65, diarrhea c.
12796, Whitmore, C, 8 cav, Co M, died March 18, '65, scorbutus.
6781, Wiley, E T,* 1, Co E, died Aug 25, dysentery.
749, Wright, Wm A, 7, Co K, died April 26, dysentery c.
1089, Woolsey, B, 22, Co E, died May 14, diarrhea c.
1701, Walker, J, 22, Co C, died June 7, diarrhea.
1920, Wolf, F, 13, Co K, died June 14, diarrhea.
3301, Wendarkly, 5, Co G, died July 14, diarrhea c.
2899, Whitlock, M, 2, Co E, died July 5, scorbutus.
3180, Willet, S, † 22, Co K, died July 11, dysentery.
3269, Wright, W, 5 cav, Co K, died July 13, diarrhea.
3137, Wolverton, C, 6, Co B, died July 17, dysentery.
3992, Woodruff, B, 1 cav, Co E, died July 26, diarrhea.
4419, Warren, H, 4, Co E, died July 31, diarrhea.
4860, Walker, Geo, 22, Co G, died Aug 6, scorbutus.
5051, Williams, M, 1, Co A, died Aug 8, diarrhea.
5786, Williams, T, 2 cav, Co L, died Aug 15, diarrhea.
1183[illegible], Wolfinger, J M, 20, Co H, died Oct 28, scorbutus.
12307, Windlass, S, 8 cav, Co K, died Dec 18, scorbutus.
5559, Warner, C, 5, Co F, died Aug 13, scorbutus.
11098, Warner, J, 5 cav, Co K, died Oct 18, debilitas.
12723, White, C, 5 cav, Co F, died March 8, '65, diarrhea c.
9844, Wheeler, E, 24, Co A, died Sept 27, scorbutus.
6930, Wisner, Jno,* 6 cav, Co I, died Aug 17, diarrhea.
8331, Wood, A O, † 9 cav, Co M, died Sept 10, scorbutus.
8076, Wilder, H S, 23, Co K, died Sept 7, scorbutus.
6996, Wolverton, J S, 5 cav, Co A, died Aug 27, diarrhea c.
7362, Way, F, 7, Co C, died Aug 31, diarrhea.
7812, Whelen, H, † 6, Co I, died Sept 4, dysentery.
7882, Wells, F, 7, Co F, died Sept 5, diarrhea.
9022, Wing, A, 17, Co G, died Sept 17, diarrhea.
9525, Whitworth, W G, 6 cav, Co A, died Sept 22, diarrhea.
12796, Whitmore, C, 8 cav, Co M, died March 18, '65, scorbutus.

2210, Yacht, E, † 22, Co E, died July 5, dysentery.
2626, Zett, J, 22, Co D, died June 23, scorbutus.

MINNESOTA.

60[illegible]4, Atkinson, Geo, 9, Co F, died March 17, scorbutus.
6537, Allen[illegible], J [illegible], 9, Co B, died March 23, ictus solis.
11977, Allman, G, 1, Co B, died Nov 12, scorbutus.

4221, Becker, G, 9, Co E, died July 29, scorbutus.
5[illegible]35, Barnard, H A, 9, Co A, died Aug 15, scorbutus.
6[illegible], B[illegible], M, 9, Co H, died Aug 23, diarrhea.
7841, B[illegible], D, 9, Co E, died Sept 4, diarrhea.
78[illegible], Brayton, J M, 9, Co B, died Sept 5, scorbutus.
80[illegible], B[illegible], J F, 9, Co G, died Sept 7, scorbutus.
82[illegible], Burrows, H, 9, Co K, died Sept 9, diarrhea.
91[illegible], Babcock, L A, 9, Co D, died Sept 21, catarrh.
9[illegible], B[illegible], 9, Co [illegible], died Sept 26, diarrhea.
127[illegible]8, Baker, J G, 1, Co A, died March 15, diarrhea c.

27[illegible]7, C[illegible], P H, Co A, died July 1, diarrhea.
[illegible], C[illegible], J, 9, Co D, died July 19, fever remittent.
41[illegible], C[illegible], 9, Co I, died July 27, diarrhea c.

6970, Coughlin E, 9, Co C, died July 27, diarrhea.
10724, Cassady, J, 9, Co F, died Oct 6, diarrhea.

7692, Dunham, R H, 9, Co K, died Sept 3, diarrhea c.
10971, Davis, E J, 9, Co E, died Oct 15, scorbutus.

8517, Fitch, W F, 9, Co F, died Sept 12, diarrhea.
12656, Fuchs, H, 9, Co D, died Feb 14, '65, diarrhea c.
9905, Freescholz, F, 9, Co F, died Sept 27, diarrhea c.

3287, Geer, O, 9, Co F, died July 14, scorbutus.
10101, Goodfellow, E C, 9, Co D, died Oct 6, dysentery.
10579, Goodwin, Geo, 9, Co A, died Oct 9, diarrhea c.
4130, Gordon, W C, 17, Co I, died July 28, dysentery.

6033, Higly, M F, 9, Co G, died Aug 18, diarrhea.
6661, Hill, C J, 9, Co K, died Aug 18, dysentery.
6605, Handy, J, musician, 9, Co I, died Aug 23, debilitas.

No. of Grave.
9144, Hearvay, J E, 9, Co K, died Sept 19, diarrhea.
4170, Holts A, 9, Co F, died July 28, diarrhea.

7809, Johnson, N, 9, Co H, July 4, dysentery.

1211, Kerrick, Samuel, 4, Co K, died May 19, diarrhea.
9127, Kloss, L, 9, Co H, died Sept 18, diarrhea.

6079, Lindley, C, 9, Co B, died Aug 8, diarrhea.
7706, Large, M, 9, Co G, died Sept 4, diarrhea.
12165, Lewis L, 9, Co E, died Nov 29, dysentery.
12510, Latimore, W H, 9, Co D, died Jan 12, '65, dysentery.
9512, Lenyer, M, 9, Co G, died Aug 30, diarrhea.

5400, Myers, J, 3, Co I, died Aug 13, diarrhea.
7288, Murder, J W, 9, Co A, died Aug 30, diarrhea.
8180, McDougal, J, 9, Co A, died Sept 8, diarrhea.
9105, Montenary, J, 9, Co G, died Sept 18, diarrhea.

2829, Nichols, John, 15, Co A, died July 3, diarrhea c.

7789, Oilman, Wm, 9, Co B, died Sept 4, diarrhea.
8384, Oreutt, J,* 2, Co C, died Sept 10, diarrhea.

2841, Pitcher, E, 5, Co B, died July 2, diarrhea.
4813, Packett, C, 9, Co K, died Aug 5, diarrhea.
6606, Pericle, Jacob, 9, Co H, died Aug 13, dysentery.
6909, Pence, Geo, 9, Co H, died Aug 16, dysentery.
83 3, Poluder, T, 9, Co B, died Sept 19, dysentery.
8323, Pettijohn, S W, 9, Co H, died Sept 14, diarrhea c.

4277, Roberts, J G, 9, Co E, died July 29, diarrhea.

5588, Roovin, J, 1, Co H, died Aug 14, scorbutus.
10627, Robertson, John, 9, Co B, died Oct 4, diarrhea.
10715, Reese, Wm, 9, Co E, died Oct 11, diarrhea c.

5941, Short, M, 9, Co K, died Aug 17, scorbutus.
6216, Sperce, C, 9, Co G, died Aug 24, scorbutus.
6276, Sontor, C, 9, Co H, died Aug 20, marasmus.
7185, Scheffer, H, 9, Co G, died Aug 20, diarrhea.
12058, Shiver, E,* 9, Co E, died Nov 17, scorbutus.
12868, Sarf, Henry, 5, Co E, died March 22, diarrhea.

8408, Thompson, W, 9, Co A, died Sept 11, diarrhea.
10186, Tittam, N M, 9, Co B, died Oct 1, diarrhea.
11603, Thomas, W R, 9, Co E, died Oct 28, scorbutus.

12166, Ulrin, A,* 9, Co E, died Nov 20, scorbutus.

11505, Vanhouse, B A,* 9, Co C, died Oct 26, diarrhea c.
11563, Vittum, E W, 9, Co B, died Oct 27, dysentery.

986, Wood, Ashley, 2, Co B, died May 9, diarrhea.
3867, Walrich, P, 1, Co C, died July 24, diarrhea c.
4198, Wheeler, A, 9, Co C, died Aug 1, diarrhea.
4688, Woodoury, Jas, 9, Co C, died Aug 2, diarrhea.
5637, Wilson, F C, 9, Co E, died Aug 14, diarrhea.
8233, Winter, G, 9, Co H, died Sept 9, dysentery.
8416, Whipple O C, 9, Co F, died Sept 11, diarrhea.
8459, Westorer, J, 9, Co E, died Sept 11, debilitas.
8777, Warron, E F, musician, 9, Co A, died Sept 14, diarrhea c.

5006, Youug, D S, 9, Co I, died Aug 8, diarrhea.

MISSOURI.

231, Borns, John, 17, Co I, died Apr 1, pneumonia.
1251, Bork, J H, 2, Co H, died May 2, anasarca.
1464, Buel, J, 4, Co C, died May 29, debilitas.
2217, Bishop, P, 16, Co I, died June 20, diarrhea.
2306, Boomker, Wm, 2, Co F, died June 22, diarrhea.
4269, Broyer, J, 2, Co E, died July 29, diarrhea c.
6355, Birley, Peter, 29, Co I, died Aug 16, marasmus.
8664, Berger, J, 2, Co I, died Sept 13, diarrhea.
8772, Eitter, H, 29, Co F, died Sept 14, dysentery.
11225, Bollard, James, 19, Co D, died Oct 20, scorbutus.
12705, Bates, P, 44, Co F, died Mar 18, '65, diarrhea c.

2861, Cline, C, 2, Co I, died July 4, catarrh.
4328, Clemants, Jas, 2 cav, Co A, died July 30, diarrhea c.
6533, Cornell, James, 9 cav, Co H, died Aug 23, diarrhea.
12351, Coon, F, 15, Co K, died Dec 28, scorbutus.
12776, Chapman, R, 24, Co B, died Mar 14, '65, pleuritis.

5263, Dickson, D, 18, died Aug 10, scorbutus.
1641, Daley, M, 10 cav, Co H, died June 6, diarrhea c.

813, Eddington, G W, 29, Co A, died Apr 2, diarrhea c.
2953, Eagler, John, 15, Co B, died July 25, diarrhea.

6987, Fogg, E F,* 1 cav, Co H, died Aug 27, diarrhea.
8633, Folk, L,* 18, Co C, died Sept 13, diarrhea.
11266, Fay, J W,* 2, Co K, died Sept 21, diarrhea.
12805, Fry, M,* 12 cav, Co L, died Mar 21, '65, scorbutus.
6914, Frick, S,* 2, Co E, died Aug 26, diarrhea.

2730, Guffy, R, 18, Co E, died July 2, diarrhea.
8725, Gallegher, F, 2, Co G, died July 21, diarrhea.

226, Houston, W E, 18, Co E, died Mar 20, pneumonia.
4506, Hunter, W, 1 cav, Co H, died Aug 1, scorbutus.
4568, Hartman, V, 20, Co G, died Aug 2, scorbutus.
4727, Huntsley, A,† 22, Co H, died Aug 4, scorbutus.
7064, Hartney, F, 2, Co K, died Aug 28, scorbutus.
226, Houston, W E, 18, Co E, died Mar 29, pneumonia.
1652, Head, B J, 28, Co B, died June 2, anasarca.
2155, Helfpen, G, 12, Co E, died June 20, dysentery.
8926, Hasse, John, 11 cav, Co L, died Sept 6, fever typhoid.
9312, Hamilton, W,* 31, Co A, died Sept 17, diarrhea c.
11941, Hanahan, A, 29, Co B, died Nov 9, scorbutus.

6140, Isonhour, J, 9, Co I, died July 31, dysentery.

6709, Keyan, M, 2, Co D, died Aug 15, diarrhea.
7414, Keller, A, 29, Co H, died Aug 21, diarrhea.
8178, Kline, C S,† 2, Co F, died Sept 5, scorbutus.
10746, Kannst, H, 18, Co G, died Oct 9, scorbutus.
12821, Kellar, I, 43, Co H, died April 1, '65, diarrhea c.
7713, Kuhn, Jacob, 15, Co E, died Sept 3, debilitas.

3249, Lowe, John, 18, Co E, died July 13, diarrhea.
4803, Lewilley, Wm, 29, Co K, died Aug 5, scorbutus.
7035, Lang, C, 10 cav, Co B, died Aug 27, diarrhea.
12232, Litch, J, 4, Co A, died Dec 6, scorbutus.
6401, Lindsay, J, 18, Co A, died Aug 12, scorbutus.

7478, Miller, W, 4 cav, Co E, died Sept 1, diarrhea.
8913, Morgan, E,* 12 cav, Co F, died Sept 16, fever typhoid.
11035, Manning, S H,† 30, Co A, died Oct 16, scorbutus.
12459, Monzt, W, 15, Co G, died Jan 15, '65, scorbutus.
12706, Martin, J, 44, Co H, died Feb 27, '65, debilitas.
12754, McGuire, O, 2 cav, Co I, died Mar 12, '65, diarrhea c.
12760, McDowell, J, 2, Co F, died Mar 12, '65, diarrhea c.

3456, Newkirk, Charles, 15, Co F, died July 17, diarrhea c.
8539, Neelout, W, 2, Co E, died July 18, diarrhea c.
4169, Nelson, John, 29, Co A, died July 28, diarrhea.

12774, O'Dell, E, 44, Co D, died Mar 14, '65, debilitas.

12823, Purcell, J R, 44, Co G, died Apr 5, '65, diarrhea.
755, Phillips, Pat, 11, Co E, died Apr 27, dysentery.
25, Payne, Joseph,* 29, Co A, died Apr 16, small pox.
4978, Perkins, A H, 29, Co L, died Aug 7, scorbutus.
6732, Plasmlue, A, 26, Co D, died Aug 24, diarrhea.
10569, Plomer, E D, 24, Co B, died Oct 8, diarrhea.

1348, Reilly, P, 29, Co B, died May 25, rheumatism.
3540, Riddle, F, 8, Co D, died July 18, diarrhea.
6110, Ritteman, Jno, 15, Co F, died Aug 9, scorbutus.
6915, Reiners, J, 4, Co G, died Aug 26, diarrhea.
2422, Robertson, J C, 10 cav, Co F, died June 25, diarrhea c.

1424, Schenck, Philip, 15, Co B, died May 26, diarrhea.
1478, Seebol, A, 12, Co G, died May 30, diarrhea.
1623, Search, Henry, 15, Co D, died June 4, diarrhea.
2464, Stickle, D, 4, Co D, died June 24, scorbutus.
2480, Stofacke, F, 15, Co D, died June 25, diarrhea c.
28, Stiner, Gotlieb, 20, Co A, died Apr 17, small pox.
5239, Storion, F, 58, Co E, died Aug 9, diarrhea.
5667, Schmas, G, 15, Co G, died Aug 14, nephritis.
6856, Sagin, C,† 2, Co H, died Aug 26, diarrhea.
6930, Shuman, Joseph, 1, Co D, died Aug 26, diarrhea.
7535, Sherman, H, 15, Co G, died Sept 1, scorbutus.
9821, Schaut, D B, 18, Co E, died Sept 26, diarrhea c.

636, Trask, Geo K, 29, Co A, died Apr 14, diarrhea.
770, Terrill, Christian, 27, Co E, died Apr 27, dysentery c.
1509, Terrell, J, 12, Co A, died May 31, diarrhea.
6072, Tresler H W, 4, Co I, died Aug 14, dysentery c.
12780, Turman, D, 44, Co B, died Mar 4, '65, debilitas.

2803, Vance, H J, 26, Co B, died July 3, dysentery.

No. of Grave.
373, Walham, H, 14, Co C, died Apr 5, diarrhea.
678, Watson, J J, 18, Co A, died Apr 22, diarrhea.
3100, Wigan, M, 2, Co F, died July 10, diarrhea.
7494, Williams, J M, 31, Co H, died Sept 1, scorbutus.

No. of Grave.
10859, Weldam, J,* 2, Co B, died Oct 14, diarrhea.
12550, Ware, J B, 40, Co K, died Jan 29, '65, scorbutus.
12739, West, J, 40, Co K, died Mar 6, '65, diarrhea c.

NEW HAMPSHIRE.

26, Ames, John O, † 2, Co F, died March 8, pneumonia.
29, Allen, E S, 2, Co H, died March 9, pneumonia.
4656, Allen, S, 9, Co C, died Aug 3, scorbutus.
4746, Abbott, C, 7, Co K, died Aug 5, diarrhea.
7130, Archus, J L, 9, Co A, died Aug 28, diarrhea.
9518, Atmore, G W, 3, Co G, died Sept 22, scorbutus.
9842, Anderson, J N, 7, Co E, died Sept 24, scorbutus.
11765, Avery, J, 1 cav, Co M, died Nov 3, diarrhea c.
5721, Austendalph, I, 3, Co D, died Aug 15, enteritis.

883, Bashby, N, 7, Co C, died May 1, diarrhea.
3316, Bailey, A D, 7, Co C, died July 15, diarrhea.
3380, Bush, A, 4, Co H, died July 16, diarrhea.
4417, Bachelor, J R, 1, died Aug 1, diarrhea.
4965, Baker, Wm, 4, Co H, died Aug 7, dysentery.
4958, Babb, James, 7, Co D, died Aug 7, wounds.
6871, Brown, W F, 2, Co B, died Aug 26, nephritis.
6765, Breakmann, A, 12, Co I, died Aug 25, diarrhea.
7857, Baker, D W, 4, Co G, died Sept 5, diarrhea.
8463, Bell, Geo, 5, Co C, died Sept 11, scorbutus.
10291, Boud, J, 12, Co F, died Oct 4, scorbutus.

2228, Clark, G M, * 7, Co C, died May 20, anasarca.
3326, Combs, John, 7, Co B, died July 14, diarrhea c.
4230, Coon, Charles, 7, Co G, died July 29, scorbutus.
5187, Colby, John N, 13, Co D, died Aug 9, diarrhea.
7072, Cooney, Thomas, 9, Co C, died Aug 28, diarrhea.
8551, Connelly, M, 4, Co C, died Sept 12, scorbutus.
2796, Chadwick, C E, 7, Co F, died July 2, diarrhea c.
11192, Carr, P, 1, Co H, died Oct 20, dysentery.

1370, Downs, E, 7, Co I, died May 25, fever remittent.
2086, Doer, S, 7, Co D, died June 17, diarrhea c.
3668, Dodge, C F, † 7, Co K, died July 24, scorbutus.
5577, Drake, Charles C, 1 cav, Co B, died Aug 14, scorbutus.

8566, Eschoymer, H, 1 cav, Co B, died July 19 dysentery.
5337, Estey, E E, 4, Co C, died Aug 10, diarrhea.
8426, Edwards, John, 9, Co F, died Sept 11, scorbutus.
12841, Elliott, A, 7, Co I, died April 21, '65, diarrhea.

1896, Fuller, Geo, 7, Co B, died May 26, diarrhea.
5210, Faucett, J, 7, Co C, died Aug 10, diarrhea.
6678, Flanders, O, 9, Co F, died Aug 24, dysentery.
6894, Ford, W, 7, Co K, died Aug 26, diarrhea.
9160, Faggerty, Jackson, 1 cav, Co A, died Sept 21, scorbutus.
12140, Felch, O P, 7, Co H, died Jan 12, '65, pleuritis.

9838, Guingwlett, H, 2, Co E, died July 3, phthisis.
4413, Gill, N, 7, Co A, died July 31, scorbutus.
4687, Gooley, J, * 7, Co G, died Aug 4, diarrhea c.
11905, Goodwin, A, 1, Co I, died Nov 7, diarrhea.
9671, Gardner, A, 4, Co C, died Sept 24, diarrhea.
6516, Gray, G H, 4, Co E, died Aug 22, fever intermittent.

6149, Hunter, C, 4, Co K, died Aug 19, diarrhea.
6875, Hood, Wm, 6, Co I, died Aug 26, diarrhea.
7869, Hartford, H, 4, Co A, died Sept 5, diarrhea.
8537, Hally, H, 7, Co C, died Sept 12, erysipelas.
10269, Hase, W, * 11, Co H, died Oct 3, diarrhea.
11156, Hamlin, O W, 1 cav, Co I, died Oct 19, scorbutus.
11439, Holmes, J, * 7, died Oct 24, scorbutus.
11468, Holmes, J, 7, died Oct 26, scorbutus.

7738, Jones, J B, 9, Co K, died Sept 3, scorbutus.
9198, Johnson, O O, 5, Co F, died Sept 18, scorbutus.
11216, Juntplute, F, 12, Co E, died Oct 20, scorbutus.
11758, Johnson, P, 9, Co E, died Nov 3, scorbutus.

4914, Keyes, C, 1 cav, Co K, died July 30, diarrhea.
5114, Kemp, C H, 7, Co A, died Aug 9, diarrhea.
5151, Kingsbury, H R, 9, Co K, died Aug 9, diarrhea.
5441, Kerson, H B, * 2, Co C, died Aug 12, anasarca.
7397, Kreaser, M, 4, Co I, died Aug 31, diarrhea.
11877, Kilnsmith, J, * 10, Co I, died Nov 6, scorbutus.
11991, Kingsbury, J M, † 1 cav, Co A, died Nov 18, scorbutus.

6144, Lawrence, A, 1 cav, Co C, died Aug 19, debilitas.
6787, Lenert, D, 9, Co K, died Aug 25, diarrhea.
8048, Libby, A O, 4, Co H, died Sept 6, gangrene.
11415, Lepott, J, 8 cav, Co L, died Oct 21, scorbutus.
11481, Lucks, P, 5, Co C, died Oct 26, scorbutus.

2687, Mumford, A, 12, Co A, died June 30, bronchitis.
3652, Mantove, J, 4, Co H, died June 20, dysentery.
4284, Miller, F, 11, Co G, died July 30, diarrhea.
4629, Miller, R, 11, Co H, died Aug 3, diarrhea.
7203, Milliot, P, 5, Co I, died Aug 29, debilitas.
7423, Morrison, O P, 9, Co C, died Aug 31, scorbutus.
7948, Marten, J, 4, Co C, died Sept 6, diarrhea c.
8573, McCann, M, 9, Co G, died Sept 12, diarrhea.
9921, Matheson, F, 7, Co B, died Sept 28, scorbutus.
11207, McCann, O, 13, Co E, died Oct 20, scorbutus.
12254, Montegan, P, 35, Co F, died Dec 6, scorbutus.

1678, O'Brien, Charles, 7, Co I, died June 6, diarrhea c.
11658, Osmore, J, 1 cav, Co C, died Oct 31, scorbutus.

6185, Patch, John, 3, Co F, died Aug 19, dysentery.
819, Poore, Sam'l, * 2, Co H, died April 30, diarrhea c.
3260, Piny, J, 3, Co G, died July 13, diarrhea.
4764, Place, J K, 7, Co F, died Aug 5, diarrhea.
7011, Patterson, N, 9, Co L, died Aug 27, scorbutus.
11121, Parsons, Sam'l, 5, Co H, died Oct 18, scorbutus.
11828, Powen, H A, 7, Co A, died Nov 5, scorbutus.
11837, Phelps, M F, 9, Co D, died Nov 5, scorbutus.
5883, Pascal, E, 7, Co E, died Aug 12, diarrhea.

1572, Reed, F K, 2, Co H, died June 3, diarrhea c.
2771, Ramsay, Wm, 7, Co G, died July 2, diarrhea c.
3406, Richards, W R, 7, Co C, died July 16, dysentery.
11300, Ringer, J K, sergeant major, 11, died Oct 22, scorbutus.

1336, Smith, John, 7, Co K, died May 24, dysentery.
2330, Sanburn, W, 7, Co H, died June 22, diarrhea c.
2505, Sanlay, E, 9, Co E, died June 26, diarrhea.
2708, Simms, S, 9, Co C, died June 30, diarrhea c.
2925, Searle, J R, 7, Co E, died July 5, diarrhea c.
3472, Smith, L F, 13, Co C, died July 17, diarrhea c.
4779, Steward, Geo, 10, Co A, died Aug 5, diarrhea.
5140, Smith, J, 7, Co B, died Aug 9, diarrhea c.
5198, Schean, W, 7, Co A, died Aug 9, diarrhea.
5405, Shorey, Ed, 1, Co C, died Aug 12, diarrhea.
5438, Salsbur, J, 4, Co K, died Aug 12, anasarca.
5621, Stanley, Jno, 9, Co A, died Aug 14, scorbutus.
6517, Smith, J, 11, Co E, died Aug 23, dysentery.
7040, Swain, C, 7, Co D, died Aug 27, scorbutus.
8629, Smith, C, 3, Co F, died Sept 13, diarrhea c.
8652, Stark, S, 15, Co A, died Sept 13, diarrhea.
8950, Smith, John, 3, Co F, died Sept 17, scorbutus.
9412, Smith, L, 12, Co B, died Sept 21, scorbutus.
10508, Shantz, J, 11, Co G, died Oct 8, scorbutus.
11587, Spaulding, T C, 4, Co K, died Nov 7, scorbutus.

3396, Taylor, A B, 5, Co H, died July 16, anasarca.
3481, Tobine, T, 6, Co A, died July 17, diarrhea c.
4072, Tilton, D B, 7, Co G, died July 26, diarrhea.
8098, Thompson, A, 9, Co K, died Sept 8, scorbutus.
10734, Tilton, L G, 11, Co B, died Oct 11, diarrhea c.

10493, Upkins, A, 1 cav, Co B, died Oct 7, diarrhea c.

5491, Valley, John, 10, Co K, died Aug 12, diarrhea.

794, Woolard, L A, 7, Co K, died April 29, diarrhea c.
1991, Williams, J, 7, Co I, died June 15, diarrhea c.
2345, Woodbury, A, 7, Co H, died June 23, diarrhea c.
2545, Whipple, John, * 11, Co C, died June 27, debilitas.
4156, Webster, J, 6, Co I, died July 28, diarrhea.
2710, Welson, W, 4, Co F, died July 1, diarrhea c.
4104, Whalen, M, 9, Co M, died July 27, dysentery.
4749, Welch, James, 7, Co I, died Aug 5, scorbutus.
4750, Weston, W W, 8, Co A, died Aug 5, dysentery.
5702, Wagner, John, 7, Co H, died Aug 15, scorbutus.
7459, Welsh, J, 7, Co C, died Sept 2, anasarca.
7834, Wolf, John D, 3, Co F, died Sept 4, diarrhea.
8083, Weitzrausen, F, 9, Co L, died Sept 7, diarrhea c.
11278, Williams, P, 3, Co H, died Oct 22, scorbutus.
11472, Wingerd, D, 3, Co G, died Oct 26, dysentery.
11768, Wilson, J, 11, Co I, died Nov 3, scorbutus.
11878, Warren, E, 1 cav, Co M, died Nov 6, diarrhea.
12734, Whitman, G, E, † 1 cav, Co B, died March 6, '65, scorbutus.

6736, York, Charles, 1 cav, Co B, died Sept 14, diarrhea.

NEW JERSEY.

No. of Grave.

3347, Aaron, Thomas, 2, Co B, died July 15, diarrhea c.
3354, Aoey, G, 1, Co K, died July 16, diarrhea.
4098, Austin, D B, 2, Co I, died July 27, diarrhea.
7138, Anderson, T, 2, Co E, died Aug 28, dysentery.
8513, A Bright, —,* 3 cav, Co I, died Sept 12, diarrhea.
11389, Alexander, W L, 3, Co C, died Oct 24, scorbutus.
12646, Amps, C, 33, Co I, died Feb 13, '65, vulnus sclop.

909, Broderick, J S, 2, Co A, died May 5, diarrhea.
1548, Beach, J, 11, Co E, died June 1, scorbutus.
2181, Brannan, Pat, 11, Co B, died June 19, debilitas.
2260, Bells, J H, 2, Co M, died June 21, diarrhea c.
2577, Buckley, John, 1, Co G, died June 27, fever intermittent.
2980, Bloun, Adam, 2, Co I, died July 4, diarrhea.
3499, Batlman, A C,* 1 artil, Co B, died July 10, diarrhea c.
5761, Bailey L, 7, Co A, died Aug 9, scorbutus.
6272, Brown, Geo, 1 cav, Co B, died Aug 10, diarrhea c.
5957, Burns, P, 3 cav, Co C, died Aug 11, diarrhea.
6379, Baker, Wm, 1 cav, Co K, died Aug 12, scorbutus.
6184, Blanchard G, 7, Co K, died Aug 13, anasarca.
5934, Bennett, C, 14, Co B, died Aug 17, scorbutus.
11682, Brant, Charles,† 1, Co E, died Oct 31, scorbutus.
12238, Buyer, A, 6, Co I, died Dec 7, scorbutus.
12640, Brewer, W H, 10, Co D, died Feb 12, '65 scorbutus.

715, Corley, Daniel, 11, Co A, died April 24, diarrhea.
1437, Creamer, E, 35, Co A, died May 28, diarrhea.
6929, Creamer, E, 10, Co B, died Aug 26, diarrhea.
3209, Chamberlain, R, 1 cav, Co D, July 12, diarrhea c.
6730, Clark, C H, 2, Co C, died Aug 15, scorbutus.
8240, Coonan, J, 2, Co C, died Sept 9, scorbutus.
10552, Collar, H, 2, Co D, died Sept 9, fever remittent.
11990, Clayton, L, 10, Co B, died, Nov 13, scorbutus.
3476, Curtis, W O,† 1 cav, Co L, died July 17, phthisis.
8041, Coykondall, D, 15, Co K, died, Sept 6, diarrhea.

335, Disbrow, J P, 14, Co K, died April 2, diarrhea.
2473, Davenport, J, 7, Co I, died June 25, fever typhoid.
3444, Davis, H, 12, Co F, died July 17, dysentery.
4926, Dayton, C, 2, Co C, died Aug 6, anasarca.
6148, Dorland, A H, 10, Co I, died Aug 9, dysentery.
6306, Dewinger, J, 2, Co G, died Aug 20, debilitas.
7076, Dunbam, L, 35, Co H, died Aug 28, dysentery.
7304, Dilan, Edward, 9, Co G, died Aug 30, diarrhea.
7469, Dermer, J L, 9, Co G, died Sept 1, scorbutus.
7734, Doremus, C, 2 cav, Co A, died Sept 3, scorbutus.
7804, Duncan H P, 2, Co G, died Sep 4, scorbutus.
8440, Doyle, H, 16, Co C, died Sept 11, scorbutus.
10533, Duno, G, 1, Co F, died Sept 8, diarrhea.

1426, Ebner, Charles, 1 cav, Co K, died May 28, diarrhea c.
1715, Egbert, James, 15, Co B, died June 8, diarrhea.
4303, Esligh, Jacob, 10, Co D, died July 30, diarrhea.

1522, Farrell, J H, 5, Co G, died May 31, diarrhea c.
3938, Folland, M,* 1 cav, Co K, died July 25, scorbutus.
4693, Fitch, F,† 35, Co F, died Aug 4 diarrhea.
5327, Fry, John, 9, Co G, died Aug 4, scorbutus.
6737, Fisher, Wm, 9, Co C, died Aug 24 diarrhea
7285, Farren, J, 3, died Aug 30, diarrhea.
9072, Fairbrother, H, 35, Co D, died Sept 28, scorbutus.
11564, Ford, A, 7, Co K, died Oct 28, scorbutus.
7338, Fisher, N O, 9, Co I, died Aug 30, dysentery

5900, Gale, B,* 9, Co D, died Aug 18, diarrhea.
7039, Galloway, F C, 12, Co K, died Aug 27, scorbutus.
11165, Glenn, C H, 4, Co I, died Oct 19, scorbutus.
11120, Guier, O, 7, Co D, died Oct 20, scorbutus.

1508, Hallman, H, 6, Co C, died May 31, diarrhea c.
3074, Hemis, Daniel, 1 cav, Co B, died July 9, diarrhea c.
3519, Hick, James, 9, Co G, July 23, diarrhea.
4151, Hegamann, J, 14, Co K, died died July 28, diarrhea.
4189, Hamoile, A, 1 cav, died July 28, diarrhea.
4744, Huber, C, 9, Co G, died Aug 5, diarrhea.
4902, Herbert, J S, 2 cav, Co I, died Aug 6, diarrhea c.
4911, Halmane, M, 1 cav, Co A, died Aug 6, fever remittent.
7821, Hull, Alexander, 7, Co C, died Sept 4, diarrhea.
7670, Howell, J, 1, Co K, died Sept 5, diarrhea.
7900, Hilgard, P F,* 10, Co A, died Sept 5, dysentery.
10701, Hutter, W, 3, Co I, died Oct 12, scorbutus.
12302, Humes, E M, 2, Co M, died Dec 17, scorbutus.
12410, Hook, J M, 2 cav, Co D, died Jan 8, '65, scorbutus.

6252, Jennings, O H, 2 cav, Co A, died Aug 10, diarrhea.
9519, Jone, A, 1 cav, Co A, died Sept 22, dysentery.
11117, Jay, H,* 5, Co K, died Oct 18, scorbutus.
11399, Jonson, G W, 6, Co G, died Oct 24, scorbutus.
12344, Johnson, A F, 9, Co D, died Dec 20, scorbutus.

3702, Krouk, Peter, 2 cav, Co H, died July 22, dysentery.
5085, Kulon, R, 9, Co A, died Aug 8, diarrhea.
8649, Ketchell, S, 7, Co K, died Sept 13, scorbutus.
12023, King, C, 15, Co G, died Nov 15, diarrhea c.

1985, Lyons, D, 1 cav, Co K, died June 15, diarrhea c.
795, Layton, Stephen, 11, Co A, died April 29, diarrhea
1769, Lindsley, Samuel, 10, Co H, died June 9, fever typhoid
3622, Lewis, S, 3 cav, Co G, died July 20, diarrhea.
4095, Leadbeater, J H, 6, Co B, died July 27, diarrhea.
5944, Leighton, Wm, 5, Co H, died Aug 17, scorbutus.
6157, Luney, Ed, 8, Co G, died Aug 19, diarrhea.
12102, Larime, C, 16, Co C, died Nov 20, scorbutus.

2019, Monnn, Jacob, 11, Co H, died June 15, debilitas.
2852, Miller, J, 1 cav, Co K, died July 4, diarrhea.
2323, McIntire, R, 8, Co I, died July 14, diarrhea c.
3548, Marks, Charles, 2 cav, Co G, died July 18, dysentery.
4594, Mulinay, I, 4, Co B, died August 3, dysentery.
4645, Miller, S S, 2 cav, Co G, died Aug 3, dysentery.
5250, Morell, A, 5, Co K, died Aug 10, scorbutus.
5832, Mahler, John, 35, Co I, died Aug 16, dysentery.
6986, Munn, Charles, 4, Co K, died Aug 27, diarrhea.
8019, McElroy, E, 10, Co I, died Sept 6, scorbutus.
8332, Mount, C H, 9, Co D, died Sept 10, scorbutus.
8592, Miller, J, 7, Co K, died Sept 13, scorbutus.
10959, Mullan, A, 39, Co B, died Oct 14, scorbutus.
11252, Mills, F, 2, Co I, died Oct 21, diarrhea.
11564, Millington, J, 1 cav, Co H, died Oct 27, scorbutus.

6780, Null, M, 9, Co A, died Aug 25, dysentery.
4983, Nichols, J, 1 s s, Co C, died Aug 7, dysentery.

7131, Osborne, F, 14, Co E, died Aug 28 diarrhea c.
10403, Osborn, J M, 9, Co H, died Oct 7, scorbutus.

1071, Pratt, J F, 1, Co M, died May 13, fever typhoid.
1072, Purdee, Charles, 11, Co C, died May 13, diarrhea c.
5206, Peterson, Henry, 3 cav, Co H, died Aug 10, diarrhea.
6298, Peer, T, 9, Co K, died Aug 20, diarrhea.
6562, Pelger, M, 10, Co G, died Aug 27, diarrhea.
7451, Peterson, G, 12, Co I, died Sept 1, diarrhea.
8017, Post, C J, 4, Co I, died Sept 6, diarrhea.
9990, Parker, W, 2, Co I, died Sept 29, scorbutus.
12221, Frank, J, 2, died Dec 4, scorbutus.

2145, Rooks, H, 5, Co H, died June 18, diarrhea c.
2821, Riley, M, 1 cav, Co L, died July 3, anasarca.
4066, Robinson, Jacob, 1 cav, Co D, died July 27, fever typhoid
4858, Radford, Wm, 18, Co B, died Aug 6, debilitas.
8282, Reed, A, 9, Co D, died Sept 9, scorbutus.
10461, Ray, J, 10, Co A, died Oct 7, diarrhea.
10708, Regan, D O, 8, Co C, died Oct 11, scorbutus.
11292, Reevis, F, 2, Co I, died Oct 21, diarrhea.

2548, Starr, N, 5, Co H, died June 27, diarrhea.
5087, Simonds, J, 9, Co K, died Aug 8, dysentery.
5807, Shanahan, W, 9, Co C, died Aug 16, scorbutus.
7364, Stout, L,† 2, Co C, died Aug 31, dysentery.
7565, Street, John J, 9, Co D, died Sept 2, scorbutus.
7577, Stiffin, H, 3, Co M, died Sept 2, diarrhea c.
7729, Skell, C W, 3 cav, Co M, died Sept 3, gangrene.
8687, Swetser, P, 9, Co G, died Sept 13, scorbutus.
8751, Stevenson, W, 2 cav, Co M, died Sept 14, diarrhea.
9328, Shay, H H, 7, Co I died Sept 19, scorbutus.
10846 Smith, A, 5, Co G, died Oct 13 dysentery.
11615, Sutton, T, 12, Co K, died Oct 28, scorbutus.
11653, Stimmell, I, 6, Co A, died Oct 30, scorbutus.
11793, Sullivan, I, 8, Co G, died Nov 4, scorbutus.
11882, Steele, Geo, 2, Co B, died Nov 6, scorbutus.
10882, Sweet, B F, 10, Co K, died Oct 13, dysentery.

1853, Tindel, E,† 1, Co B, died June 11. diarrhea c.
5112, Taylor, Peter, 9, died Aug 9, diarrhea.
6131, Townsend, J, 35, Co I, died Aug 19, diarrhea.
7937, Turner, R, 4, Co G, died Sept 5, gangrene.
9698, Townsend, F, 10, Co C, died Sept 21, dysentery.
11364, Thompson, S, 4, Co I, died Oct 21, scorbutus.
12451, Thatcher, J, 8, Co H, died Jan 14, '65, scorbutus.
12705, Toy, J, 7, Co G, died Feb 27, '65, debilitas.
10212, Thomas, Henry,† 10, Co B, died Oct 2, scorbutus.
6448, Trattman, Jas, 9, Co D, died Aug 22, diarrhea c.

No. of Grave.
2634, Utter, Stephen, 1 artil, Co B, died June 20, scorbutus.

2100, Vallett, W, 5 artil, Co A, died Nov 19, scorbutus.

1955, Weed, Wm,* 15, Co I, died June 14, diarrhea c.
2216, Wood, W J, 12, Co E, died June 20, anasarca.
4643, Wheeler, W, 5, Co G, died Aug 3, dysentery.
4698, Wainwright, 9, Co C, died Aug 7, diarrhea.
6631, Wolverton, 1, Co I, died Aug 5, diarrhea.

No. of Grave.
5099, Warner, A, 4, Co A, died Aug 9, diarrhea.
5233, Willey, J, 2 cav, Co M, died Aug 10, anasarca.
6168, Wynard, Wm, 2, Co I, died Aug 19, marasmus.
7560, Willis, A, 35, Co I, died Sept 2, anasarca.
8142, Wright, S M, 7, Co K, died Sept 8, diarrhea.
8307, Ward, J, 1 cav, Co H, died Sept 10, diarrhea.
12157, Williams, W, 1, Co D, died Nov 20, scorbutus.
12658, Wells, G, 10, Co C, died Feb 15, '65, diarrhea c.

NEW YORK.

No. of Grave.
2068, Abbey, O,* 174, died June 15, diarrhea a.
2141, Abbey, W H, 85, Co E, died June 18, diarrhea c.
4719, Abel, C, 15 artil, Co C, died Aug 4, diarrhea.
4612, Aber, J, 104, Co I, died Aug 3, dysentery c.
6629, Ackerman, Saml, 97, Co K, died Aug 14, scorbutus.
64, Ackheart, David, 20, Co A, died March 19, pleuritis.
8497, Adams, H, 98, Co G, died Sept 11, scorbutus.
4581, Adams, J A, 10, Co F, died Aug 2, pneumonia.
6467, Adams, O, 61, Co C, died Aug 22, diarrhea.
8559, Adams, S, 100, died Sept 12, scorbutus.
3226, Adams, T R, 85, Co H, died July 12, '64.
1700, Ades, Ed, 8 cav, Co C, died June 7, debilitas.
6047, Adeler, A, 8, Co D, died Aug 8, dysentery.
6575, Adney F, 85, Co K, died Aug 23, diarrhea.
4382, Ahearn, Daniel, 170, died July 31, diarrhea.
3349, Aiken, J W, 85, Co H, died July 15, pneumonia.
8001, Akerman, M, 7 artil, Co L, died Sept 6, diarrhea.
7082, Albarson, J, 42, Co C, died Aug 28, diarrhea.
6698, Albert, William, 24 battery, died Aug 24, dysentery.
7007, Alderman, F, 15 cav, Co F, died Aug 27, diarrhea.
1755, Alexander, J, 125, Co C, died June 9, diarrhea c.
11212, Alford, B C, 152, Co F, died Oct 20, scorbutus.
3293, Allen, A W, 14 artil, Co M, died July 14, diarrhea.
12472, Allen, J I, 82, Co A, died Jan 14, '65, scorbutus.
6568, Allen, W, 1 cav, Co H, died Aug 13, dysentery.
5844, Allenberger, J, 39, Co B, died Aug 16, fever typhus.
7478, Altenderens, E, 39, Co D, died Sept 1, scorbutus.
11479, Allinger, L, 48, Co I, died Oct 26, wounds.
7587, Allman, Charles, 7 artil, Co C, died Sept 2, scorbutus.
6841, Alroy, F, 111, Co K, died Aug 26, scorbutus.
5978, Alphord, J, 75, Co G, died Aug 17, scorbutus.
7739, Alsaver, S, 47, Co H, died Sept 3, scorbutus.
800, Amider, Fred, 47, Co H, died April 29, diarrhea c.
2344, Ambrose, Jacob, 9 cav, Co C, died June 23, scorbutus.
10642, Ames, Henry, 2 artil, died Oct 10, scorbutus.
4654, Ames, J R, 14 artil, Co I, died Aug 3, diarrhea.
7743, Amgere, G, 47, Co E, died Sept 3, scorbutus.
1954, Amish, A, 162, Co K, died June 14, anasarca.
3739, Anderson, A, 100, Co I, died July 21, fever intermittent.
4890, Anderson, A, 99, Co F, died Aug 6, scorbutus.
587, Anderson, B, 20 cav, Co M, died April 14, debilitas.
8819, Anderson, J, 39, Co E, died Sept 15, gangrene c.
4110, Anderson, L, 14, Co D, died July 27, diarrhea c.
1389, Andrews, G, 111, Co I, died May 30, diarrhea c.
7533, Andrews, W, 85, Co K, died Sept 1, diarrhea c.
8717, Anson, Robert, 1 cav, Co K, died Sept 14, scorbutus.
6518, Answelt, J, 15 cav, Co A, died Aug 23, dysentery.
8720, Antisdale, George, 5 cav, died Sept 14, scorbutus.
6976, Appleby, S W, 85, Co K, died Aug 27, diarrhea.
9741, Argt, C, 6, died Sept 25, dysentery.
11172, Armond W, 7, Co F, died Oct 19, scorbutus.
9175, Armstrong, H, 110, Co G, died Sept 21, diarrhea c.
10818, Armstrong, J, 164, Co C, died Oct 12, dysentery.
11571, Armstrong, W, 24 battery, died Oct 27, scorbutus.
7470, Arnold, R B, 7 artil, Co L, died Sept 1, diarrhea c.
6951, Arnold, C, 47, Co C, died Aug 26, diarrhea.
1580, Ashley, C G, 146, Co G, died June 3, diarrhea c.
12292, Auster, F, 39, Co B, died Dec 1, scorbutus.
12622, Ashley, S, citizen, died Feb 9, '65, scorbutus.
5544, Ashton, —,* 10, Co I, died Aug 3, diarrhea.
7207, Atwood, G S, 24 battery, died Aug 29, diarrhea.
950, Aubray, K, 14, Co A, died May 8, diarrhea c.
11748, Augh, J, 66, Co D, died Nov 2, scorbutus.
5027, Augustine, F, 52, Co A, died Aug 8, dysentery.
1736, Austin, A, 147, Co H, died June 8, diarrhea.
3694, Austin, J, 7 artil, Co M, died July 10, diarrhea.
8218, Austin, G, 147, Co H, Sept 3, diarrhea.
12820, Ayers, G S, 147, Co G, died March 29, '65, scorbutus.

12247, Babcock, J M, 140, Co I, died Dec 27, scorbutus.
1712, Babcock, H, 111, Co G, died May 7, anasarca.
3063, Babcock, J, 72, Co E, died July 9, scorbutus.
6235, Babcock, J, 55, Co E, died Aug 11, fever typhoid.
4658, Babcock, J S, 140, Co D, died Aug 3, diarrhea.
1898, Babcock, R, 9, Co I, died Aug 6, dysentery.
11831, Babcock, W H, 13 cav, Co L, died Nov 5, scorbutus.

No. of Grave.
6692, Babst, M, 9, Co D, died Aug 15, diarrhea.
754, Bacon, E P, 154, Co B, died Apr 27, dysentery c.
9101, Bacon, J, 154, Co E, died Sept 18, diarrhea.
2870, Bacchus, A, 100, Co A, died July 4, dysentery.
11272, Bacchus, E R, 15 artil, Co F, died Oct 22, scorbutus.
3447, Bachelder, B F, 24 battery, died July 17, fever congestive.
3115, Backley, C, 24 battery, died July 10, fever typhus.
3771, Badger, P, 47, Co E, died July 22, debilitas.
7890, Bailey, A, 5, Co K, died Sept 5, diarrhea.
10163, Bailey, C, 76, Co K, died Oct 1, scorbutus.
5697, Bailey, G W,* 154, Co G, died Aug 15, scorbutus.
7497, Bailey, John, 12 cav, Co A, died Sept 1, diarrhea c.
8215, Baker, J, 24 battery, died Sept 8, pleuritis.
10636, Baker, A, 93, Co B, died Oct 10, diarrhea c.
4468, Baker, Charles, 52, Co G, died Aug 1, diarrhea.
3550, Baker, E, 85, Co E, died July 18, dysentery.
12376, Baker, George, 40, Co H, died Jan 1, '65, scorbutus.
8759, Baker, H, 146, Co F, died Sept 14, diarrhea c.
8052, Baker, Ira, 85, Co H, died Sept 7, scorbutus.
11848, Baker, J, 24, Co F, died Nov 5, diarrhea.
11660, Baker, J,* 16 cav, Co K, died Oct 31, scorbutus.
61, Baker, Wm, 7, Co D, died March 18, pneumonia.
7591, Baldwin, C, 24 cav, Co M, died Sept 2, diarrhea.
6853, Baldwin, G, 154, Co C, died Aug 25, scorbutus.
4457, Ballard, Robert B, 85, Co C, died Aug 1, constipatio.
4364, Barnard, Wm, 65, Co K, died July 31, diarrhea.
6347, Bancroft, A H, 85, died Aug 11, diarrhea.
8102, Barrett, G M, 184, Co E, died Sept 8, diarrhea.
11605, Bandgan, A, 82, Co A, died Oct 28, scorbutus.
5536, Banker, J M, 118, Co K, died Aug 13, dysentery.
9819, Banker, J T, 152, Co G, died Sept 26, fever typhus.
8443, Bannan, H, 39, Co H, died Sept 11, scorbutus.
11056, Banuyer, F, 126, Co K, died Oct 17, scorbutus.
12315, Barber, H,* 96, Co D, died Dec 20, scorbutus.
1659, Barge, H, 120, Co A, died June 6, diarrhea c.
3748, Barnes, J, 12 cav, Co F, died July 22, dysentery.
6771, Barnes, J S, 10 cav, Co K, died Aug 25, scorbutus.
11343, Barnes, M,* 115, Co F, died Oct 23, wounds.
6963, Barnes, A C, 85, Co D, died Aug 27, diarrhea.
8821, Barnes, R W, 24 battery, died Sept 15, scorbutus.
10418, Barnes, Thomas, 76, Co B, died Oct 6, diarrhea.
1855, Barrett, J, 132, Co C, died June 11, diarrhea c.
8361, Barnum, H, 39, Co H, died Sept 10, diarrhea.
7877, Barklett, H, 24 battery, died Sept 5, diarrhea.
8192, Barrett, G M, 184, Co E, died Sept 8, diarrhea.
10153, Barratt, G, 22, Co A, died Oct 1, diarrhea.
588, Barrett, D, 13, Co H, died April 10, diarrhea.
9979, Barron, C L, 12 battery, died Sept 28, diarrhea.
3580, Barrows, M, 14, Co G, died July 19, diarrhea.
11612, Bartill, R, 164, Co F, died Oct 28, scorbutus.
4768, Bartlett, L, 118, Co I, died Aug 5, debilitas.
8409, Barton, D, 85, Co I, died Sept 11, diarrhea c.
6352, Bass, Charles, 7 artil, Co B, died Aug 23, diarrhea.
8217, Bass, George, teamster, 63, died Sept 8, diarrhea.
8097, Bassford, J, 12 cav, Co G, died Sept 7, diarrhea.
5555, Bates, G, 5, Co A, died Aug 13, dysentery.
530, Bates, J, 97, Co A, died April 13, diarrhea c.
3845, Bates, John,* 14, Co I, died July 24, diarrhea.
1069, Bates, Lester, 97, Co A, died May 13, diarrhea.
10756, Baters, W, 139, Co G, died Oct 9, dysentery.
10099, Baty, A, 132, Co K, died Oct 16, diarrhea c.
61, Bayne, Daniel, 57, Co D, died July 4, small pox.
9350, Baywood, J, 1 cav, Co I, died Sept 20, scorbutus.
6021, Beam, B, 2 cav, Co M, died Aug 17, dysentery.
4062, Beck, John, 97, Co H, died July 30, scorbutus.
6034, Beckham, F B, 10 cav, Co A, died Aug 18, fever intermittent.
9216, Beckshire, J,* 12 cav, Co F, died Sept 19, dysentery.
8472, Beckwith, C, 14 artil, Co D, died Sept 11, scorbutus.
6012, Bee, George, 119, Co F, died Aug 8, diarrhea.
8092, Beebe, J E, 11, died Sept 17.
3843, Beekman, J, 43, Co A, died July 23, dysentery.
11923, Beers, W, 82, Co B, died Nov 8, scorbutus.
8010, Belden, Wm, 82, Co E, died Sept 6, diarrhea.
3267, Bell, D S, 20, state mil, Co D, died July 13, scorbutus.
9136, Bell, J, 6, Co B, died Sept 18, scorbutus.
11124, Bell, J C, 120, Co D, died Oct 18, '64, scorbutus

No. of Grave.

8942, Bell, Wm,* 39, Co K, died Sept 16, diarrhea.
11094, B lwen, C, 179, Co F, died Oct 31, diarrhea c.
3089, Bennett, I H, 85, Co E, died July 9, diarrhea.
3138, Bennett, 140, Co B, died July 13, pleuritis.
6045, Bentley, C, 22 cav, Co L, died Aug 17, catarrh.
6670, Bentner, Joseph, 100, Co I, died Aug 24, scorbutus.
6979, Benway, C, 5 artil, Co K, died Aug 27, dysentery.
11055, Be ees, E, 146, Co D, died Oct 14, dysentery.
6598, Berdell, M L, 125, Co A, died Aug 23, diarrhea c.
6749, Best, Isaac, 42, Co G, died Aug 15, scorbutus.
6039, Bertin F, 62, Co G, died Aug 18, scorbutus.
6137, Besrha, John 15 artil, Co B, died Aug 19, marasmus.
8234, Beul, J, 85, Co B, died Sept 9, anasarca.
5230, Beyers H, 24, Co K, died Aug 10, scorbutus.
361, Bidon, S, 52, Co A, died April 2, fever typhus.
10635, Bidwell, J, 5 cav, Co O, died Oct 10, diarrhea c.
3232, Bigelow, L, 85, Co D, died July 12.
10505, Billings, J, 2 cav, Co M, died Oct 8, scorbutus.
601, Billinge, W W, 52, Co G, died April 17, debilitas.
10945, Bings, G, 5 artil, Co B died Oct 14, scorbutus.
10905, Bingham, C E, 5 cav, Co D, died Sept 29, diarrhea.
12531, Bird, M, 7 artil, Co K, died April 14, '65, diarrhea c.
4780, Bird, P,* 7 artil, Co K, died Aug 5, pneumonia.
6590, Bishop, C, 7 artil, Co M, died Aug 23, dysentery.
5786, Bissell, J S, 85, Co D, died Aug 15, diarrhea.
11018, Black, J, 42, Co G, died Oct 16, '64, scorbutus.
2574, Black L, 9, Co A, died June 27, diarrhea.
11971, Black, H C, 42, Co F, died Nov 12, scorbutus.
1885, Blackman, J, 85, died June 13, debilitas.
4076, Blackwood, W, 115, Co G, died July 27, fever typhus.
7889, Blair, D, 15, Co C, died Sept 5, dysentery.
12460, Blair, James,* 8 cav, Co K, died Jan 16, '65, scorbutus.
498, Blaize H, 3 artil, Co H, died April 12, diarrhea.
3236, Blake, W D, 24 battery, died July 22.
2439, Blake, George, 100, Co I, died June 25, diarrhea c.
6129, Blanchard, E, 12 cav, Co F, died Aug 19, dysentery.
8340, Blanchard, L, 100, Co K, died Sept 13, scorbutus.
10383 Blascott, Wm, 95, Co B, died Sept 30, diarrhea.
1861, Blink, J M, 95, Co A, died June 12, diarrhea c.
4933, Bliss, James H, 22 cav, Co I, died Aug 7, diarrhea.
8059, Block, J P, 100, Co F, died Sept 16, diarrhea c.
7205, Blood, L, 7, Co C, died Aug 29, scorbutus.
2777, Blyme, S, 85, Co G, died July 2, diarrhea.
12521, Boaman, J, 1 cav, Co D, died Jan 25, '65, scorbutus.
6371, Boates, A, 178, Co D, died Aug 21, scorbutus.
6285, Bode A, 85, Co B, died Aug 11, scorbutus.
2989, Bodishay, J, 7, Co F, died July 7, anasarca.
474, Boermaster, J, 14, Co A, died April 9, anasarca.
3073, Bohl, H, 10 cav, Co E, died July 9, anasarca.
6618, Bolan E,† 35, Co F, died Aug 17, diarrhea.
11718, Bolby, O, 14 artil, Co D, died Nov 1, scorbutus.
8267, Boles, J, 22 cav, Co D, died Sept 9, diarrhea c.
3606, Bomsteel, S A, 20, Co G, died July 19, scorbutus.
6269, Borst J, 5 cav, Co B, died Aug 10, anasarca.
4401, Bodler, D, 7, Co D, died July 31, dysentery.
51, Boughton, H, 77, Co A, died March 16, pneumonia.
7027, Boulton, T, 43, Co G, died Sept 2, diarrhea c.
11066, Bowden, P, 16 cav, Co M, died Oct 17, scorbutus.
6744, Bowen, J H, 65, Co D, died Aug 24, diarrhea.
4001, Bowin, J, 7 cav, Co K, died Aug 3, diarrhea.
11944, Bowman, H, 84, Co K, died Nov 10, scorbutus.
12521, Bowman I, 1 cav, Co D, died Jan 25, '65, scorbutus.
3635, Bowman, S, 147, Co H, died July 20, diarrhea.
1275, Box, G, 111, Co D, died May 22, diarrhea a.
9728, Boyce, A, 3 cav, Co I, died Sept 25, debilitas.
2073, Boyce, R, 6 cav, Co M, died June 30, diarrhea.
10, Boyle, Pat, 63, Co A, died March 5, pneumonia.
8912, Boyle, Pat, 48, Co F, died Sept 16, diarrhea c.
11974, Boyle, I, 10, Co D, died Nov 12, scorbutus.
4365, Bradford, D B, 7 artil, Co B, died July 31, dysentery.
5232, Bradley, John, 69, Co K, died Aug 10, diarrhea.
16685, Bradshaw, R,* 120, Co E, died Aug 24, diarrhea.
12219, Brady, J, 140, Co E, died Dec 4, scorbutus.
3979, Bragg, J C, 2 cav, Co E, died July 26, diarrhea.
12263, Bran, Wm, 5 artil, Co B, died Dec 12, diarrhea.
7704, Brandon, O, 15 artil, Co A, died Sept 3, diarrhea.
1800, Breny, James, 178, Co K, died June 10, diarrhea c.
6134, Brewer, Fred, 39, Co C, died Aug 9, diarrhea.
11655, Brewer, Henry,† 2 cav, Co G, died Oct 31, diarrhea c.
10221, Brewer, J S, 6, Co B, died Oct 2, scorbutus.
1365, Brewer, S, 15, Co K, died May 25, diarrhea c.
519, Brewer, Thomas, 111, Co F, died April 13, diarrhea.
9690, Briant, L A, 140, Co B, died Sept 24, diarrhea a.
8116, Bright, 104, Co C, died Sept 8, scorbutus.
11627, Brightman, E, 7, Co D, died Oct 28, scorbutus.
8115, Brill, C, 140, Co F, died Sept 11, diarrhea.
6953, Brink C, 109, Co K, died Aug 26, gangrene.
9787, Britonsky, J, 52, Co E, died Sept 20, diarrhea c.
2997, Brobst, J, 52, Co B, died July 7, diarrhea a.
9148, Brock, W, 76, Co F, died Sept 18, scorbutus.
6882, Broder, H, 76, Co F, died Aug 26, diarrhea.
12002, Brogan, J M, 85, Co B, died Nov 14, scorbutus.

No. of Grave.

1324, Brooks, William,* 10 cav, Co E, died May 24, diarrhea.
1221, Brott, Anthony, 1 cav, Co K, died May 19, anasarca.
9838, Broscang, C, 150, Co C, died Sept 27, scorbutus.
7517, Brought, Charles, 14 artil, Co I, died Sept 1, scorbutus.
51, Broughten, H, 77, Co H, died March 16, pleuritis.
10668, Brown, A, 140, Co K, died Oct 11, scorbutus.
5538, Brown, B M, 55, Co I, died Aug 13, scorbutus.
4112, Brown, C, 103, Co C, died July 27, bronchitis.
9556, Brown, C, 66, Co K, died Sept 23, scorbutus.
11953, Brown, C, 39, Co H, died Nov 10, scorbutus.
11928, Brown, C, 1 Cav, Co M, died Nov 8, diarrhea c.
6623, Brown, Charles, 97, Co F, died Aug 21, diarrhea.
7501, Brown, D, 118, Co B, died Sept 1, diarrhea c.
3659, Brown, E O, 7 artil, Co L, died July 20, pneumonia.
9674, Brown, G H, 85, Co H, died Sept 24, diarrhea.
7985, Brown, G H, 63, Co C, died Sept 6, diarrhea.
2465, Brown, H, 72, Co C, died June 25, diarrhea.
1879, Brown, H, 12 cav, died June 12, dysentery.
7266, Brown, H,* 39, Co F, died Aug 30, scorbutus.
1887, Brown, J, 125, died June 13, diarrhea.
7858, Brown, J, 16, Co C, Sept 3, diarrhea.
6655, Brown, James, 4 cav, Co E, died Aug 24, dysentery.
6691, Brown, James, 170, Co K, died Aug 24, debilitas.
7526, Brown, John, 66, died Sept 1, diarrhea.
7615, Brown, William, 5, Co D, died Sept 2, dysentery.
552, Brown, Warren, 120, Co K, died April 14, diarrhea.
428, Brown, William, 42, Co A, died April 8, anasarca.
7390, Broxmire, Thomas, 15, Co E, died Aug 31, scorbutus.
1559, Brumaghin, T, 125, Co E, died June 2, diptheria.
4475, Bryant, D, 170, Co B, died Aug 1, diarrhea.
7248, Bryant, H, 82, Co F, died Aug 30, anasarca.
7668, Bryan, Wm, 1 cav, Co I, died Sept 3, scorbutus.
3814, Buck, 24, Co H, died July 23, diarrhea.
9975, Buckbier, J, 7 artil, Co F, died Sept 28, diarrhea c.
10585, Buckley, W, 122, Co D, died Oct 10, scorbutus.
5714, Buel, G W, 115, Co E, died Aug 15, scorbutus.
331, Buel, S, 42, Co B, died April 2, debilitas.
12417, Buffman, L, † 100, Co K, died Jan 8, '65, dysentery.
7567, Bulkley, E A, 97, Co E, died Sept 2, diarrhea c.
12509, Burfield, C, citizen, died Jan 22, '65, pleuritis.
5953, Buller, Wm, 23 cav, Co B, died Aug 17, marasmus.
9642, Bullock, E,* 85, Co E, died Sept 24, scorbutus.
4137, Bundy, Joseph, 7 artil, Co B, died July 28, diarrhea c.
540, Bunn, W H, 132, Co F, died April 14, pneumonia.
9870, Bunnell, W, 59, Co C, died Sept 27, scorbutus.
6452, Burbanks, J, 85, Co D, died Aug 22, dysentery.
10924, Burdick, A, 85, Co C, died Oct 14, scorbutus.
978, Burdick, C, 47, Co F, died May 9, dysentery.
2134, Burdick, Samuel, 125, Co A, died June 18, diarrhea c.
7838, Burdock, L, 22 cav, Co L, died Sept 4, diarrhea c.
10316, Burleigh, L, 6 artil, Co F, died Sept 29, scorbutus.
12389, Burley, C, 3, Co B, died Jan 4, '65, diarrhea.
619, Burns, E J, † 13 cav, Co D, died April 19, ascites.
477, Burns, John, 40, Co I, died April 9, dysentery.
924, Burns, John, 99, Co H, May 6, fever intermittent.
11851, Burns, J, 118, Co F, died Nov 6, diarrhea.
8745, Burns, W, 3 cav, Co C, died Sept 14, fever typhus.
5991, Burns, Daniel, 5 artil, Co D, died Aug 17, cerebritis.
7247, Burr, H, 69, Co C, died Aug 30, diarrhea c.
6171, Bursha, Thomas, 2 artil, Co M, died Aug 19, marasmus.
3165, Burshen, F, 54, Co C, died July 11, scorbutus.
2875, Burt, J, 2 cav, Co A, July 4, debilitas.
7214, Burton, G E, 85, Co K, died Aug 29, dysentery.
217, Burton, Henry, 140, died March 29, diarrhea.
6847, Buserman, E, 97, Co E, died Aug 16, enteritis.
6457, Bush, E, 20, Co D, died Aug 22, diarrhea.
1415, Bushnell, A, 65, Co D, died May 27, diarrhea c.
487, Bushan, J R, 132, Co G, died April 11, pneumonia.
11368, Bushley, Wm,* 6 artil, Co A, Oct 23, scorbutus.
1360, Buskirk, A, 47, Co A, died May 25, diarrhea c.
2047, Buskirt, O, 13, died June 15, diarrhea a.
721, Butler, Thomas, 132, Co G, died April 25, diarrhea.
4183, Butler, W, 43, Co D, died July 28, dysentery.
12051, Butoff, R, † 124, Co C, died Feb 13, '65, diarrhea c.
10848, Butler, James, 2 cav, Co D, died Oct 13, '65, scorbutus.
9235, Butter, P, 120, Co D, died Sept 19, diarrhea c.
6805, Button, James, 24 artil, Co B, died Aug 16, dysentery.
2446, Butts, A, 111, Co C, died July 17, diarrhea.
9790, Byron, J,* 69, Co A, died Sept 26, diarrhea c.
1224 Burke, W H, 120, Co I, died May 19, diarrhea a.
5196, Burk, John, 69, Co K, died Aug 10, dysentery.
1073, Brower, John A, 5 artil, Co D, died Oct 17, diarrhea.

12190, Cademus, C, 48, Co A, died June 19, anasarca.
0765, Cady, George, 66, Co G, died Oct 12, scorbutus.
12377, Cady, J, 77, Co E, died June 23, diarrhea.
0721, Cady, J J, 14, Co H, died Oct 11, scorbutus.
3062, Cain, M, 132, Co E, died July 9, diarrhea a.
2136, Cale, J, 85, Co G, died June 18, diarrhea a.
10040, Caldham, L C, 8 cav, Co L, died Sept 17, scorbutus.
11807, Caldwell, A, 42, Co A, died Nov 4, scorbutus.
1550, Calling, E I, 7, Co D, died Oct 26, scorbutus.

No. of Grave.

9700, Calkins, S V, 120, Co D, died Sept. 25, scorbutus.
8411, Callbrook, J, 147. Co B died Sept 11, anasarca.
2848, Cameron, John, 1 cav, Co H, died July 4, diarrhea.
1770, Camp, H, 2 cav, Co F, died June 9, diarrhea c.
1238, Campbell, D, 8 cav, Co H, died May 20, anasarca.
7236, Campbell, J, 99, Co I, died Aug 29, scorbutus.
946, Campbell, L E, 104, Co B, died May 7, dysentery.
8795, Campbell, M, 169, Co K, died Sept 15, scorbutus.
11291, Campbell, W, 2, Co C, died Oct 22, scorbutus.
7378, Campbell, William, 76, Co B, died Aug 31, diarrhea.
12178, Card, A, 152, Co C, died Nov 27, scorbutus.
5031, Card, G, 103, Co F, died Aug 8, scorbutus.
8136, Carboines, W,* 39, Co C, died Sept 8, diarrhea.
6455, Cardon, E, 115, Co A, died Aug 22, dysentery.
7555, Carey, D, 57, Co A, died Sept 2, diarrhea c.
11512, Carey, F, 65, Co E, died Oct 20, scorbutus.
372, Carl, Joseph, 14, Co A, died April 5, diarrhea.
5515, Carl, L, 120, Co G, died Aug 15, catarrh.
12339, Carle, ——, 1 cav, Co D, died Dec 26, scorbutus.
12268, Carmer, F, 2, Co D, died Dec 12, scorbutus.
7655, Carmer, Andrew, 85, Co B, died Sept 3, anasarca.
11640, Carney, M, 9 cav, Co L, died Oct 30, scorbutus.
8470, Carnenan, Charles, 24 battery, died Sept 11, scorbutus.
5258, Carney, D J, 132, Co G, died Aug 10, dysentery a.
9879, Carney, Francis, 2 artil, Co C, died Sept 27, diarrhea.
3102, Carnes, P, 13 cav, Co B, died July 19, diarrhea.
10890, Carpenter, Frank, 7 art, Co C, died Oct 12, scorbutus.
8854, Carpenter, G, 7, Co D, died Sept 15, diarrhea c.
4032, Carpenter, H A, 2 Art, Co A, died Aug 3, diarrhea.
2916, Carpenter, L, 2 artil, Co B, died July 25, diarrhea c.
3977, Carpenter, M B, 85, Co B, died July 26, diarrhea.
6743, Carr, Andrew, 22, died Aug 24, dysentery.
3859, Carr, D, 25, Co B, died July 24, diarrhea c.
581, Carr, F,* 3 artil, Co K, died April 16, diarrhea.
6470, Carr, George A, 3 artil, Co K, died Aug 22, diarrhea c.
6073, Carr, William, 125, Co K, died Aug 14, scorbutus.
6304, Carr, William, 97, Co E, died Aug 20, gangrene.
4139, Carroll, James, 69. Co A, died July 28, diarrhea.
10293, Carroll, P,* 95, Co E, died Oct 4, scorbutus.
2061, Carroll, F. 132, Co F, died June 16, dysentery.
12015, Carroll, W, 42. Co. D, died Nov 15, scorbutus.
8563, Carson, J G, 100, Co B, died Sept 12, scorbutus.
8023, Cart, M A, 118, Co F, died Sept 6, diarrhea.
1987, Carter, A, 146, Co E, died June 15, bronchitis.
6212, Carter, Ed,* 7 artil, Co A, died Aug 10, scorbutus.
6433, Carson, E, 115, Co A, died Aug 22, dysentery.
11640, Carney, M, 9 cav, Co L, died Oct 30, scorbutus.
8179, Case, A F, 8 cav, Co A, died Sept 11, scorbutus.
8377, Case, E, 8 cav, Co M, died Sept 10, scorbutus.
6296, Case, H J, 12 cav, Co A, died Aug 20, scorbutus.
3832, Casey J, 100, Co G, died July 23, diarrhea.
5271, Casey, P, 174, Co A, died Aug 10, scorbutus.
8421, Cassells, Samuel, 52, Co D, died Sept 11, scorbutus.
2643, Cassine John S, 24 battery, died June 29, pneumonia.
1177, Castano, J, 104, Co H, died May 16, diarrhea c.
10482, Cashel, C, 7 artil, Co I, died Oct 7, diarrhea c.
1785, Castle, J W, 147, Co H, died June 10, diarrhea a.
6128, Castle, William, 1 artil, Co E, died Aug 19, dysentery.
1534, Cavanaugh, John, 146, Co H, died June 1, anasarca.
2071, Ceaser, D, 7 artil, Co B, died July 7, diarrhea c.
1466, Centre, A, 16, Co A, died May 29, diarrhea c.
9682, Chaffe, R A, 5 cav, Co H, died Sept 24, scorbutus.
11101, Chambers, J, 149, Co F, died Oct 18, debilitas.
6557, Chambers, J, 147, Co E, died Aug 23, diarrhea a.
5860, Chamberlain, C, 154. Co D, died Aug 16, marasmus.
4768, Champlin, W, 85, Co E, died Aug 5, diarrhea.
4726, Chapel, A, 85, Co D, died Aug 4, diarrhea.
6478, Chapel, R, 6 cav, Co A, died Aug 13, diarrhea.
5831, Chappell, A, 39, Co E, died Aug 16, enteritis.
10748, Chappell, E, 76, Co K, died Oct 12, diarrhea c.
3222, Chapin, F, 24 cav, Co A, died July 12.
3286, Chapman, J, 85, Co K, died July 14, fever remittent.
1593, Chase, A, 111, Co H, died June 3, diarrhea c.
4856, Chase, D, 98, Co I, died Aug 6, scorbutus.
6469, Chase, N F, 85, Co K, died Aug 13, diarrhea.
7450, Chase, S M, 4 artil, Co D, died Sept 1, diarrhea.
2157, Chatbrian, H, 24 battery, died June 18, fever intermittent.
8033, Chatman, C, 4 artil, Co I, died Sept 6, diarrhea.
6058, Chatman, S M, 2 Co F, died Aug 23, dysentery.
9029, Chatterton, J, 95, Co B, died Sept 28, scorbutus.
7865, Chagnon, E, 12 cav, Co F, died Sept 5, fever typhus.
7189, Chesley, P S, 10 cav, Co G, died Aug 29, scorbutus
7539, Chesley, John, 174, Co G, died Sept 2, diarrhea c.
10680, Chickchester, C H, 57, Co I, died Oct 11, dysentery.
6317, Childs, A, 85, Co I, died Aug 20, diarrhea.
4141, Childs, Wm, 73, Co A, died July 28, diarrhea.
11555, Chile, H*, 47, Co E, died Oct 27, scorbutus.
10612, Christy, J, 1 drag, Co I, died Oct 10, scorbutus.
5824, Church, C L, 5 cav, Co C, died Aug 16, marasmus.
6413, Church, F M, 2 cav, Co D, died Aug 12, diarrhea c.
4257, Churchill, C, 99, Co I, died July 29, diarrhea c.

No. of Grave.

3449, Clancey, Robert, 164, Co E, died July 17, diarrhea.
2114, Clark, A, 85, Co E, died June 17, diarrhea c.
6167, Clark, Charles, 12 cav, Co F, died Aug 9, fever typhus
2947, Clark, F, 8 cav, Co B, died July 6, dysentery a.
12114, Clark, J, 8 cav, Co K, died Nov 21, scorbutus.
12403, Clark, J B,† 7 artil, Co L, died Jan 6, '65, scorbutus
2154, Clark, John, 48, Co D, died June 18, diarrhea a.
11304, Clark, L, 100, Co G, died Oct 22, scorbutus.
10611, Clark, P, 42, Co B, died Oct 10, scorbutus.
5892, Clemons, A, 15 cav, Co F, died Aug 15, diarrhea.
6909, Clemmens, H, 65, Co F, died Aug 26, diarrhea.
11028, Cleever, W, 43, Co F, died Oct 16, diarrhea c.
813, Clifford, Charles, 16, Co B, died April 30, diarrhea c.
740, Clifford, George, 152, Co K, died April 26, dysentery.
6494, Cline, B, 85, Co K, died Aug 22, scorbutus.
11437, Cline, J W, 85, Co K, died Oct 24, scorbutus.
12021, Cline, S M, 1 drag, Co H, died Nov 15, scorbutus.
9721, Cline, W, 76, Co F, died Sept 25, diarrhea.
6243, Clingman, J, 150, Co L, died Aug 20, scorbutus.
12471, Clinton, R, 102, Co D, died Jan 17, '65, diarrhea.
1497, Clute, H V, 24 battery, died May 31, anasarca.
5955, Clyeon, J P, 147, Co B, Aug 17, diarrhea c.
7343, Coanas, W, 73, Co D, died Aug 31, wounds.
5365, Coburn, C, 122, Co E, died Aug 11, fever remittent.
10129, Coburn, A, 116, Co H, died Oct 1, anasarca.
933, Coddington, Wm, 99, Co H, died May 7, dysentery.
7992, Cochran, John, 120, Co K, died Sept 6, diarrhea.
11775, Cochran, M, 42, Co A, died Nov 3, scorbutus.
9237, Cochson, J, 140, Co C, died Sept 19, diarrhea.
10651, Cogger, M, 125, Co B, died Oct 11, scorbutus.
3715, Cogswell, L, 6 artil Co M, died July 21, diarrhea.
10062, Cole, E B, 14 artil, Co B, died Sept 30, scorbutus.
8456, Cole, George, 12 cav, Co A, died Sept 11, diarrhea c.
6241, Cole, John J, 5 cav, Co M, died Aug 20, scorbutus.
5890, Cole, M, 15 artil, Co M, died Aug 16, diarrhea c.
4142, Cole, R S, 152, Co H, died July 28, pleuritis.
11589, Cole, F, 109, Co K, died Oct 28, scorbutus.
4519, Cole, Wm, 61, Co H, died Aug 2, diarrhea,
7855, Coleby, A, 1 cav, Co M, died Sept 5, dysentery.
10553, Coleman, I, 2 artil, Co I, died Oct 9, scorbutus.
3070, Collins, A, 98, Co B, died July 9, diarrhea c.
7557, Colwell, D C, 2 artil, Co E, died Sept 2, scorbutus.
5743, Colwell, J, 120, Co A, died Aug 15, diarrhea.
6969, Comstock, G E, 2 artil, Co A, died Aug 27, diarrhea c.
3509, Condon, Thomas, 22 cav, Co F, died July 18, pneumonia
4320, Cone, R, 8, Co A, died July 30, dysentery.
9619, Conely, John, 125, Co K, died Sept 23, diarrhea.
5528, Conely, Pat, 164, Co G, died Aug 13, diarrhea.
8919, Conger, James,* 49, Co A, died Sept 16, scorbutus.
11347, Corvier, Charles, 1 cav, Co C, died Oct 25, scorbutus.
2160, Conkin, A, 69, Co A, died June 19, diarrhea c.
10690, Conlin, Daniel, 5. Co A, died Oct 11, diarrhea c.
11513, Connell, T, 130, Co C, died Oct 26, scorbutus.
2033, Connelly, F, 52, died June 15, diarrhea c.
10006, Conners, E, 43, Co D, died Sept 29, scorbutus.
4025, Connor, Henry, 62. Co D, died July 26, dysentery a.
936, Conners, John, 99, Co D, died May 7, diarrhea c.
7842, Cosgrove, F, 76, Co H, died Sept 4, debilitas.
11093, Cook, C H, 6 cav, Co E, died Oct 18, scorbutus,
11240, Cook, George, 60, Co E, died Oct 21, scorbutus.
7485, Cook, G W, 146, Co E, died Sept 1, dysentery.
5228, Coombs, B, 60, Co A, died Aug 10, diarrhea.
10626, Coombs, J, 96, Co I, died Oct 10, scorbutus.
2195, Coons, F, 52, Co B, died June 19, diarrhea a.
11418, Coon, George F, 65, Co K, died Oct 24, scorbutus.
3692, Cooney, F, 14, Co G, died July 21, dysentery.
10723, Cooney, T, 82, Co E, died Oct 11, diarrhea c.
5816, Cooper, James, 22 cav, Co G, died Aug 16, diarrhea c.
12274, Cooper, N, 22 cav, Co F, died Dec 13, scorbutus.
1150, Copeland, J, 106, Co I, died May 16, diarrhea.
1778, Corbit, B F,† 24, battery, died June 9, dysentery.
10529, Corbit, John, 64, Co C, died Oct 8, scorbutus.
6682, Corless, R, 7, artil, Co E, died Aug 24, diarrhea.
7182, Corneilus, J, 12 cav, Co F, died Aug 29, dysentery.
1995, Coroy, P, 99, Co A, died June 15, diarrhea c.
6729, Corrall O B, 1 cav, Co D, died Aug 24, dysentery.
11331, Correll, P, 100, Co C, died Oct 23, scorbutus,
11347, Corrier, Chas, 1 cav, Co C, died Oct 23, scorbutus.
7471, Costin, J, 22 cav, Co C, died Sept 1, diarrhea c.
12767, Corselman, G, 152, Co K, died March 13, '65, diarrhea c.
7786, Cottin, Z T, 85, Co E, died Sept 4, anasarca.
5329, Countryman, 120, Co A, died Aug 11, dysentery.
3899, Courtney, W, 12 cav, Co A, died July 24, diarrhea c.
8976, Cowen, J, 4, Co I, died Sept 17, diarrhea c.
7058, Cox, D, 1 cav, Co H, died Aug 28, scorbutus.
7675, Coy, John H, 1 cav, Co L, died Sept 3, diarrhea.
11158, Coyne, M, 98. Co H, died Oct 19, scorbutus.
7274, Cozin, J, 82, Co E, died Aug 30, dysentery.
3691, Craft, B, 48, Co D, died July 21, diarrhea.
8221, Craig, J, 139, Co H, died Sept 8, dysentery.
8328, Crandall, D, 85, Co E, died Sept 10, dysentery.

No. of Grave.

8399, Crandall, J,* 85, Co C, died Sept 10, diarrhea.
2950, Crandall, R, 115, Co I, died July 6, scorbutus.
3001, Crandle, J F, 120, Co K, died July 8, fever typhus.
384, Craven, J, 134, Co E, died April 2, dysentery.
3432, Crawford, John, 61, Co B, died July 17, diarrhea c.
12649, Cripman, S, 2, Co K, died Feb 13, '65, scorbutus.
8783, Crissman, Joseph, 140, Co F, died Sept 24, scorbutus.
11471, Crine, C, 6 cav, Co K, died Oct 26, scorbutus.
2311, Criswell, J, 12 cav, Co F, died June 22, diarrhea a.
2832, Crocker, J, 93, Co E, died July 3, diarrhea.
6886, Cromark, J,† 77, Co B, died Aug 16, diarrhea c.
2644, Crompter, James,† 14, Co F, died June 29, diarrhea.
8095, Cromwell, T, 6 artil, died Sept 14, scorbutus.
8324, Crosby, M, 24 battery, died July 14, fever typhus.
2273, Crouse, George, 24 battery, died June 21, dysentery.
11207, Crowley, S, 2, B, Oct 22, diarrhea c.
6993, Cuff, S, 14, Co E, died Aug 17, marasmus.
7159, Culbert, Wm, 39, Co D, died Aug 29, diarrhea.
4119, Culver N L, 24 battery, died July 26, diarrhea.
8965, Cummings, —— 22, Co D, died Sept 16, diarrhea c.
11269, Croo F, 115, Co D, died Oct 21, scorbutus.
6470, Cunningham, J, 170, Co E, died Aug 13, diarrhea.
6721, Cunningham J, 42, Co I, died Aug 24, debilitas.
1447, Cunningham, Wm, 45, Co B, died May 29, diarrhea c.
1204, Curley, P, 125, Co E, died May 19, scorbutus.
3627, Currey, John, 146, Co B, died July 20, diarrhea.
4158, Custerman, F, 47, Co G, died Aug 1, diarrhea.
9540, Cute, A, 8 cav, Co A, died Sept 22, diarrhea.
9011, Cutler, C F,* 2, Co G, died Sept 23, diarrhea.
12434, Cutler, J P, 99, Co B, died Jan 11, '65, diarrhea.
4840, Cutler, Wm, 59, Co B, died Aug 6, diarrhea.

8193, Daher, G, 66, Co D, died Sept 8, diarrhea.
8650, Daley, T, 42, Co I, died Sept 13, pneumonia.
10741, Damoo, J D, 7 artil, Co K, died Oct 11, scorbutus.
3577, Dalley, Wm, 5 cav, Co I, died July 19, scorbutus.
11122, Daniels, W O, 76, Co K, died Oct 18, scorbutus.
6509, Daratt, Louis, 111, Co G, died Aug 14, catarrh.
1480, Daly, John, 99, Co 8, died May 30, anasarca.
6641, Dawson, J, 47, Co K, died Aug 23, diarrhea a.
8095, Darley, J,† 14 artil, Co D, died Sept 7, diarrhea c.
6726, Darling, G H, 18 cav, Co F, died Aug 24, dysentery.
5083, Darling, J, 4, cav, Co C, died Aug 8, diarrhea.
7562, Dart, Charles W, 85, Co C, died Sept 2, dysentery.
6404, Davidson, M, 15 cav, Co M, died Aug 21, diarrhea.
6391 Davis, D, 164, Co G, died Aug 21, diarrhea.
6037, Davis, G, 1, Co H, died Aug 18, scorbutus.
1383, Davis, H, 85, Co I, died May 26, diarrhea c.
7670, Davis, H, 1 artil, Co D, died Sept 3, scorbutus.
8089, Davis, H J, 85, Co C, died Sept 7, scorbutus.
961, Davis, H R,* 99, Co I, died May 8, diarrhea c.
12052, Davis, H T, 5 cav, Co G, died Feb 14, '65, diarrhea c.
6129, Davis, J, 85, Co H, died Aug 9, bronchitis.
7804, Davis, J J,* 43, Co B, died Sept 5, scorbutus.
11817, Davis, John, 47, Co E, died Nov 4, scorbutus.
10241, Davis, P,* 94, Co I, died Oct 3, scorbutus.
10018, Davy, J J, 2 cav, Co A, died Sept 29, scorbutus.
6338, Day, J W, 32, Co D, died Aug 11, pneumonia.
3866, Dean, C, 43, Co E, died July 24, diarrhea.
9400, Dean, J, 3 cav, Co G, died Sept 21, diarrhea.
2305, Dean, John, 6 artil, Co K, died June 22, diarrhea c.
10523, Debras, J, 9, Co A, died Oct 8, diarrhea c.
9058, Decker, A, 82, Co I, died Sept 28, diarrhea.
3660, Deckman, J G, 104, Co B, died July 20, dysentery.
7505, Declercy, W E, 22 cav, Co E, died Sept 1, diarrhea c.
10555, Dedrich, P, 9, Co K, died Oct 9, scorbutus.
12320, Deman, W, 66, Co E, died Dec 22, scorbutus.
7050, Desatell, J, 98, Co D, died Aug 28, scorbutus.
7936, Deet, F, 90, Co D, died Sept 5, diarrhea.
4400, Deffer, Louis, 40, Co H, died July 31, anasarca.
4914, Degammo, J, 48, Co E, died Aug 6, scorbutus.
6283, Degroff, C, 115, Co H, died Aug 20, diarrhea c.
12074, Degrout, W, 7 artil, Co I, died Nov 18, scorbutus.
12228, Devit, Charles, 7 artil, Co G, died Dec 5, scorbutus.
7261, Delane, M, 111, Co C, died Aug 30, debilitas.
11206, Delany, C, 52, Co H, died Oct 20, scorbutus.
12271, Demara, John, 108, Co M, died Dec 12, scorbutus.
6680, Demerest, D, 5, Co A, died Aug 15, scorbutus.
10108, Demerest, H V, 2 cav, Co M, died Sept 30, diarrhea.
8761, Dembart, W, 111, Co F, died Sept 14, scorbutus.
9592, Demming, F M, 85, Co H, died Sept 23, diarrhea.
7278, Dempsey, John, 85, Co B, died Aug 30, diarrhea.
7623, Demming, L,* 85, Co D, died Sept 2, scorbutus.
9930, Dennis, A A, 106, Co H, died Sept 28, diarrhea.
1489, Dennis, Thomas, 132, Co G, died May 31, fever remittent.
4090, Dennison, J, 12 cav, Co A, died July 27, diarrhea.
12257, Dennison, J,† 155, Co I, died Dec 10, scorbutus.
7461, Dennison, W, 14 artil, Co M, died Sept 1, diarrhea.
13250, Denorf, F, 147, Co B, died July 13, wounds.
2320, Densamore, S F, 115, Co G, died June 22, diarrhea a.
6324, Donsmore, E,† 85, Co K, died Aug 21, anasarca.

No. of Grave.

12603, Desmond, D,* 82, Co C, died Feb 6, '65, scorbutus.
1799, Deveny, H, 99, Co I, died June 10, diarrhea c.
7508, Devlin, A, 1 artil, Co M, died Sept 2, diarrhea
5502, Devlin, J, 12 cav, Co F, died Aug 13, diarrhea c.
10077, Dewire Dennis, 7, Co E, died Sept 30, anasarca.
2839, De Witt, S C,† 120, Co E, July 3, fever typhus.
9334, Dewit, J S, sgt, 48, Co H, died Sept 20, scorbutus.
9855, Dickinson, N, 152, Co K, died Sept 27, diarrhea c.
10597, Dickerman, W B, 6 artil, Co A, died Oct 10, scorbutus.
11854, Difendorf, R, 2 artil, Co L, died Nov 6 diarrhea.
2234, Dykeman, F, 47, Co C, died June 20, diarrhea c.
10089, Dingle, J,† 122, Co G, died Sept 30, scorbutus.
1821, Dingley, C, 4 cav, Co A, died June 10, '65, diarrhea c.
8588, Dignard, F, 15 cav, Co A, died Sept 12, scorbutus.
8245, Doan, A, 85, Co C, died Sept 9, diarrhea.
3773, Dolson, E, 85, Co C, died July 22, scorbutus.
1959, Dolan, J, 46, Co E, died June 14, diarrhea a.
11805, Dolan, M, 6 cav, Co F, died Nov 4, scorbutus.
5658, Dolan, P, 30, Co I, died Aug 14, diarrhea.
11884, Domick, E, 4 artil, Co E, died Nov 6, diarrhea.
4886, Donaghen, J, 16, Co A, died Aug 8, diarrhea.
2809, Dood, Daniel, 155, Co I, died July 3, diarrhea a.
6119, Dondall, B, 111, Co G, died Aug 19, diarrhea a.
11357, Donely, M, 10, Co F, died Oct 23, diarrhea
3 81, Donovan, J, 14 artil, died July 9, diarrhea.
229, Dooley, E J, 2 M Rifles, Co K, died Mar 29, diarrhea c.
12718, Donnell, W, 4 artil, Co A, died Mar 2, '65, pleuritis.
655, Donnelly, Jas C,† 2 cav, Co D, died Apr 21, debilitas.
10102, Doolittle, W, 76, Co D, died Sept 30, diarrhea.
3583, Dorchester, H S, vet surg, 12 cav, died July 18, anasarca
12715, Dormity, M, citizen, died Mar 1, '65, debilitas.
10320, Dotsey, J, 139, Co E, died Oct 4, scorbutus,
9416, Dougherty, E S, 85, Co I, died Sept 21, diarrhea.
4650, Dougherty, J, 9, Co C, died Aug 3, dysentery.
2052, Dougherty, O, 99, Co I, June 16, diarrhea c.
10992, Doughty, E S, 48, Co A, died Oct 16, diarrhea.
9298, Downey, H, 11, Co I, died Sept 19, ulcus.
5705, Downey, J A, 85, Co H, died Aug 15, fever intermittent.
7275, Douglass, M, 48, Co D, died Aug 30, fever typhus.
10356, Douglass, P, 147, Co C, died Oct 5, diarrhea.
6149, Dondall, B, 111, Co G, died Aug 19, diarrhea a.
2561, Doyle, John, 5 cav, Co G, died June 27, dysentery.
4827, Doyle, James, 120, Co H, Aug 5, scorbutus.
9142, Doyle, W, 7 artil, Co I, died Sept 18, dysentery.
9308, Dow, M, 125, Co H, died Sept 20, diarrhea.
3929, Drake, D W, 2 artil, Co H, died July 25, dysentery.
2347, Drake, D B, 158, Co F, died June 23, debilitas.
699, Driscoll, — 52, Co B, died Apr 23 diarrhea c.
2820, Drum, A, 155, Co A, died July 3, diarrhea c.
9357, Druse, I, 15 artil, Co D, died Sept 20, diarrhea.
394, Durfee, James, 99, Co H, died Apr 6, diarrhea.
3069, Dumfrey, Dennis, 100, Co I, died July 9, diarrhea.
3499, Dudley, J C,† 10 cav, Co H, died July 17, diarrhea c.
3957, Duell, R, 6 artil, Co F, died July 25, diarrhea.
5264, Dumond, A, 85, Co E, Aug 10, fever intermittent.
6810, Dumond, C, 120, Co A, died Aug 16, diarrhea c.
6773, Dumond, S, 5, Co B, died Aug 25, diarrhea.
10144, Dumond, F, 146, Co A, died Oct 1, scorbutus.
9116, Dunlap, C, 85, Co B, died Sept 18, diarrhea.
8669, Duane, T, 95, Co E, died Sept 13, diarrhea.
8453, Dritmao William, 42, Co C, died Sept, 11, diarrhea c.
6905, Duble, Henry, 61, Co F, died Aug 26, dysentery.
6087, Dule Levi, 5, Co B, died Aug 18, diarrhea.
10948, Duger, P, 67, Co A, died Oct 14, scorbutus.
11104, Dunbam, R, 14 artil, Co G, died Oct 18, dysentery.
7621, Dunn J, 40, Co G, died Sept 2, diarrhea c.
8244, Dunn, L H, 50 Eng, Co E, died Sept 8, diarrhea.
5732, Duon, James, 88, Co D, died Aug 15, scorbutus.
1605, Dunn, J H, 90, Co I, died June 7, diarrhea c.
10948, Dwire, P, 67, Co A, died Oct 14, scorbutus.
123, Dunbar, Thomas, 2, Co F, died March 23, fever typhus.
3234, Dunn, M, 99, Co I, died July 12.
919, Dunn, Owen, 126, Co H, died May 6, diarrhea.
1083, Dunn, Pat, 149, Co A, died May 11, anasarca.
3584, Dunning, Wm, 132, Co G, died July 19, dysentery.
2972, Dunsham, Abr, 120, Co C, died July 7, diarrhea c.
7554, Durand, H, 82, Co K, died Sept 2, scorbutus.
4832, Durand, James E, 10 cav, Co E, died Aug 0, diarrhea c.
9716, Dyer, S, 7 artil, Co D, died July 27, diarrhea.
4066, Dyer, John S, 10 cav, Co M, died Sept 25, scorbutus.
3574, Dykeman, D, 22 cav, Co F, died July 19, pneumonia.
12271, Dunaram, John, 108, Co F, died Dec 12, scorbutus.

9033, Earl C, 85, Co D, died Sept 17, scorbutus.
2443, Earl, H, 174, Co H, died June 26, diarrhea c.
3203, Eastern, Thos, 5 cav, Co L, died July 12, diarrhea.
3919, Eastman, Wm, 10, Co C, died July 25, scorbutus.
4230, Easton, E E, 52, Co F, died July 29, diarrhea.
4410, Eastwood, E, 24 battery, died July 31, diarrhea c.
7449, Eber, James, 76, Co B, died Sept 1, dysentery.
3552, Edmonds, L, 5 cav, Co M, died July 18, dysentery.

No. of Grave.
4268, Edwards B, 52, Co F, died July 30, diarrhea.
7309, Edsen, John, 61, Co D, died Aug 30, diarrhea.
7852, Eden, W, 105, Co E, died Sept 5, scorbutus.
2728, Egan, John, 125, Co D, died July 1, diarrhea c.
9454, Egerton, H, 14 artil, Co L, died Sept 29, diarrhea.
2310, Elberson, J, 10 cav, Co E, died June 21, bronchitis.
7420, Eldery, B, 146, Co E, died Aug 31, diarrhea.
6507, Eldred, H, 125, Co K, died Aug 22, diarrhea c.
3597, Eldred, I, 76, Co F, died July 19, diarrhea.
10339, Ellis, J, 2, Co H, died Oct 4, scorbutus.
12071, Ellis, P M, 2, Co E, died Nov 17, scorbutus.
9736, Ellis, C, 85, Co G, died Sept 25, diarrhea.
7284, Ellis, R H, 76, Co F, died Aug 29, diarrhea.
8930, Elliott, F P, 76, Co B, Sept 16, scorbutus.
8163, Elliott, L, 3 cav, Co I, died Sept 8, fever intermittent.
1107, Ellis, William, 119, Co F, died May 15, diarrhea c.
3526, Ellis, Perry, 106, Co I, died July 18, scorbutus.
8274, Ellison, W, 95, Co F, died Sept 9, diarrhea.
6343, Elster, James, 7 artil, Co E, died Aug 21, diarrhea.
9594, Elwell, W, 47, Co B, died Sept 23, scorbutus.
8152, Emery, G Z,* 48, Co G, died Sept 8, scorbutus.
6090, Engal, W, 39, Co B, died Aug 18, scorbutus.
9080, English G, 7 cav, Co I, died Sept 18, diarrhea.
9961, Engh, John, 7 artil, Co E, died Sept 28, diarrhea.
2454, Ensley, W H, 2 cav, Co H, died June 25, dysentery a.
10375, Erd, J, 51, Co H, died Oct 4, scorbutus.
2731, Ethear, J, 13 cav, Co E, died July 1, diarrhea c.
9450, Evans, Franklin, 140, Co D, died Sept 21, scorbutus.
12365, Evans, L, 7 artil, Co I, died Dec 31, scorbutus.
6780, Evens, B, 60, Co B, died Aug 25, diarrhea.
6429, Everett, J, 58, Co K, died Aug 22, diarrhea c.
11263, Everly, G, 108, Co I, died Oct 21, diarrhea.

11352, Faggerty, C, 2 cav, Co C, died Oct 23, scorbutus.
1622, Fallum, Pat, 3 artil, Co K, died June 3, diarrhea.
11576, Fancie, E, 43, Co D, died Oct 28, scorbutus.
7666, Fairfax, Charles, 111, Co A, died Sept 3, diarrhea.
12091, Farland T, 6, Co I, died Nov 19, diarrhea.
11247, Farley, W, 14 artil, Co F, died Oct 21, diarrhea c.
10259, Farrell, James, 100, Co C, died Oct 3, scorbutus.
6840, Farn, C, 169, Co G, died Aug 16, scorbutus.
6946, Fairman, H B, 6 artil, Co M, died Aug 17, scorbutus.
6995, Fawry, John, 2 artil, Co C, died Aug 27, diarrhea c.
7415, Face, J, 115, Co E, died Aug 31, diarrhea.
10057, Faredough, R, 2, Co F, died Sept 30, scorbutus.
9609, Ferris, C, 100, Co E, died Sept 23, scorbutus.
8439, Ferris, Robert, 14 artil, Co I, died Sept 3, scorbutus.
3452, Ferris, John, 5, Co E, died July 17, diarrhea.
4769, Fetter, F, 60, Co C, died Aug 5, dysentery.
7260, Ferguson, H C, 14, Co C, died Aug 30, diarrhea.
7498, Ferguson, M, 39, Co G, died Sept 1, diarrhea.
7412, Felton, George, 164, Co C, died Aug 31, diarrhea.
8407, Fonsel, H, 7 artil, Co F, died Sept 3, dysentery.
9779, Ferguson, J M, 15 cav, Co G, died Sept 26, scorbutus.
12507, Finnerty, P, 155, Co G, died Jan 22, '65, diarrhea c.
247, Fich, John, 8, Co M, died March 30, diarrhea.
3809, Fioccum, John, 96, Co E, died July 24, diarrhea c.
6192, Fields, F, 2 artil, Co L, died Aug 19, diarrhea.
6656, Finch, Henry, 22 cav, Co L, died Aug 24, dysentery.
8699, Finch, James, 22 cav, Co L, died Sept 14, scorbutus.
10072, Findley, Andrew, 70, Co D, died Sept 30, diarrhea.
11482, Finley, A, 7 artil, Co D, died Oct 26, scorbutus.
6215, Fish, L V, 7 artil, Co B, died Aug 20, catarrh.
4412, Fish, H, 179, Co A, died July 31, dysentery.
6752, Fish, F, 52, Co K, died Aug 15, enteritis.
9723, Fish, J W, 12 cav, Co C, died Sept 25, diarrhea.
279, Fish, William, 17, Co H, died April 1, fever typhus.
11651, Fisher, C P, 124, Co C, died Oct 30, fever typhoid.
10049, Fisher, Conrad, 1 cav, Co E, died Sept 29, diarrhea.
5104, Fisher, Daniel, 45, Co F, died Aug 9, diarrhea.
2389, Fisher D, 125, Co K, died June 24, diarrhea c.
12542, Fisher, H, 59, Co K, died Jan 27, '65, ulcers.
10986, Fisher, L, 39, Co D, died Oct 15, scorbutus.
10171, Fitch, A, 3, Co F, died Oct 1, diarrhea.
4819, Fitch, C, 24 battery, died Aug 5, diarrhea.
3569, Fitzgerald, N, 111, Co C, died July 19, scorbutus.
6453, Fitzgerald, Tho, 24 battery, Co D, died Aug 22, diarrhea.
12400, Fitzpatrick, ——, 10 cav, Co G, died Jan 5, scorbutus.
6961, Fitzpatrick, O, 100, Co E, died Aug 27, diarrhea.
6500, Flagler, William, 7 artil, Co M, died Aug 22, diarrhea c.
7452, Flanigan, E I, 7 artil, Co C, died Sept 1, diarrhea.
6558, Flanigan, P, 40, Co D, died Aug 13, dysentery.
8583, Fleming, P, 22 cav, Co E, died Sept 12, fever intermittent.
390, Fletcher, Wm,* 13 cav, Co G, died March 27, fever typhus.
12537, Flintkoff, F, 102, Co E, died Jan 27, '65, scorbutus.
774, Florence, B, 40, Co H, died April 28, diarrhea c.
7690, Fluke, J, 76, Co K, died Sept 3, scorbutus.
8378, Flynn, J, 24 battery, died Sept 10, scorbutus.
11958, Flynn, J, 13, Co K, died Nov 11, diarrhea.
9242, Flynn, Wm, 71, Co E, died Sept 19, scorbutus.
9283, Fohnsbelly, C, 169, Co A, died Sept 19, diarrhea.

No. of Grave.
8942, Folden, H, 7 artil, Co B, died Sept 6, diarrhea.
3987, Folet, D, 1 cav, Co A, died July 20, dysentery.
10841, Follard, James, 1 cav, Co I, died Oct 13, scorbutus.
4807, Foulke, Peter, 100, Co F, died Aug 5, anasarca.
175, Ford, E V, 132, Co K, died March 26, dysentery.
7441, Forcher, A, 12 cav, Co F, died Aug 31, anasarca.
11730, Foley, F, 77, Co B, died Nov 2, scorbutus.
1789, Forget, G H,* 85, Co K, died June 3, diarrhea c.
2470, Foster, H, 1 cav, Co B, died June 25, scorbutus.
759, Foster, J, 5 cav, Co G, died April 27, dysentery c.
408, Foster, James, 2 cav, Co D, died April 6, diarrhea c.
6115, Fox, A, 49, Co K, died Aug 19, anasarca.
11173, Fox, D, 152, Co A, died Oct 19, scorbutus.
2850, Fox, M, 15 artil, Co K, died July 5, dysentery.
9132, Frahworth, F, 57, Co I, died Sept 21, wounds.
8393, Frake, S, 11, Co G, died Sept 10, scorbutus.
2863, Francis, P L, 2 cav, Co H, died July 4, diarrhea c.
9917, Franklin, J, 39, Co I, died Sept 28, scorbutus.
4227, Franklin, J C, 22 cav, Co L, died July 29, diarrhea.
10484, Fraser, J H, 73, Co C, died Oct 7, scorbutus.
11353, Fredlander, C, 2 cav, Co B, died Oct 23, scorbutus.
4829, Freburg, E, 52, Co F, died Aug 5, diarrhea.
6619, Fredenburg, James, 55, Co H, died Aug 23, anasarca.
6668, Free, C, 20, Co B, died Aug 24, scorbutus.
11393, French, J, 2 cav, Co H, died Oct 23, scorbutus.
10968, French, James, 22 cav, Co G, died Oct 15, scorbutus.
6989, French, John C, 5 cav, Co H, died Aug 27, dysentery.
1395, Fresser, John, 111, Co K, died May 26, dysentery.
5125, Frisby, W L,* 111, Co B, died Aug 9, dysentery c.
11421, Froster, F, 16 cav, Co L, died Oct 24, scorbutus.
3806, Fuller, A, 49, Co K, died July 22, bronchitis.
11628, Fuller, C, 52, Co H, died Oct 30, scorbutus.
3713, Fuller, J B, 85, Co F, died July 21, diarrhea c.
11050, Fuller, N, 18, Co C, died Oct 17, scorbutus.
10295, Fuller, W, 122, Co A, died Oct 4, scorbutus.
10328, Funday, F, 39, Co B, died Oct 4, diarrhea.
10140, Fricks, A, 62, Co L, died Oct 1, scorbutus.

2472, Gagan, Thomas, 85, Co C, died June 25, fever typhus.
5773, Gale, George,* 2, Co A, died Aug 15, scorbutus.
1148, Gallagher, G, 5 cav, Co D, died May 16, diarrhea.
6106, Gallagher, P, 47, Co D, died Aug 18, scorbutus.
4689, Gallewin, Thomas, 20 artil, Co F, died Aug 4, diarrhea.
10489, Galush, W, 5 cav, Co F, died Oct 7, diarrhea c.
7678, Gaudley, J, 3 cav, Co F, died Sept 3, diarrhea c.
6993, Gannon, S, 7 artil, Co E, died Aug 27, diarrhea.
365, Gansey, 94, Co B, died April 5, pneumonia.
11153, Gardner, H, 152, Co A, died Oct 19, scorbutus.
5251, Gardner, B, 155, Co K, died Aug 10, diarrhea.
982, Gardner, H, 132, Co E, died May 9, dysentery.
1323, Gardner, O, 104, Co C, died May 24, dysentery.
9206, Gardner, Wm, 7 cav, Co I, died Sept 18, scorbutus.
7926, Garlock, John, 46, Co B, died Sept 5, dysentery.
8982, Garman, J, 126, Co H, died Sept 17, scorbutus.
8383, Garney, C, 40, Co A, died Sept 10, diarrhea.
7033, Garoy, James, 95, Co C, died Aug 27, diarrhea.
2688, Garrison, J, 65, Co H, died June 30, fever remittent.
7216, Gartell, H, 22 cav, Co L, died Aug 29, dysentery.
7044, Gartland, 169, died Aug 27, diarrhea.
94, Garvey, John, 52, Co K, died March 22, diarrhea c.
10539, Gatoff, H, 52, Co D, died Oct 8, diarrhea.
5270, Gavette, C, 134, Co G, died Aug 10, dysentery.
6868, Gear, James, 142, Co A, died Aug 26, diarrhea.
7120, Gees, A, 85, Co I, died Aug 28, diarrhea.
7930, Geiser, Charles, 39, Co D, died Sept 5, diarrhea.
8878, Gemmage, J, 6 artil, died Sept 16, scorbutus.
7650, Gesler, James, 65, Co E, died Sept 3, scorbutus.
6728, Gian, Benjamin, 11, died Aug 24, dysentery.
10967, Gibbs, Charles, 4 artil, Co B, died Oct 15, scorbutus.
6259, Gibbs, M H, 22 cav, Co E, died Aug 20, cerebritis.
3218, Gibson, J, 170, Co A, died July 12.
12017, Gibson J, 82, Co I, died Nov 15, scorbutus.
6912, Giddings, J, 115, Co H, died Aug 26, diarrhea.
2042, Gifford, H N, 111, died June 15, anasarca.
4185, Gilbert, E, 143, Co D, died July 28, scorbutus.
10925, Gilbert, E, 22 cav, Co B, died Oct 14, scorbutus.
1834, Gilbert, J, 111, Co K, died June 11, diarrhea c.
11270, Gillis, G, 85, Co G, died Oct 21, scorbutus.
10160, Gill, John F, 1 cav, Co B, died Oct 1, scorbutus.
2113, Gill James, 111, Co K, died June 24, anasarca.
3339, Gillen M, 107, Co E, died July 15, diarrhea.
7898, Gillett, Wm, 85, Co F, died Sept 5, scorbutus.
12345, Gilmore, M,* 17, Co B, died Dec 27, scorbutus.
310, Gimrich, Peter, bugler, 2 cav, Co K, died July 10, debilitas.
1678, Gleick, Wm, 11 cav, Co A, died June 6, diarrhea c.
3946, Gleason, Thomas, 97, Co D, died July 25, diarrhea c.
10338, Goaner, F, 16, Co K, died Oct 4, scorbutus.
2553, Goffney, J, 104, Co D, died June 27, diarrhea a.
8639, Goldsmith, Wm, 2, Co F, died Sept 13, diarrhea c.
2962, Gond, E, 104, Co C, died July 6, diarrhea a.
7068, Goodbread, J F, 147, Co B, died Aug 28, dysentery.

No. of Grave.

12529, Goodell, F, * 122, Co K, died Jan 26, '65, scorbutus.
4145, Goodenough, Jas, * 140, Co D, died July 28, diarrhea c.
7343, Goolman, J A, 154, Co A, died Aug 31, scorbutus.
3042, Goodrich, F, 154, Co B, died July 8, diarrhea c.
4561, Goodrich, George, * 2 cav, Co D, died Aug 2, scorbutus.
1415, Gorman, G, 3 artil, Co K, died June 17, dysentery c.
8228, Goodnow, J, 64, Co I, died Sept 9, scorbutus.
12604, Got, C, 49, Co D, died Feb 7, '65, rheumatism.
2203, Oass, James, 132, Co G, died June 19, diarrhea.
3322, Gould, Richard, 61, Co D, died July 14, diarrhea c.
11985, Gough, H, 146, Co B, died Nov 13, scorbutus.
3765, Gower, J, 147, Co B, died July 22, diarrhea.
10499, Graff, F, 14 cav, Co M, died Oct 8, scorbutus.
9347, Graham, J, 15 cav, Co L, died Sept 20, diarrhea.
7089, Graham, Wm, 12 cav, Co F, died Aug 28, anasarca.
10093, Grampy, M J, 52, Co D, died Sept 30, diarrhea.
2640, Grandine, D S, 111, Co E, died June 29, bronchitis.
3048, Granger, A, 93, Co I, died July 20, bronchitis.
5798, Granger, John, 107, Co H, died Aug 15, dysentery.
4131, Granner, H, 62, Co I, died July 28, diarrhea.
3212, Grant, C, 95, Co B, died July 12, diarrhea.
3875, Grant, James, † 125, Co K, died July 24, dysentery.
6449, Grant, J K, 9, Co D, died Aug 22, diarrhea c.
9511, Grass, H, 42, Co G, died Sept 22, dysentery.
12200, Graves, E, 2 cav, Co I, died Dec 1, scorbutus.
4787, Graves, W F, 2, Co H, died Aug 5, dysentery.
5354, Gray, John, 6 artil, Co H, died Aug 11, scorbutus.
1342, Green, E, 85, Co C, died May 24, diarrhea.
12522, Green, H W, 146, Co E, died Jan 26, 1865, scorbutus.
10277, Green, J H, 109, Co K, died Oct 3, diarrhea.
6863, Greer, John, 76, Co B, died Aug 26, diarrhea.
5202, Green, O, 154, Co G, died Aug 10, dysentery.
2184, Greenman, John S, † 2 cav, Co D, died June 19, diarrhea c.
7634, Gregory, A D L, 120, Co E, died Sept 2, diarrhea c.
4322, Gregory, John, 61, Co E, died July 30, diarrhea.
7402, Gregory, L, 7 artil, Co M, died Sept 1, diarrhea.
7201, Grenals, H, 70, Co F, died Aug 29, diarrhea.
11502, Griffin, J B, 7 cav, Co D, died Oct 26, scorbutus.
3816, Griffin, John, 40, Co H, died July 23, diarrhea.
5766, Griffin, N, 52, Co F, died Aug 15, scorbutus.
3101, Griffith, A, 24 battery, died July 10, diarrhea.
11185, Griffith, E P, 85, Co D, died Oct 19, diarrhea c.
8351, Grilmartin, A, 69, died Sept 10, scorbutus.
3815, Griswold, B F, * 109, Co F, died July 23, diarrhea.
1220, Groncly, M, 47, Co E, died May 19, diarrhea.
10944, Gross, C, 68, Co E, died Oct 14, scorbutus.
9653, Gross, J, 140, Co I, died Sept 24, gangrene.
9981, Grose, J, 151, Co B, died Sept 29, bronchitis.
3092, Groven, Joseph, 49, Co F, died July 10, diarrhea c.
10997, Grundy, E J, 73, Co G, died Oct 16, scorbutus.
10813, Gunan, Wm, 8 cav, Co D, died Oct 12, diarrhea c.
5867, Gundalach, F, 95, Co A, died Aug 16, enteritis.
1459, Gunn, Calvin, 12 cav, Co G, died, May 29, diarrhea c.
6651, Gunnahan, J, 85, Co G, died Aug 23, diarrhea.
9372, Gunnell, John, 2 cav, Co B, died Sept 20, scorbutus.
8317, Gulle, A L, † 154, Co C, died Sept 10, diarrhea c.
12145, Guyer, F, 15 artil, Co A, died Nov 24, scorbutus.
12328, Gwin, Charles, 69, Co H, died Dec 24, scorbutus.

6495, Hack, J, 12, Co K, died Aug 22, scorbutus.
10194, Hackett, C, 43, Co C, died Oct 2, scorbutus.
2623, Hackett, J, 12 cav, Co F, died June 28, fever typhoid.
7113, Hackett, J, 7 artil, Co D, died Aug 28, dysentery.
6876, Hagate Jacob, 19 cav, Co F, died Aug 26, diarrhea.
4677, Hager, ——, 52, Co H, died Aug 4, scorbutus.
3646, Hager, J, 59, Co B, died July 20, diarrhea.
6909, Hagerty, Wm, 147, Co E, died Aug 26, debilitas.
8275, Hadden, C, 20, died Sept 9, diarrhea.
473, Haddish, J, 14, Co A, died April 9, diarrhea.
7721, Hadsell, F, 2 artil, Co L, died Sept 3, diarrhea c.
6024, Haight, J E, 8 artil, Co H, died Sept 14, dysentery.
2887, Hair, G, 89, Co A, died July 4, debilitas.
11036, Halbert, A H, * 85, Co D, died Oct 16, scorbutus.
3342, Halbert, L, 1, Co D, died July 15, diarrhea.
170, Haline, Gotfried, 12 cav, Co K, died March 26, fever typhus.
11310, Hall, C, 1 dragoons, Co H, died Oct 28, scorbutus.
2214, Hall, Charles, 12 cav, Co K, died June 20, anasarca.
6003, Hall, Charles, 109, Co G, died Aug 8, diarrhea c.
12370, Hall, C W, 40, Co I, died Jan 1, '65, wounds.
870, Hall, Ed, 111, Co C, died May 3, dysentery.
2846, Hall, James, 9 cav, Co E, died July 3, diarrhea c.
4459, Hall, John, 109, Co E, died Aug 1, diarrhea.
9661, Hall, S, 14 cav, Co L, died Sept 24, diarrhea.
7731, Hall, W C, 8 cav, Co K, died Sept 3, '64, scorbutus.
7819, Hall, Wm, 2, Co K, died Sept 4, anasarca.
10865, Hallenbeck, S, 145, Co H, died Oct 13, scorbutus.
4175, Holloway, J, 140, Co D, died July 28, diarrhea c.
9253, Halpin, P, 68, died Sept 19, scorbutus.
11049, Halper, John, 134, Co F, died Oct 17, diarrhea c.
8213, Hamilton, H, 132, Co D, died Sept 8, diarrhea.
12405, Hamilton J, 111, Co G, died Jan 6, '65, scorbutus.

No. of Grave.

10032, Hamilton, John, 6 artil, Co L, died Sept 29, diarrhea.
6601, Hamilton, Thomas, 6 artil, Co L, died Aug 23, diarrhea.
5634, Hammond, N, 66, Co G, died Aug 14, scorbutus.
1164, Hand, L, 5 cav, Co C, died May 15, pneumonia.
9862, Hanlon, Thomas, 180, Co F, died Sept 27, scorbutus.
11076, Hand, H S, 169, Co A, died Oct 17, scorbutus.
3589, Hanks, J, 1 cav, Co L, died July 19, dysentery c.
3857, Hanley D, 22, Co B, died July 24, anasarca.
12448, Hanley Wm, 29, Co D, died Jan 13, '65, scorbutus.
6009, Hancock, R, 2 cav, Co D, died Aug 17, diarrhea c.
1207, Hanor, Frank, 12, Co G, died May 19, diarrhea c.
6432, Hansom, C, 67, Co F, died Aug 22, diarrhea c.
11149, Hardy, J, 95, Co C, died Oct 19, scorbutus.
9353, Hardy, I, † 5 cav, Co I, died Sept 20, diarrhea.
10101, Hardy, W, 95, Co E, died Sept 30, scorbutus.
7029, Harmon, John, * 164, Co I, died Sept 5, diarrhea.
1411, Haines, Philip, 85, Co I, died May 27, diarrhea c.
2383, Harp, M, 95, Co I, died June 23, diarrhea c.
8323, Harper, J, 126, Co G, died Sept 10, diarrhea c.
10115, Harren, F J, 52, Co C, died Oct 1, scorbutus.
5550, Harris, G, 63, Co E, Aug 13, dysentery.
5182, Haines, H, 5 cav, Co I, died Aug 13, diarrhea.
6784, Harris, Thomas, 65, Co C, died Aug 25, dysentery.
4056, Harris, V S, 8 cav, Co M, July 27, dysentery.
1378, Harrington, Pat, 71, Co D, died May 29, anasarca.
10384, Harrison, Henry, 76, Co K, died Oct 5, diarrhea.
8362, Harrison, O, 14, Co K, died Sept 10, diarrhea.
2526, Harry, A, 143, Co K, died June 26, dysentery.
4705, Hart, D R, 109, Co D, died Aug 4, scorbutus.
5748, Hart, J, 12 cav, Co F, died Aug 15, ictus solis.
11524, Hart, J, 7 artil, Co K, died Oct 26, scorbutus.
8287, Hart, S, * 146, Co B, died Sept 9, scorbutus.
8337, Hart, S, 22 cav, Co M, died Sept 10, anasarca.
7432, Hartman, I N, 40, Co H, died Aug 31, debilitas.
766, Harty, John, 2 cav, Co M, died April 27, diarrhea c.
10812, Hasket, A, 39, Co I, died Oct 12, diarrhea c.
8758, Hasler, M, 119, Co C, died Sept 14, diarrhea c.
11947, Hass, J F, 49, Co F, died Nov 10, scorbutus.
1891, Hathaway, Charles, 24 battery, died June 13, diarrhea.
10878, Hause, Jno, 1 cav, Co L, died Oct 13, diarrhea.
2202, Haveland, H, 6 artil, died June 21, diarrhea c.
11461, Havens, George, 22, Co G, died Oct 25, scorbutus.
3826, Havens, H, 141, Co A, died July 23, dysentery.
4814, Havens, S, † 104, Co A, died Aug 5, dysentery.
3523, Haverslight, H, 66, Co E, died July 18, diarrhea c.
11629, Hawley, W L, 2 cav, Co D, died Oct 28, scorbutus.
10646, Hawley, F, 76, Co E, died Oct 11, scorbutus.
5355, Hayatt, L P, * 1 cav, Co A, died Aug 11, scorbutus.
11786, Hayes, C, 2, Co F, died Nov 4, diarrhea.
8022, Hayes, Edward, 69, Co G, died Sept 6, scorbutus.
9080, Hayes, J, 6, Co A, died Sept 18, diarrhea.
10004, Hayes, James, 39, Co E, died Oct 14, scorbutus.
11204, Hayes, P, 35, Co H, died Oct 21, diarrhea.
9134, Head, Thomas, 6 artil, Co A, died Sept 18, scorbutus.
3394, Haynes, W C, 6 artil, Co G, died July 16, anasarca.
10220, Hayner, L, 125, Co H, died Oct 2, scorbutus.
10662, Heacock, R, † 66, Co H, died Oct 11, scorbutus.
3581, Hecker, C, 47, Co C, died July 19, diarrhea.
6181, Heddle Wm, 5 cav, Co M, died Aug 19, cerebritis.
3155, Hefferman, D, 132, Co C, died July 11, diarrhea.
8135, Helaf-attan, J, 63, Co K, died Sept 8, scorbutus.
11382, Helf, J C, 1 cav, Co G, died Oct 24, scorbutus.
6828, Heller, D, 14 artil, died Aug 25, diarrhea.
7330, Henderson, N J, 85, Co K, died Aug 30, dysentery.
10296, Hendfest, J B, 100, Co K, died Oct 2, scorbutus.
11380, Henerites, B, 15, Co I, Oct 24, scorbutus.
11733, Hilbert G, 5, Co E, died Nov 2, scorbutus.
6336, Hennessy, M, 3 artil, Co K, died Sept 10, scorbutus.
7196, Henyon, W, 85, Co H, died Aug 29, diarrhea.
10870, Heratage, Thomas, 8, Co C, died Oct 13, scorbutus.
196, Herget, John, 111, Co A, died March 27, bronchitis.
3119, Hermance, F C, * 20 Sta Mil, Co A, died July 10, anasarca.
11990, Hermance, J, 100, Co C, died Nov 13, scorbutus.
4495, Herrick, Charles, 39, Co M, died Aug 1, scorbutus.
6627, Henning, C, 140, Co I, died Aug. 23, scorbutus.
10568, Hestolate, John, 69, died Oct 9, diarrhea.
12104, Hewes J, 1 cav, Co A, died Nov 20, scorbutus.
11193, Hewes, R, * 100, Co C, died Oct 20, dysentery.
7005, Hicks, W H, 99, Co I, died Sept 2, scorbutus.
99, Hietzel, C, 52, Co B, March 22, diarrhea.
9037, Higgins, J, 43, Co G, died Sept 28, diarrhea.
888, Higgins, Wm, 99, Co B, died May 4, diarrhea.
4058, Higley, George, 85, Co F, died July 27, diarrhea.
7652, Hildreth, H, 85, Co K, died Sept 3, diarrhea.
3698, Hildreth, L C, 85, Co D, died July 21, scorbutus.
777, Hill, A A, 44, Co G, died April 28, fever intermittent.
8648, Hill, A J, * 2, Co F, died Sept 13, diarrhea c.
3970, Hill, Frank, 2 cav, Co K, died July 25, scorbutus.
11998, Hill, L, 22, Co B, died Nov 13, scorbutus.
11912, Hill, William, 24 cav, Co E, died Nov 8, scorbutus.
3316, Hillman, George, 85, Co B, died July 14, dysentery.

No. of Grave.

4454, Hines, J, 120, Co G, died Aug 1, scorbutus.
9060, Hingman, A, 140, Co G, died Sept 17, scorbutus.
31. Hinkley, B, 9 cav, Co B, died March 9, pneumonia.
6255, Hinkley, D, 1 cav, Co E, died Aug 20, scorbutus.
6331, Hinton, J, 14 Artil, Co D, died Aug 11, diarrhea a.
2967, Hinton, Thomas, * 12 Cav, Co E, died July 6, diarrhea.
7192, Hoag, I, 169, Co A, died Aug 29, dysentery.
395, Hoag, John A, 21 cav, Co L, died April 6, diarrhea.
11670, Hoar, H J, 120, Co I, died Oct 30, scorbutus.
2085, Hobbs, J, 8, Co H, died June 17, diarrhea c.
2934, Hobson, Wm, 14 cav, Co F, died July 7, diarrhea a.
6556, Hodge, John, 22 cav, Co A, died Aug 23, diarrhea a.
6977, Hodgekiss, A, 8 cav, Co M, died Aug 27, dysentery.
1027, Hoffand, John, 132, Co E, died May 11, diarrhea c.
5010, Hoffman, Fred, 48, Co B, died Aug 8, scorbutus.
3811, Hoffman, H, 47, Co F, died July 23, dysentery.
4932, Hoffman, H, 7 artil, Co L, died Aug 7, scorbutus.
6248, Hoffman, N, 5 cav, Co F, Aug 29, diarrhea c.
7718, Hofyeneck, T, 21 cav, Co I, died Sept 3, diarrhea.
11317, Hogan, J, 63, Co F, died Oct 22, scorbutus.
5489, Hogan, John J, 6 artil, Co M, Aug 13, diarrhea.
162, Horsenton, E L, 91, Co B, died March 26, diarrhea.
6465, Holbrook, G, 76, Co K, died Aug 22, diarrhea c.
6327, Holbrook, J E, 85, Co E, died Aug 21, diarrhea
5013, Holcomb, M D, 95, Co F, died Aug 8, dysentery.
2204, Holcomb, Theo, 44, Co K, died June 19, diarrhea a.
11662, Holfe, J, 48, Co E, died Oct 30, scorbutus.
6475, Holiday, S, 85, Co E, died Aug 22, scorbutus.
2510, Hollands, H, 115, Co E, died June 26, diarrhea c.
7218, Holen, M, 152, Co A, died Aug 29, scorbutus.
2573, Hollenbeck, H J, 120, Co G, died June 27, debilitas.
7051, Holliday, S, * 85, Co K, died Aug 28, dysentery.
10624, Holmen, J, 50, Co C, died Oct 10, scorbutus.
7952, Holmes, C, 85, Co A, died Sept 6, diarrhea.
7104, Holmes, E, 7 artil, Co K, died Aug 28, diarrhea.
5531, Holmes, Henry, 99, Co H, died Aug 13, scorbutus.
12467, Holmes, J, 4 artil, Co K, died Jan 16, '65, scorbutus.
1504, Holstenstein, H, 48, Co E, died May 31, diarrhea c.
12298, Holtcamp, B, 96, Co F, died Dec 16, scorbutus.
7826, Homvighausen, F, 140, Co B, died Sept 4, dysentery.
7117, Hooker, T, 111, Co H, died Aug 28, fever typhus.
6369, Hoover, A, 15 artil, Co H, died Aug 11, diarrhea.
514, Hoppock A, 15 artil, Co H, died April 12, diarrhea.
8040, Homstead, H, 22, Co A, died Sept 6, diarrhea.
6114, Hore, R, * 15 cav, Co L, died Aug 19, diarrhea c.
2445, Hosford, W F, 24 battery, died June 25, fever typhoid.
6094, Houghtallinger, M, 120, Co D, died Aug 18, diarrhea.
10817, Houghtelling, C, 5 artil, Co A, died Oct 12, diarrhea.
5632, Hour, James, 119, Co E, died Aug 14, anasarca.
7457, Hous, A R, 96, Co C, died Sept 1, diarrhea.
11099, Housden, E, 85, Co G, died Oct 18, debilitas.
11693, Howard, A, 2 artil, Co M, died Oct 31, diarrhea
8477, Howard, J, 12 cav, Co F, died Sept 11, scorbutus.
4387, Howard, Wm, 39, Co A, died July 31, diarrhea.
10114, Howe, G, 16 cav, Co M, died Oct 1, diarrhea c.
12292, Howe, S, 59, Co C, died Dec 15, scorbutus.
11064, Howell, C R, 2 cav, Co C, died Oct 17, scorbutus.
6622, Hoye, J, 9 artil, Co I, died Aug 23, diarrhea.
7301, Hubbard, A, 76, Co B, died Aug 30, scorbutus.
10666, Hudson, J A, 148, Co A, died Oct 11, scorbutus.
9562, Hudson, S R, 15 cav, Co L, died Sept 23, scorbutus.
9387, Hull, J E, 24 cav, Co E, died Sept 20, diarrhea.
1462, Hull, W S, 140, Co C, died May 29, diarrhea c.
7931, Huganer, A, 185, Co K, died Sept 5, dysentery.
16, Huganer, D M, 64, Co I, died March 6, dysentery.
7895, Hughes, John, 93, Co K, died Sept 4, scorbutus.
11191, Hughes, M, * 82, Co K, died Oct 20, dysentery.
7287, Hughes, Thomas, 61, Co G, died Aug 30, dysentery.
2562, Hulet, W, 22 cav, Co L, died June 27, fever typhus.
7584, Hulse, G, 99, Co I, died Sept 2, scorbutus.
1474, Hulse, W. S, 47, Co G, died May 30, diarrhea c.
7153, Humphrey H, * 85, Co F, died Aug 29, diarrhea c.
2618, Humphrey, Jas, 155, Co I, died June 28, diarrhea c.
2898, Hunnell, J, 100, Co A, died July 5, dysentery.
470, Hunt, F J, 46, Co D, died April 9, diarrhea c.
3365, Hunter E, † 24 battery, died July 15, fever typhus.
10978, Hunter J, 115, died Oct 15, scorbutus.
9862, Hanlon, Thomas, 180, Co F, died Sept 27, scorbutus.
5841, Huntsmore, G, 85, Co E, died Aug 16, diarrhea.
6497, Hurlburt, S B, 100, Co E, died Aug 13, scorbutus.
4430, Hurley, John, 52, Co A, died July 31, diarrhea.
12614, Hurrell, J, 10 cav, Co E, died Feb 8, '65, diarrhea.
11851, Hutchings, H W, 1 cav, Co D, died Nov 1, diarrhea.
3112, Hutchings, S A, 5 cav, Co B, died July 10, diarrhea.
6024, Hutchings, Wm, 6 artil, Co G, died Aug 8, dysentery.
898, Hutchinson, T, 13 cav, Co D, died May 4, diarrhea.
8585, Hutchinson, J, 82, Co A, died Sept 12, scorbutus.
11019, Hutchinson, M, * 52, Co G, died Oct 16, scorbutus.
9173, Huleson, Wm E, 2 artil, Co D, died Sept 18, scorbutus.
8955, Hyde, C, 14, Co F, died Sept 10, scorbutus.

No. of Grave.

11083, Hyde, G, 42, Co C, died Oct 18, scorbutus.
8770, Hyde, J F, 76, Co B, died Sept 14, diarrhea.
7625, Hyland, O, 5, Co D, died Sept 2, diarrhea c.
2106, Hyman, J, 45, Co E, died June 17, diarrhea.

2187, Imhoff, R, 2 cav, Co G, died June 19, dysentery.
4019, Imlay, E, 195, Co A, died July 26, diarrhea
4359, Inman, J P, 1 cav, Co A, died July 31, diarrhea.
10549, Ingerson, S, 14 artil, Co G, died Oct 9, dysentery.
4685, Ingraham, C B, 85, Co B, died Aug 4, diarrhea.
3428, Inier, I, 1 cav, Co H, died July 16, diarrhea c.
4587, Irish, G, 85, Co C, died Aug 2, dysentery,
11751, Ivespack, W, 15 cav, Co E, died Nov 3, scorbutus.

8159, Jaquays, R, 9, Co L, died Sept 8, pleuritis.
7596, Jack, J W, 95, Co H, died Sept 2, diarrhea.
6558, Jackson, A, 5 cav, Co E, died Aug 23, diarrhea.
9048, Jackson, J, 43, Co K, died Sept 17, diarrhea.
11791, Jackson, T A, 122, Co E, died Oct 24, scorbutus.
5402, Jackson, John S, 109, Co F, died Aug 12, diarrhea.
7253, Jackson, William, 85, Co F, died Aug 30, diarrhea.
6966, Jarmone, James, 115, Co I, died Aug 27, scorbutus.
4795, Jamison, A, 51, Co A, died Aug 5, scorbutus.
3615, Jarvis, E, 106, Co H, died July 29, diarrhea.
11704, Jasper, C, 7 artil, Co D, died Oct 31, scorbutus.
6671, Jay, John, 8 artil, died Aug 24, scorbutus.
9389, Jay, John, 2 artil, Co G, died Sept 20, diarrhea.
3984, Jeffrey, B, 9 artil, Co D, died July 26, dysentery.
1120, Jelley, John, 99, Co K, died May 15, diarrhea c.
29, Jenner, Henry, 3 artil, Co K, died April 19, small pox.
10757, Jennings, C, 149, Co K, died Oct 12, wounds.
744, Jewell, Jas B, 3 artil, Co K, died April 26, dysentery.
9934, Johnson, A, 74, Co C, died Sept 28, scorbutus.
11182, Johnson, A, 7 artil, Co A, died Oct 19, wounds.
12121, Johnson, B, 63, Co D, died Nov 22, scorbutus.
12477, Johnson, B F, 82, Co H, died Jan 17, '65, pleuritis.
10118, Johnson, H S, 85, Co D, died Oct 1, scorbutus.
5916, Johnson H, 115, Co I, died Aug 17, diarrhea c.
6232, Johnson, H, 10 cav, Co C, died Aug 20, diarrhea a.
7712, Johnson, J, 89, Co I, died Sept 3, diarrhea.
12546, Johnson, J, 146, Co A, died Jan 27, '65, dysentery.
10043, Johnson, L W, 14 artil, Co C, died Sept 29, diarrhea.
5935, Johnson, M, 96, Co H, died Aug 17, scorbutus.
9495, Johnson, P B, 24 battery, died Sept 21, diarrhea c.
8054, Johnson, R, 111, Co A, died Sept 7, scorbutus.
3427, Johnson, R, 120, Co I, died July 16, diarrhea.
4047, Joice, Thomas, 22, Co C, died July 27, fever typhus.
7413, Jolley, F, 93, Co E, died Aug 31, diarrhea.
5980, Jones, C N, 10 cav, Co C, died Aug 17, marasmus.
6898, Jones, David, 85, Co H, died Aug 26, dysentery.
10769, Jones, E C, 147, Co E, died Oct 12, diarrhea c.
3650, Jones, E, 134, Co F, died July 20, dysentery.
4373, Jones, G C, 20, died July 31, diarrhea.
3282, Jones, G W, 47, Co F, died July 14, scorbutus.
5753, Jones, H, 10 cav, Co I, died Aug 15, diarrhea.
5582, Jones, John, 76, Co K, died Aug 14, fever remittent.
11855, Jones, John, 6 cav, Co A, died Nov 6, scorbutus.
2487, Jones, R, 99, Co B, died June 26, diarrhea c.
4403, Jones, Thomas, 116, Co B, died July 31, anasarca.
5042, Jones, Wm, 52, Co B, died Aug 8, diarrhea.
8807, Jones, Wm, farrier, 5 cav, Co C, died Sept 15, diarrhea
8771, Jones, J B, 22 Co F, died Sept 14, scorbutus
9528, Jourdan, Barry, 7 artil, Co E, died Sept 22, diarrhea.
4188, Jule, H, 51, Co E, died July 28, diarrhea
9107, Jump, O, 8 cav, died Sept 18, diarrhea c.

5198, Kahbaun, E, 12 cav, Co F, died Aug 10, scorbutus.
12170, Kane, F, 82, Co A, died Nov 26, scorbutus.
792, Kane, Peter, h s, 20 cav, died Apr, 28, diarrhea c.
8568, Kanope, C, 49, died Sept 15, diarrhea.
9194, Kapp, D, 100, Co F, died Sept 18, diarrhea.
10222, Kearsley, W, 16 cav, Co A, died Oct 2, scorbutus.
8452, Keating, M, 146, Co A, died Sept 11, diarrhea c.
4484, Keating, Thomas, 83, Co L, died Aug 1, diarrhea.
11075, Keean, W, 47, Co I, died Oct 17, scorbutus.
7387, Keers, M, 49, Co A, died Aug 31, scorbutus.
11756, Kehoo T, 155, Co A, died Nov 3, scorbutus.
10341, Kelley, M, 2 artil, Co L, died Oct 4, diarrhea.
10649, Kellar, John, 140, Co E, died Oct 11, scorbutus.
6730, Kelley, D, * 45, Co C, died Aug 24, dysentery.
11100, Kelley, J, 4 artil, Co K, died Oct 18, debilitas.
10675, Kelley, James, 140, Co K, died Oct 11, scorbutus,
6997, Kelley, James, 40, Co F, died Aug 27, diarrhea c.
10388, Kelley, M, 63, died Oct 6, scorbutus.
9670, Kelley, P, 106, Co D, died Sept 24, scorbutus.
12209, Kelley, T, † 82, Co F, died Dec 2, diarrhea,
10950, Kenarm, Alfred, 70, Co K, died Oct 14, scorbutus.
11425, Kennedy, M E, 82, Co K, died Oct 24, scorbutus.
9865, Kennedy, W, 132, Co D, died Sept 27, scorbutus.
11244, Kennion, F, 8, Co H, died Oct 21, scorbutus.
2572, Kenny, A W, 65, Co D, died July 19, dysentery c.

No. of Grave.

1250, Keany, G W, 24 battery, died May 21, fever typhus.
8671, Kenoy, M, 2, Co F, died July 20, diarrhea c.
4398, Kent, E L, 85, Co I, died July 31, diarrhea.
7403, Kenwell, R, 5 cav, Co D, died Aug 31, scorbutus.
1070, Keogh, Peter, 132, Co C, died May 14, diarrhea.
5052, Kerrit, Jacob, 132, Co D, died Aug 17, marasmus
5310, Kerr, G L, 85, Co B, died Aug 11, scorbutus.
2484, Kerr, H, 2 cav, Co L, died June 25, anasarca.
3915, Kertser, T, 178, Co K, died July 25, diarrhea c.
2797, Kester, Charles,† 141, Co F, died July 2, diarrhea c.
1622, Kettle, Sol, 2 artil, Co K, died Oct 28, scorbutus.
9015, Keys, R, 95, Co C, died Sept 17, diarrhea.
654, Keyes, O S,† 5 cav, Co E, died Apr 29, diarrhea.
1932, Kidd, Owen, 120, Co K, died June 14, diarrhea c.
4506, Killmer, Sanford, 125, Co F, died Aug 3, dysentery c.
1864, Kimmer, J, 5, Co I, died June 12 dysentery.
10614, Kilson, J, 115, Co E, died Oct 10, scorbutus.
12025, Kimball, S,† 7 artil, Co F, died Nov. 15, scorbutus.
3262, Kimberly, C, 76, Co B, died July 13, diarrhea.
7990, King, -- 99, Co I, died Sept 6, diarrhea.
9816, King N, 21 cav, Co G died Sept 26, diarrhea
8738, King, Sylvanus, 24 battery, died Sept 14, diarrhea.
3787, King, Richard,† 99, Co H, died July 22, anasarca.
3095, Kingsley, D, 12 cav, Co H, died July 10, diarrhea
9679, Kingsley, James, 5 cav, died Sept 24, diarrhea.
239, Kinney, Lucas, 99, Co H, died Mar 30, diarrhea c
11558, Kinsey, M, 42, Co C, died Oct 27, scorbutus.
8400, Kinnie, J, 73, Co F, died Sept 10, scorbutus.
564, Kinsey, B B,† 132, Co K, died Apr 15, diarrhea.
7977, Kinsman, John E 14 artil, Co I, died Sept 6, diarrhea.
12839, Kinsman, W S, 86, Co I, died Apr 20, '65, diarrhea.
4297, Kirby, Charles, 12 cav, Co F, died July 30, anasarca.
7087, Kirkland, I, 2 artil, Co D, died Aug 28, dysentery.
12742, Kirkpatrick, —, 12 cav, Co D, Mar 6, '65, diarrhea c.
5589, Kittle, E N,* 125, Co E, died Aug 14, scorbutus.
8873, Kizer, G W, 76, Co B, died Sept 15, scorbutus.
4525, Knapp, Henry, 24 cav, Co A, died Aug 2, scorbutus.
6233, Knapp, Phillip, 10 cav, Co C, died Aug 10, diarrhea.
2604, Knabe, E, 48, Co C, died June 28, diarrhea c.
7949, Knight, Wm, 142, Co C, died Sept 6, diarrhea c.
12318, Knowl, H, 66, Co C, died Dec 21, scorbutus.
11976, Kossuth, W, 54 Co F, died Nov 12, diarrhea c.
8860, Krasipars, K, 65, Co L, died Sept 15, diarrhea c.
9211, Krautz, H,* 54, Co E, died Sept 19, scorbutus.
12115, Kreit, J K,† 1 cav, Co L, died Nov 21, scorbutus.
11948, Krelar, A, 13 battery, died Nov 10, wounds.
3892, Kroom, C E, 61, Co G, died July 24, diarrhea c.
1208, Krouser, G R, 178, Co K, died May 19, diarrhea c.

8956, Lahey, P, 1, Co D, died Sept 16, diarrhea c.
8447, Lacey, P, 12 cav, Co F, died Sept 11, scorbutus.
3601, Lacey, Wm,* 85, Co K, died July 19, diarrhea.
10736, Lackley, P I, 1 cav, died Oct 11, scorbutus.
10879, Lacks, Lee, 22, Co G, died Oct 13, scorbutus.
8372, Lacoster, H, 85, died Sept 10, scorbutus.
11527, Lader, A, 9, Co E, died Oct 26, scorbutus.
7156, Lagay, Frank, 118, Co B, died Aug 29, scorbutus.
41, Lahey, Daniel, 82, Co I, died Mar 13, pneumonia.
12775, Lahiff, D, 42, Co K, died Mar 14, '65, diarrhea c.
12100, Lake, Wm, 145, Co K, died Nov 21, scorbutus.
6487, Laman, C, 39, Co H, died Aug 22, diarrhea.
6381, Lamareux, J, 76, Co K, died Aug 21, scorbutus.
11893, Lambright, A,* 7 artil, Co K, died Nov 7, diarrhea c.
11599, Lambly, J, 1, Co I, died Oct 28, scorbutus.
11318, Lampman, W S, 6 artil, Co M, died Oct 22, scorbutus.
11213, Lampert, R, 98, Co D, died Oct 20, debilitas.
9836, Larrabee, E,* 15, Co D, died Sept 27, scorbutus.
3283, Landers, C, 7 artil, died July 14, diarrhea.
12214, Lane, C, 146, Co E, died Dec 3, scorbutus.
7462, Lane, Charles, 3 cav, Co E, died Sept 1, anasarca.
2678, Lane, G W, 85, Co C, died June 30, dysentery.
11499, Lane, J W, 15 cav, Co M, died Oct 26, diarrhea c.
2288, Lang, A,* 85, Co F, June 21, '65, fever typhus.
13, Lang, William W, 1 dragoons, died Mar 6, pneumonia.
8238, Langdon, A. M, 85, Co B, died Sept 9, scorbutus.
4375, Lansing, Wm, 12 cav, Co B, died July 31, scorbutus.
3788, Lansop, J, 85, Co D, died July 22, diarrhea.
10093, Langen, A, 39, Co I, died Sept 30, diarrhea.
4871, Lappan, L H, 24 battery, died Aug 6, diarrhea.
8487, Larcks, G, 85, Co F, died Sept 7, scorbutus.
6631, Larkins, M C, 100, Co A, died Aug 23, wounds.
14, Lasar, Benjamin, 6 cav, Co F, died Mar 6, fever remit.
8956, Latey, P, 1, Co D, died Sept 16, diarrhea c.
851, Lattarretta, J,* 1 cav, Co A, died May 3, diarrhea c.
4107, Laugha, W, 1 artil, Co M, died July 27, diarrhea c.
8162, Lawton, J, 69, Co E, died Sept 8, catarrh.
10035, Lawrence, J, 7 artil, Co G, died Sept 30, diarrhea.
4101, Lawson, John, 2 cav, Co D, died July 27, dysentery.
6434, Layman, C, 120, Co K, died Aug 22, dysentery.
2374, Leabrook, John, 157, Co B, died June 23, pneumonia.
2119, Leach, S, 10 cav, Co E, died June 17, diarrhea c.

No. of Grave.

1737, Lean, W H, 21 cav, Co C, June 8, dysentery.
7142, Ledderer, William, 132, Co G, Aug 20, diarrhea c.
1914, Lee, A, 24 battery, died June 14, diarrhea c.
2169, Lee, F, 15, Co F, died June 19, scorbutus.
2572, Lee, P, 2 artil, Co A, died June 27, fever remittent.
9696, Lee, William, 6 cav, Co L, died Sept 24, scorbutus.
8514, Legrist, W, 11, Co E, died Sept 10, diarrhea.
6399, Lechinger, J, 3 cav, Co D, died Aug 21, anasarca.
3565, Leiner, A, 39, Co B, died July 19, dysentery.
11697, Leret, V, 47, Co I, died Oct 21, diarrhea.
2086, Lent, A, 24 battery, died June 30, pneumonia.
7499, Leonard, A, 52, Co B, died Sept 1, diarrhea c.
12076, Leonard, C H, 7 artil, Co A, died Nov 18, scorbutus.
8987, Leonard, J W, 85, Co K, died Sept 17, diarrhea.
10065, Lestraff, C, 7 artil, Co A, died Sept 30, diarrhea.
6150, Letch, John, 5 cav, Co C, died Aug 19, cerebritis.
8774, Levalley, C, 140, Co A, died Sept 14, scorbutus.
9045, Lewis, C, 85, Co F, died Sept 17, diarrhea c.
3727, Lewis, C F, 52, Co E, died July 21, diarrhea c.
1329, Lewis, F. A, 9, Co G, died May 24, fever typhus.
11515, Lewis, G W, 140, Co G, died Nov 8, scorbutus.
8297, Lewis, J, 1 artil, Co E, died Sept 9, bronchitis.
6115, Lewis, P W, 85, Co B, died Aug 9, diarrhea.
10365, Lickley, P, 1 cav, Co E, died Oct 5, scorbutus.
11551, Limbach, S, 7, Co D, died Oct 27, scorbutus.
8419, Litch, J H, 76, Co I, died Sept 11, fever typhus.
5845, Linchler, F, 1 cav, Co E, died Aug 15, diarrhea.
10559, Lindsay, D, 147, Co E, died Oct 9, diarrhea.
7815, Lincham, Thomas, 125, Co C, died Sept 4, diarrhea.
6759, Ling, John, 4 artil, Co F, died Aug 25, diarrhea a.
38, Link, Gottlieb, 54, Co K, died Mar 12, dysentery c.
10073, Little, C, 76, Co F, died Sept 30, scorbutus.
10963, Livingston, A, 1 cav, Co C, died Oct 14, diarrhea.
4543, Locher, Conrad, 15 artil, died Aug 2, dysentery.
5565, Lock, A, 98, Co B, died Aug 13, diarrhea c.
2142, Lodge, T, 12, Co A, died June 18, diarrhea a.
8246, Loftern, H, 12 cav, Co F, died Sept 9, diarrhea c.
9722, Loftus, M, 11 cav, Co E, died Sept 24, diarrhea.
7010, Longs, R, 2 artil, Co A, died Aug 27, scorbutus.
11591, Long, J, 75, Co A, died Oct 28, scorbutus.
7924, Long, L, 40, Co I, died Sept 5, anasarca.
4514, Longle, William, 4 artil, Co B, died Aug 1, scorbutus.
5424, Loomis, John, 14 artil, Co M, died Aug 12, scorbutus.
9712, Loony, C, 40, Co A, died Sept 25, diarrhea.
9988, Lorztran, J, 64, Co E, died Sept 29, diarrhea.
11906, Louis, C, 16 cav, Co C, died Nov 7, scorbutus.
12329, Love, J, 125, Co A, died Dec 24, scorbutus.
7146, Lovejoy, F, 1 cav, Co I, died Aug 29, scorbutus.
10248, Lovering, F, 14 artil, Co I, died Oct 3, scorbutus.
12313, Lowery, G, 7, Co A, died Dec 20, scorbutus.
2568, Lowery, James F, 140, Co A, died June 27, dysentery a.
9663, Lows, H, 22 Cav, Co E, died Sept 24, diarrhea.
8325, Loyd, S, 47, Co D, died Sept 10, dysentery.
9354, Luce, V, 140, Co D, died Sept 20, scorbutus.
10311, Lucia, A, 95, Co H, died Oct 4, scorbutus.
7268, Lureock, E, 14 artil, Co M, died Aug 30, scorbutus.
9002, Lutton, O, 14 artil, Co H, died Sept 17, scorbutus.
5772, Lynch, D, 164, Co A, died Aug 15, diarrhea.
6895, Lynch, F,* 43, Co K, died Aug 26, anasarca.
931, Lynch, Pat, 99, Co H, died May 7, diarrhea c.
12633, Lyons, Charles, 2 cav, Co M, died Feb 10, '65, debilitas.
1427, Lyons, Michael, 99, Co E, died May 28, diarrhea c.
8419, Luch, J H, 76, Co I, died Sept 11, fever typhus.
6151, Lucah, John, 5 cav, Co C, died Sept 19, cerebritis.
8342, Lyons, J H, 5 artil, died Sept 10, scorbutus.
6156, Lyons, Thomas, 6 artil, Co G, died Aug 10, diarrhea a.
7913, Lyons, W,* 47, Co A, died Sept 5, diarrhea c.

37, Mace, Jeff, 134, Co I, died March 12, diarrhea.
6665, Mace, L, 48, Co H, died Aug 24, scorbutus.
10850, Mack, J, 39, Co D, died Oct 13, diarrhea.
6616, Mackin, Wm, 85, Co F, died Aug 8, diarrhea c.
3933, Madder, P, 155, Co E, died July 25, diarrhea c
10506, Madden, F,† 132, Co E, died Oct 8, diarrhea c.
4822, Madden, 1 cav, Co D, died Aug 5, dysentery.
11257, Madezan, John, 125, Co B, died Oct 21, scorbutus.
9798, Madison, D, 75, Co D, died Sept 26, scorbutus.
11714, Magrath, G H, 61, Co D, died Nov 1, dysentery.
4028, Mahon, E, 170, Co G, died July 26, tonsilitis.
122, Mahon, James,† 132, Co K, died March 23, fever typhus.
1422, Mahon, Thomas, 120, Co C, died May 28, diarrhea c.
5812, Mailer, J R,† 134, Co E, died Aug 16, erysipelas.
11679, Maine, F O, 85, Co A, died Oct 31, scorbutus.
11580, Mainhart, F, 39, Co B, died Oct 28, scorbutus.
12069, Makay, J, 5, Co E, died Nov 17, scorbutus.
7042, Malleck, M,* 6 Cav, Co D, died Sept 5, diarrhea c.
9427, Malley, S S, 16, Co K, died Sept 21, diarrhea.
9457, Malone, Pat, 123, Co F, died Sept 21, scorbutus.
3284, Maloney, C, 6, Co C, died July 14, diarrhea c.
11447, Maloney, J, 73, Co G, died Oct 25, scorbutus.
7600, Mandeville, Wm, 85, Co F, died Sept 2, scorbutus.

No. of Grave.

2302, Mangin, M, 7 artil, Co F, died July 3, scorbutus
10623, Manning, 33, died Oct 9, scorbutus.
7139, Manning, M, 6 artil, Co D, died Aug 28, scorbutus.
10540, Manning, Thomas, 125, Co B, Oct 8, scorbutus.
2912, Mannidy, J, 71, Co C, died July 6, diarrhea a.
2856, March, J, 22 cav, Co C, died July 4, diarrhea c.
4900, Mariey, John, musician, 53, Co E, died July 26, diarrhea.
1123, Marion, J, 99, Co I, died May 15, dysentery.
11764, Martaugh, J, 6 cav, Co A, died Sept 3, scorbutus.
3824, Marsh, Ira, 6 artil, Co M, died July 23, scorbutus.
6407, Marsh, J, 104, Co D, died Aug 12, diarrhea.
11937, Marston, A, 65, Co G, died Nov 13, scorbutus.
3441, Martin A, 12 cav, Co F, died July 17, dysentery.
435, Martin, C, 10 cav, Co A, died April 8, anasarca.
6543, Martin, Charles, 42, Co G, died Aug 23, diarrhea,
11603, Martin, E A, 5 cav, Co C, died Oct 28, scorbutus.
12208, Martin, J, 39, Co G, died Dec 2, diarrhea.
4321, Martin, H, 76, Co H, died July 30, dysentery.
5083, Martin, J C, 24 battery, died Aug 8, diarrhea c.
9164, Martin, P, 99, Co H, died Sept 18, scorbutus.
6293, Martin, John, 16 cav, Co L, died Aug 20, scorbutus.
1256, Martin, Peter, 40, Co I, died May 21, diarrhea a.
8002, Martin, W, 142, Co F, died Sept 6, scorbutus.
3959, Martin, W B, 12, Co I, died July 26, scorbutus.
8746, Martin, W H, 24 artil, Co M, died Sept 14, diarrhea.
1073, Martin, Wm, 13 cav, Co D, died May 13, diarrhea c.
676, Marveney, James, 132, Co G, died Apr 22, phthisis.
10483, Mason, F,* 14 artil, Co I, died Oct 7, scorbutus.
2215, Martin, Samuel, 85, Co I, died June 22, diarrhea c.
11290, Masterson, E, 2, Co D, died Oct 22, scorbutus.
11296, Masson, H L, 86, Co C, died Oct 22, scorbutus.
10498, Maxwell, J, 85, Co D, died Oct 8, scorbutus.
1477, Maxwell, Robert, 48, Co D, died May 30, wounds
11788, Matthews, W, 155, Co I, died Nov 4, scorbutus.
4472, Matthews, H, 12 cav, Co M, died Aug 1, diarrhea.
2109, Mattice, H C, 134, Co E, died June 17, diarrhea c.
6651, Mattison, R, 85, Co D, died Aug 14, scorbutus.
4946, Maxum, S G, 12 cav, Co A, died Aug 7, diarrhea c.
10519, McAllister, J, 125, Co I, died Oct 8, scorbutus.
7093, McBride, 82, Co K, died Sept 6, scorbutus.
4598, McCabe, James, 88, Co D, died Aug 1, diarrhea.
2517, McCabe, P, 12 cav, Co F, died June 28, diarrhea c.
752, McCabe, Peter, 12 cav, Co E, died April 25, dysentery.
2196, McCabe, J, 44, Co C, died June 19, diarrhea a.
8324, McCafferty, W, 100, Co D, died Sept 10, diarrhea c.
10716, McCain, L, 18, Co G, died Oct 11, scorbutus.
9864, McCardell, W, 15 cav, Co H, died Sept 27, scorbutus.
7620, McCarten, L, 9 artil, Co B, died Sept 2, diarrhea c.
3413, McCarty, D, 155, Co G, died July 16, diarrhea a.
4180, McCarty, Denis, 2 artil, Co D, died Aug 1, diarrhea c.
6122, McCarty, I, 99, Co H, died Aug 9, dysentery c.
9683, McCarty, I, 2, m r, Co K, died Sept 24, diarrhea.
4750, McCarty, John, 69, Co K, died Aug 5, diarrhea.
6150, McCarty, John, 104, Co E, died Aug 10, cerebritis.
1055, McCarty, P, 132, Co K, died May 11, diarrhea.
2865, McCarty, S, 99, Co C, died July 6, diarrhea a.
6227, McCarty, W, 9 cav, Co L, died Aug 20, dysentery.
8242, McClusky, F, 173, Co E, died Sept 9, diarrhea.
1344, McColligan, Pat, 99, Co F, died May 24, diarrhea a.
9256, McCauley, J H, 47, Co G, died Sept 19, scorbutus.
6443, McConnell, John, 97, Co A, died Aug 22, scorbutus.
4416, McConnell, E, 9 artil, died July 31, diarrhea.
6012, McCord, H, 7 artil, Co G, died Aug 17, diarrhea.
11110, McCormic, M, 93, Co K, died Oct 18, diarrhea c.
6997, McCormick, H, 69, Co K, died Aug 29, scorbutus.
9018, McCormick, H, 178, Co F, died Sept 17, diarrhea.
3629, McCormick, J, 155, Co H, died July 20, dysentery.
6203, McCormick, J, 21 battery, died Aug 19, diarrhea.
7441, McCormick, J, 43, Co F, died Sept 1, dysentery.
10258, McCormick, P, 43, Co D, died Oct 3, scorbutus.
1483, McCormick, Peter, 39, Co I, died May 23, diarrhea a.
6208, McCormick, W, 2, Co I, died Aug 10, diarrhea.
7730, McCracker, B, 7 artil, Co B, died Sept 3, scorbutus.
8644, McCrass J, 148, died Sept 13, scorbutus.
2279, McCrember, M, 85, Co I, died June 21, diarrhea c.
8507, McCullen D, 57, Co F, died Sept 12, diarrhea.
10778, McDavid, J, 5, Co D, died Oct 12, scorbutus.
6912, McDermott, P, 164, Co H, died Aug 28, scorbutus.
8969, McDonald, A, 24 battery, died Sept 16, diarrhea c.
7745, McDonald, A B, 85, Co E, died Sept 3, diarrhea.
7140, McDonald, B, 52, Co D, died Aug 20, diarrhea.
4013, McDonald, John, 164, Co E, died July 26, dysentery.
12138, McDonald, F, 16 cav, Co L, died Nov 23, scorbutus.
10092, McDonald, F,* 95, Co A, died Sept 29, diarrhea.
7259, McDonnell, Wm, 14 artil, Co D, died Aug 20, scorbutus.
8126, McDurie, C, 71, died Sept 8, scorbutus.
4089, McElray, John, 43, Co I, died July 27, diarrhea.
9581, McErmany, P, 7 artil, Co G, died Sept 23, diarrhea.
538, McFarland, A, 72, Co I, died April 2, pneumonia.
12478, McGilben, I, 170, Co B, died Jan 17, '65, scorbutus.
11116, McGowan, Wm, 6 artil, Co L, died Oct 18, scorbutus.

No. of Grave.

4001, McFadden, Jas, 20, Co F, died July 20, dysentery.
2666, McGaln, I, 90, Co H, died June 29, diarrhea c.
354, McGeatte, 52, Co, D, died April 2, pneumonia.
3551, McGlooney, H, 85, Co E, died July 18, phthisis.
2753, McGiven Wm, 158, Co B, died July 1, scorbutus.
8225, McGowan, F, 170, Co H, died Sept 9, diarrhea.
248, McGowan, John, 132, Co K, died March 30, diarrhea
1112, McGrath, M, 12 cav, Co E, died May 15, diarrhea c.
4709, McGuckier, A, 11 cav, Co C, died Aug 4, dysentery.
4904, McGuire, P, 140, Co C, died Aug 7, diarrhea c.
6827, McGuire, P, 16, Co C, died Aug 25, diarrhea.
3230, McGuire, Pat, 101, Co F, died July 12.
8754, McHarty, M, 69, Co A, died Sept 10, scorbutus.
3239, McKabe, J, 12 cav, Co F, died July 12.
1168, McKenley, J, 59, Co I, died May 14, diarrhea.
12604, McKenna, H,* 12, Co F, died Feb 16, '65, [illegible].
5359, McKeechay, J H, 85, Co F, died Aug 11, diarrhea
8290, McKinney, John, 82, Co D, died Sept 20, diarrhea.
10292, McLane, R, 42, Co E, died Oct 6, scorbutus.
10555, McLaughlin, O, 2, Co E, died Sept 30, scorbutus.
4268, McLorens, E, 20 cav, Co M, July 29, diarrhea.
6830, McLaughlin, J,* 63, Co D, died Aug 25, dysentery.
3611, McMahon, C L, 3 cav, Co E, died July 19, diarrhea
6814, McMurrier, Wm, 2 cav, Co L, died Aug 25, diarrhea
9959, McNamara, Wm, 2 artil, Co L, died Sept 28, diarrhea
10728, McNaminto, B F, 14, Co A, died Oct 13, scorbutus.
6406, McNulty, 85, Co E, died Aug 12, diarrhea.
3724, McPeak, W, 2 cav, Co D, died July 21, diarrhea.
7271, McPearson, Wm, 14 artil, Co M, died Aug 30, scorbutus.
6868, McQuillan, A, 6 artil, Co L, died Aug 13, diarrhea.
8889, McSorley, G W, 20, Co M, died Sept 16, scorbutus.
3127, Mead P, 1 artil, Co C, died July 10, diarrhea.
153, Megrawe, W H, 99, Co E, died March 25, pneumonia.
10599, Melin, A, 14 artil, Co L, died Oct 10, diarrhea.
11167, Mellins, W, 82, Co B, died Oct 10, dysentery.
2068, Menzie, A, 3 artil, Co K, died June 14, diarrhea, c.
6042, Meritt, H P, 76, Co F, died Aug 13, dysentery.
9353, Merkle, J, 15, Co A, died Sept 20, scorbutus.
11204, Merwin, A, 2 cav, Co A, died Oct 29, diarrhea c.
11214, Merz, F A, 5, Co I, died Oct 20, scorbutus.
8906, Messing, J, 39, Co A, died Sept 16, scorbutus.
10116, Messinger, C, 1 cav, Co L, died Oct 1, scorbutus.
6462, Messitie, J M, 11 cav, Co A, died Aug 22, scorbutus.
2523, Metcalf, A, 85, Co G, died June 26, diarrhea c.
3134, Meyers, F, 45, Co G, died July 10, pneumonia.
8852, Meyer, H, 66, Co F, died Sept 19, diarrhea.
11723, Meyers, I, 57, Co F, died Nov 1, scorbutus.
2899, Meyers, W, 54, Co C, died July 5, anasarca.
4520, Michael, ——, 66, Co A, died Aug 2, diarrhea.
11780, Micello, W, 2 cav, Co B, died Nov 3, fever intermittent,
3750, Mhikan, F,* 12 cav, Co A, died July 22, anasarca,
2709, Migner, H J, 54, Co D, died June 30, diarrhea c.
6292, Miard, F J J, 12 cav, Co A, died Aug 19, diarrhea.
168, Millens, Adam, 125, Co E, died March 26, diarrhea.
5520, Miller, A W, 52, Co D, died Aug 17, diarrhea.
4617, Miller, C, 111, Co I, died Aug 3, anasarca.
6469, Miller, Chas E, 21 cav, Co E, died Aug 22, diarrhea.
3521, Miller, F, 182, Co D, died July 18, dysentery.
5155, Miller, F, 99, died Aug 9, diarrhea.
6860, Miller, F, 15 artil, Co D, died Aug 26, diarrhea.
11516, Miller, G A, 152, Co C, died Oct 26, scorbutus.
6585, Miden, George, 61, Co F, died Aug 23, diarrhea.
11522, Miller, George, 1, Co G, died Oct 26, scorbutus.
3131, Miller, H, 1 cav, Co L, died July 10, scorbutus.
10627, Miller, H W, 98, Co E, died Oct 10, diarrhea c.
8278, Miller, J, 95, Co E, died Sept 9, scorbutus.
5521, Miller, Jacob, 39, Co I, died Aug 13, scorbutus.
628, Miller, J E, Fugler, 2 cav, Co M, died April 19, pneumonia.
9565, Miller, John, 12, Co A, died Sept 22, scorbutus.
708, Miller, O, 126, Co G, died April 24, dysentery c.
9926, Miller, Wm, 2 artil, Co C, died Sept 29, scorbutus.
8063, Millerman, G, 22 cav, Co B, died Sept 7, diarrhea.
8852, Mills, J J, 85, died Sept 15, scorbutus.
2844, Mills, S, 12 cav, Co A, died July 3, anasarca.
4874, Millspaugh, Fred, 9 artil, Co A, died Aug 6, scorbutus
79, Milliner, John, 95, Co G, died March 29, pneumonia.
1889, Mindler, Peter, 1 cav, died June 13, diarrhea c.
4771, Miner, J G, 24 battery, died Aug 5, diarrhea.
2618, Minie, F, 99, Co F, died July 20, dysentery.
8080, Mitchell, J, 125, Co E, died Sept 7, diarrhea.
9630, Mitchell, John, 120, Co I, died Sept 28, diarrhea.
7396, Mitty, Samuel, 12 cav, Co L, died Aug 30, diarrhea.
2486, Moe, John, 120, Co I, died June 25, diarrhea.
4121, Moffat, J, 7 artil, Co C, died July 28, diarrhea.
6720, Monaghan, ——, 66, Co D, died Aug 15, diarrhea
4441, Monihan, J, 85, Co G, died July 31, diarrhea.
4392, Monohon, J, 73, Co D, died July 31, diarrhea.
11537, Monohan, P, 88, Co D, died Oct 27, scorbutus.
4658, Monroe, J R,* 111, Co G, died Aug 3, scorbutus.
11961, Monroe, A J, 22, Co G, died Nov 11, scorbutus.
7453, Morgan, M, 76, Co B, died Sept 1, dysentery.

No. of Grave.
8241, Mousohilz, J. 65, Co D, died Sept 9, scorbutus.
1933, Monson, Wm, 11, Co G, died June 14, diarrhea.
7830, Monson, George, 6, died Sept 4, dysentery.
6635, Monta, Henry, 52, Co B, died Aug 14, dysentery.
3512, Montag, George, 39, Co B, died July 18, scorbutus.
11050, Moran, D G, 40, Co G, died Oct 30, diarrhea.
6565, Moran, Thomas, 85, Co A, died Aug 23, ictus solis.
7732, Moram M. J, 3 cav, died Sept 3, scorbutus.
11621, Moroarty, I, 1, Co M, died Oct 28, scorbutus.
10308, Morgraff, Wm, 64, Co H, died Oct 4, diarrhea.
8461, Moody, C R, 100, Co B, died Sept 11, scorbutus.
6423, Moody, Thomas, 147, Co B, died Aug 22, scorbutus.
3108, Moody, P, 3 artil, Co K, died July 10, diarrhea c.
3651, Moony, I, 188, Co D, died July 20, diarrhea.
8417, Mooney, J. 52, Co D, died Sept 11, diarrhea.
10883, Mooney, Thomas, 139, Co. F, died Oct 14, scorbutus.
2760, Moore, Asa, bu. l. r, 22 cav, Co E, died July 12, diarrhea c.
7656, Moore, C C, 1 cav, Co B, died Sept 3, diarrhea.
11829, Moore, C, 2 artil, Co B, died Nov 5, scorbutus.
658, Moore, Martin, 74, Co C, died April 21, diarrhea.
1094, Moore, S, 46, Co H, died June 7, diarrhea c.
442, Moore, T H. 5 cav, Co M, died April 9, pneumonia.
457, Moore, W H, 125, Co F, died April 9, diarrhea.
7767, Moore, John, 39, Co H, died Sept 4, dysentery.
9778, Moore, W S, 85, Co D, died Sept 26, scorbutus.
10781, Morgan, E, 14 artil, Co S, died Oct 12, scorbutus.
7563, Morgan, E J, 179, Co C, died Sept 2, dysentery.
10631, Mortross, D H, 7 artil, Co L, died Oct 10, diarrhea c.
624, Morland, H, 21 cav, Co H, died April 19, diarrhea.
4686, Morris, E, 7 artil, Co K, died Aug 4, scorbutus.
9944, Morris T, 65, Co C, died Sept 28, scorbutus.
3730, Morris, H, 71, Co F, died July 22, diarrhea.
8031, Morris, J, 5 cav, Co D, died Sept 6, scorbutus.
11226, Morris, J, 99, Co A, died Oct 20, scorbutus.
5865, Morris, J A, 7 artil, Co G, died Aug 16, enteritis.
6069, Morris, John, 70, Co B, died Aug 18, fever typhus.
12387, Morris, R, 66, Co G, died Jan 3, '65, scorbutus.
9373, Morris, L R, 85, Co B, died Sept 20, scorbutus.
7703, Morris, T A, † 111, Co E, died Sept 3, diarrhea.
4889, Morris, Wm † 102, Co G, died Aug 6, scorbutus.
8638, Morrison, W, 5, Co I, died Sept 13, gangrene.
9371, Morrison, W, 5 cav, Co I, died Sept 20, scorbutus.
7956, Morse, E, * 5 cav, Co L, died Sept 6, diarrhea.
12511, Morse I, 1, Co L, died Jan 23, '65, scorbutus.
617, Martin, Charles, 47, Co A, died April 18, diarrhea.
10625, Martin, G H, 7 artil, Co L, died Oct 10, scorbutus.
3181, Martin, Henry, 61, Co C, died July 11, scorbutus.
7672, Mortimer Wm, 5 artil, Co A, died Sept 3, diarrhea.
7079, Mosher, E, 9 artil, Co D, died Aug 28, diarrhea.
10152, Mosier, E, 9 artil, Co E, died Oct 1, diarrhea.
11010, Mosier, M W, 4, Co G, died Oct 16, scorbutus.
2872, Moses, L, 85, Co E, died July 4, diarrhea.
12003, Motts, C, 24 battery, died Nov 14, scorbutus.
8711, Moss, W S, * 7 artil, died Sept 14, scorbutus.
11468, Mulcahy, W, † 42, Co E, died Oct 26, diarrhea.
7997, Mulcohy, D D, 76, Co F, died Sept 6, scorbutus.
11368, Mulgrave, James, 2, Co C, died Oct 23, scorbutus.
12240, Mullen, Charles, 7 artil, Co I, died Dec 7, scorbutus.
11324, Muller P, 7, Co H, died Oct 23, scorbutus.
6985, Mulligan J, 24, Co H, died Aug 27, scorbutus.
11485, Mulsh R, 48, Co A, died Oct 26, scorbutus.
12155, Mullio, J, 82, Co G, died Nov 25, scorbutus.
4720, Mullington, C, * 6 artil, Co H, died Aug 4, bronchitis.
8370, Munger, D, 2 artil, Co C, died Sept 10, diarrhea.
8404, Murcheson, D, † 4 cav, Co D, died Sept 11, diarrhea c.
146, Murphy, John, 99, Co H, died Mar 25, diarrhea.
6804, Morphy, F, 61, Co B, died Aug 16, dysentery.
5918, Murphy, L, 170, Co E, died Aug 17, dysentery.
6550, Murphy, W S, 40, Co K, died Aug 23, diarrhea.
11803, Murphy, R, * 85, Co E, died Nov 4, scorbutus.
10200, Murphy, Martin, 2 cav, Co D, died Oct 2, scorbutus.
12118, Murray, J, 23 cav, Co F, died Nov 22, scorbutus.
11273, Murray, J, 47, Co I, died Oct 22, scorbutus.
3379, Murry, A, 118, Co C, died July 16, diarrhea.
8947, Murry, J, 20, Co C, died Sept 16, scorbutus.
11519, Murry, John, 63, Co F, died Oct 26, scorbutus.
6218, Muray, M, 11 battery, died Aug 20, dysentery.
11954, Murrey, M, * 98, Co D, died Nov 10, scorbutus.
1560, Morville, S, 1, Co C, died June 2, diarrhea.
12491, Muselman, J, 2, Co K, died Jan 20, '65, scorbutus.
1384, Myers, E, 154, Co D, died May 21, diarrhea c.
4958, Myers, H, 47, Co A, died Aug 7, diarrhea c.
9913, Myers, H, 2 cav, Co G, died Sept 28, scorbutus.
5000, Myers, H L, 147, Co H, died Aug 7, dysentery.
8970, Myers, J, 20 cav, Co M, died Sept 16, dysentery.
6221, Myers, Jas, 85, Co K, died Aug 20, dysentery.

8073, Neal, J, 22, Co E, died Sept 16, diarrhea c.
10587, Nedden, J, 62, Co A, died Oct 10, scorbutus.
7922, Nellman, A, 66, Co I, died Sept 4, diarrhea.
2341, Nelson, B, 39, Co A, died June 27, diarrhea.

No. of Grave.
6051, Nelson, John, 82, Co D, died Aug 18, diarrhea.
11362, Nelson, John, 2 artil, Co D, died Oct 17, scorbutus.
3022, Nevens, C, 100, Co F, died July 7, diarrhea.
2985, Newton, L C, 14 artil, Co I, died July 7, pneumonia.
4469, Newton, R J, 24 battery, died Aug 1, diarrhea.
4943, Newton, Sam'l D, 85, Co G, died Aug 7, diarrhea c.
6227, Newton, C W, * 85, Co K, died Aug 10, constipation.
2238, Nichols, A S, 2, Co C, died June 20, diarrhea c.
5109, Nichols, D A, 125, Co D, died Aug 9, diarrhea.
7059, Nichols, F E, * 7 artil, Co F, died Aug 27, diarrhea.
9417, Nolles, E, 14, Co A, died Sept 27, diarrhea.
11533, Nolan, M, 5, Co I, died Oct 26, dysentery.
11356, Nolan, Pat, 88, Co D, died Oct 23, scorbutus.
5050, Noonan, E, † 16 cav, Co L, died Aug 8, scorbutus.
4643, Noruman, J, 15 artil, Co H, died Aug 3, dysentery.
633, Northrop, D, 125, Co H, died Apr 19, diarrhea.
5928, Northrop V, 10, Co G, died Aug 17, enteritis.
17, Norton Alonzo, 154, Co A, died Mar 7, pneumonia.
4451, Norwood, D F, 85, Co E, died Aug 1, anasarca.
4735, Nostrand C, 2 artil, Co I, died Aug 4, scorbutus.
12241, Nott, S A, 15 cav, Co E, died Dec 7, scorbutus.
2549, Nutt, M, 126, Co D, died June 27, diarrhea a.
11681, Notterville, W, 8, Co G, died Oct 31, scorbutus.

5429, O'Brien, D, 63, Co F, died Aug 12, diarrhea.
9765, O'Brien, M, 1 cav, Co A, died Sept 25, scorbutus.
8036, O'Brien, S, 5 cav, Co L, died Sept 6, diarrhea.
1553, O'Brien, W, 8 cav, Co A, died June 2, diarrhea.
6270, O'Farrell, F, 69, Co A, died Aug 20, marasmus.
7359, Oeb, S, 46, Co D, died, Aug 31, dysentery.
3530, O'Connell, Thomas, 72, Co B, died July 18, diarrhea c.
2755, O'Dougherty, J, 51, Co F, died July 1, dysentery.
12397, O'Kay, Peter, 140, Co E, died Jan 5, '65, scorbutus.
9737, O'Kelf, C, 146, Co C, died Sept 25, diarrhea.
9916, Olahan, A, 65, Co F, died Sept 28, scorbutus.
10069, Olmstead, F H, 2 artil, Co I, died Sept 30, scorbutus.
6435, Older, W M, 16 cav, Co L, died Aug 22, dysentery.
1448, Omat M, 175, Co B, died May 23, diarrhea c.
12150, Onnia James, 7 artil, Co B, died Nov 24, scorbutus.
11404, O'Neil, J, 39, Co H, died Oct 24, scorbutus.
1988, Ostenhal, L, † 73, Co C, died June 15, diarrhea c.
12, Osterstuck, W, 154, Co I, died Mar 5, dysentery c.
6456, Osborne, R B, 22, Co E, died Aug 22, diarrhea.
2714, Osterhardt, B S, 120, Co C, died July 1, diarrhea.
12269, Ostrander, J, 86, Co A, died Dec 12, scorbutus.
108, Ostrander, J H, 120, Co F, died Mar 23, fever conges.
6526, Otis, John, 94, Co A, died Aug 21, scorbutus.
8768, Otto, Charles, 100, Co F, died Sept 14, scorbutus.
656, Otto, James L, * 10 cav, Co E, died April 21, diarrhea
5447, Owens, Ed, 47, Co G, died Aug 12, dysentery.
12227, Owens, Wm, 49, Co I, died Dec 5, scorbutus.
7564, O'Reilly, Philip, 2 artil, Co I, died Sept 1, diarrhea a.

9719, Page, O D, 146, Co F, died Sept 20, diarrhea.
2325, Palmer, P H, 85, Co D, died June 22, diarrhea c.
2582, Palmer, F, 17, Co F, died June 27, diarrhea.
6753, Pallette, D, 15 cav, Co K, died Aug 24, dysentery.
20, Palmiter, R, * 85, Co D, died March 7, dysentery c.
5958, Pangerin, Wm, 71, Co H, died Aug 17, enteritis.
3359, Pardy, E, † 85, Co K, died July 15, diarrhea c.
5710, Parish, D, 146, Co E, died Aug 15, scorbutus.
12180, Parker, F * 128, Co C, died Nov 27, scorbutus.
2092, Parker, J, 85, Co I, died June 17, diarrhea c.
2819, Parker, Isaac, 124, Co G, died July 3, diarrhea.
1392, Parker, J, 85, Co I, died May 26, diarrhea c.
2952, Parker, J, 154, Co G, died July 6, diarrhea.
3386, Parker, J, 15 cav, Co F, died July 16, diarrhea.
4752, Parkinson, A, 4 artil, Co C, died Aug 4, diarrhea c.
11956, Parks, Wm, 169, Co K, died Nov 11, scorbutus.
11218, Parsons W, 64, Co E, died Oct 20, scorbutus.
9487, Patterson, D, 76, Co D, died Sept 21, scorbutus.
5880, Patterson, E, 6 artil, Co M, died Aug 16, scorbutus.
3440, Patterson, Geo W, 15 artil, Co M, died July 17, dysentery.
6165, Patterson, H, 1 cav, Co C, died Aug 19, cerebritis.
6279, Patterson, I P, 85, Co F, died Aug 11, diarrhea c.
4768, Patterson, J H, 85, Co G, died Aug 4, dysentery.
10368, Paul P, 39, Co L, died Oct 8, scorbutus.
6695, Pease, Martin, 2 cav, Co C, died Aug 24, scorbutus.
2106, Peck, J G, 22 cav, Co F, died June 19, diarrhea c.
11630, Peckins, L, 24 cav, Co A, died Oct 28, dysentery.
11673, Pedro, Francis, 12 cav, Co E, died Oct 30, scorbutus.
1542, Pellett, Ed, 15 cav, Co I, died June 1, diarrhea.
3781, Pen, R, 2 cav, Co F, died July 22, dysentery.
2703, Penablin, John, 49, Co F, died July 12, dysentery.
11348, Pen, Charles, 6 artil, Co D, died Oct 22, scorbutus.
7398, Perkey, D, 85, Co B, died Aug 31, diarrhea.
7172, Perkins, J P, 24 battery, died Aug 29, scorbutus.
10562, Perry, A, * 33, Co G, died Oct 9, scorbutus.
4527, Perry, John, 84, Co D, died Aug 2, scorbutus.
7866, Perry, W, 2 cav, Co B, died Sept 5, diarrhea.
3721, Perry, William, 99, Co I, died July 21, phthisis.

No. of Grave.
12182, Perry, William, 79, Co A died Nov 27, scorbutus.
4517, Person, A, 61, Co H, died Aug 2, diarrhea.
3082, Persons, W B, 64, Co B, died July 9, diarrhea.
5224, Peters, Fritz, 52 Co C, died Aug 10, dysentery c.
3914, Peters, J, 114, Co F, died July 25, diarrhea c.
6684, Peterson, C, 178, Co I, died Aug 15, scorbutus.
9120, Peterson, H, 48, Co B, died Sept 18, diarrhea.
5302, Pettis, L P, 100, Co F, died July 14, diarrhea.
6527, Petree, Joseph, 81, Co I, died Aug 13, scorbutus.
486, Phelps, Mortin, 132, Co G, died April 9, pneumonia.
4235, Phillips, Geo A, 85, Co B, died July 29, diarrhea.
12481, Philips, I, 6 cav, Co E, died Jan 17, scorbutus.
7657, Phillips, H, † 100, Co H, died Sept 2, scorbutus.
3318, Phillips, R,* 85, Co B, died, July 14, diarrhea c.
4152, Pierce, Albert, 2 artil, Co M, died July 28, diarrhea.
2459, Pierce, Charles, 73, Co F, died June 25, pneumonia.
5371, Pierce H, 85, Co D, died Aug 11, dysentery.
6027, Pierce, J, 85, Co D, died Aug 18, diarrhea.
11663, Pierce, J H, 8 cav, Co 8, died Oct 30, scorbutus.
6005, Pierson, J, 76, Co B, died Aug 17, dysentery.
9422, Pilsbeck, E, 61, Co I, died Sept 21, diarrhea.
1532, Pinmon, John, 99, Co I, died May, 31, diarrabea.
9994, Pitts, G, 97, Co K, died Sept 29, diarrhea.
11441, Pivant, M, 61, Co D, died Oct 25, scorbutus.
6084, Place, E, 47, Co F, died Aug 18, diarrhea.
815, Plass, H, 120, Co G, died April 30, dysentery.
11379, Plunkett, J, 146, Co A, died Oct 24, scorbutus.
9549, Polack, J, 85, Co C, died Sept 33, dysentery.
4432, Pollock R, 16 cav, Co L, died July 31, anasarca.
1843, Pomroy, C, 21 cav, Co G, died June 11, diarrhea c
4531, Ponteis, G, 16 cav, Co K, died Aug 2, scorbutus.
1830, Poppie, W G, 85, Co B, died June 11, fever typhus.
11120, Pope, James E, 15 artil, Co A, died Oct 18, scorbutus.
12291, Post, H E, 135, Co G, died Oct 15, scorbutus.
12425, Post, J A, 94, Co E, died Jan 10, '65, debilitas.
6385, Potter, H, 48, Co E, died Aug 21, dysentery.
1582, Potter, W H,† 85, Co F, died June 3, '63, diarrhea c.
5116, Powell, George, 7 art, Co H, died Aug 9, dysentery.
2048, Powers J, 24 cav, Co H, died July 6, dysentery c.
3367, Powers, J, 10, Co K, died July 15, dysentery.
6390, Powers, O, 6 artil, Co I, died Aug 21, diarrhea.
6435, Pratt, B F, 146, Co G, died Aug 12, diarrhea.
1394, Presselman, C, 4 cav, Co M, died May 26, diarrhea c.
6523, Preston, H G, 9, Co G, died Aug 13, diarrhea.
1096, Price, David, 154, Co A, died May 14, anasarca.
12346, Price, J, citizen, died Dec 27, scorbutus.
6455, Pratt, P, 24 battery, died Aug 22, diarrhea.
1651, Priest, W, 132, Co E, died June 5, pneumonia.
1479, Pratt, G B, 10 cav, Co D, died May 30, diarrhea.
7964, Pringer, Thomas W,* 148, Co A, died Sept 6, diarrhea.
6914, Prow, John, 14 artil, Co L, died Aug 26, diarrhea.
9668, Prowman, S H, 149, Co H, died Sept 24, diarrhea.
9907, Puff, I, 15 artil, died Sept 28, diarrhea.
2221, Puley, Daniel, 115, Co I, died June 22, fever typhus.
720, Pullers, U H, 132, Co E, died April 25, diarrhea c.
2305, Putman, L, 14 artil, Co L, June 24, laryngitis.
1515, Purkey, Jacob, 84, Co B, died May 31, diarrhea c.
4063, Purstle, S, 49, Co A, died July 27, dysentery.
11432, Prunan, L,* 147, Co H, died Oct 24, diarrhea.

9046, Quackenbuss, P, 11, Co K, died Sept 17, diarrhea c.
8227, Quigley, J, 99, Co I, died Sept 9, dysentery.
6064, Quinn, Edser, 10 cav, Co B, died Sept 7, diarrhea.

4305, Randolph, —, 9, Co E, died July 30, debilitas.
11648, Rafrun, W, 59, Co C, died Oct 31, scorbutus.
512, Rafferty, M, 132, Co G, died Apr 12, dysentery.
2534, Rafferty, P, 5 cav, Co M, died June 26, dysentery c.
11330, Rafferty, T, 5 artil, Co B, died Oct 23, scorbutus.
4593, Raker, L, 1 cav, Co E, died Aug 3, diarrhea.
3751, Ranch, J, 100, Co D, died July 22, diarrhea.
10875, Randall, John, 99, Co A, died Oct 13, diarrhea.
6503, Ralinger, J, 47, Co D, died Aug 22, scorbutus.
6794, Ranglcart, John, 100, Co A, died Aug 25, diarrhea.
7778, Rastifer, John, 100, Co A, died Sept 4, dysentery.
4216, Rattery, John, 104, Co I, died July 29, dysentery
10937, Ray, C, 3 cav, Co B, died Oct 14, diarrhea c.
10240, Ray, R S, 154, Co A, died Oct 3, diarrhea.
4736, Raynard, F, 125, Co F, died July 30, diarrhea c.
3435, Raitersboom, J, 3 artil, Co K, died July 17, scorbutus.
2530, Ramsay, Isaac, 66, Co I, died July 4, diarrhea.
1265, Ramsay, Hiram, 51, Co K, died May 21, diarrhea.
2186, Reamer, W C, 111, Co B, died June 19, diarrhea c.
2820, Redman, J, 3 artil, Co K, died July 8, diarrhea c.
11095, Reddo, D V, 8 cav, Co M, died Oct 31, diarrhea c.
7232, Reed, F A, 64, Co E, died Aug 30, scorbutus.
8574, Reed, J, 140, Co H, died Sept 12, diarrhea.
498, Reed, S G, 13, Co D, died Apr 6, diarrhea c.
6041, Reed, W D, 146, Co H, died Aug 18, scorbutus.
10232, Reed, W J, 41, Co I, died Oct 2, diarrhea.
6402, Reed, William, 14 artil, Co I, died Sept 11, scorbutus.

No. of Grave.
7360, Reetz, John, 52, Co A, died Aug 31, diarrhea.
6094, Reeve, O, 152, Co C, died Aug 15, scorbutus.
1680, Reeves, John, 57, Co H, died June 6, scorbutus.
10467, Redmond, J, 43, Co C, died Oct 7, scorbutus.
10911, Regler, W H, 22 cav, Co M, died Oct 14, diarrhea c.
9122, Reffey, P O, 164, Co B, died Sept 18, diarrhea.
7195, Renback, C, 29, died Aug 29, diarrhea.
12455, Rebman, J, 59, Co C, died Jan 15, '65, diarrhea c.
8451, Renecrmane, J R, 5 cav, Co B, died Sept 11, scorbutus.
9320, Randall, A B, 76, Co F, died Sept 20, diarrhea c.
3352, Remsen, C, 2 cav, Co M, died July 15, scorbutus.
8269, Reynolds, O, 155, Co E, died Sept 8, scorbutus.
6799, Reynolds, O S, 85, Co E, died Aug 25, diarrhea.
10253, Reynolds, Samuel, 92, Co H, died Oct 3, diarrhea.
6350, Reynolds, William, 140, Co I, died Aug 21, dysentery.
6546, Ready, J D, 65, Co I, died Aug 23, dysentery.
4318, Rice, F,* 59, Co I, died July 30, diarrhea c.
3077, Rich, T D, 24 battery, died July 9, diarrhea.
12289, Rich, J, 82, Co C, died Dec 15, scorbutus.
3561, Richey, R, 66, Co C, died July 18, diarrhea.
2427, Rider, E, 178, Co E, died June 24, diarrhea c.
8005, Rhenevault, R H, 21, Co B, died Sept 6, diarrhea.
11904, Rehm, W, 7 artil, Co C, died Nov 7, scorbutus.
3391, Richistine, C,* 132, Co D, died July 24, diarrhea c.
6317, Richards, A, 52, Co D, died Aug 11, diarrhea.
5674, Richards, A, 41, Co E, died Aug 14, gangrene.
12243, Richards, A, 9, Co C, died Dec 7, scorbutus.
3682, Richards, H, 47, Co E, died July 21, dysentery.
7578, Richards, N J,† 146, Co C, died Sept 2, diarrhea c.
4240, Richardson, H M, 20 cav, Co M, died July 29, diarrhea c.
12193, Ricker, M, 2 artil, Co M, died Nov 29, scorbutus.
8155, Rickhor, J, 85, Co E, died Sept 8, dysentery.
415, Rikel, Robert, 125, Co G, died Apr 7, diarrhea c.
12382, Riley, I, 73, Co E, died Jan 2, '65, dysentery.
2885, Riley, J, 99, Co C, died July 4, dysentery.
5021, Riley, John, 176, Co C, died Aug 8, scorbutus.
6347, Riley, John, 39, Co D, died Aug 21, diarrhea.
11163, Ripley, F A, 152, Co C, died Oct 19, scorbutus.
11760, Ripp, W, 42, Co E, died Nov 3, scorbutus.
3514, Rising, C, 76, Co B, died July 18, diarrhea.
10310, Risley, George W, 47, Co G, died Oct 4, diarrhea.
2558, Ritcher, F,† 132, Co D, died June 27, dysentery.
7245, Ritson, S, 18 cav, Co E, died Aug 29, dysentery.
9224, Ritzmullin, John, 115, died Sept 19, scorbutus.
1775, Roach, F, 99, Co F, died June 9, anasarca.
1842, Roach, Charles, 85, Co E, died June 11, diarrhea c.
2354, Robberger, P H, 46, Co B, died June 23, diarrhea c.
11195, Roberson, C A, 122, Co B, died Oct 20, dysentery.
2346, Robertson, W H, 134, Co B, died June 23, diarrhea c.
8554, Robertson, W M, 96, Co B, died Sept 12, scorbutus.
9970, Robinson, H, 39, Co K, died Sept 28, diarrhea.
7607, Robinson, A, 111, Co I, died Sept 2, diarrhea.
3680, Robinson, H C, 95, Co I, died July 21, scorbutus.
6419, Robinson, John, 115, Co A, died Aug 22, diarrhea.
27, Robins, L,* 154, Co K, died March 8, pneumonia.
7663, Roberts, A, 173, Co C, died Sept 3, dysentery.
7585, Rockwell, N C, 14 artil, Co D, died Sept 2, scorbutus.
3813, Rockfellar, R E, 85, Co D, died July 23, diarrhea.
11342, Rockfellar, H, 15 artil, Co M, died Oct 23, scorbutus.
3959, Rock, F, 6 artil, Co F, died July 25, dysentery.
4350, Rogers, A, 7 artil, Co I, July 31, scorbutus.
6059, Rogers A, 125, Co H, died Aug 18, scorbutus.
5791, Rogers, O, musician, 85, Co F, died Aug 15, rheumatism
3011, Rogers, James, 132, Co H, died July 7, diarrhea.
4287, Rogers, H C, 85, Co C, July 30, diarrhea.
8369, Rogers, H J, 2 artil, Co E, died Sept 10, scorbutus.
4912, Rogers, M, 43, Co D, died Aug 6, anasarca.
7098, Rogers, O S,† 85, Co C, died Aug 29, scorbutus.
6824, Rogers, Thomas, 12, Co F, died Aug 25, diarrhea.
11772, Romer, F, 9, Co A, died Nov 3, diarrhea c.
8468, Rook, G, 6 artil, Co E, died Sept 11, scorbutus.
9963, Rooney, John, 152, Co G, died Sept 28, diarrhea.
9102, Rooney, M, 132, Co F, died Sept 18, scorbutus.
8922, Rooney, P, 2 artil, Co C, died Sept 16, dysentery.
5569, Root, A N, 85, Co C, died Aug 14, anasarca.
2998, Roots, W T, 120, Co H, died July 7, diarrhea.
1785, Root, Legrand, 24 battery, died June 8, pneumonia.
10278, Rose, A, 16, Co L, died Oct 2, scorbutus
9550, Rosecrans, J E, 125, Co H, died Sept 23, dysentery.
8171, Ross, C, 23 cav, Co A, died Sept 8, dysentery.
3874, Ross, F F, 111, Co I, died July 24, fever typhus.
5591, Ross, David, 27, Co D, died Aug 11, scorbutus.
6741, Ross, G, 76, Co K, died Aug 24, diarrhea.
9751, Ross, A, 1 cav, Co M, died Sept 25, scorbutus.
11963, Ross, J H, 121, Co G, died Nov 11, scorbutus.
5939, Rosenberger, John, 4, Co D, died Aug 17, enteritis.
3616, Rosser, Lewis, 84, Co A, died July 20, dysentery.
2924, Rosenburg, J, 30, Co A, died July 5, diarrhea c.
8767, Rosson, Charles, 24 cav, Co E, died Sept 14, diarrhea.
12269, Roswell, J, 93, Co K, died Dec 10, scorbutus.
727, Ross, Jacob, 151, Co A, died April 25, diarrhea c.

No. of Grave.

1940, Row, W J, 120, Co B, died June 14, diarrhea c.
5097, Roth, Louis, 39, Co D, died Aug 9, scorbutus
8504, Rothwell, M, * 20 cav, Co M, died Sept 12, scorbutus.
8722, Rouse, William, bugler, 12 cav, Co F, died July 21, diarrhea.
7709, Rowbotham, R, 11 cav, Co L, died Sept 3, scorbutus.
5857, Rowell, J E, 70, Co G, died Aug 16, marasmus.
8432, Rowell, L N, 99, Co H, died July 17, diarrhea.
59, Roberts, A B, † 8 cav, Co B, died March 18, pneumonia.
2609, Ruddin, C '20, Co H, died June 28, diarrhea.
867, Rudler, William 120, Co M, died May 3, dysentery.
40, Rue, Newton † 5 cav, Co A, died March 13, diarrhea c.
8667, Runey, F, 69, Co H, died Sept 13, diarrhea.
12535, Russ, John, 2, Co K, died Feb 10, '65, diarrhea c.
8856, Russell, J, * 7 artil, Co A, died Sept 15, diarrhea c.
5094, Ryan, D, 106, Co D, died Aug 8, diarrhea.
8599, Ryan, J, 95, Co E, died Sept 12, scorbutus.
8741, Ryan, J, 22 cav, Co E, died Sept 14, fever typhus.
7258, Ryan, Owen, 12, Co A, died Aug 30, diarrhea.
4762, Ryench, John, 66, Co I, died Aug 5, scorbutus.
6418, Ryson, John, 7 artil, Co L, died Aug 22 scorbutus.
6206, Ryne, J M, 9, Co E, died Aug 9, diarrhea c.
684, Rush, John, 111, Co E, died April 28, dysentery c.

7284, Sackett, R S, 85, Co G, died Aug 29, diarrhea c.
1929, Sadley, M, 77, Co H, died June 14, diarrhea c.
1580, Safford, B J, 24 battery, died June 12, dysentery.
11870, Salsbury, H, 1 artil, Co M, died Nov 6, diarrhea.
10652, Salisbury, E, 16, Co D, died Oct 11, scorbutus.
10923, Samlett, ——, 18 cav, Co I, died Oct 14, scorbutus.
10880, Samet, W, 15, Co H, died Oct 13, scorbutus.
6769, Sampson, J, 100, Co K, died July 22, diarrhea.
346, Sanders, Charles, * 9 mil, Co A, died Apr 12, fever remittent.
8818, Sanders, J, 99, Co C, died July 23, diarrhea c.
9857, Sanders, J, 12 cav, Co A, died Sept 27, scorbutus.
4428, Sandford, P O, 7 artil, Co L, died July 31, diarrhea c.
2341, Sanghin, J, 12 cav, Co F, died June 28, fever remittent.
7740, Sawyer, J, 2 cav, Co L, died Sept 8, diarrhea.
11202, Sayles, A, 22 cav, Co L, died Oct 21.
3612, Seaman, A, * 85, Co H, July 19, diarrhea.
10856, Seaman, A, 2 artil, died Oct 13, diarrhea.
1372, Sears, F, 2 cav, Co H, died May 25, dysentery.
6120, Seagher, J, 8, Co M, died Aug 19, dysentery.
4025, See, Henry, 11, Co K, died July 30, dysentery.
9824, Seeley, A J, 140, Co A, Sept 15, diarrhea.
11874, Seeley, C E, 15, Co H, died Oct 24, scorbutus.
4256, Seeley, Thomas, 100, Co F, died July 29, dysentery.
10027, Segam, Ed, 5 cav, Co K, died Sept 29 diarrhea.
4204, Seigler, George, 10, died July 29, diarrhea.
7458, Seigle John R, 120, Co K, died Sept 1, diarrhea.
11880, Selson, H, 59, Co C, Nov 6, scorbutus.
3457, Serrier, R, 40, Co C, died July 17, scorbutus.
1746, Serine, C, 4 cav, Co M, died June 6, diarrhea c.
629, Settle, Henry, 99, Co H, died April 19, diarrhea.
9628, Seyman, F, 1 cav, Co A, died Sept 27, diarrhea.
6951, Seard, Louis, 77, Co E, died Aug 17, marasmus.
6868, Schayler, J W, 21 cav, Co M, died Aug 26, pneumonia.
10794, Schadt, Theodore, 160, Co A, died Oct 12, scorbutus.
3557, Scheck, B, 2 cav, Co G, died July 18, diarrhea.
3190, Schemerhorn, H, 120, Co G, died July 12, diarrhea.
11965, Schempp, M, 7 artil, Co F, died Nov 11, scorbutus.
2795, Schermashie, B, 170, Co A, died July 2, dysentery.
1325, Schlotesser, J, 91, Co H, died May 24, dysentery.
11515, Schlotesser, J, † 1, Co L, died Oct 26, scorbutus.
9578, Schmaker, John, 39, Co B, died Sept 23, diarrhea c.
10291, Schmaley, J, 1, Co G, died Oct 16, scorbutus.
10550, Schmeager, A, 39, Co A, died Oct 9, scorbutus.
5311, Schneider, Charles, 39, Co A, died Aug 11, diarrhea.
8595, Schocknoy, T T, 24 battery, died Sept 12, scorbutus.
5796, Schofield, J, 7, Co H, died Sept 15, diarrhea.
2441, Scholl, John, 54, Co D, died June 25, scorbutus.
11422, Schriber, H, 59, Co I, died Oct 24, scorbutus.
7814, Schroder, G, 7 artil, Co E, died Sept 4, diarrhea.
8550, Schrum, J, 15 artil, Co K, died Sept 12, scorbutus
1070, Schriner, Wm, 20, Co B, died May 13, diarrhea.
4280, Schware, F, 12 cav, Co K, died July 30, diarrhea.
6613, Schwick, A, 66, Co G, died Aug 23, diarrhea.
4849, Scott, J C, † 85, Co K, died Aug 6, diarrhea c.
6857, Scott, P C, 14 cav, Co G, died Aug 26, dysentery.
8622, Scott, W W, 2 cav, Co F, died Sept 13, scorbutus.
8290, Sibble, W, 148, Co G died Sept 9, diarrhea.
4362, Sick, R, 5, Co E, died July 31, diarrhea.
4557, Sickler, E, 7 artil, Co E, died Aug 2, diarrhea.
3210, Sickler, A, 120, Co D, died July 12, diarrhea.
11959, Siddell, G, 40, Co H, died Nov 10, scorbutus.
12284, Simmons, A, 8 artil, Co H, died Dec 13, scorbutus.
6764, Simmons, C G, † 85, Co B, died Aug 21, diarrhea.
8316, Simon, H, 146, Co B, died Sept 10, diarrhea.
6224, Simmons, H L, † 85, Co E, died Aug 20, diarrhea c.
142, Simondinger, B, 155, Co I, died Mar 24, dysentery.
242, Simpson, D, 99, Co H, died Mar 30, fever congestive
6345, Sisson, P V, † 22 artil, Co M, died Aug 21, diarrhea.

No. of Grave.

10067, Shaat, J, 50, Co A, died Sept 30, scorbutus.
201, Shae, Pat, drummer, 61, Co M, died Mar 28, diarrhea c.
4801, Shaffer, M, 7 artil, died Aug 5, anasarca.
4581, Shaffer, J, 66, Co E, died Aug 2, diarrhea.
782, Shafer, H, 163, Co F, died Apr 28, diarrhea c.
6747, Shaughnessey, J, 6 cav, Co A, died Aug 24, diarrhea.
4446, Shannon, E, 6 artil, Co H, died Aug 1, anasarca.
6645, Shank, S W, 24 battery, died Aug 14, diarrhea.
290, Shaw, Alexander, 3 artil, Co K, died Apr 1, pneumonia.
9067, Shaw, T J, 15 cav, Co M, died Sept 24, diarrhea.
12814, Shaw, W, 7 artil, Co F, died Mar 25, diarrhea c.
7660, Shay, John, 69, Co B, died Sept 3, diarrhea.
3360, Sheldon, M, 7 artil, Co B, died July 15, dysentery.
4217, Shepardson, L, * 22 cav, Co E, died July 29, diarrhea.
5474, Shaw, J, 2 cav, Co E, died Aug 13, diarrhea.
7788, Shuter, Chas, 52, Co G, died Sept 4, diarrhea.
8325, Shaw, M, 76, Co D, died Sept 10, scorbutus.
9924, Sheppard, W H, 9, Co F, died Sept 28, scorbutus.
8205, Shever, H, 5 cav, died Sept 6, diarrhea.
10940, Sheridan, J, 2 cav, Co F, died Oct 14, scorbutus.
4076, Sherwood, J E, 76, Co G, died Aug 4, diarrhea c.
720, Shields, Richard, 132, Co F, died Apr 25, diarrhea c.
701, Shilts, E, 52, Co K, died Apr 23, catarrh.
10495, Shibler, George, 97, Co F, died Oct 8, scorbutus.
6206, Shindler, J, 15 artil, Co E, died Sept 6, diarrhea.
7437, Shirlock, R, 85, Co K, died Sept 1, diarrhea.
6837, Shipley, F, 85, Co D, died Aug 16, diarrhea.
2340, Shirley, P, 24 battery, died June 25, dysentery.
2151, Shats, C, 111, Co F, died June 18, diarrhea c.
5775, Shorty, Robert, 164, Co B, died Aug 15, diarrhea.
5343, Shotliff, J, † 7 artil, Co L, died Aug 11, diarrhea.
2975, Shults, John, 118, Co F, died July 7, scorbutus.
6623, Shultz, F, 70, Co F, died Aug 23, dysentery.
12194, Shultz, William, 7 art, Co C, died Nov 29, scorbutus.
11822, Shultz, C, * 60, Co F, died Nov 5, scorbutus.
11813, Shumaker, P, 100, Co K, died Nov 4, scorbutus.
11280, Sholipe, F D, 125, Co K, died Oct 22, gangrene.
2462, Shuster, —, 54, Co C, died June 25, dysentery a.
2922, Slater, F, 48, Co F, died July 5, diarrhea c.
700, Slater, John, 120, Co H, died Apr 23, debilitas.
12554, Slater, James, † 7, Co K, died Jan 27, '65, scorbutus.
11162, Slater, Richard, 2, Co E, died Oct 19, scorbutus.
12811, Sleight, C, 32, Co I, died Mar 24, diarrhea c.
10377, Sleat, William, 140, Co E, died Oct 5, scorbutus.
6819, Sloates, F, 76, Co F, died Aug 25, diarrhea.
10125, Slimp, W, 146, Co A, died Oct 11, scorbutus.
7028, Smades, W, 9, Co D, died Sept 2, diarrhea.
12083, Small, S, 53, Co F, died Nov 18, scorbutus.
7783, Smarty, John, 22 cav, Co G, died Sept 4, diarrhea.
7466, Smead, L, 18 artil, Co D, died Aug 31, dysentery.
762, Smalley, George, 140, Co H, died April 27, hydro-thorax.
12503, Smith, A, 7 artil, Co F, died Jan 21, '65, scorbutus.
11371, Smith, A, 9, Co A, died Oct 23, scorbutus.
7326, Smith, A J, 85, Co D, died Aug 30, diarrhea c.
802, Smith, Bernard, * 152, Co B, died April 29, diarrhea c.
1310, Smith, Benjamin, 2 cav, Co H, died May 23, fever typhoid.
2659, Smith, Charles, 61, Co A, died June 29, diarrhea c.
3785, Smith, Charles, 52, Co E, died July 21, dysentery c.
4534, Smith, Charles, 100, Co B, died Aug 2, dysentery.
7612, Smith, Charles, 15 artil, Co K, died Sept 2, scorbutus.
10052, Smith, Charles, 9, Co G, died Sept 30, scorbutus.
11283, Smith, E, 61, Co D, died Oct 22, scorbutus.
1819, Smith, F, 48, Co F, died June 10, diarrhea c.
1246, Smith, Frank, 99, Co I, died May 20, diarrhea.
11559, Smith, G R, 2 cav, Co H, died Nov 5, diarrhea.
3372, Smith, N, 9 cav, Co C, died July 15, diarrhea c.
1247, Smith, Henry, 132, Co C, died May 20, dysentery.
3238, Smith, J, 5 cav, died July 12.
3504, Smith, J, 4 cav, Co B, died July 18, diarrhea.
4834, Smith, J, 115, Co G, died Aug 6, diarrhea c.
9300, Smith, J, 52, Co A, died Sept 20, diarrhea.
10456, Smith, J, * 13 cav, Co D, died Oct 7, scorbutus.
12627, Smith, J, 46, Co E, died Feb 10, '65, debilitas.
1245, Smith, James, 20 cav, Co M, May 20, diarrhea.
7001, Smith, James, 6, Co A, died Aug 27, diarrhea.
11787, Smith, James, 57, Co B, died Nov 4, scorbutus.
7610, Smith, Jackson, 85, Co I, Sept 2, diarrhea.
11210, Smith, J, 52, Co A, died Oct 20, scorbutus.
395, Smith, John, 71, Co C, died April 1, diarrhea c.
534, Smith, John, 3 cav, Co E, died April 14, dysentery c.
5496, Smith, John, 41, Co E, died Aug 13, diarrhea.
6602, Smith, John, 66, Co F, died Aug 14, scorbutus.
6428, Smith, John, 95, Co D, died Aug 22, scorbutus.
10587, Smith, John, 69, Co G, died Oct 9, scorbutus.
5882, Smith, John J, 169, Co C, died Aug 16, dysentery.
11434, Smith, J M, 59, Co A, died Oct 25, scorbutus.
10079, Smith, K, 22 cav, Co K, died Sept 30, scorbutus.
5809, Smith, L A, 115, Co F, died Aug 8, scorbutus.
9973, Smith, Levi, 127, Co B, died Sept 28, diarrhea.
7706, Smith, John C, * 48, Co K, died Sept 3, dysentery.
2789, Smith, S, 11, Co I, died July 2, pneumonia.

No. of Grave.

6854, Smith, S A, 132, Co F, died Aug 16, marasmus.
6709, Smith, T, 147, Co E, died Aug 24, scorbutus.
6301, Smith, Thomas, 47, Co C, died Aug 21, scorbutus.
9490, Smith, T K, 2, Co E, died Sept 21, gangrene.
139, Smith, William, 99, Co H, died March 24, dysentery.
325, Smith, Wm, 3 artil, Co K, died April 2, diarrhea.
532, Smith, Wm, 104, Co A, died April 14, diarrhea a.
812, Smith, Wm, 106, Co B, died April 20, diarrhea c.
7550, Smith, Wm, 2, Co L, Sept 2, diarrhea c.
10104, Smith Wm, 76, Co K, died Oct 1, scorbutus.
12394, Smith, H, 7, Co C, died Jan 5, '65, diarrhea.
5705, Snedegar, A J, 111, Co D, died July 21, diarrhea.
7173, Snyder, A, 25, Co E, died Aug 29, fever typhus.
4148, Snyder, B, 2, Co B, died Aug 1, scorbutus.
10076, Snyder, Wm, 1 dragoons, Co E, died Sept 30, scorbutus.
1319, Sombeck, George, 52, Co I, died May 23, anasarca.
6169, Somers, John, 2, Co E, died Aug 9, debilitas.
2773, Sopher, James, 132, Co F, died July 2, dysentery.
2103, Sopher, S, 102, Co K, died June 24, debilitas.
4352, Sotter, J M, 47, Co C, died July 31, diarrhea.
3534, Southard, H, 5 cav, Co C, died July 18, debilitas.
11526, Southard, N, 2, Co H, died Oct 8, scorbutus.
11340, Southard, W A, 18, Co I, died Oct 23, gangrene.
2877, Soutter, Henry, 69, Co K, died July 4, dysentery.
8124, Southworth, R, 22 cav, Co E, died Sept 8, diarrhea.
10488, Skall, S, 7 artil, Co L, died Oct 7, diarrhea.
12029, Skeeley, T, 66, Co H, died Nov 15, scorbutus.
9954, Spark, G, 16 artil, Co C, died Sept 28, scorbutus.
6975, Sparks, E, 10, Co B, died Aug 27, diarrhea.
6421, Spaulding, H, 1 cav, Co F, died Aug 12, scorbutus.
5567, Spellman, John, 66, Co B, died Aug 13, scorbutus.
10712, Spencer, A, 93, Co D, died Feb 28, scorbutus.
10983, Sperry, A, 51, Co F, died Oct 16, scorbutus.
5532, Span, James, 147, Co H, died July 18, diarrhea c.
6982, Spanbury, S, 14 artil, Co C, died Aug 17, diarrhea c.
6821, Sprague, E H, 10 battery, died Aug 16, scorbutus.
3593, Sprague, J, 85, Co I, died July 19, diarrhea.
10730, Sprig, James A, 24 cav, Co E, died Oct 11, scorbutus.
4877, Sprink, A, 140, Co F, died Aug 6, dysentery.
9335, Strate, John, 15, Co A, died Sept 17, scorbutus.
889, Stacey, John, 99, Co I, died May 4, fever typhoid.
4574, Stadler, J J 39, Co A, died Aug 2, scorbutus.
10078, Stancliff, A B, 106, Co H, died Sept 30, scorbutus.
2570, Stanton, H H, 22, Co E, died June 27, diarrhea c.
5187, Stark, J D,* 100, Co A, died Aug 9, diarrhea.
11740, Starkweather, L, 146, Co E, died Nov 2, dysentery.
12650, Star, C, 15, Co D, died Feb 13, debilitas.
7381, Stanton, L H 7 artil, Co K, died Aug 31, dysentery.
2520, Stark, J H, 121, Co A, died June 26, diarrhea a.
1698, Stanley, J C,* 85, Co C, died June 7, pneumonia.
10290, St Dennis, L, 16, Co F, died Oct 4, scorbutus.
9963, Stewart, Peter, 5, Co B, died Sept 27, scorbutus.
7636, Stevens, E, 120, Co C, died Sept 2, diarrhea c.
95, Stevenson, Wm, 132, Co G, died March 22, fever typhus.
8782, Sternhoff, A, 15 artil, Co C, died July 22, anasarca.
4678, Stevens, John S, 100, Co F, died Aug 4, diarrhea c.
6530, Steinour, C, 7 artil, Co M, died Aug 13, catarrh.
7028, Stevens, Wm, 99, Co I, died Aug 27, scorbutus.
2543, Stead, J, 115, Co F, died June 27, fever typhus.
6531, Stebins, C, 85, Co C, died Aug 23, anasarca.
3872, Stevenson, W, 10, Co F, died July 24, dysentery.
6443, Stead, J, 15, Co D, died Aug 22, scorbutus.
2634, Stewart, John, 83, died June 15, dysentery.
1863, Stebbins, H, 85, Co B, died June 12, dysentery.
6049, Steinbrecht, D, 22 cav, Co C, died Aug 18, cerebritis.
10149, Stickler, E, 169, Co A, died Oct 1, scorbutus.
11755, Stivers, R, 111, Co F, died Nov 2, scorbutus.
7075, Still, D, 132, Co D, died Aug 28, dysentery.
6102, Stamp, W, 6, Co K, died Aug 18, diarrhea.
4193, Still, James, 164, Co E, died July 29, phthisis.
4385, Stillwell, S, 2 artil, Co E, died July 31, dysentery.
915, Stone, John, musician, 5 cav, Co C, died May 6, dysentery.
11048, Stoddard, L, 111, Co F, died Oct 17, diarrhea c.
6722, Stone, L, 24, Co E, died Aug 24, diarrhea.
2353, Stoup, J, 15, Co A, died June 16, diarrhea.
8415, Strue, G N, 1 artil, Co B, died July 16, diarrhea c.
6991, Storing, A, 85, Co B, died July 26, diarrhea c.
8520, Strain, N W, 2 cav, Co I, died Sept 12, diarrhea.
6305, Streeter, F, 76, Co F, died July 24, scorbutus.
4365, Storms, A N, 7 artil, Co I, died Aug 4, diarrhea c.
4798, Strale, J, 178, Co B, died Aug 5, scorbutus.
5342, Strater, George, 85, Co K, died Aug 11, scorbutus.
6988, Stratten, J H, 140, Co H, died Aug 27, dysentery.
11967, Strip, W,* 42, Co E, died Nov 11, scorbutus.
116, Streight, Lewis, 127, Co A, died March 23, pneumonia.
2401, Stratten, Charles, 125, Co K, died June 21, diarrhea c.
7845, Sturdevant, G, 15 cav, Co I, died Sept 4, diarrhea.
1994, Stutzman, P, 39, Co D, died Aug 17, marasmus.
6102, Stump, W, 60, Co K, died Aug 18, diarrhea.
11882, Styler, G W, 7 artil, Co I, died Nov 5, scorbutus.
9953, Sugheim, I, 5 a, Co B, died Sept 28, scorbutus.

No. of Grave.

640, Sullivan, Ed, 69, Co A, died April 20, diarrhea.
6048, Sullivan, M, 69, Co K, died Aug 18, cerebritis.
1492, Sullivan, Pat,* 99, Co H, died May 31, debilitas.
7728, Sullivan, P C,* 155, Co E, died Sept 3, diarrhea.
5440, Susear, Fred, 39, Co I, died Aug 12, fever typhus.
10661, Sutliff, E,* 15 cav, Co M, died Oct 11, diarrhea c.
1, Swarner, J H, 2 cav, Co H, died Feb 27, pneumonia.
4005, Swarner, J, bugler, 2 cav, Co H, died July 26, anasarca.
6166, Swartz, M, 2 cav, Co M, died Aug 22, diarrhea.
12267, Swager, G, 101, Co F, died Dec 12, dysentery.
2722, Sweeney, James, 155, Co I, died June 22, diarrhea a.
1875, Sweeney, M, 122, Co C, died Aug 16, marasmus.
8727, Sweet, E, 93, Co F, died July 18, scorbutus.
2921, Sweet, L, 4 artil, Co M, died July 5, diarrhea.
4960, Sylurs, S, 140, Co E, died Aug 7, diarrhea c.
12765, Swaneent, J, 2, Co A, died March 13, '65, diarrhea c.
10559, Stratton, E, 76, Co E, died Oct 10, scorbutus.

1934, Taylor, A, 2 cav, Co F, died June 14, diarrhea c.
4867, Taylor, C, 115, Co F, died Aug 6, diarrhea.
551, Taylor, Charles B, 154, died April 14, diarrhea.
11321, Taylor, D, 149, Co D, died Oct 22, scorbutus.
2742, Taylor, R H, 125, Co F, died July 1, diarrhea c.
493, Taylor, Thomas B, 10 cav, Co E, died April 11, rheumatism.
9993, Taylor, L B,* 147, Co K, died Sept 29, scorbutus.
12290, Taylor, W, 12 cav, Co A, died Dec 15, scorbutus.
12480, Taylor, W, 42, Co B, died Jan 17, '65, scorbutus.
10370, Taylor, W H, 7 artil, Co C, died Oct 5, scorbutus.
10738, Taylor, W H, 7 cav, Co C, died Oct 11, diarrhea c.
10157, Taylor, Wm, 22 cav, Co C, died Oct 1, diarrhea.
8961, Taylor, W W, 12, Co I, died Sept 16, scorbutus.
8988, Tarvis, G W, 1 dragoons, Co K, died Sept 17, diarrhea.
9480, Ture, W, 115, Co D, died Sept 21, diarrhea.
8681, Tambrick, A, 16 cav, Co A, died July 21, scorbutus.
3976, Tanner, M, 1, Co E, died July 25, diarrhea.
4126, Tonschivit, Ed, 15 artil, Co E, died July 30, dysentery.
7019, Tell, William, 59, Co C, died Aug 27, dysentery.
9143, Thompson, A, 9, Co D, died Sept 18, diarrhea.
193, Terry, Aaron J 12, Co K, died March 24, bronchitis.
9064, Teneyck, M, 14 artil, Co E, died Sept 17, diarrhea.
4909, Tewey, J, 99, Co H, died Aug 6, scorbutus.
6445, Terwilliger, D B, 85, Co D, died Aug 22, fever intermittent.
10352, Thomas, J, 2 cav, Co D, died Oct 5, dysentery.
8598, Thomas, H J 88, Co D, died July 19, dysentery.
3711, Thomas, W, 8, Co H, died July 21, diarrhea c.
4619, Thomas, J, 85, Co G, died Aug 3, fever typhus.
10361, Thearer, J, 1 battery, died Oct 5, scorbutus.
8161, Thompson, C W, 85, Co K, died Sept 8, diarrhea.
4781, Thompson, J, 89, Co H, died Aug 5, diarrhea.
5510, Thompkins, Ira, 6 art, died Aug 13, scorbutus.
6524, Thompson, P, 10, Co E, died Aug 13, scorbutus.
5730, Thompson, N B, 146, Co A, died Aug 24, scorbutus.
5784, Thompson, J, 104, Co G, died Aug 15, diarrhea.
2613, Thompson, T, 12 cav, Co F, died June 28, diarrhea c.
820, Thompson, Daniel, 142, Co E, died April 2, diarrhea.
8539, Thresh, G, 5 cav, Co K, died July 18, dysentery.
6147, Thruston, N E, 85, Co C, died Aug 9, diarrhea.
11235, Thornton, J, 14 art, Co L, died Oct 21.
6309, Thorpe, W C, 82, Co I, died Aug 20, diarrhea.
4393, Thurston, G W, 85, Co E, died July 31, dysentery.
12869, Thayer, G, 70, Co E, died April 22, '65, diarrhea c.
679, Thierbach, P M, 89, Co D, died April 22, fever typhus.
11280, Tilton, H, 24 artil, died Oct 20, scorbutus.
8283, Tillitson, N P, 51, Co A, died Sept 9, diarrhea c.
8849, Timerson, Wm, 2 artil, Co I, died Sept 15, diarrhea.
2680, Timmish, —, 85, Co C, died June 30, diarrhea a.
650, Tiner, David, 79, Co E, died April 21, debilitas.
10422, Townsend, W, 111, Co B, died Oct 6, scorbutus.
8068, Townsend, L, 22 cav, Co G, died Sept 7, dysentery.
3583, Townsend, John, 52, Co A, died July 24, diarrhea c.
635, Townsend, Geo M, 111, Co F, died April 14, diarrhea.
9050, Tohnson, F, 22, died Sept 17, diarrhea.
4774, Toney, L, 100, Co D, died Aug 5, scorbutus.
10727, Tolaf, Pat, 164, Co K, died Oct 11, scorbutus.
6583, Tonner, L, 5 cav, Co G, died Aug 16, enteritis.
6047, Tobias, A, 120, Co G, died Aug 18, dysentery.
2112, Toomey, J F,* 85, Co I, died June 17, diarrhea c.
12465, Tourrer, P, 99, Co B, died Jan 16, '65, diarrhea c.
12630, Toedt, H, 1, Co K, died Feb 10, '65, diarrhea.
12708, Tomlinson, W F, 22, Co G, died Feb 28, '65, diarrhea c.
8193, Tripp, Ira, 177, Co B, died July 12, diarrhea.
10412, Tripp, O S, 3 artil, Co K, died Oct 7, scorbutus.
9567, Truman, A M, 2 artil, Co D, died Sept 22, scorbutus.
7629, Trueman, E, 7 artil, Co G, died Sept 2, diarrhea c.
8544, Tremor, M, 76, Co F, died Sept 12, scorbutus.
7317, Trumpp, E, 22 cav, Co F, died Aug 30, debilitas.
3882, Trumbull H, 115, Co I, died July 24, diarrhea c.
7187, Travis, T, 8 cav, Co G, died Aug 29, diarrhea.
4052, Truesdale, W J, 85, Co H, died July 27, diarrhea.
8125, Trompter, F J 140, Co B, died July 16, wounds.
100, Tracey, Pat, 99, Co I, died March 22, fever typhus.

No. of Grave.
707, Turner, Wm,* 5 cav, Co G, died April 24, dysentery c.
7970, Turner, John, 40, Co A, died Sept 5, scorbutus.
11376, Turner, J, 22 cav, Co M, died Oct 24, scorbutus.
1688, Turner, Thomas, 16 cav, Co G, died June 6, diarrhea.
2120, Turner, J B, 85, Co C, died June 17, diarrhea c.
10535, Tuthill, C, 22 cav, Co G, died Oct 8, scorbutus.
9687, Tuthill, S D, 2 artil, Co M, died Sept 24, diarrhea.
10601, Tuft, E, 29, Co C, died Oct 10, dysentery.
7915, Turden, E S, 15 cav, Co D, died Sept 5, diarrhea.
7421, Turton, W F, 2 artil, Co I, died Aug 31, diarrhea.
8796, Tubbs, W H, 85, Co D, died July 22, diarrhea c.
8084, Tupple, H, 1 154, Co H, died July 9, pneumonia.
3129, Tucker, G, 120, Co D, died July 10, diarrhea.
2893, Tuttle, W, 48, Co K, died July 4, fever typhus.
10494, Tyrrell, I, 22 cav, Co A, died Oct 8, diarrhea.

4217, Uncer, James, 15, Co H, died July 29, diarrhea c.
416, Uber, Charles, † 14, Co A, died April 7, diarrhea c.
12401, Udell, J, 7 artil, Co H, died Jan 5, '65, scorbutus.
10887, Utmer, H, 15 artil, Co K, died Oct 14, scorbutus.
2317, Underburg L W, 77, Co G, died June 22, debilitas.
254, Underhill, H, 47, Co E, died March 30, fever intermittent.
1495, Underwriter, A, 62, Co F, died May 21, pneumonia.

1091, Van Clarke, Wm, 106, Co D, died May 14, diarrhea.
9087, Van Alien, C, 7, Co E, died Sept 18, dysentery.
1025, Van Buren, J W, 3 artil, Co K, died May 11, diarrhea c.
664, Van Buren, Henry, 3 artil, Co K, died April 21, diarrhea.
10071, Van Bethysen, H, 7 artil, Co I, died Sept 30, scorbutus.
12529, Van Bramin, T, 71, Co K, died Jan 27, '65, diarrhea c.
1577, Van Derbreck, A, 132, Co B, died June 8, dysentery.
8464, Van Dugen, 24 cav, Co M, died July 17, dysentery.
6561, Van Husen, C, 95, Co A, died Aug 23, diarrhea.
10656, Van Housen, B, 12 battery, died Oct 11, scorbutus.
3176, Van Haughton, J, 124, Co C, died July 15, diarrhea.
1418, Vanderbogart, W, 101, Co F, died May 27, diarrhea c.
8657, Vanarsdale, P, 1, Co G, died Sept 16, diarrhea.
8782, Vanalstine, H, 152, Co A, died Sept 14, scorbutus.
8806, Vanclack, F, 5, Co D, Sept 15, scorbutus.
7584, Vanvelzer, J M, 85, Co I, died Sept 2, dysentery.
7635, Vanburen, J, 15 cav, Co B, died Sept 2, diarrhea.
11446, Vanscott, L, 59, Co C, died Oct 25, scorbutus.
11596, Vanarnum, J, 5 cav, Co E, died Oct 28, scorbutus.
7051, Vanwagner, C, 2 artil, Co F, died Aug 25, diarrhea.
7244, Vanesse, M, 2 cav, Co K, died Aug 29, dysentery.
7252, Vanzart, Wm, 7 artil, Co E, Aug 30, diarrhea.
6477, Varney, C, 169, Co E, died Aug 22, diarrhea.
6634, Vanalstine, C, 7 artil, Co C, died Aug 23, dysentery.
3348, Vanest, J H, 14 artil, Co B, died July 15, diarrhea.
83, Vanvelsen, J, 120, Co A, died March 21, bronchitis.
2089, Vaughan, W H, 6 cav, Co K, died June 17, diarrhea c.
973, Vespers, James W, 85, Co D, died May 9, diarrhea c.
7506, Van Osten, C, 52, Co H, died Sept 1, diarrhea.
5661, Vencot, L, 2 cav, Co H, died Aug 14, scorbutus.
4196, Veil, William, 6 artil, Co F, died July 29, diarrhea c.
1539, Vernon, S, 2 cav, Co M, died June 1, scorbutus.
7816, Vincent, R, 178, Co I, died Sept 4, diarrhea.
2782, Vincent, Richard, 1, Co K, died July 2, diarrhea c.
2879, Vinsant, G M, 14 artil, Co I, died July 4, diarrhea.
2715, Vish, O, 178, Co E, died July 1, diarrhea c.
6525, Vibbard, George, 22 cav, Co E, died Aug 22, diarrhea.
10023, Voelling, H, 15 artil, Co C, died Sept 29, diarrhea.
4623, Vogie, Anton, 10, Co C, died Aug 3, dysentery.
5563, Voorhies, A H, 1 cav, Co H, died Aug 13, diarrhea c.
11507, Voorhies, E R, 85, Co C, died Oct 26, scorbutus.
6652, Voorhies, George, 85, Co C, died Aug 23, diarrhea.

1184, Walls, Peter, 4 cav, Co D, died May 18, diarrhea c.
6001, Wall, James, † 15, Co G, died Aug 7, scorbutus.
1398, Wallace, John, 11 cav, Co B, died May 26, diarrhea.
10214, Watt, H, 12 cav, Co A, died Oct 2, scorbutus.
9977, Watts, C, 6, Co C, died Sept 28, diarrhea c.
10118, Waters, A L, 8 cav, Co F, died Oct 4, dysentery.
10477, Warner, Charles L, 2 cav, Co D, died Oct 7, diarrhea c.
4026, Warren, L, 95, Co I, died July 26, dysentery.
7851, Warner, P P, 14 artil, Co M, died Aug 31, diarrhea.
7114, Warner, A J, 76, Co F, died Sept 1, diarrhea c.
12419, Warner, Luther, 12 cav, Co A, died Jan 9, '65, diarrhea c.
10543, Ward, Patrick, 85, Co C, died Oct 8, diarrhea.
5127, Ward, J, 99, Co G, died Aug 9, ascites.
10920, Ward, J, 40, Co H, died Oct 14, anasarca.
2238, Ward, H, 95, Co I, died June 20, debilitas.
400, Ward, W A, 99, Co B, died April 6, diarrhea.
12516, Warden, H B, 5, Co B, died March 25, '65, diarrhea c.
9858, Walters, D, 125, Co E, died Sept 27, scorbutus.
1657, Walters, Nelson, † 120, Co K, died June 2, diarrhea c.
8381, Walterhouse, Ed, 9, Co I, died July 16, dysentery.
2827, Wallace, J, 2 cav, Co M, died July 3, pneumonia.
8939, Watson, G, 6 artil, Co C, died Sept 16, scorbutus.
10965, Watson, James, 15 artil, Co M, died Oct 15, scorbutus.
6947, Watson, T, 99, Co I, died Aug 26, dysentery.

No. of Grave.
9356, Wade, M, 14 artil, Co D, died Sept 20, diarrhea.
8146, Walker, J, 2 artil, Co D, died Sept 8, diarrhea.
8198, Wall, J, 61, Co I, died Sept 8, diarrhea.
7276, Warhurst, Samuel, 7 artil, Co I, died Aug 30, diarrhea.
3731, Washington, I, 76, Co G, died July 21, scorbutus.
5679, Washburn, H, 5 cav, Co D, died Aug 14, scorbutus.
2023, Wagner, C, 79, Co E, died June 15, diarrhea c.
10686, Wagner, C, 93, Co K, died Oct 11, scorbutus.
11001, Warren, P, 7 artil, Co G, died Oct 16, ulcus.
6537, Warren, E, 22 cav, Co L, died Aug 23, scorbutus.
4120, Warren, George R, 2, Co F, died July 25, scorbutus.
11082, Warrell, E C, † 57, Co I, died Oct 17, scorbutus.
11945, Waterman, S, 169, Co K, died Nov 10, scorbutus.
6978, Waldron, N, 146, Co A, died Aug 27, dysentery.
7249, Walz, M, 14 artil, Co I, died Aug 30, diarrhea.
6125, Walling, George, 76, Co E, died Aug 22, scorbutus.
6046, Watchner, J, † 119, Co G, died Aug 18, scorbutus.
4060, Wails, C H, 109, Co K, died July 27, diarrhea.
3336, Walser, John, 15 artil, Co D, died July 15, diarrhea.
1564, Walcott, G P, 67, Co D, died June 2, debilitas.
2291, Wales, J, † 85, Co D, died June 22, diarrhea c.
1537, West, James, 3 artil, Co H, died June 1, diarrhea.
9572, West, T, 13 cav, Co F, died Sept 23, diarrhea.
3964, West, William, 152, Co E, died July 25, scorbutus.
759, West, James, † 2 cav, Co E, died April 25, dysentery.
10363, Weston, L, 115, Co F, died Oct 4, diarrhea.
9731, Webster, G, 29, Co C, died Sept 25, diarrhea.
5593, Webster, E, 76, Co E, died Aug 14, scorbutus.
1598, Webster, James, 137, Co C, died June 4, diarrhea c.
9889, Wendle, John, 7 artil, Co E, died Sept 27, scorbutus.
9941, Wellstraff, C, 100, Co D, died Sept 28, scorbutus.
10013, Welch, W, 76, Co G, died Sept 29, scorbutus.
5030, Welch, C, 3 cav, Co B, died Aug 8, diarrhea.
8555, Welber, E O, 120, Co K, died Sept 15, diarrhea.
8268, Weil, E C, 164, Co B, died Sept 8, dysentery.
7561, Welson, James H, 74, Co K, died Sept 2, dysentery.
8177, Welch, C, 39, Co H, died Sept 8, diarrhea.
5181, Welch, E, 24 battery, died Aug 9, dysentery.
6692, Welch, J, 5 cav, Co K, died Aug 24, scorbutus.
2310, Welsh, L, 146, Co B, died June 22, diarrhea c.
8855, Welber, E G, 120, Co K, died Sept 15, diarrhea c.
9428, Weaver, J, 1 cav, Co E, died Sept 21, diarrhea.
7078, Weaver, B S, 96, Co I, died Aug 28, diarrhea.
9448, Webber, C H, 65, Co C, died Sept 21, diarrhea.
9506, Westerfield, P S, 7 artil, Co B, died Sept 22, scorbutus.
8731, Werting, John, 52, Co D, died Sept 14, scorbutus.
7987, Wellington, G R, 12 cav, Co A, died Sept 6, diarrhea.
8204, Weeks, J, 7, Co G, died Sept 8, diarrhea.
7472, Wells, Jeff, 9, Co H, died Sept 1, diarrhea.
12036, Wells, E, 69, Co K, died Nov 16, scorbutus.
7667, Weismere, H, 32, Co I, died Sept 3, fever typhus.
4915, Wedder, N C, 184, Co E, died Aug 6, dysentery.
11061, Wedder, C M, 22 cav, Co G, died Oct 17, dysentery.
11397, Westbrook, D, 155, H, died Oct 21, debilitas.
6927, Weafer, Charles, 115, Co A, died Aug 26, diarrhea.
7256, Wertz, James, 12 cav, Co I, died Aug 30, debilitas.
6370, Webb, M E, 14 art, Co F, died Aug 21, scorbutus.
11127, Welch, J, 5 cav, Co D, died Oct 18, diarrhea c.
6302, Welber, J, 6 artil, Co E, died Aug 17, diarrhea.
4272, Weller, W H, 85, Co E, died July 29, diarrhea.
3235, Westfall, John, 151, Co H, died July 12.
265, Weldon, Edson, 20 cav, Co M, died March 31, dysentery c.
507, Westbrop, H, 125, Co B, died April 12, diarrhea c.
6755, Webster, H, 22 cav, Co A, died Aug 24, scorbutus.
10303, Weston, L, 115, Co F, died Oct 4, scorbutus.
7543, Whitmore, D, 140, Co I, died Sept 2, dysentery.
10423, Wharton, J R, 5 cav, Co L, died Oct 6, scorbutus.
9743, Whittle, J C, 85, Co E, died Sept 25, dysentery.
9678, Whertmour, M, 15 art, Co M, died Sept 13, diarrhea.
8611, Whipple, M, 22 cav, Co D, died Sept 13, diarrhea c.
8680, White, James, 1 dragoons, Co D, died Sept 13, scorbutus.
11879, White, L, 8 artil, Co G, died Nov 6, diarrhea.
3024, White, E, 10 cav, Co D, July 8, dysentery.
8702, Whiting, M, 85, Co D, died Sept 15, scorbutus.
7417, Whitney, John, 129, Co K, died Aug 31, diarrhea.
6207, Whitney, J, 104, Co E, died Aug 10, diarrhea c.
10972, Whitman, J, 16, Co H, died Oct 15, scorbutus.
12049, Whitmans, F, 66, Co E, died Nov 16, scorbutus.
11724, Whitbeck, J,* 20, Co D, died Nov 1, diarrhea c.
6611, Wheeler, D, 147, Co H, died Aug 23, diarrhea c.
5770, Whitmore, O B, 40, Co A, died Aug 15, dysentery.
4155, Whitlock, William, 14 artil, Co I, died July 28, diarrhea.
1123, Wilson, James, 132, Co K, died May 16, pneumonia.
3757, Wilson, John, 95, Co A, died July 22, diarrhea.
6832, Wilson, M, 2 artil, Co H, died Aug 25, scorbutus.
11983, Wilson, W, 155, Co H, died Nov 13, dysentery.
5870, Wilson, A J, 57, Co A, died Aug 16, diarrhea c.
1645, Wilson, D, 48, Co H, died June 5, dysentery.
6233, Windness, A, 15 artil, Co C, died Aug 20, wounds.
4080, Williams, F, 125, Co A, died July 27, diarrhea.
4022, Williams, Ed, 42, Co A, died Aug 2, diarrhea.

No. of Grave.
11130, Williams, H, 2 cav, Co M, died Oct 18, scorbutus.
12697, Williams, S, 94, Co I, died Feb, 23, scorbutus.
9516, Williams, L D, 85, Co G, died Sept 22, diarrhea.
8478, Wilcox, T E, 85, Co B, died Sept 11, scorbutus.
7945, Williams, James, 63, Co G, died Sept 5, diarrhea.
4603, Williams, George,* 1 cav, Co K, died Aug 3, scorbutus.
4701, Williams, John, 52, Co K, died Aug 4, scorbutus.
3947, Williams, O, 24 battery, died July 25, diarrhea.
1567, Williams H, 9 state inf, Co A, died June 2, pneumonia.
6861, Williams, L, 16, Co A, died Aug 26, scorbutus.
7112, Williams, J B, 24 cav, Co C, died Aug 28, dysentery
6219, Williams, C E, 85, Co E, died Aug 20, anasarca.
3069, Winn, P, 20 cav, Co M, died July 9, diarrhea.
3273, Wicks, D, 63, Co D, died July 13, diarrhea c.
1938, Wilcox, Geo, 12 cav, Co F, died June 14, fever remittent.
2044, Wilcox, R, 14, died June 15, diarrhea.
9496, Wilcox, W, 43, Co G, died Sept 21, diarrhea c.
3570, Wilcox, J, 85, Co D, July 19, scorbutus.
11111, Wilcox, H R, 55, Co C, died Oct 18, scorbutus.
11428, Wilcox, C, 5 cav, Co G, died Oct 24, diarrhea c.
12607, Wiley, I, 59, Co B, died Feb 7, diarrhea c.
10122, Willis, J, 121, Co G, died Oct 1, scorbutus.
9057, Willsey, D, 7 artil, died Sept 17, scorbutus.
8729, Wiggins, James, 52, Co D, died Sept 14, scorbutus.
7980, Winn, James, 7 artil, Co I, died Sept 6, scorbutus.
8208, Will, E C, 164, Co B, died Sept 8, dysentery.
7622, Wiley, W, 115, Co G, died Sept 2, diarrhea c.
8728, Wilkey, S, 8, Co B, died July 21, dysentery.
10977, Wilkinson, J N,* 42, Co A, died Oct 15, scorbutus.
6063, Wicks, Frank, 1 artil, Co K, died Aug 14, diarrhea.
11474, Winney, G A, 103, Co D, died Oct 25, dysentery.
11520, Winter, G, 10 cav, Co L, died Oct 26, scorbutus.
11689, Wilds, J, 154, Co B, died Oct 31, diarrhea c.
7122, Winser, J, 117, Co I, died Aug 28, diarrhea,
7581, Wood, E G, 24 battery, died Sept 2, diarrhea,
3607, Wood, F, 5 cav, Co I, died July 19, diarrhea.
9874, Wood, H, 115, Co G, died Sept 27, scorbutus.
10063, Wood, H, 15, Co D, died Sept 30, scorbutus.

No. of Grave.
9715, Wood, J, 10 cav, Co M, died Sept 25, scorbutus.
7686, Wood, John, 97, Co D, died Sept 3, diarrhea.
3881, Wood, M, 111, Co H, died July 24, diarrhea c.
6039, Wood, J S, 6 artil, Co A, died Aug 8, diarrhea c.
9132, Woolhenney, D M, 3 cav, Co M, died Sept 18, diarrhea.
10141, Wood, W J, 95, Co H, died Oct 1, scorbutus.
8382, Woodworth, B, 56, Co D, died Sept 10, dysentery.
7884, Woodland H, 1, Co I, died Sept 5, [illegible].
5626, Woodburn, D F, 8 cav, Co E, died Aug 15, scorbutus.
12356, Wooley, G C, 7 artil, Co K, died Dec 30, scorbutus.
11801, Wolf, F, 88, Co D, died Nov 5, scorbutus.
11031, Wolfe, W, 2 artil, Co M, died Oct 16, scorbutus.
6130, Wolfe, Fred,* 24 cav, Co E, died Aug 19, debilitas.
691, Wolfram, A, 52, Co G, died April 16, diarrhea c.
4847, Wright, Charles S, 118, Co E, died Aug 6, diarrhea c.
10941, Wright, D, 41, Co G, died Oct 14, scorbutus.
5126, Wright, J J, 118, Co I, died Aug 9, scorbutus.
4281, Wing C, 39, Co E, died July 30, diarrhea.
7784, Wuelinger, John, 86, Co G, died Sept 4, diarrhea.
4589, Wyatt, James, 147, Co G, died Aug 2, diarrhea.
7334, Wyncoop, G, 12 cav, Co H, died Aug 30, scorbutus.
2104, Winegardner, L, 18, Co G, died June 17, diarrhea c.

7433, Yales, W G, 71, Co H, died, Sept 1, diarrhea.
4984, Yencer, J D, 24 battery, died Aug 7, dysentery.
12501, Yeonnard, G, 7, Co A, died Jan 21, diarrhea.
6559, Young C, 41, Co D, died Aug 23, scorbutus.
5598, Young, Charles, 15, Co C, died Aug 14, scorbutus.
8224, Young, E, 2 artil, Co L, died Sept 8, diarrhea c.
1306, Young, Eugene, 111, Co G, died May 23, diarrhea.
8723, Young, George, 22, Co H, died Sept 14, diarrhea.
6946, Young, J, 1st cav, Co B, died Aug 26, diarrhea.
7411, Young, T B, 148, Co A, died Aug 31, diarrhea.
10451, Yonker, W, 10 artil, Co B, died Oct 7, diarrhea.

7480, Zaphan, H P, 7 artil, Co E, died Sept 1, scorbutus.
12204, Zoller, F W, 40, Co D, died Dec 1, scorbutus.
12617, Zeigler, S, 145, Co G, died Feb 9, 65, scorbutus.

NORTH CAROLINA.

1596, Barker, J, 2, Co F, died June 3, dysentery.
819, Briggs, Wilson, 1, Co A, died May 3, dysentery c.

275, Collowill, B, 2, Co F, died March 31, fever congestive.
475, Cox, William, C, 2, Co F, April 9, fever intermittent.
864, Check, W F,* 2, Co F, died May 8, diarrhea c.

144, Dunbar, Alex, 2, Co F, died March 25, diarrhea c.

1057, Miller, J, drummer, 2, Co D, died May 13, phthisis.
10705, Masey, Henry, 7, died Oct 11, diarrhea.
11844, Moss, Wm, 1, Co F, died Nov 5, scorbutus.

8690, Norfield, Warren, 1, Co G, died Sept 14, diarrhea.

370, Stone, Jno A, 2, Co F, died April 5, diarrhea a.
2636, Smith, Jas, 2, Co F, died June 29, diarrhea c.
4599, Smith, Geo, 2, Co E, died Aug 5, scorbutus.

333, Turner, F, 2, Co I, died April 2, diarrhea a.
798, Turner, H, 1 colored, Co I, died April 29, diarrhea a.

204, Weeks, Nathan, 2, Co F, died March 28, diarrhea c.
712, Williams, Thos, 2, Co D, died April 24, diarrhea.

OHIO.

12846, Akers, J W, 4, Co B, died April 24, '65, diarrhea.
251, Arther, George, 7, Co B, died March 30, diarrhea.
789, Arrowsmith, W R, 45, Co K, died April 28, diarrhea c.
1118, Ames, George, 100, Co K, died May 15, dysentery.
1530, Allen, W, 45, Co B, died June 1, diarrhea c.
1569, Alinger, D, 51, Co C, died June 2, diarrhea c.
1724, Anderson, D, 111, Co B, died June 8, diarrhea.
1779, Augustus, T, 89, Co K, died June 9, pneumonia.
1805, Akers, A A, 94, Co F, died June 10, anasarca.
2040, Aldridge, C W, 83, died June 15, pneumonia.
2935, Adam, Miller, 101, Co I, died July 5, debilitas.
8046, Anderson, R, 93, Co C, died July 8, diarrhea.
3197, Aldbrook, C W, 60, died July 12, diarrhea.
8485, Arthur, J C, 89, Co A, died July 17, diarrhea.
8852, Armebrish, A, 21, Co A, died July 24, scorbutus.
8982, Almond A, 72, Co A, died July 25, diarrhea.
4520, Arnold, Charles, 9 cav, Co G, died Aug 2, diarrhea.
4990, Alles, T G, 20, Co I, died Aug 7, diarrhea.
6048, Andrews, Samuel, Co G, died Aug 8, diarrhea c.
6422, Adams, E, 2 cav, Co C, died Aug 22, scorbutus.
7429, Allen, A B,* 121, Co C, died Aug 31, scorbutus.
7482, Alward, A, 183, Co B, died Sept 1, ic us rolis.
7736, Arthur, J, 69, Co I, died Sept 3, debilitas.
7843, Arne, I, 64, Co D, died Sept 4, diarrhea.
9818, Alown A, 34, Co D, died Sept 26, diarrhea.
10393, Andrews, J R, 63, Co K, died Oct 6, diarrhea c.
10425, Adams, J, 122, Co I, died Oct 6, diarrhea.
10874, Allen, James C, 91, Co F, died Oct 13, scorbutus.
11198, Andermill, John, 24, Co K, died Oct 20, scorbutus.
12495, Allen, J W,* 1, Co G, died Jan 20, '65, scorbutus.

188, Balel, W T, 45, Co F, died March 27, diarrhea.
207, Bodin, Thomas S, 44, died March 28, dysentery a.
691, Beaver, George E, 111, Co B, died April 23, fever typhus.
829, Beeman, Richard, 125, Co E, died May 1, dysentery.
861, Biddinger, M musician, 94, Co K, died May 3, diarrhea a.
952, Brannigan, James, 82, Co F, died May 8, diarrhea.
1094, Bisugy, S, 70, Co B, died May 14, diarrhea c.
1212, Botkins, A, S, 45, Co G, died May 19, debilitas.
1226, Black, G W, 99, Co F, died May 20, diarrhea.
1366, Bates, L B, 1 cav, Co A, died May 25, dysentery.
1368, Botkin, W, 45, Co K, died May 25, anasarca.
1376, Baldwin, N, 9 cav, Co F, died May 26, dysentery.
1385, Bowers, James, 89, Co A, died May 26, marasmus.
1468, Boyd, H J, 7, Co H, died May 30, diarrhea.
1602, Bowman, John, 2, Co C, died June 4, diarrhea c.
1609, Bryan, E, 16, Co C, died June 4, diarrhea c.
1781, Balcom, H, 19, Co F, died June 9, pneumonia.
1919, Brownlees, John, 7, Co I, died June 14, anasarca.
1937, Brooks J, 135, Co I, died June 14, diarrhea a.
1970, Bolton, W J, 45, Co F, died June 15, anasarca.
1991, Bartholomew, E W, 205, Co C, died June 15, debilitas.
2065, Belding, F, 105, Co D, died June 16, diarrhea c.
2067, Brookheart, W, 45, Co I, died June 16, diarrhea c.
2087, Benor, P, 100, Co E, died June 17, scorbutus.
2110, Bishop, S, 49, Co K, died June 17, diarrhea c.
2170, Berry, J C, 90, Co F, died June 19, diarrhea c.
2264, Beers, A, 45, Co A, died June 20, diarrhea.
2292, Burnham, W, 1 artil, Co K, died June 21, anasarca.
2415, Bird, J, 45, Co A, died June 24, diarrhea c.
2402, Bratt, G, 21, Co G, died June 23, fever remittent.

No. of Grave.

2599, Boughfman, J, 39, Co C, died June 28, anasarca.
2696, Brandon, John, 15, Co F, died June 30, pneumonia.
3053, Barnes, V H, 92 Co H, died July 9, diarrhea.
3245, Brown, Charles 23, Co D died July 12, diarrhea.
3299, Burns, M G, 111 Co B, died July 13, diarrhea.
36 8, Brackneck H, 7 cav, Co A, died July 19, diarrhea.
3656, Bogart, John, 9 Co G, died July 20, scorbutus.
3706, Boutell, C, 6, Co G, died July 21, diarrhea.
3756, Batch, O, 45, Co I, died July 22, diarrhea.
3831, Bowman, S, 51, Co K, died July 23, dysentery.
4071, Borgkway, M, 2 artil, Co D, died July 27, dysentery.
4279, Boyle, W H, 11, Co H, died July 30, diarrhea.
4681, Britt n, B H, 125, Co H, died Aug 4, rheumatism.
4968, Berdy, M J, 45, Co D, died Aug 7, scorbutus.
5138, Buckle, John J, 126, Co E, died Aug 9, diarrhea.
5219, Brabham, George, 9 cav, Co B, died Aug 10, scorbutus.
5498, Baldwin, George, 9 cav, Co G, died Aug 13, diarrhea c.
5623, Bonestine, W H,* 107, Co I died Aug 14 catarrh.
5656, Barea, J M, 121, Co K, died Aug 14, diarrhea.
5758, Balmet, J, 19, Co I, died Aug 15, scorbutus.
5771, Bratch, E 10 cav, Co I, died Aug 15, dysentery.
5819, Pond, S F, 123, Co B, died Aug 16, marasmus.
5825, Boyle, H, 130, Co B, died Aug 16, marasmus.
5937, Bower F, 61, Co I died Aug 17, dysentery.
5985, Birch L F, 31, Co H, died Aug 17, marasmus.
6008, Bowman A, 104, Co E, died Aug 17, diarrhea.
6 20, Bright, N, 6, Co E, died July 17, dysentery.
6152, Brown, O S 111, Co F, died Aug 18, scorbutus.
6889, Baren, T J,* 89, Co A, died Aug 25 scorbutus.
7280, Barrett, S C, 26, Co F, died Aug 30, diarrhea.
7283, Beil, A, 70, Co B, died Aug 30, diarrhea.
7484, Baxter, P D, 121, Co D, died Sept 1, scorbutus.
7490, Brenning, C, 14 Co G, died Sept 1, dysentery.
7529, Brown W, 26, Co G, died Sept 1, scorbutus.
7806, Bear, E, 33, Co A, died Sept 4, dysentery.
7953, Bender C, 54, Co C, died Sept 6, diarrhea.
7963, Brown, M,* 110, Co F, died Sept 6, dysentery.
7994 Barnes, T S, 31, Co B, died Sept 6, scorbutus.
8365, Benent, W A, 135, Co F, died Sept 10, scorbutus.
8376 Barston, G H, 135, Co F, died Sept 10, scorbutus.
8476, Brenner N, 60, Co F, died Sept 11, scorbutus.
8496, Barnes, A, 86, Co G, died Sept 11, diarrhea.
8508, Blythe, C, 1, Co I, died Sept 12, anasarca.
8509, Brinbaner, J, 65, Co C, died Sept 12, diarrhea.
8676, Brown, D H, 41, Co A, died Sept 13, scorbutus.
8693, Bell, James, 135, Co B, died Sept 14, scorbutus.
8572, Buckley, J O, 126, Co A, died Sept 15, dysentery.
8939, Blessing, C, 9, Co F, died Sept 16, scorbutus.
9287, Baker, W C, 94, died Sept 19 diarrhea.
9446 Brookover, Geo, 135, Co B, died Sept 21, diarrhea.
9473, Brisco, J R, 122, Co C, died Sept 21, diarrhea.
9625, Bradley, A, 101, Co A, died Sept 24, diarrhea.
9679, Blackman, S, 72, Co G, died Sept 24, scorbutus.
9897, Burchfield, Eli, 14, died Sept 27, diarrhea.
9949, Beant, H T, 34, m I, Co D, died Sept 28, diarrhea.
10120, Brewer, D C, 43, Co K, died Oct 1, wounds.
10199, Brown, E N, 21, Co E, died Oct 2, scorbutus.
10251, Brum, W H,† 20, Co B, died Oct 4, diarrhea.
10590, Briggs F, 17, Co G died Oct 10, diarrhea.
11072, Baymher, L G, 153, Co A, died Oct 17, scorbutus.
11307, Boles, O, 112, Co H, died Oct 22, scorbutus.
11308, Brooker J 11, Co K, died Oct 22, scorbutus.
11313, Burns M, 12, Co K, died Oct 22, scorbutus.
11626, Bricker, J J,† 126, Co H, died Oct 28, diarrhea.
11920, Bumgardner, Joel, 3 Co C, died Nov 8, scorbutus.
11939, Barber, R, 10 cav, Co D, died Nov 9, diarrhea c.
12296, Bissel, J, 2 cav, Co E, died Dec 16, scorbutus.
12388, Beckley, G 102, Co F, died Jan 8, '65, diarrhea c.
12574, Barnes, E H, 2, Co D, died Jan 26, '65, scorbutus.
12641, Bower, A, 87, Co F, died Feb 12, diarrhea a
517, Blackwood, J 92, Co I, died April 12, diarrhea c.
12772, Bowens, W H, 100, Co A, died March 13, '65, pleuritis.

5, Carpenter, White,* 92, Co D, died March 4, pneumonia.
458, Copeland C, 1, Co A, died April 9, wounds.
561, Coates, George H, 7 cav, Co I, died April 15, diarrhea.
569, Campbell, James 7 cav, Co H, died April 15, diarrhea.
723, Callaway, Wm, 7 cav, Co F, died April 25, diarrhea c.
763, Coleman, G, 101, Co A, died April 27, diarrhea.
911, Chapman, George, 75, Co A died May 1, phthisis.
928, Crosser M, 111, Co B, died May 7, diarrhea.
965, Corey, W C, 111, Co B died May 8, diarrhea.
1269, Cruet, Wm, 59 Co C, died May 21, diarrhea.
1291, Collins, Thomas,* 21, Co G, died May 22, diarrhea c.
1521, Capeheart, H, 70 Co I, died May 31, diarrhea.
1587, Clark, H S, 62, Co E, died June 3, diarrhea c.
1631, Conklin, W, 121, Co B, died June 5, pneumonia.
1679, Clark, D V, 111, Co B died June 6, diarrhea.
1900, Childers, Wm, 89, Co B, died June 13, diarrhea.
1915 Crocker, George, 1 artil, Co A, died June 14, diarrhea.
1992, Christy, W. 53, Co K, died June 15, diarrhea c.
2017, Curtis, N, 45, Co D, died June 15, anasarca.
2025, Carnahan, G M, 65, Co F, died June 15, diarrhea c.
2101, Caldwell, J,† 15 Co D, died June 17, diarrhea a.
2162, Cornelius, B C,* 89, Co C, died June 19, cathaneties.
2207, Cochrane, James,† 22 Co G, died June 20, diarrhea c.
2463, Church, E, 2, Co G, died June 25, diarrhea.
2578, Combston, J, 7 cav, Co L died June 27, diarrhea c.
2968, Cameron, H, 69, Co B, died July 6, diarrhea c.
3002, Callahan, H, 34, Co C died July 7, dysentery.
3241, Coyner, George M, 89, Co D, died July 13, diarrhea.
3307, Canand, J Q A, 14, Co G, died July 13, diarrhea.
3356, Cruer, J W, 60, Co B, died July 15, diarrhea c.
3541, Cole, B, 52, Co A, died July 18, diarrhea.
3578, Collins, P, 15 Co I, died July 19 diarrhea.
3604, Cook, L B, 2 cav, Co C, died July 19, diarrhea.
3617, Clark, J C,† 31, Co H, died July 20, scorbutus.
3774, Clayton, D J, 9 cav, Co D, died July 22, scorbutus.
3937, Cover, L, 49, Co B died July 25, diarrhea c.
4 28, Clayton, J, 89, Co G, died July 28, diarrhea.
4342, Conway, J, 103, Co A, died July 30 diarrhea.
4493, Cordray, J J, 89 Co G, died Aug 1, scorbutus.
4965, Cahill, J N, 90, Co C, died Aug 6, diarrhea.
5105, Charles, F, 100 Co A, died Aug 9, diarrhea c.
5451, Collyer, J, 11, Co G, died Aug 12, diarrhea.
5518, Chandler, M, 121, Co E, died Aug 13, diarrhea.
5922, Clark, James, 89, Co I, died Aug 17, debilitas.
6022, Cline, K, 111, Co B, died Aug 17, diarrhea.
6108, Church, George E,† 14, Co G, died Aug 18, diarrhea.
6188, Chambers, R S, 89, Co A, died Aug 19, scorbutus.
6258, Copir, S A,* 83, Co C, died Aug 20, anasarca.
6281, Conklin, J R, 45, Co L, died Aug 20, diarrhea c.
6562, Craig, D † 2, Co D, died Aug 23, catarrh.
7483, Caswell, G 21, Co C, died Sept 1, dysentery.
7 86, Coons David, 57, Co C, died Sept 1, scorbutus.
7495, Crooks, J M, 92, Co K, died Sept 1, diarrhea.
7695, Chard, C W, 2, Co H, died Sept 3, diarrhea.
7800, Cregg J † 49, Co K, died Sept 4 diarrhea.
7835, Cline M, 2, Co E, died Sept 4, diarrhea.
7919, Clark, George, 60, Co D, died Sept 5, fever remittent.
7998, Clokie, J W, s major, 49, died Sept 6, diarrhea.
8130, Cummings, W S, 35, Co I, died Sept 8, diarrhea.
8454, Cattlebock, F 85, Co A, died Sept 14, diarrhea c.
8457, Campbell, W C, 5, Co L, died Sept 11, diarrhea.
8694, Chapin, James, 135, Co F, died Sept 14, scorbutus.
8701, Crooke, W B, 135, Co B, died Sept 14, scorbutus.
8810, Clark, J R, 135, Co F, died Sept 15, scorbutus.
9243, Corstein, W,* 93, Co C, died Sept 19, scorbutus.
9288, Crambler, A J, 123, Co H, died Sept 19, diarrhea c.
94 2, Campbell, Samuel, 74, Co G, died Sept 21, diarrhea.
9476, Cadwell, A F, 3, Co E, died Sept 21, diarrhea.
9491, Clay, O 122, Co D, died Sept 21, diarrhea.
9562, Cort, W, 11, Co D, died Sept 24, diarrhea.
9770, Cummings, A, 6 cav, Co E, died Sept 25, scorbutus.
9772, Clark, S, 24, Co H, died Sept 26, scorbutus.
9895, Conner, J B, 9 cav, Co G died Sept 27, diarrhea.
9971, Castable, I, 51, Co A, died Sept 28, diarrhea.
10381, Coates, Rufus, 2 cav, died Oct 5, diarrhea.
10796, Colts, R E, 2, Co C, died Oct 12, scorbutus.
10834, Cepp, J, 14 Co I died Oct 13, scorbutus.
10986, Carey, A, 21, Co E, died Oct 16, scorbutus.
11103, Carter, John B, 89, Co I, died Oct 18, scorbutus.
11224, Craven, A J,* 15, Co C, died Oct 20, dysentery.
11262, Cromwell, W H, 59, Co H, died Oct 21, diarrhea c.
11403, Cutsdaghner, W J, 95, Co D, died Oct 24, scorbutus.
11540, Croonlnberger, J C, 23, Co I, died Oct 27, scorbutus.
11567, Cantwright, L, 51, Co F, died Oct 27, scorbutus.
11587, Chapin, J A, 135, Co F, died Oct 28, scorbutus.
11618, Clark, H M, 21, Co A, died Oct 28, scorbutus.
11641, Clingan, A P, 26, Co K, died Oct 30, scorbutus.
11766, Cohagen, J H, 6, Co K, died Nov 3, diarrhea.
12082, Cahill, Wm, 51, Co A, died Nov 18, scorbutus.
12385, Calvington, R, 72, Co C, died Jan 3, '65, fever remittent.
12435 Chambers, J C, 15 Co C died Jan 11, '65, scorbutus.
12691, Crampton, A, 79, Co C, died Feb 22, '65, diarrhea c.
12798, Conover, S, 175, Co B, died March 19, '65, diarrhea c.

690, Davis, Wm E, 7, Co H, died April 28, bronchitis.
930, Downing, George, 45, Co C, died May 7, fever remittent.
981, Dumer, R,† 45, Co B, died May 9, debilitas.
1267, Dugan, Thomas, 1 cav, Co B, died May 21, fever typhus.
1748, Davis, I,† 7 cav, Co F, died June 9, dysentery.
2251, Decker, B F, 111, Co B, died June 21, debilitas.
2296, Dumas, J P, 2, Co H, died June 21, dysentery.
2351, Douglass, W, 24, Co F, died June 23, diarrhea c.
2674, Davis, B, 22, Co B, died June 30 scorbutus.
2909, Davis, G W, 45, Co E, died July 5 diarrhea.
2973, Dandelion, T, 3d Co, indpt cav, died July 7, anasarca.
3703, Dodson, E 7 cav, Co H, died July 21, diarrhea.
3802, Dille, Charles, 23, Co I died July 22, diarrhea c.
4455, Dodge, 2, Co I died Aug 1, diarrhea.
4501, Dicey, C, 26, Co G, died Aug 1, diarrhea.

No. of Grave
4772, Denton, John, 7 cav, Co E, died Aug 5, scorbutus.
5020, Desselhem, M, 1, Co I, died Aug 8, debilitas.
5268, Dorson, L,* 12, Co I, died Aug 10, dysentery.
5294, Duty, E E, 41, Co H, died Aug 11, diarrhea.
5368, Dyke, F, 5 cav, Co K, died Aug 11, diarrhea.
5465, Dooly, James, 1 cav, Co F, died Aug 13, scorbutus.
5620, Davis, W H, 33, Co D, died Aug 14, diarrhea.
6043, Decker, J, 111, Co B, died Aug 18, diarrhea c.
6225, Durant, B, 95, Co D, died Aug 20, diarrhea.
6312, Downer, A P, 52, Co B, died Aug 20, anasarca.
6718, Dougherty, W H, 15, Co H, died Aug 24, gangrene.
7219, Di'dine, J, 33, Co K, died Aug 29, diarrhea.
7356, Deming, W,* 111, Co B, died Aug 31, anasarca.
7409, Daley, S, 34, Co D, died Aug 31, diarrhea.
7427, Dick, Charles,† 54, Co G, died Aug 31, wounds.
7479, Drake, M, 59, Co D, died Sept 1, scorbutus.
7500, Doran, James, 60, Co A, died Sept 1, diarrhea.
7609, Dixon, John, 51, Co A, died Sept 2, diarrhea.
7631, DeMastoris, J, 54, Co B, died Sept 2, wounds.
8051, Davidson, P S, 21, Co K, died Sept 6, scorbutus.
8193, Dudley, M, 59, Co G, died Sept 11, scorbutus.
8498, Drake, John F, 125, Co C, died Sept 11, scorbutus.
8779, Diver, J, 4, died Sept 14, scorbutus.
8820, Davete, J, 49, Co D, died Sept 15, scorbutus.
9293, Diver, John, 123, Co H, died Sept 19, diarrhea c.
9605, Decker, S, 12, Co C, died Sept 23, scorbutus.
9702, Dobson, J B, 99, Co H, died Sept 25, diarrhea.
9819, Duffy, G, 45, Co C, died Sept 27, diarrhea.
10112, Dunbar, J, 122, Co F, died Oct 1, dysentery.
10113, Dixon, J, 135, Co F, died Oct 1, dysentery.
10130, Duncan, A, 49, Co K, died Oct 1, scorbutus.
10194, Dunham, James, 8 cav, Co M, died Oct 1, diarrhea.
10124, Dewitt, Joseph, 65, Co G, died Oct 6, scorbutus.
10526, Dibble, F, 105, Co H, died Oct 10, scorbutus.
11017, Diper, O, 128, Co I, died Oct 16, scorbutus.
11102, Dunton, W H, 105, Co E, died Oct 18, diarrhea.
12159, Donahue, P, 72, Co K, died Oct 25, scorbutus.
12221, Drith, C, 33, Co K, died Dec 4, scorbutus.
12615, Dunken, T, 20, Co K, died Feb 19, '65, diarrhea c.
12738, Deputy, W, 21, Co H, died Feb 6, '65, diarrhea c.
7431, Davis, G W,* 21, Co G, died Aug 31, scorbutus.
1629, De Rush, Samuel, 94, Co F, died June 5, diarrhea c.

327, Elijah, Baker, 45, Co B, died April 2, dysentery.
351, Evart, E J, 10, Co M, died April 2, diarrhea c.
1017, Eppert, Samuel, 9, Co B, died May 12, anasarca.
2421, Eatles, William, 4 cav, Co G, died June 20, diarrhea c.
3376, Ellis, Charles, 29, Co B, died July 16, scorbutus.
4594, Elliott, W,* 20, Co F, died Aug 1, anasarca.
5304, Evans, Samuel, 33, Co E, died Aug 11, scorbutus.
5319, Eastman, J, 18, Co C, died Aug 11, dysentery.
5717, Evens, Charles, 1 artil, Co D, died Aug 15, enteritis.
5887, Emsley, Wm, 135, Co F, died Aug 16, diarrhea.
6015, Eckhart, J, 2, Co B, died Aug 17, scorbutus.
7148, Ehnsan, A, 28, Co F, died Sept 1, scorbutus.
8981, Entulle, B C, 104, Co K, died Sept 17, scorbutus.
11051, Evans, W, 51, Co I, died Oct 17, ulcus.
11169, Evans, E M,† 20, Co I, died Oct 19, scorbutus.
11452, Elba, H S, Co A, died Oct 25, scorbutus.
11634, Ewing, D, 135, Co D, died Oct 30, scorbutus.
12321, Ellerman, N, 59, Co K, died Dec 22, scorbutus.

75, Falmon, A, 82, Co H, died March 20, pneumonia.
176, Fairbanks, Alph, 45, Co A, died March 26, dysentery.
246, Ferris, Joseph, 2 cav, Co H, died March 30, diarrhea.
311, Foster, A M, 100, Co A, died April 2, fever typhus.
572, Fraver, Daniel, 99, Co I, died April 5, diarrhea.
636, Facer, William, 111, Co K, died April 20, fever.
830, Fisher, Charles, 8 cav, Co C, died May 1, dysentery.
1054, Free, M, 22 battery, died May 13, dysentery.
1321, Freenough, George, 8 cav, died May 26, diarrhea c.
1786, Fraiser, James,† 2, Co E, died June 10, diarrhea.
2457, Fry, W L, 123, Co H, died June 25, diarrhea.
2479, Fenton, J M,† 75, Co I, died June 25, scorbutus.
2761, Finnan, James, 18, Co K, died July 2, diarrhea c.
4231, Fry, Jacob, 99, Co I, died July 29, diarrhea.
4317, Fitch, E P, 40, Co G, died July 30, diarrhea.
4337, Fulkinson, H, 2, Co I, died July 30, diarrhea.
4651, Fife, J, 33, Co E, died Aug 3, diarrhea.
4868, Fling, T J, 27, Co A, died Aug 6, scorbutus.
5249, Feree, R S, 2, Co C, died Aug 10, diarrhea.
5626, Falk, W, 82, Co D, died Aug 14, dysentery.
5864, Fullerston, W,* 18, Co K, died Aug 16, anasarca.
6212, Foreman, A, 64, Co E, died Aug 19, dysentery.
6308, Fisher, D, 89, Co I, died Aug 20, scorbutus.
6891, Futers, John H, 82, Co F, died April 26, fever contag.
7878, Franks, R L, 122, Co E, died Sept 5, scorbutus.
7976, Forney, W O, 123, Co D, died Sept 6, diarrhea.
9158, Firman, V, cav, died Sept 18, diarrhea c.
9225, Ferguson, H, 3 cav, Co D, died Sept 19, gangrene.
9533, Fowler, C, 100, Co A, died Sept 22, scorbutus.

9557, Finch, C, ——, Co B, died Sept 23, diarrhea.
9976, Frankinburg, C, 72, Co G, died Sept 28, diarrhea.
10045, Farshay, A, 116, Co F, died Sept 29, diarrhea.
10915, Freeley, P, 10, Co G, died Sept 14, scorbutus.
11819, Flowers, W F, 116, Co D, died Nov 5, scorbutus.
11914, Forest, Wm, 21, Co K, died Nov 8, scorbutus.
12108, Fargrove, M B, 135, Co F, died Nov 21, scorbutus.
12637, Fussleman, J, 20, Co H, died Feb 11, '65, rheumatism.
12781, Foults, M, 183, Co D, died March 15, diarrhea c.
12427, Fike, W P, 95, Co H, died Jan 9, pleuritis.

197, Gilling, Daniel, 13, Co A, died March 27, bronchitis.
245, Gardner, A, 100, Co H, died March 30, diarrhea.
386, Gresmust, S,* 6 cav, Co G, died April 2, debilitas.
611, Gillingher, B, 7 cav, Co L, died April 18, diarrhea.
681, Godfrey, Amos, 45, Co C, died April 23, dysentery c.
693, Greek, Samuel, 100, Co C, died April 23, diarrhea.
916, Gibson, Collins, 40, Co H, died May 5, diarrhea c.
1465, Greer, R J, 6 cav, Co C, died May 29, diarrhea.
2542, Gilmon, J, 85, Co K, died June 27, dysentery.
2926, Garner, C, 1 cav, Co K, died July 5, diarrhea.
3130, Golfe, P E, 19, Co K, died July 10, diarrhea c.
3251, Gaunt, Wm,* 14, Co I, died July 13, diarrhea.
3327, Gibson, R, 40, Co B, died July 15, diarrhea c.
3762, Gingeng, P S,* 21, Co E, died July 25, diarrhea.
4037, Gillette, G W, 6, Co G, died July 26, scorbutus.
4242, Gilbert, J, 19, Co B, died July 29, diarrhea c.
4301, Grafton, D, 118, Co D, died July 30, bronchitis.
4383, Graham, J W, 31, Co C, died July 31, diarrhea.
4445, Golly, P, 113, Co G, died Aug 1, anasarca.
4655, Gregger, H, 125, Co H, died Aug 3, scorbutus.
4802, Greer, G O, 49, Co D, died Aug 5, catarrh.
4902, Granbaugh, 85, Co E, died Aug 6, scorbutus.
6024, Gordon, Wm, 45, Co B, died Aug 17, diarrhea.
6075, Gallagher, James, 30, Co F, died Aug 18, scorbutus.
6207, Green, E, 4 cav, Co D, died Aug 19, fever typhus.
6346, Gordon, W, 10, Co G, died Aug 21, diarrhea.
6465, Graff, A J, 13, Co E, died Aug 22, catarrh.
6486, Gates, H, 13, Co G, died Aug 22, diarrhea.
6821, Greens, L, 12, Co C, died Aug 25, scorbutus.
7111, Gilland, A, 27, Co F, died Aug 28, wounds.
8330, Goodrich, J S, 9, Co A, died Sept 10, diarrhea.
8367, Gannold, L, 60, Co A, died Sept 10, scorbutus.
9566, Gould, J M, 121, Co A, died Sept 23, diarrhea c.
9813, Graft, P, 20 battery, died Sept 26, diarrhea.
9927, Galbraith, J S,† 6 cav, Co M, died Sept 28, diarrhea.
11215, Gunther, J, 60, Co B, died Oct 20, scorbutus.
11850, Gardner, G, 1, Co K, died Nov 5, scorbutus.
12033, Glissin, A,† 2 cav, Co M, died Nov 15, scorbutus.
12064, Gillenback, J, 77, Co E, died Nov 17, scorbutus.
12109, Goodbrath, C, 28, Co G, died Oct 21, scorbutus.
12560, Griffith, J H, 58, Co C, died Jan 31, '65, diarrhea c.
12842, Gassler, P, 61, Co A, died April 22, diarrhea c.

85, Hall, J W, 4, Co A, died March 9, pneumonia.
295, Hochenburg, N, 45, Co C, died April 1, diarrhea.
420, Hawney, W F, 45, Co A, died April 7, diarrhea c.
424, Hill, J,† 7 cav, Co L, died April 7, diarrhea c.
437, Henry, James, 7 cav, Co L, died April 8, diarrhea c.
464, Hauer, Jacob, 45, Co B, died April 9, diarrhea c.
527, Hickcox, M R, 2 cav, Co B, died April 13, pleuritis.
580, Holdman, F, 1 battery, Co D, died April 16, pneumonia.
748, Hanning, Mark, 7 cav, Co I, died April 26, diarrhea.
748, Harvey, Charles, 76, Co E, died April 26, dysentery c.
875, Henry, G W, 95, Co E, died May 4, diarrhea.
949, Hawkins, W W,* 108, Co G, died May 8, fever typhus.
1129, Hulsampilfer, R L, 7 cav, Co L, died May 15, diarrhea c.
1354, Hend, George, 103, Co H, died May 25, diarrhea.
1390, Holloway, G W, 1, Co C, died May 28, diarrhea c.
1524, Harrison, J, 21, Co I, died May 31, dysentery c.
1666, Hazlett, Wm, 2, Co K, died June 6, fever intermittent.
1822, Hull, S,† 21, Co E, died June 10, diarrhea c.
1979, Harris, E D,† 99, Co I, died June 15, diarrhea.
2029, Hogle, John, 1 cav, Co C, died June 15, dysentery.
2185, Humphreys, Wm, 45, Co C, died June 19, pleuritis.
2263, Hanley, C, 15, Co F, died June 20, diarrhea.
2300, Henderson, S W,† 40, Co H, died June 22, diarrhea c.
2369, Howard, J, musician, 70, Co D, died June 23, diarrhea c.
2424, Hayford, A E, 125, Co C, died June 24, diarrhea.
2597, Harrington, S J, 108, Co I, died June 28, bronchitis.
2671, Horles, I, 126, Co C, died June 30, fever intermittent.
2775, Hurlburt, O, 14, Co H, died July 2, diarrhea c.
2842, Hudson, J,* 111, Co B, died July 3, diarrhea.
3185, Hall, T,† 2, Co H, died July 11, diarrhea.
81, Heaton, Ames, 45, Co F, died April 20, small pox.
3388, Hudsen, Wm, 74, Co G, died July 16, diarrhea.
3420, Hunt, W H, 113, Co G, died July 16, dysentery.
3736, Harman, L, 9, Co F, died July 21, diarrhea c.
4030, Hansbury, E A, 6, Co G, died July 26, scorbutus.
4408, Hendershot, John, 45, Co D, died July 31, scorbutus.
4411, Harris, J, 1, Co E, died July 31, diarrhea.

No. of Grave.
4506, Hartman, H, 18, Co K, died Aug 1, diarrhea c.
4599, Harrison, J M, 105, Co M, died Aug 3, diarrhea c.
4993, Hendrickson, O, 19, Co F, died Aug 7, scorbutus.
5293, Holfbaugh, J A, 23, Co E, died Aug 11, diarrhea.
5296, Hatfield, George W, 126, Co K, died Aug 11, dysentery.
5396, Holman, A, 65, Co K, died Aug 12, wounds
5551, Hemmill, F B, 9, Co G, died Aug 13, diarrhea.
5636, Huey, B F, 89, Co C, died Aug 14, scorbutus.
5813, Hicks F, 40, Co H, died Aug 16, diarrhea
5858, Hibbet, Wm, 21, Co D, died Aug 19, marasmus.
5858, Hoi , P, 116, Co B, died Aug 16, marasmus.
6058, Hamm, E J, * Co K, died Aug 18, cerebritis.
6123, Huggins, J W, † 14, Co C, died Aug 18, diarrhea.
6174, Houser, W R, 89, Co K, died Aug 18, cerebritis.
6522, Hicks, J, H, Co D, died Aug 22, dysentery.
6625, Hughes, Henry, 33, Co A, died Aug 24, scorbutus.
6639, Henricks, E, 34, Co H, died Aug 23, scorbutus.
6647, Hartman, J, 2, Co K, died Aug 23, scorbutus.
6794, Herrig, N, 7 cav, Co D, died Aug 25, catarrh.
6802, Hine, T E, 2 cav, Co D, died Aug 25, diarrhea.
7022, Hall, O, 89, Co B, died Aug 27, diarrhea.
7388, Hubbell, W A, 2, Co A, died Aug 31, scorbutus.
7446, Hurdnell, O, 72, Co C, died Sept 1, fever typhus.
7825, Holley, V H, † 100, Co B, died Sept 4, scorbutus.
7946, Hughes, J, 12, Co E, died Sept 5, diarrhea.
8060, Herbolt, Daniel, 115, Co F, died Sept 7, diarrhea.
8067, Harper, J H, 60, Co I, died Sept 7, diarrhea.
8284, Halshult, A, 12, Co C, died Sept 9, diarrhea.
8481, Hechler, John, 86, Co G, died Sept 11, scorbutus.
8696, Hitchkock, G, 34, Co G, died Sept 14, scorbutus.
8725, Hifner, G, 56, Co C, died Sept 14, scorbutus.
9189, Hoyt, B, 7, Co K, died Sept 18, scorbutus.
9210, Hart, E, 10, Co H, died Sept 19, scorbutus.
9348, Hall, S, 126, Co F, died Sept 20, scorbutus.
9415, Hood, F, 13, Co F, died Sept 21, diarrhea
9510, Hamilton, J, 13, Co A, died Sept 22, diarrhea.
9582, Hoover, J, 18, Co K, died Sept 23, diarrhea
9632, Hurley, John C, 124, Co C, died Sept 23, diarrhea.
10094, Holmes, Wesley, 135, Co F, died Sept 30, diarrhea.
10207, Harrison, J, 2 cav, Co A, died Oct 2, scorbutus.
10208, Holcomb, L, 7, Co L, died Oct 2, scorbutus
10225, Harkins, M, 60, Co D, died Oct 2, diarrhea.
10390, Hinton, Wm, 72, Co A, died Oct 5, diarrhea
10492, Hererlin, B, 82, died Oct 7, diarrhea.
10518, Hoobert, Wm, 4, Co L, died Oct 8, scorbutus.
10524, Hounich, C, 110, Co D, died Oct 8, scorbutus.
10647, Herman, R, 135, Co F, died Oct 11, scorbutus.
11029, Hillyard, J, 98, Co F, died Oct 16, diarrhea.
11032, Hubber, D, 5, Co A, died Oct 16, scorbutus.
11058, Heymers, B, 2, Co G, died Oct 17, scorbutus.
11209, Hanard, J B, 123, Co C, died Oct 20, dysentery.
11228, Hoyt, W B, 49, Co A, died Oct 20, scorbutus.
11235, Henderson, D, 122, Co H, died Oct 23, scorbutus.
11588, Hintz, D, 1, Co B, Oct 28, scorbutus.
11592, Hutchins, G W, 135, Co A, died Oct 28, scorbutus.
11696, Hutchins, J W, 153, Co A, died Oct 31, diarrhea.
11856, Hasner, B, 135, Co A, Nov 6, scorbutus.
11948, Hatfield, A G, 114, Co E, died Nov 9, debilitas.
12350, Hume, J A, * 32, Co F, died Dec 29, marasmus.
12370, Haines, N S, * 72, Co E, died Jan 1, '65, scorbutus.
12404, Hell, W L, 54, Co A, died Jan 6, '65, scorbutus.
12446, Hill, E P, 89, Co G, died Jan 13, '65, scorbutus
12512, Hagerman, R, 31, Co B, died Jan 23, '65, diarrhea.
12569, Hart, H C, 2, Co C, died Feb 1, '65, scorbutus.
12611, Hagerly, D G, 72, Co E, died Feb 7, '65, debilitas.
12743, Hoitz, W, 101, Co I, died March 7, '65, debilitas.
1129, Hudson, R L, * 7 cav, Co L, died May 15, diarrhea c.
1132, Hank, George B, 7 cav, Co L, died May 16, pneumonia.
2607, Hands, L C, 92, Co E, died June 28, diarrhea c.

1280, Irving, Ester, 114, Co H, died May 22, fever.
1967, Ingler, Wm, 81, Co G, died June 14, diarrhea c.
7479, Imboden, J, 44, Co E, died Sept 1, dysentery.
9744, Irwin, A, 1, Co I, died Sept 14, debilitas.
10700, Idold, A, † 7 cav, Co C, died Oct 11, diarrhea.
12579, Ishnm, D, 89, Co G, died Feb 8, '65, scorbutus.

854, Justice, George W, 45, Co B, died April 2, diarrhea c.
1697, Johnson, J H, 98, Co D, died June 5, fever typhus.
3590, Jacobs, P O, 45, Co E, July 19, scorbutus.
3754, Jones, R, 45, Co C, died July 22, scorbutus.
3908, Jones, S, 111, Co B, died July 24, fever intermittent.
4381, Jewell, I, 93, Co F, died July 31, dysentery.
5120, Johnston, John W, 8, Co H, died Aug 9, diarrhea.
5508, Johnson, M, 126, Co C, died Aug 13, dysentery.
5591, Jones, H, 40, Co G, died Aug 14, dysentery c.
5624, Jewell, W A, 126, Co G, died Aug 14, diarrhea.
5839, Jolly, G, 21, Co K, died Aug 16, scorbutus.
6265, Jeffeles, H, 36, Co I, died Aug 20, ictus solis.
6810, Jones, John, * 40, Co G, died Aug 25, scorbutus.
7308, Johnson, E, 124, Co I, died Aug 30, diarrhea.

No. of Grave.
7861, Jones, R W, 118, Co F, died Sept 5, diarrhea.
8647, Jenkins, Wm, 3 battery, died Sept 13, scorbutus.
8757, Johnson, D, 43, Co B, died Sept 14, diarrhea.
8760, Johnson, I, 51, Co A, died Sept 14, diarrhea.
9306, Jordan, A, 103, Co G, died Sept 20, scorbutus.
9700, Jones, I B, 90, Co M, died Sept 25, diarrhea.
9744, Johnson, I B, 2, Co C, died Sept 25, diarrhea c.
9850, Jones, Wm, * 84, Co B, died Sept 27, diarrhea.
11014, Jones, S D, 135, Co F, died Oct 16, dysentery.
11203, Jennings, John, * 24, Co K, Oct 29, scorbutus
11912, Jones, G L, 105, Co G, died Nov 9, scorbutus.
12126, Jarvitt, W, 15, Co A, died Nov 22, scorbutus.
12231, Johnson, A S, * 45, Co I, died Dec 6, diarrhea c.
12325, Jones, W H, 2, Co C, died Dec 26, scorbutus.
12428, Jackson, S, 72, Co E, died Jan 10, '65, pleuritis.
7947, Jacobs, H, * 26, Co F, died Sept 6, diarrhea.

886, Kelley, Josiah, 45, Co C, died May 1, pneumonia.
4615, Kimble, S, 98, Co A, died Aug 1, debilitas.
4718, Knight, J, 21, Co E, died Aug 4, anasarca.
5381, Relley, E, 21, Co D, died Aug 12, diarrhea.
5448, Knidler, J W, 33, Co H, died Aug 12, dysentery.
5576, Kelly, H J, Co I, died Aug 14, dysentery.
6195, Kelsey, John, * 3, Co I, died Aug 19, debilitas
7177, Kenedy, S J B, 45, Co E, died Aug 29, scorbutus.
7424, Kelley, G, 15, Co E, died Oct 31, anasarca.
9377, Kelly, Wm, 46, Co C, died Sept 20, anasarca.
9436, Kerr, J H, 122, Co C, died Sept 21, diarrhea.
9680, Knapp, J, 51, Co K, died Sept 24, diarrhea.
10139, Killar, J, 15, Co D, died Oct 1, scorbutus
10607, Kirby, A, 4 cav, Co A, died Oct 10, scorbutus.
10853, Keanshoff, L, 28, Co I, died Oct 13, diarrhea.
11055, Kerr, A, 13, Co I, died Oct 17, diarrhea c.
11732, Kingkade, S, 18, Co C, died Nov 2, scorbutus.
12661, Kennedy, J, 70, Co K, died Nov 16, bronchitis.
12746, Kuler, J, 72, Co B, died March 8, '65, diarrhea c.
12802, Karch, J, 183, Co B, died March 20, '65, pleuritis.
765, Kinner, John, * 67, Co F, died April 27, diarrhea c.
2406, Knowlton, E, 6 cav, Co B, died June 24, diarrhea c.
13, Kiger, J H, * 45, Co E, died April 9, small pox.

834, Lowry, James, 49, Co I, died May 1, diarrhea.
935, Lewis, Frank, 103, Co D, died May 7, diarrhea c.
1256, Larme, Charles, 45, Co K, died May 22, diarrhea c.
1364, Larkin, Joseph, 1 artil, died May 25, diarrhea c.
1170, Logan, Frank, 89, Co F, died May 30, diarrhea.
1615, Logan, H, 6 cav, Co E, died June 4, diarrhea c.
1828, Leonard, John, 21, Co A, died June 11, scorbutus.
2173, Lever, H B, 2, Co C, died June 19, dysentery
2372, Lisure, Samuel, 7, Co A, died June 23, fever typhus
2426, Lemons, M, 89, Co E, died June 24, fever typhus.
3195, Lutz, M, * 14, Co C, died July 18, scorbutus.
3197, Love, John, 96, Co E, died July 18, diarrhea.
3649, Linsay, J, 21, Co D, died July 29, diarrhea.
4097, Lyon, L L, 1 artil, Co F, died July 27, diarrhea.
4351, Law, S S, 124, Co I, died July 31, diarrhea.
4262, Lawsen, J, * 2, Co E, died July 29, anasarca.
4641, Lucas, J, 89, Co H, died Aug 3, anasarca.
4628, Legrand, D, 111, Co B, died Aug 3, scorbutus.
4692, Long, John, 45, Co H, died Aug 4, diarrhea.
5193, Lightfoot, Wm, * 9 cav, Co G, died Aug 10, scorbutus.
5246, Latta, W H, 89, Co H, died Aug 10, diarrhea c.
5449, Lehigh, W, 22, Co B, died Aug 12, dysentery.
5665, Lamphare, G W, 125, Co K, died Aug 14, diarrhea.
5676, Larisen, A, 63, Co D, died Aug 14, wounds.
6066, Lowe, G H, 72, Co C, died Aug 18, cerebritis.
6844, Leasure, Isaac, 122, Co K, died Aug 21, wounds.
7123, Leasure, F, 45, Co K, died Aug 28, scorbutus.
7744, Linway, J, 2, Co H, died Sept 3, scorbutus
8016, Lambert, James, 89, Co A, died Sept 6, diarrhea.
8789, Licklilter, Henry, 135, Co B, died Sept 14, scorbutus
8874, Lindsley, A K, 99, Co K, died Sept 16, diarrhea.
9336, Leonard, T M, 12, Co H, died Sept 20, scorbutus.
9358, Lovely, John, 100, Co K, died Sept 20, diarrhea.
9361, Lawyer, J B, 89, Co L, died Sept 20, diarrhea.
9119, Lefarer, W E, citizen, Gardner, Athens Co.
10039, Laley, ——, 28, died Sept 29, diarrhea.
11161, Lepe, A, 7, Co K, died Oct 19, scorbutus
11196, Lantz, A W, 45, Co A, died Oct 20, scorbutus.
11344, Lachner, M, 72, Co E, died Oct 23, scorbutus.
11440, Laughlin, M W, 1, Co L, died Oct 24, scorbutus.
11190, Lips, F, * 2, Co H, died Oct 26, scorbutus.
11816, Lane, D, 91, Co D, died Nov 4, scorbutus.
12027, Lay, John, 123, Co K, died Nov 19, scorbutus.
12201, Lohmeyer, H, 35, Co K, died Nov 30, shot by the guard.
12297, Livingood, C B, * 35, Co G, died Dec 16, scorbutus.
12525, Langstreet, W F, 31, Co A, died Jan 26, '65, scorbutus.
12698, Lewis, D, 7, Co A, died Jan 23, '65, diarrhea a.
12826, Little, Wm, 175, Co D, died April 7, '65, diarrhea.

66, Metcalf, Milo R, 100, Co E, died March 19, fever congestive.

No. of Grave.

86, Malsbrar, Asa, 40 cav, Co A, died March 22, fever typhus.
118, Moore, T J, † 2, Co D died March 23, pneumonia.
141, McKeever James, 8 Co G, died March 24, scorbutus.
165, Mickey, Samuel, 4, Co F, died March 26 diarrhea.
215, Murphey, John, 7 cav, Co L, died March 28, diarrhea.
412, Mitchell J, 120, Co F, died April 7, diarrhea.
441, McKindry, M, 7, Co I died April 9, diarrhea.
575, Malone, R J, † 40, Co H, died April 16, diarrhea.
883, McCormick J W E, 34, Co B, died May 4, fever congestive.
981, Musser, D, 45, Co B, died May 9, diarrhea
998, Meek, David, 111, Co K, died May 10, diarrhea.
1262, McKnight, H, 11, Co G, died May 21, diarrhea.
1283, McMurray, George † 21, Co G, died May 22, diarrhea.
1650, Moore, Charles, 19, Co H, died June 5, diarrhea c.
1849, Masters, Samuel, 17, Co I, died June 11, anasarca.
1930, Martin G, 105, Co F, died June 14, anasarca.
2075, McClung, B, 7 cav, Co I died June 17, diarrhea.
2129, Maloney A, 4 Co H, died June 18, dysentery.
2150, Mitchell W H, 31, Co D died June 18 diarrhea c.
2290, Massey, J C, 33, Co A, died June 21, diarrhea c.
2471, Mullin, J, 65, Co K, died June 25, anasarca
2667, McCloud A, 35, Co G, died June 29, diarrhea.
2682, Miller, T, 4 cav, Co A, died June 30, dysentery.
2743, McFarland, L, 2, Co I, died July 1, diarrhea.
2806, McInness, A, 45, Co B, died July 3, diarrhea.
2873, Moriatt, Joseph, 5, Co K, died July 4, scorbutus
2991, Mitchell, James, 17, Co D, died July 7, anasarca.
3104, Malone L B 7 cav Co L, died July 10 diarrhea.
3122 Mitchell, C, 1 Co K, died July 10, diarrhea
3137 Minshall, R, 45, Co C died July 10 anasarca.
3290, Matin, B 51, Co I, died July 13, dysentery.
3491, Master, J, 13 Co A, died July 7, diarrhea.
3718, Miller E, 4, Co E, died July 21, diarrhea
4040 Marshall, T, * 21, Co G, died July 26, dysentery.
4199, Myer, C 21, Co I, died July 29, diarrhea.
4252, Meek J, 19, Co E, died July 29, dysentery.
4298, McNeill, M J, † 89, Co D died July 30 anasarca.
4361, Mooney, James 50 Co D died July 31, diarrhea.
4421, Morris C E, 11 Co H, died July 31, scorbutus.
4531, McCann, A, 33, Co C died Aug 3, dysentery.
4657, Maher, P, 7, Co E, died Aug 3, diarrhea
4789, Martin, D, 3 cav, Co L, died Aug 5, scorbutus.
5748, McCabe, H, 12 Co C, died Aug 15, diarrhea.
5777, Mausen, W, 9 Co G, died Aug 15, bronchitis.
5883, McIntosh, D, 50, Co D, died Aug 16, diarrhea.
6026, Monahan, Thos, 21, Co D, died Aug 18, diarrhea.
6040 McKee, James, 51, Co A, died Aug 18 debilitas.
6035, McHugh, W S, 2, Co D, died Aug 18, cerebritis.
6063, McClair, P M, 27, Co A, died Aug 18, dysentery.
6478, McCabe, J, 66, Co C, died Aug 22, scorbutus
6841, McCormick, W P, 2, Co G, died Aug 25 diarrhea.
6855, McSorley, D, 49, Co F, died Aug 26, diarrhea.
6862, McCoy, J B 98, Co A, died Aug 26, diarrhea
6925, McDell, Wm, 81, Co K, died Aug 26, dysentery.
7108, McDonald, J, 99, Co H died Aug 28, diarrhea.
7134 Mason J, 45, Co H, died Aug 28 scorbutus.
7136, More, John H, 63, Co D, died Aug 28, dysentery.
7515, Myers, L H, 135, Co B, died Sept 1, scorbutus.
7896 Morris, J, 105, Co A, died Sept 5, diarrhea
8021 Merk, Robert, 111, Co K, died Sept 6, scorbutus.
8011, Myers A 51, Co I died Sept 6, wounds.
8185 Mavmer, R, 68, Co D, died Sept 10, fever typhus.
8408, McCabe J 70, Co C, died Sept 11, scorbutus.
8482, Morens, H 51, Co A, died Sept 11, scorbutus.
8658, Moore, T H, 59, Co C, died Sept 13, scorbutus
8706, Miller, Samuel, 135 Co F, died Sept 14, scorbutus.
8838 Mackell, R, 50, Co I, died Sept 15, scorbutus.
8885 Maulig, S 60, Co A, died Sept 16, diarrhea.
9039 Miller, C, 28, Co I died Sept 17, scorbutus.
9106, McMillan, J F, 123, Co A died Sept 18, diarrhea.
9111, McComb, J S, 14, Co K died Sept 19, scorbutus.
9348, Maxwell P, 12, Co A died Sept 20, diarrhea
8036, Moor, D D, 2, Co A, died Sept 9, diarrhea
9559, Manley, J, 7 Co M, died Sept 24, scorbutus.
9867, Mitchell, R C, 10 cav, Sept 27, scorbutus.
10064, Morgan, R O 12 cav, Co H, died Sept 30, diarrhea.
10081, McIntosh, Wm, † 25, Co I, died Sept 30, scorbutus.
10106, Morris, Wm, 15 Co F, died Sept 30, diarrhea.
10517 Montgomery, J, 2, Co G died Oct 8, scorbutus.
10563, Myer, L, blacksmith, 1, Co A, died Oct 9, diarrhea.
10926 Martin, F, 10 cav, Co A died Oct 14, scorbutus.
11016, McElroy, John 92, Co B died Oct 18 scorbutus.
11200, Martin, W, 15, Co A, died Oct 24, scorbutus
11341, McQuilken, F, 1, Co I died Oct 23, scorbutus.
11360, Mark, J, 135, Co B died Oct 24, scorbutus.
11810, Miller, J, 135, Co I, died Nov 4, scorbutus
12050, Moore, R F, 101, Co C died Nov 16 scorbutus.
12054 Mills, G W, 60, Co F, died Nov 16, debilitas
12184, Morrison, J H, 21, Co H, died Nov 28, scorbutus.
12534, McDonald, H H, citizen, died Jan 27, '65, diarrhea.
12717, Milliband, R, 183, Co B, died March 1, '65, diarrhea

12872, McGrath, D, * 115, Co G, died March 15, '65, scorbutus.
12875, Martin, M, * 135, Co B, died March 16, '65, diarrhea.

983, Neal, John, 45, Co C, died May 9, diarrhea
2328, Nash, C D, 45, Co B, died May 22, diarrhea c.
4994, Nelson, J, 1 cav, Co K, died Aug 7, scorbutus.
5897, Neff, B, 95, Co H, died Aug 16, diarrhea
7103, Nelson, Thomas, 1 cav, died Aug 25, diarrhea.
10584, Nelder, S, 89, Co G, died Oct 10, dysentery.
11012, Nott, J, 153, Co H, died Oct 16, diarrhea.
11148, Norman, G L, 135 Co B, died Oct 25, scorbutus.
12815, Norris, E J, 102, Co K died March 25, '65, diarrhea c.
2153, Niver, Edward, 8 cav, Co I, died June 19, diarrhea

2245, Ostrander, E W, 100, Co A, died June 20, diarrhea c.
2442, Ott, C, 51, Co C, died June 25, diarrhea.
4552, O'Neil, James, 126, Co F, died Aug 2, dysentery.
12024, O'Conner, F, 103, Co F, died Nov 15, diarrhea.
12247, Oliver, J, 122, Co C, died Dec 8, scorbutus.
12429, Olinger, J, 61, Co F, died Dec 10, '65, scorbutus.
12855, Orung, J B, 101, Co I, died April 17, '65, diarrhea.
11349, O Brien, John, 2, Co D, died Oct 24, scorbutis.

65, Pusey, James, 45, Co H, died March 19, fever congestive.
724, Parker, Wm E, 45, Co H, died April 25, fever typhus.
913, Penny, A, * 59, Co C, died May 6, diarrhea c.
1326, Prouty, Wm, 9 cav, Co L, died May 24, diarrhea c.
2692, Phenix, A H 21, Co H, died June 20, scorbutus.
9, Price, Barney, 45, Co I, died April 5, small pox.
3391, Pile, Wilson, * 34, Co F, died July 16, scorbutus.
3555, Pierce, H, 100, Co A, died July 18, diarrhea.
4120, Perkins, W B, 89, Co G, died July 26, scorbutus.
5190, Pitler, G, 123, Co A, died Aug 9 fever typhus.
5377, Parker, W, * 124, Co H, died Aug 11, scorbutus.
5426, Perrin, N, 72, Co A, died Aug 12, diarrhea.
6163, Purlice, George W, 94, died Aug 22, scorbutus.
6589, Potter, H, 72, Co F, died Aug 23, debilitas.
6690 Pullen, Samuel, 33, Co B, died Aug 24, diarrhea.
6717, Post, J, 1 artil, Co D, died Aug 24 diarrhea.
6984, Palmer, Samuel, 135, Co I, died Aug 27, diarrhea.
7021, Pease, G E, 10 cav, Co I, died Aug 27, diarrhea.
7157, Plunket, M, * 124 Co E, died Aug 29, diarrhea.
7329, Peltersen, F, 113, Co G, died Aug 30, wounds.
7368, Purcell, John, 72, Co D died Aug 31, diarrhea c.
7384, Pierson, J, 125, Co B, died Aug 31, scorbutus.
4299, Palmer, F G, 2 cav, Co D, Aug 31 diarrhea.
7519, Patten, W, 21, Co D, died Sept 1, pneumonia.
7644, Pierce, Wm, 75, Co H, died Sept 3, diarrhea.
7701, Pruser, H, 1, Co B, died Sept 3, diarrhea.
7724, Payne, J, 89, Co E, died Sept 3 diarrhea.
8009, Potts, James, 122, Co E, died Sept 7, dysentery.
8278, Phillips, H, 83 Co I, died Sept 9, scorbutus.
8531, Powell, F, 9, Co G, died Sept 12, scorbutus.
8597, Pror A M, † 135 cav, Co B, died Sept 12, scorbutus.
8620, Pinert, F, 21, Co C, died Sept 13, diarrhea c.
8753, Parker, Z 124, Co E, died Sept 14, diarrhea c.
9111, Parks J W, 6 cav, Co G, died Sept 18, scorbutus.
9327, Parker, J, 40, Co H, died Sept 20, scorbutus.
9470, Perrin, G, 3, Co B, died Sept 21, diarrhea c.
9768, Pipenbring, George, 13, Co K, died Sept 25, scorbutus.
9822, Preston, Wm, 84, m I, Co B, died Sept 27, diarrhea.
10056, Parks, E F, 36, Co D, died Sept 30, scorbutus.
11221, Piper, E A, 23, Co B, died Oct 20, scorbutus.
11453, Patterson, F, 28 cav, Co F, died Oct 25, scorbutus.
11676, Prouse P L, 1, Co I, died Oct 30, scorbutus.
11779, Preshall, J A, 116, Co C, died Nov 3, scorbutus.
12038, Peasley, J, † 65, Co H, died Nov 16, scorbutus.
12040, Porter, W C, 40, Co H died Nov 16, scorbutus.
12452, Powers, J, 21, Co K, Dec 28, scorbutus.
12551, Poistan, J, 183, Co F, Jan 29, 1865, scorbutus.
12645, Piper, I, 64, Co F, died Feb 18, '65, diarrhea c.

844, Ricker, Henry, 2 cav, Co E, died April 2, diarrhea c.
908, Rush, D, 107, Co H, died May 5, diarrhea c.
1642, Radabaugh, W H, 33, Co A, died June 5, diarrhea.
2080, Ralston, W J, † 89, Co C, died June 15, diarrhea.
2124, Rawlings, S, 45, Co E, died June 17, diarrhea c.
2156, Rancey, A K, 111, Co B, died June 18, diarrhea.
2281, Rickards, W Y, 33, Co B, died June 20, diarrhea c.
2410, Rowe, A, 124, Co F, died June 24, diarrhea c.
2878, Rees, Thomas, * 98, Co C, died July 4, scorbutus.
3074, Rix, William, 2, Co K, died July 9, dysentery.
49, Reed, Harmon, 108, Co E, died May 25, small pox.
3400, Rogers, T, 51, Co C, died July 16, diarrhea c.
3426, Ralston, J M, 89, Co C, died July 16, dysentery.
3618, Russell, L F, 111, Co B, died July 20, diarrhea.
3862, Regman, O, 2, Co D, died July 24, dysentery.
3961, Robinson, H H, † 110, Co H, died July 25 diarrhea.
4061, Reiggs H, 21, Co F, died July 27, diarrhea c.
4335, Rex J W, 3 cav, Co K died July 30, diarrhea
4777, Robbins, A, 6 cav, Co D, died Aug 5, rheumatism.

OHIO.

No. of Grave.

5570, Reichardson, G, 82, Co G, died Aug 14, scorbutus.
5631, Russell, J O, 116, Co G, died Aug 14, scorbutus.
5639, Read, George H, 21, Co H, died Aug 14, scorbutus.
5641, Redder, G, 45, Co G, died Aug 14, scorbutus.
6418, Robbins, D B, 89, Co I, died Aug 22, diarrhea.
6511, Ross, J, 59, Co A, died Aug 22, diarrhea c.
6835, Reidgway, John, 23, Co D, died Aug 25, dysentery.
6948, Redd, C, 122, Co H, died Aug 26, diarrhea.
7174, Ross, A, 45, Co H, died Aug 29, scorbutus.
7353, Roberts, E I, 75, Co K, died Aug 31, diarrhea.
7639, Rutain, E B, 44, Co E, died Sept 2, diarrhea.
7841, Russell, James, 9, Co E, died Sept 4, diarrhea.
8521, Rhottn, W, 2, Co C, died Sept 12, scorbutus.
8747, Riley, W M,* 89, Co B, died Sept 14, diarrhea.
8818, Robertson, R, 120, Co D, died Sept 15, dysentery.
9614, Robinson, J, 65, Co D, died Sept 23, scorbutus.
9617, Rose, John, 72, Co H, died Sept 23, diarrhea.
10165, Ryper O H, 110, Co G, died Oct 1, scorbutus.
10354, Rogers, C, 13, Co H, died Oct 5, scorbutus.
10658, Rochelle, John,* 135, Co F, died Oct 11, fever typhus.
11079, Romain J, 59, Co H, died Oct 21, diarrhea.
11360, Reece, A, 80, Co C, died Oct 28, scorbutus.
11418, Reese, R, 59, Co D, Oct 24, scorbutus.
11646, Rapp, N, 19, Co A, died Oct 30, scorbutus.
11657, Robins, P, 122, Co H, died Oct 30, scorbutus.
11672, Robinson, C J, 2 cav, Co E, died Oct 30, scorbutus.
11859, Rourk, J, 6, Co G, died Nov 6, scorbutus.
12366, Repan, A, 47, Co A, died Dec 31, scorbutus.
12647, Rapp, D C, 2, Co C, died Feb 13, 1865, diarrhea.
12692, Rawsbottom, A F, 99, Co D, died Feb 22, '65, diarrhea c.
1763, Rel, J, 124, Co K, died June 6, diarrhea c.

83, Smith, J E, 7 cav, Co C, died March 9, pneumonia.
44, Smith, H B, 82, Co B, died March 14, fever typhus.
58, Strill, Michael, 100, Co K, died March 18, diarrhea.
231, Sears, Samuel, 2 cav, Co F, died March 29, debilitas.
260, Stephen, H, 100, Co B, died March 31, diarrhea.
263, Shields, George, 7 cav, Co L, died March 31, diarrhea c.
284, Saughessy, John, 45, Co B, died April 1, diarrhea.
481, Steel, Abraham, 50, Co H, died April 9, diarrhea.
594, Swench, W, 45, Co A, died April 16, diarrhea.
658, Snyder, Lewis, 89, Co C, died April 20, diarrhea c.
726, Sweeny, Samuel, 7 cav, Co G, died April 25, diarrhea.
771, Shannon, Charles, 45, Co I, died April 28, diarrhea c.
804, Starbuck, F, 62, Co E, died April 29, diarrhea.
937, Storer, John, 17, Co A, died May 7, diarrhea.
962, Smith, John, 7 cav, Co F, died May 8, diarrhea.
994, Smith, William, 103, Co E, died May 10, anasarca.
1160, Sames, Wm, 14, Co H, died May 17, diarrhea.
1179, Smith, Conrad, 100, Co A, died May 18, diarrhea.
1183, Smith, William, 2, Co G, died May 18, scorbutus.
1229, Spangler, A, 45, Co E, died May 20, fever intermittent.
1251, Swineheart, J W, 111, Co B, died May 22, fever intermittent.
1404, Seyman, Aaron, 89, Co D, died May 27, scorbutus.
1672, Sprague, W L, 6 cav, Co K, died June 6, dysentery.
1773, Simmons, John, 22 battery, died June 9, diarrhea.
2220, Shannon, E, 35, Co A, died June 20, scorbutus.
2280, Stanett, J, 45, Co C, died June 20, diarrhea c.
2370, Stiver, J, 93, Co C, died June 23, diarrhea c.
2524, Smith, G W, 11, Co K, died June 26, diarrhea.
2575, Sampson, C, 89, Co D, died June 27, scorbutus.
2688, Stolts, P, 45, Co F, died June 29, diarrhea.
2789, Shiver, L, 81, Co B, died July 2, pneumonia.
2792, Smith, N H, 1, Co H, died July 2, diarrhea c.
3116, Smith, G, † 21, Co I, died July 10, diarrhea.
42, Sabine, Alonzo, 100, Co A, died May 11, small pox.
3252, Short, James,† 4 cav, Co A, died July 13, diarrhea.
3288, Smith, D, 7, Co H, died July 13, scorbutus.
3361, Saffle, J, 2, Co E, died July 15, scorbutus.
3536, Steward, C S, 33, Co K, died July 18, diarrhea.
3602, Stevenson, D, 111, Co B, died July 19, scorbutus.
3298, Squires, Thomas, 49, Co C, died July 20, diarrhea.
3744, Snyder, Thomas,† 9, Co G, died July 21, diarrhea c.
3770, Smith D,* 2, Co I, died July 22, diarrhea c.
3794, Sever, H H, 2, Co C, died July 22, dysentery.
4249, Shephard, J H,* 2, Co E, died July 29, diarrhea.
4275, Smith, J B,† 1, Co B, died July 29, diarrhea c.
4294, Steward, J,† 2, Co K, died July 30, diarrhea c.
4745, Steiner, M J, 72, Co F, died Aug 5, diarrhea.
5018, Snock, A, 93, Co D, died Aug 6, dysentery.
5054, Smarz, A, 93, Co E, died Aug 8, scorbutus.
5066, Shipple, John, 6 cav, Co G, died Aug 8, anasarca.
5183, Scott, S E, 4, Co I, died Aug 9, scorbutus.
5287, Stevenson, John, 111, Co B, died Aug 11, scorbutus.
5380, Spegle, F, 14, Co D, died Aug 11, scorbutus.
5378, Schem, J, 101, Co K, died Aug 11, dysentery.
5455, Stevens, G W, 101, Co K, died Aug 12, scorbutus.
5896, Sullivan, W, 78, Co D, died Aug 16, diarrhea c.
6010, Staley, G, 89, Co A, died Aug 17, diarrhea.
6032, Smith, Wm, 9 cav, Co G, died Aug 18, diarrhea.
6178, Simpson, W J, 82, Co F, died Aug 19, wounds.

6199, Sheddy, G, 9, Co K, died Aug 19, dysentery.
6214, Shaw, George W, 105, Co A, died Aug 20, diarrhea.
6258, Shoulder, I, 24, Co F, died Aug 20, scorbutus.
6179, Super, P, 72, Co G, died Aug 25, dysentery.
6870, Scarberry, O, 89, Co D, died Aug 26, diarrhea.
7031, Sutton, J, 4, Co A, died Aug 27, diarrhea.
7065, Shoemaker, J,† 47, Co E, died Aug 28, dysentery.
7436, Stinebear, F E,† 101, Co A, died Sept 1, diarrhea.
7475, Shafer, J, 9, Co G, died Sept 1, scorbutus.
7510, Sell, Adam, 125, Co E, died Sept 2, diarrhea.
7788, Stewart, John S, 19, Co B, died Sept 4, diarrhea.
7897, Smith, H H, 2 cav, Co A, died Sept 5, diarrhea.
7986, Selb, Jacob, 28, died Sept 6, diarrhea.
8014, Shriver, George, 45, Co K, died Sept 6, diarrhea.
8015, Snider, James, 4, Co C, died Sept 6, anasarca.
8156, Sturdevant, W, 72, Co A, died Sept 8, debilitas.
8197, Shrouds, J, 6 battery, died Sept 8, diarrhea.
8200, Strouse, A, 7, Co E, died Sept 8, scorbutus.
8229, Shaw, W, 15, Co I, died Sept 9, diarrhea.
8300, Smith N, 121, Co H, died Sept 9, scorbutus.
8319, Sheldon, W, 49, Co E, died Sept 10, diarrhea.
8442, Sullivan, John, 135, Co F, died Sept 11, scorbutus.
8728, Sisson, P B, 18, Co H, died Sept 14, scorbutus.
8752, Sickles, J, 51, Co I, died Sept 14, diarrhea.
8914, Simmonds, S P, 1, Co A, died Sept 16, ulcus.
8931, Stull, G, 15, Co G, died Sept 16, scorbutus.
9009, Sharp, F S, 64, Co K, died Sept 17, diarrhea.
9244, Semall, J D, 12, Co E, died Sept 19, diarrhea.
9386, Smith, L, 153, Co H, died Sept 20, scorbutus.
9645, Scott, J H, 33, Co H, died Sept 24, gangrene.
9649, Skiver, J, 114, Co H, died Sept 24, diarrhea.
10250, Sheets, W, 81, Co A, died Oct 3, anasarca.
10312, Spencer, S M,* 89, Co E, died Oct 4, scorbutus.
10434, Shingle, D, 2 cav, Co L, died Oct 6, diarrhea.
10437, Stanford, P W,† 2 cav, Co A, died Oct 6, diarrhea.
10576, Stonehecks, J D, 51, Co F, died Oct 9, scorbutus.
10618, Schafer, P, 101, Co I, died Oct 10, diarrhea.
10708, Stouts, Samson, 2, Co F, died Oct 11, scorbutus.
10833, Sheppard, John, 84, Co D, died Oct 13, scorbutus.
11139, Shork, H, 72, Co F, died Oct 17, scorbutus.
11146, Smith, G A,* 45, Co F, died Oct 19, scorbutus.
11249, Sullivan, F, 76, Co C, died Oct 21, diarrhea.
11439, Swaney, E, 124, Co A, died Oct 24, scorbutus.
11579, Smith, P, 69, Co I, died Oct 28, scorbutus.
11595, Sapp, W N,† 20, Co E, died Oct 28, diarrhea.
11711, Spiker, J, 122, died Nov 1, scorbutus.
11797, Shaler, F,* 72, Co E, died Nov 4, scorbutus.
12105, Sly, F, 89, Co G, died Nov 20, scorbutus.
12281, Singer, J, 6, Co G, died Dec 18, scorbutus.
12305, Sweet, M,† 49, Co F, died Dec 18, scorbutus.
12441, Shoemaker, C, 8, Co F, died Jan 12, '65, pleuritis.
12538, Stewart, A F, 2 Co D, died Jan 27, '65, diarrhea c.
12562, Sponcerlar, George, 71, Co B, died Jan 31, '65, diarrhea.
12668, Shorter, W, 59, Co K, died Feb 17, '65, diarrhea c.
12769, Sloan, L, 123, Co D, died March 18, diarrhea c.
12759, Stroup, S, 50, Co B, died March 17, '65, diarrhea c.
12793, Seeley, N, 132, Co D, died March 18, '65, diarrhea.
12810, Scott, R, 75, Co G, died March 24, '65, diarrhea c.

780, Tweede, R, 1 cav, Co A, died April 25, diarrhea.
743, Trescott, Samuel, 2, Co C, died April 26, diarrhea.
999, Trimmer, Wm, 40, Co H, died May 10, dysentery.
1156, Turney, U S, 2 cav, Co G, died May 18, dysentery.
1496, Thomas, Wm, 10 cav, Co M, died May 30, fever remittent.
2860, Thomas, W B, 89, Co C, died July 4, diarrhea.
4784, Thompson, J, 2, Co E, died Aug 5, diarrhea.
4931, Toromian, W R, 18, Co E, died Aug 7, scorbutus.
5356, Tierney, W, 1 artil, Co L, died Aug 11, diarrhea.
5552, Tensley, M, 90, Co B, died Aug 13, scorbutus.
5668, Terilliger, N, 12, Co C, died Aug 14, scorbutus.
6380, Tanner, A,† 82, Co G, died Aug 21, wounds.
7224, Thompson, V B, 26, Co C, died Aug 29, diarrhea.
7246, Turner, S B, 45, Co B, died Aug 30, catarrh.
7640, Thomas, James, 44, Co C, died Sept 2, diarrhea.
8850, Talbert, R, 135, Co F, died Sept 15, fever typhus.
9774, Thomas, N, 103, Co B, died Sept 26, scorbutus.
9945, Townsend, J, 26, Co C, died Sept 28, diarrhea.
10471, Tattman, B, 153, Co C, died Oct 7, diarrhea.
10800, Tinway, P, 93, died Oct 12, diarrhea.
11820, Townsley, E M,† 89, Co B, died Nov 5, scorbutus.
12577, Teasdale, T H, 2 cav, Co E, died Feb 3, pleuritis.

12251, Uebre, S, 12, Co E, died Dec 9, scorbutus.

2194, Vining, W H H, 45, Co G, died June 19, diarrhea c.
8902, Valentine, C, 127, Co H, died July 24, scorbutus.
4330, Vaugh, B, 125, Co F, died Aug 1, diarrhea.
4497, Vangrider, H, 103, Co H, died Aug 1, diarrhea.
5268, Vatler, J F, 6 cav, died Aug 10, diarrhea.
6170, Vail, John L,† 17, Co C, died Aug 19, cerebritis.
6659, Vanaruso, M, 21, Co E, died Aug 26, scorbutus.

No. of Grave.

6985, Vandervеer, A. 6. Co H, died Aug 27, diarrhea.
7756, Victor, H. 1 artil. Co D, died Sept 4, gangrene.
9576, Vo'is, J, 81, Co H, died Sept 23, scorbutus.
10252, Vall, N. 12 Co K, died Oct 3, scorbutus.
10389, Vail, G M, 7 Co D, died Oct 5, scorbutus.
10172, Van Fleet, H. 14 Co I, died Oct 7, scorbutus.
11035, Vankirk, G, 135, Co B, died Oct 18, scorbutus.
11097, Van Malley, J M, 89, Co G, died Oct 18, debilitas.
125 4, Vanhorn, S, 9 cav, Co C, died Jan 30, '65 scorbutus.

7, W'l'ey, Samuel, 82, Co A, died March 5, pneumonia.
185, Wickman, William, 111, Co B, died March 27, fever typhus.
779, Woolley, John, 45, Co B, died April 28, diarrhea c.
807, Wetts, Louis, 45, Co D, died April 30, diptheria.
1083, Wood, William, 89, Co A, died May 11, diarrhea c.
1449, Wentling Joseph, 109, Co K, died May 29, anasarca
1604, Wood, Joseph, 15, Co B died June 4, dysentery.
1836, Wilkinson, W.* 89, Co D, died June 11, dysentery.
1913, Wilson, James, 93, Co I, died June 13, diarrhea c.
2020, Way, John, 44, Co I, died June 15, diarrhea.
2041, Windgrove, S R, 15, died June 15, diarrhea c.
2172, Webb, E 45, Co A, died June 19, diarrhea.
2358, Walters, F 9, Co E, died June 23, diarrhea c
2576, Wing, F, 2 cav, Co M, died June 26, diarrhea c.
2815, Willis, A, 89, Co A, died July 3, diarrhea.
2840, Wroten, L, 89 Co H, died July 3, dysentery c.
3188, Williams, D, 94, Co A died July 12, anasarca.
31, Wright, Wm, 7, Co H, died April 24, small pox.
3310, White, H, 15, Co A, died July 15 fever remittent.
8325, Whitton, G, 75, Co K, died July 14 diarrhea c.
4211, West, J B, 89, Co B, died July 29, diarrhea.
4681, Witt, John T, 93, Co G, died Aug 4, dysentery.
4688, Win, J,* 111 Co E, died Aug 4, scorbutus.
4695, Wile A,* 31, Co D, died Aug 4, dysentery.
5121, Winder, P, 70, Co D, died Aug 9, scorbutus.
5211, Wood, N L, 4 cav, Co L, died Aug 10, diarrhea.
5726, Winters, George, 115, Co K, died Aug 15, scorbutus.
6314 Wainwright, S G, 89, Co H, died Aug 20, scorbutus.
6318, Wisser, F J, 35, Co A, died Aug 20, diarrhea.
6362, Wistman, N, 9 cav, Co G, died Aug 21, diarrhea.
6397, Wilson E, 4 Co A, died Aug 21, debilitas.
6700, Watson, G, 21, Co A, died Aug 21, dysentery.

No. of Grave.

6761, Wood, S, 123, Co A, died Aug 25, diarrhea.
7056, Wood, W H, 59, Co E, died Aug 28, diarrhea.
7373, Wyatt, J, 90 Co B, died Aug 31, diarrhea.
7582, Wentworth, L, 72, Co A, died Sept 1, diarrhea c.
8298, Wright, J S, 89, Co E, died Sept 9, diarrhea c.
8396, Warner, 7, 14, Co C, died Sept 10, scorbutus.
8997, Wyckman, D, 78, Co G, died Sept 16, scorbutus.
9384 Worte, J, 116, died Sept 20, scorbutus.
9527, Woodruff, J M, 135, Co F, died Sept 22, diarrhea.
9691, Wagner, J, 93, Co F, died Sept 24, diarrhea.
10007, Whitney, E, 21, Co K, died Sept 29, anasarca.
10230, Williams, Orland, 7 cav, Co K, died Oct 2, diarrhea.
10309, Weaver, M, 72, Co H, died Oct 4, gangrene.
10402, Ward, Francis, 21, Co H, died Oct 6, dysentery.
10464, Whitehead, A B, 83, Co E, died Oct 7, scorbutus.
10528, Wiley, A, 26, Co I, died Oct 8, scorbutus.
10713, White, I, 73, Co E, died Oct 11, scorbutus.
10844, Westbrook R L,* 135, Co F, died Oct 13, diarrhea.
11014, Walker, C, 65, Co I, died Oct 16, scorbutus.
11024 Waldron, H, 14, Co A, died Oct 16, scorbutus.
11418, Williams, S M, 60, Co F, died Oct 24, diarrhea c.
11770, Worthen, D, 122, B, died Nov 3, scorbutus.
11874, Wesson, J, 36, Co F, died Nov 6 scorbutus.
12042, Wickham, J, 14, Co H, died Nov 16, scorbutus.
12073, White, R M, 15, Co D, died Nov 18 scorbutus.
12158, Warner, B F, 35, Co E, died Nov 25, scorbutus.
12584 Whitaker, E, 72, Co A, died Feb 4, '65, rheumatism.
12722, Wells, E, 57, Co A, died March 3, rheumatism.
12759, Winkiet, T, McLaughlin's squadron, died March 12, '65 s.
12786, Warner, M 102, Co G, died March 16, '65, diarrhea a.
4583, Webricks, Joseph H, 9, Co G, died Aug 6, dysentery.

638, Yuterler, W A, 45, Co E, died April 20, diarrhea.
5477, Younker, S, 80, Co F, died Aug 13, scorbutus.
6 08, Young, John, 7, Co E, died Aug 18, dysentery.
7816, Yeager, John, 7 cav, Co B, died Sept 4, diarrhea.
7876, Young, J, 9, Co F, died Sept 5, diarrhea.
10583, Young, W, 6, Co G, died Oct 10, dysentery.
12659, Young, W, 15, Co A, died Feb 16, '65, pleuritis.

8225, Zubers, J M, 100, Co B, died July 12.
11253, Zink, A J, 72, Co E, Oct 21, scorbutus.

PENNSYLVANIA.

224, Altwood, Abraham, 18 cav Co 1, died Mar 29, diarrhea.
250, Armidster, M, 4 cav, Co A, died Mar 30, diarrhea.
468, Ackerman, C, 5, Co B, died Apr 9, diarrhea c.
758, Ash, Simon, 4 cav Co C, died Apr 27, dysentery.
846, Allbeck, G B,† 62, Co F, died May 3, wounds.
975, Algert, H K, 54, Co F, died May 9, bronchitis.
1382, Arble, Thomas, 13 cav, Co A, died May 26, diarrhea c.
1837, Alt, M, 21, Co K, died June 11, ictus solis.
2348, Akers, George, 90, Co H, died June 23, diarrhea c.
2398, Allison, E, 55, Co K, died June 24, dysentery.
2547, Anderson, D,† 103, Co K, died June 27 fever typhus.
2648, Able, J, 54, Co F, died June 29, dysentery.
2954, Amagart, Eli,† 103, Co F, died July 6, diarrhea c.
3018, Ackley, G B, 3 artil, Co B, died July 7, diarrhea.
3317, Alexander, M 1 cav, Co F, died July 14, dysentery.
3361, Ardray, J F,† 13, Co F, died July 25, diarrhea.
4055, Anderson, J,* 79, Co I, died July 27, dysentery.
4143, Aches, T J, 7, Co H, died July 28, diarrhea.
4149, Alcorn, George W, 145, Co F, died July 28, diarrhea.
4195, Archart, H, 51, Co C, died July 29, diarrhea c.
4673, Allen, C, 8 cav, Co K, died Aug 4, scorbutus.
4973, Andertin, J, 4 cav, Co L, died Aug 7, diarrhea.
5286, Aler, B, 103, Co D, died Aug 11, diarrhea c.
5511, Ault, J L, 101, Co C, died Aug 13, scorbutus.
5862, Armstrong, Charles,† 4 cav, Co C, died Aug 16, diarrhea.
6 29, Anersen, John, 91, Co C, died Aug 18, marasmus.
7163, Arnold, Daniel, 181, Co C, died Aug 29 diarrhea.
7887, Angeledt, George W, 1, Co F, died Sept 5, dysentery.
8185, Allen, J L, 101, Co I, died Sept 8, scorbutus.
8232, Ambler, C, 18 cav, Co D, died Sept 9, diarrhea c.
8389, Alexander, W, 2 reserve, Co I, died Sept 10, diarrhea.
8653, Armstrong, A, 7, Co K, died Sept 13, diarrhea c.
8655, Arnold, L, 73, Co A, died Sept 13, scorbutus.
8765, Altimus, Wm, 7, Co E, died Sept 14, diarrhea.
1743, Alnley, Wm, 8 cav, Co F, died June 9, anasarca.
9150, Alcorn, J W, 18 cav, Co D, died Sept 18, scorbutus.
9896, Allison, D B, 55, Co K, died Sept 27, diarrhea.
10487, Andersen, A, 135, Co F, died Oct 7, diarrhea.
10470, Allen, D, 126, Co A, died Oct 9, diarrhea c.
10823, Allin, S, 7 cav, Co H, died Oct 13, wounds.
11419, Appleby, T M, 149, Co K, died Oct 24, scorbutus.
11607, Antill, F 61, Co I, died Oct 28, scorbutus.
11710, Anger, W, 118, died Nov 1, scorbutus.

11852, Afflerk, T, 2, Co F, died Nov 6, scorbutus.
11860, Aunandt, J, 154, Co D, died Nov 6, scorbutus.
12520, Atchinson, W P, 142, Co F, died Jan 25, '65, scorbutus.

228, Ball, Frank, 4 cav, Co H, died Mar 29, diarrhea c.
243, Bunton, Lafayette, 18 cav, Co D, died Mar 30, dysentery.
332, Briggs, Andrew, 13 cav, Co H, died Apr 2, diarrhea c.
427, Beagler, A, 27, Co C, died Apr 8, diarrhea c.
543, Breel, Jacob,* 27, Co H, died Apr 14, pneumonia.
569, Black, James A, 14 cav, Co D died Apr 15, pneumonia.
661, Bradley, Alex, 8 cav, Co F, died Apr 21, diarrhea.
671, Burns, Samuel, 73, Co K, died Apr 22, fever typhus.
673, Barns, J, 54, Co F, died Apr 22, diarrhea.
822, Bayne, Wm, 145, Co I, died May 1, dysentery.
874, Bradley, M, 3 artil, Co A, died May 4, dysentery.
897, Brown, Henry, 94, Co H, died May 5, diarrhea c.
938, Brown, D, 4, Co C, died May 7, diarrhea c.
974, Falling Isaac,* 8 cav, Co H, died May 9, diarrhea.
1048, Baker, J D, 57, Co F, died May 12, diarrhea c.
1188, Butler, Wm, 90, Co B, died May 18, scorbutus.
1300, Boyd, Thomas, 9, Co D, died May 23, diarrhea c.
1309, Bryson, J, 2 cav, Co D, died May 23, dysentery.
1327, Brining, J, 13 cav, Co B, died May 24, dysentery.
1375, Burney, J, 13 cav, Co G, died May 26, dysentery.
1393, Brown, J B, 4 cav, Co K, died May 26, diarrhea c.
1576, Boman, Samuel, 3 artil, Co B, died June 3, diarrhea.
1601, Berferl, R, 103, Co B, died June 4, fever typhus.
1654, Brumley, George, 4 cav, Co I, died June 5, diarrhea.
1790, Butler, J D, 76, Co B, died June 10, diarrhea.
1859, Berkhawn, H, 73, Co G, died June 12, scorbutus.
1872, Brooks, D S, 79, died June 12, diarrhea.
1923, Brian, Charles, 183, Co F, died June 14, diarrhea c.
1999, Bixter, R, 73, Co C, died June 15, diarrhea.
2026, Burns, Owen, 13 cav, Co C, died June 15, diarrhea.
2046, Begler, M, 4 cav, died June 15, diarrhea.
2127, Brown, C, 3 cav, Co B, died June 17, diarrhea.
2131, Buckbannan, W, 3 artil, Co B, died June 18, debilitas.
2180, Ball, L, 26 Co K, died June 19, diarrhea.
2236, Barr, J T, 4 cav, Co K, died June 20, diarrhea c.
2323, Baker, Henry, 18 cav, Co I died June 22, diarrhea.
2483, Bisel, John,† 18 cav, Co K, died June 25, diarrhea c.
2538, Babley, Wm, 20 cav, Co F, died June 26, diarrhea a.
2610, Brown, M, 14 cav, Co C, died June 28, diarrhea.

No. of Grave.
2727, Brenn, J, 73, Co K. died July 1, dysentery.
2738, Bolt, J H,† 18 cav, Co E. died July 1, diarrhea c.
2741, Beam, John, 76 Co E, died July 1, scorbutus.
2816, Burns, John, 13 cav. Co A. died July 3. diarrhea c.
2913, Bish, J, 104, Co F, died July 5, dysentery.
2918, Belford, John, 145, Co F, died July 5, diarrhea.
3005, Bryan, P. 3 artil, Co A, died July 7, diarrhea.
3019, Barr. S, 103, Co G, died July 7. diarrhea.
3027, Braney, J, 43, Co K, died July 7, diarrhea.
3051, Barnes, W,* 101 Co H, died July 8, scorbutus.
3097, Butler, L J, 118, Co E, died July 10, pneumonia.
3109, Brant, A, 115. Co G, died July 10, anasarca.
3216, Beraine, A A, 101, Co E. died July 12
3294, Burns, James, 103, Co F. died July 14, diarrhea.
3412, Brinton, J, 157, Co D, died July 17, dysentery.
3477, Baker, Wm, 103, Co F, died July 17, diarrhea.
3535, Burnside, J,† 57, Co H, died July 18, diarrhea.
3600, Black, W O, 103, Co G, died July 19, diarrhea c.
3693, Bittig, J L, 3 cav, Co H, died July 21, scorbutus.
3716, Brenlinger, Wm E, † 4 cav, Co D, died July 21, scorbutus.
3808, Butler, C P, 148, Co A, died July 22, scorbutus.
3821, Batchell, D, 55, Co D, died July 23, diarrhea.
3917, Bright, E, 90, Co I, died July 25, diarrhea.
• 3988, Bradford, L, 10, Co I died July 26, dysentery.
4002, Berkley, M, 50, Co I, died July 26, dysentery.
4054, Backner, Adam, 116, Co G, died July 27, fever intermittent.
4330, Barrett, J, 6, Co K, died July 30, diarrhea c.
4363, Brown, J 53, Co G, died July 31, diarrhea c.
4402, Butler, D, 53, Co G, died July 31, fever intermittent.
4494, Barton, James, 4 cav, Co B, died Aug 1, scorbutus.
' 4500, Burke, J, 90, Co A, died Aug 1, diarrhea.
4610, Baker, E, * 4, Co K, died Aug 3, diarrhea
4667, Behrens, A, 7, Co E, died Aug 4, scorbutus.
4752, Bennett, George, 55, Co D, died Aug 5, scorbutus.
4989, Bowers, J, 2 artil, Co I died Aug 7, wounds.
5010, Bammratts, ——, 73, Co D, died Aug 8, diarrhea.
5071, Barber, C, 6, Co D, died Aug 8, scorbutus
5084, Buck, B F, 2 cav, Co K, died Aug 8, diarrhea.
5118, Brown, M, 50, Co D, died Aug 9, scorbutus.
5324, Berlingame, A J, 141, Co K, died Aug 11, scorbutus.
5391, Bear, John, 79, Co D died Aug 12, scorbutus.
5416, Bruce, John, 101, Co C, died Aug 12, fever remittent.
5526, Bower, Benjamin, 6 cav, Co L, died Aug 13, scorbutus.
5587, Barnbaum, H, 143, Co F, died Aug 14, scorbutus.
5592, Broadbuck, Adam, 11 cav, Co A, died Aug 14, catarrh.
• 5662, Buck, B F, 2 cav, Co K, died Aug 14, dysentery.
5577, Browning Thomas, 103, Co A, died Aug 16, enteritis.
5948, Bohnaberger, A, 115, Co G died Aug 17, marasmus.
5969, Boyer, F, 43, Co E, died Aug 17, diarrhea
6061, Baker, James, 101, Co C, died Aug 18, diarrhea.
6074, Bower, G W, 103, Co K died Aug 18, dysentery.
6099, Bailey, J F, 18, Co D, died Aug 18, diarrhea.
• 6127, Benhand, J A, 103, Co D, died Aug 19, dysentery.
6229, Bear, Samuel, 55, Co G, died Aug 20, diarrhea.
6244, Boles M S, * 4 cav, Co K, died Aug 20, fever typhus.
6279, Bower, C, 101, Co C, died Aug 20, scorbutus.
6319, Birney, J, 4 cav, Co C, died Aug 20, scorbutus.
6359, Bennett, A, 67, Co K, died Aug 21, scorbutus.
6512, Blackman, W, 18, Co D, died Aug 23, diarrhea.
6551, Brannon, P, 7, Co A, died Aug 23, dysentery.
6554, Baldwin, C H, 2 cav, Co K, died Aug 23, scorbutus.
6604, Barnett, E T, 149, Co I, died Aug 23, diarrhea.
6621, Bell, Thomas, 11, Co E, died Aug 23, diarrhea.
6660, Blair, John G, 46, Co F, died Aug 24, diarrhea.
6663, Brecklnridge, W, 78, Co K, died Aug 24, diarrhea.
6688, Bowman, A, 63, Co B, died Aug 24, scorbutus
6701, Boyd, J W, 101, Co C, died Aug 24, dysentery.
• 6704, Beemer, Wm, 145, Co K, died Aug 24, scorbutus.
6887, Brown, T, * 11 cav, Co I, died Aug 26, dysentery.
6928, Bryan, L, 106, Co F, died Aug 26, diarrhea.
7125, Bridaham, H W, 55, Co H, died Aug 28, scorbutus.
7161, Bemer, S, 184, Co E, died Aug 29, diarrhea.
7347, Ball, P, 49, Co H, died Aug 31, diarrhea c.
7460, Barnes, W, 119, Co G, died Sept 1, diarrhea.
• 7477, Bennett, J, 55, Co D, died Sept 1, scorbutus.
7541, Barnett, M, 145, Co K, died Sept 2, diarrhea.
7684, Black, J, 143, Co I, died Sept 3, diarrhea.
7747, Blair, J G, 49, Co E, died Sept 3, dysentery.
7775, Brink, F, 11 cav, Co M, died Aug 4, diarrhea.
7940, Browers, J A, 151, Co F, died Sept 5, debilitas.
7963, Brumley, Frederick, 54, Co K, died Sept 6, diarrhea.
8078, Bright, Adam, * 101, Co K, died Sept 7, dysentery.
8075, Boland, Daniel, 183, Co I, died Sept 7, diarrhea c.
• 8256, Barr, P, 103, Co C, died Sept 9, diarrhea.
8286, Brown, L, 8 cav, Co C, died Sept 9, diarrhea.
8356, Brown, A, 101, Co H, died Sept 10, diarrhea c.
8358, Brickenstaff, W, 101, Co I, died Sept 10, diarrhea.
8363, Bruce, J B, † 101, Co F, died Sept 10, diarrhea.
8413, Blosser, Jonas, 7 reserve, Co H, died Sept 11, diarrhea.
8434, Bowsteak, T D, † 106, Co H, died Sept 11, scorbutus.
• 8499, Bicklet, E H, 57, Co K, died Sept 11, scorbutus.

No. of Grave.
8606, Boots, E N, 101, Co H, died Sept 12, scorbutus.
8719, Beatie, Robert, 95, Co D, died Sept 14 scorbutus.
8769, Boyer, J M, † 7 cav, Co F, died Sept 14, scorbutus.
8795, Bentley, T, 54, Co H, died Sept 14 diarrhea c.
8794, Brown, P, 55, Co A, died Sept 15, scorbutus.
8902, Baker, J, 184, Co C, died Sept 16, scorbutus.
8917, Baker, Wm, 11 cav, died Sept 16, scorbutus.
9147, Blake, E, 69, Co K, died Sept 18, scorbutus.
9520, Boyler, James, 7, Co E, died Sept 22, scorbutus.
9682, Baldwin, A, 61, Co K, died Sept 24, diarrhea.
9745, Bowers, F, 5 cav, Co A, died Sept 25, diarrhea.
9809, Honewell, W W, 14 cav, Co C, died Sept 26, diarrhea.
9952, Blair, George, 7 artil, died Sept 28, scorbutus.
10201, Burdge, H L, 3 cav, Co D, died Oct 2, ulcus.
10226, Byers, J, 22, Co E, died Oct 2, scorbutus.
10260, Burns, J, 103, Co E, died Oct 3, scorbutus.
10292, Brown, G M, 10, Co I, died Oct 4, scorbutus.
10357, Burgess, H, 27, Co C, died Oct 5, scorbutus.
10584, Buck, D C, 2 cav, Co L, died Oct 8, diarrhea.
10577, Ballinger, George, 87, Co D, died Oct 9, scorbutus.
10671, Blackman, W, 84, Co A, died Oct 11, scorbutus
10758, Beightel, J F, 51, Co G, died Oct 12, scorbutus.
10779, Boies, J M, 145, Co G, died Oct 12, diarrhea.
10783, Bouling, J, 3, Co A, died Oct 12, diarrhea c.
10943, Barthart, I, 116, Co H, died Oct 14, scorbutus.
10980, Baney, George, 4, Co I, died Oct 15, scorbutus.
10983, Baoyar, J S, 55, Co E, died Oct 15, scorbutus.
11024, Bunker, F, 55, Co K died Oct 16, scorbutus.
11087, Boman, G, 149, Co E, died Oct 18, gangrene.
11322, Bisel, B, 142, Co F, died Oct 22, scorbutus.
11379, Bruce, A, 11, Co I, died Oct 23, scorbutus.
11434, Berk G, 51, Co A, died Oct 24, scorbutus.
11445, Ball J, * 19, Co K, died Oct 25, gangrene.
11504, Bohn, G, 183, Co G, died Oct 26, scorbutus.
11528, Baney, I, 4 cav, Co I, died Oct 26, scorbutus.
11556, Baker, B H, 148, Co B, died Oct 27, scorbutus.
11563, Brock, C, 46, Co A, died Oct 27, scorbutus.
11569, Feighley, W, 103, Co C, died Oct 27 scorbutus.
11597, Blair, John, 106, Co H, died Oct 28, scorbutus.
11611, Boyer, T, 11, Co F, died Oct 28, scorbutus.
11635, Burr, E, 145, Co K, died Oct 28, scorbutus.
11674, Bolinger, O, 87, Co D, died Oct 30, scorbutus.
11818, Bayley, H, 66, Co K, died Nov 4, scorbutus.
11894, Burch, W, 2 artil, Co F, died Nov 7, scorbutus.
11929, Burke, J D, 22 cav, Co D, died Nov 9, gangrene.
11972, Bupp, L, 119, Co G, died Nov 12, scorbutus.
12039, Bailey, J J, 2 artil, Co F, died Nov 16, scorbutus.
12059, Bogar, David,† 184, Co C, died Nov 17, diarrhea c.
12079, Bond, C C, 20, Co K, died Nov 18, scorbutus.
12096, Brady, N, 5 cav, Co M, died Nov 19, diarrhea c.
12168, Brubaker, B P,* 79, Co D, died Nov 26, scorbutus.
12177, Braddock, T, 77, Co C, died Nov 27, scorbutus.
12418, Barrens, J, 5 cav, Co G, died Jan 9, '65, scorbutus.
12812, Barnett, J, 6, Co D, died March 25, '65, diarrhea.
2917, Brinn, James, 56, Co I, died July 5, diarrhea.
12665, Bennett, J, 184, Co E, died Feb 16, '65, pleuritis.

45, Carter, William, 139, Co H, died Mar 14, dysentery c.
97, Chase, Wm B,† 15 cav, Co C, died March 22, pneumonia.
156, Conpsey, James, 14 cav, Co H, died March 25, dysentery.
335, Carman, F H, 54, Co F, died April 2, diarrhea c.
415, Coyle, P, 45, Co A, died April 9, pleuritis.
466 Crouch, Levi, 40 Co I, died April 9, pneumonia.
479, Croghan, John,† 3 cav, Co A, died April 9, diarrhea c.
518, Case, Daniel, 8 cav, Co M, died April 14, diarrhea
734, Conner, Andrus, 4 cav, Co L, died April 25, diarrhea.
837, Cravener, S P, 14 cav, Co K, died May 1, diarrhea.
869, Curry, A, 119, Co E, died May 3, anasarca.
1015, Campbell, Wm, 8 cav, Co E, died May 10, dysentery.
1099, Case, Silas,* 2 cav, Co L, died May 14, diarrhea.
1138, Carmicheal, George, 18 cav, Co K, died May 16, anasarca.
1156, Crisholm, J H, 150, Co H, died May 18, scorbutus.
1206, Caldwell, S A, 14 cav, Co E, died May 19, anasarca.
1282, Coburg, M C, 6 cav, Co L, died May 20, diarrhea c.
1490, Conn, J H, 18 cav, Co K, died May 31, diarrhea.
1498, Campbell, H B, 103, Co E, died May 31, pneumonia.
1530, Clatter, F, 18 cav, Co C, died May 31, diarrhea.
1702, Callihan, Thomas, 14 cav, Co H, died June 7, diarrhea c.
1731, Cephas, L, 145, Co I, died June 8, diarrhea.
1829, Carter, Wm, 101, Co K, died June 11, pneumonia.
1832, Calvert, R R,† 6, Co B, died June 11, anasarca.
1871, Coombs, John, 3 artil, died June 12, diarrhea.
1873, Cox, J A, 113 cav, died June 12, diarrhea c.
2069, Cooper, T, 18 cav, Co K, died June 16, dysentery.
2349, Curry, R, 73, Co F, died June 23, diarrhea c.
2399, Coyle, H, 8 cav, Co F, died June 24, anasarca.
2455, Crouse, E, 141, Co A, died June 25, diarrhea.
2695, Copple, F, 54, Co H, died June 30, diarrhea c.
2743, Chapman, J, 7, Co H, died July 1, diarrhea.
2849, Carron, James, 4 cav, Co C, died July 4, diarrhea.
2884, Calean, Samuel, 103, Co K, died July 4, dysentery.
2995, Coleman, J,† 18 cav, Co K, died July 7, dysentery.

No. of Grave.

8320, Chase, F M, 72, Co G, died July 14, pneumonia.
8362, Clark, N, 8 cav, Co D, died July 15, diarrhea.
8407, Caton, W T, 49, Co D, died July 16, diarrhea c.
8490, Couch, Benjamin, 50, Co H, died July 17, anasarca.
3918, Coyle, Ed, 68, Co E, died July 25, dysentery.
3993, Carter, L, 10, Co I, died July 26, dysentery.
4015, Carpenter, L, 42, Co K, died July 27, diarrhea c.
4117, Cantrill, M, 6, Co B, died July 28, diarrhea.
4263, Conklin, N, 90, Co K, died July 29, scorbutus.
4338, Chapman, J, 3 artil, Co B, died July 30, diarrhea.
4353, Crawford, M, 11 cav, Co G, died July 31, diarrhea.
4357, Cox, James, 103, Co A, died July 31, dysentery.
4369, Claybaugh, G W, 2 artil, Co F, died July 31, catarrh.
4512, Crock, D,* 45, Co A, died Aug 1, diarrhea.
4682, Croup, W S, 103, Co L, died Aug 4, dysentery.
4729, Cochran, C, 103, Co I, died Aug 4, diarrhea.
4963, Clew, John,* 18, Co F, died Aug 6, diarrhea.
5177, Crames, E, 4 cav, Co M, died Aug 9, scorbutus.
5375, Campbell, James, 3 cav, Co F, died Aug 11, diarrhea.
5417, Cregy, J G, 54, Co I, died Aug 12, scorbutus.
5423, Cumberland, Thos, 14 cav, Co B, died Aug 12, diarrhea.
5484, Conahan, M, 145, Co B, died Aug 13, scorbutus.
5518, Carpenter, W C, 145, Co G, died Aug 14, diarrhea.
5581, Campbell, R D, 11, Co E, died Aug 14, scorbutus.
5628, Cox, H,* 7 cav, Co B, died Aug 14, diarrhea.
5828, Cummings, Benj, 8, Co A, died Aug 16, enteritis.
5979, Conner, J N, 184, Co C, died Aug 17, marasmus.
6237, Corbin, W, 49, Co C, died Aug 20, scorbutus.
6269, Campbell, R G, 11, Co C, died Aug 20, marasmus.
6320, Coon, George, 2, Co F, died Aug 21, diarrhea.
6346, Cameron, Wm,* 101, Co A, died Aug 21, diarrhea.
6395, Connelly, Wm, 55, Co C, died Aug 21, dysentery.
6440, Conner, J, 6, Co D, died Aug 22, diarrhea.
6502, Cline, J, 3, Co H, died Aug 22, diarrhea.
6615, Crawford, J, 77, Co E, died Aug 23, diarrhea.
6645, Coleman, C, 19, Co E, died Aug 23, dysentery.
6746, Comly, John, 101, Co A, died Aug 24, diarrhea.
6913, Craft, A, 90, Co G, died Aug 26, scorbutus.
7045, Cobert, F C, 11 cav, Co L, died Aug 27, diarrhea.
7095, Carr, J, 51, Co G, died Aug 28, scorbutus.
7116, Cathcart, Robt, 103, Co H, died Aug 29, diarrhea.
7209, Crain, J, 4 cav, Co H, died Aug 9, scorbutus.
7456, Craig, Wm, 103, Co D, died Sept 1, scorbutus.
7463, Clay, Henry, 184, Co A, died Sept 1, scorbutus.
76 7, Curry, S, 140, Co C, died Sept 2, scorbutus.
7632, Carroll, A, 2 cav, Co A, died Sept 2, diarrhea.
7669, Campbell, Geo T, 3 artil, Co A, died Sept 3, scorbutus.
7696, Criser, M, 54, Co F, died Sept 3, diarrhea.
8117, Crawford, J A, 103, Co B, died Sept 8, diarrhea.
8121, Collins, M, 101, Co K, died Sept 8, scorbutus.
8169, Cole, J C, 118, Co K, died Sept 8, diarrhea.
8260, Chapman, —, 18, Co A, died Sept 9, diarrhea.
8512, Coyle, M,* 79, Co B, died Sept 12, scorbutus.
8594, Culver, J, 69, died Sept 12, scorbutus.
8665, Cutler, L, 11, Co C, died Sept 13, scorbutus.
8700, Cavender, J L, 149, Co E, died Sept 14, scorbutus.
8884, Cysey, A, 3 hvy artil, died Sept 15, diarrhea.
9094, Coffman, Wm, 18, Co F, died Sept 18, scorbutus.
9134, Cramer, E, 55, Co F, died Sept 18, diarrhea.
9141, Church, C H,* 45, Co B, died Sept 18, diarrhea c.
9269, Clark, J, 101, died Sept 19, anasarca.
9396, Coats, S R, 135, Co C, died Sept 20, scorbutus.
9410, Combs, S, 1, Co H, died Sept 21, diarrhea.
9508, Clossy, J, 145, Co F, died Sept 22, scorbutus.
9554, Crum, C, 149, Co G, died Sept 23, diarrhea c.
9639, Cline, J, 118, Co A, died Sept 24, diarrhea c.
9778, Coulter, O, 45, Co K, died Sept 25, scorbutus.
9823, Cummings, R, 65, Co K, died Sept 27, diarrhea.
9846, Callahan, M, 52, Co D, died Sept 27, scorbutus.
9931, Conrad, W, 14 cav, Co M, died Sept 28, dysentery.
10104, Campbell, Wm, 13 cav, Co D, died Sept 30, diarrhea.
10120, Coats, L R, 139, Co H, died Oct 1, scorbutus.
10214, Crawford, George, 1, Co F, died Oct 3, scorbutus.
10276, Cantler, J L, 13, Co A, died Sept 3, scorbutus.
10283, Cromlch, F, 7, Co H, died Oct 4, scorbutus.
10386, Cornelius, Wm, 7 cav, died Oct 5, diarrhea.
103 9, Collingford, P, 55, Co C, died Oct 6, diarrhea.
10443, Clarke, W, 5 cav, Co K, died Oct 7, diarrhea c.
10462, Canby, G C, 2 cav, Co E, died Oct 7, scorbutus.
10497, Coperbewer, Wm,* 1, Co D, died Oct 8, diarrhea.
10541, Culberton, Louis, 73, Co B, died Sept 9, scorbutus.
10842, Corbin, M, 184, Co D, died Oct 13, scorbutus.
10847, Clark, G, 1 cav, Co H, died Oct 13, scorbutus.
11005, Coe, George W, 145, Co E, died Oct 16, scorbutus.
11025, Clark, J, 3, Co D, died Oct 16, scorbutus.
11250, Clark, H, 184, Co F, died Oct 21, diarrhea c.
113 9, Clark, E B, 101, Co B, died Oct 22, scorbutus.
11370, Carol, W, 145, Co B, died Oct 23, scorbutus.
11436, Crawford, L, 184, Co B, died Oct 24, pleuritis.
11438, Cole, H O, 2 cav, Co L, died Oct 24, scorbutus.
11477, Campbell, C A, 11 cav, Co C, died Oct 26, scorbutus.
11565, Creagan, G, 1 cav, Co F, died Sept 27, diarrhea c.
11614, Crawford, M, 14, Co K, died Sept 28, scorbutus.
11656, Coyle, H, 54, Co K, died Oct 30, scorbutus.
11659, Craney, George, 20 cav, Co L, died Oct 30, scorbutus.
11800, Cregger, W H, 5 cav, Co G, died Nov 4, scorbutus.
11815, Chacon, A W, 106, Co B, died Nov 4, diarrhea c.
11826, Colebaugh, W, 69, Co K, died Nov 5, scorbutus.
11876, Crandall, L, 145, Co I, died Nov 6, scorbutus.
11922, Cleaveland, E, 10 cav, Co I, died Nov 8, diarrhea c.
11993, Crampton, A B, 143, Co B, died Nov 13, scorbutus.
12120, Cullen, T P, 81, Co I, died Nov 22, gangrene.
12141, Conway, C C, 2 artil, Co A, died Nov 23, scorbutus.
12255, Crampton, F G, 71, Co F, died Dec 10, scorbutus.
12295, Cone, S, 115, Co E, died Dec 16, scorbutus.
12301, Culp, P K, 135, Co B, died Dec 17, scorbutus.
12368, Connor, S, 112, Co H, died Jan 1, '65, shot by the guard.
12424, Clark, J, 89, Co D, died Jan 9, '65, bronchitis.
12487, Collins, G, 118, Co E, died Jan 19, '65, scorbutus.
12599, Cassell, D, 20, Co E, died Feb 6, '65, pleuritis.
12672, Clark, F D, 7, Co C, died Feb 20, '65, rheumatism.
12818, Copeland, B, 14 cav, Co D, died March 29, '65, scorbutus.
1961, Culbertson, John, 13 cav, Co B, died June 14, diarrhea.

152, Davidson, H, 57, Co I, died March 25, diarrhea.
866, Dorr, Phineas, 119, Co K, died May 3, dysentery.
1020, Doran, McK, 63, Co D, died May 11, diarrhea.
1161, Duntler, Henry,* 51, Co K, died May 16, diarrhea.
1338, Donner, M, 2, Co K, died May 24, dysentery.
1463, Davis, Richard, 3 cav, Co L, died May 29, rheumatism.
1541, Deamott, J K, 45, Co C, died June 1, diarrhea c.
1545, Davis, Isaac, 8 cav, Co H, died June 1, diarrhea c.
2630, Dun, R B, 101, Co B, died June 29, pneumonia.
2657, Donovan, J, 139, Co K, died June 29, bronchitis.
2716, Delly, William, 53, Co H, died July 1, diarrhea c.
2938, Davis, M, 22 cav, Co B, died July 6, diarrhea c.
3378, Degret, N, 15 cav, Co M, died July 15, diarrhea.
3563, Davidson, Charles, 100, Co M, died July 15, diarrhea.
3741, Dallin, James, 8 cav, Co H, died July 21, diarrhea c.
379 , Davis, J, 103, Co A, July 22, dysentery a.
3873, Davis, M H, 103, Co E, died July 24, diarrhea.
3985, Dougherty, J, 7, Co E, died July 26, dysentery.
4087, Deron, Robert P, 149, Co B, died July 27, dysentery.
4202, Drenkle, J A, 79, Co K, died July 29, scorbutus.
5292, Decbman, John, 184, Co G, died July 29, diarrhea.
4481, Dodrick, Louis, 50, Co I, died Aug 1, debilitas.
4491, Denton, M, 9 cav, Co B, died Aug 1, diarrhea.
4497, Day, Wm, 97, Co A, died Aug 1, diarrhea.
4625, Davis, J, 101, Co E, died Aug 3, diarrhea.
4711, Dort, C R, 4 cav, Co H, died Aug 4, diarrhea.
4786, Dendle, Robert, 101, Co A, died Aug 5, diarrhea.
4792, Davy, H,* 68, Co K, died Aug 5, fever intermittent.
4806, Davenbrook, J J, 101, Co G, died Aug 5, anasarca.
4885, Delaney, J, 101, Co A, died Aug 6, diarrhea.
4897, Dunbar, John, 14 cav, Co M, died Aug 6, diarrhea.
4910, Dean, J, 148, Co F, died Aug 6, scorbutus.
5028, Dawlin, L, 110, Co D, died Aug 8, diarrhea.
5256, Ditzell, L, 73, Co I, died Aug 10, anasarca.
5431, Davidson, George, 57, Co C, died Aug 12, diarrhea c.
5468, Dougherty, 101, Co I, died Aug 13, diarrhea c.
5664, Decker, J, 45, Co B, died Aug 14, diarrhea.
5743, Day, And H, 2 cav, Co H, died Aug 15, diarrhea.
5746, Doran, P, 99, Co I, died Aug 15, dysentery.
6017, Deal, F, 63, Co A, died Aug 17, dysentery.
6045, Degrood, H,† 13 cav, Co A, died Aug 18, diarrhea.
6176, Defree, James, 15, Co G, died Aug 19, cerebritis.
6226, Dodd, J, 18, Co F, died Aug 20, anasarca.
6316, Davis, Wm, 153, Co A, died Aug 20, diarrhea c.
6568, Dawney, George, 148, Co B, died Aug 23, ictus solis.
6679, Donovan, D, 90, Co B, died Aug 24, dysentery.
6678, Dunn, Johnes, 69, Co F, died Aug 25, diarrhea.
6797, Dailey, M, 7, Co I, died Aug 25, diarrhea.
6879, Dunn, John, 184, Co A, died Aug 26, diarrhea.
7053, Dakenfelt, J, 55, Co D, died Aug 28, diarrhea.
7077, Deets, R, 3, Co A, died Aug 28, diarrhea.
7282, Day, S,* 18, Co A, died Aug 30, gangrene.
7360, Dively, J, 110, Co C, died Aug 31, dysentery.
7488, Dilks, C, 1, Co K, died Sept 1, diarrhea.
7651, Dewell, Samuel, 50, Co G, died Sept 3, diarrhea.
7828, Daugherty, J, 184, Co D, died Sept 4, diarrhea.
8211, Dixon, J, 105, Co B, died Sept 8, fever typhus.
8331, Doherty, J,† 73, Co F, died Sept 10, scorbutus.
8569, Duff, J,† 4 cav, Co B, died Sept 12, diarrhea.
8579, Dougherty, F, 90, Co C, died Sept 12, diarrhea.
8718, Durharse, B, 11 cav, Co G, died Sept 14, scorbutus.
8828, Donnelly, J, 97, Co H, died Sept 15, scorbutus.
8887, Dean, R, 2 cav, Co M, died Sept 15, scorbutus.
9109, Davidson, C, 90, Co G, died Sept 18, diarrhea.
9146, Driscoll, N C, 26, Co I, died Sept 18, scorbutus.
9191, Duffie, J, 52, Co F, died Sept 18, fever typhus.
9289, Delaney, E, 7, Co G, died Sept 19, scorbutus.
10004, Davidson, G,* 12, Co K, died Sept 29, scorbutus.

No. of Grave.

*10193, Dougherty, M, 3 cav, Co D, died Oct 2, ulcos.
10436, Durkale John, 1 cav, Co F, died Oct 6, diarrhea.
10917, Dalzell, J G, 139 Co I died Oct 14, scorbutus.
11295, Derry, Frederick, 20, Co C, died Oct 22, scorbutus.
11350, Diehell, Espy, 55, Co D, died Oct 24, scorbutus.
11894, Dewitt, M, 1 cav, Co E, died Oct 24, scorbutus.
11628, Davidson, S, 184 Co A died Oct 28 scorbutus.
*11988, Dickens Charles, 2 artil, Co A, died Oct 13, diarrhea.
12186, Dalrymble, J E, 145, Co K, died Oct 23, scorbutus.
12399, Donley, P, 120, Co G, died Jan 5, '65, wounds.
12575, Deeds, J, 13 cav, Co H, died Feb 2, diarrhea.
11181, Dixon, B, 145, Co K, died Oct 19, scorbutus.

972, Ellers, Henry, 13 cav, Co H, died May 9, diarrhea.
1081, Elsley, John, 18 cav, Co K, died May 14, diarrhea.
1416, Engle, Peter, 14 cav, Co K, died May, 28, diarrhea.
2105, Elliott, John, 13 cav, Co F, died June 17, dysentery.
2794, Elliott, J, 69, Co D, died July 2, diarrhea c.
3038, Erwin, C, 78, Co D, died July 8, debilitas.
3052, Epsey, James,† 145, Co H, died July 9, fever remittent.
3295, Elliott, J P, 103, Co D, died July 14, diarrhea.
3823, Ebright, Benj, 9 cav, Co A, died July 23, scorbutus.
4278, Eaton, Nat, 1 rifle, Co E, died July 30, diarrhea.
*4761, Eleuberger, P, 145, Co D, died Aug 5, diarrhea.
5687, Ennies Andrew, 145, Co K, died Aug 15, scorbutus.
6424, Ewetts, James, 103, Co G, died Aug 22, scorbutus.
6607, Ellis, F, 53, Co G, died Aug 23, diarrhea c.
6572, Eckles, E, 77, Co E, died Aug 26, dysentery.
6589, Ensley, C, 184, Co A, died Aug 26, dysentery.
7300, Ellis, H H, 18 cav, Co I, died Aug 30, diarrhea.
*7657, Egan, John, 55, Co C, died Sept 3, debilitas.
8066, Exline, Jacob, 55, Co K, died Sept 7, diarrhea.
8513, Eichnor, C, 149, Co F, died Sept 12, scorbutus.
8964, Earlman, J, 7, Co K, died Sept 16, diarrhea.
10009, Elfrey, B S, 7, Co K, died Sept 29, diarrhea c.
10694, Elliott, John H, 84, Co D, died Oct 11, diarrhea.
10731, Erdibach, C,* 5 cav, Co B, died Oct 11, diarrhea.
10799, Ervingfelts, Jacob, 187, Co D, died Oct 12, diarrhea c.
11831, Edgar, W H,† 7, Co G, died Nov 5, scorbutus.
11838, Erebedier, J,† 5, Co B, died Nov 5, scorbutus.
2001, Etters, D, 145, Co D, died Nov 14, scorbutus.
2673, Ebhart, J,* 87, Co E, died Feb 18, '65, diarrhea c.
9490, English, J C, 100, Co K, died Sept 21, diarrhea.

200, Fluhr, John, 73, Co D, died March 28, diarrhea.
*511, Fleh, John, 83, Co B, died April 12, diarrhea c.
791, Fry, L, † 4 cav, Co D, died April 28, diarrhea c.
1010, Fuller, H, 13 cav, Co H, died May 10, diarrhea c.
1098, Fifer, Charles, 27, Co I, died May 14, erysipelas.
1411, Fry, Alexander, * 4 cav, Co B, died May 28, diarrhea c.
1728, Fink, Peter, 73, Co C, died June 8, scorbutus.
1957, Freeman, W M, † 4 artil, Co A, died June 14, dysentery a.
*2078, Fulton, Thomas A, 103, Co H, died June 17, diarrhea.
2099, Friday, S D, 101, Co H, died June 17, diarrhea c.
2147, Fish, Charles W, 101, Co B, died June 18, diarrhea c.
2155, Farley, James, 54, Co F, died June 18, diarrhea c.
2261, Fox, George, 73, Co E, died June 21, diarrhea.
2477, Flay, L, 26, Co G, died June 25, diarrhea.
2530, Funkhanna, Jas, 101, Co C, died June 26, fever typhus.
2587, Falloun, A, 50, Co D, died June 26, diarrhea c.
2591, Fugartus, T, 90, Co K, died June 28, scorbutus.
2851, Faney, George, 18 cav, Co F, July 4, scorbutus.
3088, Ford, M, 53 Co K, died July 9, scorbutus.
3258, Fisher, B M, *101, Co H, died July 13, diarrhea.
3582, French, A, 2 artil, Co G, died July 19, dysentery.
3712, Forsyth, J, 18 cav, Co H, died July 21, diarrhea c.
3870, Fingley, John, 14 cav, Co D, died July 24, diarrhea.
*4307, Flick, L, 184, Co G, died July 30, diarrhea.
4439, Filey, J H, 53, Co E, died July 31, wounds.
4452, Foreman, G S, *1 cav, Co B, died Aug 1, pneumonia.
4521, Flasharse, H, 12 cav, Co A, died Aug 2, diarrhea.
4586, Flynn, M, 18 cav, Co B, died Aug 2, diarrhea.
4612, Fewer, E, 87, Co H, died Aug 3, dysentery.
4668, File, C, 116, Co D, died Aug 4, scorbutus.
*5062, Fish, J, 85, died Aug 8, dysentery.
5172, Fleming, W, *97, Co E, died Aug 9, scorbutus.
5586, Flickinger, Jno, 50, Co B, died Aug 14, scorbutus.
5788, Ferry, W, 79, Co A, died Aug 15, anasarca.
5873, Fee, George M, 103, Co G, died Aug 16, scorbutus.
6092, Fates A, 145, Co E, died Aug 18, cerebritis.
6184, Farman, E, 57, Co E, died Aug 19, cerebritis.
6155, Felthansen, 145, Co G, died Aug 19, scorbutus.
6180, Fantlenger, F, 53, Co K, died Aug 19, scorbutus.
6365, Fanen, James F, 7 reserve, Co G, died Aug 21, diarrhea.
6496, Finlaugh, S, 14 cav, Co G, died Aug 21, dysentery.
6619, Fox, E, 155, Co H, died Aug 23, scorbutus.
6675, Fritzman, J W, † 18, Co K, died Aug 24, scorbutus.
6694, Flinn, Thomas, 143, Co G, died Aug 24, diarrhea.
6881, Fuller, G, 2 cav, Co A, died Aug 26, diarrhea.
6884, Frederick, L, 148, Co B, died Aug 26, scorbutus.
6890, French, James, 101, Co H, died Aug 26, dysentery.
6892, Ford, Thomas, 7, Co I, died Aug 26, dysentery.
7041, Fullerton, E, 99, Co E, died Aug 27, scorbutus.
7097, Fester, John, 103, Co B, died Aug 28, debilitas.
7169, Fisher, W, 54, Co I, died Aug 29, diarrhea c.
7198, Fry, S, 101, Co E, died Aug 29, diarrhea c.
7575, Fitzgerald, M, 145, Co K, died Sept 2, diarrhea c.
7588, Fahy, John, 13 cav, Co B, died Sept 2, dysentery.
7776, Fritz, D, * 18 cav, Co K, died Sept 4, dysentery.
8006, Felter, H M, † 18 cav, Co K, died Sept 6, dysentery.
8149, Fullerton, J, 118, Co I died Sept 8, anasarca.
8175, Fetterman, J, 48, Co H, died Sept 8, diarrhea.
8324, Francis, N, 69, Co G, died Sept 10, diarrhea.
8631, Fagan, E, 118, Co F, died Sept 13, scorbutus.
9062, Fisher, C, 4 cav, died Sept 17, diarrhea.
9099 Floyd, B, 67, Co K, died Sept 18, diarrhea.
9232, Farr, J C, 107, Co H, died Sept 19, scorbutus.
9869, Faith, Alexander, 183, Co C, died Sept 27, scorbutus.
10176, Fessenden, N E, 149, Co F, Oct 1, diarrhea.
10408, Fingley, S, 14, Co B, died Oct 6, diarrhea.
10639, Fisher, W, 101, Co E, died Oct 10, dysentery.
10667, Flynn, S, * 76, Co C, died Oct 11, scorbutus.
10688, Free, J, 145, Co H, died Oct 11, diarrhea.
11026, Flemming, J, 97, Co E, died Oct 16, scorbutus.
11112, Flanney, J, 106, Co K died Oct 18 scorbutus.
11164, Ferguson, J R, 11 cav, Co D, died Oct 19, scorbutus.
11367, Fox, M, 8 cav, Co H, died Oct 23, scorbutus.
11378, Frill, D, 55, Co C, died Oct 24, scorbutus.
11601, Ferguson, John, 134, Co A, died Oct 25, scorbutus.
11802, Frishl, H, 115, Co E, died Nov 4, scorbutus.
11916, Freed, S, 53, Co B, died Nov 8, scorbutus.
11962, Fairbanks, E, 149, Co A, died Nov 11, scorbutus.
12000, Fagley, C, * 14 cav, Co I, died Nov 14, scorbutus.
12025, Foust, S L, 149, Co I, died Nov 15, scorbutus.
12207, Foster, C W, 76, Co B, died Dec 1, scorbutus.
12244, Falkenstine, F, 148, Co C, died Dec 8, scorbutus.
12386, Fruce, J, 52, Co A, died Dec 26, scorbutus.
12145, Fisk, J, 67, Co H, Jan 13, '65, scorbutus.
12605, Falle, W D, 20 cav, Co A, died Feb 7, '65, debilitas.

71, Goodman, Robert, 18 cav, Co M, died March 19, diarrhea.
131, Gesse, Christian, 54, Co F, died March 23, fever conges.
314, Graffell, Wm, 73, Co B, died April 2, pneumonia.
529, Guley, J, 145, Co G, died April 12, diarrhea.
573, Green, Wm, 3 cav, Co A, died April 16, diarrhea c.
968, Garman, B, 18 cav, Co E, died April 9, dysentery.
1001, Greer, J A, * 3 cav, Co E, died May 10, dysentery.
1008, Graham, W J, 4, Co C, died May 10, diarrhea c.
1063, Goodman, Henry, 27, Co I, died May 13, pneumonia.
1302, Gray, M, 7, Co B, died May 23, diarrhea c.
1373, Gilbert, John, 29, Co G, died May 25, diarrhea c.
1399, Gilroy, Berney, 73, Co F, died May 26, scorbutus.
1528, Getts, B, 54, Co G, died May 31, anasarca.
1649, Griffil, G W, 13 cav, Co L, died June 5, diarrhea.
1761, Genst, J W, 57, Co I, died June 9, diarrhea c.
1793, Gardner, (negro,) S, Co F, died June 10, diarrhea.
1911, Gensle, John, 19 cav, Co F, died June 13, diarrhea c.
1939, Goerlt, E, 73, Co H, died June 14, diarrhea.
2060, Galliger, F, 13 cav, Co B, died June 16, dysentery.
2084, Gilmore, James, 110, Co E, died June 17, diarrhea c.
2297, Gunn, Alex, 4 cav, Co D, died June 21, diarrhea.
2356, Greenwald, G, 127, Co H, died June 23, diarrhea.
2531, Guinbert, A, *103, Co B, died June 26, diarrhea.
2557, Gettings, J H, 1 rifle, Co C, died June 28, diarrhea c.
2944, Gross, Samuel, 51, Co E, died July 6, diarrhea.
2955, Gotwalt, H, *55, Co D, died July 6, diarrhea.
2988, Griffin, J, 103, Co I, died July 7, diarrhea.
2992, George, A, 149, Co G, died July 7, diarrhea.
2996, Gists, H, 103, Co H, died July 7, diarrhea c.
3037, Gilleland, Wm, 14 cav, Co B, died July 8, diarrhea c.
3528, Gorsuch, M A, 110, Co B, died July 18, scorbutus.
3590, Gibbs, E, 18 cav, Co K, died July 19, diarrhea.
4944, Gost, W H, 5 cav, Co K, died Aug 7, dysentery.
5422, Gregg, T, 139, Co K, died Aug 12, dysentery.
5655, Gross, John, 62, Co K, died Aug 14, diarrhea c.
5735 Gregg, D, 142, Co A, died Aug 15, dysentery.
5737, Graham, Wm, 103, Co F, died Aug 15, diarrhea c.
5808, Graham, D,* 4 cav, Co K, died Aug 16, diarrhea c.
5851, Growre, G, 145, Co C, died Aug 16, diarrhea c.
5885, Gettenher, D M, 103, Co I, died Aug 16, dysentery.
6006, Geand, C,* 4 cav, Co M, died Aug 17, scorbutus.
5288, Gladen, A, 21, Co C, died Aug 11, scorbutus.
6140, Garrett, James, 51, Co K, died Aug 19, dysentery.
6158, Gunn, J W, 101, Co H, died Aug 19, diarrhea.
6384, Gamble, O J,* 77, Co A, died Aug 21, scorbutus.
6389, Gallagher, E, 48, Co A, died Aug 21, diarrhea.
6897, Green, J C, 13 cav, Co D, died Aug 26, dysentery.
7224, Gibson, D, 56, Co A, Co A, died Aug 29, diarrhea.
7320, Graham, J, 56, Co H, died Aug 30, scorbutus.
7340, Geary, D, 151, Co G, died Aug 30, scorbutus.
7357, Groves, A T, 45, Co A, died Aug 31, scorbutus.
7352, Glass, Wm, 55, Co C, died Aug 31, diarrhea.

No. of Grave.
7527, Griffith, A, 54, Co F, died Sept 1, diarrhea.
7589, Granger, E H, 55, Co C, died Sept 2, diarrhea.
7679, Goslin, E H, 4, Co G, died Sept 3, diarrhea.
7773, Gies, C, 7, Co K, died Sept 4, diarrhea.
7889, Gross, G W,* 79, Co A, died Sept 4, anasarca.
8109, Galbraith, C,† 11, Co K, died Sept 6, diarrhea.
8311, Garrison, W, 8, Co K, died Sept 10, scorbutus.
8418, Gallagher, Wm, 5 cav, Co F, died Sept 11, scorbutus.
8765, Griffin, J C, 5 cav, Co D, died Sept 14, diarrhea.
9005, Gearhart, S, 142, Co C, died Sept 17, scorbutus.
9210, Griffin, D, 11, Co E, died Sept 19, scorbutus.
9326, Gilbert, H, 57, Co F, died Sept 20, scorbutus.
9437, Gorby, F J, 19 cav, Co M, died Sept 21, anasarca.
9503, Goodman, F, 55, Co H, died Sept 21, diarrhea.
9764, Grubbs, J, 103, Co F, died Sept 25, scorbutus.
9776, Gibson, J, 11, Co D, died Sept 26, scorbutus.
9792, Glenn, Wm, 101, Co C, died Sept 26, scorbutus.
9811, Great, R, 73, Co H, died Sept 26, diarrhea c.
9966, Gilbert, D, 138, Co B, died Sept 28, diarrhea.
9989, Garrett, F, 149, Co G, died Sept 29, scorbutus.
10051, Gibson, D G, 16 cav, Co A, died Sept 30, anasarca.
10127, Gemperling, Wm, 79, Co A, died Oct 1, scorbutus.
10468, Grant, M, 18 cav, Co I, died Oct 7, dysentery.
10613, Grullin, J, 56, Co A, died Oct 10, scorbutus.
10709, Gimberling, I, 184, Co F, died Oct 11, diarrhea.
11060, Greathouse, E, 14, Co B, died Oct 17, scorbutus.
11197, Grabb, M P, 83, Co H, died Oct 20, scorbutus.
11299, Gilbert, A F, 14 cav, Co F, died Oct 20, scorbutus.
11496, Grant, J, 6, Co E, died Oct 26, dysentery.
11573, Gasse, R, 22, Co B, died Oct 27, dysentery.
11806, Gordon, R, 65, Co F, died Nov 4, scorbutus.
11904, Green, W S, 12, Co I, died Nov 7, diarrhea.
12181, Gilher, P, 73, Co H, died Nov 27, scorbutus.
12247, George, F,† 18 cav, Co D, died Dec 6, diarrhea.
12337, Garrety, Thomas, 106, Co C, died Jan 2, '65, froze to death.
12411, Gates, J, 11 cav, Co E, died Jan 7, '65, diarrhea.
12432, Grunnell, John, 26, Co H, died Jan 11, '65, dysentery.
5843, Gillespie, J, 11, Co A, died Aug 6, diarrhea.
5118, Gibbons, Wm, 11, Co H, died Aug 9, diarrhea.
6228, Gallagher, T,* 101, Co A, died Aug 21, scorbutus.
6971, Gray, L,† 163, Co D, died Aug 17, diarrhea.

423, Hanson, T R, 119, Co E, died April 7, diarrhea.
470, Herbert, Otto, 73, Co A, died April 9, pneumonia.
455, Hoffmaster, L, 16, Co H, died April 14, diarrhea.
654, Hamilton, J G,* 4 cav, Co L, died April 20, diarrhea.
711, Holt, J, (negro), 8, Co E, died April 24, diarrhea c.
769, Hessinger, P, 73, Co E, died April 27, diarrhea.
988, Hammons, J, 3 artil, Co A, died May 10, dysentery.
990, Heager, J, 2, Co B, died May 10, diarrhea.
1080, Huff, Arthur, 54, Co F, died May 14, diarrhea.
1118, Hates, Charles, 2, Co H, died May 15, diarrhea c.
1225, Henderson, Robert, 18 cav, Co D, died May 20, diarrhea.
1311, Heckly, M,† 4 cav, Co M, died May 24, diarrhea.
1420, Hull, H C,† 18, Co K, died May 28, diarrhea c.
1488, Holtenstein, G W, 18 cav, Co I, died May 30, diarrhea c.
1552, Heuen, Pat, 145, Co E, died June 2, diarrhea c.
1650, Hendricks, N, 4 cav, Co D, died June 5, dysentery.
1768, Holmes, Robert, 12 cav, Co H, died June 9, diarrhea c.
2011, Hannah, Thomas,† 4 cav, Co D, died June 15, diarrhea.
2153, Hammer, P C, 18 cav, Co D, died June 18, diarrhea c.
2189, Harts, John, 51, Co H, died June 19, diarrhea.
2387, Hooks, T, 103, Co D, died June 24, fever typhus.
2450, Hiler, H, 50, Co C, died June 25, dysentery.
2551, Hammer, John,† 73, Co G, died June 27, diarrhea c.
2707, Howard, James, 83, Co I, died June 30, diarrhea.
2728, Henderson, A, 58, Co F, died July 1, scorbutus.
2786, Hollibaugh, W, 57, Co C, died July 2, anasarca.
2808, Hastings, J, 118, Co D, died July 2, dysentery.
2916, Homer, D,* 18 cav, Co F, died July 5, diarrhea.
3020, Hedley, E, F,* 57, Co A, died July 7, diarrhea.
3201, Harrington, John, 55, Co C, died July 12, scorbutus.
2, Headley, J D, 18, Co G, died Mar 15, small pox.
3379, Height, S C, 55, Co H, died July 16, diarrhea.
3439, Hughes, John, 118, Co A, died July 17, phthisis.
3525, Heenan, John, 14 cav, Co F, died July 18, scorbutus.
3554, Hadlet, J, 4 cav, Co G, died July 18, dysentery.
3563, Hester, I P, 7, Co H, died July 18, diarrhea.
3676, Heth, R, 2, Co A, died July 20, diarrhea.
3785, Harrington, J W, 3 cav, Co A, died July 22, diarrhea.
3792, Haller, Peter, 139, Co K, died July 22, scorbutus.
3836, Harvey, P D, 57, Co B, died July 23, diarrhea.
3853, Hollenbeck, J A, 55, Co B, died July 24, scorbutus.
3920, Hall, Henry, 53, Co H, died July 25, scorbutus.
3953, Haller, A, 73, Co A, died July 25, scorbutus.
4105, Hartlick, C, 99, Co E, died July 27, diarrhea.
4130, Helfelinger, V, 14, Co K, died July 28, diarrhea.
4147, Hobbs, A, 141, Co H, died July 28, diarrhea.
4154, Hill, P,* 101, Co B, died July 28, diarrhea.
4222, Hoover, John, 18 cav, Co E, died July 29, diarrhea c.

No. of Grave.
4232, Holland, J, 143, Co I, died July 31, diarrhea.
4370, Hill, John, 73, Co I, died July 31, diarrhea.
4379, Hardinger, W, 147, Co B, died July 31, scorbutus.
4431, Hill, Thomas, 18, Co L, died July 31, diarrhea.
4474, Hayes, John, 116, Co K, died Aug 1, diarrhea.
4790, Hallinger, J, 91, Co C, died Aug 5, diarrhea.
4921, Hick, G, 12, Co G, died Aug 6, diarrhea.
5045, Huber, C, 14 cav, Co B, died Aug 8, scorbutus.
5080, Haf, H, 149, Co I, died Aug 8, diarrhea.
5082, Hunter, L, 63, Co C, died Aug 8, diarrhea c.
5151, Hardis, J L, 11, Co A, died Aug 9, dysentery.
5178, Harden, M, reserve bucktails, Co F, died Aug 9, scorbu
5281, Hoffman, Charles, 7 cav, Co K, died Aug 11, scorbutus.
5284, Hickey, D C, 3 cav, Co C, died Aug 11, scorbutus.
5289, Hanson, J, 76, Co B, died Aug 11, dysentery.
5486, Horder, —, 184, Co C, died Aug 13, scorbutus.
5575, Hoffmaster, G,† 20, Co F, died Aug 14, anasarca.
5688, Heinback, S, 116, Co H, died Aug 15, diarrhea.
5954, Holinbeck, D, 101, Co E, died Aug 17, marasmus.
6175, Honigan, C, 55, Co C, died Aug 19, dysentery.
6302, Henry, R W, 4, Co H, died Aug 20, diarrhea.
6367, Hill, J E, 2 cav, Co L, died Aug 21, scorbutus.
6481, Hollingworth, J, (negro), 8, Co A, died Aug 22, diarrhea.
6597, Hofmaster, L, 73, Co I, died Aug 23, diarrhea c.
6635, Hazenflucey, J, 26 lettery, died Aug 23, scorbutus.
6711, Hoch, John, 103, Co K, died Aug 24, scorbutus.
6752, Haden, R, 119, Co A, died Aug 24, pneumonia.
6793, Hogan, Thomas, 103, Co K, died Aug 25, scorbutus.
6845, Hurling, A, 57, Co C, died Aug 25, dysentery.
6901, Hammer, John, 3 artil, Co B, died Aug 26, diarrhea.
7000, Hoy, J, 101, Co F, died Aug 27, dysentery.
7102, Houseman, G, 118, Co I, died Aug 28, diarrhea.
7286, Holloman, Wm, 102, Co G, died Aug, 30, dysentery.
7328, Hopes, W, 2 artil, Co A, died Aug 30, dysentery.
7422, Havert, B, 52, Co I, died Aug 31, scorbutus.
7491, Helliger, C, 63, Co D, died Sept 1, diarrhea.
7531, Hill, E, 110 died Sept 1, dysentery.
7537, Henry, A B, 103, Co E, died Sept 1, anasarca.
7568, Hobson, B F, 7, Co G, died Sept 2, dysentery.
7571, Harman, John, 14, Co H, died Sept 2, diarrhea.
7588, Harris, A, 2 cav, Co K, died Sept 2 scorbutus.
7613, Honiker, J, 119, Co H, died Sept 2, scorbutus.
7661, Hockenbroot, J, 2 artil, Co F, died Sept 3, scorbutus.
7665, Hughes, J, 11 cav, Co B, died Sept 3, diarrhea.
7682, Hoover, S P, 7, Co H, died Sept 3, diarrhea.
7687, Hunter, Charles, 3, Co A, died Sept 3, diarrhea.
7881, Holmes, S,* 140, Co B, died Sept 5, diarrhea.
7965, Hutton, James, 118, Co I, died Sept 6, diarrhea.
7990, Hazel, George, 2 cav, Co D, died Sept 6, diarrhea.
8254, Hecker, G, 6 reserves, Co C, died Sept 9, diarrhea c.
8462, Henry, O H, 2 cav, Co L, died Sept 11, scorbutus.
8525, Heselport, J F, 68, Co G, died Sept 12, diarrhea.
8532, Hopkins, G R,† 50, Co K, died Sept 12, diarrhea.
9088, Halsey, —, 90, Co C, died Sept 18, diarrhea c.
9118, Hooker, Wm, 8, Co G, died Sept 18, diarrhea.
9123, Holdhane, C, 63, Co E, died Sept 18, diarrhea.
9404, Houghbough, J, 143, Co D, died Sept 21, diarrhea c.
9434, Hanks, J, 1, Co A, died Sept 21, diarrhea c.
9443, Hartzel, J, 7, Co I, died Sept 21, diarrhea c.
9532, Houston, D, 4, Co B, died Sept 22, scorbutus.
9579, Harmony, J, 169, Co H, died Sept 23, diarrhea.
9843, Hollinshalt, W, 149, Co E, died Sept 27, scorbutus.
9884, Hibblare, J, 99, Co H, died Sept 27, scorbutus.
9904, Hughly, John, 69, Co D, died Sept 27, scorbutus.
10022, Hamilton, B, 183, died Sept 29, diarrhea.
10070, Holden, Isaac, 7, Co G, died Sept 30, diarrhea.
10169, Harper, R, 103, Co B, died Sept 30, scorbutus.
10239, Hicks, J F, 14 cav, Co A, died Oct 2, diarrhea.
10340, Hammood, J, 10, Co D, died Oct 5, scorbutus.
10386, Hill, S M, 14, Co D, died Oct 5, scorbutus.
10430, Haldwell, P, 7 cav, Co E, died Oct 6, wounds.
10448, Hiller, S, 64, Co D, died Oct 7, gangrene.
10474, Howe, M A, 12 cav, Co B, died Oct 7, dysentery.
10535, Hand, H, 58, died Oct 8, diarrhea.
10571, Holden, P, 12 cav, Co B, died Oct 9, diarrhea.
10574, Hayes, J,† 15 cav, Co G, died Oct 9, diarrhea.
10610, Hands, J, 106, Co A, died Oct 10, diarrhea.
10670, Hull, Ed, 77, Co G, died Oct 11, scorbutus.
10804, Hennessy, P, 49, Co H, died Oct 12, scorbutus.
10814, Hunsbach, J, 116, Co G, died Oct 12, diarrhea.
10862, Hoberg, A J, 2 cav, Co M, died Oct 13, scorbutus.
10903, Hennessy, A, 55, Co I, died Oct 14, scorbutus.
10906, Hall, A, 118, Co E, died Oct 14, scorbutus.
10952, Hoover, S, 79, Co G, died Oct 14, diarrhea.
10962, Huffman, S, 64, Co C, died Oct 15, scorbutus.
11083, Happy, G, 101, Co K, died Oct 16, scorbutus.
11092, Harty, James, 148, Co I, died Oct 18, scorbutus.
11113, Horton, S, 106, Co I, died Oct 18, scorbutus.
11183, Hess, O, 118, Co D, died Oct 19, scorbutus.
11194, Hepsey, M, 73, Co K, died Oct 20, dysentery.
11383, Hunter, T, 5 cav, Co M, died Oct 24, scorbutus.

No. of Grave.

11481, Hart, J, 7, Co I, died Oct 26, scorbutus.
11219, Hunter, J, 14 cav, Co M, died Oct 20, scorbutus.
11495, Hardinlvck, J, 2, Co C, died Oct 20, dysentery.
11609, Hossflock, H A, 6 cav, Co E, died Oct 28, diarrhea c.
11643, Hicket, J, 30, Co D, died Oct 31, scorbutus.
11702, Hoover, J, 90, Co A, died Oct 31, scorbutus.
11799, Hagerty, W B, 7, Co G, died Nov 4, scorbutus.
11897, Hart, M, 11, Co K, died Nov 7, scorbutus.
12215, Hyatt, J F, 118, Co F, died Dec 3, diarrhea.
12260, Healy, J B, 100, Co M, died Oct 11, scorbutus.
12308, Hammond, W, 20, Co K, died Dec 18, scorbutus.
12610, Heneman, E L, 5, Co C, died Feb 7, '65, debilitas.
12632, Healey, J,* 143, Co K, died Feb 10, '65, diarrhea.
12719, Hummell, J, 87, Co D, died Mar 2, '65, diarrhea c.
7020, Hazen, M J, 101, Co H, died Aug 22, dysentery.
2474, Hall, B, 105, Co F died July 17, scorbutus.
10227, Haman, I, 118, Co E, died Oct 1, diarrhea.

124, Isheart, N, 18 cav, Co G, died Mar 23, dysentery.
1401, Illy, Tobias, 27, Co C, died May 27, dysentery.
10534, Irvin, T J 15 cav, Co M, died Oct 8, anasarca.
10616, Ireton, S R, 138, Co I, died Oct 10, dysentery.
11560, Irwin, W, 184, Co A, died Oct 27, scorbutus.
831, Ingersoll, Sam'l, 3, Co D, died May 1, diarrhea.

233, Johnson, John J, 45, Co I, died Mar 20, debilitas.
463, Johnson, Charles, 93, Co C, died Apr 9, diarrhea.
665, Johnson, John, 2 cav, Co G, died Apr 15, diarrhea.
976, Jacobs, Jacob, 2 cav, Co M, died Apr 9, diarrhea.
1703, Jones, William, 145, Co A, died May 23, diarrhea c.
1595, Jones, J, 147, Co C, died June 3, diarrhea.
1840, Jones, Wm, 26, Co C, died June 11, diarrhea c.
2108, Jones, O, 4 cav, Co D, died June 17, diarrhea c.
2312, Johnston, Wm, 3 artil, Co A, died June 22, diarrhea.
2500, Jones, R, 103, Co D, died June 28, diarrhea.
2914, Jordan, D W, 103, Co B, died July 5, diarrhea.
3409, Johnson, D, 45, Co I, died July 18, pneumonia.
3510, Jennings, H, 45, Co G, died July 18, pneumonia.
3885, Jones, Wm, 55, Co C, died July 24, diarrhea.
4057, John, Thomas 54, Co E, died July 27, wounds.
4093, Jones, J, 79, Co A, died July 27, diarrhea c.
4540, Johnson, J W, 50, Co G, died Aug 2, diarrhea.
4590, Jameson, Wm, 103, Co H, died Aug 3, diarrhea.
4817, Johne, Robert, 101, Co I, died Aug 5, diarrhea.
5295, Johnson, H, 2 artil, Co I, died Aug 11, scorbutus.
5516, Jacobs, B G, 150, Co F, died Aug 13, diarrhea.
5871, Jones, Robert, 100, Co A, died Aug 16, enteritis.
6197, Jones, T, 101, Co I, died Aug 19, diarrhea.
6200, Jones, W E, 27, Co B, died Aug 19, scorbutus.
6817, Jones, S, 49, Co G, died Aug 22, fever intermittent.
6700, Joslin, J, 145, Co I, died Aug 25, anasarca.
6817, Joher, J, 77, Co B, died Aug 25, dysentery.
6031, Jrmuter, C, 7, Co A, died Aug 28, scorbutus.
7506, Johnson, Charles, 53, Co G, died Sept 2, scorbutus.
8818, Johnson, J, 45, Co I, died Sept 10, diarrhea.
8853, Jolly, James, 101, Co H, died Sept 15, diarrhea.
9103, Jones, P, 63, Co F, died Sept 20, diarrhea.
9351, Jordan, J M, 149, Co D, died Sept 20, scorbutus.
9378, Jacobs, J S, 6 cav, Co F, died Sept 20, anasarca.
9952, Jeffres, C, 4, Co B, died Sept 29, diarrhea.
9909, Jones, T, 101, Co B, died Sept 29, scorbutus.
10735, Jubin, James, 55, Co E, died Oct 11, scorbutus.
10987, Jones, A, 27, Co D, died Oct 16, diarrhea c.
11058, Johnson, Wm, 184, Co D, died Oct 17, scorbutus.
11420, Jordan, Thomas, 145, died Oct 24, scorbutus.
11539, Jenks, J C, 115, Co H, died Oct 27, dysentery.
12007, Jobson, L, 118, Co C, died Nov 4, scorbutus.
12231, Jack, J P, 7, Co E, died Dec 24, scorbutus.
2869, Johnson, A G,* 103, Co I, died July 4, fever remittent.

2, Kelley, Charles H, 71, Co H, died March 1, phthisis.
238, Kelley, H S, 13 cav, Co H, died Mar 30, diarrhea.
266, Kuntyelman, J, 63, Co E, died Mar 31, fever typhus.
1024, Kenny, Wm, 12, Co F, died May 11, diarrhea c.
1824, Kyle, Wm, 5, Co H, died June 10, diarrhea.
1875, Kelly, Peter, 73, died June 12, anasarca.
2076, Knight, John, 7 cav, Co K, died June 17, diarrhea.
2385, Kehoe, Moses, 8, Co H, died June 22, diarrhea c.
2639, Kennan, M A, 14 cav, Co L, died June 29, diarrhea.
3048, King, C, 6, Co C, died July 8, debilitas.
3187, Koich, N,* 54, Co A, died July 12, anasarca.
3265, Klink, A, 101, Co C, died July 13, debilitas.
3471, Kemp, E, 103, Co A, died July 17, diarrhea c.
3634, Keeston, E, 103, Co I, died July 20, diarrhea.
4162, Kagman, J T, 45, Co B, died July 28, diarrhea.
4293, Kuffman, S D, 45, Co E, died July 30, dysentery.
4545, Kanf, J, 2 artil, Co B, died Aug 2, scorbutus.
4895, Kelley, O F, 148, Co B, died Aug 6, dysentery c.
5058, Kock, H, 21, Co H, died Aug 8, diarrhea.
5145, Kawell, John H, 18 cav, Co E, died Aug 9, scorbutus.
5154, Keys, Alex C,* 16 cav, Co H, died Aug 9, diarrhea.

6208, Kester, L, 140, Co F, died Aug 10, bronchitis.
5443, Kelley, T, 13 cav, Co H, died Aug 12, anasarca.
5851, Kalm, R, 96, Co K, died Aug 13, dysentery.
5718, Kester, John M, 103, Co A, died Aug 15, dysentery.
5744, Keeley, Wm, 13 cav, Co A, died Aug 15, scorbutus.
6028, Kauffman, B F, 45, Co K, died Aug 18, diarrhea.
6084, Kemper, J, 73, Co D, died Aug 18, scorbutus.
6459, Kiger, Wm, 3 cav, Co C, died Aug 22, scorbutus.
6497, Kenter, A W, 67, Co B, died Aug 22, diarrhea c.
6514, Kniver, S, 184, Co F, died Aug 22, fever typhus.
6628, Krigle, H, 11, Co K, died Aug 23, diarrhea.
6965, Krader, W O, 55, Co H, died Aug 27, scorbutus.
7005, King, M, 3 cav, Co A, died Aug 27, diarrhea.
7372, Keller, A, 9, Co M, died Aug 31, diarrhea.
7553, Keller, M, 105, Co G, died Sept 2, scorbutus.
7781, Kyle, Wm, 118, Co F, died Sept 4, diarrhea.
8210, Kinsman, F P, 184, Co F, died Sept 8, fever typhus.
8731, Kantard, John C, sgt major, 5 cav, died Sept 14, diarrhea.
8799, Kaufman, J, 45, Co E, died Sept 17, anasarca.
9039, Kipp, W, 12 cav, Co D, died Sept 18, diarrhea c.
9563, Klmnick T,* 145, Co K, died Sept 23, scorbutus.
9630, Kearney, L, 50, Co F, died Sept 24, scorbutus.
10335, Kerr, B, 140, Co B, died Oct 4, diarrhea.
10367, Kirby, J A, 101, Co E, died Oct 5, scorbutus.
10429, Kline, Ross, 184, Co F, died Oct 6, scorbutus.
10502, Kennedy, J, 152, Co A, died Oct 8, diarrhea.
10698, King, M, 11, Co K, died Oct 11, diarrhea c.
10747, Kirkwood, H, 101, Co C, died Oct 11, scorbutus.
10926, Kreiper, C, 80, Co F, died Oct 14, scorbutus.
11258, Kurtz, J, 55, Co K, died Oct 21, scorbutus.
11322, King, J R, 55, Co K, died Oct 23, scorbutus.
11384, Kelley, E, 7 cav, Co F, died Oct 24, scorbutus.
11463, King, R, 6, Co E, died Oct 26, scorbutus.
11645, Kramer, George,* 116, Co G, died Oct 30, scorbutus.
12695, Knox, J J 184, Co A, died Feb 23, '65, diarrhea c.
3670, Kerer, H N, 63, Co E, died July 20, '64, scorbutus.

88, Liesen, Lewis, 13 cav, Co A, died Mar 21, bronchitis.
243, Lancaster, E, 14 cav, Co F, died Mar 30, fever congestive
297, Luck, W, 11 cav, Co H, died Apr 1, pneumonia.
549, Lynch, Adam, 6 cav, Co L, died Apr 14, diarrhea.
1403, Levy, Frank, 3 cav, Co H, died May 27, diarrhea.
1429, Lieene, Wm,* 13, Co E, died May 28, diarrhea c.
1579, Lindine, J, 3 artil, Co A, died June 3, diarrhea.
1588, Little, M, 106, Co F, died June 3, diarrhea.
1621, Lubars, Melter, 145, Co A, died June 4, diarrhea.
2250, Lackey, James, 183, Co D, died June 21, debilitas.
2379, Leach, J, 3 cav, Co D, died June 23, diarrhea c.
3091, Larimer, J, 11, Co E, died July 9, fever remittent.
3734, Ladbeater, James, 7, Co K, died July 21, diarrhea c.
3305, Link, P, 98, Co H, died July 14, scorbutus.
3300, Long, A, 118, Co H, died July 14, scorbutus.
3360, Lanigan, N, 13 cav, Co L, died July 15, anasarca.
3403, Lewis, Ed, 101, Co I, died July 16, dysentery.
3448, Leonard, George, 40, Co G, died July 17, fever remittent.
3489, Logan, B, 90, Co B, died July 17, diarrhea c.
3546, Lee, James, 13 cav, Co B, died July 18, diarrhea.
4312, Long, D F B, 101, Co I, died July 30, diarrhea.
4434, Lambert, W, 4 cav, Co K, died July 31, diarrhea.
4696, Larrison, Wallace, 14 cav, Co C, Aug 4, diarrhea.
4818, Lewis, A, 3 cav, Co D, died Aug 5, pneumonia.
4857, Laughlin, J, 101, Co E, died Aug 6, diarrhea.
4907, Lohman, C, 73, Co C, died Aug 6, diarrhea.
4929, Livingston, J K, 2, Co B, died Aug 6, anasarca.
5199, Long, Augustus, 55, Co H, died Aug 10, diarrhea.
5225, Londin, H N, 14, Co H, died Aug 10, scorbutus.
5314, Lacock, Hugh, 116, Co E, died Aug 11, scorbutus.
6252, Lodiss, H, 90, Co A, died Aug 20, cerebritis.
6636, Leach, James, 49, Co E, died Aug 23, anasarca.
6783, Light, S,* 143, Co H, died Aug 25, dysentery.
7145, La Bolt, J, 21, Co F, died Aug 20, dysentery.
7938, Lemon, John E, 4 cav, Co I, died Sept 5, anasarca.
7950, Lockhard, J, 145, Co B, died Sept 6, diarrhea.
8405, Lepley, Charles, 108, Co E, died Sept 10, diarrhea.
8754, Laymen, F, 49, Co B, died Sept 14, diarrhea.
8823, Laughlin, J L, 1, Co H, died Sept 15, scorbutus.
8895, Lester, W H, 7 cav, Co I, died Sept 16, diarrhea.
8904, Lippoth, J, 5, Co E, died Sept 16, diarrhea.
9085, Logue, S, 26, Co A, died Sept 18, diarrhea.
9191, Leary, C, 83, Co K, died Sept 19, dysentery.
9647, Lolen, J, 4 cav, Co C, died Sept 24, debilitas.
10066, Laytin, P, 110, Co D, died Sept 30, scorbutus.
10086, Lutz, P M, 21, Co G, died Sept 30, scorbutus.
10091, Lebos, C, 116, Co D, died Sept 30, scorbutus.
10273, Limar, W, 140, died Oct 3, scorbutus.
10295, Long, W, 67, Co G, died Oct 4, dysentery c.
10372, Long, P,* 11 cav, Co C, died Oct 5, dysentery.
10549, Lancaster, C, 119, Co B, died Oct 8, scorbutus.
10572, Lynch, W J, 3 cav, Co I, died Oct 9, diarrhea.
10580, Labor, R, 7, Co F, died Oct 10, diarrhea.
10667, Luchford, R, 143, Co F, died Oct 11, scorbutus.

No. of Grave.

10873, Lang, I, 110, Co C, died Oct 13, scorbutus.
11094, Lenchtles, J, 5, died Oct 16, scorbutus.
11255, Lantz, Wm, 7, Co C, died Oct 21, diarrhea.
11165, Lewis, J, 4 cav, Co L, died Oct 26, diarrhea c.
11728, Luther, I, 4 cav, Co L, died Nov 1, scorbutus.
11803, Lugo, George, 12, Co A, died Nov 6, dysentery.
11907, Lat[illegible], A, 53, Co M, died Nov 7, diarrhea c.
12192, Lape, J, 18, Co K, died Nov 23, diarrhea.
12210, Lewis, D S, 63, Co K, died Dec 2, scorbutus
12419, Linsey, D, 77, Co G, died Jan 19, '65, scorbutus.
5601, Ledwick, F M, 139, Co C, died Aug 15, scorbutus.
7081, Latchem, David, 4 cav, Co K, died Aug 28, diarrhea.
7197, Lochery, A, 14 cav, Co E, died Aug 30, diarrhea.
1985, Logan, W, 97, Co A, died, Aug 17, dysentery.
6030, London, S, 101, Co A, died Aug 18, marasmus.
6054, Leyton, Samuel, 181, Co A, died Aug 18, scorbutus.
6071, Leach, C, 71, Co B, died Aug 18, diarrhea.
6082, Lane, Amos, 6 cav, Co E, died Aug 18, cerebritis.
6152, Lohnich, John, 2 artil, Co F, died Aug 19, marasmus.
753, Leonard, M, 13 cav, Co D, died April 26, dysentery.
761, Lord, G W, 141, Co E, died April 27, rheumatism.
871, Louden, Samuel,* 2, Co F, died May 4, bronchitis.

183, Maynard, John, 105, Co G, died March 27, pneumonia.
208, Massile, Val, 47, Co C, died March 28, dysentery.
225, Miller, Daniel, 13 cav, Co H, died March 29, pneumonia.
361, Martin, J F, 14 cav, Co K, died April 2, diarrhea.
461, McEntire, W, 41, Co F, died April 9, diarrhea c.
638, Mine, Joseph, * 54, Co F, died April 14, diarrhea.
685, Marple, S L, 14, Co A, died April 17, rheumatism.
695, McKissick, John, 23, Co F, died April 18, diarrhea.
667, Myers, G, 1 cav, Co E, died April 22, diarrhea.
736, McKeever, E L, † 71, Co F, died April 25, diarrhea.
773, McDonald, R, 23, Co C, died April 28, diarrhea c.
780, McCartny, James, 18 cav, Co E, died April 28, diarrhea c.
969, McQueeny, W, 79, Co B, died May 9, dysentery.
1005, Moyer, John, 2 cav, Co E, died May 10, diarrhea.
1128, McKey, J, 1 cav, Co I, died May 15, anasarca.
1139, McMahon, J, 73, Co F, May 16, diarrhea c.
1147, McKnight, J E, 57, Co B, died May 16, diarrhea.
1151, McHale, J, 14 cav, Co D, died May 18, diarrhea.
1185, Moser, John, 13 cav, Co B, died May 18, scorbutus.
1273, McCollin, W, † 4 cav, Co L, died May 22, dysentery.
1287, Milligan, J, 61, Co F, died May 22, diarrhea.
1308, McCartney, M, 73, Co H, died May 23, anasarca.
1460, Murray, John, 13 cav, Co E, died May 29, diarrhea c.
1586, Miles, Lewis, 4 cav, Co I, died June 3, diarrhea c.
1633, Myers, J R, * 13 cav, Co M, died June 5, diarrhea c.
1722, Marshall, M M, 78, Co E, died June 8, diarrhea c.
1748, Moyer, Thomas, 103, Co E, died June 9, diarrhea a.
1792, Miller, M, 118, Co A, died June 10, fever typhus.
1858, McHose, J, 4 cav, Co A, died June 12, diarrhea c.
1907, Miller, Henry, 8, Co G, died June 13, diarrhea c.
1982, Mucholland, J, 101, Co K, died June 15, diarrhea c.
2050, Monny, W H, 3 cav, Co A, died June 16, pneumonia.
2056, Mitchell, J J, 101, Co K, died June 16, pneumonia.
2109, Monay, J, 101, Co C, died June 19, scorbutus.
2265, McCutcheon, J, 4 cav, Co C, died June 21, diarrhea.
2278, Milton, Wm, 19 cav, Co H, died June 21, diarrhea.
2335, Myers, F, 1 27, Co H, died June 22, diarrhea c.
2364, Meers, Peter, 76, Co G, died June 23, diarrhea.
2388, Morton, T, 79, Co I, died June 24, diarrhea c.
2399, McCabe, J, 3 cav, Co L, died June 24, pneumonia.
2411, McKay, M J, 163, Co B, died June 24, fever typhus.
2485, Merry, James, 67, Co E, died June 26, dysentery.
2495, Martin, A J, * 4 cav, Co E, died June 26, dysentery.
2508, Morris, J, 18 cav, Co A, died June 26, dysentery.
2613, McManes, 77, Co B, died June 29, debilitas
2634, Mines, J, 101, Co B, died June 30, diarrhea c.
2690, Morris, G, 77, Co G, died June 30, diarrhea.
2795, Marsh, D, 50, Co D, died July 2, diarrhea
2841, McCune, Charles, 14, Co C, died July 3, diarrhea.
2917, McKeith, J, 48, Co C, died July 7, diarrhea c.
3065, Morris, Calvin, 53, Co D, died July 9, scorbutus.
3133, McCalasky, J E, 14 cav, Co K, died July 10, diarrhea.
3141, Mattser, B 57, Co F, died July 11, diarrhea.
3172, Malden, Daniel, 140, Co G, died July 11, pneumonia.
3250, Myers, M, 138, Co E, died July 13, diarrhea.
3374, Mink, H, 2 artil, Co A, died July 16, diarrhea.
3467, Meaker, E N, 155, Co H, died July 17, dysentery c.
3481, McKeon, John, 101, Co H, died July 17, diarrhea.
3498, Milton, J, 138, Co D, died July 17, dysentery.
3559, Marony, John, 1 cav, Co D, died July 20, dysentery.
3633, McCarton, J, 4 cav, Co A, died July 21, anasarca.
3733, Myers, John, 116, Co D, died July 23, scorbutus.
3971, Martin, G 45, Co I, died July 25, diarrhea.
4116, McDermott, J M, 79, Co F, died July 28, diarrhea.
4123, McGee, James, 153, Co I, died July 28, anasarca.
4137, Moore, M G, 1 artil, Co A, died July 29, catarrh.
4343, Marquet, M, 6, Co M, died July 30, diarrhea.

No. of Grave.

4407, McKever, John, 100, Co A, died July 31, catarrh.
4414, McFarland, Jas, 55, Co E, died July 31, dysentery.
4546, Moan, James, 101, Co K, died Aug 2, diarrhea.
4607, Martin, Bryant, 7, Co F, died Aug 3, scorbutus.
4635, McKeral, James, 14, Co K, died Aug 3, diarrhea.
4710, Mathews, C W, * 145, Co B, died Aug 4, scorbutus.
4731, Moore, M, 71, Co I, died Aug 4, scorbutus.
4790, McDevitt, J, 3 artil, Co D, died Aug 5, diarrhea.
4824, Miller, H, 14 cav, Co I, died Aug 5, diarrhea.
4876, Mills, Wm, 150, Co G, died Aug 6, scorbutus.
4898, Muldany, M, 96, Co K, died Aug 6, diarrhea.
5008, Martain, John, 103, Co E, died Aug 8, dysentery.
5069, Measler, James, 103, Co E, died Aug 8, scorbutus.
5139, McCaffrey, John, hospital steward, 3 artil, Co A, died Aug diarrhea.
5159, Martin, C, 8 cav, Co A, died Aug 9, scorbutus.
5266, Marey, H F, 103, Co F, died Aug 10, dysentery.
5291, Mohr, J R, 11, Co G, died Aug 11, diarrhea.
5415, McCarty, Dennis, 101, Co K, died Aug 12, fever intermittent
5433, McGee, J, 14, Co H, died Aug 12, anasarca.
5595, Mickelson, B, 16 cav, Co B, died Aug 14, dysentery.
5612, McClough, L C, 18, Co C, died Aug 14, anasarca.
5704, Miller, John, 101, Co G, died Aug 15, dysentery.
5723, McCann, John, 3 artil, Co A, died Aug 15, scorbutus.
5781, Miller, S, 143, Co B, died Aug 16, diarrhea.
5809, Montgomery, R, 62, Co A, died Aug 16, anasarca.
5868, McQuillen, A, 6 artil, Co L, died Aug 16, diarrhea.
5893, McCuller, S, 4 cav, Co B, died Aug 16, diarrhea.
5926, Mutchy, J A, 50, Co D, died Aug 17, diarrhea.
5988, Mann, James, * 119, Co G, died Aug 17, diarrhea c.
6014, McPherson, D, 103, Co F, died Aug 17, scorbutus.
6038, Moore, C, 103, Co G, died Aug 18, scorbutus.
6148, McCracker, J, 53, Co K, died Aug 19, fever remittent.
6294, McLaughlin, Jas, 4 cav, Co A, died Aug 20, scorbutus.
6441, McWilliams, H, 82, Co I, died Aug 22, scorbutus.
6480, Martin, John, 103, Co D, died Aug 22, diarrhea.
6532, McGan, J, 18 cav, died Aug 23, diarrhea.
6664, McKee, ——, 144, Co C, died Aug 24, scorbutus.
6689, Marner, M, 73, Co K, died Aug 24, diarrhea
6910, McGlann, H, 143, Co B, died Aug 26, diarrhea.
6925, McGuigan, H C, 7, Co K, died Aug 26, diarrhea.
7026, Marks, P, 143, Co B, died Aug 27, dysentery.
7061, Moore, M J, 107, died Aug 28, dysentery.
7107, Moyer, Wm M, 55, Co H, died Aug 28, diarrhea.
7109, Miller, John L, 53, Co K, died Aug 28, fever intermittent.
7127, McAfee, Jas, 72, Co F, died Aug 28, scorbutus.
7175, Moore, Thomas, 69, Co D, died Aug 29, scorbutus.
7263, Martin, John, 77, Co C, died Aug 30, dysentery.
7265, Musser, John, 77, Co D, died Aug 30, scorbutus.
7305, Moser, S, 103, Co E, died Aug 30, dysentery.
7323, Morris, John, 183, Co G, died Aug 30, diarrhea.
7407, Marchin, Wm, 50, Co E, died Aug 31, scorbutus.
7512, Millinger, John H, 7, Co C, died Sept 1, dysentery.
7602, Moorhead, J S, 103, Co D, died Sept 2, diarrhea.
7719, Myers, H, 9, Co A, died Sept 3, scorbutus.
7875, Mayer, W, 8, Co M, died Sept 5, diarrhea.
7925, Mays, N J, 103, Co H, died Sept 5, diarrhea.
8027, Murphy, A, 13 cav, Co I, died Sept 6, fever typhus.
8047, McKnight, J, 18 cav, Co I, died Sept 6, diarrhea c.
8122, Miller, J,* 101, Co C, died Sept 8, scorbutus.
8123, Mullings, W, 145, Co G, died Sept 8, scorbutus.
8128, Mussager, W, 13 cav, Co L, died Sept 8, diarrhea.
8134, Mehaffey, J M, 16 cav, Co B, died Sept 8, scorbutus.
8153, McCautley, W, 2 artil, Co A, died Sept 8, diarrhea.
8158, McLane, T, 12, Co E, died Sept 8, scorbutus.
8194, McKink, J,* 110, Co D, died Sept 8, diarrhea.
8216, Mansfield, J, 101, Co G, died Sept 8, diarrhea.
8322, Myers, A, 118, Co I, died Sept 10, diarrhea.
8469, Magill, H, 103, Co I, died Sept 11, scorbutus.
8596, Morrison, J, 140, Co E, died Sept 12, scorbutus.
8627, McKinney, D, 90, Co C, died Sept 13, scorbutus.
8691, Mortze, A, 118, Co D, died Sept 14, diarrhea c.
8802, McCulloyt, 101, Co F, died Sept 15, scorbutus.
9071, Maynard, A, 3 artil, died Sept 17, diarrhea.
9090, McCall, Wm, 22 cav, Co B, died Sept 18, diarrhea.
9228, McCullough, S, 138, Co K, died Sept 19, wounds.
9270, Mayhan, F, 20 cav, died Sept 19, anasarca.
9316, Marsh, W, 149, Co K, died Sept 20, scorbutus.
9329, Meyers, J A, 138, Co C, died Sept 20, scorbutus.
9526, McQuigley, John, 101, Co C, died Sept 22, scorbutus.
9583, Mead, H J, 184, Co B, died Sept 23, scorbutus.
9598, Martin, J, 17 cav, Co C, died Sept 23, scorbutus.
9644, Morris, J, 14, Co I, died Sept 24, scorbutus.
9646, Morgan, J E, 2, Co A, died Sept 24, gangrene.
9651, McCook, B, 118, Co A, died Sept 24, scorbutus.
9761, McMurray, Wm, 1 cav, Co I, died Sept 25, scorbutus.
9871, Mason, John, 112, Co A, died Sept 27, scorbutus.
4378, McKerner, S, 73, Co E, died Aug 2, anasarca.
10050, Mean, James,* 10, Co F, Sept 30, scorbutus.
10060, Morgan, C, 45, Co A, Sept 30, scorbutus.
10119, McClany, J, 101, Co C, died Oct 1, scorbutus.

No. of Grave.
10154, McElroy, Wm, 13 cav, Co L, died Oct 1, diarrhea.
10300, Meese, J, 48, Co A, died Oct 4, diarrhea.
10396, McGraw, John, 3 artil, Co A, died Oct 6, scorbutus.
10407, Miller, H, 79, Co K, died Oct 6, scorbutus.
10486, Miller, Washington, 18 cav, Co C, died Oct 7, diarrhea.
10610, McKearney, J W, 118, Co K, died Oct 10, scorbutus.
10620, McClief, Wm, 7, Co A, died Oct 10, diarrhea.
10641, Marker, W H, 118, Co D, died Oct 10, diarrhea.
10678, Martin, J P, 7, Co I, died Oct 11, scorbutus.
10684, Miller, James, 7, Co I, died Oct 11, diarrhea.
10803, Mattis, Aaron, 133, died Oct 12, scorbutus.
10825, Moore, C H, 13 cav, Co C, died Oct 13, dysentery.
10820, Mortin, Geo H, 108, Co I, died Oct 14, scorbutus.
10981, Maxwell, S, 14 cav, Co B, Oct 15, scorbutus.
10991, Moses, W, 16 cav, Co H, died Oct 16, scorbutus.
10993, McKnight, Jas, 118, Co K, died Oct 16, scorbutus.
11081, Mitchell, J O, 55, Co H, died Oct 18, scorbutus.
11142, Mansfield, George, 101, Co I, died Oct 19, fever remittent.
11229, McClay, J, 11 cav, Co D, died Oct 20, scorbutus.
11305, McBride, J, 2 cav, Co H, died Oct 22, scorbutus.
11326, Marshal, L, 184, Co A, died Oct 23, scorbutus.
11357, Moore, S, 101, Co F, died Oct 24, scorbutus.
11459, Moore, J, 13 cav, Co B, died Oct 25, scorbutus.
11464, McNelse, J H,* 100, Co E, died Sept 26, scorbutus.
11542, Miller, F, 54, Co K, died Oct 27, scorbutus.
11655, Midz, J, 20 cav, Co A, died Oct 30, scorbutus.
11658, Mcnk, W, 12 cav, Co F, died Oct 30, scorbutus.
11682, Morrow, J C, s maj, 101, Co E, died Oct 31, scorbutus.
11684, McCann, J, 11 cav, Co L, died Oct 31, scorbutus.
11689, Moore, W, 184, Co B, died Oct 31, diarrhea.
11692, Mulligan, J, 7, Co H, died Oct 31, pneumonia.
11909, McCuno, J, 67, Co E, died Nov 8, scorbutus.
11913, McClush, N, 97, Co E, died Nov 8, scorbutus.
11982, Maceo, M, 53, Co H, died Nov 13, scorbutus.
12008, McCray, J, 145, Co A, died Nov 14, scorbutus.
12088, Maher, D, 118, Co E, died Nov 18, scorbutus.
12103, Miller, W, 31, Co I, died Nov 22, gangrene.
12248, Murray, W, 14 cav, Co H, died Dec 8, scorbutus.
12326, McIntire, J, 55, Co C, died Dec 24, scorbutus.
12331, Myers, A D, 52, Co A, died Dec 26, scorbutus.
12554, Matthews, J, 6 cav, Co F, died Jan 30, '65, scorbutus.
12595, Maloy, J M, 184, Co D, died Feb 6, '65, scorbutus.
12625, McGeoger, J, 20, Co C, died Feb 9, '65, diarrhea c.
12696, Myers, H, 87, Co E, died Feb 23, '65, diarrhea c.
12771, McDonald, —, 9, Co G, died March 13, '65, debilitas.
12506, McGarrett, R W, 193, Co F, died Feb 21, '65, diarrhea c.

1134, Nicholson, John, 3 cav, Co H, died May 16, debilitas.
1298, Nelson, Wm, 76, Co H, died May 23, diarrhea c.
2832, Nolti, Wm, 6, Co F, died July 3, diarrhea c.
3653, Newell, G S, 183, Co A, died July 20, anasarca.
4246, Nicholson, W, 1 cav, Co H, died July 29, dysentery.
4489, Nelson, George, 2, Co K, died Aug 1, scorbutus.
4936, Nayler, G W,† 13 cav, Co L, died Aug 7, diarrhea.
5100, Nichols, D A, 125, Co D, died Aug 9, scorbutus.
6001, Neal, H G, 90, Co B, died Aug 17, diarrhea.
6012, Nickle, C, 37, Co G, died Aug 17, diarrhea.
6702, Nickeim, James, 77, Co G, died Aug 24, scorbutus.
8154, Naylor, S, 20 cav, Co H, died Sept 8, diarrhea.
8907, Noolo, J, 73, Co D, died Sept 16, scorbutus.
9124, Nice, Isaac, 11, Co L, died Sept 21, diarrhea.
9468, Neff, J, 4 cav, Co D, died Sept 21, scorbutus.
10146, Nelson, G, 55, Co A, died Oct 1, diarrhea.
10286, Nelson, J A, 145, Co G, died Oct 4, diarrhea.
10764, Newberry, John, 20 cav, Co A, died Oct 12, gangrene.
11107, Nelson, A, 160, Co E, died Oct 18, diarrhea c.
11254, Noble, Thomas, 19 cav, Co G, died Oct 21, diarrhea c.
11776, Nichols, G, 20, Co C, died Nov 3, diarrhea.

414, Osborne, S R, 4, Co K, died April 7, dysentery.
622, Ogelsby, J, 4 cav, Co K, died April 19, diarrhea.
1318, O'Brien, P, 13, Co A, died May 23, diarrhea c.
1403, Ottinger, I, 8 cav, Co I, died May 27, diarrhea.
1897, O'Neil, John,† 69, died June 12, diarrhea c.
2580, Oswald, Stephen, 55, Co G, died June 28, diarrhea c.
3101, O'Conor, ——, 63, died July 11, scorbutus.
3193, O'Neil, J, 63, Co I, died July 12, anasarca.
3704, Olmar, H,† 2 cav, Co H, died July 21, diarrhea.
3861, O'Connor, H, 49, Co E, died July 24, dysentery.
4161, Owens, G H, 7, Co A, died July 28, diarrhea.
5110, Offlehack, Z, 90, Co K, died Aug 8, diarrhea c.
5184, Oliver, W, 103, Co D, died Aug 9, diarrhea.
5939, O'Hara, M, 101, Co E, died Aug 17, scorbutus.
6254, O'Connell, Wm, 183, Co G, died Aug 20, scorbutus.
6535, O'Hara, John, 150, Co E, died Aug 23, scorbutus.
6628, Oiler, Samuel, 103, Co G, died Aug 24, dysentery.
6908, O'Rourke, Charles, 109, Co C, died Aug 26, dysentery.
7102, Otte, John, 5 cav, Co B, died Aug 28, diarrhea.
7557, [illegible] J M,† 101, Co I, died Sept 2, scorbutus.
[illegible], 164, Co A, died Sept 18, scorbutus.
[illegible] N V B, 149, Co K, died Sept 20, diarrhea.

No. of Grave.
9330, Owens, E, 69, Co D, died Sept 20, scorbutus.
10895, Osborn, E,* 11 cav, Co A, died Oct 13, scorbutus.

33, Peck, Albert, 57, Co K, died March 9, pneumonia.
62, Patterson, Rob't, 2 res, Co E, died March 18, fever typhus.
125, Parker, James M,* 76, Co B, died March 23, dysentery c.
500, Petrisky, H, 54, Co F, died April 12, diarrhea.
1110, Patterson, Thomas, 3 cav, Co A, died May 15, diarrhea c.
1119, Patent, Thomas, 73, Co G, died May 16, diarrhea.
1258, Powell, Wm, 14 cav, Co D, died May 21, diarrhea.
1556, Powers, John, 26, Co I, died June 2, diarrhea c.
1780, Preso, Thomas, 26, Co E, died June 9, pneumonia.
1884, Powell, Frank, 18, died June 12, diarrhea c.
2566, Page, J, 183, Co G, died June 27, fever typhus.
2590, Porter, David, 101, Co H, died June 28, diarrhea.
2903, Parsons, J T, 103, Co D, died July 5, diarrhea.
3197, Painter, J G, 26, Co F, died July 11, diarrhea.
3415, Painter, S, 63, Co A, died July 17, scorbutus.
4049, Patterson, R, 101, Co H, died July 27, diarrhea.
4157, Pickett, J C, 3 cav, Co A, died July 28, diarrhea.
4177, Pratt, F, 14 cav, Co I, died July 28, dysentery.
4191, Plymeer, W, 20 cav, Co B, died July 28, diarrhea.
4415, Page, John, 112, Co A, died July 31, diarrhea.
4473, Powell, H, 102, Co H, died Aug 1, scorbutus.
5323, Prosser, J, 63, died Aug 11, scorbutus.
5579, Pyers, Isaac, 72, Co G, died Aug 14, diarrhea.
5610, Phillips, Jas B, 101, Co I, died Aug 14, diarrhea.
5947, Parish, J A, 184, died Aug 17, scorbutus.
6341, Prenos, H, 149, Co K, died Aug 21, scorbutus.
6439, Palmer, H, 140, Co D, died Aug 22, scorbutus.
6527, Poole, G, 52, Co B, died Aug 22, diarrhea.
6530, Piter, M, 13, Co G, died Aug 23, scorbutus.
6574, Phillips, J W, 1 cav, Co F, died Aug 23, scorbutus.
6843, Peterson, G, 103, Co D, died Aug 25, scorbutus.
6844, Penn, John, 5 cav, Co E, died Aug 25, scorbutus.
6885, Pattin, H W, 2 artil, Co F, died Aug 26, diarrhea c.
7118, Potts, Edward, 183, Co H, died Aug 28, bronchitis.
7232, Perkins, N, 103, Co D, died Aug 29, diarrhea c.
8030, Powell, A T, 149, Co C, died Sept 6, diarrhea.
8160, Pricht, F, 87, Co H, died Sept 8, scorbutus.
8763, Peck, C W, 145, Co H, died Sept 14, diarrhea.
8877, Persil, Frederick, 101, died Sept 15, scorbutus.
9220, Palmer, A, 143, Co D, died Sept 19, fever typhus.
9684, Perego, W, 143, Co G, died Sept 24, scorbutus.
9754, Phipps, J H, 57, Co E, died Sept 25, scorbutus.
10074, Price, G, 106, Co H, died Sept 30, diarrhea.
10573, Penstock, A, 144, Co B, died Oct 9, diarrhea.
10858, Powell I, 101, Co I, died Oct 13, scorbutus.
11108, Price, O, 109, Co C, died Oct 19, scorbutus.
11261, Phay, M, 69, Co C, died Oct 21, scorbutus.
11637, Phillips, F, 61, Co K, died Oct 28, scorbutus.
11737, Pees, M T, 145, Co H, died Nov 2, diarrhea.
11883, Penn, J, 18 cav, Co I, died Nov 6, scorbutus.
11918, Phelps, W, 4 cav, Co G, died Nov 8, scorbutus.
11328, Porterfield, J K, 5 cav, Co M, died Oct 23, scorbutus.
12075, Pemer, W, 18, Co C, died Nov 18, scorbutus.
12191, Pryor, Wm, 11, Co C, died Nov 28, scorbutus.
12359, Poleman, H, 1 cav, Co F, died Dec 30, scorbutus
12378, Perry, H, 121, Co C, died Jan 2, '65, dysentery.
12388, Pritchett, J, 72, Co C, died Jan 3, '65, debilitas.
12479, Potter, B F, 148, Co I, died Jan 17, scorbutus.

6756, Quinby, L C, 76, Co E, died Aug 24, scorbutus.

47, Reed, Sam'l, 4 cav, Co D, died March 15, pneumonia.
126, Robertson, J, 119, Co K, died March 23, diarrhea.
132, Rosenburg, Henry, 49, Co K, died March 24, diarrhea.
171, Reign, John, 83, Co K, died March 26, anasarca.
608, Richpeder, A, 13, Co B, died April 2, diarrhea.
610, Ray, Wm, 8 cav, Co F, died April 18, diarrhea.
847, Rhinehart, J, 8 cav, Co D, died May 8, anasarca.
895, Russell, F, 4, Co D, died May 5, diarrhea.
907, Rhinebolt, J, 18 cav, Co I, died May 5, diarrhea c.
940, Robinson, C W,† 150, Co E, died May 7, diarrhea c.
1152, Randall, H, 4 cav, Co H, died May 16, diarrhea c.
1218, Rigney, Chas, 4 cav, Co G, died May 19, dysentery.
1454, Raleigh, A, 51, Co G, died May 29, diarrhea c.
1485, Rudolph, S,* 13 cav, Co K, died May 30, diarrhea c.
1599, Rhine, George, 69, Co I, died June 4, diarrhea.
1624, Rosenburg, H, 18 cav, Co H, died June 4, diarrhea c.
1719, Raymond, John,† 18 cav, Co H, died June 8, scorbutus.
1808, Rheems, A,† 73, Co I, died June 10, debilitas.
1838, Ramsay, J D, 103, Co F, died June 11, scorbutus.
1922, Rush, S, 18, Co G, died June 14, diarrhea.
1942, Robinson, Wm, 77, Co D, died June 14, diarrhea c.
2225, Roush, Peter, 102, Co E, died June 20, diarrhea c.
2528, Rupert, F, 2 cav, Co H, died June 26, diarrhea.
2602, Roat, J, 54, Co F, died June 28, scorbutus.
2735, Rhodes F, 79, Co E, died July 1, diarrhea.
2911, Rock, J E, 5, Co M, died July 5, bronchitis.
2979, Regart, John, 16 cav, Co E, died July 7, diarrhea.

No. of Grave.
2101, Ray, A,† 11, Co E, died June 17, diarrhea c.
8024, Rugh, M J, 103, Co D, died July 7, scorbutus.
3270, Robins, R, 69, Co B, died July 13, diarrhea.
3468, Ransom, H, 148, Co I, died July 17, dysentery.
3827, Rinner, L, 5 cav, Co A, died July 23, dysentery.
4074, Ringwalk, F J, 79, Co H, died July 27, dysentery.
4241, Roger, L, 115, Co L, died July 29, fever typhus.
4309, Rogers, C, 78, Co C, died July 30, diarrhea.
4476, Ray, James R, 184, Co B, died Aug 1, dysentery.
4507, Riese, S, 103, Co D, died Aug 1, diarrhea c.
4844, Riche, James, 103, Co B, died Aug 6, diarrhea.
4940, Ruthfer, J, 2 artil, Co F, died Aug 7, diarrhea.
5319, Rice, Sam'l, 101, Co K, died Aug 11, catarrh.
5189, Rose, David, 103, Co B, died Aug 12, diarrhea.
5180, Robinson, John, 99, Co D, died Aug 12, diarrhea.
5537, Rose, B, 13, Co I, died Aug 13, dysentery.
5800, Robins, J, 2 cav, Co M, died Aug 15, fever typhus.
5879, Render, H, 7 cav, Co L, died Aug 16, diarrhea.
5894, Richards, E, 143, Co E, died Aug 16, diarrhea.
5912, Resse, Jacob, 103, Co B, died Aug 17, diarrhea.
5940, Richards, John,* 1 cav, Co G, died Aug 17, scorbutus.
6321, Robbins, O, 106, Co G, died Aug 21, pneumonia.
6378, Roger, John L, 110, Co H, died Aug 21, scorbutus.
6520, Reynolds, J, 14, Co H, died Aug 22, scorbutus.
6725, Rowe, E,* 103, Co A, died Aug 24, diarrhea.
6777, Rangardener, J, 149, Co H, died Aug 25, diarrhea.
6789, Richards, G, 13 cav, Co A, died Aug 25, diarrhea.
6794, Runels, John, 6 cav, Co L, died Aug 25, dysentery.
6822, Rum, A, 188, Co C, died Aug 25, scorbutus.
6838, Reese, D, 148, Co K, died Aug 25, gangrene.
6896, Raiff, T, 1, Co A, died Aug 26, scorbutus.
6933, Richardson, ——, 61, died Aug 26, diarrhea.
7067, Reese, D, 143, Co F, died Aug 28, dysentery.
7202, Roeff, J, 103, Co F, died Aug 29, diarrhea.
7232, Redmire, H, 98, Co B, died Aug 30, diarrhea.
7293, Robins, George, 62, Co A, died Aug 30, diarrhea.
7410, Richardson, H, 103, Co K, died Aug 31, diarrhea.
7462, Richard, D, 18 cav, Co D, died Sept 1, scorbutus.
7716, Rice, E, 1, Co B, died Sept 3, diarrhea.
7738, Roads, Frederick, 101, Co E, died Sept 3, dysentery.
8139, Rathburn, K, 2, Co F, died Sept 8, scorbutus.
8510, Russell, S A,* 79, Co A, died Sept 12, scorbutus.
8545, Ray, A, 149, Co D, died Sept 12, dysentery.
8602, Richards, J, 106, Co H, died Sept 12, scorbutus.
8685, Rhaugmen, G,† 138, Co D, died Sept 13, scorbutus.
8742, Root, D, 48, Co B, died Sept 14, diarrhea.
9019, Ret, George, 18, Co A, died Sept 17, diarrhea.
9272, Ramsay, J I, 149, died Sept 19, anasarca.
9585, Richie, H, 11, Co F, died Sept 23, scorbutus.
9590, Reamner, W H, 57, Co H, died Sept 23, diarrhea.
9612, Richards, John, 113, Co D, died Sept 23, diarrhea.
9653, Reed, B, 103, Co A, died Sept 24, diarrhea.
9786, Ramsay, R, 84, Co D, died Sept 25, scorbutus.
9882, Richards, J, 53, Co K, died Sept 27, diarrhea.
10174, Reed, J, 55, Co A, died Oct 1, diarrhea.
10864, Ramsay, Wm, 87, Co B, died Oct 18, scorbutus.
10622, Reedy, E T,† 87, Co B, died Oct 10, diarrhea c.
10935, Roundabush, H B, 55, Co A, died Oct 14, diarrhea.
10947, Rockwell, A, 2 cav, Co L, died Oct 14, scorbutus.
11071, Raeff, J B, 72, Co E, died Oct 17, scorbutus.
11118, Rinkle, John A, 26, Co A, died Oct 18, scorbutus.
11293, Rolston, J, 18, Co F, died Oct 22, scorbutus.
11147, Rudy, J, 13, Co F, died Oct 19, scorbutus.
11414, Rifle, S G,* 189, Co C, died Oct 25, scorbutus.
11566, Richardson, A, 144, Co E, died Oct 27, scorbutus.
11868, Rowland, N, 111, Co F, died Nov 6, scorbutus.
12018, Rapp, A E, 18 cav, Co I, died Nov 15, scorbutus.
12048, Ruth, B S, 23, Co I, died Nov 16, scorbutus.
12206, Rothe, C, 101, Co A, died Dec 1, scorbutus.
12355, Reese, D, 7, Co A, died Dec 29, diarrhea.
12372, Reed, W S, 128, Co H, died Jan 1, '65, debilitas.

377, Smith, M D, 18, Co B, died April 5, diarrhea a.
788, Smith, George, 5 cav, Co H, died April 28, diarrhea c.
881, Smith, Wm, 4, Co A, died May 4, diarrhea c.
882, Smith, T, 19, Co G, died May 4, diarrhea.
921, Stettler, W J,† 12 cav, Co G, died May 6, diarrhea.
1014, Serena, H, 4 cav, Co D, died May 10, dysentery.
1030, Shebert, Gotlieb, 73, Co C, died May 11, dysentery.
1058, Spilyfiter, A, 54, Co F, died May 13, anasarca.
1105, Sullivan, D, 101, Co K, died May 15, diarrhea c.
1114, Shlude, S R,† 140, Co K, died May 15, diarrhea.
1156, Stearnes, E K, 14 cav, Co A, died May 16, diarrhea c.
1168, Stoat, D, 76, Co I, died May 16, diarrhea.
1175, Scott, Wm, 4, Co B, died May 16, diarrhea c.
1216, Severn, C, 139, Co A, died May 19, diarrhea.
1258, Summers, H,† 2 cav, Co B, died May 21, diarrhea.
1349, Smith, Charles, 20, Co A, died May 24, anasarca.
1453, Soldenbough, C, 4 cav, Co G, died May 29, diarrhea c.
1503, Smith, Martin, 18 cav, Co H, died May 31, diarrhea c.
1585, Stone, Samuel, 26, Co F, died June 1, debilitas.

No. of Grave.
1543, Shoemaker, M,† 13 cav, Co H, died June 1, diarrhea.
1605, Swearer, G, 13, Co H, died June 4, diarrhea c.
1620, Schiefelt, Jacob, 54, Co F, died June 4, diarrhea.
1632, Schmar, R, 45, Co F, died June 5, diarrhea.
1963, Smith, D, 11 cav, Co H, died June 14, dysentery.
2039, Slough, H, 53, died June 15, fever typhus.
2070, Stevens, A, 13 cav, Co M, died June 16, dysentery.
2121, Sherwood, C H,† 4 cav, Co M, died June 17, diarrhea c.
2123, Stall, Samuel, 75, Co D, died June 17, pneumonia.
2126, Sey, J R, 4 cav, Co K, died June 17, diarrhea c.
2165, Steel, J S, 7 cav, Co F, died June 19, diarrhea.
2259, Scoles, M, 27, Co K, died June 21, diarrhea c.
2331, Sims, B, 14 cav, Co G, died June 22, diarrhea c.
2412, Shoop, Jacob, 2, Co M, died June 24, fever typhus.
2622, Springer, John, 101, Co E, died June 28, fever typhus.
2650, Stewart, J B, 103, Co A, died June 29, diarrhea c.
2725, Scott, Allen, 150, Co H, died July 1, dysentery.
2758, Schimgert, J, 73, Co G, died July 1, scorbutus.
2791, Shimer, J A, 13 cav, Co A, died July 2, diarrhea c.
2864, Scott, Wm, (negro), 8, Co D, died July 4, diarrhea.
2905, Stump, A, 11, Co I, died July 5, dysentery.
2941, Smith, Jacob, 51, Co H, died July 6, diarrhea.
2952, Shaw, W, 140, Co B, died July 7, diarrhea c.
2999, Smalley, Jno, 112, Co K, died July 7, fever remittent.
3057, Sutton, R M, 103, Co I, died July 9, diarrhea.
3113, Sweet, H, 57, Co K, died July 10, dysentery.
3136, Shoemaker, M, 148, Co G, died July 10, scorbutus.
3154, Sellers, Wm, 77, Co D, died July 11, scorbutus.
3214, Stone, W F, 53, Co G, died July 12, scorbutus.
3480, Sweitser, J, 103, Co D, died July 17, diarrhea c.
3507, Smalley, L, 58, Co K, died July 19, diarrhea.
3508, Stevens, S G, 150, Co H, died July 19, scorbutus.
3580, Sickles, Daniel, 116, Co K, died July 19, dysentery.
3032, Serders, J S, 142, Co K, died July 20, dysentery.
3670, Stopper, Wm, 16, Co B, died July 20, anasarca.
3763, Stillenberger, F, 72, Co F, died July 22, dysentery.
3775, Strance, D, 11, Co H, died July 22, scorbutus.
3855, Smith, J, 79, Co F, died July 24, diarrhea c.
3906, Smith, O C,† 77, Co G, died July 24, diarrhea c.
3956, Seilk, A, 144, Co D, died July 25, dysentery.
3960, Sullivan, T, 77, Co F, died July 25, diarrhea.
4006, Smith, F, 64, Co K, died July 26, anasarca.
4009, Shafer, J H, 84, Co E, died July 26, diarrhea c.
4012, Shapley, Geo, 103, Co G, died July 26, dysentery.
4047, Strichley, C, 53, Co H, died July 27, diarrhea.
4064, Shrively, E S, 19 cav, Co M, died July 27, dysentery.
4113, Sheppard, E, 145, Co G, died July 28, diarrhea.
4164, Smith, S W, 101, Co B, died July 28, diarrhea c.
4213, Shaffer, Peter, 52, Co F, died July 29, diarrhea.
4223, Shister, F, 3 cav, Co A, died July 29, scorbutus.
4228, Stein, J, 7, Co G, died July 29, diarrhea.
4274, Sloan, J, 11, Co E, died July 29, anasarca.
4285, Soone, P, 4 cav, Co D, died July 30, scorbutus.
4345, Stubbs, W W,* 101, Co E, died July 30, diarrhea.
4348, Scott, A, 22 cav, Co F, died July 31, debilitas.
4351, Scundler, J, 67, Co A, died July 31, diarrhea.
4372, Smith, P, 72, Co C, died July 31, diarrhea.
4506, Sale, Thomas, 15, Co M, died Aug 2, scorbutus.
4775, Shank, James, 81, Co F, died Aug 5, scorbutus.
4791, Sullivan, Ed, 67, Co H, died Aug 5, scorbutus.
4797, Sear, C, 14 cav, Co L, died Aug 5, diarrhea.
4845, Sheomber, Jno, 11 cav, Co D, died Aug 6, diarrhea.
4928, Slicker, J, 77, Co D, died Aug 6, scorbutus.
4931, Sheit, P, 61, Co G, died Aug 7, diarrhea.
4945, Swarts, P,* 27, Co I, died Aug 7, dysentery.
5160, Stiner, John, 22 cav, Co G, died Aug 9, scorbutus.
5189, Striker, F, 14 cav, Co C, died Aug 9, scorbutus.
5215, Sworeland, Wm, 184, Co A, died Aug 10, diarrhea.
5232, Speck, A, 118, Co A, died Aug 10, dysentery.
5411, Shaffer, Daniel, 13 cav, Co F, died Aug 12, pneumonia.
5529, Shangrost, A, 108, Co D, died Aug 12, diarrhea.
5437, Shears, J S, 140, Co K, died Aug 12, diarrhea.
5463, Stubbs, W, 50, Co H, died Aug 13, dysentery.
5494, Shape, F, 18 cav, Co A, died Aug 13, diarrhea.
5603, Somerfield, W, 69, Co E, died Aug 14, diarrhea.
5700, Stineback, A, 150, Co C, died Aug 15, diarrhea.
5750, Spears, W M,† 2 cav, Co K, died Aug 15, pneumonia.
5874, Sheppard, N, 79, Co F, died Aug 16, scorbutus.
5965, Shultz, F, 13 cav, Co K, died Aug 17, diarrhea.
6205, Shoop, G, 103, Co K, died Aug 19, scorbutus.
6289, Smith, H, 26, Co K, died Aug 20, fever typhus.
6337, Smith, W, 18 cav, Co B, died Aug 21, debilitas.
6382, Swager, M, 101, Co F, died Aug 21, diarrhea.
6436, Spain, Thomas, 118, Co H, died Aug 22, diarrhea.
6523, Stover, J, 49, Co F, died Aug 22, scorbutus.
6526, Stahler, S, 140, Co G, died Aug 22, anasarca.
6534, Snyder, John, 118, Co C, died Aug 23, scorbutus.
6584, Sloate, E, 50, Co D, died Aug 23, dysentery.
6593, Shirley, Henry, 185, Co I, died Aug 23, diarrhea c.
6669, Sherwood, P, 64, Co I, died Aug 24, dysentery.
6776, Shellito, R, 150, Co C, died Aug 25, dysentery.
6823, Spain, Richard, 118, Co H, died Aug 25, anasarca.

No. of Grave

6829, Sturgess, W A,* 79, Co G, died Aug 25, scorbutus.
6880, Stabler, D, 4 cav, Co A, died Aug 26, anasarca.
7029, Strickler, J W, 11, Co F, died Aug 27, dysentery.
7103, Smith, John F, 55, Co C, died Aug 28, icterus.
7137, Sloan, J M, 18 cav, Co D, died Aug 28, dysentery.
7141, Springer, J, 103, Co F, died Aug 29, dysentery.
7292, Shriver, B, 18 cav, Co K, died Aug 30, diarrhea.
7302, Singer, J, 2 art l, Co A, died Aug 30, diarrhea.
7358, Scoleton, J, 53, Co F, died Aug 31, scorbutus.
7363, Sweeney, D, 14 cav, Co E, died Aug 31, diarrhea c.
7379, Scott, W B, 4 cav, Co D, died Aug 31, diarrhea.
7631, Streetman, J, 7, Co E, died Sept 2, diarrhea.
7638, Steele, J, 62, Co M, died Sept 2, diarrhea.
7648, Spencer, Geo, 20, Co C, died Sept 3, diarrhea.
7662, Snyder, M S, 183, Co A, died Sept 3, dysentery.
7705, Swartz, Geo, 5 cav, Co A, died Sept 3, fever remittent.
7770, Stockhouse, D,* 18 cav, Co I, died Sept 4, diarrhea.
7905, Sellers, H, 149, Co G, died Sept 5, diarrhea.
7930, Shultz, John, 4 cav, Co I, died Sept 5, anasarca.
7939, Smith, A C, 7, Co F, died Sept 6, diarrhea.
8038, Simpson, T, 53, Co K, died Sept 6, diarrhea.
8103, Stump, J, 105, Co I, died Sept 7, diarrhea.
8112, Slade, E,* 150, Co H, died Sept 7, scorbutus.
8444, Shirk, M B, 142, Co A, died Sept 11, scorbutus.
8567, Simons, Wm H, 76, Co K, died Sept 12, scorbutus.
8659, Spauld, E, 90, Co E, died Sept 13, scorbutus.
8773, Smith, Wm, 2, Co K, died Sept 14, gangrene.
8795, Stella, J F, 1, Co B, died Sept 15, diarrhea.
9236, Signall, ——,* 79, Co H, died Sept 19, scorbutus.
9012, Steadman, W, 54, Co F, died Sept 17, diarrhea.
9123, Shably, J, 54, Co A, died Sept 18, diarrhea c.
9138, Stoup, S, 16 cav, Co B, died Sept 18, diarrhea c.
9310, Smith, Charles, 7, Co H, died Sept 20, diarrhea.
9365, Stebbins, Z, 7, Co H, died Sept 20, diarrhea.
9411, Scott, D, 149, Co G, died Sept 21, scorbutus.
9507, Snyder, A, 148, Co I, died Sept 23, diarrhea.
9593, Sternbolt, Wm, 58, died Sept 23, diarrhea.
9742, Supple, C M,* 63, Co B, died Sept 25, dysentery.
9780, Stirpus, W,† 13 cav, Co L, died Sept 26, diarrhea.
9800, Shirk, Christian, 145, died Sept 27, scorbutus.
9898, Sweeny, W P, 13 cav, died Sept 27, scorbutus.
9912, Sanford, C, 69, Co H, died Sept 28, anasarca.
9955, Sheppard, C,† 118, Co E, died Sept 29, scorbutus.
10088, Snow, P, 115, Co A, died Aug 30, scorbutus.
10132, Smith, J S, 22 cav, Co B, died Oct 1, diarrhea.
10299, Strong, H, 55, Co E, died Oct 4, scorbutus.
10323, Smith, E, 10, Co H, died Oct 4, scorbutus.
10516, Snyder, Wm, 54, Co H, died Sept 8, dysentery.
10525, Stones, T, 121, Co K, died Oct 8, dysentery.
10539, Sandiwood, C, 7, Co F, died Oct 8, scorbutus.
10609, Small, H, 101, Co H, died Oct 10, scorbutus.
10720, Smallman, J W, 63, Co A, died Oct 11, diarrhea.
10808, Steele, F F, 20 cav, Co A, died Oct 12, scorbutus.
10837, Shank, A, 184, Co C, died Oct 13, scorbutus.
11044, Smith, Andrew, 22 cav, Co B, died Oct 17, diarrhea.
11069, Stevens, C P, 11, Co A, died Oct 17, scorbutus.
11233, Smith, H W, 53, Co B, died Oct 21, scorbutus.
11246, Smith, James, 57, Co E, died Oct 21, fever typhus.
11355, Silvy, David, 18 cav, Co I, died Oct 23, scorbutus.
11368, Seyoff, H, 81, Co C, died Oct 23, scorbutus.
11458, Sunderland, E, 11, Co D, died Oct 26, scorbutus.
11529, Stevenson, John, 111, Co I, died Oct 26, scorbutus.
11661, Speck, Olive, 67, Co H, died Oct 30, scorbutus.
11741, Smith, H, 183, Co D, died Nov 2, scorbutus.
11785, Snodgrass, R J, 145, Co H, died Nov 4, scorbutus.
11792, Bellentine, M, 145, Co C, died Nov 4, scorbutus.
11825, Seltzer, D, 20, Co K, died Nov 5, scorbutus.
11885, Smith, W B, 14 cav, Co E, died Nov 6, scorbutus.
11890, Shure, J P, 184, Co F, died Nov 7, scorbutus.
11895, Snively, G W, 20 cav, Co F, died Nov 7, scorbutus.
11928, Stover, J H, 79, Co G, died Nov 8, scorbutus.
11951, Sheffley, W, 118, Co G, died Nov 9, scorbutus.
12057, Stitzer, G, 2, Co E, died Nov 16, scorbutus.
12081, Stensley, D,* 184, Co A, died Nov 18, scorbutus.
12217, Smith, J S, 118, Co F, Dec 3, diarrhea.
12218, Skinner, S O,* 77, Co A, died Dec 4, scorbutus.
12282, Shafer, T, 184, Co E, died Dec 13, scorbutus.
12308, Stafford, W, 67, Co H, died Dec 19, scorbutus.
12384, Sourbeer, J E, 20, Co A, died Jan 3, '65, scorbutus.
12590, Sipe, F, 87, Co C, died Feb 5, '65, diarrhea c.
12598, Stauffer, J, 1, Co K, died Feb 6, '65, diarrhea c.
12648, Stain, G W, 20 cav, Co K, died Feb 13, '65 debilitas.
12669, Slough, E B,* 1 cav, Co D, died Feb 17, '65, pleuritis.
12670, Scott, A J, 14, Co D, died Feb 17, '65, diarrhea c.
12676, Sheridan, M, 103, Co F, died Feb 19, '65, diarrhea c.
12817, Starks, J N, 14, Co D, died March 27, '65, diarrhea.
12834, Shultz, H H, 87, Co A, died April 5, '65, diarrhea.

778, Thistlewood, J, 73, Co F, died April 28, fever congestive.
785, Toland, D, 13 cav, Co D, died April 28, laryngitis.
1141, Taylor, J F, 13, Co E, died May 16, fever typhus.
1145, Tull, D,* 4, Co D, died May 16, pneumonia.
1153, Toner, Peter, 19, Co A, died May 16, diarrhea c.
1814, Thompson, H, 57, Co C, died June 10, diarrhea c.
2182, Thompson, A, musician, 4 cav, Co C, died June 19, debilitas.
2302, Townsend, D, 18 cav, Co D, died June 22, diarrhea c.
2635, Tyser, L, 145, Co D, died June 29, diarrhea c.
2897, Terwilliger, E,† 103, Co H, died July 5, dysentery.
3003, Thompson, R, 103, Co F, died July 7, diarrhea.
47, Taylor, C W, 84, Co D, died May 24, small pox.
3329, Titus, W, 171, Co D, died July 14, debilitas.
3473, Todd, Wm, 103, Co K, died July 17, scorbutus.
3571, Thompson, J S, 183, Co H, died July 19, dysentery.
3768, Terrell, A, 12 cav, Co B, died July 22, diarrhea.
3948, Trumbull, H, 3, Co E, died July 25, scorbutus.
4116, Thompson, James,† 18 cav, Co G, died July 28, diarrhea.
4160, Tinsdale ——, 149, Co E, died July 28, diarrhea.
4713, Thompson, J, 3 artil, Co A, died Aug 4, scorbutus.
5179, Thompson W W, 101, Co E, died Aug 9, scorbutus.
5345, Thomas F, 7, Co F, died Aug 11, scorbutus.
5906, Thompson J B, 100, Co H, died Aug 17, scorbutus.
6146, Thompson, F A B, 69, Co I, died Aug 19, cerebritis.
6447, Tubbs, E, 143, Co I, died Aug 23, scorbutus.
6476, Toll, Wm, 11 res, Co I, died Aug 22, scorbutus.
6791, Turner, John, 118, Co H, died Aug 25, diarrhea.
7250, Thomas, E, 23, Co F, died Aug 30, diarrhea c.
7409, Thorpe, L, 61, Co E, died Aug 31, diarrhea.
7904, Trash, Seth, 81, Co A, died Sept 6, diarrhea.
8232, Truman, E W, 9, Co G, died Sept 9, scorbutus.
8531, Tift, W, 115, Co A, died Sept 12, diarrhea.
8619, Tutor, C, 184, Co A, died Sept 13, scorbutus.
9027, Tite, P, —, Co C, died Sept 17, scorbutus.
9212, Thorpe, D, 18, Co D, died Sept 19, diarrhea.
9302, Thompson, H, 18 cav, Co I, died Sept 20, diarrhea.
9726, Tonson, J, 99, Co B, died Sept 25, diarrhea.
9775, Tbuck, I, 7, Co C, died Sept 26, scorbutus.
9981, Tones, E, 145, Co F, died Sept 26, diarrhea.
10008, Thompson J, 90, Co H, died Sept 29, scorbutus.
10725, Tibbels, Geo,* 69, Co K, died Oct 11, scorbutus.
11002, Thatcher, R, 14, Co C, died Oct 16, diarrhea c.
11407, Thompson, J, 12 cav, Co E, died Oct 24, diarrhea.
11754, Treppin, P, 67, Co H, died Nov 2, scorbutus.
12080, Townsend, C,* 103, Co E, died Nov 18, scorbutus.

971, Ulrick, John, 17, Co E, died May 9, typhus fever.
4184, Urodragh, W, 4, Co B, died July 28, diarrhea.
12133, Utler, Wm, 45, Co H, died Nov 23, diarrhea.

1369, Veutter, Chas,† 73, Co G, died May 25, rheumatism.
7739, Vogel, L,* 150, Co A, died June 8, diarrhea c.
2428, Vernon, S, 7, Co K, died June 24, debilitas.
4265, Vanbolt, T, 18, Co A, died July 29, diarrhea.
5392, Vandeby, E,† 7, Co A, died Aug 12, diarrhea.
6877, Vanderpool, F, 57, Co B, died Aug 26, diarrhea.
7716, Vancampments, George, 52, Co I, died Sept 4, diarrhea.
8270, Vail, G B, 77, Co G, died Sept 9, diarrhea.
8791, Vaughan, J, 108, Co A, died Sept 15, diarrhea.
8948, Varndale, J, 112, Co A, died Sept 16, diarrhea.
9688, Vaudier, Wm, Phila, died Sept 24, scorbutus.

57, Wilkins, A, 12 cav, Co L, died March 17, fever congestive
128, Waterman, John, 88, Co B, died March 23, dysentery.
193, Wise, Isaac, 18, Co G, died March 27, pleuritis.
496, Wheeler, J, 150, Co I, died April 12, diarrhea.
516, Warren, J, 76, Co A, died April 12, diarrhea.
587, Weed, A B, 4, Co K, died April 17, dysentery.
657, Wentworth Jas, 83, Co G, died April 21, fever typhus.
665, Watson, F F, 2, Co H, died April 22, dysentery.
686, Wahl, John, 73, Co C, died April 23, rheumatism.
764, Wilson, John, 14 cav, Co H, died April 27, diarrhea.
852, Williams, S, 18 cav, Co I, died May 3, diarrhea c.
941, Wolf, J H, 13 cav, Co H, died May 7, diarrhea c.
1021, Wright, J, 12 cav, Co B, died May 11, diarrhea c.
1067, Whitton, Robt, 145, Co C, died May 13, diarrhea c.
1093, Wright, Wm, 16 cav, Co A, died May 14, diarrhea c.
1386, Wyomns, Jas,* 150, Co C, died May 26, diarrhea c.
1387, Wilson, James, 13 cav, Co D, died May 26, diarrhea c.
1443, Williams, F, 3 cav, Co G, died May 28, diarrhea c.
1494, Williams, Fred, 101, Co K, died May 30, diarrhea.
1525, Wallace, H, 13 cav, Co H, died May 31, pneumonia.
1563, Wolfermeyer, H, 76, Co H, died June 2, diarrhea c.
1721, Whitney, W, 83, Co A, died June 8, diarrhea.
1749, Woodsides, W I, 18, Co E, died June 9, diarrhea c.
1791, Wolf, Samuel, 77, Co A, died June 10, diarrhea.
1903, Woodward, G W, 3 cav, died June 13, diarrhea.
1977, Wyant, H, 103, Co G, died June 15, diarrhea c.
2228, Walters, C, 73, Co B, died June 22, diarrhea c.
2615, Williams, J, 83, Co F, died June 28, dysentery.
2669, Wike, A, 96, Co B, died June 30, diarrhea.
2760, Whitaker, —, (negro), 8, died July 2, diarrhea.
2937, Whisinger, S, 96, Co E, died July 6, diarrhea.
3023, Weider, L, 60, Co H, died July 7, diarrhea c

No. of Grave.

3135, Wallace, A, 116, Co I, died July 10, diarrhea c.
3277, Wri[illegible], W A, 20 cav, Co G, died July 14, diarrhea.
3384, Wo[illegible]f, W D, 103, Co B, died July 16, diarrhea.
3[illegible], Wa[illegible] Geo, 1 cav, Co G, died July 16, diarrhea c.
[illegible], Walker, E, 7, Co A, died July 19, dysentery.
[illegible], Wi[illegible], E D, 12 cav, Co H, died July 21, diarrhea.
4181, W[illegible], 18 cav, Co K, died July 28, diphtheria.
4[illegible], W[illegible], 148, Co F, died July 30, diarrhea.
[illegible], White, M, 7, Co C, died July 24, diarrhea.
[illegible], W[illegible] A[illegible]rew, 103, Co H, died July 23, diarrhea.
40[illegible], W[illegible], A, 145, Co D, died July 27, diarrhea.
4[illegible], W[illegible]r, A, 73, Co G, died July 27, diarrhea.
[illegible], W[illegible], Wm, 4[illegible], died July 25, diarrhea.
4[illegible], Williams, Geo, 54, Co H, died July 21, diarrhea.
4[illegible], W[illegible], E, 148, Co I, died Aug 4, scorbutus.
4[illegible], Ward, P, 1[illegible], Co B, died Aug 6, diarrhea.
4[illegible], W[illegible], C, 54, Co F, died Aug 7, debilitas.
4981, W[illegible], G, 4 cav, Co I, died Aug 7, diarrhea.
49[illegible], W[illegible], S, 1[illegible] cav, Co B, died Aug 7, diarrhea.
5105, W[illegible], James, 93, Co K, died Aug 9, scorbutus.
[illegible], W[illegible], S, 77, Co G, died Aug 11, pleuritis.
5458, W[illegible], Wm, 7, Co K, died Aug 12, dysentery.
5677, W[illegible], D, 53, Co G, died Aug 14, dysentery c.
60[illegible], Williams, J, 7, Co A, died Aug 18, diarrhea.
6[illegible], W[illegible]house, W, 3 cav, Co L, died Aug 18, cerebritis.
6[illegible], Workman, A, 118, Co D, died Aug 19, diarrhea.
6[illegible], W[illegible], P,* 18, Co B, died Aug 20, debilitas.
6427, Ward, C, 143, Co E, died Aug 22, scorbutus.
6[illegible], W[illegible]erman, Jas, 77, Co A, died Aug 23, scorbutus.
6563, W[illegible], Paul, 57, Co A, died Aug 23, ictus solis.
6[illegible], W[illegible], S A, 1[illegible], Co I, died Aug 23, scorbutus.
6818, W[illegible], E C, 1[illegible]3, Co E, died Aug 25, dysentery.
6884, Wo[illegible]r, W H,* 77, Co C, died Aug 27, scorbutus.
6981, W[illegible], Jas P, 14[illegible], Co D, died Aug 27, debilitas.
7023, Woodford, J A, 101, Co E, died Aug 27, diarrhea.
7[illegible], White Ed, 10[illegible], Co K, died Aug 30, diarrhea.
7382, Web[illegible], J S, 69, Co K, died Aug 31, dysentery.
738[illegible], Walton, A, 14 cav, Co A, died Aug 31, scorbutus.
7680, Wallwork, T, 118, Co D, died Sept 3, diarrhea.
7714, Warner, L, 5 cav, Co C, died Sept 3, diarrhea c.
77[illegible], Wynn, H, 131, Co F, died Sept 4, diarrhea.
7803, Wiggins, D, 2 artil, Co D, died Sept 5, diarrhea c.
7[illegible], Wee[illegible]and, F, 101, Co K, died Sept 5, diarrhea.
79[illegible], Wade, George W, 118, Co E, died Sept 5, diarrhea.
8081, Weber, W, 116, Co F, died Sept 7, diarrhea.
8[illegible], White, D, 2 artil, Co F, died Sept 10, diarrhea c.
8879, Wheeler, J, 7, Co C, died Sept 15, scorbutus.
9091, Wheeler, C C, 14 cav, Co M, died Sept 18, diarrhea.
9[illegible]43, Williams, W, 20 cav, died Sept 20, scorbutus.
9[illegible]4, Wilson, W H, 3, Co I, died Sept 21, diarrhea.
95[illegible], Woodman, H, 18 cav, Co A, died Sept 22, scorbutus.
9[illegible]3, W[illegible], C, 111, Co I, died Sept 23, wounds.
9[illegible], Wi[illegible]er, J, 103, Co A, died Sept 24, diarrhea.
9657, Wilson, G M, 7 cav, Co M, died Sept 24, diarrhea.
9825, Wilke, G, 4 cav, Co K, died Sept 27, diarrhea.
1909, Wentley, J, 155, Co G, died Sept 28, diarrhea.
10092, Watson, Wm, 99, Co I, died Sept 30, diarrhea.

10217, Wocks, C, 70, Co F, died Oct 2, diarrhea.
10229, Waltz, J, 7, Co H, died Oct 2, diarrhea.
10236, Weekly, John, 14, Co A, died Oct 2, diarrhea.
10253, Weeks, C, 76, Co F, died Oct 3, scorbutus.
10315, Wolfhope, J, 184, Co A, died Oct 4, dysentery.
10400, Wilson, G, 55, Co C, died Oct 6, diarrhea.
104[illegible]6, Wilson J, 118, Co D, died Oct 6, diarrhea.
10521, Williams, W, 46, Co K, died Oct 8, dysentery.
10568, Walk, W, 87, Co E, died Oct 9, diarrhea c.
10632, Weirs, John M,* 116, Co E, died Oct 10, diarrhea c.
10659, Watts, A J, 12 cav, Co I, died Oct 11, scorbutus.
10729, White, J M, 21, Co G, died Oct 11, scorbutus.
10797, Walker, Wm, 148, Co B, died Oct 12, scorbutus.
9464, Warner, Cyrus W, 184, Co B, died Oct 21, scorbutus.
10840, Wright, Wm, 16, Co I, died Oct 13, scorbutus.
10932, Wolford, D, 54, Co K, died Oct 14, scorbutus.
10974, Watson, C, 184, Co E, died Oct 15, scorbutus.
11048, Wilderman, E, 14, Co D, died Oct 17, scorbutus.
11108, Walker, A, 45, Co D, died Oct 18, diarrhea.
11129, Wilson, G, 140, Co F, died Oct 18, scorbutus.
11493, Warrington, J H, 106, Co H, died Oct 26, diarrhea.
11503, Walter, W, 184, Co F, died Oct 26, scorbutus.
11557, Wood, J, 119, Co C, died Oct 27, scorbutus.
11722, Woodburn, D J, 7, Co G, died Nov 1, scorbutus.
11750, Wyncoop, F P, 7, Co I, died Nov 2, scorbutus.
11899, Webster, J, 20 cav, Co L, died Nov 7, diarrhea c.
11978, Wilkinson, C, 104, Co I, died Nov 12, scorbutus.
11987, Weaver, J, 53, Co K, died Nov 13, diarrhea.
12095, Walder, John, 5 cav, Co L, died Nov 19, scorbutus.
12098, Wider, N H, 184, Co F, died Nov 19, scorbutus.
12128, Weatherald, H W, 7, Co H, died Nov 22, scorbutus.
12129, Webb, C M, 101, Co H, died Nov 23, scorbutus.
12222, Williams, J, 145, Co A, died Dec 4, scorbutus.
12137, Wood, J M, 2, Co A, died Nov 23, scorbutus.
12380, Watson, H, 184, Co A, died Jan 2, '65, diarrhea c.
12485, Williams, B, 75, Co B, died Jan 19, diarrhea.
12493, Walker, N C, 87, Co B, died Jan 20, debilitas.

10158, Van Dyke, D L, 103, Co A, died Oct 1, diarrhea.
11810, Vanmarkes, D, 5, Co E, died Nov 4, scorbutus.
12154, Vanbatterman, I, 4, Co G, died Nov 25, scorbutus.
3958, Vogle, V, 78, Co D, died July 25, scorbutus.

3700, Yocumbe, W B, 93, Co B, died July 22, diarrhea c.
4900, Yocum, D, 1 cav, Co M, died Aug 6, diarrhea c.
6103, Yingbug, E, 78, Co E, died Aug 13, diarrhea.
6545, Yeager, Sam'l, 158, Co D, died Aug 23, diarrhea.
10264, Young, J B, 49, Co G, died Oct 2, dysentery.
11040, Young, W H, 145, Co F, died Oct 17, diarrhea c.
11572, Yeager, J, 49, Co C, died Nov 6, dysentery.

1806, Zerphy, J, 79, Co E, died June 10, diarrhea c.
4255, Zimmerman, B, 148, Co B, died July 29, diarrhea.
6573, Zane, Wm, 19, Co K, died Aug 23, ictus solis.
6818, Zerl, S, 103, Co F, died Aug 25, scorbutus.
11327, Zane, M, 118, Co E, died Oct 23, scorbutus.

RHODE ISLAND.

8200, Austin, J A,† 1 cav, Co H, July 13, diarrhea.
6231, Allen, Charles, 1 cav, Co D, died Aug 21, diarrhea c.

1744, Bosley, Wm, 1 cav, Co M, died June 8, diarrhea c.
1958, B[illegible], James, 1 cav, Co G, died June 14, dysentery.
2[illegible]21, Blake, J F, 1 cav, Co M, died June 26, diarrhea.
2647, Burk, James, 1, Co C, died July 20, dysentery.
4261, Bel[illegible], J, 2, Co C, died July 29, scorbutus.
4576, Baine, H, 5, Co A, died Aug 2, diarrhea c.

1[illegible], Carpenter, P, 1 cav, Co E, died May 24, anasarca.
1413, C[illegible], B F, 1 cav, Co K, died May 27, dysentery.
2810, Callahan, James, battery, died July 23, dysentery.
7961, Colvin, E O,† 5 artil, Co A, died Sept 6, scorbutus.
12802, Collins, J H, 1 cav, Co A, died April 16, '65, diarrhea c.

6[illegible]1, Deb[illegible]ah, E B,† 1 cav, Co G, died April 20, diarrhea.
1217, D[illegible]z, George, 1 cav, Co M, died May 19, pneumonia.
1425, Dickinson, [illegible], 1 cav, Co K, died May 29, diarrhea.
3[illegible]8, Dearborn, G, 1 cav, died July 8, fever remittent.
4[illegible], Dard[illegible], Robert, 1 cav, Co F, died Aug 5, scorbutus.
4[illegible], Doolittle, G S, 2 artil, Co B, died Aug 8, diarrhea.
55[illegible], Doyle, James, 5 artil, Co A, died Aug 14, diarrhea.

821, En[illegible], Geo C, 1 cav, Co M, died May 1, diarrhea.
10203, Eaton, A, 5 artil, Co A, died Oct 1, scorbutus.

9[illegible], Freelove, H, 1 cav, Co H, died May 7, diarrhea.
4533, Farrell, James F, 1 artil, Co A, died Aug 2, diarrhea.

4672, Fay, John, 2, Co G, died Aug 4, fever typhus.
7336, Fey, A, 5 artil, Co A, died Aug 31, scorbutus.

1868, Goudy, John, 5 artil, Co A, died June 12, diarrhea c.
4866, Gallagher, C, 5, Co A, died Aug 6, dysentery.
6561, Garvey, Wm, 5 artil, Co A, died Aug 13, anasarca.
8308, Green, R, 2, Co B, died Sept 10, diarrhea c.
9978, Green, Daniel, 2, Co H, died Sept 29, diarrhea.

1075, Henry, T, 1 cav, Co F, died May 13, diarrhea.
2655, Healy, A, 1 cav, Co D, June 29, fever typhus.
2746, Hunt, C W, 1 cav, Co A, died July 1, diarrhea.
3904, Hampstead, J, 5 artil, Co F, died July 24, scorbutus.
7032, Hooker, A, 1 cav, Co G, died Aug 27, diarrhea.
11843, Hawkins, D F, 5, Co A, died Nov 6, wounds.
12016, Hanley, T, 5 artil, Co A, died Nov 15, scorbutus.

1962, Ide, S R, 1 cav, Co H, died June 14, dysentery.

3049, Johnson, A G, 5 artil, Co A, died July 8, diarrhea.

2068, Kettell, James, 1 cav, Co B, died, July 6, diarrhea.
8006, Kiney, J, 2, Co B, died July 10, dysentery c.

4215, Lewis, Edward, 5 artil, Co A, died July 29, dysentery.
6827, Littlebridge, W H,* 5 artil, Co A, died Aug 16, diarrhea.
6793, Lee, Cornelius, 5 artil, Co A, died Aug 25, diarrhea.
7849, Leach, L D, 1 cav, Co F, died Sept 5, diarrhea.
11686, Livingston, John, musician, 5 artil, Co A, died Oct 31, diar

No. of Grave.

1750, Miner, S, 1 cav, Co D, died June 9, diarrhea c.
7393, McKay, Thomas, 2, Co F, died Aug 31, diarrhea.
6306, McKenna, J, 3 artil, died Sept 10, diarrhea.

5192, Northorp, E, 1 cav, Co H, died July 12, diarrhea.
7904, Navon, G, 5, Co K, died Sept 5, diarrhea.

607, Peterson, John, 1, Co D, died April 18, dysentery.

7210, Rathburn, J, 1 cav, Co A, died Aug 29, debilitas.

2382, Sword, M, 1 cav, Co D, died June 23, diarrhea.
2563, Spunk, J, 1 cav, Co H, died June 27, diarrhea.
2859, Slocum, George T, 2d lieut, 1 cav, Co A, died July 4, fever typhus.
4158, Smith, P, 1 cav, Co A, died July 28, diarrhea.
4949, Staford, J, 1 battery, Co A, died Aug 7, scorbutus.

No. of Grave.

6186, Sisson, Charles T, 5 artil, Co A, died Aug 19, dysentery.
6157, Seymour, H, 5 artil, Co A, died Aug 19, diarrhea.
6351, Sullivan, J, 5 artil, Co A, died Aug 21, diarrhea c.
7129, Sander, Charles, 5 artil, Co A, died Aug 28, anasarca.
7425, Slocum, C A,* 5 artil, Co A, died Aug 31, anasarca.

3075, Turner, Charles, 7, Co E, died July 9, diarrhea.
8522, Thomas, J, 5, died Sept 12, scorbutus.

19, Wright, Moses, 2 cav, Co A, died March 7, fever remittent.
1788, West, H, 1, Co A, died June 10, diarrhea c.
3173, Wallace, Wm, 5 artil, Co A, died July 11, diarrhea c.
5908, Wood, J B, 5, Co A, died Aug 16, diarrhea c.
6222, West, J, 2 cav, Co A, died Aug 21, diarrhea c.
6766, Wayne, S, 1 cav, Co A, died Aug 25, diarrhea.
7831, Wilson, J, 5, Co A, died Sept 4, anasarca.
9273, Witham, D, 1 light artil, died Sept 19, anasarca.

TENNESSEE.

883, Allen, James W, 11, Co B, died May 4, diarrhea c.
987, Amos, F G, 2, Co C, died May 10, diarrhea.
2318, Allison, B F, 13 cav, Co D, died June 22, diarrhea c.
2631, Andrewson, Joseph, 2, Co C, died June 29, diarrhea.
3167, Anderson, S, 8 cav, Co B, died July 11, diarrhea.
3194, Aber A, 7 cav, Co A, died July 12, diarrhea.
3334, Anglon, Wm, 7 cav, Co A, died July 15, diarrhea.
4094, Athens, J H, 2 cav, Co C, died July 26, anasarca.
6411, Alkin, George W,* 7, Co K, died Aug 22, scorbutus.
6474, Ashby, J F, 7 cav, Co B, died Aug 22, fever typhus.
6541, Antoine, P, 13 cav, Co H, died Aug 23, dysentery c.
7572, Aspray, Wm,† 13, Co B, died Sept 2, diarrhea.
7907, Anderson, C S,† 10, Co D, died Sept 5, dysentery.
9151, Achley, A, 3, Co A, died Sept 18, scorbutus.
9010, Atkins, L, 2, Co D, died Sept 28, scorbutus.
1895, Arrowood, James, 8 cav, died June 13 diarrhea.
8495, Alexander, P S, 13 cav, Co D, died Sept 11, diarrhea.
12710, Allen, G W, 7, Co I, died Feb 28, '65, pleuritis.

639, Boling, Wm, 11, Co E, died April 14, diarrhea.
685, Benson, Benjamin, 2, Co E, died April 17, pneumonia.
663, Rood, Jas J T, 2, Co F, died April 21, diarrhea.
695, Baker, T K, 5 cav, died April 23, dysentery c.
705, Batey, W H, 2, Co B, died April 24, dysentery c.
772, Burton, Wm, 1 artil, Co A, died April 28, diarrhea c.
808, Brannon, Ellis, 2, Co F, died April 30, diarrhea c.
845, Browder, H V, 2, Co K, died May 1, diarrhea.
859, Byerly, W H, 1, Co A, died May 3, diarrhea.
920, Brewer, M, 2, Co E, died May 6, diarrhea.
1053, Boyden, A L, 2, Co B, died May 13, diarrhea.
1137, Beatty, Thomas, 2, Co B, died May 16, diarrhea.
1242, Bryant, James A, 8, Co I, died May 20, pneumonia.
1244, Barnard, W H, 2, Co A, died May 20, diarrhea.
1248, Boyd, A D,* 2, Co F, died May 20, diarrhea c.
1527, Butler, J J,† 7, Co B, died May 31, dysentery.
1538, Bradshaw, A G, 2, Co B, died June 1, diarrhea.
1610, Browning, J, 2, Co F, died June 4, diarrhea c.
1635, Brown, J, 13 cav, Co E, died June 5, diarrhea.
1847, Branon, Wm, 2, Co F, died June 11, anasarca.
1876, Birket, W D,* 7, died June 12 diarrhea.
1883, Burchfield, W R, 2, died June 12, diarrhea c.
1976, Berger, W, 2, Co B, died June 15, diarrhea c.
2037, Berger, W M, 2, died June 15, diarrhea.
2555, Boutwright, A,† 7, Co A, died June 27, diarrhea.
2744, Brewer, W T, 7 cav, Co D, died July 1, diarrhea.
2939, Bibbs, Alexander, 7 cav, Co D, died July 6, diarrhea a.
2963, Bright, John, 8, Co G, died July 7, dysentery.
3176, Blalock, H, 2, Co D, died July 11, abscess.
3198, Brown, J D,† 2, Co F, died July 12, anasarca.
6, Brandon, G, 4, Co D, died April 4, small pox.
16, Burke, John, 2, Co D, died April 12, small pox.
52, Brummell, A D, 2, Co H, died June 3, small pox.
57, Bralts, S, 4, Co F, died June 20, small pox.
58, Beeler, Daniel, 5, Co D, died June 25, small pox.
3328, Barton, F F, 13 cav, Co A, died July 14, diarrhea c.
3330, Bynom, J W, 13 cav, Co C, died July 14, diarrhea c.
3414, Brennan, James, 2, Co I, died July 16, diarrhea.
3636, Burris, D B, 13, Co B, died July 20, anasarca.
3643, Bracoan, J, 2, Co A, died July 20, diarrhea c.
3726, Billings W, 6, Co 1, died July 21, diarrhea.
3786, Bowman, J, 7 cav, Co C, died July 22, diarrhea c.
3934, Boles, H, 13, Co C, died July 25, diarrhea.
4108, Boyd, W H, 9 cav, Co C, died July 27, diarrhea.
4221, Barnes, A C, 15, Co H, died July 29, wounds.
4770, Bryant, Wm, 2, Co D, died Aug 5, diarrhea.
5017, Butler, W W, 7 cav, Co B, died Aug 8, anasarca.
4371, Bradfield, E L, 7 cav, Co C, died July 31, anasarca.
5049, Brummell, R, 11 cav, Co C, died Aug 8, scorbutus.
5277, Barnhart, D F, 7 cav, Co B, died Aug 11, diarrhea.
5294, Baker, Isaac, 13, Co B, died Aug 11, dysentery.
5313, Blackwood, G W, 11, Co B, died Aug 11, pleuritis.
5533, Boles, G W, 13 cav, Co B, died Aug 13, scorbutus.
5617, Baker, M A, 13 cav, Co E, died Aug 14, dysentery c.
6003, Boles, W G, 13 cav, Co B, died Aug 17, anasarca.
6142, Bayles, K, 2, Co C, died Aug 19, dysentery.
6194, Burnett, S H, 6, Co H, died Aug 19, anasarca.
6287, Butler, W J, 7, Co B, died Aug 20, diarrhea c.
6509, Barnes, Wm, 7 cav, Co M, died Aug 23, ictus solis.
6572, Bishop, W, 7 cav, Co H, died Aug 23, fever typhus.
7430, Brewer, J, 2, Co D, died Aug 31, gangrene.
7064, Bales, Henry, 2, Co K, died Sept 2, diarrhea.
7943, Boyer, D, 15, Co D, died Sept 5, scorbutus.
8222, Bird, S H, 13 cav, Co D, died Sept 8, anasarca.
8998, Blackner, Thomas, 7 cav, Co L, died Sept 17, anasarca.
9023, Bell, F, 5, Co I, died Sept 17, diarrhea.
9079, Boyle, R C, 7 cav, Co I, died Sept 17, scorbutus.
9149, Bean, C S, 3 cav, Co E, died Sept 18, scorbutus.
9478, Bowlen, C F, 13, Co B, died Sept 21, scorbutus.
9543, Bromley, H,† 7, died Sept 23, scorbutus.
4888, Brannon, L, 2, Co A, died Aug 6, scorbutus.
10098, Byerly, James, 1, cav, Co A, died Sept 30, scorbutus.
10452, Bible, W, 8, Co D, died Oct 7, diarrhea.
10617, Blackney, B, 7, Co E, died Oct 10, diarrhea c.
10826, Bartholomew, John, 7 cav, Co H, died Oct 13, scorbutus.
11015, Bosworth, W H, 7 cav, Co E, died Oct 16, scorbutus.
11298, Brogan, John,* 2, Co C, died Oct 22, diarrhea.
11372, Brown, J B,* 2 Co K, died Oct 23, scorbutus
12171, Bradford, H A, 7, Co E, died Oct 26, scorbutus.
12565, Brown, J W, 13, Co B, died Jan 31, '65, scorbutus.
12613, Barnhart, G, 7, Co C, died Feb 8, '65, diarrhea c.
12662, Barnes, F B, 7 cav, Co D, died Feb 16, '65, diarrhea c.
462, Bell, E S, 4, Co C, died April 9, diarrhea c.
4782, Barnes, G, 10, Co D, died Aug 6, constipatio.

189, Cardwell, W C, 6, Co C, died March 27, diarrhea.
216, Conaster, Philip, 2, Co D, died March 28, dysentery c.
230, Chimney, Jesse,† 2, Co A, died March 29, diarrhea a.
375, Colwell, J H, 2, Co C, died Apr 15, diarrhea c.
436, Croswell, Samuel, 2, Co K, died April 8, diarrhea c.
459, Childers, J M, 2, Co D, died April 9, diarrhea.
482, Clark, Lewis, 2 cav, Co B, died April 9, diarrhea a.
615, Covington, A, 2, Co K, died April 18, diarrhea.
717, Chitwood, J H, 2, Co G, died April 24, diarrhea.
811, Carden, Robert, 2, Co C, died April 30, diarrhea c.
840, Cardwell, W C, 6, Co G, died May 2, diarrhea.
1050, Cooper, C, 2, Co B, died May 12, diarrhea.
1213, Clark, Alexander, 2, Co C, died May 19, anasarca.
1425, Cross, M C, 2, Co F, died May 28, diarrhea.
1574, Childers, J, 13, Co A, died June 3, rubeola.
1636, Clemens, J D, 7 cav, Co D, died June 5, diarrhea c.
1751, Campbell, W, 2, Co A, died June 9, dysentery a.
1859, Carden, A K, 7 cav, Co E, died June 11, diarrhea c.
2031, Covington, J B, 2, Co K, died June 15, diarrhea.
2062, Carwin, James, 1, died June 16, diarrhea.
2071, Crow, J,† 2, Co F, died June 16, scorbutus.
2280, Crawford, A, 13 cav, Co B, died June 21, diarrhea.
2468, Childers, Thos L, 2, Co C, died June 25, constipatio.
2632, Cooper, E, 1, Co A, died June 29, anasarca.
2789, Cook, W P, 2 c, Co A, died July 1, diarrhea.
2858, Cooper, G W, 7, Co B, died July 4, diarrhea.
2886, Collins, W, 2, Co H, died July 4, scorbutus.
2940, Carter, H C, 13 cav, Co E, died July 6, diarrhea c.
3687, Cross, N, 2, Co H, died July 21, diarrhea c.
3953, Corwine, J, East Tenn, G, died July 26, diarrhea
4691, Cornish, A, 13 cav, Co C, died Aug 4, anasarca.
5298, Chase, A P, 7 cav, Co I, Aug 11, scorbutus.
5829, Collins, R, 7 cav, Co K, died Aug 16, marasmus.
5895, Clyne, E T,† 11 cav, Co E, died Aug 16, dysentery.

No. of Grave.

6310, Crews, G, 7 cav, Co B died Aug 20, diarrhea.
7523, Childers, E, 13, Co E, died Sept 1, scorbutus.
7525, Clark, James, 13, Co A, died Sept 1, anasarca.
7691, Cunlse, E, 7 cav, Co I, died Sept 2, diarrhea.
7702, Childers, W E, 7 cav, Co E, died Sept 3, diarrhea.
7857, Cothrain, S, 13, Co E, died Sept 5, gangrene.
7871, Camp, W W, 7, Co K, died Sept 5, dysentery.
7884, Cottered, G W, 7, Co C, died Sept 5, diarrhea.
8219, Creesy, S P, 7 cav, Co K, died Sept 8, anasarca.
9121, Crum, A, 4, Co F, died Sept 17, diarrhea.
9238, Cooley, J, 7 cav, Co L, died Sept 18, anasarca.
9393, Chadwick, M, 16, Co I, died Sept 24, scorbutus.
10137, Cole, Geo M, 9, Co C, died Oct 1, scorbutus.
10258, Clay, H, 13, Co H, died Oct 3, diarrhea.
10403, Cleaver, W, 7, Co G, died Oct 6, dysentery.
10654, Churchill, E, 13, Co A, died Oct 11, scorbutus.
11230, Check, R, 6 cav, Co D, died Oct 20, scorbutus.
11312, Carter, W B, 11, Co E, died Oct 22, scorbutus.
12643, Camway, H, 6, Co K, died Feb 13, '65, rheumatism.

302, Dodd, Benjamin, 2, Co D, died April 1, diarrhea c.
399, Doss, J W, 2, Co C, died April 6, diarrhea c.
485, Dalley, Samuel, 1 cav, Co A, died April 0, dysentery.
645, Dutrom, Irdell, 2, Co G, died April 20, dysentery c.
759, Duncan, G W, * 2, Co B, died April 27, diarrhea c.
850, Doak, I V, 2, Co F, died May 3, diarrhea.
894, Davis, Leroy, 7, Co K, died May 5, pneumonia.
1016, Diggs, J G, 2, Co C, died May 9 dysentery.
43, Dykes, Pleasant, 2, Co K, died May 11, small pox.
1182, Duff, J W, 16, Co H, died May 18, diarrhea.
1581, Davis, J W, 2, Co C, died June 3, diarrhea c.
2266, Dabney, B, 1, Co A, died June 20, diarrhea c.
2366, Daniel, Suttrell, 2, Co K, died June 23, dysentery.
2419, Diggs, John G, 2 cast, Co C, died June 25, diarrhea c.
3518, Deer, H, 7, Co M, died July 18, scorbutus.
3647, Davis, J, 3, Co A, died July 20, scorbutus.
5398, Deney, E W, 11 cav, Co C, died Aug 12, scorbutus.
6261, Dunn, B, 19, Co I, died Aug 20, scorbutus.
6991, Dyn, Wm, 7 cav, Co K, died Aug 27, diarrhea.
4821, Dean, R H, 10, Co I, died Aug 5, scorbutus.
8423, Davie, Levi, 7 cav, Co K, died Sept 11, scorbutus.
7219, Davis, James, 7, Co C, died Aug 20, debilitas.
7808, Diel, S F, 7 cav, Co B, died Sept 2, diarrhea.
8329, Dyer, W, 7 cav, Co K, died Sept 10, dysentery.
9373, Dodd, Chas, citizen, Decat'r Co, Tenn, died Sept 20, scorbutus.
9453, Dort, R, 7, Co G, died Sept 21, diarrhea.
9701, Duke, Wm, 7, Co E, died Sept 25, diarrhea.
10014, Dyer, H, 4 cav, Co A, died Sept 29, diarrhea.
10244, Davis, Wm, 7, Co D, died Oct 3, scorbutus.
12119, Dodd, J A, 1 cav, Co M, died Nov 22, scorbutus.
12379, Dykes, L, 2, Co K, died Jan 2, '65, scorbutus.
12498, D—, E, 8, Co C, died Jan 21, diarrhea.
12794, Doty, 1, citizen, died Jan 18, diarrhea.

293, Edwards, I, 5, Co B, died April 1, diarrhea c.
360, Everitt, A T, 2, Co A, died April 2, diarrhea.
610, Evans, S D, 8, Co C, died April 12, diarrhea c.
657, Everitte, John, 2, Co G, died April 14, diarrhea.
848, Evans, W, 7, Co C, died May 3, pneumonia.
873, Edwards, C S, 5, Co B, died May 4, fever intermittent.
970, Evans, J M, 7, Co M, died May 9, pneumonia.
979, Etier, Valentine, 11, Co D, died May 9, diarrhea.
1886, Emmert, J C, 4, died June 13, anasarca.
55, Eddins, James C, 2, Co E, died June 16, small pox.
3701, Ellison, Isaac, 2 cast, Co F, died July 22, scorbutus.
4785, Ellis, G O, 13 cav, Co C, died Aug 5, scorbutus.
6944, Ethridge, Wm, 13, Co B, died Aug 16, diarrhea.
7402, Ebler, P, 2, Co F, died Aug 31, scorbutus.
9075, Escue, H, * 6 cav, died Sept 17, diarrhea.
10560, Elliott, Wm, 4, Co A, died Oct 9, diarrhea c.
10985, Easton, J, 13 cav, Co B, died Oct 16, scorbutus.
11629, Ellington, J, 13 cav, Co B, died Oct 30, scorbutus.

353, Fairchilds, Jesse, 2, Co B, died April 2, diarrhea.
683, Fryer, W L, 2, Co H, died April 23, diarrhea.
697, Fagen, Parker, 8, Co I, died April 23, diarrhea.
1445, Fannon, G H, Tenn State Gd, died April 28, anasarca.
2408, Fisher, C N, 2, Co K, died June 24, catarrh.
2506, Francisco, R, 7 cav, Co B, died June 26, diarrhea.
62, Friar, John, 2, Co H, died July 9, small pox.
2835, Fox, E, Tenn State Gd, died July 3, diarrhea c.
6320, Firestone, 1 cav, Co M, died Aug 11, fever intermittent.
6997, Frazier, —, John, 8, Co H, died Aug 17, diarrhea c.
6289, Flowers, W P, 13 cav, Co B, died Aug 20, diarrhea c.
7244, Franks, W W, 2, Co B, died Aug 29, debilitas.
7782, Fields, R G, 1, died Sept 4, diarrhea.
8555, Finch, A, 7 cav, Co L, died Sept 12, scorbutus.
10133, Finch, J B, 7, Co B, died Oct 1, scorbutus.
12502, Franshier, J D, 8, Co K, died Jan 21, '65, debilitas.
3006, Fowler, I, 4, Co A, died July 7, diarrhea a.
3733, Finch, H, 7 cav, Co I, died July 21, diarrhea.

No. of Grave.

578, Goddard, John, 2, Co B, died April 16, diarrhea.
1831, German, P, 2, Co C, died June 11, debilitas.
2043, Gorman, James, 6, died June 15, diarrhea.
2571, Graham, J D, 7 cav, Co D, died June 27, diarrhea c.
2891, Goodling, James, 2, Co D, died July 4, diarrhea.
3, Gould, James, 11, Co B, died March 18, small pox.
15, Graves, Henry, 2, Co E, died April 11, small pox.
69, Gray, John W, 2, Co I, died June 29, small pox.
3291, Gorman, F, 6, Co B, died July 14, scorbutus.
3357, Grays, L, 12, Co F, died July 15, scorbutus.
9238, Gamon, I A, 7 cav, Co A, died Sept 19, scorbutus.
3624, Grundee, Alex, 4, Co D, died July 20, dysentery.
3719, Girler, J O, * 7, Co B, died July 21, diarrhea c.
3887, Gibson, C G, 1, Co B, died July 24, diarrhea c.
4531, Grevett, S P, 7 cav, Co C, died Aug 1, bronchitis.
6182, Given, I A, 9, Co I, died Aug 9, diarrhea.
5146, Griswell, Thos J, 7 cav, Co H, died Aug 0, diarrhea.
5374, Garrett, M T, 7 cav, Co L, died Aug 11, diarrhea.
5288, Green, S G, 7 cav, Co I, died Aug 12, diarrhea.
6370, Grams, Wm, 2, Co A, died Aug 21, diarrhea c.
6490, Graves, J C, 2, Co E, died Aug 21, dysentery.
6498, Grisson, C, 8, Co B, died Aug 22, diarrhea c.
7221, Green, J C, 7, Co I, died Aug 29, scorbutus.
7454, Gunter, R C, 13, Co A, died Sept 1, dysentery c.
7908, Griswold, W H, 7 cav, Co K, died Sept 5, diarrhea.
8612, Gibbs, J A, 7 cav, Co L, died Sept 6, diarrhea c.
8093, Griffin, W A, 2 cav, Co C, died Sept 7, scorbutus.
8940, Gill, G W, 1 cav, Co L, died Sept 16, scorbutus.
9271, Gaff, R, 1 cav, Co C, died Sept 19, anasarca.
9875, Gibson, James, 13 cav, died Sept 27, scorbutus.
10224, Gardner, H, 14 cav, Co C, died Oct 4, diarrhea.
10599, Garrison, A, * 7, Co E, died Oct 1 , scorbutus.
11063, Galbraith, G W, 7 cav, Co E, died Oct 17, scorbutus.
11632, Grier, J, 7, Co B, died Oct 28, scorbutus.
11925, Giles, M C, 7, Co I, died Nov 8, scorbutus.
12402, Ganon, T, 4 cav, Co I, died Jan 6, '65, scorbutus.
12438, Gilbert, Wm, 7 cav, Co C, died Jan 12, '65, scorbutus.
12464, Golden, J H, 7 cav, Co C, died Jan 18, '65, scorbutus.
1000, Grey, Thomas, 11, Co E, died May 19, diarrhea.
433, Graves, James, 2, Co E, died April 8, pneumonia.

58, Hampton, I A, 8, Co D, died March 16, pneumonia.
85, Henlger, Peter, 11, Co I, died March 21, diarrhea.
163, Hoover, Samuel, 2, Co B, died March 26, diarrhea.
316, Huff, Benjamin, 2, Co K, died April 2, diarrhea c.
357, Huckleby, Thomas, 2, Co C, died April 2, diarrhea.
467, Hickson, George, 11, Co E, died April 9, pneumonia.
616, Hurd, William, 2, Co B, died April, 18, diarrhea.
660, Head, Daniel, 12 cav, Co B, died April 21, diarrhea.
682, Hixton, John, 2, Co F, died April 23, dysentery c.
714, Henderson, Robert, 2, Co B, died April 24, bronchitis.
805, Hayes, J, 7, Co E, died April 29, diarrhea c.
844, Hughes, E, 2, Co I, died May 2, diarrhea c.
958, Hickley, Thomas, 2, Co K, died May 8, dysentery.
1036, Hickson, Henry, 2, Co L, died May 12, dysentery.
1124, Hall, John, 2, Co B, died May 15, anasarca.
1159, Heatherby, John, 1, Co C, died May 19, anasarca.
1491, Hickson, Daniel, 2, Co F, died May 31, diarrhea c.
1551, Hopkins, A, 1 artil, Co A, died June 2, diarrhea c.
1554, Hunt, J, 2, Co B, died June 2, debilitas.
1766, Harris, Wm, 8, Co I, died June 9, diarrhea c.
1774, Hodges, I M, 2, Co F, died June 9, diarrhea c.
1846, Harman, A B, 4, Co A, died June 11, debilitas.
1925, Hendson, J S, 2, Co K, died June 14, diarrhea c.
1950, Hickerman, T, 9 cav, Co B, died June 14, diarrhea.
2276, Hilton, A F, 2, Co H, died June 20, diarrhea a.
2376, Hugely, C W, 13 cav, Co D, died June 23, dysentery a.
2491, Hawn, E A, 2, Co B, died June 26, diarrhea a.
2642, Hale, R H, 3, Co F, died June 29, rubeola.
2851, Hall, B A, 2, Co A, died July 4, fever typhus.
2949, Hudson, J A, 8 cav, Co F, died July 9, diarrhea.
3012, Haines, J A, 13, Co E, died July 7, diarrhea.
4855, Hall, J J, 13 cav, Co E, died Aug 6, diarrhea c.
4836, Heimsen, Wm, 13 cav, Co B, died Aug 6, diarrhea c.
4805, Haywood, J G, 7, Co I, died Aug 5, diarrhea.
3098, Hawkins, S D, 3, Co E, died July 10, diarrhea.
3121, Hodges, —, 7, Co K, died July 10, diarrhea c.
3248, Hopson, Thomas, 3 cav, Co E, died July 13, diarrhea.
3421, Howard, A, 2, Co F, died July 16, dysentery.
3672, Heckman, Wm, * 2 cast, Co G, died July 20, dysentery
3712, Henderson, J R, 6, Co D, died July 21, diarrhea c.
3729, Hendley, J, 9, Co A, died July 21, diarrhea c.
3807, Hayes, J C, 7 cav, Co C, died July 22, anasarca.
4535, Henry, Wm, 7, Co C, died Aug 1, fever intermittent.
5278, Hudson, John, 55, Co I, died Aug 11, diarrhea.
5326, Harvey, Morgan, 2, Co F, died Aug 11, scorbutus.
5535, Hensley, James M, 3, Co E, died Aug 13, scorbutus.
5604, Hicks, M, 2, Co I, died Aug 14, diarrhea.
5607, Hasborough, J H, 13 cav, Co E, died Aug 14, scorbutus
6393, Haines, G, 13 cav, Co A, died Aug 21, dysentery.
6553, Hughes, Wm, 2, Co F, died Aug 23, diarrhea.

No. of Grave.
6561, Hibbrath, M H, 7 cav, Co I, died Aug 23, ictus solis.
6648, Harris, A G, 5, Co E, died Aug 23, anasarca.
6681, Horton, W C, 7 cav, Co H, died Aug 24, diarrhea.
7808, Hanson, John, 7 cav, Co H, died Sept 4, dysentery.
8094, Hallford, J A, 13, Co A, died Sept 7, scorbutus.
8115, Hicks, E, 9, Co F, died Sept 7, scorbutus.
8486, Hale, Ira, 7 cav, Co C, died Sept 11, scorbutus.
8529, Haywood, A J, † 7, Co I, died Sept 12, scorbutus.
9044, Henderson, A G, 13, Co C, died Sept 17, diarrhea c.
9788, Hodges, John, 13, Co E, died Sept 20, diarrhea c.
9797, Herbs, D, 1 cav, Co D, died Sept 26, scorbutus.
9805, Haney, H, 7 cav, Co A, died Sept 26, scorbutus.
9802, Hauks, A, † 11, Co D, died Sept 27, dysentery.
10003, Hall, W R, 2, Co D, died Sept 29, scorbutus.
10145, Halliwacke, 7, Co E, died Oct 10, scorbutus.
10329, Hooks, John L, 7 cav, Co A, died Oct 4, diarrhea.
10810, Holler, W, 6 cav, Co E, died Oct 12, scorbutus.
10956, Holloway, H B, 2, Co G, died Oct 14, scorbutus.
11377, Herman, H, 4, Co K, died Oct 23, scorbutus.
11791, Hickman, D, 2, Co I, died Nov 4, scorbutus.
11801, Howard, 16, died Nov 4, scorbutus.
11861, Higgs, L, 7, Co D, died Nov 6, scorbutus.
12028, Hazzie, Wm, 7, Co C, died Nov 13, scorbutus.
12146, Hall, J M, 1, Co A, died Nov 24, scorbutus.
12212, Hanley, T, 2, Co E, died Dec 2, scorbutus.
12423, Horg, B F, 7, Co E, died Jan 9, '65, scorbutus.
12655, Hullaker, J, 2, Co K, died Feb 14, '65, scorbutus.
12693, Hanbuck, J, 7, Co K, died Feb 22, '65, rheumatism.

1041, Israel, S, 21, Co B, died June 14, anasarca.
9515, Irwin, P P, 49, Co F, died Sept 22, diarrhea.

52, Jones, Rufus, 2, Co I, died March 16, dysentery.
291, Jones, Warren T, 11, Co C, died April 1, diarrhea.
358, Jeffers, J, 2, Co C, died April 2, diarrhea.
491, Jones, J E, 2, Co G, died April 11, diarrhea.
584, Jack, Benjamin S, 2, Co B, died April 17, dysentery.
668, Jones, H D, 4, Co F, died April 22, diarrhea.
1181, Johnson, E A, † 2, Co A, died May 18, anasarca.
1227, Johnson, S L, 2, Co A, died May 19, diarrhea.
1536, Jones, John J, 13 cav, Co C, died June 1, diarrhea.
3805, Jones, H, 2, Co H, died July 22, scorbutus.
3980, Johnson, A, 10, Co C, died July 26, diarrhea c.
4571, Jones, D, 6, Co C, died Aug 2, anasarca.
6517, Johnson, C F, 7, Co K, died Aug 13, diarrhea.
6921, Jones, J M, 2, Co K, died Aug 17, diarrhea c.
7447, Jones, Albert, † 13 cav, Co B, died Sept 1, dysentery.
8013, Joiner, J M, 7 cav, Co B, died Sept 6, fever typhus.
8503, Jones, J, 13 cav, Co B, died Sept 12, scorbutus.
8500, Johnson, J, † 3 cav, died Sept 12, scorbutus.
8764, Johnson, C, M, Co K, died Sept 14, scorbutus.
9552, Jones, D, 11, Co E, died Sept 23, scorbutus.
9018, Jones, Wm T, * 11 cav, died Sept 23, diarrhea.
10479, Johnson, M, 13 cav, Co G, died Oct 7, scorbutus.
12319, Johnson, E W, 7 cav, Co C, died Dec 21, scorbutus.
12702, Johnson, W, 13, Co D, died Feb 26, '65, scorbutus.

32, Kirby, James, Co M, died March 11, pneumonia.
434, Kilpatrick, R, 2, Co E, died April 8, diarrhea c.
605, Kelsey, John, 12, Co A, died April 17, dysentery c.
600, Keutzler, Henry, 2, Co G, died April 17, dysentery c.
85, King, James T, 2, Co D, died April 25, small pox.
3702, Kirk, B J, 7 cav, Co B, died July 21, diarrhea c.
3749, Keesee, Hoza, 7 cav, Co C, died July 22, dysentery.
7367, Kean, J S, 7 cav, Co C, died Aug 31, diarrhea.
7641, Kirk, J P, 3, Co D, died Sept 2, diarrhea.
8183, Kingsley, S, 2, Co D, died Sept 8, dysentery.
8714, Keoser, Joseph, 2 cav, died Sept 14, scorbutus.
9407, Kelley, J W, † 2, Co E, died Sept 21, diarrhea.
11241, Kissinger, F, 7, Co I, died Oct 21.
12570, Kidwell, J, 4, Co C, died Feb 2, '65, scorbutus.
1157, Kuner, E B, 3, Co E, died May 16, diarrhea.

627, Long, Jonathan, 2, Co H, died April 19, fever typhus.
658, Lane, L E, 2, Co I, died April 23, pneumonia.
713, Lofty, R J, 2, Co I, died April 24, diarrhea.
1223, Lovette, W T, 18 cav, Co A, died May 19, rubeola.
1252, Langley, E G, 11, Co B, died May 21, scorbutus.
1362, Long, C C, 2, Co C, died May 25, anasarca.
1597, Long, John, 2, Co C, died June 3, diarrhea c.
2193, Looper, E, 2, Co D, died June 19, diarrhea a.
8, Lanen, Thomas, 2, Co H, died April 6, small pox.
45, Lingo, James, 2, Co C, died May 17, small pox.
63, Levi, J N, 2, Co I, died June 3, small pox.
3698, Lamphey, J, 7 cav, Co C, died July 21, diarrhea.
3760, Little, E D, 7, Co A, died July 22, scorbutus.
3830, Lemmar, J E, † 13 cav, Co A, died July 23, diarrhea.
4114, Lawrence, J C, 13 cav, Co I, died July 28, diarrhea a.
4292, Lewis, R, 1 battery, Co B, died July 30, dysentery.
4575, Long, John, 13, Co H, died Aug 2, scorbutus.
8640, Lawson, M, 8, Co H, died Sept 13, diarrhea c.

No. of Grave.
8926, Lawson, H G, 8, Co I, died Sept 14, scorbutus.
9594, Lester, James, 7 cav, Co M, died Sept 27, diarrhea.
9641, Lewis, J, 3, Co G, died Sept 24, diarrhea c.
11827, Lapriut, J, 11, Co K, died Nov 5, scorbutus.
1352, Long, C C, 2, Co C, died May 25, anasarca.
11970, Leonard, J, 7, Co C, died Nov 12, diarrhea.

388, McCune, Robert, 2, Co E, died April 5, diarrhea c.
405, Meyers, W J, 12, Co F, died April 6, fever intermittent.
558, Miller, W H, 2, Co F, died April 15, diarrhea.
562, Macklin, John, 2, Co H, died April 15, diarrhea.
683, Malcolm, S A, 4, Co B, died April 16, diarrhea.
722, Maines, Wm, 1, Co D, died April 27, diarrhea c.
801, McCart, Wm, 2, Co B, died April 29, diarrhea c.
845, McDowell, G I, 2, Co D, died April 26, diarrhea.
1051, Myrick, E I, 2, Co A, died May 12, diarrhea.
1176, May, W, 10, Co C, died May 16, diarrhea.
1289, Meyers, D, 2, Co H, died May 22, diarrhea.
1402, Martin, F A, 2, Co A, died May 27, diarrhea.
1451, McLane, H C, 2 cav, Co I, died May 29, diarrhea c.
1561, Massie, Eli, 2, Co C, died June 1, diarrhea c.
1668, Myers, John, * 2, Co H, died June 6, diarrhea c.
1703, Moulden, Wm, 2, Co A, died June 7, scorbutus.
1725, Mecart, J, 2, Co B, died June 8, rheumatism.
1960, McDonald, L M, 12, Co G, died June 14, pneumonia.
2050, Meyers, Wm, 12, Co H, died June 16, diarrhea c.
2171, Matheny, D C, 7, Co D, died June 19, anasarca.
2224, Melterberger, M, 2, Co G, died June 20, diarrhea a.
2277, Morris, J, * 2 cav, Co E, died June 20, diarrhea c.
2475, Mitchluer, H, 13, Co H, died June 25, fever typhus.
2506, Mackin, W, 7 cav, Co K, died June 26, fever remittent.
2516, Moss, J, 2, Co A, died June 26, diarrhea c.
3124, McAllister, W H, 4 cav, Co H, died July 10, diarrhea c.
24, Mayes, William, 2, Co E, died April 15, small pox.
38, Mee, Thomas, 2, Co F, died April 29, small pox.
46, Mergen, H S, 2, Co G, died May 18, small pox.
3243, McGee, Wm, 7 cav, Co B, died July 3, scorbutus.
3642, Maynard, W J, 13, Co A, died July 20, dysentery.
4567, Miller, J W, 8 cav, Co G, died Aug 2, diarrhea.
4523, McLean, A G, 3, Co C, died Aug 1, scorbutus.
3897, McCoy, W C, 2, Co G, died July 24, diarrhea c.
4236, McDover, H, 2, Co C, died July 29, diarrhea c.
4237, Montgomery, Wm, 1, Co C, died July 29, diarrhea.
4751, McGuin, M, 7 cav, Co C, died Aug 5, scorbutus.
4905, Mussurzo, M, 9 cav, Co H, died Aug 6, bronchitis.
4496, Mulanox, A C, * 2, Co B, died Aug 1, scorbutus.
5008, Myers, A, 13 cav, Co C, died Aug 8, diarrhea.
5064, Miles, Samuel, 2, Co A, died Aug 8, catarrh.
5282, Morris, H S, 13 cav, Co C, died Aug 11, diarrhea.
5594, Mitchell, James, 7 cav, Co K, died Aug 14, diarrhea.
5782, Mitton, Wm, 13, Co B, died Aug 15, diarrhea.
6555, Maddro, James, 2, Co C, died Aug 23, scorbutus.
7435, Mefford, J, * 8 cav, Co C, died Sept 1, diarrhea.
7574, Moore, James, 13, died Sept 2, diarrhea.
7764, McGee, A, 13, Co B, died Sept 4, diarrhea.
8059, Mayher, J W, 2, Co E, died Sept 7, diarrhea.
8174, Martin, J S, 7 cav, Co H, died Sept 8, fever typhoid.
8954, Mackey, S, 7, Co D, died Sept 16, diarrhea c.
9140, McKeese, Samuel, 8 cav, Co G, died Sept 17, diarrhea c.
9542, McDonald, W, 7, Co D, died Sept 23, diarrhea.
9559, Montgomery, C F, 1 cav, Co L, died Sept 20, dysentery.
9783, Metheney, V V, 13 cav, Co A, died Sept 26, scorbutus.
9861, Macart, R, 2, Co B, died Sept 27, scorbutus.
10795, Martin, S, 7 cav, Co G, died Oct 12, scorbutus.
10976, Meare, J H, 7 cav, Co I, died Oct 15, fever typhus.
11532, Mays, L, 9 cav, Co A, died Oct 26, scorbutus.
11544, McCaslin, M C, 7, Co D, died Oct 27, scorbutus.
11649, Myracle, C, 7, Co C, died Oct 30, scorbutus.
11667, Morris, William, 7 Cav, Co I, died Oct 30, diarrhea.
11845, Moore, Wm P, 11, Co D, died Nov 6, scorbutus.
12277, McNealy, W, 7 cav, Co C, died Dec 3, scorbutus.
12338, Moore, T, 7 cav, Co I, died Dec 26, scorbutus.

7497, Norton, J, 10, Co K, died Sept 1, scorbutus.
163, Newman, Jesse, 2, Co K, died March 25, fever typhus.
826, Norris, Thomas, 2, Co D, died May 1, dysentery.
1237, Norman, James, * 13 cav, Co C, died May 20, rubeola.
3191, Newport, H, 11 cav, Co E, died July 12, scorbutus.
50, Neely, A, 8, Co H, died June 2, small pox.
6262, Nichols, W T, 7 cav, Co A, died Aug 20, ictus solis.
7818, Newman, T A, † 4, died Sept 4, diarrhea.
9068, Norwood, Wm, 7 cav, Co I, died Sept 17, scorbutus.
9447, Norris, P W, 7 cav, Co B, died Sept 21, diarrhea.
9640, Needham, F, 13, Co C, died Sept 24, diarrhea c.
9996, Neighbour, M, 7, Co E, died Sept 29, scorbutus.
10223, Norris, W, 2, Co D, died Oct 2, diarrhea.
12642, Neighbors, A, 7, Co B, died Feb 13, '65, rheumatism.

4680, Odorn, John, † 8, Co B, died Aug 4, scorbutus.
1753, Owen, A, 2, Co D, died June 9, diarrhea c.
10743, Oliver, L, 13, Co C, died Oct 11, diarrhea.

No. of Grave.
923, Ollenger, John, 2, Co I, died May 6, dysentery.
2697, Overton, J S, 2, Co C, died June 30, pneumonia.

689, Palmer, Wm, 2, Co K, died April 23, bronchitis.
806, Perkins, G W, 17, Co M, died April 29, dysentery.
1141, Penix, John, 5, Co G, died May 16, fever intermittent.
1365, Perry, James, 6 cav, Co L, died May 25, diarrhea c.
1517, Profett, James, 13, Co C, died May 31, diarrhea c.
1638, Powers, H, 17 cav, Co A, died June 5, diarrhea.
2146, Pander, E H, 11, Co K, died June 18, diarrhea c.
2748, Perry, Thomas, 11, Co B, died July 1, dysentery.
2767, Pursly, W B, 11 cav, Co C, died July 2, diarrhea.
3170, Pankey, A J, 13, Co B, died July 11, diarrhea.
505, Pilot, Joseph, 2, Co K, died April 12, diarrhea c.
4392, Pascall, J B, 13, Co B, died Aug 3, diarrhea.
4572, Powell, A N, 17, Co K, died Aug 2, diarrhea.
8695, Pavies, S, 7 cav, Co C, died Sept 12, scorbutus.
1, Polivar, Martin, 2, Co E, died March 12, small pox.
10, Phillips, N, 2, Co H, died April 5, small pox.
32, Parker, Wiley, 3, Co B, died April 25, small pox.
4041, Parmer, E, 7, Co I, died July 26, debilitas.
4380, Palmer, D P, 7 cav, Co I, died July 31, scorbutus.
6191, Parks, R T, 7 cav, Co I, died Aug 19, scorbutus.
6335, Prison, E T, 7, Co B, died Aug 21, fever typhus.
6485, Prices, Nelson, 15, Co B, died Aug 22, debilitas.
6610, Phillips, T, 2, Co G, died Aug 23, anasarca.
7290, Park, James, 7 cav, Co E, died Aug 30, debilitas.
9020, Penn, W H, 2, Co E, died Sept 17, diarrhea.
9121, Padcock, D W, * 2 cav, Co I, died Sept 17, diarrhea.
9310, Pennington, G W, * 11, died Sept 21, diarrhea.
10304, Pegram, W, 7, Co A, died Oct 4, scorbutus.
10318, Powers, H M, * 7, Co A, died Oct 4, scorbutus.
10364, Poster, N P, 13, Co E, died Oct 4, scorbutus.
10655, Pomeroy, John, 7, Co K, died Oct 11, scorbutus.
10852, Pierce, Wm, 8, Co A, died Oct 13, scorbutus.
10907, Partean, W, 7, Co K, died Oct 14, scorbutus.
11285, Pickering, E, 4 cav, Co G, died Oct 22, scorbutus.
11406, Pickley, J, 7, Co B, died Oct 24, diarrhea.
11501, Powers, J, 7 cav, Co A, died Oct 26, scorbutus.
12644, Powers, R, 7 cav, Co H, died Feb 13, '65, diarrhea c.
675, Perry, Wesley, 2, Co I, died April 22, bronchitis.
1978, Pope, F, 7 cav, Co D, died June 15, diarrhea c.

2232, Quiller, T, 7 cav, Co D, died June 20, diarrhea c.

271, Ragan, J, 2, Co B, died March 28, diarrhea c.
380, Rowden, Wm, 2, Co A, died April 5, diarrhea c.
382, Reynolds, Henry, 11 cav, Co L, died Apr 15, diarrhea c.
454, Russell, R, 2, Co K, died April 0, diarrhea c.
4344, Roberts, John, 2, Co F, died Aug 3, dysentery.
5815, Rouser, A, * 1, Co A, died Aug 16, diarrhea.
2519, Reed, John, C, 7, Co A, died June 26, diarrhea c.
523, Robinson, James M, 3, Co A, died April 13, diarrhea.
646, Robinson, Isaac, 3, Co A, died April 20, debilitas.
951, Robinson, William, 1, Co G, died May 8, pneumonia.
1438, Ryle, F, 1 artil, Co C, died May 28, diarrhea c.
1464, Reece, James, 13, Co C, died May 29, diarrhea c.
1783, Ralph, J F, 13, Co E, died June 10, diarrhea c.
1924, Reel, G W, 7, Co A, died June 14, diarrhea c.
2005, Ringoland, W H, 2, Co D, died June 15, anasarca.
2008, Robb, G W, 13, Co A, died June 15, diarrhea c.
2083, Ryan, Wm, 3, Co K, died June 17, diarrhea c.
2219, Robinson, J C, 2, Co B, died June 20, diarrhea c.
2314, Roberts, T, 2, Co H, died June 22, bronchitis.
2691, Riley, J M, 6, Co G, died June 30, diarrhea.
2753, Ryan, C P, 2, Co G, died July 1, diarrhea.
17, Riddle, Robert, 2, Co F, died April 12, small pox.
3752, Ritter, John, 3, Co C, died July 22, diarrhea c.
3755, Rodins, T, 2, Co D, died July 22, debilitas.
3772, Reeves, George W, 4, Co F, died July 22, debilitas.
4086, Robinson, A, 2, Co B, died July 27, dysentery.
4254, Renshaw, H G, 7 cav, Co C, died July 29, fever typhus.
4368, Rainwater, A, 7, Co F, died July 31, diarrhea.
5974, Rater, Henry, 7 cav, Co E, died Aug 17, diarrhea c.
4616, Roberts, Chas, 7, Co A, died Aug 3, scorbutus.
6267, Reeves, A, 11 cav, Co B, died Aug 20, ictus solis.
6409, Rider, W R, 1, 13, Co C, died Aug 22, diarrhea.
6837, Rogers, A G, 7 cav, Co B, died Aug 25, gangrene.
7082, Russell, J S, 7, Co E, died Aug 28, scorbutus.
7091, Ross, John, 7 cav, Co B, died Aug 28, diarrhea.
7099, Roach, J W, 7 cav, Co K, died Aug 28, anasarca.
7191, Riter, John, 7, Co E, died Aug 29, scorbutus.
7774, Reynolds, W, 3, Co G, died Sept 4, diarrhea.
7978, Rogan, Geo W, 3, Co G, died Sept 6, diarrhea.
8151, Rose, M L, 2 east, Co A, died Sept 8, diarrhea.
8523, Ramsey, W, Co A, died Sept 12, scorbutus.
9513, Renneger, Jeff, 13 cav, died Sept 22, dysentery.
10107, Richardson, R, 13 cav, Co E, died Sept 30, scorbutus.
10869, Rushing, W R, 7, Co B, died Oct 13, scorbutus.
11995, Roberts, J G, 7, Co L, died Nov 13, scorbutus.
12101, Riley, J, 6, Co E, died Nov 20, scorbutus.

12758, Robins, W, 7, Co B, died March 12, '65, diarrhea c.
8978, Reeder, C, sutler, 51, died Sept 16, fever intermittent.

298, Stinger, A E, 2, Co K, died Apr 1, diarrhea c.
319, Sane, Joseph, 8, Co B, died Apr 2, debilitas.
374, Sukirk, J F, 2, Co B, died Apr 5, diarrhea a.
390, Smith, John, 2 cav, Co I, died Apr 6, diarrhea c.
776, Scott, R S, 2, died Apr 28, diarrhea c.
985, Southpater, Eli, 11, Co K, died May 9, diarrhea.
1140, Seals, John, 2, Co D, died May 16, diarrhea.
1191, Stepp, Preston, 2, Co D, died May 18, diarrhea c.
1254, Stafford, Wm, 13 cav, Co C, died May 21, rubeola.
1278, Sisson, James, 2, Co E, died May 22, diarrhea.
1284, Smith, T A, 2, Co C, died May 22, pneumonia.
1313, Short, L H, 7 cav, Co C, died May 29, diarrhea c.
1354, Smith, C, 2, Co B, died May 25, diarrhea.
1408, Simpkins, Thomas, 9, Co A, died May 27, diarrhea c.
1475, Smith, Joel, 2, Co A, died May 30, diarrhea.
1481, Strawberry, A, 8, Co A, died May 30, diarrhea.
1488, Sutton, John, 2, Co I, died May 31, diarrhea c.
1526, Stover, A, 2, Co C, died May 31, erysipelas.
1670, Smith, Wm, 2, Co D, died June 6, diarrhea c.
2280, Stevens, R, 2, Co D, died June 20, diarrhea c.
2284, Smith, J, 13 cav, Co E, died June 21, diarrhea c.
2558, Smith, J B, 20, Co I, died July 6, diarrhea.
11, Stanton, W, 4, Co F, died Apr 5, small pox.
12, Sutton, Thomas, 2, Co I, died Apr 8, small pox.
39, Sandusky, G, 2, Co B, died Apr 29, small pox.
56, Stout, D D, 2, Co F, died June 18, small pox.
8038, Scarbrough, S N, 13, Co E, died July 8, dysentery.
8276, Shrop, J B, 2 east, Co E, died July 14, diarrhea.
3298, Sells, W, 2 east cav, Co D, died July 14, dysentery.
8332, Swappols, O B, 4, Co A, died July 15, diarrhea.
8520, Slaver, A, 11 cav, Co C, died July 18, diarrhea.
3865, Smith, John M, 12, Co M, died July 24, diarrhea c.
4048, Sapper, S, 8, Co H, died July 26, diarrhea.
4170, Snow, W, 7 cav, Co M, died July 28, diarrhea.
5462, Smith, L, 13, Co L, died Aug 13, scorbutus.
5633, Sutton, Andrew, 13 cav, Co E, died Aug 14, diarrhea.
5878, Swan, John, 2, Co D, died Aug 16, marasmus.
5962, Scott, John, 18, Co B, died Aug 17, diarrhea c.
6643, Sutton, D, 1 cav, Co H, died Aug 28, scorbutus.
7086, Smith, J, 6, Co M, died Aug 28, gangrene.
7296, Stewart, J W, 13 cav, Co K, died Aug 30, dysentery.
7314, Smidney, E, 1 cav, Co E, died Aug 30, diarrhea c.
7787, Scobey, L A H, 13 cav, Co B, died Sept 2, dysentery.
7923, Barret, James D, Tenn State Guard, died Sept 5, dysentery.
8667, Smith, J, 8 cav, Co E, died Sept 18, diarrhea.
9192, Smith, T A, 13, Co C, died Sept 18, diarrhea.
9381, Southerland, J, 13 cav, Co C, died Sept 20, scorbutus.
9395, Stewart, E, 13 cav, Co D, died Sept 20, scorbutus.
9555, Smith, W H, 7, Co B, died Sept 23, diarrhea c.
9719, Swatzell, W L, 8 cav, Co E, died Sept 25, scorbutus.
9803, Stratten, J L, 7 cav, Co M, died Sept 25, scorbutus.
10409, Stafford, S, 13, Co A, died Oct 6, anasarca.
10454, Shonall, John, 13, Co C, died Oct 7, scorbutus.
11594, Shay, D, 11, Co E, died Oct 28, diarrhea.
12558, Smith, H, 2, Co E, died Jan 30, '65, scorbutus.
12749, Stevens, J F, 2 cav, Co E, died March 8, '65, scorbutus.
12756, Smith, J D, 4, Co C, died March 12, '65, diarrhea c.
12784, Stewart, R H, 7, Co C, died March 15, '65, pleuritis.
12800, Shook, N A, 7, Co B, died March 19, '65, rheumatism.
12880, Smith, George, 2, Co B, died Apr 18, '65, diarrhea c.
36, Selner, W H, 2, Co E, died Apr 28, small pox.
8995, Slover, A W, 2, Co C, died July 26, diarrhea.

211, Tompkins, T B, 2, Co F, died March 28, dysentery c.
258, Thompson, W D, 2, Co F, died March 31, diarrhea c.
793, Thompson, Charles, 2, died Apr 29, diarrhea c.
992, Thomas, W H, 2, Co K, died May 7, anasarca.
1657, Tomlin, A, 7 cav, Co M, died June 6, diarrhea c.
1704, Thauton, S A, 1 artil, Co H, died June 7, diarrhea.
2229, Tice, S J, 7, Co B, died June 20, diarrhea c.
2718, Tipton, W H, 2, Co I, died July 1, dysentery c.
8460, Taylor, J, 13, Co D, died July 17, scorbutus.
4122, Tyttle, John, 1 cav, Co A, died June 28, dysentery.
4778, Templeton, G W, 2, Co C, died Aug 5, diarrhea.
5646, Tue, W S, 13, Co C, died Aug 14, diarrhea.
7052, Thomas, W H, 7 cav, Co A, died Aug 28, debilitas.
9203, Tolley, D, 8, Co H, died Sept 19, scorbutus.
9375, Terry, D, 9 cav, Co D, died Sept 20, scorbutus.
10780, Tinnn, R A, 7 cav, Co B, died Oct 12, diarrhea c.
12694, Tidwell, T, 13, Co D, died Feb 22, '65, pleuritis.
4825, Tidwell, J W, 13, Co C, died Aug 5, fever remittent.

2592, Usley, T R, 2, Co A, died June 28, bronchitis.
4518, Undergrate, A, 2, Co I, died Aug 2, scorbutus.

885, Vaugh, I, 8, Co H, died May 5, debilitas.
1203, Vanhorn, J, 2, Co H, died May 19, diarrhea c.
2915, Varner, T W, 11 cav, Co E, died July 5, scorbutus.

No. of Grave.
7217, Vanhook, J M,* 11 cav, Co H, died July 29, anasarca.
4530, Vaughry, Frederick, 2, Co D, died Aug 1, rheumatism.

60, Wolfe, John, 11, Co E, died March 18, '64, diarrhea.
259, Woolen, I. 2, Co A, died March 31, diarrhea o
339, Webb, Robert, 2, Co B, died April 2, fever typhus.
359, Woas, M, 2, Co I, died April 2 pneumonia.
601, Watts, C C. 2 Co A, died April 12, dysentery.
670, Ward, Jordan, 2, Co A, died April 15, diarrhea.
810, White, John, 2, Co B, died April 30, diarrhea c.
932, William, C, 7, Co B, died May 5, phthisis.
1052, Ward, A, 3, Co I, died May 12, debilitas.
1756, Watts, J W, 7, Co M, died June 9, fever typhus.
1794, White I, 2, Co D, died June 10, dysentery.
1865, Wallace, L, 2, cavl, Co C, died June 12, anasarca.
2057, Ward, C, 2, Co H, died June 16, diarrhea c.
2066, Watts, T,* 2, Co I, died June 16, diarrhea c.
2132, Wray, Samuel, 13, Co C, died June 18, scorbutus.
2496, Wilson, A, 8 cav, died June 26, dysentery a.
2764, Winningham, J, 2, Co B, died July 2, diarrhea c.
2810, Wolls, E, 8, Co H, died July 3, scorbutue.
3021, Watkins, J M, 4, Co I, died July 7, scorbutus.
3031, Woodsend, T, 7, Co K, died July 8, scorbutus.
3169, Webb, D, 8 cav, Co G, died July 12, scorbutus.
21, Winchester, J D. 1 cav, Co E, died April 15, small pox.
19, Weaver, P, 2, Co D, died April 13, small pox.
4554, West, W F, 2, Co H, died Aug 2, anasarca.
4869, Ward, John, citizen, died Aug 6, diarrhea.
22, Whitby, R B, 2 Co C, died April 15, small pox.
83, Weese, W, 2, Co I, died April 23, small pox.
3297, Weir, I, 1 cav, Co B, died July 14, diarrhea o.
3304, Wilson, H, 2, Co B, died July 14, scorbutus.
3319, Wolf, A, 10, Co C, died July 14, pneumonia.
3468, Williams, A, 3 cav, Co E, died July 17, scorbutus.
3615, Willis, James, Tenn State G, died July 20, dysentery.
3714, Webbe, J, 2, Co B, died July 21, debilitas.
3737, Wilson, J, 12, Co F, died July 21, diarrhea.
3932, Wilson, B L, 2, Co D, died July 26, scorbutus.

No. of Grave.
4033, Watford, W, 7, Co A, died July 26, diarrhea o.
4704, Wallace, L, 2, Co C, died Aug 4, constipatio.
5207, Wright, J W, 7 cav, Co B, died Aug 10, constipatio.
5572, Withyde, S, 1, Co A, died Aug 14, scorbutus.
6108, Wood, P D, 3, Co B, died Aug 19, diarrhea.
6580, Webb, Robert, 2, Co B, died Aug 23, diarrhea.
6608, Wortell, H H, 7 cav, Co I, died Aug 23, diarrhea c.
7618, White, R O M, 13, Co B, died Sept 2, diarrhea c.
8740, Wicks, N, 7, Co H, died Sept 14, diarrhea.
7231, Wood, J, 7, Co C, died Aug 29, anasarca.
9103, Woolsey, J, 2, Co F, died Sept 18, debilitas.
9479, Walker, John, 13 cav, Co C, died Sept 21, diarrhea.
9658, Williams, C S, 9 cav, Co B, died Sept 24, scorbutus.
9670, Whittle, H W, 7 cav, Co C, died Sept 24, diarrhea.
9730, Webb, T, 6, Co G, died Sept 25, diarrhea.
9929, White, L S, 11 cav, Co D, died Sept 28, diarrhea.
10337, Wiggins, G W, 11 cav, Co C, died Oct 4, diarrhea.
10338, White, H, † 7 cav, Co A, died Oct 4, scorbutus.
10739, Warrell, J W,* 7 cav, died Oct 11, diarrhea.
10605, Webb, W, 3, Co A, died Oct 10, scorbutus.
11386, Worden, J W, † 7, Co E, died Oct 24, ulcus.
12107, Wineing, J, 7, Co M, died Nov. 21, scorbutus.
12125, White, Wm M, 11, Co D, died Nov 22, scorbutue.
12139, Watson, I C, 1 cav, Co C, died Nov 23, scorbutus.
12570, Walker, C H, 6, Co H, died Feb 3, '65, scorbutus.
12699, Woodruff, J, 4 cav, Co B, died Feb 24, '65, debilitas,
12779, Woods, Thomas, 13, Co B, died March 15, '65, scorbutus
8190, White, J, † 7 cav, Co A, died Sept 8, diarrhea.
5669, Wilson, Wm A, 6, Co A, died Aug 14, diarrhea.
4717, Westbrook, J H, 6 cav, Co A, died Aug 4, diarrhea
4793, Wilson, J M, 13 cav, Co D, died Aug 6, scorbutus.

383, Yarber, Wiley, 5, Co I, died April 6, diarrhea c.
878, Young, James, 2, Co D, died May 4, diarrhea c.
1142, Young, James, 2, Co F, died May 16, anasarca.
14, Yerant, Samuel, 3, Co E, died April 10, small pox
5662, Yarnell, J E, 3, Co E, died Aug 14, scorbutus.

VERMONT.

3975, Averill, T E, 9, Co I, died July 25, diarrhea.
4579, Adams, Daniel, 1 cav, Co L, died Aug 2, fever intermittent.
6301, Albee, S, † 11, Co G, died Sept 9, diarrhea c.
9960, Atwood, A, 1, Co C, died Sept 28, diarrhea.
10664, Aldrich, L E, † 11, Co A, died Oct 11, diarrhea.
11250, Aldrich, H B, 1 artil, Co A, died Oct 21, scorbutus.
12092, Aiken, M A, 1, Co A, died Nov 19, diarrhea.
12766, Avery, B F, 3, Co C, died March 13, '65, diarrhea o.

2135, Bloomer, J, 2 battery, died June 15, diarrhea c.
3166, Bailey, James, 2, Co A, died July 11, diarrhea c.
4036, Brown, George, 16, Co B, died July 20, scorbutus.
4173, Bailey, S P, 1 cav, Co H, died July 28, diarrhea c.
4200, Beadle, H H, 9, Co G, died July 29, dysentery.
4509, Bucker, James, 1, Co M, died Aug 1, diarrhea c.
4631, Boyd, A M, 1 cav, Co L, died Aug 3, diarrhea.
4954, Bentley, M W, 6, Co A, died Aug 7, diarrhea.
5671, Bacom, A M, 8, Co G, died Aug 14, diarrhea.
5728, Bliss, J H, 1 cav, Co L, died Aug 15, scorbutus.
6134, Burchard, C, 11, Co L, died Aug 21, debilitas.
6249, Benson, A, 1, Co C, died Aug 21, diarrhea c.
6416, Bonnvile, J, 4, Co D, died Aug 22, scorbutus.
6594, Barnes, W, 1 cav, Co F, died Aug 23, dysentery.
7886, Burton, W, 11, Co K, died Sept 5, diarrhea.
8029, Beady, Wm, 9, Co I, died Sept 6 dysentery.
8086, Barker, F, 1 artil, Co A, died Aug 7, diarrhea.
8316, Burrows, H, 11, Co F, died Sept 10, diarrhea c.
8591, Brainard, J B, 1 cav, Co L, died Aug 12, scorbutus.
10305, Brown, G, 9, Co D, died Oct 4, diarrhea.
10371, Bowles, L H, 7, Co A, died Oct 5, scorbutus.
10431, Burton C, 4, Co A, died Oct 6, dysentery.
10745, Barker, C, 4, Co D, died Oct 11, diarrhea o.
11068, Brown, J B, 1, Co A, died Oct 17, scorbutus.
11225, Batch, B F, 4, Co C, died Oct 20, dysentery.
11375, Bohamar, J, 9, Co I, died Oct 24, scorbutus.
11469, Baker, John, 11, Co E, died Oct 26, scorbutus.
11747, Boulon, A, 2, Co B, died Nov 2, scorbutus.
11841, Babcock, T, 1, Co K, died Nov 5, diarrhea.
12055, Barber, W H, 1, Co C, died Nov 16, diarrhea.
12185, Burns, J, 7, Co B, died Nov 28, scorbutue.
12239, Butter, A F, 1 artil, Co L, died Dec 7, scorbutus.
12406, Baxter, G, 4, Co A, died Jan 6, '66, scorbutus.
12412, Bishop, E, 11, Co E, died Jan 8, '65, rheumatism.
12585, Bailey, E, 4, Co B, died Feb 4, '65, scorbutus.

1044, Corey, C A, 1 cav, Co F, died May 12, diarrhea o.
1170, Clifford, Jas, 4, Co F, died May 17, dysentery.
1228, Chatfield, Wm,* 10, Co F, died May 20, diarrhea.

1973, Collitt, Jas, 1 cav, Co H, died June 15, diarrhea c.
2675, Caswell, F, 9, died June 30, diarrhea.
2694, Clough, B, 9, Co A, died June 30, dysentery.
2811, Chase, M, 6, Co H, died July 3, bronchitis.
3351, Cole, A H, 9, Co H, died July 16, scorbutue.
3817, Crocker, D, 5, Co D, died July 23, diarrhea.
3918, Clough, John D, 11, Co A, died July 24, diarrhea o.
4205, Chamberlain, 6, Co A, died July 29, diarrhea.
4883, Crouse, N, 5, Co C, died Aug 6, wounds.
5108, Chester, A, 11, Co K, died Aug 9, diarrhea.
5480, Corey, Thos, 1 artil, died Aug 13, scorbutue.
6806, Carmine, P, 1 artil, Co L, died Aug 25, diarrhea.
6932, Conner, W A, † 4, Co A, died Aug 26, diarrhea.
7345, Clark, M L, 11, Co F, died Aug 31, diarrhea.
7361, Clark, John, 11 artil, Co M, died Aug 31, scorbutus
7698, Cunningham, J, 1 cav, Co F, died Sept 3, scorbutus.
8320, Cook, J J,* 1 cav, Co I, died Sept 10, diarrhea c.
8923, Chase, E L, 1 artil, Co C, died Sept 16, dysentery
9724, Crowley, D, 11, Co F, died Sept 25, diarrhea.
11738, Cross, E F, 11, Co L, died Nov 2, scorbutus.
11769, Carter, J, 11, Co A, died Nov 3, scorbutus.
10330, Colburn, W, 1 artil, Co M, died Oct 4, scorbutue.

3068, Drew, F, 1 cav, Co F, died July 9, diarrhea.
5927, Donohue, P, 1 cav, Co D, died Aug 17, dysentery.
6104, Dunn, G E,* 1, Co G, died Aug 18, scorbutus.
6338, Doying, F W, 1 artil, Co F, died Aug 21, diarrhea.
6840, Darey, F, 4, Co D, died Aug 25, scorbutus.
7974, Day, George, 11, Co H, died Sept 6, fever remittent.
8271, Davis, O F, 9, Co I, died Sept 9, diarrhea c.
10420, Dunn, W W, 1 cav, Co G, died Oct 6, diarrhea.
10458, Day, J D, 1 cav, Co A, died Oct 7, dysentery.
12375, Dragoon, N, 1 cav, Co G, died Jan 1, '65, diarrhea c

6353, Ennison, G, 11, Co A, died Aug 21, diarrhea c.
10316, Eliot, C, 4, Co F, died Oct 4, scorbutus.

821, Farmer, E L, 14, Co H, died May 1, diarrhea
3464, Freeman, C R, 9, Co H, died July 17, scorbutus.
4077, Farnsworth, M, 1, Co B, died July 26, diarrhea.
5851, Farnham, L B, 1 artil, Co A, died Aug 16, marasmus.
6014, Foster, A, 17, Co K, died Aug 17, diarrhea.
6758, Fuller, W, 1 cav, Co G, died Aug 25, diarrhea.
7165, Forrest, S, 3, Co I, died Aug 29, anasarca.
8096, Fox, W, 11, Co K, died Sept 7, diarrhea.
8201, Foster, H B, 11, Co L, died Sept 8, diarrhea c.
10784, Feast, Geo, 1 artil, Co K, died Oct 12, diarrhea.
10960, Fisk, W P, 4, Co K, died Oct 15, diarrhea c.
11314, Farrell, J H, 4, Co D, died Oct 2[illegible], scorbutus.

No. of Grave.
11351, Flint, C B, 4, Co D, died Oct 23, scorbutus.
11458, Foster, H C, 1 artil, Co D, died Oct 25, scorbutus.
12317, Ferand, A, 1 artil, Co B, died Dec 21, scorbutus.
12322, Ferrett, J, 1, Co K, died Dec 23, scorbutus.
12065, Fairchild, G L, 1 artil, Co A, died Nov 17, scorbutus.
6264, Farnham, L D, † 11, Co A, died Aug 20, ictus solis.

1770, Gelo, A, 8, Co B, died June 8, diarrhea c.
6273, Green, E, 2 battery, died Aug 10, diarrhea c.
6572, Gleason, C W, 1 artil, Co H, died Sept 12, dysentery.
9799, Gillman, S A, 4, Co G, died Sept 26, diarrhea.
11598, Graves, J, 11, Co E, died Oct 28, scorbutus.
12531, Gerry, E B, * 4, Co H, died Jan 26, '65, diarrhea c.

2176, Hubbard, F, 2 battery, died June 19, diarrhea c.
3851, Humphrey, John, 1 cav, Co A, died July 24, diarrhea c.
5218, Hill, Benj, 11, Co A, died Aug 10, scorbutus.
6145, Hyde, E, * 11, Co L, died Aug 18, diarrhea.
6657, Havens, E W, 9, Co H, died Aug 24, dysentery.
7294, Hazen, W, 9, Co H, died Aug 31, dysentery.
10824, Hines, L, 11, Co A, died Oct 13, diarrhea.
10843, Hart, S L, 2, died Oct 13, diarrhea c.
10910, Hudson, J B, 11, Co A, died Oct 14, scorbutus.
10958, Hudson, J M, 11, Co A, died Oct 16, diarrhea c.
11442, Howard, J, 1 cav, Co K, died Oct 25, scorbutus.
11730, Holmes, Joseph, 1 artil, Co K, died Nov 2, scorbutus.
11810, Howard, J, 11, Co A, died Nov 4, diarrhea c.
1206, Hall, C A, 1, Co A, died Nov 17, scorbutus.
12300, Hodges, J, 1 cav, Co H, died Dec 17, scorbutus.

3309, Jones, H L, 6, Co B, died July 14, diarrhea.
3858, Joslin, H, 1, Co B, died July 24, diarrhea c.
3886, Jordan, A E, 17, Co A, died July 24, scorbutus.
4699, Johnson, D W, 11, Co H, died Aug 4, scorbutus.
10183, Johnson, John, 1 artil, Co K, died Oct 1, diarrhea.

4007, Knapp, L, 1, Co G, died July 25, anasarca.
6968, Kelsey, L C, 1 artil, Co F, died Aug 27, scorbutus.
7762, Kingsley, S, 1, Co D, died Sept 4, scorbutus.
8901, Knowles, C W, 4, Co H, died Sept 16, scorbutus.
6239, Knight, Chas, 1 artil, Co K, died Aug 26, scorbutus.

4597, La Boney, H, 1, Co M, died Aug 3, diarrhea.
4694, Laraway, H, 6, Co A, died Aug 3, dysentery.
7653, Lapcain, A, 1 cav, died Sept 3, debilitas.
7891, Ladderbush, J, 17, Co A, died Sept 5, diarrhea.
8355, Leoport, C, 11, Co L, died Sept 10, diarrhea.
10180, Lungershan, W C, 1 cav, Co F, died Oct 1, diarrhea.
11074, Lacker, H, 11, Co A, died Oct 17, scorbutus.
12916, Lunsden, C, 4 cav, Co D, died Feb 8, '65, scorbutus.

1335, Mitchell, Jacob, 2d bat, died May 24, anasarca.
1544, Mosey, A, 1 cav, Co K, died June 1, diarrhea c.
2068, McIntire, John, 7, Co F, died June 17, diarrhea c.
2294, Macian, P, 9, died June 24, diarrhea.
4617, Morse, W, 1, Co F, died Aug 3, diarrhea.
6073, Martin, Jas, 1, Co M, died Aug 8, fever congestive.
6949, Mills, Wm, 1, Co E, died Aug 17, marasmus.
7324, Merrill, B J, 1, Co B, died Aug 30, dysentery.
8475, Mayhim, J, 6, Co C, died Sept 11, diarrhea.
8965, Manchester, J M, 1 cav, Co I, died Sept 16, diarrhea.
9352, McGager, J, 2, Co G, died Sept 20, scorbutus.
9405, Montgomery, O A, 10, Co A, died Sept 21, diarrhea c.
11227, McAllister, W B, 3, Co I, died Oct 20, scorbutus.
11735, Martin, M, 1 artil, Co A, died Nov 2, diarrhea.
12631, Monroe, A, 11 artil, Co L, died Feb 10, '65, diarrhea c.
9901, Morgan, Charles, 11 artil, Co M, died Sept 27, '64, scorbutus.
4478, McCrillis, Edw, 1 cav, Co C, died Aug 1, anasarca.
7289, Milcher, Wm, 9, Co F, died Aug 30, diarrhea.

6559, Nownes, Geo H, 1 cav, Co C, died Aug 23, diarrhea.
11067, Nichols, H L, 1 artil, Co A, died Oct 17, diarrhea c.
12253, Nelson, S H, 4 artil, Co I, died Dec 13, scorbutus.

704, O'Brien, Wm, 1, Co H, died April 23, catarrh.
4300, O'Neil, J M, 10, Co A, died July 30, diarrhea.

3183, Plude, John, 2d bat, died July 11, rheumatism.
3213, Pev, Jas, 17, Co D, died July 12.
4981, Preston, F, 1 artil, died Aug 7, diarrhea.
5135, Phelps, H W, 9, Co H, died Aug 9, diarrhea.
5605, Poppins, Frank, 3, Co I, died Aug 14, diarrhea.
6586, Parmor, E, 4, Co C, died Aug 23, diarrhea.
7290, Park, Jas, 7 cav, Co E, died Aug 30, debilitas.
10040, Pillsbury, F, 4 cav, Co C, died Sept 29, diarrhea.
10237, Paul, John C, 4 cav, Co G, died Oct 2, scorbutus.
11041, Page, E, 4, Co I, died Oct 17, scorbutus.
11397, Powers, A, 4, Co H, died Oct 22, scorbutus.
11992, Packard, M G*, 1 artil, Co A, died Nov 13, diarrhea.
12198, Pike, N N, 4, Co I, died Nov 30, diarrhea c.
12721, Perry, A B, 4, Co H, died March 3, '65, diarrhea c.

1888, Reed, D W, 1 cav, died June 17, diarrhea c.
6699, Ransom, Geo W, 1 artil, Co L, died Aug 24, dysentery.
7697, Reese, C, 11, Co H, died Sept 3, diarrhea.
8158, Roberts, J M, 11, Co K, died Sept 8, diarrhea.
8173, Richards, J, 1 cav, Co L, died Sept 8, diarrhea.
9402, Raynor, Louis, 4 cav, Co C, died Sept 21, scorbutus.
9894, Ross, H E, 11 bat, Co K, died Sept 27, diarrhea.
11009, Reynolds, F, 11, Co F, died Oct 16, scorbutus.
11426, Raney, A, 4, Co A, died Oct 24, scorbutus.
11691, Rice, F W, 14, Co F, died Oct 31, dysentery.
12519, Rouncerver, E T, 9, Co D, died Jan 25, '65, scorbutus.

648, Spoore, W O, 1 cav, Co B, died April 20, diarrhea.
2913, Smith, J C, 1, Co H, died July 6, pneumonia.
2382, St John, A, 11, Co A, died July 16, dysentery.
4580, Seward, O, 5, Co C, died Aug 2, diarrhea.
5707, Skinner, F A, 4, Co H, died Aug 15, scorbutus.
5963, Stone, Jas A, 1 artil, Co H, died Aug 17, diarrhea.
6640, Simons, L, 1, Co G, died Aug 23, diarrhea.
7509, Seaton, T B, 4, Co F, died Sept 1, diarrhea.
7810, Sweeney, Henry, 11, Co C, died Sept 4, dysentery.
7813, Sprout, A, 17, Co F, died Sept 4, diarrhea.
8444, Stockwell, A, 11, Co H, died Sept 11, scorbutus.
10690, Sanburn, H, 4, Co G, died Sept 11, diarrhea c.
10811, Styles, A B, * 4, Co K, died Sept 12, diarrhea c.
10897, Sheldon, H, 1 cav, Co M, died Sept 14, scorbutus.
11282, Sarlett, L, 1, Co M, died Oct 22, scorbutus.
11470, Swaddle, W, 4, Co G, died Oct 26, scorbutus.
11966, Sanborn, M L, 1 artil, Co A, died Nov 11, diarrhea.
12266, Scott, R O, 4, Co F, died Dec 12, dysentery.
12514, Shay, J, 1 cav, Co K, died Jan 23, '65, diarrhea c.
12552, Sheldon, G, 1, Co K, died Jan 29, '65, scorbutus.
12567, Stewart, E W, 11, Co A, died Feb 1, '65, scorbutus.
5911, Scott, Geo W, 1 cav, Co C, died Aug 17, diarrhea.
8136, Suppes, T E, 1 cav, Co K, died Sept 11, scorbutus.

3784, Tuttle, C S, 1 cav, Co F, died July 22, diarrhea c.
5833, Tatro, Alfred, 9, Co F, died Aug 16, marasmus.
6587, Taylor, H C, 1 artil, Co L, died Aug 23, diarrhea.
6659, Trow, H, 17, Co D, died Aug 24, debilitas.
9374, Tanner, H, * 11, Co I, died Sept 20, scorbutus.
9574, Talmao, W C, † 11, Co F, died Sept 23, dysentery.
11171, Taylor, J W, 1 artil, Co A, died Oct 19, scorbutus.
11220, Thompson, W A, 1 artil, Co I, died Oct 20, scorbutus.

5693, Varnum, E G J, 11, Co F, died Aug 15, scorbutus.

3177, Weller D, 9, Co B, died July 11, fever typhus.
4370, Whitehall, Geo, 6, Co D, died July 31, diarrhea.
4435, Wilson, A, 6, Co B, died July 31, diarrhea c.
4585, Wilder, L F, 11, Co H, died Aug 2, wounds.
5075, Whitney, A, 9, Co D, died Aug 8, diarrhea.
5307, Warner, Geo O, 10, Co E, died Aug 11, scorbutus.
5751, Woodard, S P, 1 artil, Co H, died Aug 15, enteritis.
7063, Wells, Geo A, 4, Co F, died Aug 28, diarrhea.
7322, Wright, E S, 11 artil, Co A, died Aug 30, debilitas.
7689, Witt, T, 1 cav, Co F, died Sept 3, scorbutus.
7920, Ward, Alfred, 11, Co A, died Sept 5, diarrhea.
8239, Watkins, G C, 1, Co C, died Sept 9, dysentery.
9264, Woodmance, G, 11, Co F, died Sept 9, scorbutus.
9178, Welles, C, 11, Co H, died Sept 18, diarrhea.
10510, White, A, 11, Co A, died Oct 8, scorbutus.
10711, Webster W A, † 4, Co A, died Oct 11, diarrhea c.
11289, Wakefield, J W, 4, Co H, died Oct 22, scorbutus.
11398, Woods, J M, 1, Co F, died Oct 24, scorbutus.
11783, Wheeler, B, 11, Co K, died Nov 3, diarrhea c.
11840, Warden, G, 3, Co B, died Nov 5, diarrhea.
11865, Worthers, S T, 1 cav, Co D, died Nov 6, dysentery.
12158, Willey, J S, 1 artil, Co A, died Nov 25, scorbutus.
4533, Washburn, Tru, 1 cav, Co D, died Aug 2, dysentery.

VIRGINIA.

824, Anderson, A, 2, Co H, died May 1, dysentery.
876, Armstrong, †, 8 mil, Co C, died May 4, diarrhea.
942, Ayers, S V, 11, Co C, died May 7, diarrhea c.
1968, Armstrong, G D, 8, Co C, died June 14, anasarca.
2769, Armhult, W H, * 10, Co I, died July 1, diarrhea c.
6011, Armstrong, J, 3, Co C, died Aug 8, scorbutus.
6341, Arbogast, C W, 1 artil, Co C, died Aug 11, scorbutus.
8865, Abercrombie, W H, 12, Co G, died Sept 15, scorbutus.
11525, Allison, G, 1, Co F, died Oct 26, dysentery.

221, Burns, S A, 18, Co C, died March 29, diarrhea c.
255, Brooks, Sam'l F, 10, Co I, died March 30, fever intermittent.

VIRGINIA.

No. of Grave.

448, Boore, Jas, 1 cav, Co L, died April 9, diarrhea c.
756, Bennett, L J, 11, Co C, died April 27, dysentery c.
943, Brake, J, † 6, Co C, died May 7, pneumonia.
950, Blackburn, Geo, 10, Co I, died May 9, diarrhea.
1765, Bates, T E, 11, Co F, died June 7, diarrhea.
2518, Brown, M, 14, Co E, died June 20, diarrhea c.
2627, Bowermaster, S R, bugler, 3 cav, Co D, died June 25, scorbutus.
3407, Bateman, D P, 2, Co B, died July 16, dysentery.
4427, Barber, Jas, 1 cav, Co F, died July 31, diarrhea c.
5495, Bishop, J C, 3, Co C, died Aug 12, diarrhea.
6706, Bearer, P, 10, Co I, died Aug 24, scorbutus.
10297, Bontnell, O, 4, Co F, died Oct 3, diarrhea.
7126, Beasley, P, 9, Co G, died Aug 28, scorbutus.
7909, Bogard, Jno R, * 14, Co A, died Sept 5, scorbutus.
8539, Batt, M, 18, Co E, died Sept 12, anasarca.
9796, Butcher, Peter, 14, Co F, died Sept 26, diarrhea.
10198, Boom, J, 1 cav, Co B, died Oct 2, fever remittent.
11090, Bessing, P, 15, Co K, died Oct 18, scorbutus.
11337, Bush, H H, 14, Co B, died Oct 23, scorbutus.
11411, Burton, W B, 8 cav, Co A, died Oct 24, diarrhea.
11669, Barrett, J, 6 cav, Co K, died Oct 30, scorbutus.
11921, Beach, J F, 14, Co K, died Nov 8, scorbutus.
12045, Boggs, H C, * 6 cav, Co E, died Nov 16, scorbutus.
12414, Burton, N, 3 cav, Co B, died Jan 8, '65, rheumatism.

110, Corbett, L B, W Va mil, Co C, died March 23, diarrhea.
403, Carr, Wm, 8, Co B, died April 6, fever typhus.
835, Clendeman, C L, 4 cav, Co D, died May 1, diarrhea.
1032, Coste, Jesse, 8, Co E, died May 11, diarrhea.
1100, Coon, Nathan, 11, Co K, died May 14, diarrhea c.
2013, Carrington, Jas, 2, Co A, died June 15, anasarca.
2[illegible], Coffman, F, 3 cav, Co A, died June 20, phthisis.
2569, Cunderson, —, 8, Co D, died June 27, dysentery.
2661, Carnes, H, 10, Co E, died June 20, diarrhea.
2817, Conrad, H, 3, Co F, died July 3, diarrhea c.
2930, Cunningham, J, 8, Co E, died July 5, dysentery.
3315, Cox, T A, † 8 cav, Co A, died July 14, diarrhea.
4263, Cool, J B, * 3 cav, Co H, died July 31, diarrhea.
4741, Crook, E H, † 7, Co I, died Aug 5, anasarca.
5174, Cuppett, J, 3, Co H, died Aug 9, dysentery.
5384, Covil, Wm, 3, Co I, died Aug 12, debilitas.
6674, Clements, L, 3 cav, Co A, died Aug 24, dysentery.
6809, Curtin, B, 4 cav, Co B, died Aug 25, diarrhea c.
7091, Clark, —, 7, Co E, died Aug 28, diarrhea.
7179, Cremones, D, 9, Co D, died Aug 29, scorbutus.
8990, Cook, J, 7 cav, Co I, died Sept 17, diarrhea.
9406, Campbell, O H, 14, Co F, died Sept 21, diarrhea.
9755, Christian, J, 15, Co C, died Sept 25, scorbutus.
9762, Catnill, L, 9, Co B, died Sept 25, scorbutus.
9957, Cubin, J M, 14, Co B, died Sept 28, diarrhea.
10598, Childs, S P, 1 cav, Co C, died Oct 10, diarrhea.
11561, Castle, C H, 1, Co A, died Oct 27, scorbutus.
11830, Cooper, A H, * 7 cav, Co I, died Nov 5, diarrhea.
12174, Campbell, B, 12, Co I, died Nov 26, scorbutus.

24, Deboard, H A, 5, Co G, died Mar 8, fever typhus.
202, Douglas, Geo, 8, Co C, died Mar 28, diarrhea c.
347, Dean, Samuel, 5, Co H, died April 2, dysentery.
632, Deffbaugh, W R, * 1 artil, Co G, died April 19, diarrhea.
647, Davis, S, 3, Co D, died April 20, pneumonia.
843, Duncan, J M, 5, Co D, died May 2, dysentery.
2081, Daley, Jas, 3 cav, Co A, died June 17, dysentery.
3105, Duckworth, W B, 14, Co A, died July 10, diarrhea.
3246, Dyer, Jas, 19, Co I, died July 13, pneumonia.
5507, Drake, Samuel, 9, Co B, died Aug 13, scorbutus.
6588, Dorsey, A L, 15, Co K, died Aug 23, diarrhea.
6745, Darer, J, 10, Co L, died Aug 24, fever typhus.
6836, Darsey, M, 9, Co L, died Aug 26, scorbutus.
6949, Dodd, S, † 9, Co F, died Aug 26, scorbutus.
7092, Dunberger, Geo, 9, Co C, died Aug 28, diarrhea.
8248, Divers, G, 15, Co D, died Sept 9, scorbutus.
8487, Dant, Jno M, 7 cav, Co H, died Sept 10, scorbutus.
8562, Dason, N, 8 cav, Co L, died Sept 12, dysentery.
9159, Dunn, I, 2, Co K, died Sept 18, diarrhea.
12235, Duncan, W M, 8 cav, Co C, died Dec 6, scorbutus.
12807, Donohue, S, 9, Co C, died Mar 21, '65, pleuritis.
12508, Doty, John, 8 cav, Co A, died Jan 23, '65, diarrhea.

10975, Estuff, Jno, 1 cav, Co L, died Oct 12, diarrhea c.

117, Fuller, Irwin, militia, died March 23, pneumonia.
613, Foster, Charles K, 9, Co H, died April 18, dysentery.
955, Fox, H C, * 1, Co D, died May 8, diarrhea c.
6765, Fawkes, Wm, 14, Co D, died Aug 15, wounds.
7203, Foster, S, 8, Co A, died Aug 29, dysentery.
7941, Feather J B, 14, Co B, died Sept 5, diarrhea c.
8608, Feasley, Len, 1 artil, died Sept 14, scorbutus.
8723, Furner, J E, 6 cav, Co D, died Sept 14, diarrhea.
10206, Freeborn, R L, † 14, Co B, died Oct 2, fever remittent.
10709, Furr, E, 10, Co K, died Oct 11, diarrhea.
11922, Fleming, W W, 6 cav, Co A, died Oct 16, scorbutus.
10314, Forth, R, 8, Co D, died Sept 3, scorbutus.

No. of Grave.

2485, Grey, P, 3 Va, Co A, died June 25, diarrhea.
2649, Greshoe, M, 11, Co C, died June 29, bronchitis.
2712, Golden, J, 2 cav, Co G, died July 1, diarrhea.
4738, Gordon, S, 2, Co G, died Aug 4, scorbutus.
6348, Guonant, A, 2, Co I, died Aug 21, diarrhea.
10581, Garton, Wm, * 2, Co I, died Oct 10, scorbutus.
11574, Gluck, A F, 10, Co D, died Oct 28, scorbutus.
11864, Gibson, A, 1, Co A, died Nov 6, scorbutus.

84, Hollingshead, S, 1, Co G, died March 8, fever typhus.
294, Harrison, D, 10, Co I, died April 1, diarrhea c.
365, Henry, Robt O, 8, Co C, died April 2, diarrhea c.
398, Hunter, G W, 8, Co A, died April 9, bronchitis.
508, Heller, Wm, * 3, Co D, died April 15, diarrhea.
839, Halpin, Jno, 2, Co D, died May 2, dysentery.
997, Hoffman, G W, 8, Co E, died May 10, diarrhea.
1013, Hess, J, 11, Co C, died May 10, diarrhea.
1421, Hatfield, J, 1, Co B, died May 28, diarrhea c.
1854, Harkins, H, 2, Co F, died June 11, scorbutus.
2702, Hoover, W H, 3, Co A, died June 30, debilitas.
2902, Howell, A, 14, Co E, died July 5, diarrhea c.
2957, Howe, S, 2, Co I, died July 6, diarrhea c.
3930, Horant, E A, 3, Co C, died July 25, diarrhea c.
4739, Hane, Wm, 2, Co A, died Aug 5, diarrhea c.
5061, Hammer, S, 3 cav, Co G, died Aug 8, dysentery.
5412, Hartly, Isaac, 3, Co I, died Aug 12, dysentery.
5649, Hall, Henry, 10, Co F, died Aug 14, scorbutus.
6538, Harper, W, 8, Co H, died Aug 23, anasarca.
8061, Hushman, W, 10, Co I, died Sept 7, diarrhea.
8208, Hardway, D B, 9, Co G, died Sept 9, diarrhea.
8341, Harden, G W, 8 cav, Co A, died Sept 10, scorbutus.
8344, Hutson, J, 14, Co A, died Sept 10, scorbutus.
9160, Hauslan, B, 6 cav, died Sept 18, scorbutus.
9537, Hudgins, J, 14, Co B, died Sept 22, anasarca.
9794, Handland, H, 1, Co H, died Sept 26, diarrhea.
10990, Hollinbeck, W H, * 1 cav, Co B, died Oct 14, diarrhea.
11316, Hubert, W C, 12, Co G, died Oct 22, scorbutus.
11396, Hendershot, F F, 7, Co E, died Oct 24, scorbutus.
11739, Hurn, R, 8, Co E, died Nov 2, scorbutus.
12014, Hartzel, S, 1, Co D, died Nov 15, dysentery.
12153, Hickman, E, 11, Co B, died Nov 24, scorbutus.

312, Johns, E K, 8 mil, Co C, died April 2, diarrhea c.
3045, Jake, A R, 8, Co I, died July 8, anasarca.
3969, Jackson, S E, 2, Co F, died July 25, scorbutus.
6098, Jones, G, 2 cav, Co D, died Aug 18, diarrhea.
7681, Johnston, I A, 1 cav, Co D, died Sept 3, dysentery.
8371, Jenkins, W, 1 artil, Co D, died Sept 10, diarrhea.

323, Kane, J, 4 cav, Co L, died April 2, pneumonia.
5822, Kimball, Jno, 14, Co K, died Aug 16, enteritis.

589, Lodibing, W, 2, Co A, died April 17, diarrhea.
1565, Langstan, N H, 1 cav, Co A, died June 2, diarrhea c.
1592, Lanham, Henry, 8, Co C, died June 3, debilitas.
1949, Logger, J, 3 cav, Co B, died June 14, diarrhea c.
2734, Lysbon, Wm, 2, Co I, died July 1, anasarca.
2739, Loud, George, 9, Co D, died July 1, diarrhea c.
6924, Lansbury, W, † 15, Co E, died Aug 26, diarrhea.
7237, Lough, H, 1 cav, Co L, died Aug 29, scorbutus.
10564, Liston, David, 6 cav, Co C, died Oct 9, diarrhea.
10569, Lowe, J, 9, Co C, died Oct 9, diarrhea.
11021, Lowe, W G, 13, Co G, died Oct 16, scorbutus.
11325, Laymon, W F, 14, Co C, died Oct 23, scorbutus.
11624, Laughlin, D, * 9, Co E, died Oct 28, wounds.
11989, Lucas, J, 9, Co D, died Nov 13, scorbutus.
12262, Lowring, J, 1 artil, Co D, died Dec 12, diarrhea.

41, Maddons, W L, 4 cav, Co K, died May 3, small pox.
280, Mason, Peter, 10, Co G, died April 1, diarrhea c.
387, Magaher, J, 3 cav, Co A, died April 5, dysentery.
422, McNeily, Jas, 8 cav, Co A, died April 7, anasarca.
582, McCormick, R, 2, Co F, died April 16, ascites.
786, McConnaughy, D, 11, Co F, died April 28, diarrhea c.
820, McGitton, J, 6, Co G, died May 1, dysentery.
1068, Morris, J M, 3 cav, Co E, died May 13, diarrhea c.
1419, Murphy, J, 8, Co D, died May 28, dysentery.
1675, Moore, M, 14, Co K, died June 6, anasarca.
2932, Milum, Jas, 8, Co I, died July 5, diarrhea.
3955, Mokie, R, 7 cav, died July 20, scorbutus.
6060, Miller, C W, 2, Co C, died Aug 27, diarrhea.
7018, Meiner, H, 12, Co I, died Aug 27, diarrhea.
9698, Mencar, L B, 14, Co B, died Sept 24, scorbutus.
9767, Morris, O, 14, Co A, died Sept 25, scorbutus.
9955, Miller, D, 14, Co C, died Sept 28, scorbutus.
10567, Moody, R W, 6 cav, Co E, died Oct 9, scorbutus.
10578, McKinney, Wm, 1 cav, Co L, died Oct 9, scorbutus.
10934, McConkey, A L, * 6 cav, Co B, died Oct 14, diarrhea.
10970, McLoughlin, R, 1 artil, Co D, died Oct 15, diarrhea.
11546, Mousan, J F, 14, Co C, died Oct 27, scorbutus.
12090, Matt, Henry, 12, Co E, died Nov 19, scorbutus.
12272, McCausland, R, 1, Co G, died Dec 12, scorbutus.

No. of Grave.

9488, McGregor, P, 1, Co E, died Sept 21, diarrhea.
12068, McWilson, J, 14, Co F, died Nov 17, scorbutus.

2857, Norman, H, 2, Co I, died July 4, diarrhea.
5395, Newman, A, 1 cav, Co B, died July 16, anasarca.
6442, Nichols, L D, 9, Co F, died Aug 22, scorbutus.
12472, Nicholson, J, 3 cav, Co B, died Jan 17, '65, scorbutus.

241, Oxley, Robert, 14, Co C, died Mar 30, diarrhea c.
1767, Osborne, Thomas, 5, Co H, died June 9, dysentery.

39, Packard, Myron C, 2 cav, Co I, died Mar 13, pleuritis.
1707, Porterfield, Jno, 4, Co F, died June 7, diarrhea c.
2133, Porrellson, C D, 10, Co I, died June 24, dysentery.
2645, Patey, J, 8, Co G, died June 29, diarrhea.
2731, Painter, C,† 9, Co F, died July 1, anasarca.
3055, Petit, J,* 1 cav, Co L, died July 9, diarrhea.
4707, Payne, M,* 8, Co F, died Aug 3, debilitas.
5004, Pugh, L, 3, Co I, died Aug 8, diarrhea
5213, Pollard, Jno, 10, Co I, died Aug 10, scorbutus.
6004, Polley, J, 8, Co C, died Aug 17, anasarca.
6100, Perkins, James A, 12, Co K, died Aug 19, diarrhea c.
11267, Palmer, Jno,† 1 cav, Co L, died Oct 21, scorbutus.

349, Reakes, Wm, 8 m, Co C, died Apr 2, diarrhea.
521, Rice, A, 4 cav, Co G, died April 13, dysentery.
600, Randall, Jas A, 9, Co K, died Apr 15, dysentery c.
959, Rinker, F A, 3 cav, Co A, died May 8, dysentery.
1040, Robb, M, 2, Co A, died May 12, fever typhus.
1916, Richards, G L, 14, Co D, died June 14, diarrhea c.
3459, Rummer, L, 5, Co A, died July 17, scorbutus.
3465, Read, J, 12, Co B, died July 17, scorbutus.
3641, Reddon, J, 9, Co F, died July 20, diarrhea.
4163, Romsey, Wm, 9, Co C, died July 29, diarrhea.
7257, Rutroff, Jacob, 7, Co H, died July 30, diarrhea,
8082, Roush, James, 7, Co B, died Sept 7, diarrhea.
10527, Reed, J M,* 12, Co B, died Oct 7, scorbutus.
11518, Rock, J H, 12, Co C, died Oct 20, scorbutus.
11794, Raleigh, S, 1 cav, Co I, died Nov 4, scorbutus.
7005, Richardson, W, 14, Co K, died Aug 27, diarrhea.

278, Sayre, Michael, 14, Co I, died March 31, diarrhea.
680, Sprague, Geo, 11, , Co F, died April 23, diarrhea.
927, Stackleford, S, 3 cav, Co A, died May 7, dysentery.
1510, Scott, Z,† 8, Co D, died May 31, diarrhea.
2238, Seward, C, 2 cav, Co I, died June 20, diarrhea.
2350, Stagg, Wm, 10, Co I, died June 23, scorbutus.
2437, Stutter, J N, 3 cav, Co D, died June 25, diarrhea a.
2831, Skillington, G, 4 cav, Co D died July 5, diarrhea.
3321, Stephenson, A, 1 cav, Co B, died July 16, anasarca.
3588, Shilber, C A, 3, Co A, died July 19, diarrhea.
3747, Shaub, F, 2, Co E, died July 22, diarrhea.
3805, Simons, C E, 8, Co C, died July 24, diarrhea c.
3865, Stewart, Wm A, 14, Co I, died July 25, icterus.
4463, Steele, A, 2 cav, Co C, died Aug 1, scorbutus.
4812, Solder, S, 3, Co K, died Aug 5, scorbutus.

No. of Grave.

4865, Sturn, E E, 12, Co F, died Aug 7, wounds.
5130, Smith, 2, Co F, died Aug 8, scorbutus.
5237, Simmons, E, 8, Co C, died Aug 10, scorbutus.
5727, Sprouse, A, 11, Co F, died Aug 15, scorbutus.
5975, Smith, J W, 8, Co G, died Aug 17, fever typhus.
6173, Sprouse, W, 11, Co F, died Aug 22, diarrhea.
6610, Squares, Samuel, 6 cav, Co D, died Aug 23, diarrhea.
7391, Stratton, B B, 1 artil, Co F, died Aug 28, diarrhea.
7944, Stoker, S, 3 cav, Co C, died Sept 5, diarrhea c.
8011, Sands, Wm, 10, Co F, died Sept 6, scorbutus.
8164, Scritchfield, W, 10, Co F, died Sept 8, diarrhea.
8390, Stuck, H M, 14, Co B, died Sept 10, diarrhea.
8516, Smith, B, 9, Co H, died Sept 12, diarrhea.
8646, Sturgiss, W T, drummer, 14, Co B, died Sept 12, scorbutus
9217, Smith, G H, 7 cav, Co G, died Sept 19, scorbutus.
9714, Sullivan, E, 2, Co A, died Sept 25, scorbutus.
9786, Snyder, J V, 13, Co D, died Sept 20, diarrhea.
9872, Semeir, G S, 4 cav, died Sept 27, scorbutus
9906, Sands, G W, 1, died Sept 28, diarrhea c.
10151, Smith, J, 14, Co B, died Oct 1, scorbutus.
11276, Smith, J A, 9, Co B, died Oct 22, scorbutus.
11625, Slee, R,† 1 cav, Co D, died Oct 25, diarrhea c.
11824, Spaulding, F, 1 cav, Co A, died Nov 5, scorbutus.
11836, Stockwell, C H, 3, Co B, died Nov 5, scorbutus.
7291, Saylor, C M, 9, Co B, died Aug 30, diarrhea.

1103, Thatcher, J P, 2, Co A, died April 15, dysentery.
3404, Trobridge, S, 6, Co B, died July 10, dysentery.
5136, Tyrm, T, 8, Co H, died Aug 8, scorbutus.
6379, Thurston, C C, 1, Co I, died Aug 21, scorbutus.
8033, Taylor, J, 8, Co G, died Sept 13, diarrhea.
12332, Thorpe, S S, 3, Co I, died Dec 26, scorbutus.
3840, Tomlinson, S,† 3, Co I, died July 24, dysentery.
8119, Tatro, L, 11, Co B, died Sept 8, diarrhea.

244, Vincent, Jas, 8, Co C, died March 30, dysentery.
814, Very, W, 1 cav, Co C, died April 30, dysentery.
1149, Vanscoy, A,* 3 cav, Co E, died May 16, diarrhea c.
1322, Virts, R, 3 cav, Co A, died May 23, diarrhea c.

945, Wilson, Walter, 11, Co F, died May 7, diarrhea c.
1757, Weaver, M, 1 cav, Co C, died June 7, diarrhea c.
2854, Worp, J, 3, Co F, died July 6, diarrhea c.
3723, Wich, J, 1 cav, Co L, died July 21, debilitas.
3925, Whitney, W A, 8, Co F, died July 25, dysentery.
3996, Whit, A, 5, Co F, died July 26, diarrhea.
7542, Wilson, J, 3, Co B, died Sept 2, dysentery.
7832, Warwicke, E, 2, Co D, died Sept 4, diarrhea.
8598, Wells, E, 7, Co F, died Sept 12, scorbutus.
9628, Wolfe, C, 14, Co B, died Sept 24, gangrene.
10554, White, J N, 6 cav, Co C, died Oct 13, dysentery.

148, Young, A, 8, Co C, died March 25, diarrhea.
456, Young, A D, 8, Co C, died April 9, diarrhea.
694, Young, Ed, 8 cav, Co C, died April 23, diarrhea.

WISCONSIN.

2113, Allwise, J R, 24, Co E, died June 17, diarrhea c.
4477, Austin, Isaac, 25, Co G, died Aug 1, diarrhea.
5241, Abbott, A,† 21, Co D, died Aug 10, scorbutus.
5453, Allen, C P, 2, Co G, died Aug 12, wounds.
8092, Adams, A F, 36, Co F, died Sept 14, scorbutus.
10880, Adams, P, 10, Co A, died Oct 13, scorbutus.
11492, Aultin, E V,* 13, Co E, died Oct 26, scorbutus.
12728, Antone, C, 31, Co D, died March 4, '65, diarrhea c.

1341, Bower, H, 1, Co A, died May 24, dysentery.
1838, Burk, O, 15, Co B, died June 11, diarrhea.
2009, Bawgarder, B, 2, Co K, died June 15, diarrhea.
2055, Ball, H, 7, Co A, died June 16, diarrhea.
2128, Bowban, H A,† 10, Co F, died June 18, fever typhus.
2334, Brooks, E, 1 cav, Co H, died June 22, diarrhea c.
2451, Brunner, B F,* 10, Co I, died June 25, dysentery a.
2891, Brown, O, 15, Co G, died June 30, diarrhea c.
3253, Brown, J, 4, Co H, died July 13, diarrhea.
3673, Bruce, H, 24, Co H, died July 20, diarrhea.
4870, Brumsted, G,† 15, Co A, died Aug 6, diarrhea.
5026, Briggs, H, 1 cav, Co L, died Aug 8, dysentery.
5103, Budson, John, 1 cav, Co L, died Aug 9, scorbutus.
5161, Bemis, H, 10, Co C, died Aug 9, scorbutus.
5322, Briggs, E, 1 cav, died Aug 11, scorbutus.
5504, Bailey, W,* 25, Co E, died Aug 13, wounds.
6204, Hancock, S, 17, Co I, died Aug 19, scorbutus.
7205, Bailey, J, 36, Co I, died Aug 30, dysentery.
7323, Burk, J, 10 cav, Co E, died Aug 30, gangrene.
7755, Borden, E,* 21, Co K, died Sept 3, diarrhea.
7759, Boyle, P, 25, Co D, died Sept 4, diarrhea
8576, Batchelder, J, 1, Co I, died Sept 12, diarrhea.

8641, Bushell, C C, 2, Co B, died Sept 13, dysentery.
9607, Brinkman, J, 2, Co A, died Sept 23, scorbutus.
10686, Britton, H,† 15, Co I, died Oct 11, scorbutus.
10919, Bohnsen, N, 15, Co I, died Oct 14, scorbutus.
11754, Butler, M, 10, Co K, died Nov 2, scorbutus.
12032, Blakeley, R, 7, Co F, died Nov 15, scorbutus.
11610, Batterson, L, 10, Co K, died Oct 28, diarrhea.

2360, Church, A, 7, Co H, died June 23, anasarca.
2063, Chapman, J, 2, Co G, died June 29, dysentery.
2959, Cowles D, 10, Co B, died July 6, diarrhea c.
3292, Cummings, S, 21, Co A, died July 14, diarrhea.
3828, Crane, R, drummer, 7, Co D, died July 23, dysentery.
4390, Chapel, C, 1, Co E, died July 31, dysentery.
5102, Cavanaugh, John, 1 cav, Co H, died Aug 9, scorbutus.
8105, Chase, F M,* 1, Co A, died Sept 7, diarrhea.
9418, Corrier, C C, 21, Co F, died Aug 22, wounds,
9169, Carlintyre, G, 23, died Sept 18, scorbutus.
10752, Castle, C, 1 cav, Co C, died Oct 12, scorbutus.
11020, Cofam, W, 10, Co A, died Oct 16, scorbutus.
11088, Chusterson, F, 15, Co E, died Oct 18, hemorrhoids.
11535, Chamberlain, J, 21, Co I, died Oct 27, scorbutus.
11744, Clark, W C, 10, Co E, died Nov 2, scorbutus.
10346, Crommings, H, 7, Co C, died Oct 5, scorbutus.

1591, Duffey, E, 1, Co L, died June 3, diarrhea c.
2522, Damhocker, E, 20, Co I, died June 26, wounds.
3244, Daggo, John, 1 cav, Co L, died July 13, scorbutus.
5830, Destler, Fred, 26, Co G, died July 16, diarrhea.
6867, Dick, Benj, 30, Co G, died Aug 27, scorbutus.
7455, Davis, J, 36, Co B, died Sept 1, scorbutus.

No. of Grave.
8530, Decker, G,† F battery, died Sept 12, scorbutus.
8587, Depas, A, 21, Co A, died Sept 12, scorbutus.
8905, Daryson, W, 7, Co C, died Sept 15, scorbutus.
9739, Dicey, G, 12, Co I, died Sept 25, diarrhea.
10771, Davis, John, 1, Co B, died Oct 12, diarrhea c.
12750, David, D P, 26, Co B, died March 8, '65, diarrhea n.

2419, Eozer, J, 15, Co K, died June 24, dysentery c.
5247, Egan, John, 7, Co A, died Aug 10, scorbutus.
6160, Erickson, C, 15, Co B, died Aug 19, dysentery.
8001, Ellwood, S,† 10, Co C, died Aug 13, scorbutus.
8337, Errickson, S, 50, Co D, died Sept 20, dysentery.
11087, Ellenger, P, 21, Co K, died Oct 31, diarrhea.
12286, Eukhart, H, 36, Co G, died Dec 14, scorbutus.

36, Fordrury, G W, 7, Co C, died March 12, dysentery.
1260, Fuller, C W,* 7, Co E, died May 21, diarrhea c.
2283, Fountain, W F, 10, Co A, died June 20, diarrhea n.
6007, Forsnay, W K, 8, Co K, died Aug 8, scorbutus.
5759, Fieine, Oscar, 1 cav, Co H, died Aug 15, scorbutus.
6811, Fisk, J B,† 1 cav, Co H, died Aug 10, diarrhea.
6097, Fischnor, D,† 36, Co H, died Aug 18, icterus.
6236, Fanon, Wm, 1, Co A, died Aug 20, dysentery.
8460, Farnham, M B, 4, Co K, died Sept 11, scorbutus.
9664, Ferguson, J,† 15, Co G, died Sept 24, diarrhea.
10234, Fagan, M, 15, Co G, died Oct 2, diarrhea.
12618, Frost, A, 7, Co B, died Feb 8, '65, scorbutus.
12653, Ferguson, W R, 24, Co D, died Feb 14, rheumatism.

1529, Gilbert, O,† 16, Co K, died May 31, diarrhea.
2392, Gruab, Fred, 15, Co I, died June 24, diarrhea
8164, Guth, H, 1, Co D, died July 11, diarrhea.
8390, Greenman, D,† 21, Co K, died July 16, dysentery.
5557, Greenwall, M, 1 cav, Co C, died Aug 13, dysentery.
7355, Ornods, L, 15, Co I, died Aug 31, diarrhea c.
8326, Groupe, D, 4, Co F, died Sept 10, diarrhea.
10691, Gundusen, H,† 15, Co I, died Oct 11, scorbutus.
6614, Goon, John E, 8d, died Aug 23, diarrhea.

803, Helt, Carl, 26, Co E, died Apr 1, dysentery.
710, Hale, A C, 21, Co I, died Apr 24, fever typhus.
1002, Haskins, J, 1, Co E, died May 10, dysentery.
1655, Hoffland, ——, 1 sgt, 15, Co K, died June 5, anasarca.
1678, Harvey, D M, 1, Co I, died June 6, fever typhus.
2384, Hanson, J, 15, Co K, died June 23, diarrhea c
2556, Hough, B J * 10, Co K, died June 27, diarrhea c.
3720, Henderson, O, 15, Co F, died July 21, fever intermittent.
4542, Hewick, Nelson, 10, Co B, died Aug 2, bronchitis.
4570, Halts, S, 26, Co C, died Aug 2, scorbutus.
6312, Howard, F B, 10, Co K, died Aug 11, pleuritis.
6628, Holenback, A, 25, Co D, died Aug 14, wounds.
6468, Hall, A W, 21, Co I, died Aug 22, diarrhea.
7081, Hanley, T, 3 artil, Co D, died Aug 28, scorbutus.
7149, Hutchings, B, 1 cav, Co E, died Aug 29, diarrhea c.
7649, Hanson, L, 15, Co B, died Sept 3, scorbutus.
7791, Harding, W F,† 21, Co C, died Sept 4, scorbutus.
8584, High, M, 25, Co E, died Sept 12, wounds.
9498, Halter, D, 22, Co D, died Sept 20, scorbutus.
10427, Hans, P, 10, Co D, died Oct 6, scorbutus.
11443, Holenbock, C, 18, Co A, died Oct 25, scorbutus.
11927, Hanson, ——, 1, Co B, died Nov 9, scorbutus.
12167, Harris, N, 12, Co D, died Nov 26, wounds.
12586, Hardy, E L, 6, Co E, died Jan 4, '65, scorbutus.
12848, Hanson, E, 1, Co F, died Apr 28, '65, diarrhea.
12468, Hand, G, 10, Co D, died Jan 16, '65, scorbutus.

6614, Ingham, J, 10, Co K, died Sept 18, scorbutus.
9506, Irwin, A, 25, Co C, died Sept 26, scorbutus

2008, Jacobson, O,* 15, Co D, died June 15, diarrhea.
8281, Jackson, T, 4, Co H, died July 13, diarrhea.
8478, Jillett, J, 7, Co H, died July 17, diarrhea.
6938, Jennings, J R * 45, Co G, died Aug 30, diarrhea.
11284, Johnson, W H, 6, Co H, died Oct 22, scorbutus.

1165, Kemmett, J, 1, Co H, died May 17, scorbutus.
2498, Knudson, J, 15, Co E, died June 26, dysentery c.
4133, Kellett, John B,* 21, Co B, died July 27, fever intermittent.
4405, Kull, L, 24, Co C, died July 31, diarrhea
4614, Klepps, C H, 1 cav, Co E, died Aug 8, scorbutus.
6592, Kendall, W, 32, died Sept 12, scorbutus.
9068, Keerroger, Wm, 26, Co G, died Sept 17, diarrhea.
10536, Kane, F, 26, Co E, died Oct 8, diarrhea.
10692, Knowles, H, 21, Co D, died Oct 11, diarrhea.
6299, Kinds, M O, 21, Co A, died Sept 9, scorbutus.

2009, Lack, Peter, 7, Co A, died July 7, diarrhea c.
5397, Livingston, J H, 3 artil, Co E, died Aug 12, anasarca.
6642, Lansing, G, 10, Co A, died Aug 23, scorbutus.
7235, Lowe, F, 16, Co G, died Aug 29, scorbutus.
7522, Lawson, M, 15, Co B, died Sept 1, dysentery.

No. of Grave.
8914, Laleh, F, 26, Co K, died Sept 16, scorbutus.
9097, Largen, E, 15, Co A, died Sept 29, scorbutus.
8977, Latch, F, 26, Co K, died Sept 17, diarrhea.

1752, Manger, James,* 24, Co H, died June 9, anasarca.
1896, Mulligan, J, 1, died June 13, diarrhea.
2742, McMann, W, 8 battery, died July 1, dysentery.
2951, McCormick, E, 1 cav, Co L, died July 6, diarrhea.
2981, McKenzie, J, 1, Co F, died July 7, diarrhea.
3625, McLaulin, C, 36, Co I, died July 20, diarrhea.
4925, Mathison, E N, 2, Co E, died Aug 6, diarrhea.
5038, Many, J, 21, Co D, died Aug 8, diarrhea.
5165, McFadden, H, 1 cav, Co F, died Aug 9, diarrhea.
5658, Mortes, B, 10, Co D, died Aug 15, scorbutus.
5739, Main, Henry, 30, Co F, died Aug 15, diarrhea.
6231, McClury, A, 10, Co I, died Aug 20, diarrhea.
6377, Messet, F, 5, Co B, died Aug 21, diarrhea.
10289, Myers, S, 15, Co G, died Oct 4, scorbutus.
11956, Molusky, E, 21, Co B, died Nov 9, scorbutus.

4289, Nelson, E, 15, Co B, died July 30, scorbutus.
4980, Northam, S E,† 10, Co C, died Aug 7, scorbutus.
6690, Nichols, Wm, 10, Co I, died Aug 18, dysentery.
10369, Neff, Wm, 33, Co I, died Oct 6, scorbutus.

8162, Olson, O, 15, Co B, died July 11, diarrhea.
11545, Oehle, F, 26, Co E, died Oct 27, wounds.
11931, Olston, M, 15, Co B, died Nov 7, diarrhea.

604, Palmer, John,* 7, Co C, died April 18, diarrhea.
2535, Plum, A, 4 cav, Co K, died June 26, diarrhea c.
2847, Peterson, A,* 15, Co K, died July 4, diarrhea.
3510, Picket, T B,* 1, Co F, died July 18, diarrhea.
4310, Purdy, M, 10, Co E, died July 30, diarrhea.
6406, Piriris, J, 17, Co F, died Aug 22, wounds.
7530, Pardee, J, 10, Co I, died Sept 1, scorbutus.
7893, Peterson, S, 15, Co K, died Sept 5, diarrhea c.
8515, Pillsbury, A J, 1 cav, Co H, died Sept 12, gangrene
8651, Patterson, J, 21, Co A, died Sept 13, scorbutus.
9014, Painter, H,† 10, Co F, died Sept 17, diarrhea.
9902, Patterson, S,* 15, Co I, died Sept 27, scorbutus.,
9161, Peterson, C, 15, Co I, died Sept 21, scorbutus.

2028, Roach, A, 21, Co F, died June 15, diarrhea.
3624, Renseler, H, 2, Co G, died July 20, diarrhea.
3605, Reynolers, F S, 10, Co K, died July 20, dysentery.
4997, Reed, G, 1, Co K, died Aug 7, dysentery.
5792, Rasmusson, A, 1 cav, Co L, died Aug 15, dysentery.
6988, Robinson, W M,* 10, Co C, died Aug 18, scorbutus.
9860, Rice, J, 7, Co C, died Sept 27, diarrhea.
11812, Randles, J, 25, Co D, died Nov 4, scorbutus.
12233, Richmond, B,† 1 cav, Co L, died Dec 6, scorbutus.
12242, Randell, P D, 1 cav, Co K, died Dec 7, scorbutus.

68, Schleassen, J J, 7, Co F, died March 19, dysentery
440, Shrigley, H, 10, Co G, died April 8, diarrhea.
2814, Suffus, R, 15, Co F, died July 3, diarrhea c.
8078, Sirbirth, F, 24, Co E, died July 9, anasarca.
3393, Shoop, W, 1, Co G, died July 18, diarrhea.
3583, Sutton, J, 10, Co B, died July 19, diarrhea
4363, Sharp, J W, 2, Co G, died July 30, diarrhea.
4378, Smith, W F, 10, Co B, died July 31, diarrhea.
4336, Shun, J, 24, Co H, died July 31, diarrhea.
4788, Scott, E G,† 21, Co D, died Aug 5, scorbutus.
4882, Slingerland, John, 1 cav, Co B, died Aug 6, fever intermittent.
6943, Starr, E, 16, Co F, died Aug 26, wounds
7614, Seaman, M,† 21, Co D, died Sept 2, dysentery.
8068, Smith, L, 4 cav, Co K, died Sept 8, diarrhea.
9603, Snyder, M, 26, Co E, died Sept 24, scorbutus.
11097, Smith, S M,* 21, Co F, died Oct 17, scorbutus.
11047, Sales, A D, 4, Co K, died Oct 17, anasarca.

2148, Tung, S W, 21, Co D, died June 18, scorbutus.
2385, Tay, S, 1, Co K, died June 24, diarrhea s.
2588, Tomlinson, Robt, 6, Co B, died June 28, diarrhea c.
3120, Thompson, D D, 36, Co B, died June 10, diarrhea.
3375, Tyler, J,* 10, Co A, died July 10, diarrhea.
3611, Tucker, C P, 1, Co I, died July 20, diarrhea.
4467, Taylor, A L, 25, Co E, died Aug 1, diarrhea.
6858, Taylor, L, 6, Co E, died Aug 26, dysentery.
7160, Thorn, P C, 1 cav, Co L, died Aug 29, diarrhea.
8500, Troutman, A, 2, died Sept 12, scorbutus.
11236, Thurber, D,* 36, Co G, died Oct 21, scorbutus.
11420, Tyler, E P, 10, Co F, died Oct 24, scorbutus.
11475, Thorson, P, 24, Co G, died Oct 26, scorbutus.
12374, Thompson, O, 15, Co K, died Jan 1, '65, scorbutus.

2309, Updell, J S, 15, Co B, died June 22, diarrhea c.

2954, Vohoss, O H, 1, Co L, died July 6, bronchitis.
3076, Vitter, J, 6, Co F, died July 9, diarrhea.

No. of Grave.
6859, Vancuster, H, 1 cav, Co C, died Sept 10, gangrene.
8427, Vanderbilt, J, 86, Co D, died Sept 11, scorbutus.
11890, Voelee, F,* 10, Co E, died Oct 24, scorbutus.

929, Webster, A C,† 7, Co E, died May 7, bronchitis.
884, Winlow, P, 1, Co M, died May 5, diarrhea.
1007, Wilder John, 1 cav, Co F, died May 10, diarrhea c.
1520, Welenne, E D, 1 cav, Co L, died May 31, diarrhea.
1693, Walter, S P, 21, Co G, died June 7, diarrhea.
1909, Welton, M S, 1 cav, Co L, died June 13, diarrhea c.
2591, Winchester, Geo, 21, Co I, died June 28, scorbutus.

No. of Grave.
2894, Weaver, H, 10, Co F, died July 4, diarrhea.
8378, Wens, Charles, 7, Co B, died July 16, diarrhea c.
4700, Wakefield, D, 25, Co K, died Aug 4, diarrhea.
9484, Woodward, W B, 1, died Sept 21, scorbutus.
9938, Wick, J, 1 cav, Co H, died Sept 28, scorbutus.
10213, Willis, E, 7, Co E, died Oct 2, scorbutus.
10895, Winchell, S, 1, Co D, died Oct 6, scorbutus.
12111, Whalen, M, 12, Co B, died Oct 21, scorbutus.
12363, Ward, A, 1 cav, Co C, died Dec 31, scorbutus.

12526, Yessen, A, 24, Co A, died Feb 10, '65, scorbutus.

UNITED STATES ARMY.

1798, Anderson, A, 16, Co C, died June 10, diarrhea c.
3866, Atwell, Thos,† 6 cav, Co M, died July 20, phthisis.
4349, Allen, Chas, 18, Co H, died July 31, scorbutus.
4537, Ashley, D B, 10, Co C, died Aug 2, fever intermittent.
6077, Arnold, H, 18, Co H, died Aug 18, cerebritis.
6089, Adams, G, 14, Co C, died Aug 18, dysentery.
8369, Austin, Jas,† 4 cav, Co K, died Sept 7, dysentery.
11523, Amis, Chas, 8 colored, Co I, died Oct 26, scorbutus.
9250, Alfka A H, 2 cav, Co D, died Sept 19, diarrhea.

102, Blossom, Chas, 6 cav, Co E, died March 22, dysentery.
1122, Boughten, M, 15, Co E, died May 15, anasarca.
1153, Bailey, Andrew, 16, Co K, died May 16, diarrhea.
1199, Britner, A, 16, Co K, died May 18, anasarca.
1201, Banks, E E, 17, Co C, died May 19, diarrhea.
1266, Burton, George, 8 colored, Co I, died May 21, diarrhea.
1397, Barden, Chas S, 15, Co E, died May 26, scorbutus.
1442, Beal, H, 15, Co C, died May 28, diarrhea c.
1461, Becker, L, 2, Co B, died May 29, diarrhea.
1762, Brown, C, 16, Co D, died June 9, anasarca.
2122, Bates, E L, 5 cav, Co E, died June 17, diarrhea.
2434, Braenagan, J, 18, Co D, died June 24, debilitas.
2486, Bigler, N M, 2 cav, Co B, died June 25, diarrhea c.
2749, Bradshaw, H, marine corps, died July 1, diarrhea.
3370, Bush, W, 15, Co E, died July 15, diarrhea c.
4861, Baldwin, G, 19, Co A, died Aug 6, dysentery.
4969, Baker, F, signal corps, died Aug 7, diarrhea c.
5657, Boyd, S,* 4, Co C, died Aug 14, diarrhea.
5774, Breer, A, 2, Co F, died Aug 15, dysentery.
6126, Boyd, John B, 4, Co K, died Aug 19, diarrhea.
6628, Bradman, A M,† 6 cav, Co M, died Aug 23, diarrhea c.
6652, Burd, W H, 6, Co E, died Aug 23, anasarca.
6937, Bowers, J, 4, Co K, died Aug 26, anasarca.
7717, Burk, James, 1, Co K, died Sept 3, diarrhea.
7921, Cressesault, M, 2 artil, Co M, died Sept 5, diarrhea.
8909, Banvall, J, 4, Co F, died Sept 16, scorbutus.
9477, Bartlett, E K, 2 s s, Co D, died Sept 21, scorbutus.
9631, Barstow, J, 18, Co D, died Sept 24, diarrhea c.
9848, Barrett, J, 18, Co D, died Sept 27, scorbutus.
10621, Britzer, L B,* 15, Co C, died Sept 10, diarrhea.
11577, Brown, J, 12, Co H, died Oct 28, scorbutus.
11706, Brickley, H, 1, Co K, died Nov 1, scorbutus.
12077, Ball, W, 12, Co C, died Nov 18, scorbutus.
12112, Boyer, J, 1 cav, Co K, died Nov 21, scorbutus.
12564, Bromley, J, 18, Co G, died Jan 31, '65, scorbutus.

700, Chisholm, J M,† marine corps, died April 27, diarrhea c.
1947, Clemens, D, 6, Co L, died June 14, diarrhea c.
2174, Clemburg, J, 16, Co D, died June 19, diarrhea.
2216, Cassman, A, marine corps, died June 20, diarrhea.
2726, Carter, Thos, 15, Co H, died July 1, diarrhea c.
3126, Cavanaugh, P, 16, Co A, died July 10, diarrhea.
3500, Conden, H, 12, Co A, died July 18, dysentery.
3911, Crookey, S,* 15, Co H, died July 24, diarrhea.
4346, Chase, V, 16, Co C, died July 30, diarrhea.
4930, Campbell, S L, 15, Co C, died Aug 7, anasarca.
5107, Croy, J, 18, Co B, died Aug 9, diarrhea.
5156, Cussey, Jas, 15, Co A, died Aug 9, diarrhea.
5234, Casey, J, 15, Co A, died Aug 10, anasarca.
5436, Champney, P A, signal corps, died Aug 12, dysentery.
6420, Cammell, J, 12, Co H, died Aug 22, dysentery.
7532, Coolidge, M, 17, Co B, died Sept 1, diarrhea c.
7722, Connor, H, 15, Co H, died Sept 3, diarrhea.
7996, Corst, James, 14, Co D, died Sept 5, diarrhea c.
8161, Connell, J, 14, Co D, died Sept 8, scorbutus.
8243, Chamberlain, C, 17, Co B, died Sept 9, diarrhea.
8570, Collins, M, 4 cav, Co H, died Sept 12, scorbutus.
8767, Carter, C A, 1, Co B, died Sept 14, scorbutus.
9034, Clifford, J, 6 cav, Co B, died Sept 17, scorbutus.
9113, Chase, L, 10, Co C, died Sept 18, diarrhea c.
9180, Carroll, L, 2 cav, Co G, died Sept 18, diarrhea c.
9295, Congreve, E, 5, Co A, died Sept 19, diarrhea.
9482, Cuyler, W, 16, Co B, died Sept 21, anasarca.
9814, Crocker, Chas, 2 Co A, died Sept 26, diarrhea.
10210, Cargill, C, 12, Co F, died Oct 2, scorbutus.

10557, Clark, R W, 2 s s, died Oct 9, diarrhea.
11176, Casey, Jno, 19, Co A, died Oct 19, scorbutus.
11201, Childs, G, 16, Co B, died Oct 20, dysentery.
11653, Cramer, A,† 19, Co C, died Oct 25, scorbutus.

914, Dunn, John, 6, Co A, died May 6, dysentery.
910, Dangler, W G, 5, Co M, died May 5, diarrhea c.
1255, Doney, J W, 6 cav, Co D, died May 21, diarrhea.
1653, Dunn, Wm, 19, Co F, died June 5, dysentery.
2274, Dunn, John, 18, Co H, died June 20, diarrhea c.
2495, Donahan, M, 2 cav, Co L, died June 26, dysentery.
3025, Deyer, H,† 18, Co D, died July 7, dysentery.
4377, Darvin, W W, 2 s s, Co B, died July 31, diarrhea.
4490, Dunslow, B F, 12, Co G, died Aug 1, scorbutus.
4626, Delaney, Jacob, 5 artil, Co F, died Aug 3, scorbutus.
5348, Doll, R, 14, Co C, died Aug 11, diarrhea.
5459, Dolan, P, 19, Co F, died Aug 12, phthisis.
5756, Davis, G,* 19, Co A, died Aug 15, scorbutus.
6025, Decker, James, 10, died Aug 18, dysentery.
6210, Davis, J, W,* 15, Co E, died Aug 19, diarrhea c.
6297, Doran, J M, 19, Co E, died Aug 20, diarrhea c.
6770, Doughty, D B, 3 artil, Co C, died Aug 25, scorbutus.
6805, Davidson, J H, 15, Co C, died Aug 25, anasarca.
6955, Delaney, E, 19, Co F, died Aug 26, anasarca.
7049, Davis, O, 15, Co F, died Aug 27, diarrhea.
7241, Delaney, J, 2, Co F, died Aug 29, dysentery.
7792, Dean, Samuel, 4 cav, Co B, died Sept 3, scorbutus.
8214, Downing, M, 10, Co D, died Sept 8, diarrhea.
8832, Doule, J, 10, Co D, died Sept 15, scorbutus.
10255, Davis, Clarke, 1 battery, Co K, died Oct 2, diarrhea.
10883, Draper, L, 14, Co F, died Oct 14, scorbutus.
11554, Davy, H, 18, Co G, died Oct 27, scorbutus.
11613, Diller, O M, 5 cav, Co I, died Oct 28, scorbutus.
12140, Drummond, J, 18, Co F, died Nov 23, scorbutus.
12591, Dunn, C, 15, Co C, died Feb 4 '65, scorbutus.

5648, Evans, T, 14, Co F, died Aug 14, dysentery.
6813, Edwards, Wm, (negro,) 6, Co A, died Aug 25, diarrhea.
7576, Erick, J, 2, Co K, died Sept 2, dysentery.
7616, Ellerton, N, 16, Co D, died Sept 2, scorbutus.
12689, Emmiet, S S, 5, Co C, died Feb 22, '65, scorbutus.

42, Ferguson, J, 6 cav, Co E, died March 15, catarrh.
1243, Fitzgibbons, Thos, 2, Co C, died May 20, diarrhea.
1509, Ferrell, J, 12, Co A, died May 31, diarrhea c.
2155, Fifley, H, 18, Co E, died May 23, diarrhea a.
2888, French, George, 1st Lieut, 37, died July 3, fever remittent.
3007, Feed, G, 6 cav, Co D, died July 7, diarrhea.
3250, Frenchy, D, 2, Co F, died July 13, dysentery.
5543, Fielding, A, 13, Co E, died July 18, diarrhea c.
5487, Firestine, S, 16, Co C, died Aug 12, anasarca.
6804, Felps, Daniel, (negro,) 8, Co H, died Aug 25, diarrhea.
7167, Flanigan, M, 2, Co I, died Aug 20, debilitas.
8536, Fannton, H, 14, Co F, died Sept 12, scorbutus.
9154, Flanery, M, 1 cav, Co H, died Sept 18, diarrhea.
9725, Frum, E, 3 cav, Co C, died Sept 25, diarrhea.
9083, Flarety, O, 16, died Sept 29, scorbutus.
10655, Fenall, J, 14, Co G, died Oct 11, diarrhea.
10839, Flonagan, P, 4 cav, Co D, died Oct 13, scorbutus.
11402, Fritz, A, 119, Co A, died Oct 24, scorbutus.
12312, Foster, J, 4, Co H, died Dec 19, scorbutus.

272, Gilligan, Mat,* 1, Co I, died March 31, dysentery.
1639, Gardener, C, signal corps, died June 5, diarrhea a.
2801, Gutterman, S, † 16, Co D, died July 2, diarrhea.
4977, Gray, Wm, 18, Co C, died Aug 7, diarrhea.
6182, Gale, Walter, 11, Co F, died Aug 19, diarrhea c.
7230, Gulvere, David, 4, Co C, died Aug 29, scorbutus.
8057, Griffith, S, 11, Co F, died Sept 7, scorbutus.
8671, Gunter, John, 4 cav, died Sept 13, diarrhea.
8857, Grace, Thomas, 1, Co B, died Sept 15, wounds.
9851, Gilbert, A, 5, Co K, died Sept 27, scorbutus.
12086, Getts, F, 19, Co E, died Nov 16, dysentery.
7335, Golton, R, 16, Co B, died Aug 30, diarrhea.

397, Hatch, T C, 11, Co A, died April 6, pneumonia.

No. of Grave.
533, Halbert, F, 2, Co H, died April 13, dysentery.
1547, Halpin, P, 5 artil, Co H, died June 1, diarrhea c.
1585, Hawey, H, 16, Co D, died June 3, diarrhea c.
1698, Hurman, J H, 4 cav, Co E, died June 4, diarrhea c.
2096, Hendricks, J, 16, Co D, died June 17, anasarca.
2209, Hogan, M, 16, Co A, died June 20, diarrhea c.
2706, Henry, Wm, 2, Co B, died June 30, diarrhea c.
2730, Hurley, D, marine corps, died July 1, dysentery.
2987, Hulit, Wm, 16, Co D, died July 7, diarrhea c.
3753, Hill, George, 17, Co H, died July 22, diarrhea c.
4593, Hopkins, W, (negro,) 17, Co C, died July 24, anasarca.
4429, Hill, D S, (negro,) 16, Co C, died July 31, diarrhea.
7238, Heddington, W, 15, Co F, died Aug 29, dysentery.
7405, Hausham, J R, 15, Co G, died Aug 31, anasarca.
8004, Halley, J, 13, Co B, died Sept 6, diarrhea.
9104, Hook, H, 19, Co F, died Sept 18, diarrhea c.
9155, Heir, J, 14, Co A, died Sept 18, scorbutus.
9665, Hildreth, Jas, 12, died Sept 24, diarrhea.
9918, Haney, J, 12, Co C, died Sept 28, scorbutus.
10054, Hasler, C, 13, Co M, died Sept 30, gangrene.
10439, Hirshfeld, G, marine corps, died Oct 7, scorbutus.
10867, Harman, J, 15, Co E, died Oct 14, diarrhea.
11136, Hamilton, S, 2 s s, Co D, died Oct 18, diarrhea c.
12369, Hill, M A, 2, Co G, died Jan 1, '65, debilitas.
12601, Hoit, E, (negro,) 35, Co H, died Feb 6, '65, diarrhea c.
10322, Hammun, W H, 15, Co F, died Oct 4, scorbutus.

6532, Imhoff, I, 15, Co E, died Aug 13, pleuritus.
7647, Ireland, George, 14, Co E, died Sept 3, diarrhea.
10742, Ireson, I, 4 cav, Co A, died Oct 11, scorbutus.

1111, Johnson, P, 6, Co C, died May 15, diarrhea c.
8125, Johnson, P, 2 battery, died Sept 8, scorbutus.
8566, Jones, W, 1 artil, Co K, died Sept 10, scorbutus.
10319, Jones, C B, 1 cav, Co H, died Oct 3, scorbutus.
11923, Jerald, W H, † 18, Co F, died Nov 8, scorbutus.

495, Klogeny, J, 1, Co K, died, April 12, diarrhea.
912, Kelly, John, 16, Co C, died May 5, diarrhea c.
1062, Kain, P F, † 15, Co A, died June 6, dysentery.
3250, Kenley, D, 2, Co F, died July 13, dysentery.
3341, Kerkoey, F, 18, Co F, died July 15, diarrhea.
3685, Kilbride, J, 15, Co F, died July 21, diarrhea.
4245, Kane, Wm, 18, Co H, died July 29, dysentery.
4266, Kalkrath, C, 3, Co I, died July 29, diarrhea.
4271, Kelly, D, 4, Co H, died July 29, diarrhea.
4694, Koster, J, 15, Co F, died Aug 4, diarrhea.
5649, Kay, Robert, 4, Co F, died Aug 14, scorbutus.
5643, Kelly, J, marine corps, died Aug 14, scorbutus.
6271, Kochel, J, * 19, Co G, died Aug 20, marasmus.
6577, Kelly, Wm, 9, Co I, died Aug 23, dysentery.
6764, King, I, 7, Co K, died Aug 25, diarrhea.
7465, Kinney, G W, 1 battery, Co D, died Sept 1, scorbutus.
8261, Kilbaty, H, 1 artil, Co K, died Sept 9, scorbutus.
8490, Kricka, F, 14, Co C, died Sept 11, scorbutus.
8527, Kripp, J, 16, Co D, died Sept 12, scorbutus.
9082, Knapp, C, 11, Co A, died Sept 18, gangrene.
11268, Kain, Pat, 15, Co A, died Oct 21, scorbutus.
11767, Kelly, J S, 2, Co D, died Nov 8, catarrh.
11949, Kennedy, J, 12, Co A, died Nov 10, scorbutus.
12205, Kahl, Chas, 2 artil, Co M, died Dec 1, scorbutus.
12532, Kemp, J W, 2, Co K, died Jan 27, '65, diarrhea c.

65, Love, Wm, 16, Co F, died March 17, pneumonia.
2252, Larreby, G, 16, Co D, died June 20, diarrhea.
2774, Little, J, 19, Co E, died July 21, dysentery.
3099, Lackey, J, 16, Co B, died July 26, diarrhea c.
4463, Langstaff, R, 10, Co F, died Aug 1, diarrhea.
5711, Lake, Horace, 4 cav, Co K, died Aug 15, diarrhea.
5891, Lynch, B, 18, Co E, died Aug 16, diarrhea.
6116, Lattio, E, 12, Co A, died Aug 19, cerebritis.
6300, Lawrence, C, 11, Co E, died Aug 20, diarrhea.
6352, Lyons, E, signal corps, died Aug 21, diarrhea c.
6561, Little, R, 19, Co F, died Aug 23, scorbutus.
9732, Larqiell, Wm, † 14, Co A, died Sept 2?, diarrhea.
10317, Louby, O, 4 cav, Co H, died Oct 3, scorbutus.
10379, Lockwood, H, negro, 8, Co D, died Oct 5, diarrhea.
11038, Lyons, R, 1 cav, Co E, died Oct 17, scorbutus.
1543, Lyman, O S, 18, Co A, died Oct 27, scorbutus.
11978, Lewis, Wm P, 8, Co B, died Nov 12, scorbutus.

180, McCoy, Augustus, 6, Co M, died March 26, diarrhea.
267, McClellan, J, 6 cav, Co D, died March 31, fever typhus.
829, Mason C H, 12, Co I, died May 1, dysentery.
948, Murphy, D, 12, Co B, died May 8, dysentery.
1012, McEvers, T L, 18, Co C, died May 10, diarrhea.
1048, McGuire, J, 8, Co C, died May 12, diarrhea.
1332, Murray, Thomas, 1 artil, Co L, died May 24, diarrhea.
147, Mulhall, Peter, † marine corps, died May 30, diarrhea.
1823, Marze, James, 12, Co D, died June 10, diarrhea.
1946, McLaughlin, J, 2, Co H, died June 14, diarrhea c.

No. of Grave.
1965, McConaghy, P, marine corps, died June 14, scorbutus.
2141, Meadow, John, 6 cav, Co E, died June 25, scorbutus.
3054, Muller, J, marine corps, died June 30, dysentery.
2920, Miller, C H, 6 cav, Co E, died July 5, scorbutus.
3054, McKinney, J, marine corps, died July 9, diarrhea c.
3088, Maloney, R, 10, Co B, died July 9, diarrhea c.
3950, Merkill, Peter, 14, Co H, died July 25, diarrhea.
4712, March, Wm, 11, Co C, died Aug 4, diarrhea.
4823, McClintock, J S, 18, Co H, died Aug 5, diarrhea c.
4863, Martin, M, marine corps, died Aug 6, diarrhea.
5363, Martin, J, 1 cav, Co K, died Aug 11, diarrhea c.
5364, McCann, B, 12, Co B, died Aug 11, diarrhea.
5456, Michols, R, 1 cav, Co K, died Aug 12, scorbutus.
5581, McLean, P, 17, Co C, died Aug 14, scorbutus.
5769, McCoslin, Robert, 1 artil, Co B, died Aug 15, enteritis.
6073, McDonald, 4 cav, Co E, died Aug 18, dysentery.
6081, McClair, R, 11, Co G, died Aug 18, scorbutus.
6313, Munson, C, 12, Co D, Aug 20, scorbutus.
6407, Mulhern, C, 4 cav, Co C, died Aug 22, scorbutus.
6515, Mantle, J, M, * 15, Co F, died Aug 22, fever typhus.
6851, Marston, B, 51 s s, Co G, died Aug 25, diarrhea.
6972, McKinley, E W, marine corps, died Aug 27, diarrhea.
7311, McGuire, J, 12, Co D, died Aug 30, scorbutus.
8293, Mun, W, 18, Co H, died Sept 9, scorbutus.
8473, McGinness, A, 4 artil, Co E, died Sept 11, scorbutus.
9110, Montgomery, C, 13, Co G, died Sept 13, diarrhea.
9231, McCoy, J M, † marine brigade, died Sept 19, diarrhea.
9368, Miller, H, 2 artil, died Sept 20, diarrhea.
9172, Morris, G J, 18, Co I, died Sept 21, diarrhea.
9580, McDermott, H, 16, Co E, died Sept 26, scorbutus.
10135, Manning, J, 15, Co A, died Oct 1, scorbutus.
10321, McCoy, J, 4, Co F, died Oct 3, scorbutus.
10157, Mills, A, 15, Co G, died Oct 7, scorbutus.
10554, McCord, G, 14, Co E, died Oct 9, scorbutus.
10855, McGee, P, * 2, died Oct 13, scorbutus.
11008, Murray, James, 17, Co G, died Oct 16, scorbutus.
12148, Mizner, W, 1st signal corps, Co K, died Nov 24, scorbutus.
12151, Moran, J, 4 cav, Co F, died Nov 24, scorbutus.
7341, McGuire, J, 12, Co D, died Aug 31, scorbutus.
12364, McGorren, J, 17, Co C, died Dec 31, scorbutus.

2876, Northrop, H E, 4, Co H, died July 3, diarrhea.
6803, Newcombe, John, 18, Co G, died Aug 20, anasarca.
6954, Nichols, H, * 12, Co A, died Aug 26, diarrhea.
10240, North, Jacob, 15, Co A, died Oct 8, scorbutus.
12386, Neise, J, 6, Co F, died Jan 2, '65, debilitas.
12833, Nuff, V, bugler, 1 artil, Co B, died April 16, diarrhea.
12790, Newel, L, 18, Co G, died March 17, '65, diarrhea c.

2368, O'Reilly, Theodore, † 8, Co K, died June 23, scorbutus.
7086, Ott, John, 10, Co A, died Aug 27, scorbutus.
11846, Osrans, J, 4 cav, Co I, died Nov 5, scorbutus.

492, Partridge, J W, signal corps, died April 12, diarrhea.
1607, Pace, J F, 18, Co C, died June 4, diarrhea.
1893, Pulliam, Wm, 1 cav, died June 13, diarrhea c.
3219, Pigott, J, marine corps, died July 12, diarrhea.
3669, Ponter, ——, 1 artil, Co I, died July 18, diarrhea.
4631, Pearson, S C, 40, Co C, died Aug 3, diarrhea.
5309, Pratt, C E, 1 artil, Co M, died Aug 11, scorbutus.
5729, Pike, Wm, * 5 cav, Co G, died Aug 15, scorbutus.
5731, Poulton, Henry, 19, Co A, died Aug 15, scorbutus.
6392, Page, J E, 18, Co B, died Aug 21, dysentery.
7068, Phillips, C, 14, Co D, died Aug 27, scorbutus.
7267, Pruet, Jas M, 19, Co A, died Aug 30, scorbutus.
7311, Plummer, G, 2 s s, Co D, died Aug 30, diarrhea.
2611, Preston, John, marine corps, died June 28, diarrhea.
7752, Pratt, J, 3, Co B, died Sept 8, diarrhea.
9571, Post, A, 1 artil, Co F, died Sept 28, diarrhea.
10951, Palmer, Wm E, † 15, Co F, died Oct 14, scorbutus.
11170, Pattit, J S, 11, Co F, died Oct 19, scorbutus.
12142, Puck, C, 15, Co G, died Nov 24, scorbutus.

4022, Quinback, J, 18, Co G, died July 26, scorbutus.

11, Ross, ——, 19, Co A, died March 5, phthisis.
194, Rooney, Mark, 14, Co F, died March 27, pneumonia.
404, Reardon, D, 13, Co G, died April 6, dysentery.
702, Reynolds, Edward, marine corps, died April 23, dysentery c.
2855, Rooney, F J, 18, Co E, died July 15, diarrhea c.
8820, Ritzer, Geo A, 5 cav, Co H, died July 21, diarrhea.
4276, Robison, W R, 6 cav, Co H, died July 30, diarrhea.
4957, Rhodes, A, 18, Co B, died Aug 7, scorbutus.
5910, Rinkle, George, 2 cav, Co G, died Aug 10, diarrhea.
5964, Rouke, J, 10, Co D, died Aug 17, diarrhea.
7154, Richards, Theodore, 2 cav, Co D, died Aug 29, diarrhea.
8438, Rogers, Wm, 18, Co G, died Sept 11, scorbutus.
9268, Reynolds, D, 4 cav, Co C, died Sept 19, anasarca.
10792, Reilly, J, 3, Co B, died Oct 2, scorbutus.
2701, Rawson, J, 16, Co K, died June 30, diarrhea c.

No. of Grave.

363, Striff John, 2, Co F, died April 2, diarrhea.
1236, Shelton, C, 8, Co F, died May 20, diarrhea.
1253, Spabling, Wm, 8 cav, Co H, died May 21, diarrhea.
1295, Scripter, C E, 5 cav, Co D, died May 23, diarrhea.
1647, Sweltzer, M, 19, Co H, died June 5, scorbutus.
1714, Smith, H W, 15, Co G, died June 7, diarrhea.
2073, Stoltz, † 16, Co C, died June 17, scorbutus.
2082, Smith, James 16, Co D, died June 17, anasarca.
2298, Styles, J N, 13, Co A, died June 22, diarrhea.
2530, Sumser, J, 19, Co G, died June 27, diarrhea.
3110, Spaulding, James, 13, Co B, died July 10, diarrhea.
3114, Sclumer, L, 13, Co C, died July 10, diarrhea.
3838, Smartkash, C, * 15, Co C, died July 23, diarrhea c.
3978, Somers, P, 4 cav, Co C, died July 26, diarrhea.
4258, Seybert, J S, * 1 s s, Co H, died July 29, diarrhea.
4310, Smith, Allen, 4, Co H, died July 30, anasarca.
4666, Striper, M, 18, Co D, died Aug 4, scorbutus.
5023, Sutgen, F, 16, Co G, died Aug 8, diarrhea c.
5365, Sorg, A, 1 artil, Co M, died Aug 11, scorbutus.
5393, Swagger, H, 4 cav, Co D, died Aug 12, diarrhea.
5801, Sisson, J, 4, Co D, died Aug 15, scorbutus.
6620, Slaughterback, B, 15, Co H, died Aug 23, anasarca.
6833, Sutgen, F, 16, Co C, died Aug 25, scorbutus.
7377, Smith, F, 14, Co E, died Aug 31, scorbutus.
7606, Starr, Darius, † 2, s s, Co F, died Sept 2, dysentery.
7874, Snider, J, 11, Co B, died Sept 5, diarrhea c.
8839, Scott, Jas H, 2 cav, Co B, died Sept 15, scorbutus.
9215, Stansbury, E, marine corps, died Sept 19, diarrhea.
9514, Sauls, J H, 15, Co F, died Sept 22, anasarca.
10214, Sullivan, T, 11, Co C, died Oct 2, scorbutus.
11144, Schroder, F, 15, Co C, died Oct 19, scorbutus.
11301, Smith, J, 8, Co D, died Oct 22, scorbutus.
11333, Stanton, R, 14, Co K, died Oct 23, scorbutus.
11661, Spencer, J H, 2, Co D, died Oct 30, scorbutus.
11690, Shortman, J, 14, Co E, died Oct 31, dysentery.
12186, Streeter, J, 16, Co B, died Nov 28, scorbutus.
12211, Stanton, C, 2, Co I, died Dec 2, diarrhea.

93, Tooley, Michael, 13, Co G, died March 21, diarrhea c.
489, Taylor, Amos, 17, Co H, died April 12, diarrhea c.
2603, Thompson, Wm, 19, Co G, died June 28, scorbutus.
2662, Truman, J, 5 cav, Co D, died June 29, dysentery.
3466, Tyson, E S, 14, Co D, died July 17, pleuritus.
4716, Tredridge, A, musician, 13, died Aug 4, anasarca.
7366, Taylor, M D, 18, Co E, died Aug 31, diarrhea.

No. of Grave.

7801, Turk, H, 16, Co H, died Sept 4, diarrhea.
8258, Thomas, J, 1 cav, Co D, died Sept 9, diarrhea c.
8259, Trainer, M, 6, Co F, died Sept 9, diarrhea.
8279, Thomas, L, (negro) 8, Co D, died Sept 9, fever intermittent.
9115, Taylor, E, * 18, Co I, died Sept 18, diarrhea c.
11393, Topper, J, 11, Co B, died Oct 24, scorbutus.

7929, Unmuch, C, 1 artil, Co K, died Sept 4, dysentery.

3657, Volmore, J, 8, Co K, died July 18, scorbutus.
7012, Vancotten, Wm, 16, Co D, died Aug 27 scorbutus.
7105, Vickery, Wm, 1, Co H, died Aug 28, diarrhea.
12041, Van Buren, W H, 16, Co B, died Nov 16, scorbutus.

1259, Walker, Wm, 6, Co D, died May 21, diarrhea.
1299, Worster, Chas B, 5 cav, Co H died May 23, diarrhea c.
2752, White, Thomas, 1, Co D, died July 1, diarrhea.
4023, Williams, D, 18, Co D, died July 26, scorbutus.
4248, Warner, S, 16, Co E, died July 29, diarrhea c.
4306, Williams, John, 4, Co D, died July 30, diarrhea.
5425, Walmor, 10, Co D, died Aug 12, diarrhea.
6125, Wickham, G H, 16, Co B, died Aug 19, scorbutus.
6637, Wills, S, 13, Co E, died Aug 23, dysentery.
7048, Wright, C S, 12, Co C, died Aug 27, fever congestive.
7109, Wadsworth, B H, 12, Co C, died Aug 28, diarrhea.
7264, Warner, H, 2, Co D, died Aug 30, diarrhea.
9105, Whitney, J W, * 4 cav, Co K, died Sept 18, scorbutus.
9181, White, Samuel, 8, Co F, died Sept 18, diarrhea.
9677, Walker, John, (negro) 8, Co F, died Sept 24, scorbutus.
9854, Walter, I, 17, Co B, died Sept 27, scorbutus.
10355, Wigley, E, 17, Co C, died Oct 5, dysentery.
10374, Waters, † 8, Co C, died Oct 5, diarrhea.
10756, Waldo, J M, 1 artil, Co K, died Oct 12, scorbutus.
11137, Williams, C, 1 artil, Co K, died Oct 19, scorbutus.
11295, Wizmaker, G, 2, Co M, died Oct 21, scorbutus.
12009, Wilson, C W, 15, Co A, died Nov 14, scorbutus.
12027, Wise, G B, 6, Co F, died Nov 15, anasarca.

6496, Yarger, A, 18, died Aug 22, scorbutus.
7101, Young, Robert, 1 cav, Co K, died Aug 28, diarrhea.
10754, Young, F B, 2 artil, Co M, died Oct 12, scorbutus.
11378, Young, J C, 19, Co A, died Oct 23, scorbutus.

7793, Zimmerman, J, 17, Co D, died Sept 4, scorbutus.
10428, Zing, P, † 10, Co C, died Oct 6, scorbutus.
10450, Zimmerman, M, 14, Co I, died Oct 7 scorbutus.

UNITED STATES NAVY.

2610, Akinson, A, G B Nepsin, died June 27, diarrhea.
4698, Anker, George, Schooner Norman, died Aug 4, diarrhea.
8071, Anderson, Chas, G B Saithfield, died Sept 7, diarrhea.
2919, Bradley, John, G B Southfield, died July 3, diarrhea.
3475, Broderick, W, U S Navy, died July 17, diarrhea.
6074, Bowers, W H, G B Water Witch, died Aug 8, diarrhea c.
12047, Boucher, W, G B Shawsheen, died Nov 16, scorbutus.

1914, Carnes, Wm, U S Navy, died June 13, diarrhea c.
2149, Conant, G S, U S S Southfield, died June 18, diarrhea.
2580, Carter, W J, G B Montgomery, died June 27, diarrhea c.
6301, Collins, Thomas, G B Southfield, died Aug 19, dysenteria.
7144, Corbet, E, U S Navy, died Aug 29, debilitas.
7508, Connor J, U S Navy, died Sept 1, scorbutus.
9644, Culbert, J, U S Navy, died Sept 23, diarrhea.

104, Dillingham, J N, G B Housatonic, died March 26, phthisis.
6437, Duffney, J, U S Navy, died Aug 22, diarrhea.

3086, Ellis, J R, U S S Columbine, died July 9, fever typhus.
4134, Evans, John, G B Shawsheen, died July 28, diarrhea c.
4462, Earl Jas H, paymaster stw'd U S Navy, died Aug 1, scorbutus.
5419, Foley, Daniel, G B Southfield, died Aug 12, diarrhea c.
4605, Green, G C, G B Southfield, died Aug 3, scorbutus.
8871, Goundy, Thomas, U S Navy, died Sept 15, diarrhea.
1087, Heald, Wm, G B Canandaigua, died April 14, diarrhea c.
1489, Hunter, John, seaman, died May 30, anasarca.
2215, Hilton, John, steamer Johans, died June 20, diarrhea.
3448, Hodges, L, schooner Norman, died July 17, bronchitis.
3791, Hughes, Benj, U S S Wabash, died July 22, fever typhus.
5875, Heald, H H, merchantman, died Aug 16, diarrhea c.
9284, Holms, Thomas, Water Witch, died Sept 19, diarrhea.

1432, Jones, Wm, U S S Underwriter, died May 28, diarrhea c.
2178, Jones, Theodore, U S S Underwriter, died June 19, diarrhea c.
2206, Journeny, John, fireman U S Navy, died June 19, diarrhea c.
6417, Jackson, J, G B Shawsheen, died Aug 22, scorbutus.
8291, Johnson, G P, U S Navy, died Sept 9, diarrhea.
8858, James, F A, U S Navy, died Sept 15, dysentery.
9292, Johnson, M, U S Navy, died Sept 20, diarrhea.
10218, Joseph, F, U S Navy, died Oct 2, diarrhea.

602, Keefe, John, G B Housatonic, died April 18, dysentery.
698, Kultz, A, U S S T Ward, died April 23, dysentery.
1546, Kelly, James, U S S Underwriter, died June 7, diarrhea c.
3650, Kinney, John, G B Water Witch, died July 24, diarrhea c.

7375, Lodi, John, U S Navy, died Aug 31, diarrhea.
2843, Lindersmith, E, U S S Montgomery, died July 3, diarrhea.
4291, Lawton, James, U S S Ladona, died July 30, dysentery.

275, Mays, A H, mate schr Norman, died March 23, dysentery.
2452, McDonald, John, U S Navy, died June 25, diarrhea.
2581, Moore, A, schr Anna, died June 27, scorbutus.
3128, Malaby, P, U S S Montgomery, died July 10, dysentery.
3348, Murphy, M J, U S Navy, died July 15, diarrhea.
3529, McDonald, John, U S Navy, died July 17, diarrhea.
3804, Matthews, John, U S S Underwriter, died July 22, diarrhea c.
4208, Mc Henry, Daniel, G B Southfield, died July 29, diarrhea.
4324, McCarty, T, G B Housatonic, died July 30, diarrhea c.
4396, McVey, K, U S Navy, died July 31, dysentery.
4679, McTier, J, U S Navy, died Aug 4, dysentery.
4800, McLaughlin E, U S Navy, died Aug 5, dysentery.
5485, Meldon, J, U S Navy, died Aug 13, pneumonia.
6355, Marshall, N B, G B Leipsig, died Aug 21 diarrhea.
6571, McDermott, P, U S S Montgomery, died Aug 23, debilitas.
6825, Mathews, W C, U S Navy, died Aug 25, diarrhea.
6917, McLaughlin, B, U S Navy, died Aug 26, scorbutus.
7251, McGowan, J, U S S Powhattan, died Aug 30, diarrhea.
11603, Muston, J, G B Ratler, died Nov 6, scorbutus.

7624, Noe, M, U S Navy, died Sept 4, fever intermittent.

2227, O'Brien, Wm, U S Navy, died June 20, diarrhea.
3208, Ottinger, M, G B Water Witch, died July 12, scorbutus.

3153, Pace, Lyman, U S Navy, died July 11, scorbutus.
5325, Parkham, Jas C, G B Shawsheen, died Aug 11, diarrhea.
9024, Peterson J, U S Navy, died Sept 17, diarrhea.

2460, Quinlan, N, U S Navy, died June 25, scorbutus.
7867, Quade, M, U S Navy, died Sept 5, scorbutus.

No. of Grave.
2237, Ragan, John, U S S T Ward, died June 20, fever intermittent.
4661, Raymond, W, U S S T Ward, died Aug 3, scorbutus.
5108, Roland, John, U S S Underwriter, died Aug 9, scorbutus.
7003, Reynolds, T J, U S Navy, died Aug 27, diarrhea.

160, Stark, John, U S Navy, died March 26, diarrhea c.
2010, Sullivan, J, U S S Underwriter, died June 15, diarrhea.
2883, Smith, John W, G B Southfield, died July 3, fever typhus.
3201, Sampson, J R, Naval Battalion, died July 11, diarrhea.
4611, Smith, B N, G B Mendota, died Aug 3, scorbutus.
6592, Stanley, Wm, G B Southfield, died Aug 23, diarrhea c.
11299, Smith, Wm, G B Water Witch, died Oct 22, scorbutus.

1713, Thomas, Samuel, G B Southfield, died June 7, diarrhea c.
1851, Thomas, John, G B Southfield, died June 11, diarrhea c.
2787, Turner, Wm, U S Navy, died July 1, fever remittent.

No. of Grave.
4169, Trymer, James, G B Southfield, died July 28, diarrhea.
7445, Tobin, Michael, U S Navy, died Sept 1, diarrhea.
8302, Ta, B F, G B Southfield, died Sept 10, diarrhea.

1646, Willis, J P, U S Navy, died June 5, diarrhea.
3004, Wilson, A, G B Southfield, died July 7, diarrhea c.
3878, Williams, M W, U S Navy, died July 24, diarrhea.
4118, Willis, M, G B Southfield, died July 28, scorbutus.
4198, Williams, C, U S S Aries, died July 29, diarrhea c.
5820, Wordell, G K, U S Navy, died Aug 16, Marasmus.
6080, Warren, W H, U S Navy, died Aug 17, diarrhea.
6458, Wooley, M, U S Navy, died Aug 22, scorbutus.
7503, Walsh, James, U S Navy, died Sept 1, diarrhea.
8104, Welch, V, G B Southfield, died Sept 7, diarrhea.
10565, West, John, G B Southfield, died Oct 9, diarrhea.

MISCELLANEOUS.

11460, Addley, A, citizen, died Oct 25, scorbutus.
887, Amos, J, Ringold battery, Co F, died May 4, fever typhus.
2977, Augar, A, died July 7, diarrhea.

282, Bane, Sample, Ringold batt'y, Co A, died April 1, pneumonia
2072, Beatty, D, * Ringold battery, Co F, died June 17, diarrhea c.
4327, Baker, John, citizen teamster, died July 30, diarrhea c.
4974, Bemmer, L, died Aug 6, diarrhea.
5747, Butterfield, James, citizen, died Aug 15, dysentery.
6100, Blair, H, citizen, died Aug 18, anasarca.
6360, Bidwell, C, citizen teamster, died Aug 21, dysentery.
8102, Burkhead, W, Prunell's legion, died Sept 7, diarrhea.
9344, Blood, G P, died Sept 20, scorbutus.
9591, Brogdin, D C, died Sept 23, diarrhea.
10500, Burk, C, citizen, died Oct 8, scorbutus.
10602, Bishop, J, citizen teamster, died Oct 10, dysentery.
10903, Brown, Geo, * Bridge's battery, died Oct 15, scorbutus.
12342, Boland, James, Prunell's cav, died Dec 28, diarrhea c.

177, Cannon, Wm, teamster, died March 26.
389, Campbell, Daniel, Ringold bat'y, Co E, died April 6, diarrhea.
431, Childers, C H, died April 8, diarrhea c.
1195, Cobb, J, citizen teamster, died May 18, pleuritus.
1881, Clark, M, citizen teamster, died June 12, diarrhea a.
3309, Cable, C, citizen, died July 16, debilitas.
3972, Cregger, J F, musician, died July 25, diarrhea.
6315, Crowley, Pat, died Aug 20, scorbutus.
9245, Carroll, C, teamster, 19 army corps, died Sept 19, scorbutus.
10485, Corbit, J, died Oct 7, wounds.
10872, Carey, Thomas, died Oct 13, scorbutus.
11726, Collins, J, citizen teamster, died Nov 1, scorbutus.
12449, Carroll, James, citizen teamster, died Jan 13, '65, scorbutus.

752, Deems, P, Ringold battery, Co E, died April 29, diarrhea c.
2820, Delp, Geo, citizen teamster, died June 28, diarrhea.
4334, Davis, J, citizen, died July 30, diarrhea.
6866, Danforth, Geo A, died Aug 16, diarrhea.
8202, Delmore, W, citizen, died Sept 8, diarrhea.
11084, Dubin, M, citizen teamster, died Oct 18, scorbutus.
11243, Delhanta, Wm, citizen, died Oct 21, diarrhea.

182, England, E, died March 27, pneumonia.
3923, Evans, M, citizen, died July 25, diarrhea.
Everett, T S, citizen, Md, died Aug 30, diarrhea.

157, Freeman, John, died March 25, dysentery.
453, Fenley, R, citizen, died April 9, diarrhea c.
1116, Fannon, A, citizen, died May 15, dysentery.
2332, Foster, W, telegraph operator, died June 22, diarrhea c.
2435, Farrell, M, citizen, died June 25, anasarca.
10478, Flckison, J, died Oct 7, diarrhea.
4808, Fitzgerald, ——, died Aug 5, diarrhea.
5078, Frank, F M, Wilder's battery, died Aug 8, scorbutus.
5009, Fox, Henry, citizen teamster, died Aug 14, scorbutus.
7643, Ford, P, teamster, died Sept 3, diarrhea.
9084, Foncks, H C, Keye's Ind't cav, died Sept 18, dysenteria.
11315, Ferrall, M C, teamster, died Oct 22, scorbutus.

2729, Gilden, D, citizen, died July 1, scorbutus.
4115, Grogran, D, died July 28, diarrhea c.
4747, Gisbart, J, died Aug 5, fever typhus.
6139, Graham, E, citizen, died Aug 10, diarrhea.
7854, Gorb, S, died Sept 5, scorbutus.
9747, Goodman, J O, died Sept 25.
10672, Gilman, John, died Oct 11, diarrhea c.
11862, Goodyear, F, citizen, died Nov 6, scorbutus.
10717, Graves, Wm E, died Oct 11, scorbutus.

219, Heartless, S, died March 29.
244, Hammond, S, teamster, died March 31, diarrhea c.
606, Hoffman, Charles, citizen teamster, died April 18, dysentery.
1274, Harkins, John, teamster, died May 22, diarrhea c.
2370, Hammond, J, citizen teamster, died June 23, diarrhea.
3227, Hudson, G W, citizen teamster, died July 12, diarrhea.
4244, Hughes, P, died July 29, wounds.
6070, Hannay, D, citizen teamster, died Aug 18, fever typhus.
8055, Herilage, J, teamster, died Sept 7, scorbutus.
8756, Harkins, D S, * m m b, died Sept 14, diarrhea.
9006, Hyatt, J, died Sept 17, scorbutus.
9051, Hulbert, J H S, died Sept 17, diarrhea.
9297, Hall, M, n a s, died Sept 19, scorbutus.
9425, Hart, Isaac, citizen teamster, died Sept 21, diarrhea.
10262, Hines, Daniel, died Oct 3, diarrhea.
10331, Hopkins, John, died Oct 4, diarrhea.
11934, Heckinbridge, died Nov 9, scorbutus.
12456, Harrington, J, † died Jan 15, '65, diarrhea c.

8722, Imbagg, ——, died Sept 14, diarrhea.

4794, Jones, Charles, citizen teamster, died Aug 5, diarrhea c.
8854, Jacobs, W C, citizen, died Aug 26, dysentery.
12714, Johnson, J, citizen, Canada, died March 1, '65, diarrhea c.

2208, Kingland, W H, citizen, died June 20, diarrhea.
3515, Kerr, E, citizen teamster, died June 18, diarrhea.
6273, Kins, W H, citizen teamster, died Aug 20, marasmus.
7364, Knight, J B, citizen teamster, died Sept 5, anasarca.
9467, Kellogg, E L, citizen, Springfield, Mass, died Sept 21, diarrhea.

546, Lee, James, citizen teamster, died April 14, dysentery c.
1772, Lafferty, Wm, Ringgold battery, died June 9, scorbutus.
3689, Lummo, Robt, citizen, died July 21, scorbutus.
10353, Linton, E, Ringgold battery, died Oct 5, dysentery.

76, Morton, J B, Ringgold cav, Co A, died March 20, fever typhus
208, McMahon, Pat, died March 28, diarrhea.
220, Morrison, F, citizen teamster, died March 29, diarrhea.
865, Mower, W, citizen, died May 3, debilitas.
2285, McAtie, M, teamster, died June 21, diarrhea c.
2432, Manning, B F, citizen teamster, died June 24, diarrhea.
2373, McEusbon, Peter, died June 23, dysentery.
3450, Moyer, J, died July 17, diarrhea.
4017, Messenger, H M, citizen, died July 26, dysentery.
5387, Morland, J S, citizen teamster, died Aug 12, diarrhea.
5996, McGee, J, died Aug 17, diarrhea.
6380, McKenna, F, died Aug 21, scorbutus.
8039, McGuire, J, citizen, died Sept 6, scorbutus.
9135, Myers, John, died Sept 18, diarrhea.
9247, McDonald, J, died Sept 19, scorbutus.
9616, Munch, Christian, topog engineer, died Sept 23, diarrhea.
12535, McDonald, H H, citizen (Ohio), died Jan 27, '65, diarrhea.
6666, Monteith, M, citizen teamster, died Aug 24, diarrhea.

184, Newton, Wm, teamster, died March 27, pneumonia.
7074, Norton, E, citizen, died Aug 28, dysentery.
8510, Nichols, J, teamster 15 army corps, died Sept 12, diarrhea.
4190, Osborne, J, citizen, died July 28, dysentery.
5414, Oliver, W W, died Aug 12, scorbutus.

719, Pringle, Wm, citizen teamster, died April 25, fever typhus.
1855, Podzas, L, citizen teamster, died June 12, diarrhea.
5920, Poole, C, died Aug 17, scorbutus.
8893, Powers, G, citizen, died Sept 16, scorbutus.
9010, Potter, S D, died Sept 17, diarrhea.
9366, Phillips, B B, teamster, died Sept 20, diarrhea.
12364, Parker, James, citizen teamster, died Dec 29, diarrhea c.
10100, Parkhurst, W L, 1 m m b, died Sept 30, diarrhea.

858, Quinn, James, citizen, died May 3, diarrhea c.
5394, Quinlan, Pat, citizen teamster, died Aug 12, scorbutus.

No. of Grave.

5768, Quinn, —, citizen, died Aug 15, scorbutus.

3542, Reed, A R, Independent, died July 18, diarrhea.
3770, Rand, J, citizen teamster, died July 22, scorbutus.
5966, Rooley, J, died Aug 17, diarrhea.
10111, Reddig, C H, citizen, died Oct 1, scorbutus.
10453, Ryan, John, citizen, died Oct 7, gangrene.
11131, Reiss, R, citizen, died Oct 18.
11703, Richardson, J C, 1 m m b, Co I, died Oct 30, scorbutus.

440, Scott, Blair, citizen, died April 9, diarrhea c.
2431, Smith, P, m m b, died June 24, diarrhea.
2440, St Clair, Benj, citizen teamster, died June 25, diarrhea.
2552, Slater, Charles, citizen teamster, died June 27, diarrhea.
2959, Spicer, W, citizen teamster, died July 6, pneumonia.
3000, Stout, Chas, citizen, died July 7, debilitas.
3662, Shunk, J, citizen, died July 20, dysentery.
4008, Smith, H, Bridges Battery, died July 26, nausarca.
4843, Sawyer, J D, died Aug 6, dysentery.
9720, Stanton, J, citizen, died Sept 25, diarrhea.
10815, Sinayo, David, died Oct 12, diarrhea.

136, Thompson, Jno, teamster, died March 24, pneumonia.
1531, Tullis, L B G, citizen, died June 1, diarrhea c.

No. of Grave.

2693, Thompson, Geo, died June 30, scorbutus.
3409, Thomas, J H, citizen teamster, died July 16, diarrhea.
3896, Taylor, J W, citizen, died July 24, constipatio.
12337, Tucer, B, citizen, Indiana, died Dec 28, scorbutus.

9397, Ulmgender, G, m m b, Co C, died Sept 21, diarrhea.

799, Wilkins, A, * Ringgold Battery, died April 29, diarrhea a.
1092, Welsh, G L, citizen teamster, died May 14, diarrhea a.
1121, White, Geo, citizen, died May 15, dysentery.
2784, Wilson, D E, Ringgold Battery, died July 2, debilitas.
10953, Weir, J, citizen teamster, died Oct 14, diarrhea.
11006, Woods, R C, Knapp's Battery, died Oct 28, scorbutus.
4730, Wright, Chas, citizen teamster, died Aug 4, dysentery.
4869, Ward, John, citizen teamster, died Aug 6, diarrhea.
9043, Williams, F G, died Sept 17, diarrhea c.
10075, Wentgel Thomas, died Sept 30, diarrhea.

9497, Vankirk, W, Ringgold Battery, died Sept 21, scorbutus.
9388, Vandier, W M, citizen, Phila, Penn, died Sept 24, diarrh

4127, Young, Henry, citizen teamster, died July 28, dysentery.
12246, Young, D, citizen teamster, died Nov 8, scorbutus.

MEN THAT WERE HUNG.

1, Sarsfield, Jno, 144 N Y, July 11, hung.
2, Collins, Wm, 88, Pa, Co D, July 11, hung.
3, Curtis, Chas, 5 R I artil, Co A, July 11, hung.
3, Delaney, Pat, 83 Pa, Co E, July 11, hung.
5, Muir, A, U S Navy, July 11, hung.
6, Rickson, W R, U S Navy, July 11, hung.

NUMBER OF GRAVES CONTAINING UNKNOWN U. S. SOLDIERS.

101	3142	4815	5492	8564	8756	8890	8979	9066	9181	9359	9601	9863	10168	10383
103	3143	4837	5500	8565	8757	8891	8984	9069	9182	9360	9608	9876	10173	10387
104	3144	4839	5804	8566	8759	8892	8986	9070	9107	9364	9610	9877	10175	10391
105	3145	4840	6031	8600	8790	8894	8959	9072	9109	9382	9613	9881	10177	10420
106	3146	4841	6939	8604	8800	8896	8991	9074	9200	9391	9615	9883	10178	10432
107	3147	4842	7030	8609	8801	8915	8995	9076	9201	9393	9620	9887	10182	10470
111	3148	4851	7047	8610	8803	8916	8996	9077	9203	9394	9666	9891	10185	10475
115	3171	4852	7545	8660	8808	8918	8997	9124	9204	9440	9669	9900	10188	10507
120	3186	4864	8000	8672	8809	8920	9000	9126	9207	9442	9672	9906	10189	10532
127	3200	4873	8179	8673	8811	8921	9007	9128	9255	9149	9673	9922	10191	10544
138	3221	4891	8191	8674	8813	8927	9008	9130	9257	9455	9675	9923	10195	10628
140	3229	4924	8251	8675	8816	8928	9016	9133	9259	9466	9683	9956	10209	10629
147	3265	4936	8327	8677	8817	8929	9026	9152	9261	9485	9685	9959	10238	10630
232	3364	4989	8394	8678	8825	8930	9029	9157	9262	9489	9695	9964	10261	10633
326	3454	4972	8412	8679	8826	8932	9030	9160	9264	9493	9697	10012	10263	10643
345	3404	5032	8420	8683	8820	8933	9031	9161	9267	9522	9749	10020	10264	10697
2072	3502	5033	8424	8684	8831	8934	9032	9163	9275	9523	9756	10021	10266	10701
2710	4016	5052	8482	8702	8842	8935	9036	9165	9276	9524	9769	10025	10282	10704
2721	4282	5006	8435	8703	8843	8936	9038	9167	9277	9529	9771	10034	10324	10707
2722	4600	5111	8471	8704	8844	8940	9047	9168	9279	9565	9782	10038	10325	10712
2779	4609	5157	8485	8705	8845	8941	9049	9171	9280	9569	9802	10041	10326	10713
2865	4671	5168	8489	8706	8846	8945	9052	9172	9281	9586	9804	10090	10333	10714
2806	4758	5204	8491	8707	8847	8949	9053	9174	9283	9587	9806	10105	10343	10718
3117	4764	5206	8494	8708	8870	8950	9064	9176	9285	9588	9810	10159	10344	10719
3118	4755	5209	8535	8709	8880	8951	9055	9177	9288	9589	9815	10162	10345	10722
3125	4756	5300	8552	8710	8881	8952	9056	9170	9346	9595	9837	10166	10363	10732
3140	4757	5301	8558	8784	8883	8963	9058	9150	9355	9596	9841	10167	10378	10755
3141	4758	5302	8561	8785	8889	8978	9061							

www.ingramcontent.com/pod-product-compliance
Lightning Source LLC
Chambersburg PA
CBHW020322090426
42735CB00009B/1371

9783337307240